AF600373

Karaite Judaism and Historical Understanding

Studies in Comparative Religion
Frederick M. Denny, Series Editor

Karaite Judaism and Historical Understanding

Fred Astren

University of South Carolina Press

Published in Columbia, South Carolina, by the
University of South Carolina Press

Manufactured in the United States of America

24 23 22 21 20 6 5 4 3 2

Library of Congress Cataloging-in-Publication Data

Astren, Fred.
Karaite Judaism and historical understanding / Fred Astren.
p. cm. — (Studies in comparative religion)
Includes bibliographical references and index.
ISBN 1-57003-518-0 (cloth)
1. Karaites—History. 2. Karaites. I. Title. II. Studies in comparative religion (Columbia, S.C.)
BM185.A88 2004
296.8'1—dc22

2003023745

The author thanks the editors and publishers of the following publications for their permission to use materials originally printed by them: "History or Philosophy? The Construction of the Past in Medieval Karaite Judaism," *Medieval Encounters* 1, no. 1 (1995): 114–43; "Karaite Approaches to History in Medieval Islam," in *Judaism and Islam: Boundaries, Communication, Interaction: Essays in Honor of William Brinner,* ed. Benjamin H. Hary, John L. Hayes, and Fred Astren, 321–34, (Leiden: E. J. Brill, 2000), and "Islamic Contexts of Medieval Karaism" and "Karaite Historiography and Historical Consciousness," in *Karaite Judiasm: A Guide to Its History and Literacy Sources,* ed. Meira Polliack, 145–77 and 25–69, respectively (Leiden: E. J. Brill, 2003).

Contents

Series Editor's Preface

Several decades ago, while I was studying early Islamic history in graduate school, I became deeply absorbed by the creative ways in which the emerging Islamic civilization drew from and interacted with the rich and varied cultures, religions, scientific legacies, as well as the theological, legal, philosophical, and exegetical discourses of the Nile to Oxus region. One of the most arresting developments to me was the rise of Karaite Judaism and the ways in which it resonated with certain Islamic schools of scriptural interpretation, legal argument, and rational theology as it sustained an ongoing dispute with the dominant Rabbanite Judaism of the dual Torah (written and oral) in favor of upholding the written Torah as the supreme authority for Jewish faith and order.

When I first read Fred Astren's manuscript for *Karaite Judaism and Historical Understanding* I was transported back to my grad school study pleasures and reintroduced to Karaism in a manner that I never could have imagined back then. The study of Karaism has progressed enormously in the past thirty to forty years. Astren's study is not, in his view, a historiographical undertaking so much as an expedition into sacred history. The goal of his study is the of understanding Karaite sectarian expression in its own terms along a diachronic route of a thousand years through such diverse regions as Egypt, Jerusalem, Constantinople before and during the Ottoman period, the Crimea, Poland, Lithuania, and Russia.

The rich variety of textual resources that the author utilizes, some of which are drawn upon for the first time in modern scholarship, strongly contribute to this work's pace-setting importance in advancing our knowledge of Karaism. Of greatest significance is the author's liberating of the discourse from its traditional and somewhat misleading focus on biblical scripturalism as the be-all and end-all of the movement—a view that misses the equally important ritual, social, messianic-millenarian, and legal (*halakhic*) dimensions, which eventually came to utilize methods of argument and application similar to Rabbinic standards and practices.

This book will be of considerable interest to comparative religion scholars, because much of what the author has provided in the way of historical analysis and theoretical modeling—particularly with respect to sect theory, heresy as a scholarly category, and notions of what he calls "sacred history"—

may be applied in parallel fashion to studies of Islam, Christianity, Buddhism, Hinduism, and beyond. Indeed, Astren's profoundly insightful opening chapter addresses Islamic influences on Judaism in general and Karaism in particular in a manner that significantly advances our knowledge and understanding of religious minorities in the religiopolitical world of classical Islamic civilization. Later in the book we see how Karaism fared in other contexts, such as Europe during the Protestant Reformation when an obscure Jewish community focusing on the written Torah would understandably attract the attention of advocates of Luther's doctrine of *sola scriptura.*

Frederick Mathewson Denny

Acknowledgments

This book could not have been completed without the assistance and support of many people. I would like to thank Philip Miller and Daniel Frank, with whom I have had important conversations regarding the Karaites and Jewish history. Special thanks to Daniel Lasker, whose knowledge of Karaism impelled me to reconsider much that I had taken for granted or overlooked and whose interest in my work has been, and remains, extremely supportive. His close readings of my writing have been instrumental in the process of putting this book together. Gordon Newby has also provided challenging historical insight for me as I grappled with the Islamic Middle Ages. Special thanks go to him for inviting me to publish an article on al-Qirqisānī in *Medieval Encounters.* Similarly, I am grateful to Meira Polliack for inviting me to make two contributions to a new handbook in Karaite Studies entitled *Karaite Judaism.* Her support made the publication of this book possible. Peter Brown's interest and participation in my work has provided me with a much deeper and wider historical perspective. And Lawrence Schiffman impelled me to look more closely into the origins of Karaism by inviting me to write entries in the *Encyclopedia of the Dead Sea Scrolls* and an article in *Dead Sea Discoveries.* Barry Walfish's careful reading of the manuscript prevented me from making many errors, and the anonymous reader DT changed my entire view on many matters.

Acknowledgment goes to Aryeh Grabois, David Sklare, Sumaiya Hamdani, Michael Cook, Shaul Shaked, Ariel Bloch, Ronald Kiener, and Rachel Havrelock, each of whom contributed to specific, key matters connected with the book. David Biale has supported this work from its beginnings and helped move it toward publication. And Elliot Wolfson showed interest in the book in its early stages. Thanks to Joshua Holo and Dina Stein of the Richard S. Dinner Center for Jewish Studies at the Graduate Theological Union for permitting me to subject the participants of a small graduate seminar to my writings.

Most of all, Ze'ev Brinner has offered intellectual and academic guidance as well as personal encouragement over the course of many years, some of which were especially trying. I would not have discovered the Karaites without his guidance, nor would I have embarked on the long journey that has culminated in this book. I offer him my most profound gratitude.

Special mention must be made of the fellowship of a group of scholars from whom I have derived great benefit and pleasure through both personal association and professional interaction. This circle includes Roger Brooks, Reuven Firestone, Ronald Kiener, Gordon Newby, and Steven Wasserstrom. All of them knowingly or unwittingly have made contributions to this project. I hardly know how to begin to thank my close friend and fellow scholar Samuel Wineburg, without whose friendship, encouragement, and intellectual support this book truly would never have been completed. None of the aforementioned colleagues and associates are responsible for errors or inadequacies in this book; all such inadequacies are wholly mine.

The most important element of material support for this book came from the Koret Jewish Publications Program of the Koret Foundation, which awarded me a publication subsidy in spring 2000. Thanks also to the Jewish Theological Seminary of America in New York, the Bibliotheek der Rijksuniversiteit Leiden, and the Manuscript Department of the Jewish National and University Library in Jerusalem for permission to use manuscripts in their collections. Over the years my writing has been supported by the University of North Carolina at Wilmington and, more recently, by San Francisco State University, whose release-time program has permitted me over latter years to continue to pay attention to this book.

Others whose participation and assistance were helpful in many ways include John Simmons, Mona Moxley, and my parents, Alex and Lorraine Astren. I am indebted in the most profound way to Pat Bourdelle, my wife, whose patience and support established the widest and deepest foundation for life and for the writing of this book.

Abbreviations

Citations for biblical books and rabbinic literature follow standardized abbreviations.

BT	Babylonian Talmud
EJ	*Encyclopaedia Judaica,* 16 vols. Jerusalem: Encyclopaedia Judaica. 1971–72. 2d [corrected] printing, 1973.
Ḥilluk	*Ḥilluk ha-Kara'im veha-Rabbanim*
HUCA	*Hebrew Union College Annual*
JE	*The Jewish Encyclopedia.* 12 vols. New York: Funk & Wagnalls, 1902–5.
JJS	*Journal of Jewish Studies*
JQR	*Jewish Quarterly Review*
KA	*Kitāb al-anwār wa'l-marāqib, Code of Karaite Law.* Ed. Leon Nemoy. 5 vols. New York: Publications of the Alexander Kohut Foundation, 1939–43.
M	Mishnah
ME	*Me'irat 'Einayim,* Simhah Isaac ben Moses Lutzki.
MGWJ	*Monatsschrift für Geschichte und Wissenschaft des Judentums*
n.s.	New series
o.s.	Old series
OṢ	*'Oraḥ Ṣaddikim,* Simhah Isaac ben Moses Lutzki.
PAAJR	*Proceedings of the American Academy for Jewish Research*
PT	Palestinian Talmud
REJ	*Revue des études juives*

Introduction

Representing One's Past

The idea that representation of the past is something different from history informs much literary and historical study of the last generation. This idea is illustrated by Patricia Nelson Limerick in a study of the American West:

> Celebrating one's past, one's tradition, is a bit like hosting a party: one wants to control the guest list tightly. . . . To celebrate the western past with an open invitation is a considerable risk: the brutal massacres come back along with the cheerful barn raisings, the shysters come back with the saints, contracts broken come back with contracts fulfilled.[1]

One who would examine the history of any people must necessarily take the preceding words to heart. Portrayal of the American West in writing and film has been demonstrated to be a reflection of the cultural and historiographical assumptions of its authors.[2] To cite an example, responsibility for the debacle of the dust bowl in the 1930s has been ascribed to poor planning and exploitative policies by the region's new European inhabitants or, alternatively, to the irresistible forces of nature moving through its own cycles in the arid stretches of the Great Plains.[3] Where to place the blame? Needless to say, the representation of this phenomenon has explicit and implicit ramifications for one's overall view of the history of the American West, for its meaning in the larger context of American and world history, and for the understanding of the American present—as an explanation of immediacy for explaining the world around us. To extend Limerick's metaphor, the host of a party that will represent the past must always and will necessarily have a carefully screened

1. *The Legacy of Conquests: The Unbroken Past of the American West,* 330, cited in Brian W. Dippie, "The Winning of the West Reconsidered," 80.

2. See the review article by John Mack Faragher, "The Frontier Trail: Rethinking Turner and Reimagining the American West."

3. William Cronon, "A Place for Stories: Nature, History, and Narrative."

list of invitees. Put in other words, historical representation is always constructed.[4]

Even human nature itself points toward the past as something that is constructed. There is a natural human psychological impetus to use the past for self-explanation. To some degree, a person is the result of the accumulated experiences of his or her past. In our day, the "recovery" of repressed memories by abused individuals has in some cases found standing in the courts of law. However, it has led to a debate in the professional psychological community regarding the veracity of these newly realized personal histories, whether they are truly personal epiphanies, implanted memories, or the result of autosuggestion. In a sense, we believe what we want to believe about our childhood and past experiences. Our personal histories are constantly being "rewritten" in our minds, and, most importantly, through the process of telling and retelling.

When examining the historical expression of a religio-cultural group, one faces interpretive problems of similar import, but of decidedly different consequences. In terms of groups—communities, whether in the form of societies or civilizations—these problems are fundamental to ways of thinking about history and the past. Recent writing that distinguishes between memory and history comments on difficulties of representing the past.[5] At the heart of the matter is the idea that representations of the past inform us as much, if not more, about the times in which they were constructed as the times about which they are concerned.[6]

Jewish Tradition and the Past

In the case of the history of religion, specific epistemological and theological assumptions shape self-explanations that rely on and represent a picture of

4. Foundational to this view are Peter L. Berger and Thomas Luckmann, *The Social Construction of Reality: A Treatise in the Sociology of Knowledge;* and Benedict Anderson, *Imagined Communities: Reflections on the Origin and Spread of Nationalism.*

5. Some of these problems come to light in Steven Zipperstein's chapters in *Imagining Russian Jewry: Memory, History, Identity.* One of the earliest approaches to this topic—perhaps the best—is Yosef Hayim Yerushalmi, *Zakhor: Jewish History and Jewish Memory,* and there are now also essays by others in his festschrift, *Jewish History and Jewish Memory: Essays in Honor of Yosef Hayim Yerushalmi.* See David Lowenthal, *The Past Is a Foreign Country,* for a careful analysis of many of the problems of representing and dealing with the past, as well as his *Possessed by the Past: The Heritage Crusade and the Spoils of History.*

6. In general historiography, one must consult the work of Hayden White, esp. *Metahistory: The Historical Imagination in Nineteenth-century Europe;* also the essays in *The Content of the Form: Narrative Discourse and Historical Representation.* Other approaches can be found in R. Layton, ed., *Who Needs the Past? Indigenous Values and Archaeology.* A recent work, Michel-Rolph Trouillot, *Silencing the Past: Power and the Production of History,* discusses how history is written.

the past. Revelatory religions—like Judaism, Christianity, and Islam—are established in part on the narratives and commands of canonical texts, whose authenticity is believed to be divinely guaranteed. In this regard, all forms of Judaism recognize the Hebrew Bible in this or a related capacity. For the Judaism that is based upon the teachings of the rabbis and is "dominant" or "normative" in many historical settings, other literatures also fall into this category: the Mishnah, the Talmuds, and associated genres of Late Antiquity and the Middle Ages. Jacob Neusner calls this "the Judaism of the dual Torah," to describe "the myth of divine revelation to Moses at Sinai in two media, oral and written."[7] For Rabbanites (that is, those who have historically followed this version of Judaism) the past is found in these books—in narratives of biblical antiquity that are part of the inherited ancient past of the Hebrew Bible, and in a distinct, "later" past, constructed by using scattered data selected from the vast corpus of rabbinic literature.

Whereas the past found in the Bible is explicit and usually based in narrative, rabbinic texts are characterized by an ahistoricity that necessitates a process of selection and collation in order to realize any kind of a picture of a postbiblical past derived from this literature. This lack of historical specificity is the result of a literature that appears to have a communal authorship, described by Neusner as purposefully "framed as implicitly to deny historical development of ideas,"[8] thereby obscuring or excising event, personality, and cause and effect from the literary record. The lack of individual authorship helps present a Judaism that is normative—whose pronouncements appear to be consensual—seemingly coherent and logical in presentation. This effacement of author and history permits a seamless presentation of rabbinic law and theology. Law supported the creation of guidelines for the immediacy of human behavior in this world, while theology contextualized other-worldly concerns from a Jewish point of view. Such concerns include morality, reward and punishment, and resolution for the current Jewish condition, which was characterized by minority marginalization, political powerlessness, and future hope. With these guiding principles operating as part of what was believed to be a divine plan, the rabbis constructed a view of human and earthly activity that centered on the righteousness and ritual observance of the people of Israel as guiding determinants in history. In such a schema, specificity is superfluous—the particular features and sequence of events are unnecessary. What is important is how Israel acted and will act.

It is important to emphasize that for the rabbis in general there is no concern for recording an event for the sake of posterity. There could be nothing further from the historical philosophy of the Greeks as expressed by Herodotus: "In this book, the result of my inquiries into history, I hope to do two things: to preserve the memory of the past by putting on record the

7. *Introduction to Rabbinic Literature,* xix.
8. Ibid., xxiii.

astonishing achievements both of our own and of the Asiatic peoples; secondly, and more particularly, to show how the two races came into conflict."[9] The works of a few Jews who wrote in accordance with this Greek mode of historical thought precede, or are beyond the confines of, rabbinic literature. Only Josephus, the Jewish historian of the late first century C.E., has left posterity a "Greek" supplement to the ahistorical views of the rabbis.[10] The influence of these Jewish authors on late antique and medieval rabbinic Judaism is mostly negligible. In fact, the study of history is discouraged, if not repudiated by rabbinic writers.[11]

The prevalence of the rabbinic point of view has resulted in a lack of worldly historical specificity in traditional Jewish cultural understanding, which makes the problem of studying premodern Jewish history particularly complex. For example, a comment from a modern popular work, which refers to Jewish life in the small communities of Eastern Europe, points to the Rabbanized sociocultural milieu and its representation of the past:

> Half the time the *shtetl* just wasn't there: it was in the Holy Land, and it was in the remote past or the remote future, in the company of the Patriarchs or prophets or of the Messiah. Its festivals were geared to the Palestinian climate and calendar . . . it prayed for the subtropical (early and late) rains indifferent to its neighbors, whose prayers had a practical, local schedule in view.[12]

Removed from the perceived source of spirituality by thousands of miles and thousands of years, these Jews had little concern for modern notions of history. This point of view is ancient in origin and has persisted for centuries.

Then how does one use rabbinic writings to study the Jewish past? The rabbinic picture of the past makes it very difficult to "do history," yet the themes of rabbinic writers tell us what they were concerned with at specific times (datable by text, document, and sometimes by the context of ideology). These themes reflect essential components of rabbinic Jewish identity as it is constructed at a given time. What can be done in terms of approaching a model for Jewish history is to focus on Jewish uses and constructions of the

9. *The Histories,* trans. Aubrey de Sélincourt, 13.

10. See Carl Holladay, *Fragments from Hellenistic Jewish Authors,* 1: *Historians;* and H. W. Attridge, "Historiography." On Josephus, see H. W. Attridge, "Josephus and His Works." See the recent interpretive reappraisal of these materials by Eric Gruen, *Heritage and Hellenism: The Reinvention of Jewish Tradition.*

11. For example, see Maimonides, *Mishnah ʿim perush rabbenu Moshe ben Maimon* (Commentary to Mishnah), commentary on Sanhedrin, 10:1, where he states that the study of history is a "waste of time."

12. Conor Cruise O'Brien, *The Siege: the Saga of Israel and Zionism.* Compare the title of Jacob Neusner's *The Presence of the Past, The Pastness of the Present: History, Time, and Paradigm in Rabbinic Judaism.*

past. In the first chapter of this book is analysis of the historical sensibilities of the rabbis, especially in light of the impact that their historical expression would have on the Karaites, the primary subjects of investigation. For indeed, although the Karaites were not rabbinic Jews, they also inherited the antique history of the Bible, but then found different expression from that of the rabbis in articulating a historical vision. The scope of this difference changed through the centuries and can be measured in a given historical period by the halakhic variances that distinguished these two Judaisms and by the Karaites' use of rabbinic literature for their own historical purposes. The purpose of this book is to describe and analyze this difference.

Describing Sectarianism and Karaite Judaism

Sects and Jews. According to Leon Nemoy, one of the twentieth century's masters of Karaite studies, Karaism is "a Jewish sect that recognizes only the Hebrew scriptures as the source of divinely inspired legislation, and denies the authority of the postbiblical Jewish tradition (the oral law) as recorded in the Talmud and in later rabbinic literature."[13] Along with others who have treated this topic extensively, Nemoy identifies Karaism as a sect without offering a definition of the word *sect.* It is assumed that the reader understands its meaning. Through deduction, one may further assume that the relationship of a sect to a dominant movement has something to do with disagreement and size. Beyond that, we learn much in descriptive terms from the pioneers of Karaite studies, but little about the idea of sect is elaborated from these studies.

We can go further along this line of inquiry by examining the monumental study by Zvi Ankori, *Karaites in Byzantium,* which wholly lacks a definition for the term *sect.* In fact, in his methodological remarks, Ankori quite correctly notes the importance of going beyond "dissident books or nonconformist observances" in an effort to understand "the sectarian way of life and philosophy of life." And, beyond that, Ankori looks for the "dynamics of sectarian life within (or against) its normative environment."[14] The notion of the normative is as difficult as the idea of sect.

In the context of modern Jewish studies, most educated readers are familiar with a somewhat well-known "map" of sectarianism.[15] With recourse to putative ideas of sectarianism, students in universities are taught about religious, historical, and social constructs. We easily identify as sects Sadducees,

13. Leon Nemoy, s.v. "Karaites," in *The Encyclopedia of Religion,* 8:254.

14. Zvi Ankori, *Karaites in Byzantium: The Formative Years, 970–1100,* 8–9.

15. For some of the following remarks, I am grateful to Sumaiya Hamdani, with whom I coauthored a brief electronic publication entitled "A Prolegomenon to the Topic of Sectarianism; or, 'I Never Met a Sectarian I Didn't Like!'" which was distributed through e-mail to members of the Carolina Seminar in Comparative Islamic Studies in 1995.

Boethusians, Sabbateans, and Frankists. Additionally, we are able to identify salient features of the respective beliefs, social structure, and history of these entities, yet the result is a mostly static model of these phenomena. A theoretical formulation of sectarianism evades us.

Shaye J. D. Cohen offers a definition of sectarianism that is based upon static socio-theological observations. He says that a sect is (1) small; (2) organized; (3) separates itself from the larger body; (4) alone embodies ideals of the larger group; and (5) alone understands God's will.[16] Cohen has taken the unarticulated assumptions of earlier scholars of sectarianism and created categories that correspond to the old discussions. In fact, this typology places restrictions on a historical understanding of sects as entities which change dynamically through time. In this regard, Ankori was right. A sect should not be viewed from a static perspective that is based upon reductive analysis, such as theological or legal differences. Invariably, these differences themselves are transformed through time as the sect and its co-religion adapt to societal change and internal development. In an effort to supplement such a fixed view of sectarianism, and to avoid monolithic representations of Karaism in particular, I have selected the development of historical expression among the Karaites as a gauge for measuring the scope of distance that "separates" what can properly be identified as two Judaisms.

Further difficulty emerges when we recognize that contemporary treatments of sectarianism are often shaped in part by our own religious and cultural biases. Early treatments of Karaism utilized such denigratory terms as *schismatic*, which echoes both orthodox Christian perspectives of heresy and a notion of separation on the part of the sect that may or may not correctly describe the situation at a given historical moment. The term *separation* needs to be interrogated for historical truthfulness.[17] Yesterday's sect may become today's mainstream religion. Perhaps there was a time when it was as yet unclear as to which group would later be designated mainstream, or normative, and which would be declared a sect, or heresy.[18]

16. *From the Maccabees to the Mishnah*, 124ff.

17. For an example of terminological confusion, see Ankori, *Karaites in Byzantium*, s.v. "Sectaries, Sectarians [Schismatics]" in the index.

18. A good example of this problem appears in Islamic historiography of the period of the Second Fitnah (often understood to mean "civil war"), 680–92 C.E. By 683, the rebel Ibn al-Zubayr was generally recognized as caliph of the Muslim empire, a position of supreme political power and significant religious influence. At the same time, the Umayyad house, which had held power since 660, had a caliph in Syria. Many Muslims withheld their allegiance from one or both of these caliphs. Which of the two held religious authority that is best characterized as "normative" or "mainstream"? We are often lured toward one position in such dilemmas when we are influenced by hindsight. In this case, Ibn al-Zubayr would fail to establish a viable caliphate, while the Umayyads would defeat their enemies and maintain their ascendancy until 750. Scholars usually privilege the Umayyads by

The ideas of separation or dissidence demand some kind of methodological explanation for describing the religious community with which the sect has its tension-filled relationship. In this regard, Cohen has identified *normative* as embodying a historical judgment that may obscure useful historical description.[19] *Mainstream* also bears such a judgment. Even more problematic is *orthodox,* which connotes a theological judgment that is problematic to the historian and, in the case of Jewish history, inappropriate on account of its Christian theological context. By and large, Jews have eschewed notions of orthodoxy, while embracing varieties of orthoprax criteria for assigning membership in the community.

As we engage these methodological categories, problems of religious, historical, and cultural bias intrude upon attempts at going beyond such formulations. It becomes clear that a "blueprint" would be more useful than the current "map." A dynamic, multidimensional model is needed, one that seeks to identify the pieces, observe their interactions, and, at the same time, takes into account the many religious, social, and historical transformations that make up the whole. Most importantly, even as these groups "construct themselves" from within, they are themselves "being constructed" by others from the outside. In the case of Jewish sectarianism, the so-called outside is composed of both Jewish and non-Jewish worlds, thereby requiring a multileveled, comparative approach. Often these seemingly opposing developments are mutually influential. Clearly, the two dimensions described by a map are inadequate.

A blueprint for working toward a dynamic and complex model for sectarianism, in general, and Jewish sectarianism, in particular, can be investigated in interdisciplinary contexts, in terms of religious studies, history, sociology, anthropology, political science, and economics:

1. Religion. Traditionally sects and sectarianism are associated with the denunciatory term of the "true" believer, *heresy.* In this regard, theological and doctrinal differences inform constructs of the Other, separating

---

referring to Ibn al-Zubayr as a usurper or pretender, thereby overlooking the indeterminacy of the situation in the middle of the eighth decade of the eighth century. For an interpretive treatment of the Second Fitnah, see Marshall G. S. Hodgson, *The Venture of Islam,* 1:217–23. Comparisons could likewise be drawn to the popes and antipopes of the fourteenth century.

In Jewish history, the Pharisees are likewise privileged because they are the intellectual and societal predecessors of rabbinic Judaism. Such a reading of the past obfuscates the complexity and fluidity that characterized the relationship of several Judaisms in the period of the Second Temple, when no single Judaism was clearly culturally dominant. In the first century C.E., the inevitability of the survival and dominance of Pharisaic/rabbinic Judaism was hardly assured.

19. On the other hand, Shaye J. D. Cohen more recently has approached these topics with much more nuance. See his *The Beginnings of Jewishness: Boundaries, Varieties, Uncertainties.*

groups one from another. A heresiological understanding of sectarianism often colors the study of Samaritans, Karaites, and other Judaisms, emphasizing doctrinal divergence from rabbinic Judaism. To only engage the idea of heresy to the exclusion of other constructions of religious difference is one-sided and incomplete.[20] Also, heresy in the host cultures can become reflected in inner-Judaic relationships of difference. On a wider civilizational level, the evocation of sectarianism also informs intrareligious interaction and conflict. The locus classicus is found in apologetic and polemical literature of the three "Abrahamic" religious traditions. It can also be seen in Muslim-Christian relations in Lebanon and in Muslim-Hindu relations in South Asia. In Jewish studies, the study of Sabbateanism is colored by the rabbinic confessionalism of the primary sources and even of contemporary scholars themselves. The modern historian needs to read through the face value of heresiology and polemic to uncover the historical identities obscured by theological purpose.

2. Minority. In certain contexts, sectarianism has been invoked to identify a minority stance or identity. For example, Karaites in modern eastern Europe consciously moved toward an ethnic identity, while diminishing Judaic religious particularity. Certainly, the identity of Ethiopian Jews is constructed more as a Jewish ethnicity than as a sectarian phenomenon. Appositely, in the Arab Middle East, sects often coincide with minorities, including the Druze, Yazīdīs, and ʿĀlawīs. Nonetheless, the minoritarian identity is relative. For example, although Shī'ites are a minority in the Muslim world, in Iran they are in the majority. Notions of ethnicity and sectarianism are often reflexive, predicated upon overlapping constructions of identity. The Arab Shī'ites in southern Iraq found themselves in a difficult position in the war against Iran, a Shī'ite nation of non-Arab ethnicity. Obviously, social minorities and creedal minorities may or may not coincide. Karaites can be located throughout history as a minority within a minority, a situation of enormous sociopolitical complexity.
3. Political opposition. Often when social groups cannot attain power, prestige, or wealth within the larger societal system, they have recourse to sectarian self-definition, wherein such goals are attainable. According to Julius Wellhausen, sects are religio-political groups who engage in active opposition to the establishment.[21] Hence the use of the term *sect* in Islam in regard to Khārijism, Shī'isms, and even competing Sunnī *madhāhib* (law schools). In many cases, only hindsight and the judgment of historians creates what appears to be a clear identification of who is the opposition (schismatic) and who is the establishment (normative).

20. See John B. Henderson, *The Construction of Orthodoxy and Heresy: Neo-Confucian, Islamic, Jewish, and Early Christian Patterns.*

21. Julius Wellhausen, *The Arab Kingdom and Its Fall.* See the historical reasoning in his introduction, esp. 60–68.

Even in minoritarian Jewish society, sects represent opposition and resistance to the political dominance of the rabbis.

4. Boundaries. The question of boundaries further emphasizes the fluid character of this topic. When do the Mourners for Zion *(avele ṣion)* become sectarian Karaites? When does a *ṣūfī* order become sectarian? That is, by what categories of definition does a community-within-a-community become recognized and/or self-defined as a sect? In political terms, when does dissent become revolt (or secession)? Boundaries, of course, are never clearly drawn, and a Muslim Shīʿite doctrine such as *taqiyya* (often translated from the Arabic as *pious dissimulation*) may make boundaries difficult to perceive. Similarly, at what point do sects become separate autonomous religions in their own right? Are Samaritans members of a Jewish sect? The Bahāʾī and Druze define themselves differently than the ways they are defined from an Islamic point of view. Alternately, sects and other marginal groups often act as intermediaries between civilizations and societies, functioning as preservers and transmitters of ideas, specific knowledge, and commerce, a role the Jews performed in the interstices of early medieval Europe and the Muslim world.
5. Economy. Often sectarian groups are married to particular resources or occupations. Caste-like social constructions have compartmentalized economies to the extent that in the Lebanon the Druze were traditionally landowners, while Maronite Christians were often tenant farmers and merchants. The impact of colonialism in the Islamic world furthered social differentiation associated with economic function as European powers sought out client groups to further their own interests in the colonial enterprise. Some medieval Karaites criticized the economic success of the Jewish merchant class; others excelled as members of that class.

Karaism as Sect. Even in its medieval beginnings in the Islamic world, Karaism's rejection of things rabbinic is, in fact, a form of participation. As Karaite society develops, it interacts with contemporary Rabbanite societies, and as Karaite thought develops it interacts with contemporary Rabbanite Jews *and* their texts. These rabbinic texts bring to the reader embedded notions of the past—notions with which the Karaites were forced to seek some accommodation.

Because Karaite halakhah and much Karaite history is seen to be partially dependent upon rabbinic forms and content, a literary model for Karaism *as a sect* emerges from this study. This model for Karaite sectarianism—that is, for Karaism's umbilical connection to dominant rabbinic Judaism—includes more than the fundamental belief in the Hebrew Bible shared by Rabbanite and Karaite Jews, and goes beyond secondary conflicts over its interpretation. From its beginnings in the early Middle Ages, the sectarian relationship increasingly was marked by accommodation from one or both parties and, on the part of the Karaites, was characterized by an increased willingness to adopt certain aspects of Rabbanite practice and thought. Historical expression found in Karaite literature exhibits a direct correspondence to the accommodation and co-optation of rabbinic halakhah, its literature, and the rabbinic worldview.

An additional level of complexity is added to these formulations when relationships with the host cultures are taken into account. Not only does Judaism interact with the religions of host cultures in which it finds itself, but Judaisms interact with the host culture at the same time that they interact with each other. Interaction of particular Judaic subcultures with a host culture (and even its subcultures) presents particularity within the generality of pan-Judaic interactions with the host culture. Such complexity suggests a dynamic sociohistorical model in which static monolithic representations of Karaism simply will not suffice.

In this study, Karaite identity as reflected in historical expression will be described, but more importantly it will be framed against the background of rabbinic culture and contextualized within the historical environment of the day. With an eye to the host cultures, whether Islam and Orthodox Christianity in the Middle East or Roman Catholic and Protestant Christianity in eastern Europe, the larger environment will then be drawn into the analysis in order to write this "history of history."

History and Sacred History

In a way, it is easier to do a "history of Karaite history" than to do a history of the Karaites. The questions that arise from such a study are at times limited by the fragmentary and obscure nature of the textual sources. Little is known for many periods, and modern scholarship is at best speculative in regard to particular problems. Nonetheless, the reader will find that this study does indeed engage questions of history. To speak about Karaite historical thinking by necessity means that one takes a position vis-à-vis Karaite history. Nonetheless, it should be emphasized that this volume is not a history of the Karaites.

I have eschewed, for the most part, the use of the term *historiography*, which implies a kind of modern approach to the writing of history—that is, a critical analysis of sources of information with an eye to extracting some kind of reasonable model and explanation for historical phenomena. This is usually done with an eye at establishing continuity through time, often by identifying cause-and-effect relationships. It begins with evidence. The historical expression of the Karaites begins with its own believed truths, objective and pragmatic within the Karaite worldview, and only then proceeds to construct a representation of the past. In addition, the term *historiography* also implies literary genre. In the case of the Karaites, and for much of Jewish historical expression in general, such expression is a *mixtum compositum*, not a literature in itself, but is embedded in the larger corpus of Karaite literature.[22] It must be emphasized that we are not discussing history as we understand it in a modern academic manner but, on the contrary, are examining other types of intellectual worlds. These worlds are consistent unto themselves and should not be denigrated because they do not stand up to modern critical definitions and expectations of "history."

Then one must ask: How can Karaite historical expression be characterized? It can be seen that the historical conclusions of the Karaites are the result of the interaction of historiosophic assumptions, sectarian apologetics, and external influences. It is, in part, my intention that these historical expressions, whether Karaite or Rabbanite, be viewed as more than what Collingwood or Barnes might describe as a Jewish equivalent of ecclesiastical, or sacred, history.[23] In this light, it is more interesting and more useful to go beyond identification and description of the philosophies and polemical ideologies that are present in an effort at contextualizing them into their historical environments and, in the case of the Karaites, outlining the relationship of the historical discourse to the rabbinic mainstream and the non-Jewish host environment. To characterize these "creative histories" simply as "uses of history" or "evocations of history" is to undervalue the interesting and complex claims to temporality, chronological priority, and the truth that are present, and to overlook the philosophies, polemical and otherwise, that inform them.

Nonetheless, the idea of sacred history does present a starting place for a characterization of Karaite historical expression. For example, in the case of nascent Christianity there came into being a religious culture without a historical tradition of its own. Theological dependence on Judaism supported Christian co-optation of Jewish and biblical notions of the past to establish foundational "historical facts," such as the existence and lives of the prophets.

22. Cf. Steven M. Wasserstrom, "Species of Misbelief: A History of Muslim Heresiography of the Jews," 42.

23. In *The Idea of History,* R. G. Collingwood examines early Christian and medieval European historiography in ways that could be used to describe Karaite Jewish historiography. However, he does not go beyond recognition of the presence of a divine plan and the periodization inherent in a religiocultural outlook that postulates a historical divine revelation. In his rush toward "scientific history," he barely seems aware of the implications that are evident from close analysis of such texts. See esp. 46–56. Similarly, Harry Elmer Barnes, in *A History of Historical Writing,* identifies literary historical forms for these periods, but does little to connect them to the sociopolitical realities of their times. See 41–98. A more interesting analysis is found in Eric Cochrane, *Historians and Historiography in the Italian Renaissance.* Cochrane distinguishes "sacred history" as one of the "lateral disciplines" accompanying the new humanistic history of the era. See 445–78. This is an example of fruitful study derived from observing content and form in literary historical production within religiocultural and sociopolitical contexts.

From such foundational data followed fully articulated Christian historical formulations of the past—the prophets were transformed into proto-Christians who lived among erring Jews, and their prophecies were reinterpreted to fit the new theology. In general, sacred history follows a method based upon the establishment of doctrinal and theological "facts." Once the facts are established, questions of continuity and relationship emerge.[24] To illustrate the point, one can look at the many origin legends and traditions among the far-flung Jewish communities of the Middle East. Communities in marginal locations often lay claim to an antique ancestry, perhaps from the so-called Ten Lost Tribes—a foundational "fact" from the past.[25] For example, the twelfth-century Jewish traveler Benjamin of Tudela reports that the Jews of Nishapur, in Persia, were descended from the biblical tribes of Dan, Asher, Zebulun, and Naphtali.[26] To cite another example, the Jews of Yemen traditionally maintain that their beginnings go back to the time of the First Temple. Once this "historical fact" is established, it is only logical to ask correlative questions. Why did they not heed the later call of Ezra to return to the land? The requirement for an answer that is consonant with theological principles and with notions of the past leads to the creation of "creative history."[27] In the various answers that are offered, Jewish tradition is harmonized with the professed antiquity of the Yemenite community.[28]

This leads one to the core of sacred, creative history. Once facts of identity are constructed—having to do with community, practice, ritual, or belief—then the logic of sacred history demands the connection of those facts with the authoritative and more esteemed past. In the world of Late Antiquity, when new religious forms were active and insecure political realities rested upon the questionable foundations of old empires, an assertion of great antiquity was a statement of prestige and authority for a community or religious

24. For an example from Islam, see G. R. Hawting, *The Idea of Idolatry and the Emergence of Islam: From Polemic to History*, 36–39, for a discussion of Arab historicizing of Abrahamic descent.

25. For examples, Louis Isaac Rabinowitz, s.v. "Ten Lost Tribes," *EJ* 15:1003–6.

26. Benjamin of Tudela, *The Itinerary of Benjamin of Tudela*, 83 [Heb.], 59 [Eng.].

27. See D. Mendels, "'Creative History' in the Hellenistic Near East in the Third and Second Centuries B.C.E."

28. One of the answers given to this question in Yemeni Jewish tradition is that the Jews of Yemen foresaw the destruction of the Second Temple and the futility of return. They judged Ezra's call to be premature and decided to stay in their exile and worship God. This is recorded by the nineteenth-century Rabbi Yehia Salih (Yeḥiyah Sāliḥ) in *Megillat Teman*, 1–14, cited in Reuben Ahroni, *Yemenite Jewry: Origins, Culture, and Literature*, 5. Ahroni discusses the elaboration of the Ezra story and the many purposes for which it was used. In addition, it is noted that the story appears in the traditions of many Jewish communities. See also Yehuda Ratzaby, "Ezra the Scribe and the Yemenites," 108–11 [Heb.]; and idem, "Additions to 'Ezra the Scribe and the Yemenites,'" 382 [Heb.].

tradition. As evidenced in Pausanias, the etiological legends that proliferate in the late Roman Empire represent a historicization of the Greek myths that seek to harmonize the practice and belief of the day with the canon of antiquity.[29] The evocation of antiquity could take different forms. Among the Greeks, sacred history might develop a connection to the heroic past and its personalities. Within the religious traditions whose sacred history goes back to the Hebrew Bible, these creative histories appear in two forms. One is characterized by a focus on genealogy—that is, a tribal-"biological" model for a connection with the past. For example, the Romans and, later, the Arab caliphs recognized the prestige attached to the antiquity of the House of David. The other form displaces the tribal model and redefines the link with the past in terms of a connection to God's revelation to the ancient Israelites. This model appears in various guises among Jews, Christians, and Muslims.

Although the primary concern of sacred history is association with an esteemed past, several concomitant results emerge, and in this regard this study proposes to go beyond the idea of sacred history. Internal aspects of doctrinal or communal accommodation and co-optation to external cultures on the part of the Karaites are explained by means of historicized explanations of relations with other communities found in their texts. Similarly, the boundaries of the group can be defined through etiological constructions within the narratives. Also, the authority of communal leadership and the constitution of the community is justified either through its portrayal within sacred history or as the preserve of the expositors of tradition itself. Equipped with these approaches, Karaite representation of the past can be seen in Karaism's interdependent role, as a sect of rabbinic Judaism and as a society immersed in a non-Jewish, "foreign" host culture. In the case of the Karaites, sociohistorical concerns of the Middle Ages and early modernity shape and reshape sacred history, permitting the modern observer richer and more productive analyses of the texts. The etiological parameters of Karaite historical expression are not simple site-specific narratives of place and space as known in so many ancient narratives; they go beyond local, limited concerns, to global representations of identity.

Studying Karaite History and Karaite Notions of the Past

This study seeks to chart the growth of historical self-explanation among the Karaites for a millennium, beginning with their origins in the eighth century. Medieval Islamicate Karaite scripturalism and anti-Rabbanism lent themselves to an indifferent attitude toward history or any idea of tradition.[30] However, as Karaite halakhah evolved toward the end of the eleventh and into the

29. Pausanias, *Guide to Greece.*

30. The term *Islamicate* was coined by Marshall G. S. Hodgson to provide an adjective to describe the civilizational in distinction from the term *Islamic,* which describes the religious. See Hodgson, *Venture of Islam,* 1:45ff.

twelfth centuries, it became increasingly engaged with rabbinic formulations of halakhah and tradition. Correspondingly, Karaite urges toward self-explanation began to engage rabbinic historiosophical assumptions, leading to the development of a Karaite version of the rabbinic chain of tradition, a primary way for the rabbis to model the past. That is, the antitraditionist Karaites developed their own historicized expression of tradition. One is not astonished at this development if one understands that Karaite halakhah is not purely scripturalist, and that, furthermore, the engagement with rabbinic halakhah and rabbinic literature provided fertile ground upon which to nurture Karaite historical expression. In the end, Karaite historical pronouncements offered variations and alternative readings to what were understood as historical materials derived from the Mishnah, Talmud, and other works of the rabbinic canon, as if to say that the rabbis simply did not understand their own texts. The new readings justified the status of the Karaites and their imagined archaic "proto-Karaitic" ancestors in relationship to God's revelation and Jewish law.

The evolution of Karaite halakhah and Karaite antirabbinic polemic depends upon the very existence of rabbinic law and literature, indicating a sectarian model for understanding the Karaites. Even as the rabbis extracted scattered data from their literary canon to create a vague historical vision, so the Karaites began to select and utilize data that could be used to describe the past from rabbinic literature. Especially after the center of Karaite intellectual activity shifted to Byzantium in the eleventh century, a growing body of materials were regarded by Karaites as having some historical validity. Eventually, the Karaites developed their own chain of tradition, which logically required questions of historical relationship and of continuity embedded in the chain to be answered. Just as the Yemenite Jews needed to answer questions of continuity that resulted from their claim to origins in the time of the First Temple, so the Karaites needed to address questions that arose as a result of their specific historical claims. If Simeon ben Shetah is elevated as the proto-Rabbanite and archenemy, then, one might ask, who was the proto-Karaite of the period? If, in answering that question, one grasps Judah ben Tabbai as the ancient father of the Karaites, then questions of continuity arise. Does Judah transmit his understanding of Judaism to others? Can such a transmission be posited as a legitimate Karaite activity? Who are the intermediate figures in such a transmission? Thus, rabbinic data were reinterpreted in answer to these questions to become Karaite history. These data existed as a kind of metatext long before they were compiled and collated into a literary form. This metatext provided the arguments for intra-Jewish polemics, for the historicization of halakhic decisions, and simply to satisfy historical curiosity.

This historicizing process culminated in the eighteenth century among a few Karaite scholars of Poland-Lithuania, who are considered in chapter 6. Their efforts begin to approach some critical methods of modern historiography. Through examination and careful citation of texts, both Rabbanite and

Karaite, they sought to harmonize inconsistencies and offer a historical presentation that appeared to be based on logical historical reasoning and prudent archival methodology. Nonetheless, their conclusions were simply more fully articulated literary expositions of the Karaite historical metatext; that is, sacred history. Karaism was postulated *as* Judaism, while a historical continuity was offered that satisfied the curious, especially among Protestant scholars of the seventeenth and eighteenth centuries.

This study is intrinsically synoptic in character. Each of the chapters seeks to present a survey of the important periods of Karaite history. Some parts of these chapters offer close readings of Karaite texts, especially where these have been unappreciated or unknown by scholars. As mentioned above, the textual sources are fragmentary and sometimes obscure, so other sections of the book cover broader ground and are more tentative and speculative regarding Karaite history and literature. In the final analysis, this study presents for the first time in more than eighty years an examination of the evolution and changing historical context of Karaite historical expression. Samuel Poznanski, acknowledged master of geonica and Karaitica, wrote a survey of Karaite historical writing in the early part of the century in his introduction to Mordecai Sultanski's *Zekher Ṣaddikim.*[31] This study was adequate for its time and for the available sources, but today new sources have become available and, more significantly, new questions can be asked of the material, as indicated above.

Significant portions of this work represent a discussion with Zvi Ankori's *Karaites in Byzantium: The Formative Years, 970–1100.*[32] Ankori's magnum opus is as much an encyclopedia of medieval Karaitica as it is a synthesized analysis and presentation of Karaite history in the Byzantine Empire. Echoing the very encyclopedism that characterizes the Byzantine Christian and Karaite subjects of his book, Ankori has bequeathed to scholars a vast compilation of Karaite and rabbinic primary texts (many as yet unpublished) as well as references to scholarly secondary literature, most of which are found in the book's extensive footnotes.[33] Correspondingly, one will find reference to Ankori often in this book's endnotes. Above and beyond Ankori as a repository of historical data and source information, a portion of my writing is framed in conversation with Ankori's arguments and ideas, variously accepting, rejecting, or qualifying such propositions as Palestino-centrism, the "Golden Age"

31. Samuel Poznanski, ed., *Zecher Caddikim: Kronika Historyczna Karaity Mordechaja Sultanskiego.*

32. Ankori, *Karaites in Byzantium.*

33. The book's index is so deeply constructed that it is unwieldy and often not useful. In this sense, one needs to work through *Karaites in Byzantium* as one would work through a premodern text that lacks a proper table of contents and index. In spite of this and other criticisms one can direct against this book, it remains one of the most significant contributions to Karaite studies.

of Karaism in Palestine, the Karaite interlinear reading of rabbinic literature, the "tenth-century revision" of Karaism, and the relationship of Karaism and Mishawism in the Byzantine Empire.

In the early twenty-first century, we now understand Karaism in different ways than in previous decades, asking more sophisticated questions when examining Karaite history and literature. The search for historical facts and the assumed reality that accompanied them (a kind of positivist notion of history) is important, but limited, if not unsatisfying. This study supplements old models of historiography to study the Karaites by using literary and cultural approaches in combination with historical method to model a Judaism and its Jews within greater Jewish and non-Jewish societies. Such modeling may be in part speculative due to the thinness of historical evidence. Nonetheless, to ignore a historical period or phenomenon because evidence is lacking betrays the intellectual enterprise of the historian, which bears an obligation to construct the past. Furthermore, literary and other nonhistorical methodologies (such as sociology), which I use on occasion, may not only enhance historical speculation, but also provide avenues for thoughtful analysis. In the end, I hope to suggest compelling models that can lead to further scholarly inquiry.

In regard to sources, I have utilized manuscripts that were unknown or unavailable to Poznanski. Where he cited the sixteenth-century Moses Bashyachi by way of the eighteenth-century Mordecai ben Nisan, I have used a manuscript of the work itself.[34] The oft-quoted *ʿAsarah Maʾamarot* of Caleb Afendopolo has been utilized by earlier scholars from extracts found in other works. Again, I have used a manuscript of the original work.[35] By using these and other primary sources, this study brings scholarly attention to otherwise obscure and unknown materials. In a small way, this study heeds the "Plea for the Publication of Texts and Translations" of Daniel Frank,[36] by producing, for the first time, an English translation of the Karaite chain of tradition from Moses Bashyachi's *Matteh ʾElohim*.[37] Similarly, a reading of ancient history as represented by the eighteenth-century Simhah Isaac Lutzki is based upon his major work, *Meʾirat ʿEnayim*, which is all but unknown to scholars.[38]

34. See chapter 5, below. Moses ben Elijah Bashyachi's *Matteh ʾElohim* has recently been edited by Yosef ben ʿOvadyah Algamil and published under the auspices of the Karaite community of Israel (Ramlah, Israel: Tiferet Yosef, 5761 [2000 or 2001]).

35. See chapter 5, below. Caleb ben Elijah Afendopolo's *Sefer ʿAsarah Maʾamarot* has recently been published under the auspices of the Karaite community of Israel (Ramlah, Israel: Mekhon Tiferet Yosef le-Ḥeker ha-Yahadut ha-Karait, 5760 [1999]).

36. Daniel Frank, "The Study of Medieval Karaism, 1959–1989: A Bibliographical Essay."

37. See chapter 5, below.

38. See chapter 6, below.

I decided that the terminus ante quem for this examination would lie with Simhah Isaac Lutzki, one of whose historical works is dated 1757. His historical writing represents both the ultimate elaboration of the engagement with rabbinic literature and the most complete and thoughtful exposition of the Karaite historical metatext. It is important to note that a few short decades later saw the introduction of a new Karaite approach to history. At that time, some eastern European Karaites would adopt an entirely new, nonbiblical historical paradigm to distance themselves from rabbinic Jews and to claim antique origins for their community in Russia. This nineteenth-century Russian Karaite approach to history does not fall under the purview of this book.

Jewish History beyond Sect

Descriptions of Karaism are often defective because observers maintain simple notions of definition that ultimately become reductionist. When one or two primary elements of Karaism are used to define the whole, then the great variety found in Karaite practice, belief, and historical experience cannot be incorporated into the description. For example, the scripturalism of early Karaites is often taken by later interpreters to be fundamental to Karaism as a whole. In fact, the Karaites went beyond literalist scripturalism to develop a wide-ranging legal system that echoes the talmudism of their opponents. The banner of scripturalism that led the charge of dissidence against the rabbis during the early Islamic period was of limited use later in formulating a consistent systematic law to govern complex communities. What we can say is that the relationship between halakhah and Scripture works differently in rabbinic and Karaite Judaism. In another example, the messianic intensity of early Karaism in Palestine is virtually absent from the Karaism of seventeenth- and eighteenth-century Lithuania and Poland. Are the Karaites to be described as focused on the Holy Land with the immediacy of active messianic belief, or are they diasporic and messianically quietistic? The answer for both parts of the question is yes, but is only correct for some periods, not for others.

This error of perspective has been identified by Efraim Shmueli as one of three fallacies found in the study of Jewish history. He describes this fallacy as *pars pro toto,* whereby the observer is guilty of "taking one set of ideas from a significant period, and making it representative of *all* Jewish cultures."[39]

More naive approaches to Karaism are taken when the action of any single Karaite is used to describe Karaism as a whole. One might think that a movement that exhibited a wide range of legal and doctrinal variety might not be best understood by using such undisciplined consideration. By such a measure, any nonrabbinic practice or belief could be called Karaite. In fact, there were other nonrabbinic Judaisms in the medieval and early modern periods with which the Karaites skirmished and against which they formed

39. *Seven Jewish Cultures: A Reinterpretation of Jewish History and Thought,* 2.

their identity. Shmueli calls this "radical relativism," characterized by a "lack of consistency, a diversity of sources incapable of forming a unity."[40] Jacob Neusner names this problem as "nominalism." In the larger context of study of Judaism, the nominalist would say, "Judaism is the sum of the attitudes and beliefs of all the members of an ethnic group; each member of the group serves equally well to define Judaism." Neusner goes on to say, "The result is that the questions of the social order—for example, which particular group or social entity of persons held this view—are dismissed."[41] That is, the societal context that is necessary for interpretive results is absent, and Karaism might be presented as an entity that lived in a vacuum, lacking a set of parameters with which to name it and look for its boundaries.

Neusner identifies another flawed approach to Jewish history, which he calls "harmonistic." He says that "all Jewish data—writings and other records—together tells us about a single Judaism, which is to be defined by appeal to the lowest common denominator among all the data."[42] In the context of Karaite studies, only a portion of belief and practice gleaned from the wide variety of Karaism might be seen to indicate shared perspectives or some kind of unity. This approach overlooks that the aforementioned doctrinal and practical variety was encompassed in self-conscious ways by Karaites. It virtually negates development and sometimes dramatic change that mark the history of Karaism. Harmonism obstructs useful historical inquiry.

Both Shmueli and Neusner identify a problem in studying religion that, in fact, informs much of the worldview of the rabbinic and Karaite writers considered in this book. It is described by Shmueli as viewing "the totality of tradition as transhistorical, i.e., that each idea in Judaism is as valuable as any other."[43] Named by Neusner as "theological," it "ignores all questions of context and social relevance. Its 'Judaism' came into existence for reasons we cannot say, addressed no issues faced by ordinary people, and constituted a set of disembodied, socially irrelevant ideas that lack history and consequence."[44] This approach is founded on religious predicates and is without accident. It speaks to believers from inside a world view of belief.

Although the purely theological perspective is of little use for an inquiry into Judaism and Karaism in terms of the academic study of religion, it frames much of the literature that the Karaites and their premodern describers wrote—the primary sources for a great deal of this book. The necessary challenge is to penetrate this worldview in order to provide an interpretive framework by which to understand the context of Karaite notions of the past in relationship to Karaite doctrine, practice, and the relationship of Karaite ideas

40. Ibid.
41. *Rabbinic Judaism: Structure and System,* 1.
42. Ibid.
43. Shmueli, *Seven Jewish Cultures,* 2.
44. Neusner, *Rabbinic Judaism,* 2.

to the world in which Karaites lived—relations with Rabbanite Jews, Muslims, and, later, Christians.

Some Notes on Terminology and Transliteration

I have chosen to use *halakhah* to refer to Karaite law, although one could argue that the term is technically specific to rabbinic Judaism. However, Karaite scholars followed strategies similar to those of the rabbis in seeking to develop a legal system that was both coherent, systematic, and of practical application, while at the same time, basing their decisions on the law of the Torah. By using *halakhah* more as a generic term to describe legal exegesis of Scripture, one can then speak of the halakhah of the Samaritans or of the Dead Sea Scrolls. It is hoped that this convenience will not obfuscate the real differences that distinguish these religio-legal systems from one another in terms of methods, conclusions, and sociohistorical context.

Some Hebrew terms and names have been transliterated with a limited use of diacritical marks. Those who know Hebrew will have no problem following the transcriptions. For Arabic, the standard diacriticals have been used following the system of the *Encyclopaedia of Islam* (new edition), except the *ḳ* has been replaced by *q*.

Names derived from Hebrew and Arabic have been anglicized when they are commonly known or found in scripture. Otherwise I have transliterated using diacritical marks.

Part One

~ 1

The Islamic Context of Jewish History, Seventh through Eleventh Centuries

Research and scholarship in recent years has yielded new approaches in the fields of Jewish and Islamic history, as in medieval studies in general. This chapter develops significant portions of a blueprint for understanding Jewish history in the Islamic world of the eighth through the eleventh centuries. With this blueprint as a background, a far-reaching model for understanding the birth and early growth of Karaism is suggested, and this is supported both by widely accepted scholarship in Karaite studies and by my own comparative approach to Jewish history, which, for the seventh through eleventh centuries, takes into account the Islamic host environment. Also, rabbinic Jewish constructions of the past will be interrogated, in particular the idea of the *shalshelet ha-kabbalah,* or chain of tradition. This historicization of tradition and use of the past is axiomatic to medieval rabbinic claims to the authenticity of the Oral Law. With these wide considerations in mind, Karaite Judaism is considered in light of its rejectionist stance vis-à-vis rabbinic tradition and of the Islamic environment in which it developed. The Karaites made rabbinic concepts of tradition a primary concern in their polemic against the rabbis and the construction of their own, nonrabbinic Judaism. And although the idea of tradition and its historicized foundation, the chain of tradition, were antithetical to the fundamentals of Karaite Judaism, Karaites found themselves moving toward accommodation to the idea by dint of halakhic necessity and the social and historical realities of the era.

The transformation of the rabbis of the Mishnah and Talmud into a social class with moral and legal authority began long before the Islamic period. From the third through fifth centuries, the leadership of many Jewish communities in both Roman Palestine and Persian Mesopotamia was assumed by the rabbis. At the grassroots level, rabbis might act as small local administrators, judges, and holy men, and at the regional and transregional level, leadership and authority were institutionalized by the academies and the exilarchate (and the patriarchate in Palestine until its demise in 429).[1] The extent to which this social transformation and its accompanying institutionalization resulted in wide political hegemony over the Jews of the Mediterranean and the Middle East is assumed in Jewish sources of Late Antiquity and is generally accepted by many modern Jewish studies scholars. Such a broad historical assumption needs to be questioned due to lack of extensive corroborative evidentiary support. Reevaluation of this historical premise is central to the new presentation of Jewish history in the early Islamic period presented in this volume.

The advent of Muslim rule follows closely upon the redaction of the Babylonian Talmud, marking a fullness in the development of late antique rabbinic literature and culture, but also presenting new challenges and arenas for action. The implications of this contemporaneity are important for Jewish legal and social history. Concurrently, rabbinic leadership and institutions began to be transformed gradually as the impact of Muslim rule was felt, beginning after the fifth decade of the seventh century. These transformations are background to the growth of a serious alternative and challenge to rabbinic Judaism in the Middle Ages.

Karaism is born and takes form in the Islamic world. The period selected, from the advent of Islam in the seventh century until the Crusader conquest of Palestine in 1099, constitutes for Karaism its formation and florescence. The formative is located in two centuries of unconnected or loosely connected proto-Karaitic phenomena that came together in the late ninth century to become a more unified movement. In the tenth and early eleventh centuries, Jerusalem became a center for Karaism and Karaite literary production, inaugurating what has been called a "golden age" of Karaism, characterized by intellectual achievement and challenge to rabbinic dominance. The Crusader conquest, following shortly on the heels of the Turkoman conquest of 1071–73, marks the end of a process of decline that had begun earlier in the century. The stories of Crusaders burning the Jews alive in their synagogues, while not able to be corroborated, certainly stand as testimony to the wholesale massacre and taking of captives that marked the end of a vibrant Jewish community in Jerusalem, composed of both Rabbanites and Karaites. For Karaism, the end of this period is signaled by a note found in a Torah codex in the possession of the Karaite synagogue in Cairo. It states that it "was brought over from the ransom [books] of the spoils of the Holy City of Jerusalem to the

1. On Jewish institutions and history in the rabbinic period, see Gedaliah Alon, *The Jews in their Land in the Talmudic Age (70–640* c.e.), which is an edited translation of *Toldot ha-Yehudim be-ereṣ Yisrael bi-tekufat ha-Mishnah veha-Talmud* (Jerusalem, 1980 and 1984); M. Avi-Yonah, *The Jews of Palestine: A Political History from the Bar Kokhba War to the Arab Conquest*; and Jacob Neusner, *A History of the Jews of Babylonia*, 5 vols. See also appropriate sections in George Foot Moore, *Judaism in the First Centuries of the Christian Era: The Age of the Tannaim;* and Ephraim E. Urbach, *The Sages: Their Concepts and Beliefs.*

community of Egypt, to the synagogue of the Jerusalemites."[2] Surely, this book was looted and then ransomed by the Crusaders.

The historical conditions described in this chapter set the stage for the Karaite relationship to Rabbanism and also acted as powerful influences on Karaite thought, literary expression, and social organization. These conditions include the broad and deep historical background established by the advent and growth of Islam and Islamic civilization against which Judaism and Jewish life is transformed and against which Karaism emerges. Major aspects of these historical conditions are summarized in sections of this chapter below.

Lack of Documentary Sources

The early Islamic centuries (7th–10th C.E.) have been described as constituting a "dark age" of sources for Jewish history. Even in terms of Islamic history, it is not until the emergence of a scribal and jurisprudential class in the late eighth and the ninth centuries that extensive and useful literary sources are available in Arabic.[3] In terms of Jewish history, some few halakhic and liturgical works are known before the tenth century, but the appearance of important historical testimony is found in documents from the Cairo Genizah, beginning sparsely in the late ninth century and offering more substantive information in the tenth century. The tenth century also marks the florescence of new literary production by Jewish intellectuals, including Saadia Gaon (882–942).[4] Other tenth-century Jewish writers of prominence in the Islamic world include Isaac ben Solomon, Sherira Gaon, and Jacob ben Nissim Ibn Shahin, as well as the first Hebrew poets of Spain and the Masoretes of the Levant. Jewish literary output explodes in the eleventh century, with more important authors than can be noted here. The eleventh century also offers a rich variety of sources for historical analysis from the documentation in the Cairo Genizah, which portrays a vibrant Jewish mercantile class in the Mediterranean and the Middle East.

Whether from the perspective of analyzing the Jewish or Muslim past, history in the early Islamic centuries is necessarily incomplete and speculative.[5] This period has been portrayed by a scholar of Muslim religious history

2. P. E. Kahle, *The Cairo Genizah*, ii, 109, cited in Joshua Prawer, *The History of the Jews in the Latin Kingdom of Jerusalem*, 30.

3. See R. Stephen Humphreys, *Islamic History: A Framework for Inquiry*, 25–65 ("Analysis of Sources"); and Hodgson, *Venture of Islam*, esp. 1:315–58.

4. See Moshe Zucker, *Rab Saadya Gaon's Translation of the Torah: Exegesis, Halakha, and Polemics in R. Saadya's Translation of the Pentateuch;* and Rina Drory, *The Emergence of Jewish-Arabic Literary Contacts at the Beginning of the Tenth Century*, summarized in English in Drory's *Models and Contacts: Arabic Literature and Its Impact on Medieval Jewish Culture.*

5. On Jewish history in the early Islamic period, see Norman A. Stillman, *The Jews of Arab Lands: A History and Source Book*, esp. 22–39; Moshe Gil, *A History of Palestine, 634–1099*, esp. 490–776, trans. from idem, *The Land of Israel in the Early*

as a "black box." "We know the cultural, religious and intellectual currents that 'go into' the box in the beginning of this period. And, we know the threads that 'come out,' but we do not understand what went on 'inside' this box."[6] Consequently, models for the history of the first three centuries of the Islamic era are contingent and speculative. It is appropriate that this contingency should make the careful observer question old assumptions that come from a historical model based upon traditional rabbinic points of view. The subject of early Karaism, theologically and halakhically subversive in its day, offers alternate interpretive models that subvert inherited and unquestioned historical discourses on this period.

Unification of the Jewish World

After the Arab-Muslim conquests of the mid-seventh and eighth centuries, the vast majority of world Jewry came under Muslim rule.[7] Jewish communities that had been isolated by political, geographical, and cultural factors were now able to have increased contact with each other. Before the Arab conquests, the Jewish communities of Byzantine Egypt and the Levant, including Palestine, conceivably would have been eradicated through the policies of the state and the Orthodox Church.[8] Not only were they "saved," but they were brought into contact with their Babylonian brethren and coreligionists. In addition to any mutual integration experienced by Jewish communities formerly under Byzantine and Persian rule, other Jewish communities that had previously existed on the margins of the empires in isolation from mainstream developments were now brought into contact with the Jewish world of the exilarchate, the academies, and the attendant rabbinic leadership. One of the important implications of such a sociogeographical phenomenon for this study is that traditions that had been otherwise forgotten or repudiated

Muslim Era (634–1099); and idem, *In the Kingdom of Ishmael in the Era of the Geonim,* 4 vols. See also Jacob Mann, "The Responsa of the Babylonian Geonim as a Source for Jewish History"; sections in Simhah Assaf, *Be-'Ohale Ya'akov;* and idem, *Tekufat ha-Ge'onim ve-Sifrutah;* and S. D. Goitein, "Jewish Society and Institutions under Islam."

6. Arthur Buehler, 1995, meeting of the Carolina Seminar for Comparative Islamic Studies, University of North Carolina, Chapel Hill.

7. It was stated by Zvi Ankori in lectures at the University of California, Berkeley, in 1982 that 80 to 90 percent of the world Jewish population came under Muslim rule in the seventh and eighth centuries. This is generally accepted among historians of the Jews. The figure of 90 percent is repeated by Robert Brody in *The Geonim of Babylonia and the Shaping of Medieval Jewish Culture,* xx, and in Menahem Ben-Sasson, "Varieties of Inter-Communal Relations in the Geonic Period."

8. See appropriate sections in Alon and Avi-Yonah cited above in note 1. See also James Parkes, *The Conflict of the Church and Synagogue,* esp. 225–70.

by the rabbis but were preserved in isolated hinterlands were reintroduced into the Jewish milieu of the new, Islamic-dominated society.[9] The resulting cultural stew posed serious challenges for the rabbis, who sought to consolidate their own social and religious system. This phenomenon will help to explain environmental and halakhic factors that influenced Jewish heterodoxy and the beginnings of Karaism in the eighth and ninth centuries.

At the same time, the Islamic state not only united the Jews but eventually recognized them as a tolerated minority. For Jews, Christians, and other minorities, treaty-like conditions defined an exchange of special taxes and some social limitations for *dhimmah*, a juridical state that for Jews defined Judaism as a *religio licita* and gave them the right to self-governance.[10] This benefited Jews not only in terms of religious and social toleration but also of internal organization, since later the only legal corporate entities recognized by Muslim law would be religious communities. *Dhimmah* created a strong external encouragement for the Jewish community to organize systematic and competent leadership in order to act effectively under the terms of this corporate recognition offered by Islam. In terms of taxation and other bureaucratic and governmental considerations, a consolidation of leadership among the empire's Jewish communities was in the interest of the caliphate. Thus, it was in the interest of the rulers and the ruled to have an organized institutional structure for Jewish governance.

Furthermore, in the first centuries of the caliphate, the exilarch was recognized by the caliphal court as a prince of the Jews. For the Arabs, whose origins were geographically and historically marginal to the great societies that they conquered, and even admired, the Davidic exilarch represented charisma emanating from a generally acknowledged antiquity that was even mentioned, and thereby sanctified, in the Qurʾān.[11]

Finally, it is to be noted that scholars have identified a relative openness and, in medieval terms, tolerance on the part of medieval Middle Eastern Islamic societies in their general relations toward non-Muslims. S. D. Goitein went so far as to identify a "creative symbiosis" experienced by Jews and

9. For a hypothesis on the survival of "Enochian Judaism" in Late Antiquity, see Yoram Erder, "When Did the Karaites First Encounter Apocryphal Literature Akin to the Dead Sea Scrolls?" Cf. idem, "The Karaites' Sadducee Dilemma"; and "The Origin of the Name Idris in the Qur'an: A Study of the Influence of Qumran Literature on Early Islam."

10. On *dhimmah,* the "protected" status of Jews and Christians under Islam, see Hodgson, *Venture of Islam,* 1:242–43; Bat Ye'or, *The Dhimmi: Jews and Christians under Islam;* and Youssef Courbage and Philippe Fargues, *Christians and Jews under Islam.* On the financial aspects of *dhimmah,* see A. Ben Shemesh, *Taxation in Islam,* 2 vols., passim.

11. Which is not to say that the treatment of Jews in the Qur'an is positive. See Moshe Gil, "The Exilarchate."

Muslims in most Islamic societies in the Middle Ages. He characterized this symbiosis by postulating mutual influence of Judaism and Islam in historical and religious development.[12] This widely accepted model is flawed as a broad generalization and is increasingly being criticized by historians.[13] Nonetheless, its continued usage by modern scholars points to important features of the Jewish experience under Islam in this period.

In general, when *dhimmah* developed to be a recognized component of the Muslim social constitution, Jews and Christians (and Zoroastrians in the earliest centuries) experienced a great degree of noninterference on the part of Muslim authorities in regard to religious observance and communal autonomy. This meant for Jews that liturgy and law could develop based on inter-Jewish concerns, while communal organization and leadership were often free of direct outside intervention. Boundaries between Judaism and Islam seem to be clearly demarcated when considered in this manner. On the other hand, the openness of Muslim societies often blurred communal boundaries as Jews, Muslims, and Christians simultaneously experienced the linguistic transformation of Arabicization and the cultural transformation of Islamization. Arabicization allowed modes of communication that had been particularist-communal and linked to now-displaced political worlds to be replaced by a cosmopolitan koine that facilitated intercommunal discourse and ultimately provided the foundations for mutual interaction among Jews, Muslims, and Christians in such arenas as philosophy, science, medicine, and even law. It also paralleled and supported the Arabization of social mores, such as cuisine, dress, and notions of hospitality and personal honor. At the same time that the Muslim social constitution provided a great degree of communal and intellectual autonomy for Jews, it also created openings for *dhimmīs* to participate in society at large. Jews are found at one time or another in various Muslim societies as merchants, artisans, and princely officials, as well as members of the urban proletariat and villagers. In most of these societies, the marketplace and the city were open to Jews.

However, since this koine was also a scriptural language to Muslims, it also implied a particular religious discourse whose features were transmitted to North African and Middle Eastern populations along with social and intellectual markers. More on this below.

12. See S. D. Goitein, *Jews and Arabs: Their Contacts through the Ages,* passim. The concept of Jewish-Muslim symbiosis is interrogated by Steven M. Wasserstrom in *Between Muslim and Jew: The Problem of Symbiosis under Early Islam;* see esp. his introduction, 3–14.

13. See Mark R. Cohen, *Under Crescent and Cross: The Jews in the Middle Ages.* Medieval Jewish-Arab and Jewish-Muslim symbiosis and notions of medieval Islamicate tolerance are ideas often used to support modern political and cultural agendas, including those of Sephardic Jews and of Palestinian and other Arab nationalists.

Increased Dominance of the Talmudic System and Rabbinic Leadership

It can be postulated that rabbinic leadership, under its newly canonized "constitution," the Talmud, was able to capitalize on the new geographic unity.[14] With political recognition from the caliphate, the exilarch and rabbinate were able to increase the proliferation of talmudic teaching, reinvigorating the trend that had developed earlier under the Romans and Persians. If successful, this meant that the Talmud would be accepted as the governing "constitution" of local communities, and the rabbis would become the only authorized interpreters of this text. It is logical that the rabbis would seek to capitalize on the new environment afforded by Muslim rule in order both to spread rabbinic Judaism and to attract financial support that was traditional to the relationship of outlying communities with the rabbinic centers. Such a rabbinic movement would seek to create political hegemony, monetary supply, theological orthodoxy, and legal conformity. Similarly, Muslims sought alternatives to the imperial, absolutist Islam that was established as much by military force as by pious means in the first two centuries A.H. Muslim pietists and others began to imagine a Muslim society that would be marked by theological consistency and legal conformity to be governed by religious, nonimperial elites. The emergence of scholarly, pietistic, and mystical cadres led to conflicts marked by tension between universal legitimacy and local realities.

On the other hand, local communities were the primary building blocks of Middle Eastern Jewish societies. There would always be tension between the supercommunal organizations (the exilarchate and academies) and local communities and their leadership.[15] In some cases, resistance and opposition would naturally develop. At the local level, this social movement might conflict with long-established regional customs to create friction. Some of the many forms of Jewish heterodoxy attested to in the eighth and ninth centuries, including the beginnings of Karaism, likely emerged from the many forms of local and regional resistance against the social, political, and legal dimensions of the reinvigorated rabbinic movement. In addition, sincere intellectual disagreement with aspects of rabbinic interpretation and theology would also generate heterodoxy. The Islamic environment provided fertile Jewish ground for the propagation of "talmudism," but also for the germination of other varieties of Judaism as well.

14. On rabbinic notions of the end of *hora'ah* (authoritative instruction associated with the Amoraim) and geonic self-consciousness, see Brody, *Geonim of Babylonia,* 4–11.

15. See Menahem Ben-Sasson, "Varieties of Inter-Communal Relations in the Geonic Period." Ben-Sasson limits his discussion to Rabbanite communities, assuming a rigidity for inner-Judaic confessional boundaries, thereby missing the complete Jewish historical context.

Islam did not emerge fully developed in the seventh century but required perhaps three hundred years to become fully elaborated and to have worked out solutions to problems of community, theology, and law. Even as the Muslims worked out a theological rationalization for their society and government, so the rabbis sought to establish their own "imperial system" as a subculture within the larger Middle Eastern society. It is noteworthy that the growth and eventual fragmentation of Islamic law in concert with a similar fate suffered by the Islamic state is mirrored by efforts on the part of the rabbis to fix the Talmud as the "constitution" of Jewish society, followed by a dissolution of central authority and the proliferation of regional versions of Rabbanism. In the first centuries A.H., the rabbis and the academies tolerated a good deal of variety in Jewish law, yet opposed many centrifugal forces.[16] At the same time, Islam was "throwing off heavier elements" from the theological and legal center. In both cases, conflict was inevitable.[17]

Thus, it is seen through time that what begins in Late Antiquity as a less-than-completely-dominant rabbinic Jewish entity among many other Judaisms becomes, by the central Middle Ages, a Rabbanism that was mostly dominant surrounded by a small constellation of sectarian orbits.

The Legal Context: Increased Individuality in the Expression of the Law

Since the only permitted form of corporate organization in Islam is based on religion, Jews and Christians, among others, found themselves granted a great degree of autonomy in organizing and governing their own communities. For Judaism, a religion of law and orthoprax expectation, this social condition created an environment for judicial activism that eventually led to the dominance of rabbinic halakhah. It should be emphasized that the final Rabbanization of Judaism on a world-historical plane occurred in the Islamic Middle Ages. In Late Antiquity, the rabbis were often transformed into local administrators and judges by dint of halakhic inclination and the pleasure of ruling regimes. In the first Islamic centuries, the union of diverse Jewish communities within a large empire often led the rabbinic leadership of remote areas to

16. See Gideon Libson, "Halakhah and Reality in the Gaonic Period: Taqqanah, Minhag, Tradition, and Consensus: Some Observations"; and idem, "Halakhah and Law in the Period of the Geonim."

17. See Garth Fowden, *Empire to Commonwealth: Consequences of Monotheism in Late Antiquity.* Fowden submits an intriguing treatment of Late Antiquity and the ideologies of empire and religion found in the Roman Catholic West, Orthodox Byzantium, and the Islamic world. The place of Judaism in these societies and its internal development are barely touched upon, but the broad categories that Fowden establishes for historical inquiry are highly suggestive for thinking about Jewish history. Clearly, the transformation of empires into commonwealths is mirrored in parallel developments in the Jewish subculture. Fowden's thesis presents serious challenges to historians of medieval Jewry, suggesting fruitful avenues for future inquiry.

pragmatic decision making enacted without recourse to written texts or the orthodox guidance of the academies. They had quasi-official responsibilities to the Islamic government in the form of census taking and tax collection, as well as local intercommunal relations. What could have been an otherwise academic or parochially confessional profession was fully embedded within the pragmatic business of day-to-day life. The leadership and individual interpretation of an isolated rabbi could become locally the rule for understanding and observing the norms and boundaries of Jewish society and religion. The world of the rabbis had enlarged, yet the exigencies of communication and transportation in this premodern world often left the individual rabbi to his own means in solving halakhic and societal problems.[18] In many areas, the importance of *individual* decision making without the help of official written texts accompanied the centralization of Islamicate rabbinic Judaism.

The situation among the Jews reflects the judicial conditions of the early Islamic milieu. Islam inherited the imperial mantle in the Middle East without having yet developed a fully elaborated legal system. Judges, assigned to posts by the government, were required to decide on cases based upon their own "opinion" *(ra'y)*. Later, juridical opinion was transformed through systematic methodologies into a coherent and useful legal system.[19] The evolution of rabbinic leadership and posttalmudic law parallels similar trends in the evolution in Islam of the religious leadership of the *ʿulamāʾ* and the systematization of law. Even as the exilarchate lost prestige and power, to be replaced by the academies, so the caliphate declined and religious leadership devolved to the newly emerging clergy.

Proclaiming the talmudic text and its interpretation, the overarching structures of the exilarchate and the academies began to bind together Jews located in disparate and far-flung locales. The magnification and success of the Talmud was the magnification and success of the rabbis. However, the Talmud would not be expanded upon at this time in the same way as the Mishnah had been by the Talmud. The canonization of the Talmud precluded continuation of the late antique literary model, which is characterized by collective authorship with an emphasis on halakhah and midrash. By the Islamic period, the emphasis on halakhah, midrash, and liturgy overshadowed direct concern with the biblical text, a fact that was often noted by Karaites when criticizing rabbinic Judaism.[20]

18. Although describing a different period and only a portion of the Middle East, see Fernand Braudel, *The Mediterranean and the Mediterranean World in the Age of Philip II* for carefully considered remarks on premodern communications and transportation, 276–312, and esp. 355–94 ("Distance: The First Enemy"). Cf. Harold A. Innis, *Empire and Communications.*

19. For remarks on this, see N. J. Coulson, *A History of Islamic Law,* 29–30, and 39–40; and Joseph Schacht, *An Introduction to Muslim Law,* 23–27.

20. On this change in emphasis, see Drory, *Models and Contacts,* 133.

Case law and the individualistic character of halakhic decision making characterize halakhic exposition in the geonic period. This is the halakhah of responsa, of the question addressed to an individual and his academy. Increase in the importance of the individual in rabbinic halakhah is reflected in a move toward case law, succeeding and superseding the talmudic process, whereby the "discussions" of authorities over decades and centuries had been canonized into authoritative texts. This halakhah is extracanonical and resists codification, finding its literary form in the *she'elot* and *teshuvot* of the rabbis. It is truly incremental and agglutinative and depends more than earlier halakhah upon case precedent.[21] Even within the rabbinic milieu, the responsa of the geonim—as heads of the academies, authoritative interpreters of the Law—exhibit a kind of individualism and lack of coherence not seen before or after in rabbinic literature.[22]

One result of these developments mirrors legal development in Islam: that individual writers now penned their own works.[23] Oppositely, the centrifugal nature of these conditions was balanced by a centripetal response. The accumulation of legal opinions begged for a higher level of systematization, which came to be expressed, like in Islam, in works of methodology and, eventually, codification.

THE LONG-TERM CHALLENGE OF ISLAMIZATION

Scholars of medieval Jewish history under Islam have given little attention to the problem of conversion, part of the larger processes of Islamization in the Middle East, North Africa, and Spain.[24] Since Muslim law forbids conversion to any religion other than Islam, documented instances of conversion to Judaism are rare. On the other hand, we know a bit more about the conversion of Jews to Islam. Although I am interested in this topic in the specific context of its impact on those who remained as Jews, conversion must be seen as part of larger processes of Islamization.

21. See Libson, "Halakhah and Law in the Period of the Geonim."

22. On geonic roles, see Brody, *Geonim of Babylonia*, 54–66. On variety in geonic halakhah, see Libson, "Halakhah and Reality in the Gaonic Period."

23. Anan ben David, the putative "founder" of Karaism, was the first to write under his own name, while Saadia was the first Rabbanite. See Drory, *Models and Contacts*, 126–77.

24. On the other hand, see S. D. Goitein, *A Mediterranean Society: The Jewish Communities of the Arab World as Portrayed in the Documents of the Cairo Geniza*, s.v. "conversion," in the index, vol. 6, and see esp. vol. 2, 299–311. See also brief remarks by Mark R. Cohen in *Under Crescent and Cross*, 175–77; and Bernard Lewis, *The Jews of Islam*, 92–102. Under Islam, incidents of forced conversion were rare, notwithstanding the Almohad invasion of North Africa and Spain in 1146, which was characterized by mass forced conversion of Jews and Christians, and a few other examples that prove to be exceptions that prove the rule.

Conversion to Islam is supported by acculturation to Arab–Islamic social norms, including such factors as dress, music, cuisine, and language. For Jews of Muslim lands, the acquisition of Arabic as a language—first for immediate and pragmatic means of communication and later for intellectual discourse—proceeded fairly rapidly after the initial Muslim conquests of the seventh century. During the caliphates of ʿAbd al-Mālik (685–701) and his immediate successors, the language of chancery records was changed from Greek and Persian to Arabic and Islamic coinage was first minted using Arabic inscriptions. This represented the beginning of a replacement of bureaucratic personnel from *dhimmis* to Arabs.[25] Over the next century, Arabic also became the language of local elites, intellectuals, and merchants. The emergence of Arabic as a lingua franca suggests a model for acculturation that is nonconfessional, yet Arabic was also a holy language, and thus bore an implicit confessional valence. In contrast to an earlier proliferation of a lingua franca, the Greek language of Hellenism did not suggest Hellenistic religion in the way that Arabic suggested Islam. The process of acculturation to Arabic language and social mores facilitated other factors that led to conversion. I intend to investigate the process of conversion here only to the extent that it helps explicate the growth in this period of a variety of Jewish movements, including Karaism.[26] To begin with, the best approach is to ask how conversion to Islam might have had an impact on Jewish communities.

In the Middle East, conversion to Islam took place gradually. Richard Bulliet suggests it reached a critical mass of 50 percent of the population in many regions in the ninth and tenth centuries, 80 percent at the beginning of the eleventh, and approached 100 percent in many regions in the twelfth and thirteenth centuries.[27] If such a conversion curve is accurate, it presents a framework in which to consider the question. If Bulliet's figures are used to mark three periods for Jews in early Islamic history, then the earliest period probably produced little conversion, since, on the one hand, Jewish self-governance was consolidating and even spreading, and, on the other hand, Islam represented the faith of only a small military elite that ruled much larger indigenous populations. Early *dhimmah* was set up in such a way as to increase revenues from *dhimmī* taxes, establishing a situation that benefited the Muslim community financially and thereby discouraged conversion to Islam. In addition, since Islam was associated with the ethnic identity of Arab,

25. Philip K. Hitti speaks of "nationalizing the state" in *History of the Arabs,* 217f.

26. Cf. appropriate essays in Nehemia Levtzion, ed., *Conversion to Islam;* and Michael Gervers and Ramzi Jibran Bikhazi, eds., *Conversion and Continuity: Indigenous Christian Communities in Islamic Lands, Eighth to Eighteenth Centuries.*

27. See Richard W. Bulliet, *Conversion to Islam in the Medieval Period: An Essay in Quantitative History.*

conversion at this time required formal association with an Arab tribe and adoption of the subservient tribal status of *mawlā* (pl. *mawālī*).[28]

With the enfranchisement of the *mawālī* as Muslims after the ʿAbbasid revolution in 750, Islam began to be transformed from an Arab ethnic religion into a universal religion. Concurrently, society experienced the growth of Muslim institutions and the emergence of Muslim clergy, the *ʿulamā*ʾ, whose authority was based on correct legal and scriptural interpretation. This consolidation of leadership corresponded to a florescence of Muslim heterodoxy, but also led to a politics and theology of identity that "othered" non-Muslims and generated anti-*dhimmī* sentiment. At the same time, Muslim law had not become so elaborated that conversion entailed onerous demands on individuals. Muslims could claim that military success, political superiority, and wealth indicated God's favor for Islam and his disregard for Jews and Christians. By the second Muslim century, bureaucrats were required to convert to Islam to retain their positions,[29] thus completing the process mentioned above that began with Arabicization under the Umayyads. In addition, the financial burden of *dhimmī* taxes would have become increasingly difficult to bear, especially for farmers. The social and economic situation would become unbearable for many during the decline of political and social order in the caliphate after the reign of al-Mutawakkil, who was assassinated in 861.

These conditions explain in outline the conversion of mass numbers of Jews, Christians, and Zoroastrians and supply the corollaries for a sociological proposition put forth by Bulliet: Individuals do not willingly change religions unless their existing social status is either threatened or can be maintained or improved through conversion.[30] It is likely that in this period the majority of Jewish conversions to Islam occurred and the threat to Jewish communities became discernible.

Jewish conversions most likely occurred on an individual basis. The types of mass conversions associated with the dictum *cuius regio, eius religio* take place when the state and religion are closely interconnected. Thus, Zoroastrianism was replaced by Islam, since the Persian Sassanian state was interlocked with religion. Furthermore, Greek Christianity's association with the Byzantine Empire led to its decline in Islamic domains. This proposition would lead us to believe that Jews and monophysite Christians might be "immunized" against conversion, but this would be mistaken. The proposition only goes so far as to explain a relative vibrancy of these religions *among those who did not convert* since the movement toward Islam on the part of Jews and Christians followed a different path.

28. On *mawālī,* see Richard W. Bulliet, "Conversion to Islam and the Emergence of a Muslim Society in Iran."

29. Ibid.

30. Ibid., 33. For other views, see also William Sims Bainbridge, *The Sociology of Religious Movements,* 54–58; and Rodney Stark and William Sims Bainbridge, *A Theory of Religion.*

Useful generalizations for thinking about Jewish conversion to Islam in our period can be posited by comparing it to Jewish conversion to Christianity in Late Antiquity. Contrary to traditional Jewish and Christian notions of the past, it is likely that the Christian mission to the Jews in Late Antiquity was a success. In *The Rise of Christianity,* Rodney Stark demonstrates this using three propositions: The first is that "new religious movements mainly draw their converts from the ranks of the religiously inactive and discontented, and those affiliated with the most accommodated (worldly) religious communities."[31] Jewish response to the Islamization engulfing society and the loss of Jews to the newer religion would likely turn some Jews toward disenchantment with Jewish ideology and disillusion with Jewish authority. It is unlikely that Jews of early Islam experienced an acculturation to cosmopolitan, areligious societal norms as did many Hellenistic Jews. Consequently, the worldliness factor should be discounted. However, religious inactivity and discontent should be given serious consideration. Religious disenchantment and concomitant inactivity would be brought on by a seeming lack of meaning in Jewish ideology in the face of the superiority of Islam. This condition of malaise would be exacerbated when Muslim discourse and its exponents evolved to be able to provide coherent and systematic meaning to people. Discontent would be intensified by the inability of Judaism and Jewish leadership to protect social status and provide opportunity.

Stark's second proposition is that "people are more willing to adopt a new religion to the extent that it retains cultural continuity with conventional religion(s) with which they are already familiar."[32] Early Christianity was, in part, based directly on Judaism and its Scripture, while its Greek facets created a "double appeal" for Hellenistic Jews. Similarly, Islam began by understanding itself as one religion (albeit, the correct one) among others. Its monotheism and textuality are informed by a multitude of details and modes of thought that would be familiar to most Jews and Christians of Late Antiquity and the early Middle Ages. As Islam developed, it increasingly looked more like its predecessors in many ways—legal elaboration paralleled Jewish legalism, mysticism mirrored aspects of Christian spirituality, and theology reinscribed much territory previously considered by Christianity—looking more attractive by offering a sense of continuity. The former Jew would find Abraham centrally located in the Muslim narrative, while a Christian convert would not be required to relinquish Jesus.

Thirdly, Stark states that "social movements grow much faster when they spread through preexisting social networks."[33] Although a comparison of Christianization to Islamization partially breaks down over this point, it is instructive to keep the idea of social networks in mind. Unlike the Christianity

31. Rodney Stark, *The Rise of Christianity,* 19f.
32. Ibid., 55.
33. Ibid.

of Late Antiquity (perhaps more like some medieval European Christianities), Islam was established at the top, as the faith of a ruling elite in regions that it would eventually convert. The subtle and gross encouragements of the ruling class and the benefits it would eventually bestow upon new Muslims created a different dynamic to conversion when compared to Christianity before 312, a year marked monumentally by Constantines's Edict of Toleration but that subtly and more importantly locates the moment when a critical mass of Christians could transform the meaning of society and empire. Nonetheless, it is social networks that are the instrumentalities for massive demographic transformations in religion. Stark expresses this more precisely in the following proposition: "Conversion to new, deviant religious groups occurs when, other things being equal, people have or develop stronger attachments to members of the group than they have to nonmembers."[34]

If the first Jewish converts to Islam were Jewish Arabs in the time of Muḥammad, the next wave of converts would come after the conquests of the seventh century from among bureaucrats who had been recruited under the first ʿUmayyads to fill positions in the official infrastructure inherited from the Byzantines and Persians. Conversion for them would create opportunities for advancement in the government. We also would expect to see Jewish merchants who catered to the Arabs in the military cities such as Basra and Kufa, the *amṣār*, to be drawn toward Islam in order to benefit fully in their commercial endeavors. Most significant for this study, we would expect to find Jews who were unhappy with the aggrandizement of rabbinic power as described above to turn to Islam. In Iraq (Babylonia), there would also be local Jewish elites in towns and landowners in the countryside whose social networks would become dominated by Muslim peers.[35] By the ninth and tenth centuries, these conditions explain the conversion of mass numbers of Jews, Christians, and Zoroastrians, when individuals were willing to change religions because their existing social status was either threatened or could be maintained or improved through conversion.[36] We would also find an occasional spiritualist or intellectual who found the content of Muslim scripture and doctrine to be appealing.

By the early ninth century, when the shift toward Muslim religious identity in the Middle East and North Africa reached critical mass, an end had come to resistance in the form of non-Muslim uprisings (and, significantly, politically active Jewish messianism).[37] It is likely that in the ninth and tenth centuries, the majority of Jewish conversions to Islam occurred and the threat

34. Ibid., 18.

35. See Michael Morony, *Iraq after the Muslim Conquests*, esp. 306–31; and now Chase F. Robinson, *Empire and Elites after the Muslim Conquest: The Transformation of Northern Mesopotamia.*

36. Ibid., 33. For another view, see Bainbridge, *Sociology of Religious Movements*, 54–58.

37. Gil, *History of Palestine*, 280–84 and 292–97; cp. Hodgson, *Venture of Islam*, 1:488–91.

to Jewish communities became discernible. In the second half of the tenth century, the Karaite Yefet ben ʿElī testifies to Muslim Ismāʿīlī efforts at conversion that would decimate the Jews.[38]

As sparse as these first Jewish converts to Islam might seem, they would all have been part of existing Jewish social networks comprised of the nuclear and extended family, locality, class, occupation, and religious congregation. With enormous cultural and religious capital to back them up, these individuals, new Muslims, would be able to influence others in their social networks to understand Islam and gain a level of comfort with its teachings and ways.[39] If the example of early Christianity is applicable, individual conversions in the context of existing social networks eventually increased to generate momentum, whereby Islam would by its very success attract more converts. Such momentum might be perceived on the part of the general population in many regions during the ninth and tenth centuries, if Bulliet's projections are worthwhile. By this time, Jews might have developed stronger attachments to Muslims in many social contexts than they had to fellow Jews. Also, Jews in such intermediate cultural locations might be easily influenced by Muslim theological and legal notions. Alternatively, new Muslims with Jewish cultural baggage and subject to influence from their Jewish coreligionists would contribute teachings to the new religious tradition, some of which would be rejected or marked as heresy in the elaboration of Islam in the ninth and tenth centuries. This subtle and complicated reflexive process generated conditions conducive to the existence of hybrid identities whose complete Jewish or Muslim character appears unclear in hindsight.

Intermediacy of identity, which combines social and religious behaviors, created a world in which a multiplicity of religious phenomena abounded. Recent work on Christianization in Late Antiquity calls into question the existence of clearly polarized religious identities, especially during centuries of religious elaboration and identity formation. The existence of hybrid identities that were both Jewish and Christian seems to have lasted until at least the fourth century, and perhaps to the sixth,[40] although Shlomo Pines wrote several articles on Judeo-Christian identity in medieval Islam.[41] More to the point, Christian–Muslim ʿIbādī identity has been located in ninth-century North Africa by Elizabeth Savage,[42] and Mazdakite-Muslim hybridities are

38. S. M. Stern, "Fāṭimid Propaganda among Jews According to the Testimony of Yefet b. ʿAlī the Karaite." See also Wasserstrom, *Between Muslim and Jew,* 132–33.

39. The figure Kaʿb al-Aḥbār in Muslim tradition represents a cultural awareness of the Jew as convert, both in positive and problematized contexts.

40. Daniel Boyarin, *Dying for God; Martyrdom and the Making of Christianity and Judaism,* esp. 22–41.

41. See bibliography, s.v. Shlomo Pines; cf. Wasserstrom, *Between Muslim and Jew,* 37–41.

42. Savage, *A Gateway to Hell, a Gateway to Paradise,* esp. 89–105.

well-known in early Islamic Iran.[43] Consequently, notions of hybrid identity suggest that Jews formally could have accepted triumphant imperial Islam in various ways, while remaining participating Jews within their existing local communities. Such a strategy is described by the Muslim jurist Muḥammad ibn al-Ḥasan al-Shaybānī (d. 804), who states that "today the Jews in the areas of Iraq recognize that there is no god but God and Muḥammad is the Prophet of God, but they claim that he was sent as a prophet only to the Arabs, and not to the Jews."[44] Such a statement permits acquiescence of fundamental Muslim truth that could be perceived by Muslims as authentic, while openly or clandestinely maintaining Jewish particularism. In the mid-tenth century, the Karaite Salmon ben Yeruḥim reported, "I have learned that the Jews of Samarqand and the region, when they say 'God is One,' [people who hear it] testify that by [saying] so they have become Muslims."[45]

From the Muslim perspective, widely embracing definitions of Muslim identity are known from this era, demonstrating that hybridity was enmeshed in the discourse of Islam itself. Boundaries of the community were hardly rigid even at the late date of the early eleventh century, when al-Baghdādī reported that a "lenient interpretation of the credo was held by several Muslim groups." These included some Khārijites, the Shīʿite Muḥammad ibn al-Ḥanafiyyah, and Murjiʿites.[46]

Hybridization thus creates possibilities for intermediate identities whose investment in Jewish and Muslim matters varied. Those Jewish–Muslims who resisted the hegemony of an increasingly legalized Islam that demanded clear allegiance and a complete lifestyle might "return" to a Judaic identity that they felt had authenticity. Nonetheless, they might also feel that rabbinic hegemony among Jews was too demanding, if not somewhat alien. This combination of attitudes created conditions for sectarian identities whose characteristics might appear to be Jewish, Muslim, or Jewish–Muslim. Among Jewish sectarians, features of hybrid identity are signal in the messianic movements of Abū ʿĪsā al-Isfahānī (d. ca. 750), who taught that Jesus and Muḥammad were prophets,[47] and of Meshwī (Mishawayh) al-ʿUkbarī (after the mid-ninth century), whose syncretism is obscured in the story of his apostasy.[48]

From the eleventh century on, a truly Muslim society as defined by Bulliet existed: numerical preponderance and the influence of social institutions

43. Madelung, *Religious Trends in Early Islamic Iran,* 1–12.

44. Wasserstrom's trans., *Between Muslim and Jew,* 78.

45. Haggai Ben-Shammai, "The Attitude of Some Early Karaites towards Islam," 10.

46. Cited in Wasserstrom, *Between Muslim and Jew,* 78.

47. On Abū ʿĪsā al-Isfahānī, see al-Qirqisānī, *Kitāb al-anwār wal-marāqib,* section 1, chapter 2, number 12, and chapter 11 [trans. Lockwood in Chiesa and Lockwood, *Yaʿqūb al-Qirqisānī on Jewish Sects,* 102–3 and 144–45]; and Wasserstrom, *Between Muslim and Jew,* 71–89.

48. Ankori, *Karaites in Byzantium,* 403, n. 141.

defined the society as a whole. By this time, the *ʿulamāʾ* and *ṣūfī* holy men had become leaders and spokesmen for the population at large, thus attracting the last wave of converts. It is likely that by this time fewer Jews were converting because with the elaboration of Muslim law and thought demands made upon Muslims became heavier. The sense of continuity that a Jew or Christian might perceive in previous centuries now was replaced by the otherness of Islam. As Islam consolidated, the possibility of Jewish–Muslim hybridity lost meaning. In fact, the ʿĪsāwiyyah disappeared in this period.

It is noteworthy that in the thirteenth century, when much of the Middle East and North Africa was fully Islamized, Jews and Christians began to lose social status and economic opportunity as the marketplace and the street became more Muslim. In addition, Islamdom suffered from the disruption of the Mongol invasions and the short-sighted ruling policies of the Mamlukes in Egypt, so that in a world of decreasing resources, Jews and Christians were increasingly left out.

In the end, Jews did not record in their writings direct evidence for the impact of Islamization on their world, even as they did not record the effects of Christianization centuries earlier. There are two reasons for this. First, Jewish literature of this period comes primarily from the rabbis, whose lack of interest in history has already been alluded to in the introduction (the topic is further discussed in the next section of this chapter). Second, the rabbis as hegemons would have little use for writing about the losses and humiliation of Islamization—a literature that would reveal weakness and failure. Alternatively, Christian writers were interested in history and hegemony and, therefore, discuss their losses, providing indirect support for the model of history suggested herein.[49] Ironically, Muslim records of Islamization are nonexistent for the earlier periods because there was as yet no literary class to generate such writings. Muslim writers of the later period provide shaky historical testimony for Islamization because they are concerned with either historical triumphalism or use history to project contemporary legal concerns into the past. Although the history is ill-documented, there can be no doubt that a large portion of the Jewish population converted to Islam in the first three or four centuries A.H.

The massive demographic shift toward Islam on the part of Jews provides an important context for understanding the rise of a variety of Judaisms in these centuries. The new Karaite movement emerged at the end of the ninth and tenth centuries as a nonhybrid alternative to both Islam and rabbinic

49. Humphreys, *Islamic History: A Framework for Inquiry*, 277–78. Also Cynthia Villagomez, "Christian Salvation through Muslim Domination: Divine Punishment and Syriac Apocalyptic Expectation in the Seventh and Eighth Centuries"; and John Iskander, "Islamization in Medieval Egypt: The Coptic–Arabic 'Apocalypse of Samuel' as a Source for the Social and Religious History of Medieval Copts."

Judaism. As a revitalization movement within Judaism it offered meaning in a world fractured by the political dissolution of the caliphate, by the economic decline of Iraq and the East, and by the demographic decline of Jewry as a consequence of Islamization. By locating itself in opposition to rabbinic institutionalization and halakhic particularity, Karaism was able to attract remnants from Jewish and other sectarian movements as well as Judeo–Muslim hybrids who were unwilling to make the final commitment to Islam. However, this successful gathering together of disparate elements of Middle Eastern society brought with it a great variety of contradictory law and theology.

Notions of the Past

Rabbinic Judaism developed a variety of approaches to the past, most of them ahistorical. Central to the rabbinic worldview was the concept of the Oral Law premised upon a link to the authoritative past of the Torah. Early vague notions of this link ultimately were expressed in the idea of a *shalshelet ha-kabbalah,* mentioned above. This literary and quasi-historical construction posited that the rabbis were inheritors of a genealogy of divine knowledge that began with Moses and proceeded in time to the rabbis themselves. Rabbinic construction of attitudes toward the past in the first centuries of the Common Era were the result of both an intra-Judaic hermeneutic and the influence of external factors, especially the conflict with Christianity in the Roman Empire. This idea became especially important later, in the first Islamic centuries, because Islam generated similar models of the past to rationalize its own sociolegal worldview. Thus the idea of a chain of tradition continued to develop in Judaism of the Islamic period both as a result of internal Jewish ideological development and from external influence.

Karaism, as a Jewish heresy, represents a critique of rabbinic Judaism, and as such developed its own notions of the past in reaction to and in engagement with rabbinic Jewish notions. That is to say, rabbinic Jewish treatment of the past and modeling of history is the basis for much Karaite counterideology in the era of its formation and florescence in the Middle East before the period of the Crusades.

Rabbinic Grand Strategies and the Past. What would become the normative expression of Judaism in the centuries after the destruction of the Jerusalem Temple in 70 C.E. was the Judaism of the rabbis and the Oral Torah.[50] The destruction of the Temple created a crisis that raised serious questions for the Jews. What to do with a religious system that had previously depended upon a central institution and its officiating priesthood? How were elements of ritual, personal practice, and theology to survive without the Temple?

50. Another way to describe this is used by Jacob Neusner, who in *Judaism and Its Social Metaphors,* 3, refers to the Judaism of the "dual Torah."

The rabbis' solutions to these and concomitant problems evolved until they received their first written expression in the redaction of the Mishnah in about 200 C.E. The rabbis needed to establish continuity with the past by trying to recapitulate their idea of an "original Judaism," while at the same time they needed to enforce changes of a pragmatic nature to deal with the entirely new situation.[51] In the apodictic laws of the Mishnah, the rabbis imagined a Judaism where the foci of purities, ritual sanctification, and the nexus of personal and corporate affairs were transferred from the Temple to the community and, by extension, to the home and the synagogue. The project of the Mishnah as described by Jacob Neusner was concerned with *sanctification.*[52]

History and the events that affect nations and individuals are of little consequence to the immediacy of the process of sanctification. The careful adherent of the regulations of rabbinic Judaism is concerned with daily observances and their meaning. In this view, Israel has no history except that which was inherited from the Hebrew Bible. Israel becomes a social construct living in the here and now, and sanctioned biblical history becomes deep background to the religious process of sanctification. The historical past is not needed for the completion of its project. The Mishnah rarely resorts to a kind of history that might support its halakhic conclusions.[53] Even the destruction of the Temple and the Bar Kokhba rebellion are barely given mention.[54] When the past is evoked, it is marshaled in support of sanctification to generate historicizations that provide proofs for case law. Other incidental uses of the past in the Mishnah suggest models for exemplary conduct, supply genealogical information, or teach the lessons regarding reward and punishment and the ultimacy of the divine plan in the world. The latter is often demonstrated with taxonomies of "historical" patterns in which historical memory eradicates the specificity of an event by categorizing it together with other similar

51. See Neusner, *Judaism and Its Social Metaphors,* 16f. Centuries later the Karaites would also seek to harmonize cultural and religious change with ideas of continuity and eternal truth.

52. For a summary of sanctification in the Mishnah, see Neusner, *Death and Birth of Judaism: The Impact of Christianity, Secularism, and the Holocaust on Jewish Faith,* 42ff.

53. See Neusner, *Judaism and Its Social Metaphors,* 32ff.

54. See Nahum Glatzer, "The Tannaim and History"; and Jacob Neusner, "History Transcended: The Mishnaic Uses of the Past." A good example that illustrates this point is the mention of the loss of the Temple in M R.H. 4:1–4. The importance of this great caesura in Jewish history is contextualized only within changes in halakhah that resulted: the *shofar* (ram's horn) could be blown on Shabbat, the *lulav* (palm branch) could be waved for seven days, and details were changed regarding testimony on the appearance of the New Moon.

events ("Five things befell our fathers on the 17th of Tammuz and five on the ninth of Ab."[55]).

Less than two centuries later, another problematic emerged. In Late Antiquity, the position of the Jewish people and the rabbis declined dramatically in Palestine and the Roman Empire. The success of Christianity brought new questions to the fore. To the rabbis, an offshoot of Judaism now dominated the Roman world, a world where the Jews were being definitively deprived of national self-determination. How could Christianity's false expression of Judaism have emerged triumphant among humankind? What is the meaning of the idea of the "chosen people" in light of these developments? Both religious cultures claim to be the true Israel: How can this be? How can the Hebrew Bible now be claimed as the birthright of another religion? Who is the messiah?

Concomitant with the intellectual crisis posed by Christianity were more concrete conditions imposed upon the community from without—persecution and decline, especially under Roman rule. Beginning with the conversion of Constantine and the accompanying Edict of Toleration in 312 C.E., followed by the dissolution of the Jewish patriarchate in 429, and culminating in Novella 146 of Justinian in 553, the feeling of imminent danger and anxiety is in evidence in some of the rabbinic literature. Certainly, an enhanced ideology of exile emerged as a consequence of continued threat and the absence of the Temple in Jewish life. The new characteristics of national identity forming in this period resulted from real conditions on the ground as much as from the philosophical agenda of the Mishnah.[56]

The rabbis' response to this ongoing crisis is indicated by changes in the rabbinic problematic in the fourth century. Christianity had not posed a special problem for the Jewish scholars of the Mishnah, whose expression of Judaism neither indicates the presence of a new religion that began as an offshoot of Judaism nor intersects with topical and theological concerns of the early church. This is hardly the case for the second stage of the development of the Oral Torah. In documents written from 200 to about 450 C.E., such as the

55. M Taan. 4:6; the translation is by Herbert Danby, *The Mishnah,* 200. This Jewish use of history is not restricted to Late Antiquity. Jews of eastern Europe contextualized the Chmielnicki massacres of 1648 against the Blois massacre of 1171. Both are understood to have taken place on 20 Sivan, and *seliḥot* and other liturgical poems of the later persecution are based upon or borrowed from the Blois incident. See Yosef Hayim Yerushalmi, *Zakhor: Jewish History and Jewish Memory,* 49–52.

56. On the history of the Jews in this period, see Gedaliah Alon, *The Jews in Their Land in the Talmudic Age,* although one should consult the more complete two-volume Hebrew edition; M. Avi-Yonah, *The Jews of Palestine: A Political History from the Bar Kokhba War to the Arab Conquest;* and Jacob Neusner, *A History of the Jews in Babylonia.*

Palestinian Talmud, Genesis Rabbah, and Leviticus Rabbah, the presence of Christianity is in evidence.[57] The new problematic of this phase of rabbinic literature is *salvation*, a concept that, compared with sanctification, requires a more concrete idea of who Israel is and what the meaning is of events in which it participates. Adding dimension to the legal and ritual immediacy of the Mishnah, the literature of the second phase of the Oral Torah constructs (1) a moral understanding of repentance as a way to individual salvation; (2) the messiah as the mechanism for corporate salvation; and (3) an eschatological framework into which these salvific ideas *and* the Mishnah's project of sanctification are incorporated. This phase, which sets the agenda for the development of most of the later authoritative Babylonian Talmud, both builds upon and goes beyond the mishnaic perspective.[58]

It must be emphasized that the salvific concerns of this rabbinic literature are congruent and parallel to the concerns of the church fathers. Theological problems, such as who is Israel (the genealogical descendants of the Israelites or the spiritual inheritors of the Prophets?), who is the messiah (one yet to come or Jesus of Nazareth?), and what are the paths to salvation (works or grace?), are shared by these two claimants to the biblical identity of Israel.[59] Needless to say, the answers as they are worked out in the two religious communities are different. What concerns us in this study are the ways that this conceptual framework embodied ideas and uses of history.

Working from the problematic of salvation, the rabbis set aside the completely ahistorical context of the Mishnah for a different understanding of time and Israel's place in it. The immediacy of halakhic observance in the here-and-now gained an added dimension by way of a moral construct, whereby people are rewarded or punished for their deeds. In the Mishnah, such a concept is hinted at as a determinant on the ultimate fate of individuals. Yet even in the Bible the correspondence of both worthiness and reward, on the one hand, and transgression and punishment, on the other, is expressed in a national context, whereby the fate of Israel is directly linked to

57. This is part of a thesis put forth by Neusner in several works in which he outlines the relationship between Judaism and Christianity and its implications for rabbinic literature and Jewish life. See the relevant sections in *Judaism and Its Social Metaphors* and especially in *Judaism in the Matrix of Christianity* and *Judaism and Christianity in the Age of Constantine.* The material is summarized in *Death and Birth of Judaism: The Impact of Christianity, Secularism, and the Holocaust on Jewish Faith,* 33–72.

58. See Neusner, *Judaism and Its Social Metaphors,* 99f.

59. See Jaroslav Pelikan, *The Christian Tradition: A History of the Development of Doctrine,* vol. 1: *The Emergence of the Catholic Tradition, 100–600,* 12–27; and vol. 2: *The Spirit of Eastern Christendom, 600–1700,* 199–215. See also William Klassen, "Anti-Judaism in Early Christianity: The State of the Question"; and Wayne A. Meeks, "Breaking Away: Three New Testament Pictures of Christianity's Separation from the Jewish Communities."

the community's proper or improper behavior.[60] In the postmishnaic literature, one now understands that beyond sanctification there are goals to be realized at the end of one's days and at the End of Days of the entire world. Whether individually or corporately, the mechanisms of sanctification as expressions of a moral imperative now lead the individual and community toward the fulfillment of a divine plan. The moral construct, based upon reward and punishment, and expressed through ideas of *zekhut* (worthiness) and sin, becomes in many ways the principle through which history unfolds. These ideas then explain the fate and role of individuals and nations in the historical scheme.[61]

The Rationale for Rabbinic Law. In an astonishing departure from the ahistorical and moralistic ideology of the bulk of rabbinic discourse, the rabbis posited a type of extended linear historicization that made specific claims to the past. In its expression, this historicization comments upon the place of the Law in Jewish society, but in its construction suggests a powerful historical contextualization of both the Law and the rabbinic caste itself. After examining historical understanding expressed in these literatures, we turn logically to an as yet unmentioned supplement to the Mishnah. Pirke Avot, now considered part of the Mishnah, was in fact written some fifty years after the Mishnah's redaction.[62] In it, we see the first systematic apology for the rabbinic agenda. Pirke Avot, or Chapters of the Fathers, is in essence an ethical tract consisting of a compilation of maxims attributed to the rabbis of the period from the restoration of the Second Temple to the immediate generations after Judah the Prince in the third century C.E. This mishnaic "Book of Proverbs"[63] reveals the "authors" of halakhah in light of their moral and ethical teachings, of their expectations of Jewish society, and of their implicit sociological assumptions. It is to be contextualized within the same stratum of rabbinic literature as the *Midreshe Halakhah* and the Tosefta, which were written to provide the Mishnah with biblical and dialectical foundations, respectively. In contrast to the rest of the Mishnah, Avot does not engage in dialectic discussions, halakhic debates, or the establishing of points of law.

Although the problematic of the Mishnah as a whole is expressed in a rather homogeneous manner, the text of Avot presents itself as if it were the

60. In Lev. 26, the fate of Israel depends upon obedience to the Covenant. In Deut. 28, the enumeration of blessings and curses describes the possible fates awaiting Israel.

61. See A. Marmorstein, *The Doctrine of Merits in Old Rabbinic Literature;* and Solomon Schechter, *Aspects of Rabbinic Theology,* chapter 12, "The Zacuth of the Fathers: Imputed Righteousness and Sin," 170–98.

62. For a summary of scholarship on Avot, see M. B. Lerner, "The Tractate Avot." Cf. Jacob Neusner's comments in *Introduction to Rabbinic Literature,* 571–90.

63. Quoting Judah Goldin, *The Living Talmud: The Wisdom of the Fathers,* 37.

result of generations of legal compilation and accumulation. Although it is outside the confines of this study to include a close discussion of the early development of rabbinic law, it is important to note some of the characteristics of that development inasmuch as they have influence on the expression of later historical notions.

The laws of the Torah, as numerous as they seem, are not complete enough to govern a complex dynamic society such as that of Judea in the Hellenistic and Roman periods. The basic requirements are present without the particulars.[64] The system of law that was in place in Late Antiquity was no doubt based in part on the scriptural heritage embodied in the Torah and maintained by the hereditary class of Levites and priests and in part on traditional or common law as practiced by judges, elders of the communities, and other communal leaders. In addition, the Hellenistic period is witness to the growth of both a scribal class and a scholarly milieu in Jewish society, among whom would naturally arise an impetus for self-explanation in terms of class identity, the legal system, and history.[65] The cosmopolitan and intellectual impact of Hellenism no doubt influenced the manner in which these self-explanations evolved. The obvious example is found in the writings of Hellenistic–Jewish historians, who tried to harmonize the Bible and Jewish history with new knowledge from the larger world that was imported with Hellenism.[66]

Hypothetically, the ancient question might have been: How can we explain these laws and regulations that we follow that are clearly not in the Torah, the recognized, divinely given source of the Law? A rhetorical way to answer is to evoke the authority of the elders. In response, an expositor of law might evoke a homiletic hyperbole: "I swear by the Torah! These are things that were said to Moses at Sinai."[67] With this claim, traditional nontoraitic law is given equal weight with the Law of the Torah. This rationalization becomes formalized and is given jurisprudential weight with the expression *Torah le-Mosheh mi-Sinai* (Law of Moses from Sinai). This expression appears in many places in rabbinic literature in order to support laws whose toraitic foundation might be questionable.[68] Ultimately, this formulation became a

64. See Moore, *Judaism,* 251f.

65. Ibid., 40f.

66. On Hellenistic-Jewish historiography, see Holladay, *Fragments from Hellenistic Jewish Authors,* vol. 1: *Historians;* H. W. Attridge, "Historiography"; and Erich S. Gruen, *Heritage and Hellenism: The Reinvention of Jewish Tradition.* Cf. Bezalel Bar-Kochva, *Pseudo-Hecataeus, "On the Jews": Legitimizing the Jewish Diaspora.* On Josephus, see H. W. Attridge, "Josephus and His Works."

67. Tos. Pea. 3:2.

68. All the occurrences of this phrase are studied by Wilhelm Bacher, "Satzung von Sinai," cited by Moore, *Judaism,* 3, 76, n. 19.

basis for the entire rabbinic hermeneutic: "Bible, Mishnah, Talmud, and haggadah, even what a senior disciple is due to teach in the presence of his master, was already stated to Moses at Sinai."[69]

The distinction between toraitic law and traditional law was not merely recognized but developed into a central principle for the construction and understanding of rabbinic law; namely, the concept of the Oral Law, *Torah she-beʿal peh.* The idea emerged that Moses received a second revelation at Mount Sinai in addition to the Torah. That additional revelation was not written down, as was the Torah, but was learned by heart and transmitted orally.[70] Thus a sense of connection with the authoritative ultimately signified past was established, that all of the Law, both written and oral, originated with God's revelation to Moses in distant antiquity.

Josephus elucidates the character of the transmission of law when he distinguishes the Pharisees from the Sadducees with this principle:

> The Pharisees have delivered to the people a great many observances by succession from their fathers, which are not written in the Law of Moses; and for that reason it is that the Sadducees reject them, and say, that we are to esteem those observances to be obligatory which are in the written word, but are not to observe what are derived from the tradition of our forefathers.[71]

In this testimony, long before the concept of the Oral Law emerged, the idea of the authority of the fathers and a succession of their teachings is emphasized. The New Testament also witnesses the idea of "traditions of the elders" in association with the Pharisees.[72] In the determination of the Law, the evocation of transmitted authority is paramount. In PT Pesahim 6:1, 31a, Hillel taught that the Passover sacrifice should take place on 14 Nissan even if it falls on Shabbat. He expounded on the biblical bases of the halakhah all day using his seven hermeneutical principles,[73] but was rejected by the Bene Bathyra until he finally evoked the authority of his teachers: "May it befall me, if this is not the way I heard it from Shemaiah and Abtalion."

Having posited such a duality in the Law, it was only logical to ask questions of continuity. How was the Law transmitted from Moses to the sages of our day? How did the perfect unity of the Law in Moses's day become fragmented by multiple differences of opinion in our day, even among the sages? It is highly significant that the rabbis actually did provide answers to these questions. It is somewhat surprising, given the rabbis' lack of concern for

69. PT Peah. 2:6.

70. First mention of the Oral Law: Sifre Deut. 351; also Midrash Tanna'im, 215; BT Shab. 31a.; cited in Urbach, *The Sages,* 290.

71. William Whiston, trans., *The Works of Flavius Josephus,* 13:11, §6, 454.

72. Matt. 15:2; and Mark 7:3, 5.

73. See Tos. San. 7:11.

historical specificity and their uses of historicization, that this matter of continuity would merit their attention. As mentioned above, the immediacy of halakhic concerns contextualized events into taxonomies of meaning and into the cycle of the ritual calendar. History was inherited from the Bible but was not important for the rabbinic jurisprudential project. "There is no 'before' or 'after' in Torah."[74] Nonetheless, principles of linear historical continuity do begin to inform the rabbinic mindset through the idea of the transmission of the Oral Law.

The succession and transmission from Sinai to the present is given credence in a number of rabbinic pericopae. "R. Joshua said: I have received as a tradition from Rabban Johanan b. Zakkai, who heard it from his teacher, and his teacher from his teacher, as a halakhah given to Moses at Sinai, that . . ."[75] Here the formula "Law of Moses from Sinai" is not simply evoked but is embedded within a chain of tradition. The authority of R. Joshua's statement is linked to the ultimately signified past, the revelation at Sinai, through intermediaries of seemingly authentic historicity.

Pirke Avot, Chapters 1 and 2. When the aggadic method characteristic of much of the postmishnaic material discussed above was used to establish the authority of the Law and the place of Israel in the world through scriptural and hermeneutical exegesis, the result generated a largely ahistorical worldview. In contrast, Avot uses the aggadic approach to focus its concerns on the expositors of the Law themselves in accompaniment with their moral formulations. Avot provides an exegesis of history with the intent of establishing the authority of the rabbis as a class, of their third-century "constitution," the Mishnah, and of the expectations of the rabbinic method upon that class and upon Israel as a whole. The presence of an extratoraitic Oral Law, the evocation of the authority of the elders, and of the revelation at Sinai are contextualized into a powerful historicization of the rabbinic class and of the authority of its pronouncements in the first chapters of Pirke Avot. This historical representation becomes paradigmatic in rabbinic Judaism and would later be used as a stalk upon which later rabbis would graft branches of historicized genealogies of knowledge, becoming the basis of an entire literary genre, the *shalshelet ha-kabbalah,* or chain of tradition. Centuries later and in a similar fashion, the Karaites would use the texts known by that name as a model for their own historical formulations, at the same time, adopting and reinterpreting it for their own purposes.

The rabbinic claim upon history is an obvious attempt to connect the rabbis of latter days to the original revelation at Mount Sinai. The hyperbolic justification for traditional and other nontoraitic law that emerged in early rabbinic discourse, "Law of Moses from Sinai," became concretized in a very specific manner into a claim of continuity from Moses to the rabbis. In this

74. BT Pes. 6b.

75. M Eduy. 8:7. Other attestations are found in M Peah 2:6; M Eduy. 1:6, 5:7; BT Ber. 27b; and BT Yom. 66b.

way, the authority of the law of the Mishnah and the rabbis is equated with written Law from Sinai. This schematization does not tell the reader very much about how the Law works, but it is an image of the rabbinic class and its relationship to the Law.

In the Greco-Roman world, the great antiquity of the Jews was generally acknowledged by virtue of the history embodied in the Hebrew Bible. Such a claim carried great prestige in a world where the ruling power, Rome, was an "upstart" when compared to the long and venerable histories of such peoples as the Greeks, Egyptians, or Persians. Other "chains" of historicized traditions are known from antiquity. Eupolemus, the Hellenistic Jewish historian, posited a succession of prophets, while some of the mystery religions claimed a lineage that extended into mythical history. Roman jurists traced their "lineage" back to T. Corunicianus in the third century B.C.E., while in Greek thought a scheme of *diadoche*, or successors, represents the continuation through history of specific philosophical schools.[76] With a chain of tradition, the rabbis portray themselves in the same manner as Greco–Roman philosophers, and by positing a transmission of "pairs" an explanation is offered for the existence of two Pharisaic schools, those of Hillel and Shammai.[77]

After the third century, the growth and influence of Christianity in the Mediterranean world presented a conflicting claim to Jewish antiquity as Christians sought to establish continuity with God's revelation and the Hebrew Bible. In concert with the contests fought by Jews and Christians over the question of the messiah, the role of the Law, and the nature of redemption, Christian polemic and internal ecclesiastical discourse sought to discredit the Jews as God's people.[78] Christian thought was faced with the problem of maintaining continuity with the biblical past while at the same time proclaiming a new dispensation. Its historical discourse was centered around the succession of the Christian church, the "New Israel," to the Old

76. These ancient chains of tradition are discussed in Elias Bickerman, "Le Chaine de la Tradition Pharisienne." See also Jaap Mansfeld, *Heresiography in Context: Hippolytus'* Elenchos *as a Source for Greek Philosophy.*

77. This interpretation is supported by the organization of Abot. See Louis Finkelstein, *Mavo le-Massekhtot' Avot ve-'Avot d'Rabbi Natan* (Introduction to the Treatises of Avot and Avot of Rabbi Nathan). According to Finkelstein, the second section, roughly corresponding to chapter 2, is largely a Hillelite addition that was interpolated before the Shammaite continuation of traditions in the third section, approximate to chapter 3.

78. On Christian anti-Jewish ideology, see the collections of articles in Ernest S. Frerichs and Jacob Neusner, eds., *"To See Ourselves as Others See Us"; Christians, Jews, "Others" in Late Antiquity;* Peter Richardson, ed., *Anti-Judaism in Early Christianity,* vol. 1, *Paul and the Gospels;* and Stephen G. Wilson, ed., *Anti-Judaism in Early Christianity,* vol. 2, *Separation and Polemic.*

Israel, the Jews.[79] The rabbinic claim to antiquity in Avot creates a history that establishes Jewish continuity with the past and that later would be used to deflect elements found in Christian and Muslim polemics.

The chain of tradition posited in Abot goes beyond being a mere schematized claim to continuity with antiquity. The chain begins in Avot 1 with Moses and links Joshua, the elders, the prophets, the men of the Great Assembly,[80] and pairs of individual sages to the first-century pair of Hillel and Shammai, and then to Hillel's immediate familial and rabbinic successors, Rabban Gamaliel I and Simeon ben Gamaliel. The chain then abruptly breaks off, and in Avot 2 the next scholar to be mentioned is Judah the Patriarch, the compiler of the Mishnah, who lived almost two centuries after his ancestor Hillel. This forms one branch of the chain, representing the authority of the Palestinian patriarchate, the princely administrative and legislative institution of Palestinian rabbinic Judaism. Hillel is both the genealogical ancestor and toraitic predecessor of Judah and the other patriarchs. The gap in the sequence of transmission only emphasizes that the authority of the patriarchate resides not in the individuals and their specific claims to the transmission of the Law, but in the office itself.[81]

Significantly, another branch in the chain of tradition is represented in 2:8. The transmission of the Law from Hillel to Yohanan ben Zakkai "occurs" sequentially within the gap left in the first branch of the chain. After this, Yohanan's five disciples are named, who are among the most important authorities in the Mishnah. Yohanan ben Zakkai is signified not simply because he was a transmitter to those worthy students but also because of historical events. Yohanan ben Zakkai was able to keep Pharisaic (rabbinic) teaching alive by having himself spirited out of the city of Jerusalem during the Roman siege in 70 C.E. Subsequently, he came to an understanding with the Romans authorities and was able to establish an academy at Yavneh. Only

79. On Christian history, see Pelikan, *The Christian Tradition,* 1:108–20; and Glenn F. Chestnut, *The First Christian Historians: Eusebius, Socrates, Sozomen, Theodoret, and Evagrius.* It is important to note that Eusebius in *The History of the Church* (ed. G. A. Williamson) places emphasis on the succession of bishops in establishing for the church and its doctrine. In another context, the cult of the saints was utilized in the geohistorical appropriation of the past. See Peter Brown, *The Cult of the Saints: Its Rise and Function in Latin Christianity;* and R. A. Markus, *The End of Ancient Christianity.*

80. Preferred over Great Synagogue.

81. On the forms and expressions of authority in rabbinic law, see Dov Zlotnick, *The Iron Pillar-Mishnah: Redaction, Form, and Intent.* In M Eduy. 1:3, the attestation of a halakhah by two weavers in the name of Shemaiah and Abtalion could be authoritative only if confirmed by the sages. See also Michael S. Berger, *Rabbinic Authority.*

later did the academy come under the leadership and authority of a descendant of Hillel, Gamaliel II.[82]

At face value, the second branch in the chain of tradition apparently offers credentials for the individuals mentioned in the Mishnah. But the point here is that Avot claims for the authority *of the text,* not for the individual tradents themselves. The Mishnah itself is the recipient of the chain of tradition. There is no explicit chain of tradition that connects the individual redactor of the text, Judah the Patriarch, with the ancient root of the Law. His connection is indirect in both cases, through his unnamed patriarchal descendants and through the Mishnah itself. Although the rabbinic claim to authority is conflated with the claims of the patriarchal line, Judah is as much the recipient of the Law *from the text* as is any other later sage. Thus "two pillars" for mishnaic authority are established.[83]

To what degree does Avot represent a claim to history? The construction of the chain of transmission in the form of a linear conception, an image of historical time, replicates the generational progression of genealogy, and at the same time exemplifies the master-disciple relationship characteristic of the society of rabbis. The connection to Moses and to the important nexus of the Great Assembly fulfills a halakhic function, but also explicitly makes a claim to history. In spite of the ahistorical inclinations of the rabbis, the Jews were the possessors of a historical inheritance separate from but connected to the Hebrew Bible. The chain of transmission suggests a continuation of biblical history, but eschews specificity by remaining divorced from the meaning of events or the lives of individuals. At its simplest, the chain of transmission connects myths of origin to the rabbinic religio-social world of the present.[84] What is most important for understanding this historicization is that it remains married to rabbinic ahistoricity. The specificity of the *shalshelet hakabbalah* is subsumed under the symbolic meaning that it employs.

In Late Antiquity, the chain of tradition in Avot spoke evocatively to the sources of authority, not as a narrative on the expositors themselves. Although its place in the rabbinic discourse planted the seeds for more specific, later expressions of history, it continued the historical philosophy of the Tannaim, who "make use of history in order to answer questions that originate in the present."[85]

The Evolution of the Chain of Tradition. Historiographical topics contextualized against religio-legal concerns have been addressed only slightly in

82. The story of Yohanan ben Zakkai's "escape" from Jerusalem is found in Avot de-Rabbi Natan 1, 4:22–24; Avot de-Rabbi Natan 2, 6:19, Lam. Rab. 1.5, 31; and BT Git. 56a–b. A good summary of the material on Yohanan ben Zakkai is found in *EJ*, 10:148–54. See also Neusner, *A Life of Rabban Yohanan ben Zakkai.*

83. See Neusner, *Judaism and Its Social Metaphors,* 78.

84. See Bronislaw Malinowski, *Magic, Science, and Religion,* 67f., and 111ff.

85. Nahum Glatzer, "The Tannaim in History," 135.

Jewish studies. Broadly conceived, such topics include the historicized claims for rabbinic authority, the place and meaning of those claims in rabbinic literature, and their relationship to religious and historical events in surrounding environments. The idea of the chain of tradition is often glossed over or referred to perfunctorily by scholars as something that is easily understandable and only marginally important for the understanding of religion and halakhah;[86] only in studies on particular works do we see more substantive attention paid to such topics.[87] Scholars who have paid attention to these materials are often unconcerned with connections between history, on the one hand, and religious development and halakhah, on the other. Interestingly, this lack of serious inquiry into the rabbinic expression of historical continuity reflects that of the rabbis themselves, who often offered apologies in their historical writings in order to deflect criticism against such an "unimportant" enterprise.[88] The chain of tradition is seen to offer a simple meaning. It is accepted at its face value: the record of a genealogy of divinely granted religio-legal knowledge going back to the source, God's revelation to Moses at Mount Sinai. However, the configuration and character of a particular exposition of the chain of tradition is related to theology, halakhah, and philosophy in the context of the social and historical environment in which it originates. Rabbinic versions of the chain of tradition tell us much about the times and environments of their provenance. They also stand as background to the development of parallel historical expression in the Karaite milieu.

86. See Isidore Twersky's slight treatment of Maimonides introduction to the *Mishneh Torah* in *Introduction to the Code of Maimonides* (Mishneh Torah), 28–30. However, note 41 on page 28 provides some references to the appearance of the *shalshelet ha-kabbalah* in rabbinic literature.

87. The outstanding example is Gerson Cohen's translation and introduction to Abraham Ibn Daud's *Sefer ha-Qabbalah: The Book of Tradition by Abraham Ibn Daud: A Critical Edition with a Translation and Notes.* See below for Cohen's thesis regarding the Islamic influence on Ibn Daud and the importance of his work. Others who deal with the idea of the chain of tradition include Kalman Kahana in his German translation and commentary of *Seder Tanna'im ve-'Amora'im,* and Nosson Dovid Rabinowich in his English translation and commentary of *'Iggeret Rav Sherira Gaon,* as well as his New York University doctoral dissertation, which I have not seen. On these, see below, this chapter.

88. See Maimonides, Commentary to Mishnah Sanhedrin, 10:1, cited by Yosef H. Yerushalmi in *Zakhor: Jewish History and Jewish Memory,* 126, n. 5. The standard edition is Yosef Kafah, ed., Maimonides, *Mishnah 'im perush rabbenu Mosheh ben Maimon,* Seder Nezikin, see 195f. To quote Yerushalmi (*Zakhor,* 66f.) regarding early modern Jewish historiographers who inherited the rabbinic prejudice against historical writing: "Most of the historical works under consideration are preceded by introductions overflowing with apology for the very fact that the writer is dealing with history at all, and offering a host of reasons to justify such a concern."

With the redaction of the Babylonian Talmud, the final form of the rabbinic "constitution" was completed. This Talmud would eventually become the authoritative source of halakhah for most Jews worldwide. The layers of literary construction represented both within this document and within other genres of rabbinic literature before the Islamic period posed innumerable methodological and epistemological questions, very few of which might be answered by reference to history, and none by the historicization of the chain of tradition in Avot. The general ahistorical worldview first posited by the Mishnah continued to remain of significant centrality. The halakhic project was one of timeless observance without historical specificity. Historicized narrative in rabbinic literature remained limited to certain types of contextualization, such as didactic taxonomy, symbolic representation, or any number of expressions of a moral construct that regards eschatology, the messiah, and reward and punishment as the governing forces in the life of Israel and all human events. This has been briefly outlined above.

It is with these concerns in mind that we begin the "biography of an idea"—the development of a historical ideology and, eventually, a *shalshelet ha-kabbalah* within Karaite literature, beginning in the Islamic period. First it is necessary to sketch briefly the outlines of that idea's appearance, context, and uses in the rabbinic literature of the period in order to lay the foundation of a similar study of Karaite claims to history. It becomes clear that as the centuries pass the Karaites become increasingly inclined to refer to and depend upon rabbinic formulations of history to construct their own versions. Thus the rabbinic development of the chain of tradition and associated claims upon history create much of the material for the Karaites to contend with and to co-opt.

A work that functions as a *gemara,* or talmudic development, to the Mishnah of Avot is Avot de-Rabbi Natan, found in the standard editions of the Babylonian Talmud at the end of the order of *Nezikin.*[89] The text cannot be dated with certainty, but is medieval in the form that it is known today.[90] It has been shown that despite the late provenance of the text, it represents a version of Avot that antedates the version in the Mishnah. It is significant for our purposes that, unlike Mishnah Avot, this alternate version maintains a chronological arrangement for the sayings of the rabbis without a break, embracing a consistent, linear conception of history.[91] The editors of the "later" version of Avot found in the Mishnah undoubtedly possessed the earliest version of what would later be known as Avot de-Rabbi Natan, and chose

89. The standard scholarly edition is Solomon Schechter, ed., *Avot de Rabbi Nathan.* In this first modern scholarly edition of any rabbinic text, Schechter identified two recensions of Avot de-Rabbi Natan.

90. Avot de-Rabbi Natan was known to the geonim and was a source for the commentary on Abot found in *Maḥzor Vitry,* dated before 1105.

91. See Judah Goldin, "Avot de-Rabbi Natan"; and Finkelstein, *Mavo le-Massekhtot' Avot ve-'Avot d'Rabbi Natan.*

to construct a broken chain of tradition. As discussed above, the nonlinear arrangement in Abot was intentional and needs to be appreciated and interpreted accordingly, while Avot de Rabbi Natan represents an early antecedent to the fully developed chain of tradition.

A work reminiscent of the ancient rabbinic chronological text *Seder Olam Rabbah* is *Seder ʿOlam Zuta,* which maintains a particular agenda beyond chronology for its own sake.[92] Although beginning its history with Adam, this work focuses on the Davidic line of the exilarchs in Babylonia, which *Seder ʿOlam Zuta* maintains began with the biblical Zerubbabel. The family line is extended from biblical antiquity to the eighth century C.E.; hence, the text is tentatively dated to that time. In *Seder ʿOlam Zuta,* the blend of chronology and genealogy indicates the importance of the Davidic line in the late antique and medieval Jewish world. Both the patriarchs of Palestine and the exilarchs of Babylonia claimed this birthright, evoking it as a source for their authority. By contrast, the chain of tradition in Avot and in subsequent rabbinical-historical works only resembles the genealogical in form, whereas a portion of *Seder ʿOlam Zuta* is explicitly so. Conflicts that occur between the rabbinate and claimants to various Davidic lines call into question the primacy of each interpretation of historical authority. The origins of Karaism are traditionally attributed to one such conflict, and the Karaites of the Arabic-speaking world maintained a patriarchate until the destruction wrought by the First Crusade. They, too, maintained genealogical lists of their Davidids.[93] The blend in *Seder ʿOlam Zuta* of chronological and genealogical elements suggests that the uses of the past had moved beyond the ahistorical formulations of the rabbis of Late Antiquity toward a new formulation (perhaps to be called medieval). The new literary form, although only hinted at here, moves from the symbolic to the concrete. The chronology is an exercise in precision, and much of the genealogy is specific to the exilarchate, a contemporary institution with a living leader.

The first important literary expression of the chain of tradition is found in the *Seder Tannaʾim ve-ʾAmoraʾim,* a geonic work possibly dating from the late eighth century.[94] It is variously attributed, to Naḥshon ben Ṣadok Gaon and Ṣemaḥ ben Paltoi Gaon (late 9th c.) or to Jacob ha-Kohen ben Mordecai

92. *Seder ʿOlam Zuta* is published in Adolf Neubauer, ed., *Medieval Jewish Chronicles,* 68–88.

93. On the conflict between Davidic claims and rabbinic spiritual and intellectual leadership, see Urbach, 602f. See also BT Hor. 11b for a *baraita* on the branches of the Davidic family. On Hillel's Davidic claims, see BT Yeb. 9a. On Karaite *nesiʾim,* see chapter 2, below.

94. *Seder Tannaʾim ve-ʾAmoraʾim* is published in Neubauer, *Medieval Jewish Chronicles,* but more usefully in Kalman Kahana, ed., *Seder Tannaʾim ve-ʾAmoraʾim,* with notes and a German translation. See the remarks of Gerson Cohen on the relationship of *Seder Tannaʾim ve-ʾAmoraʾim* to Ibn Daud in *Sefer ha-Qabbalah,* lii.

Gaon (d. 811). *Seder Tanna'im ve-'Amora'im* is comprised of two parts, the chain of tradition and a methodological section for interpreting halakhah from rabbinic sources, including specific genealogical information on some rabbis. The combination of these two elements points to the important methodological use the chain of tradition came to have in rabbinic works in the early Islamic era. Hermeneutical devices from the Talmud, such as the saying "All anonymous sayings are attributed to Rabbi Meir"[95] do not constitute complete enough guidance for the development of a fully evolved jurisprudential system. Taking into account the vast amount of material in the Talmud and other rabbinic literature, a need for method became increasingly important for elaborating halakhah (as well as for other types of interpretation). The pragmatic nature of individual rabbinic decision-making mentioned above required conventionalized means of legal and textual exegesis. One aspect of these methodological considerations was based on temporal priority. Some legislative concerns revolved around the question of whether a legal authority was anterior or posterior to another. In such cases, a clearly defined chain of tradition would provide the agreed upon matrix by means of which such a question might be answered.

I believe that these types of concerns become more important as halakhah moves out of the classical rabbinic period into the geonic and later periods. As indicated above, the voice of the Mishnah is in many ways monovocal, and although the Talmuds move away from this stance, their expression is typified as one where rabbis conduct legal discussions with each other over centuries. That is, the content is "massaged" without regard to the temporality of the discussion. The ahistorical view of a religio-legal tradition that is eternal and does not change through time remains central in this contextualization. In the geonic period, with the Talmud "canonized" and "constitutionalized," the continued development of halakhah required a means for the elucidation of the law of the Talmud, encouraging the development of methodology and systematization. *Seder Tanna'im ve-'Amora'im* offers material to approach a solution to some of these problems. In addition, the rabbinate of the Islamic period sought authority for its expositors, as Avot had provided for the rabbis of the Mishnah. *Seder Tanna'im ve-'Amora'im* offers a supplement for contemporary rabbinic authority similar to the chain of tradition of Avot and in parallel to the evolution of *ḥadīth* literature and its analysis in Islam.[96]

The fully elaborated version of the chain of tradition in *Seder Tanna'im ve-'Amora'im* is based on Avot. By the late eighth or ninth century, the face value of the chain of tradition—that is, the informational components about

95. BT Sanh. 86a. On such attributions, see Chajes, *The Student's Guide through the Talmud,* 111–17.

96. See Gerson Cohen on the relationship of Muslim constructions of tradition in relation to Ibn Daud in *Sefer ha-Qabbalah,* lv–lvii.

who passed on the law to whom—had become as important as the symbolic meaning of the tradent as proxy for Moses, as described above regarding Avot. As would then be expected, the elements of the chain that are absent in Avot are supplied, in addition to the inclusion of occasional chronological data that fills out the material. Not only are the names and order of scholars delineated but events associated with those individuals are sometimes mentioned. The chain extends to the time of the text's composition, thus filling in the intervening centuries between Judah ha-Nasi and the geonic period. The document also represents a change in the literary form in which the chain of tradition is found. *Seder Tanna'im ve-'Amora'im* begins to resemble a medieval chronicle, citing events in chronological order, each as a kind of historical "note," but without context or reference to cause and effect.[97] The gradual accretion of historical information that is first seen in *Seder ʿOlam Rabbah* and *Seder ʿOlam Zuta* is more important to the purpose and structure of *Seder Tanna'im ve-'Amora'im.*

This brings us to another important difference between *Seder Tanna'im ve-'Amora'im* and the chain of tradition in Avot. In Avot, the chain has been constructed to provide authority to the text of the Mishnah and its hermeneutic, not expressly to the individuals mentioned or any descendants, real or intellectual, that might be represented at a later time. In *Seder Tanna'im ve-'Amora'im,* the importance of the teachers of the Talmud and the geonic expositors is paramount. These rabbis are not simply the representatives and expositors of a text but are representatives and expositors of a social group with a religio-legal tradition. The character of this transformation is highlighted by the nature of the historical "notes" included in the text. Although some of these notes refer to events of historical noteworthiness, such as the founding or destruction of an academy or the murder of an exilarch, many others associate the day of a scholar's death with natural wonders or catastrophes. On the day Mar Zutra died there was an earthquake. On the day Aḥa ben Rabbah died there was an eclipse of the sun, "and the stars were seen in the daytime."[98] In this way, the importance of the expositors of the law, even as individuals, is given a kind of divine approbation. The symbolic association of Moses to the rabbis, as expressed in Avot, is secondary to this kind of divine validation. This type of miraculous accompaniment to human events within the religious world is not uncommon. The miraculous story of the translation

97. See Hayden White, "The Value of Narrativity in the Representation of Reality."

98. Papa ben Nasr (Odenathus) destroys Nehardea in 570 (Seleucid era), in Kahana, ed., *Seder Tanna'im ve-'Amora'im,* 4; and the murder of Huna ben Mar Zutra and deliverance of Jews into the hands of the Persian state in 782 (Seleucid era), ibid., 5–6.

of the Septuagint imparts divine approbation to the new Greek text.[99] A better example is the thunder and lightning that accompanied Jonathan's translation of the Torah.[100] In *Seder Tanna'im ve-'Amora'im,* the rabbis *themselves* are the recipients of approbation, not only of revelation per se or of a text. The value of the ancient revelation in this later time relies upon the tradents as bearers of traditon to such an extent that they become associated with divine interventions and thereby revelation itself. In these settings, the rabbis look like the holy men of Late Antiquity.[101]

Like the chain of tradition in Avot, the image of the master–disciple relationship is replicated, but becomes particularly important in this period, when an expositor's intellectual pedigree is a halakhic determinant. The rabbis are connected through the chain of tradition, as they were in Avot, to antiquity. This was especially important in the first three Islamic centuries, since the Muslims recognized that, although they were themselves the bearers of a venerable and respected history, it did not have an antiquity comparable to that of the Persians or Jews.

The completely revised exposition of the *shalshelet ha-kabbalah* in *Seder Tanna'im ve-'Amora'im* is the source for most later expositions of the chain of tradition. In the Middle Ages, versions appear in works of historical content, some of which are specifically concerned with an exposition of the chain of tradition. The *shalshelet ha-kabbalah* also appears in works and chapters on rabbinic methodology, both in instances where the *shalshelet ha-kabbalah* is found in commentaries and where the chain of tradition is utilized for making historical arguments in philosophical works.

Medieval Chains of Tradition. Another early example of the idea of a chain of tradition was written by Saadia Gaon (d. 942), one of the most important opponents of Karaism.[102] His *Sefer ha-Galui* included a chronology of history in order to provide proof for the transmission of tradition. Unfortunately, this work is extant only in fragments.[103] An important, but small, Karaite

99. BT Meg. 9a. See also the *Letter of Aristeas,* a new translation and introduction by J. H. Shutt, in James H. Charlesworth, ed., *The Old Testament Pseudepigrapha,* vol. 2: *Expansions of the "Old Testament" and Legends, Wisdom and Philosophical Literature, Prayers, Psalms, and Odes: Fragments of Lost Judeo-Hellenistic Works,* 7–34.

100. BT Meg. 3a.

101. See Peter Brown, "The Rise and Function of the Holy Man in Late Antiquity." Cf. Garth Fowden, "The Pagan Holy Man in Late Antique Society."

102. See Samuel Poznanski, "The Karaite Literary Opponents of Sa'adiah Gaon," 129–34.

103. The larger fragments are published in A. Harkavy, ed., *Zikhron la-Rishonim,* 5: 133–235. See also H. Malter, "Saadia Studies," 491, 497; idem, *Saadia Gaon: His Life and Works,* 387–94; and S. M. Stern, "A New Fragment from the 'Sepher Ha-Galuy' of R. Saadyah Gaon," 133f. [Heb.].

fragment is known that refutes these claims of Saadia's.[104] Although Saadia's history of tradition comprised only one of several chapters in this work, from what is known it can be said to represent the kinds of concretization of rabbinic notions related to historical transmission as described above in regard to *Seder Tanna'im ve-'Amora'im.*

The most important work of the geonic period to develop the rabbinic chain of tradition is *'Iggeret Rav Sherira Ga'on.*[105] Written in 987, this historical work is extant in two recensions, a Spanish and a French version.[106] *'Iggeret Rav Sherira Ga'on* was written in response to a series of queries from Jacob ben Nissim of Kairouan. The scholar from North Africa asked: How was the Mishnah written? What is the reason for the arrangement of the tractates? What is the purpose of the Tosefta? How was the Talmud written down? What is the chain of tradition for the saboraim and the geonim? As indicated by the questions, the character of the Oral Law was in need of explication. The chain of tradition in this text begins with Hillel and proceeds to the author and his son, Hai Gaon. Far more developed than *Seder Tanna'im ve-'Amora'im, 'Iggeret Rav Sherira Ga'on* is a primary source for modern academic study of the saboraic and geonic periods and for rabbinical studies in general relating to history, chronology, and the chain of tradition.[107]

The chroniclization of the exposition of the *shalshelet ha-kabbalah* is more evident in *'Iggeret Rav Sherira Ga'on* than in *Seder Tanna'im va-'Amoraim.* The high level of Sherira's scholarship is indicated in the inclusion of

104. Published in Harkavy, *Zikhron la-Rishonim,* vol. 5, 194–95.

105. On *'Iggeret Rav Sherira Ga'on,* see Rabinowich, *The Iggeres of Rav Sherira Gaon,* for a noncritical but annotated edition and English translation of the epistle. See his planned dissertation at New York University (cited in the unpaginated preface) for a critical study of the text and a planned Hebrew translation with full annotations. It traditionally appears in editions of Abraham Zacuto's *Sefer Yuḥasin,* first published in Constantinople, 1566 (see below), with modern editions in Neubauer, *Medieval Jewish Chronicles,* 1:2–46; and other editions by A. Hyman, *'Iggeret Rav Sherira Ga'on;* and B. M. Lewin, *Iggeret Rav Sherira Ga'on,* with addenda and corrections.

106. The primary difference between the two versions is on the question of whether Judah ha-Nasi's arrangement of the Mishnah was written or oral. The two versions correspond to the positions respectively maintained in the Middle Ages by the philosophically oriented Spanish school and the dialectically oriented French Tosafist schools.

107. See Jacob E. Ephrati, *The Savoraic Period and its Literature* for a comparison of *Seder Tanna'im ve-'Amora'im* and *'Iggeret Rav Sherira Ga'on* on saboraic chronology. In addition, see Jacob Neusner, *A History of the Jews of Babylonia,* 5: *Later Sasanian Times,* 135–46, on the differing chronologies for the fourth through seventh centuries found in *Seder 'Olam Zuta, Seder Tanna'im ve-'Amora'im, Iggeret Rav Sherira Ga'on,* and Ibn Daud. See esp. the chart on 144–45. For a summary, see Brody, *Geonim of Babylonia,* 3–34.

anecdotes from rabbinic literature and accounts of important events. *'Iggeret Rav Sherira Ga'on* also follows the previously indicated trend of magnification of the rabbinate. The text, whether Mishnah or Talmud, was by this time a centuries-old document. Requirements for interpretation were paramount, so the prestige and value of the individual tradent was all the more important. All that was indicated above regarding *Seder Tanna'im ve-'Amora'im* is more true in the tenth century for *'Iggeret Rav Sherira Ga'on.* A response to the Karaite challenge, central to Gerson Cohen's analysis of *Sefer ha-Kabbalah,* is also recognizable in this text.[108]

The most complete and conceivably most important rabbinic work to develop the chain of tradition is Abraham Ibn Daud's *Sefer ha-Kabbalah,* written in 1161. The rabbinical and genealogical agendas that typify *Seder Tanna'im ve-'Amora'im* and *'Iggeret Rav Sherira Ga'on* are supplemented and expanded upon, with the addition of regional concerns of the rabbinate in Spain. In fact, *Sefer ha-Kabbalah* is based upon *'Iggeret Rav Sherira Ga'on,* and later supplanted it to become the main historical source for rabbinic scholarship.[109] Cohen's annotated edition and translation of *Sefer ha-Kabbalah* is a model of critical historical scholarship. His analysis demonstrates the complexity of meaning found in such historical works. The previously indicated chroniclization exemplified in expositions of the chain of tradition is not merely the imposition of anecdotal reports onto the genealogical-like matrix of the chain of tradition but contains particular polemical and philosophical agendas. Cohen states that in the face of many challenges to Spanish rabbinic Judaism from the Babylonian rabbinate, Karaism, Islam, and Christianity, *Sefer ha-Kabbalah* provides "detailed evidence for Ibn Daud's contention that Judaism is validated principally by its claim to being an uninterrupted tradition."[110]

Cohen indicates three methodological themes used in *Sefer ha-Kabbalah* that supplement fundamental, inner-rabbinic theological and halakhic concerns:[111] (1) The harmonization of biblical and rabbinic chronology: Used to support other arguments in his text, this differentiation reflects Ibn Daud's political theory whereby Israel's leadership is divided between the political and religious. This is represented by linked pairs of kings and prophets, patriarchs/exilarchs and heads of the academies, and, in Spain, Jewish courtiers and the rabbinate. (2) The synchronization of Jewish history with the history of gentile nations: This method not only develops external "confirmation" of rabbinic historical data but encompasses world history within the historiosophy of the rabbis. The fate of the nations is dependent upon how they treat

108. See the introduction to Lewin's edition, op. cit., vif.

109. On the differences between *Sefer ha-Kabbalah* and *'Iggeret Rav Sherira Ga'on,* see Cohen, *Sefer ha-Qabbalah,* 177–88.

110. Ibid., xxxi.

111. The following themes are explicated in ibid., 149ff.

Israel. In Ibn Daud's political theory, the moral construct of the rabbis informs the course of empires. (3) The contextualization of heresy: This category is most important for a study of Karaite historiography. Through particular details in chronology Ibn Daud is able to distinguish his history from that of the Karaites. In his historical scheme, all heresy comes from the same source, the Samaritans, whose errors are the result of the continued presence of unreformed idolatry.[112] Ibn Daud connects subsequent manifestations of heresy in connection with the original schism. When Zadok and Boethos broke with Antigonus, they found refuge among the Samaritans and assumed leadership at Mount Gerizim.[113] Later, Anan ben David is portrayed as reinvigorating these latent heretical elements in Israel to create Karaism.[114] In linking political theory to these three historical contextualizations, Ibn Daud blames the occurrence of bad events in Israel to the presence of "lawless men" and the accession of non-Davidids to leadership. When the correct leadership, usually rabbinic, is in place, it is honored by the gentiles. Such an explanation supports a sympathetic attitude toward most Muslim hegemony, linking the success of the geonic and postgeonic rabbinate to Islam.[115]

The main purpose of *Sefer ha-Kabbalah* is to validate the authority of the Spanish rabbinate to the exclusion of the Babylonian academies. If the chain of tradition that concludes with the Spanish rabbis can be shown to have roots as solid as that of other rabbinical milieus, then the Spanish rabbis can adjudicate and legislate without recourse to the imprimatur of the Babylonian academies.[116] The fragmentation of rabbinic Judaism of this period represents the breakup of the centralized medieval rabbinate. The success of the rabbis in establishing their constitution and leadership coincided with the tenth-century beginnings of fragmentation in the Islamic world, coinciding with the breakup of the ʿAbbāsid Caliphate. Even as the Muslim imperium transformed itself into a commonwealth, so the Jewish world moved toward regional specificity in custom, halakhah, and self-rule.[117] Jewish communities

112. Ibn Daud's treatment of the Samaritans in *Sefer ha-Kabbalah* follows *Josippon.* See ibid., 16ff. In his handling of heresy, Ibn Daud approaches the purpose of much heresiography in Christian and Muslim traditions; that is, that the history of error is, in fact, a history of the truth.

113. Ibid., 17–18, 113.

114. Ibid., 49–50, esp. n. 54.

115. Ibid., 156–58.

116. For the origin of the Spanish rabbinate, see the story of the Four Captives in chapter 7 of *Sefer ha-Qabbalah,* in Cohen, 63–65. The largest chapter of the work, the seventh, and the larger part of the work as a whole, is devoted to the Spanish rabbis, ibid., 63–80. See esp., "The Four Empires and Jewish History," ibid., 223–62.

117. See Fowden, *Empire to Commonwealth,* 138–68. Cf. Mark R. Cohen, *Jewish Self-government in Medieval Egypt: The Origins of the Office of the Head of the Jews, ca. 1065–1126.*

in such areas as Spain, Provence, northern France and the Rhineland, the Byzantine Empire, Tunisia, and Egypt began to move in independent orbits. The idea of the exilarch had become as remote to the Jews as the concept of the emperor had become in the West, and the academies of Babylonia suffered decline and dissolution in concert with the decline of the caliphate and the subsequent amirate, culminating in the wholesale destruction of the Mongol invasion in 1258.

Cohen has laid the basis for understanding the Islamization of rabbinic notions of tradition in his edition of Ibn Daud's *Sefer ha-Kabbalah.*[118] He has demonstrated that the methods, forms, and sources of jurisprudence in Islam influenced Ibn Daud's theory of the Law and his exposition of the rabbinic chain of tradition. One of the important points of Cohen's work is that the *shalshelet ha-kabbalah* had become "Islamized" under the influence of Muslim jurisprudential method.[119] The chain of tradition inherited from Late Antiquity was reconfigured to represent for the rabbis a "complete and accurate record of the history of their non-scriptural tradition."[120] Mirroring the concerns of Muslim *ḥadīth* scholars, whose attention was focused on the tradents individually and their moral qualifications for representing tradition, rabbinic expositions of the chain of tradition in the Islamic period began to adopt such organizing concepts of categorization *(ṭabaqāt)* as generation *(qarn)*[121] or jurisprudential principles such as consensus *(ijmāʿ).*[122] Even as a rabbinic claim to continuity with the Bible and antiquity could defend against Christian claims of supersession so it deflected Muslim claims that God's law in the Jewish Scriptures had been abrogated thus paving the way for a new revelation and law in the form of Islam.[123] Similarly, it will be seen below that Muslim influence on Karaite jurisprudence was significant.

118. Cohen, *Sefer ha-Qabbalah.*

119. On Muslim jurisprudence, see Louis Milliot, *Introduction a l'étude du droit musulman;* Joseph Schacht, *The Origins of Muhammadan Jurisprudence;* idem, *Introduction to Muslim Law;* Coulson, *History of Islamic Law;* and Mohammad Hashim Kamali, *Principles of Islamic Jurisprudence.* For an analysis of *ḥādīth* and its chains of transmission, see I. Goldziher, *Muslim Studies;* J. Fueck, "The Role of Traditionalism in Islam"; and Muhammad Zubayr Siddīqī, *Hadith Literature: Its Origin, Development, Special Features, and Criticism.*

120. Cohen, *Sefer ha-Qabbalah,* lxii.

121. On the Islamic idea of a chain of transmission, or *isnād,* see ibid., l–lii. On *ṭabaqāt* and *qarn* in the shalshelet ha-kabbalah, see ibid., l and lv–lvi.

122. Consensus as a legal principle is not wholly an Islamic borrowing. Ideas of the consensus of Israel and scholars are found in talmudic literature, as well as Roman law. See Chajes, *Student's Guide,* 96–102. For the relationship of *ijmāʿ* to Jewish law in the Islamic period, see Cohen, *Sefer ha-Qabbalah,* xxxi and liii. On Muslim and Karaite uses of consensus, see the conclusion to part 1, below.

123. Ibn Daud took up the polemic against Muslim doctrines of abrogation in *Emunah Ramah,* his philosophical work. See Cohen, *Sefer ha-Qabbalah,* xxix–xxx.

It should be noted that the chain of tradition is also found in sections of introductions, works of methodology, commentary, and philosophy. As mentioned above, innerdiscursive formulations from the canon of rabbinic literature, such as the dictum referring to Rabbi Meir, do not provide enough material for a complete systematization of halakhah. *Seder Tanna'im ve-'Amor-a'im* is rudimentary in comparison with later works whose whole or partial intent is toward systematization. Early examples from the eleventh century of works that address halakhic methodology and include a chain of tradition are the *Mevo la-Talmud* of Samuel ben Ḥofni Gaon (d. 1013)[124] and the *Mevo ha-Talmud* of Samuel ibn Nagrela ha-Nagid (d. 1055).[125] Although methodological works usually included a description of the tradition, such is not the case for another eleventh-century introduction, that by Nissim ben Jacob Ibn Shahīn (d. 1062), *Sefer ha-Mafteaḥ*.[126] The author is supposed to have written a complete description of the chain of tradition elsewhere, but it is not extant.[127] A younger contemporary of Ibn Daud, Samuel ben Hananiah, nagid of Egypt, wrote an "Introduction to Talmud," which included an epitome of the chronology from *Sefer ha-Kabbalah*.[128] In the late twelfth or early thirteenth centuries, Joseph ben Judah ben Jacob Ibn Aknīn (d. 1220) composed *Mavo la-Talmud* that incorporated a chain of tradition.[129]

Cf. the translation of *'Emunah Ramah* by Norbert M. Samuelson, *The Exalted Faith: Abraham ibn Daud.*

124. On this work, extant only in fragments, and Samuel b. Hofni, see Shraga Abramson, *Ha-Rav Shemu'el ben Ḥofni (Geon Sura), Perakim min Sefer 'Mevo ha-Talmud,'* esp. the bibliography; idem, "Le-Mavo ha-Talmud li-Rav Shemu'el ben Ḥofni"; idem, "Milon ha-Talmud la-Rav Shemuel ben Ḥofni"; idem, "Min ha-Perek ha-Ḥamishi shel Mevo ha-Talmud li-Rav Shemuel ben Ḥofni." See also Ernst Roth, "Keta' le-Shalshelet ha-Kabbalah mi-Tekufat ha-Geonim." Now see David E. Sklare, *Samuel ben Hofni Gaon and His Cultural World: Texts and Studies.*

125. The "Introduction to the Talmud" found at the end of tractate Berakhot in the standard Vilna edition of the BT is attributed to Samuel, but is likely not his work. His introduction as described in other medieval rabbinic works contained an exposition of the chain of tradition. For another *shalshelet ha-kabbalah* by Samuel set within a poem of thanksgiving, see his *Diwan* (Habermann, ed.) 1, pt. 1, 96; also in a newer edition by D. Yarden, *Divan Shemu'el ha-Nagid,* with complete bibliography. On Samuel as a halakhist, see M. Margalioth, ed., *Hilkhot Hannagid.*

126. Edited by J. Goldenthal.

127. Entitled *Sefer Seder Mekable ha-Torah.* See Samuel Poznanski, *Esquisse Historique sur les Juifs de Kairouan,* 38 [Heb.]. Nissim was erroneously considered the author of the fragments of a description of the chain of tradition now attributed to Samuel ben Ḥofni. On Nissim, see Shraga Abramson, *Rab Nissim Gaon.*

128. Cohen, *Sefer ha-Qabbalah,* 182–83.

129. Published by H. Graetz as *Einleitung in den Talmud* in *Festschrift . . . Zacharias Frankel.*

Commentaries also offer an opportunity for writers to discuss methodology and utilize the chain of tradition. Nathan ben Abraham II (d. before 1102), *av bet din* (head of the court) of the academy of Palestine, wrote a commentary on the Mishnah whose introduction includes a survey of the development of the Oral Law.[130]

The chain of tradition and arguments for transmissional continuity with biblical antiquity are also found in philosophical works. In the eleventh century, Judah Halevi's *Kuzari* includes a description of tradition that played an important role in later Karaite historical development. Not only does he put forth the argument of historical continuity but, like Ibn Daud, he also uses the history of tradition to contextualize heresy.[131] For him, the Karaites are understood to have emerged at the time of Simeon ben Shetah and Judah ben Tabbai: "Rabbanism was laid low for some time"; that is, the well-established tradition had been obstructed by the persecution of the sages at the hand of the Hasmonean king Jannai. Those who tried to maintain the Law without recourse to tradition resorted to their own rational faculties, but this resulted in many errors.[132] In this way, Zadok, Boethos, and Jesus are understood to have deviated from the true tradition.[133] By dissociating the Karaites from Zadok and Boethos, Halevi adopts an intellectually honest posture, acknowledging that there were differences between these two groups.[134]

In the twelfth century, Maimonides also incorporated a close discussion of tradition in his introduction to his commentary on the Mishnah. Positioning his material before the entire commentary (i.e., not simply appearing in Abot), he presents a description of tradition that is used to contextualize his theory of prophecy. Also included is methodological and historical information.[135] In addition, Maimonides uses a description of tradition to introduce

130. On Nathan, see Simha Assaf, *Tekufat ha-Geonim ve-Sifrutah,* 296f. The Mishnah commentary in its Hebrew translation was edited by Yosef Kafah and published along with the mishnaic text and other commentaries (Jerusalem, 1955–56).

131. The Judeo–Arabic text of *Kitab al-Khazari* is edited by D. H. Baneth (Jerusalem, 1977). There are many other Hebrew editions, some incorporating rabbinic commentary.

132. Thus the beginnings of Karaism are described. For Halevi's description of tradition, see *Kitab al-Khazari,* 64–67. For a somewhat outdated English translation, see Hartwig Hirschfeld, trans., *Judah Hallevi's Kitab al Khazari.* An abridged translation by Isaak Heinemann is found in *Three Jewish Philosophers.*

133. On heresiography and historical contextualization, see chapter 2, below. On Judah Halevi and Karaism, see chapter 4, below.

134. Not only might Halevi have read the works of medieval Karaite philosophers, but he also knew that, unlike the Sadducees, the Karaites believed in the world-to-come and reward and punishment.

135. See Yosef Kafah, ed., *Mishnah ʿim perush rabbenu Mosheh ben Maimon,* Seder Nezikin, 1–58. There are two nonscholarly English translations: Zvi Lampel,

the *Mishneh Torah,* a systematic exposition of the laws of the Torah. The chain of tradition becomes a preface, in contrast to previous codes such as *Halakhot Gedolot* or *Halakhot Pesukot,* which used the 613 commandments. The traditional enumeration of 613 commandments was useful as an introductory device, but it does not provide a methodologically sound basis for an inquiry into the Law.[136]

The rabbinical "project" for extending and refining the chain of tradition, as mentioned above, extended beyond the Islamic world and was maintained beyond the Middle Ages. Although the primary form for the chain of tradition based on Abot is found in *Seder Tanna'im ve-Amora'im,* most of the works of historical-rabbinical and related literary genres are based to a great degree upon Ibn Daud's *Sefer ha-Kabbalah.* Abraham ben Solomon Ardutiel (often erroneously indicated as Torrutiel) completed a "supplement" to Ibn Daud's work in Fez, 1510.[137] The most important of these is *Sefer Yuḥasin,* the continuation of *Sefer ha-Kabbalah* by Abraham Zacuto (d. 1515), which improves greatly upon the historicity of the material.[138] Later, Gedaliah Ibn Yaḥya (d. 1587) intended to replace Ibn Daud's work with his *Shalshelet ha-Kabbalah.*[139] Many other historical-rabbinical works from the Renaissance and early modern periods depend upon Ibn Daud's *Sefer ha-Kabbalah* and Zacuto's *Sefer*

---

trans., *Maimonides' Introduction to the Talmud;* and Fred Rosner, trans., *Moses Maimonides' Commentary on the Mishnah: Introduction to Seder Zeraim and Commentary on Tractate Berachoth.*

136. On the structure and relationship of these two early codes, see the introduction of S. Sassoon, ed., *Halakhot Pesukot;* and Neil Danzig, *Introduction to Halakhot Pesuqot with a Supplement to Halakhot Pesuqot.* In spite of Maimonides' influence on subsequent legal codification, few of his successors in this enterprise utilized a chain of tradition in their works. In the mid-thirteenth century, the tosafist Moses ben Jacob of Coucy followed the discussions of Maimonides' *Mishneh Torah,* but maintained the traditional arrangement of 613 commandments divided between the positive and negative commandments. He did not incorporate a description of tradition in his *Sefer Miṣvot Gadol,* first printed in 1480 (Rome?). In another context, the Spaniard, Menaḥem ben Aaron Ibn Zeraḥ (d. 1385), did not utilize a chain of tradition in his code, *Ṣedah la-Derekh,* first published in Ferrara in 1554. Later editions include Lemberg, 1859, and Warsaw, 1880. The Karaites also found the enumeration of 613 commandments to be methodologically unworthy. Eschewing an argument from tradition, they often embraced a scheme of categorization based upon the Ten Commandments.

137. Published in Neubauer, *Medieval Jewish Chronicles,* 101–14; and A. Harkavy as an appendix in Heinrich Graetz, *History of the Jews.* Cited in Yerushalmi, *Zakhor,* 135, n. 10.

138. First edition published in Constantinople, 1566. On Zacuto, see A. A. Neuman, "Abraham Zacuto, Historiographer," 597–629.

139. First edition published in Venice, 1587. On Ibn Yahya, see Avraham David, "The historiographical work of Gedaliah Ibn Yahya, author of shalshelet ha-kabbalah."

Yuḥasin; these will be discussed below in relation to the Karaite historical works of the seventeenth and eighteenth centuries.[140]

The preceding remarks are by no means a complete description of the chain of tradition in medieval rabbinic literature. The purpose has been to indicate the barest outlines of its literary development and to comment on some of its historical implications, thus laying the foundation for a closer analysis of parallel phenomena in the Karaite literary milieu.

140. Mention should be made of two, whose importance for the exposition of the shalshelet ha-kabbalah are significant: David Conforte, *Kore ha-Dorot,* and Jehiel Heilprin, *Seder ha-Dorot.*

2

The Past in Early Karaite Judaism

The Middle East of the second and third Islamic centuries is the setting for the emergence and development of Karaite Judaism. Leadership of the Jewish world was increasingly being gathered into the hands of the rabbis, whose "constitution" was embodied in the Oral Law and was supported by vague approaches to the past. Different strands of opposition, rejection, and innovation eventually came together in the late ninth and early tenth centuries to coalesce into what is identifiable as Karaism. For the subsequent two centuries, the Karaites were engaged in an increasingly sophisticated and successful intellectual and social development, marked by the florescence of a scholarly center at Jerusalem and vibrant communities in Palestine, Egypt, and elsewhere.[1] Classical Islamicate Palestinian Karaism was characterized by five main features: an anti-rabbinic ideology, a claim to scripturalism, Palestinocentrism, quasi-ascetic rigorism, and millenarian messianism.[2]

1. See Haggai Ben-Shammai, "The Karaites," in Joshua Prawer and Haggai Ben-Shammai, eds., *The History of Jerusalem: The Early Muslim Period, 638–1099,* 201–24; Haim Hillel Ben-Sasson, "The Karaite Community of Jerusalem in the Tenth–Eleventh Centuries"; and Samuel Poznanski, "Reshit hityashevut ha-qara'im bi-yerushalayim" (The beginning of Karaite settlement in Jerusalem). The standard references on Karaism of this period are Jacob Mann, *The Jews in Egypt and in Palestine under the Fatimid Caliphs;* idem, *Texts and Studies in Jewish History and Literature,* 2: *Karaitica;* and now Gil, *History of Palestine,* which is an English translation of the first volume of *Palestine during the First Muslim Period, 634–1099* [Heb.], including many primary sources relating to the Karaites in vol. 2:511–65. See also relevant primary texts translated into English in Leon Nemoy, *Karaite Anthology: Excerpts from the Early Literature.*

2. Moshe Zucker notes the first three in "Responses to the Karaite Mourners of Zion Movement in Rabbanite Literature." On Karaite messianism, see Yoram Erder, "The Negation of the Exile in the Messianic Doctrine of the Karaite Mourners of Zion"; and Daniel Frank, "The *Shoshanim* of Tenth-Century Jerusalem: Kara-

By the eleventh century, the center of activity in Palestine declined as a consequence of Fāṭimid Egyptian weakness and the resulting Turkoman, Sāljūq, and Crusader conquests of the twelfth century. In 1099, the Crusader destruction of Jewish communities of Jerusalem, both Rabbanite and Karaite, marked an end to what has been described as the "classical" period of Karaism.[3] Although Karaite intellectuals of the Islamicate world would continue to make a contribution to the movement, by the thirteenth century the focus of intellectual and social activity shifted to Constantinople and the Byzantine Empire.

Palestino-centrism, Scripturalism, Quasi-ascetic Piety, and Messianism in Islamdom

One of the most important features of Middle Eastern Karaism at its height was what Zvi Ankori described as Palestino-centrism.[4] A call for the return of Jews to the Land of Israel, and especially Jerusalem, characterized the classical Karaite ideology of Daniel al-Qūmisī (fl. late 9th century) and his successors in Palestine, who combined in this ideology Jewish antecedents with contemporary opportunity.[5]

Scholars have noted that the political hegemony of Egypt over Palestine under the Ṭūlūnids and Ikhshīdids (868–905 and 935–69) was conducive to the call to immigration of al-Qūmisī and his fellow Karaites.[6] By the end of the ninth century, the political anarchy at Samarrā (861–70) in Iraq was worsened by the growth of Ṣaffārid power coming out of Sīstān in eastern Iran and the by the decline of Ṭāhirids, the main military support for the caliphate.[7] A lack of confidence in the political institution of the caliphate was

ite Exegesis, Prayer, and Communal Identity." On antirabbinic ideology, see Poznanski, "Karaite Literary Opponents," 129–234.

3. Ankori speaks of a "Golden Age of Karaism in Palestine": *Karaites in Byzantium,* 7f., 25, 206, 455. He also mentions a "Golden Age of Jewish Sectarianism" out of which originate several of the elements that come together in tenth-century Karaism. It is described as the "Golden Age of anti-talmudic dissent in the Palestinian-led countries of the East Mediterranean littoral." Ibid., 381–82. On the Crusader debacle, see Joshua Prawer, *The History of the Jews in the Latin Kingdom of Jerusalem,* esp. 1–45.

4. Ankori, *Karaites in Byzantium,* 22–24, and passim.

5. Zucker, "Responses," 387–401 [Heb.]; Jacob Mann, "A Tract by an Early Karaite Settler in Jerusalem"; and Leon Nemoy, "The Pseudo-Qumisian Sermon to the Karaites."

6. See Moshe Gil, "More about Palestine during the First Muslim Period"; Thierry Bianquis, "Autonomous Egypt from Ibn Ṭūlūn to Kāfūr, 868–969"; and Jere L. Bacharach, "Palestine in the Policies of Tulunid and Ikhshidid Governors of Egypt (a.h. 254–358/868–969 a.d.)."

7. Haggai Ben-Shammai, "Fragments of Daniel al-Qūmisī's Commentary on the Book of Daniel as a Historical Source."

felt widely. Caliphal weakness opened up opportunity for a bedouin resurgence along the boundaries of the desert and the sown and created political space for the independence of provinces. Political decline was driven, in part, by economic decline, which was the result of excessive taxation, the emergence of military regimes, and the incorporation of the *iqṭāʿ* system, a feudal-like distribution of land and resources by princes and lords to military subordinates. Muslims and Jews turned to apocalyptic and millenarian ideologies to grapple with the uncertainties of social and political turmoil. Jewish apocalyptic responses from this period are read in *Maʿaseh Daniel* and *Ḥazon Daniel,* but are also found in Karaite messianic and millennial ideology.[8] The call to return to Zion is millenarian, whereby immigration to the Land of Israel would hasten the coming of the messiah, whose presence was much needed in an age of troubles.[9]

By the ninth century, the focus of political action in the Middle East became the province, with the decline of what Marshall Hodgson calls the caliphal "absolutist tradition."[10] Outer provinces were being reorganized as Muslim societies, and new elites were establishing themselves to lead these societies. The cosmopolitanism of early multicultural society under the caliphate gave way under the transformation of Islamization to localism.[11] Egypt emerged as a province of political importance through Ṭūlūnid and Ikhshīdid policies that reinvigorated the agrarian economy and capitalized on new trade routes that centered on Egypt. Palestine benefited as a protectorate of Egypt, buffered from the impact of decline in Iraq and the East. After the conquest of Egypt in 969, the Fāṭimids would continue policies that focused attention on Palestine.[12] Even as the caliphate was being pulled apart, Rabbanite institutional leadership struggled with the centrifugal pull of the provinces. Some Jews turned to local rabbinic and commercial elites to lead them from a regional base.[13] Others looked to rabbinic Palestine for leadership after centuries of Babylonian dominance. Still others lived in a nonrabbinic Jewish Palestine, inhabited by sectarians, including a branch of the family of Anan ben David, whose participation in the Babylonian-Palestinian struggle over halakhic hegemony in the Jewish world reveals that the line

8. Avraham Grossman, "Jerusalem in Jewish Apocalyptic Literature."

9. Qarmatian wars led Yefet ben ʿEli ha-Levi to messianic hopes, cited in Gil, *History of Palestine,* 784, n. 4.

10. Hodgson, *Venture of Islam,* 1:241–47, 1:280–89, and s.v. "absolutist ideal" in the index.

11. Hodgson, *Venture of Islam,* 1:473–95; and Hugh Kennedy, *The Prophet and the Age of the Caliphates,* 200–211.

12. Paula A. Sanders, "The Fāṭimid State, 969–1171."

13. For example, see Cohen, *Jewish Self-government in Medieval Egypt.*

between sectarian and rabbinic Jew in this period is fluid and indeterminate.[14]

In a civilizational context, the progress of Islamization and the concomitant development of Muslim institutions meant that Muslim society could be something other than caliphal. The old pan-Muslim imperial-caliphal monopolies on legitimacy were undermined by mosques, as centers of the community, by the administration of Muslim law by religious clerics instead of government officials and by the symbolic appropriation of the land by holy men and holy places. New Muslim elites, detached from imperial power, rose to lead new institutions and constituencies. Identified by Hodgson as the "*sharʿīah*-minded" (*sharʿīah* = Muslim law), the *ʿulamāʾ*, along with early *ṣūfī*-mystic leaders, became the definers of Muslim religious and social life.[15] In like manner, some Jews perceived rabbinic hegemony to be no longer meaningful and began to imagine a reformulated Jewish society free from rabbinic leadership. The rise of new Muslim elites, especially the ʿulamāʾ, is mirrored both within the rabbinic milieu by the decline of central Babylonian (Iraqi) institutions and the emergence of regional rabbinic leadership and within the sectarian milieu by the rise of Karaism and the decline of activistic messianic movements.

Accompanying the rise of *sharʿīah*-minded leadership was a new symbolic Muslim appropriation of the land through the dispersal of relics of Muḥammad, but more importantly through the dispersal of knowledge of the Prophet's tradition, or *sunnah*, from Mecca and Medina to the many new urban centers of Islam.[16] In Islam, this diffusion of identity and knowledge to cities outside of Arabia was rejected by the early Khārijites, who retained a strong sense of tribal identity. They maintained a concrete sense of center, reified in the manner by which one converted to their brand of Islam through enacting a *hājj*, or pilgrimage, to their encampments. Even as the *hājj* was becoming normative in *sharīʿah*-minded Islam as a link between the Meccan center and the new diffuse urban environment, the Khārijites particularized the idea to create their own centeredness.[17] In addition, early Khārijite scripturalism centrally located the Qurʾān in their own version of Islam to the exclusion of other forms of reading and interpretation that were developing among Muslims. Similarly, Karaism would mobilize biblical scripturalism as a means for repudiating rabbinic tradition and leadership, as well as

14. See Moshe Gil, "Karaite Antiquities," *Teʿudah* 15.

15. Hodgson, *Venture of Islam,* 1:238, 345–50, and s.v. "sharīʿah-minded" in the index.

16. Brannon M. Wheeler, "From *Dār al-Hijra* to *Dār al-Islām:* The Islamic Utopia."

17. W. Montgomery Watt, "Khārijite Thought in the Umayyad Period."

the Rabbanite diaspora.[18] Return to the Bible was accompanied by return to the land.

In contradistinction to new Muslim notions of the city,[19] the Palestinocentric orientation of early Karaism evokes archaic Jewish notions of topocosm, while perhaps vaguely conjuring up a Hellenistic conception of the city as a place that possesses an essential religious and communal identity. The survival of such a Hellenistic construction of the city and its culture in early Islam is known from polytheistic Sabian Ḥarrān.[20]

The symbolic appropriation of Jewish diasporic space was simultaneously being completed as Rabbanite Jews and Muslims together engaged religiously in a shared worldview whose past (and therefore whose space) was inhabited by many of the same regal and prophetic personalities, whom for the Jews were their own biblical forebears. This hybridized diasporic space was littered with tombs and other holy places that could be shared by Jews and Muslims. The Muslim literature known as *qiṣaṣ al-anbiyāʾ* (tales of the prophets) is testimony to this shared worldview. Early Karaites would have eschewed this Rabbanite–Muslim cultural and religious syncretism by rejecting aggadah, which laid out the narrative foundations for this shared conception of space,[21] but also by refocusing Jewish concern for space and place to the traditional ancient homeland. The rejection of aggadah and new approaches to halakhah were firmly founded on Karaite scripturalism. For example, Palestinocentrism could be mobilized both scripturally and halakhically in rules for determining the leap year through observation (in the land!) of the *aviv* (ear of barley).[22] Like the Khārijites, Karaites would particularize and parochialize the notion of the sacred center, which in rabbinic Judaism was universalized and in proto-Sunnī Islam was becoming so. Unlike the Khārijites, who located the center in their own communities, centeredness would remain fixed on the traditional place—Jerusalem and the Land of Israel.

The Karaites sought a way to appropriate both symbolically and concretely a land that was and had been under the political hegemony and religious dominance of non-Jews for centuries. They turned to rigorous and

18. Cp. Haggai Ben-Shammai, "Return to the Scriptures in Ancient and Medieval Jewish Sectarianism and in Early Islam."

19. See Paul Wheatley, *The Places Where Men Pray Together: Cities in Islamic Lands, Seventh through the Tenth Centuries.* Cf. the articles in A. H. Hourani and S. M. Stern, eds., *The Islamic City.*

20. See G. W. Bowersock, *Hellenism in Late Antiquity,* 29–40; and Garth Fowden, *Empire to Commonwealth: Consequences of Monotheism in Late Antiquity,* 62–65. On the Sabians, see note 183, below.

21. See Miller, "Was There Karaite Aggadah?"; Vajda, "Quelques aggadōt critiquées"; and Mann, *Texts and Studies,* 1:49–57.

22. Gil, *History of Palestine,* 796–98.

quasi-ascetic attitudes and practices, based in part on the Bible and in part on ancient Jewish antecedents attested to in rabbinic literature in the aftermath of the destruction of Jerusalem and the Temple in 70 C.E. Known as Mourners for Zion *(abele ṣiyyon),* Jews responded to the loss of homeland and the cosmic injustice of the Exile.[23] In Late Antiquity, the rabbis had cut the link between rigorism and centralized notions of place by rejecting such practices as naziritism and excessive mourning.[24] In addition, Karaites referred to themselves as "the poor" *(ʾanavim* and *ʾevyonim),* as an evocation of rigor but also in connection to their rejection of diasporic commercialism and the accumulation of wealth associated with the Rabbanite establishment:[25]

> Woe to you, o Rich Men of the Dispersion and the Wealthy of Israel in Babylonia, you who plant gardens and orchards [in the Diaspora] and establish summer-houses for yourselves . . . , and forget God's Torah and the Mourning of Jerusalem. Your money shall be an abomination at the End of Days and the retribution for [your] sins will descend upon you.[26]

Karaite rigor also corresponded to aspects of early Muslim mysticism, often characterized by asceticism and self-denial. As *ṣūfī* and other holy men left their locational mark across the Muslim world in the form of tombs and

23. Barry Dov Walfish, "The Mourners of Zion ('Avelei Siyyon): A Karaite *Aliyah* Movement of the Early Arab Period"; and Haggai Ben-Shammai, "Poetic Works and Lamentations of Qaraite 'Mourners of Zion'—Structure and Contents." See Pesiqta Rabbati 34.1 and 34.2 (158ab). Cf. Ankori, *Karaites in Byzantium,* s.v. "Mourners of Zion" in the index; and Gil, *History of Palestine,* 617–22, for a review of Karaite participation in the movement. The term is first used in *Halakhot Keṣuvot,* a ninth-century legal compendium. In the ninth-century *Chronicle of Aḥimaʿaṣ,* donations are recorded for the *avele bet ʿolamim* and *avele ha-hekhal.* The movement may have been inspired by Jewish mystical and messianic materials of the early Islamic period. See Zvi Avneri in *EJ* 3:945–46, s.v. "Avelei Zion." Daniel al-Qūmisī is credited (probably erroneously) with a sermon encouraging immigration to Palestine. See A. Marmorstein, "Daniel al-Qūmisī's Homilies," 31ff.; and Nemoy, "Pseudo-Qumisian Sermon." Sahl ben Maṣliaḥ in his "Epistle" also provides important information on the Karaites in Jerusalem and their posture as Mourners for Zion. See Pinsker, *Likkute Kadmoniyot,* 2:25–43.

24. For rabbinic reactions to excessive mourning after the destruction of the Temple, see BT B.B. 60b and B.K. 59b; cf. similar reactions to naziritism, BT Ned. 10a and 77b, Naz. 19a, and Taʿan. 11a. See also *Megillat Ahimaʿaṣ* 18c and 20c.

25. For example, see Daniel ben Moses al-Qūmisī, *Pitron Shenem-ʿAsar,* 66. For similar ideas and language, cf. *Pitron Shenem-ʿAsar,* 14 (on Hosea 8:14); 21 (on Hosea 12:9); 63 (on Zechariah 2:1–4); and 61 (on Haggai 2:17).

26. Daniel ben Moses al-Qūmisī, *Pitron Shenem-ʿAsar,* 34 (on Amos 3:15), translated in Ankori, *Karaites in Byzantium,* 312.

other shrines, Karaites sanctified the center, Jerusalem and the Land of Israel, through their holy practices, even though the majority of Karaites repudiated mystical and gnostic tendencies of the larger Mourners for Zion movement. They also rejected worship at tombs, a diasporic, syncretistic, universalizing practice.[27]

The Karaite call for return to the Land of Israel was millennial-messianic and sought what Yoram Erder calls the "negation of the Exile."[28] Palestino-centrism situated the Karaites in diametric opposition to the rabbis, by taking hold of the center while objecting to the diaspora. The diaspora was characterized as increasingly corrupt and was led by diasporically committed rabbinic leaders, often referred to as "shepherds of the Exile," a variation on a Qumranic epithet.[29] The inner-Jewish context for Karaite resistance was directed against rabbinic hegemony, but paralleled and echoed a necessary sense of resistance to Muslim hegemony. Karaites further opposed rabbinic legal liberalism by inhabiting the space of Israel (both conceptually and in practice) with quasi-ascetic rigorism, mirroring aspects of the *ṣūfī* trend of appropriating spiritual space by rejecting religious orthodoxies and political hegemony. Immigration starting in the late ninth and early tenth centuries brought Jews, both Karaite and Rabbanite, from all over the Islamic world to Palestine,[30] where many of the variegated practices and beliefs of the previous two centuries came together.[31]

For the rabbis, there was no specific doctrine of the messiah: the idea of the messiah could serve different functions.[32] Rabbinic literature contains much material that seeks to diminish apocalyptic and millennial tendencies associated with messianism, and correspondingly would resist Karaite millennialism. The predominance of rabbinic halakhah in Jewish societies represented a religious model for *this* world, not for the one to come. As Judaism

27. For example, Sahl ben Maṣliaḥ in Pinsker, *Likkute Kadmoniyot,* 2:32.

28. Erder, "Negation of the Exile," 109–40.

29. For example, it is used repeatedly by Daniel al-Qūmisī in his ninth-century commentary on the Minor Prophets. See Daniel b. Moses al-Qūmisī, *Pithrōn Shenem ʿAsār; Commentarius in Librum Duodecim Prophetarum,* 4, 8, 9, 45, 67, 72. See also Judah Hadassi, *Eshkol ha-Kofer,* alphabet 125, *he*; alphabet 358, *vav*; alphabet 85, *alef*; and Elijah ben Abraham in Pinsker, *Likkute Kadmoniyot,* appendix, 101, 1:3f. Cf. Naphtali Wieder, *The Judean Scrolls and Karaism;* and A. Paul, *Écrits de Qumran et sectes juives aux premiers siècles de l'Islam.* See note 6 of the conclusion to part 1, below.

30. Haggai Ben-Shammai, "Rabbanite and Karaite Attitudes Toward Aliya"; Avraham Grossman, "Aliya in the Seventh and Eighth Centuries"; and Moshe Gil, "Aliya and Pilgrimage in the Early Arab Period, 634–1009." Cf. Shmuel Safrai, "Talmudic Sources on Aliya and Pilgrimage," 188–89.

31. Gil, *History of Palestine,* 609–30, esp. 617–22, on Karaites.

32. See Jacob Neusner, *Messiah in Context: Israel's History and Destiny in Formative Judaism,* 227–31.

invested increasingly in rabbinic halakhah, efforts were made to place messianic potentialities on the peripheries of mainstream thought. To "press the End"—that is, to seek to hasten the coming of the messiah, as the Karaite project was seeking—was considered inappropriate. In the Babylonian Talmud, three different rabbis are attributed with the statement "May he come, but I do not want to see him."[33]

For the rabbis, God's plan begins with creation, and revelation and is concluded with the coming of the messiah and the End of Days. All of history flows from the one to the other, and everything that takes place between these two poles of existence is to be understood by means of covenantal morality in a halakhic context. Having been born before the creation of the world, and being an agent for the End of Days, the messiah stands as a symbol of the conceptual perimeter in which all human history must unfold.[34] Biblical Creation and Revelation stand in the beginning, and the messiah stands at the end. For the rabbis, what remains in between are the operating results of the mechanisms of sanctification and salvation.

For Karaites and others to embrace an activistic messianism meant that they sought to distance themselves from the diasporically oriented here and now of the rabbis and make efforts to move toward the End. When Jews felt the imminence of redemption, the danger of antinomian or charismatic activity could threaten the social order. Rabbinic thought emphasized counter-arguments to balance against these tendencies, imprinting the rabbinic legal philosophy and halakhic project with the immediacy of sanctification, while salvation could only be the result of sanctification or a far-off telos for the course of human events.[35] The rabbis, as hegemons, sought to maintain social order and keep the End distant. Karaites seized immediacy, but redirected it through pietistic rigor and Palestino-centrism to "press the End," working toward more imminent messianic results. The Karaites seamlessly cohered messianic time and sacred space.

Polemic and Halakhah: The Karaite Struggle against Rabbinic Tradition

Many of the characteristics that distinguish Karaism of the tenth and eleventh centuries and that separate it from mainstream rabbinic Judaism are centered around ritual and the legal interpretation of the laws of the Torah. The Judaic arena in which the Karaite-Rabbanite struggle often took place is defined by a pietism that placed value in human action and by a law-defined orthopraxy that set up specific expectations on human action. Much Karaite attention

33. BT San. 98a.

34. See Pesik. Rab. 33, 34; BT Pes. 54a; and BT Ned. 39a.

35. See BT A.Z. 9b; cited in Silver, *Messianic Speculation*, 26: "If 400 years after the destruction a man says to you, 'Buy my field, which is worth one thousand dinars, for one dinar,' do not buy it."

was directed against rabbinism in a struggle over numerous particular halakhic points, but also engaged social aspects of Middle Eastern Jewish life. Anti-Rabbanism was a thread that wove its way through much of the fabric of Karaite discourse.

One of the most important Karaite writers of the tenth century is Abū Yūsuf Yaʿqūb al-Qirqisānī. His *Kitāb al-anwār wal-marāqib,* written in 937,[36] includes extended descriptions and refutations of rabbinic law.[37] Some of the significant legal differences separating Rabbanism from Karaism are indicated in specific points of halakhah that the author uses to critique Rabbanite practice. A list of some examples of disagreement includes the appropriate use of the psalms for prayer;[38] the prohibition of prostration; Sabbath practices, including buying, selling, writing, cooking, the use of candles, and sexual activity;[39] details of purities laws, including corpse uncleanness, degrees of impurity, and menstruation; dietary laws, including minimum amounts of contaminant, forbidden portions of meat, and methods of slaughter;[40] calendrical methodology, including intercalation, the date of Shavuot, the calculation of the New Moon, and counting the Omer; matters of consanguinity, marriage, and rape;[41] and the rabbinic introduction of the festival of Hanuk-

36. Edited by Leon Nemoy under the title *Kitāb al-anwār wal-marāqib [KA].* I have followed Nemoy's system for citations from the text: where general topics or references are represented by sections, they are cited in terms of al-Qirqisānī's arrangement; i.e., section, chapter, and subsection (e.g., 1:2.11); where the reference is to a specific line, phrase, or word, it is designated by the page and line number in Nemoy's edition (e.g., 594.13). For important references, I have tried to supply both methods of citation when appropriate. Pages in Wilfrid Lockwood's translation are noted in parentheses following the citation from Nemoy's edition.

37. *KA* 1:3–4 (Lockwood, 105–33). See also several chapters of the second section for al-Qirqisānī's philosophical refutations of principles of rabbinism, *KA*, esp. 2:10–18, vol. 2, 87–149. For a discussion of these sections, see Georges Vajda, "Etudes sur Qirqisânî," 87–98. Nemoy translated *KA* 1:3–4 in "al-Qirqisānī's Account of the Jewish Sects and Christianity," 317–97. A better translation by Wilfrid Lockwood is now found in Bruno Chiesa and Wilfrid Lockwood, *Yaʿqūb al-Qirqisānī on Jewish Sects and Christianity: A Translation of "Kitāb al-anwār," Book 1, with Two Introductory Essays,* 91–188.

38. See *KA*, 608.16. Cf. Uriel Simon, *Four Approaches to the Book of Psalms, from Saadiah Gaon to Abraham Ibn Ezra;* Jonathan Shunary, "Salmon ben Yeruhim's Commentary on the Book of Psalms"; and Frank, "The *Shoshanim* of Tenth-century Jerusalem."

39. Cf. Samuel al-Maghribī, *al-Maqālah al-thānīyah min al-kitāb al-musamma bil-murshid fīl-shabbat,* Nathan Weisz, ed. And now Samuel ben Moses al-Maghribī *Sefer ha-Miṣvot (Kitāb al-murshid),* Yosef ben ʿOvaydah Algamil, ed.

40. See Leon Nemoy, "Israel Maghribi's Tract on Ritual Slaughtering."

41. Cf. Samuel al-Maghribī (David Weiss, ed.), *al-Maqālah al-tāsīʿah fī al-ʿarawūt min al-kitāb al-musamma bil-murshid.* Cf. the recent edition, see note 39, above.

kah. In addition to halakhic matters, al-Qirqisānī mentions several matters of belief: adherence to anthropomorphic beliefs found in such texts as *Shiʿur komah*, the *Alphabet of Rabbi Akiva*, and the *Book of Ishmael* (these include ideas that God weeps, prays, can mourn, is a priest, and exhibits humility);[42] belief in angels, including Metatron; belief in amulets and magic;[43] that there is reward for the study of rabbinic texts; and that the rabbis of the Talmud performed miracles. These are by no means complete lists of al-Qirqisānī's halakhic and theological points, but they permit the observer to get a feel for the landscape of Karaite-Rabbanite polemic.

The constant engagement with rabbinic halakhah along the lines indicated above continued to inform the development of the legal hermeneutic of Karaism.[44] With an established schedule of halakhic points whereby Karaism differed with the rabbis, the foundation and form for a complex polemical and apologetic stance was possible. The emergence of classical Karaism in the late ninth and tenth centuries coincided with a well-executed attack on the nascent movement by Saadia Gaon.[45] Even as a consensus of some non-rabbinic practice was being acknowledged by the adherents of Karaism and cognate groups, and as deviations from rabbinic halakhah were recognized as a threat to rabbinic leadership and social life, the contestants began to devise attacks and defenses, denunciations and justifications. In the tenth century Karaite anti-rabbinic polemic exploded in response to Saadia's challenge.[46] In a sense, the discourse with Saadia fueled Karaite polemic and apology for centuries.[47] Gerson Cohen has summarized the Karaite complaints against Rabbanism with four points:

42. Cf. extracts from Daniel al-Qūmisī in Mann, *Texts and Studies*, 2: *Karaitica*, 75ff.

43. See *KA*, 574.4 and 586.12. See also Vajda, "Etudes sur Qirqisânî, 1. La magie, la mantique et l'astrologie selon le 'Livre des Lumières et des Vigies' "; Ira Robinson, "Jacob al-Kirkisani on the Reality of Magic and the Nature of the Miraculous: A Study in Tenth-century Karaite Rationalism"; and Mann, *Texts and Studies* 2: *Karaitica*, 55–57.

44. These halakhic issues are repeated and amplified in later Karaite "Books of Precepts," or compendia of halakhah. The issues are summarized comprehensively from a modern Karaite work in Leon Nemoy, "Mourad Farag and His Book *The Karaites and the Rabbanites*." See also the important 1913 doctoral thesis of Bernard Revel, "The Karaite Halakah and Its Relation to Sadducean, Samaritan and Philonian Halakah."

45. See Henry Malter, *Saadia Gaon: His Life and Works*, esp. 380–94; and Salo W. Baron, "Saadia's Communal Activities."

46. Poznanski, "Karaite Literary Opponents," 132.

47. This had been summarized in a comprehensive biographical and bibliographical format, ibid., passim; and Ankori, *Karaites in Byzantium*, 23f., where he speaks about the "Saadyah complex" of the Palestinian Karaites of the period. See also, ibid., 80, 390, 394. Karaites refer to Saadia using many euphemisms, such as

> (1) Scripture itself gave no indication that any laws not recorded in it are to be enacted and fulfilled; in other words, the so-called "Oral Torah," the Mishnah and its cognate literature, was merely human legislation, not of Mosaic or prophetic origin. (2) The rabbis of the Talmud often flatly contradicted the explicit provisions of Scripture by the type of practice which they ordained; e.g., though the Bible had expressly forbidden the use of fire in Jewish homes on the Sabbath, the rabbis established that the day should be ushered in by the kindling of "Sabbath lights." (3) The rabbis themselves betrayed the falsehood of their tradition by the countless and endless disputes among them on the correct application of the prescriptions of the Torah, and, what is more, by the flagrant differences in practice between them. If talmudic law was indeed of divine origin, why was it not as anonymous and as peremptory as the law of Moses; why, on virtually every point, did one find that the school of Hillel, for example, ordained one form of practice and the school of Shammai the very opposite? (4) The Rabbanite claim to be the heir to the Mosaic-prophetic tradition was not attested by the common consensus of Jews, for while all Jews testified by their agreement on the divinity of Scripture to the validity of its commands, the same consensus of opinion did not obtain with regard to rabbinic law.[48]

The Karaite threat to rabbinic orthopraxy is indicated most obviously in the second and third points—in the second, in terms of the sources of law, and in the third, methodologically, in terms of legal hermeneutic. But the historical assumptions of Rabbanism are primary targets for Karaite attack in the first and fourth points. This brief summary of halakhic and theological issues that defined much Karaite anti-rabbinic polemic in the tenth and eleventh centuries helps outline what Leon Nemoy identifies as, "a Jewish sect that recognizes only the Hebrew scriptures as the source for divinely inspired legislation and denies the authority of the postbiblical Jewish tradition (the oral law) as recorded in the Talmud and later rabbinic literature."[49] Because the postbiblical Jewish tradition was supported by a historical ideology embedded in the Oral Law and later in the idea of the chain of tradition, any opposition group such as the Karaites could either reject historicizing the

---

"that man" or the "Pithomite," in a wordplay on the region of his origin, the Fayyum. See Poznanski, "Karaite Literary Opponents," 149, 180. For other ad hominem arguments used in the controversy between Sahl ben Maṣliaḥ and Jacob ben Samuel, see, ibid., 166, 168. Likewise, the Rabbanites are often designated as "those people" or as "tyrants," among other derogatory names. See Mann, *Texts and Studies,* 2: *Karaitica,* 24.

48. Cohen, *Sefer ha-Qabbalah,* xliv.

49. Nemoy, in *The Encyclopedia of Religion,* 8:254–59, s.v. "Karaites."

group's connection to the past altogether or adopt an alternate historical identity. For tenth- and eleventh-century Karaites, the impulse toward the former was influenced by scripturalism, millennialism, and anti-tradition.

Karaite Approaches to the Past in Medieval Islam

When Samuel Poznanski, the early twentieth-century master of Karaite studies, reviewed historical writing in Karaite literature,[50] he described such writing in the period of early Islam "meager and thin"[51] in one instance, and in another as "comical."[52] Such views are echoed and repeated in the writings of other early scholars of Karaitica, such as Bernard Revel, who says, ". . . there is a marked lack of historical sense among them. They have no tradition as to their origin, and their opinions are conflicting."[53] Underlying such remarks is a supposition that there should exist a notion of history that can be identified as Karaite. In addition, it may be implied that a lack of historical sense is a mark of Karaite inferiority. This judgmental view of Karaite historical sensibilities privileges by implication Western notions of the past, and even rabbinic Jewish historiography. Thereby, it denies Karaism historical specificity, ignoring the possibility that its notions of the past and history can be described. Moreover, it denies Karaism a history that is nuanced and undergoes change. Presumably, a Jewish sect which challenged rabbinic Judaism so forcefully for centuries must have generated particular images and uses of the past. Critical study of Karaism, as of any religious community, yields to the scrupulous observer a complicated sense of history that undermines simple and biased views of the Karaites as a Jewish sect.

Historians of an earlier era might have researched in Karaite literature to debunk historical untruths or find embedded historical data that supported a sense of history that could only be fact-based and true or false. Historical inquiry based on such an approach might work well for studying the Roman Empire or the Dutch Republic, but is problematic for studying the Jews, for whom history was of little general concern. As a minority people, they lacked states, kings, and battles to memorialize in historical writing or architectural monuments. And, although it is true that the past was not of primary concern to most Karaite writers of the classical period, after decades of scholarship in Karaitica and related fields we can now ask different questions of their literature. How literary and historically framed writing within Karaite literature

50. The only monograph devoted to the topic of Karaite historiography is Samuel Poznanski's 1920 introduction to Mordecai Sultanski's *Zekher Ṣaddikim.* See Samuel Poznanski, ed., *Zecher Caddikim, Kronika Historyczna Karaity Mordechaja Sultanskiego* (henceforth, *Zekher Ṣaddikim*).

51. *"Dalot ve-razot."* Ibid., 13.

52. Ibid., 17.

53. Revel, "Karaite Halakah," 2. Cf. Simhah Pinsker, *Likkute Kadmoniyyot,* 2:98.

reflects the material's origin and the document's provenance goes beyond the positivist approaches of earlier historiography. We are now interested in the historical settings of texts, whether its facts are "true" or not. Within texts embedded attitudes and constructions of the past may be non-historical in an older sense, but now interest historians and scholars of religion. In this study, we must ask how such literary creations fit into a model for understanding Karaism from the late ninth through the eleventh century.

It is true that concern with the past was not of primary importance to Karaite writers of the Islamic world before the transfer of the movement's intellectual leadership to Constantinople in the thirteenth century. But, by the sixteenth century Karaites imagined a chain of tradition much like the rabbis which linked the past to the present. Moreover, in the seventeenth and eighteenth centuries Karaite scholars in Poland-Lithuania wrote historiography in response to contacts from Protestant Christian academics. The attitude shared by Poznanski and Revel is derived from their understanding of Karaism before the dissolution of its center in Jerusalem in the eleventh century to the exclusion of these later periods. In the classical period, Karaite writers lack consensus on the past, eschewing history as a means toward self-definition. This can be accounted for by two reasons: anti-Rabbanism and millenarian messianism.

Karaite Scripturalism and the Rabbinic Past. The Karaite, Salmon ben Yeruḥim, who flourished in tenth-century Jerusalem, said regarding the Rabbanite Jews:

> Know that there is no difference in learning between them and me.
> When they say, "Rabbi So-and-so said thus-and-so,"
> I answer and say, I, too, am the learned So-and-so.
> Thine escape has been cut off by this argument, else answer me, if thou canst.[54]

Salmon acknowledges and attacks an important characteristic of rabbinic authority, the generation-to-generation transmission of the divinely revealed Oral Law, which is one of the principles of the rabbinic idea of tradition embodied in the idea of the chain of tradition. The Karaites, on the other hand, admitted only a single divine revelation, that of the Hebrew Bible. Salmon equates himself and his abilities with that of the sages of the Mishnah and Talmud, striking a blow at the heart of the rabbis' historical support for their "constitution" and authority.[55] In the Middle Ages versions of the chain

54. *Book of the Wars of the Lord,* canto 2, v. 13, trans. in part in Nemoy, *Karaite Anthology,* 77. See the Hebrew edition edited by Israel Davidson, *Sefer Milḥamot Adonai,* 42.

55. This is not an entirely new attack on rabbinic tradition; e.g., see Matthew 7:28–29.

of tradition were utilized in defense against Karaite attacks upon the transmissional basis of rabbinic jurisprudence.[56] Correspondingly, because traditionalism and its idea of a chain of tradition was anathema to medieval Karaites, they found their relationship with the past to be problematic. That is, since the rabbis utilized a historicized argument to support rabbinic legitimacy, Karaites would be inclined to keep away from historical claims to support their own ideology.

Much of the sentiment of classical medieval Karaism can be summed up in the oft-repeated dictum attributed to the eighth-century Anan ben David, often acknowledged as the "founder" of Karaism by later Karaites: "Seek diligently in the Torah, and do not rely on my opinion."[57] Although the veracity of the dictum's attribution to Anan is questionable, nonetheless, it is useful as an illustration of fully developed Karaite doctrine of the tenth and eleventh centuries. The first part of the statement speaks for a kind of scripturalism that rejects the Mishnah, Talmud, or any expression of an extra-biblical Law. It lays claim to the sufficiency and uniqueness of the Torah as a source of law. The second part is a direct repudiation of the rabbinic chain of tradition, whose authority is based on the rulings and opinions of masters transmitted to disciples, and thereby to posterity.

Karaism and the Jewish Past. Although early Karaites would deny a rabbinic construction of the past, they would not deny particular models gleaned from the Jewish past. As Palestino-centric Mourners for Zion, Karaites called for Jews to return to Zion in order to hasten the coming of the messiah. The space between the distant past of mourning and expected future of messianism left little room for close consideration of history. The millennial future was understood to be imminent—its arrival could be facilitated by immigration and mourning. The past was another question. When it was mobilized by these Karaites, it was a distant biblical past, and not a recent one. Like so much of Judaism, the biblical past was all the past that was needed. However, some of the Karaite literature of this period is marked by the use of an interpretive method also present in the Dead Sea Scrolls, the pesher. By using the pesher, one reads biblical texts as signs for describing and understanding contemporary events.[58] Karaites were able to read in the Bible about rabbis, their own movement, Muslims, and signs for interpreting the imminent end of time.[59]

56. Cohen, *Sefer ha-Qabbalah,* xliii–l.

57. This motto first appears in the late tenth century in the Karaite Yefet ben 'Eli ha-Levi's commentary on Zechariah, 5:8. See Haggai Ben-Shammai, "Between Ananites and Karaites: Observations on Early Medieval Jewish Sectarianism," 22f.

58. William H. Brownlee, *The Midrash Pesher of Habakkuk.*

59. Naphtali Wieder, "The Dead Sea Scrolls Type of Biblical Exegesis among the Karaites"; idem, *The Judean Scrolls and Karaism,* 1962; and Ben-Shammai, "Fragments of Daniel al-Qūmisī's Commentary."

The pesher may be a reading of the Bible, but it is also a reading of history that can obliterate the past. It creates immediacy in the moment of reading, and obviates the necessity of using other ways to understand the past. What is important in history is a kind of eternal now that reaches for the biblical past, which at the same time embraces the immediate future. Such a focus on *illud tempore* means that history is of little value, even a waste of time. The need to connect the present to the past is precluded by immediate concerns (such as strict observance of biblical commandments, ascetic-like practices associated with mourning, and immigration to Palestine).

One approach to the study of Karaism borrows from sociology, whereby efforts are made to make theoretical and general notions of sectarianism more precise, seeking a definition and model for the phenomenon in general. In the 1970s, Bryan R. Wilson developed a taxonomy of sects, describing seven types, each according to a *response to the world* and how it approached the problem of divine or holy power and the presence of evil. His labels are: conversionist, revolutionist, introversionist, manipulationist, thaumaturgical, reformist, and utopian.[60] When studying Karaism, one notes before the decline of the Jerusalem center in the eleventh century a clear theoditic perspective that accompanies mourning, immigration, and millenarianism. Many Karaites engaged conversionist strategies through the call for immigration and adoption of the ways of the Mourners for Zion, while simultaneously maintaining a utopian stance in regard to the imminent future of restoration and salvation which would result from messianic developments toward which many Karaites were working. In contrast, the rabbis adopted the stance of societal dominance, seeking social and theological stasis in relationship to the Muslim authorities and the days of the messiah. The rabbis explained themselves, in part, through their notion of tradition and the past. In contrast, medieval Islamicate Karaism focused on the immediacy of its ideological positions by using the dual lenses of conversionism and utopianism to avoid recourse to a historical past.

When the available Karaite sources for this period are examined it becomes clear that in their adherence to a rejectionist stance toward transmitted tradition the Karaites by and large failed to come to a consensus regarding history and continuity with the past. Historical allusions and historicizations which have survived were offered *en passant* in order to fulfill ancillary intellectual and literary functions.

Salmon ben Yeruḥim, born around 910, exemplifies the absence of a consistent historical ideology among the Karaites. In one case, he denies antiquity for the Karaites, claiming they are *ḥadashim*, "newcomers."[61] He also parodies

60. Bryan R. Wilson, *Magic and the Millennium: A Sociological Study of Religious Movements of Protest among Tribal and Third-World Peoples*, 1–69.

61. Pinsker, *Likkute Kadmoniyyot*, 1:19. Cf. Revel, "Karaite Halakah," 4, n. 1, where he cites Salmon's commentary on Psalm 69:1. On this verse, see below.

rabbinic claims to antiquity by reminding the rabbis that other villains such as Sisera and Haman of the Hebrew Bible are rooted in the ancient past.[62] In another instance he equates the *bene mikra,* "people of the Book" (the Karaites), with *ahl al-kitāb,* the Muslim designation for peoples who had received a revelation from God in previous eras, and who were eligible for the status of *dhimmī* in Muslim society. This enigmatic statement can be understood as an allusion to antiquity (as acknowledged by the dominant Muslim society), or also as an innovation of the historically recent Islamic culture. Such a contradictory evocation of a characteristically Muslim concept of "comparative religion" reflects the Muslim idea of an ancient chain of prophecy culminating in the mission of Muḥammad.[63]

Salmon's claims to history are necessarily apologetic and polemical.[64] He used historical arguments gleaned from the rabbinic construction of the past to further his anti-rabbinic claims. Both Shammai and Hillel, rabbinic sages of the Mishnah, are denounced.[65] It is claimed that their followers had violent

62. *Sefer Milḥamot 'Adonai,* 113; cited in Ankori, *Karaites in Byzantium,* 362, n. 18.

63. Salo W. Baron, *A Social and Religious History of the Jews,* 5:400, n. 31. On the Islamic concept of a chain of prophecy, see Richard Bell, "Muhammad and Previous Messengers"; Arthur Jeffery, *A Reader on Islam: Passages from Standard Arabic Writings Illustrative of the Beliefs and Practices of Muslims,* 333–36, a section entitled "Muḥammad among the Prophets," from Jalāl al-Dīn Abū al-Faḍl ʿAbd al-Raḥmān al-Suyūṭī, *al-La'ālī al-maṣnūʿa,* 137–40; and Helmut Gätje, *The Qur'ān and Its Exegesis: Selected Texts with Classical and Modern Muslim Interpretations,* 53–55, which is a commentary on Sura 27:52/51 from Abū al-Qāsim Maḥmūd ibn ʿUmar al-Zamakhsharī, *Tafsīr al-kashāf ʿan haqā'iq ghawāmiḍ al-tanzīl wa-ʿuyūn al-ʿaqāwil fī wujūh al-ta'wīl.*

64. See Daniel J. Lasker, *Jewish Philosophical Polemics against Christianity in the Middle Ages,* who states that arguments made by a social group or caste within a larger group are universally understood to be types of apology and polemic. In his introduction (3f.), he describes three types of polemical argument: (1) exegetical, (2) rational, and (3) historical. Although he rightly recognizes the historical argument as the weakest of the three, it should be acknowledged that the three types of argument are not completely independent. Respectively, they are able to address a wide variety of concerns. For a more general statement, see B. Malinowski, *Magic, Science and Religion,* 67f. (cited in Cohen, *Sefer ha-Qabbalah,* li).

65. *Sefer Milḥamot 'Adonai,* 45; other general denunciations of the Mishnah and Talmud are found elsewhere, 40–42, 45–46. See Luzatto, *Kerem Ḥemed,* 4:1; cited in Revel, "Karaite Halakah," 6, n. 4. Hillel and Shammai are the objects of polemical attack in other Karaite works. See Yūsuf al-Baṣīr, *Sefer Miṣvot* in Abraham Harkavy, ed., *Zikhron la-Rishonim,* vol. 4, *Zikhron kamah geonim,* 394; and Yashar ben Ḥesed, *Sefer Miṣvot* in *le-Korot ha-kitot be-Yisra'el,* 9; cited in Poznanski, *Zekher Ṣaddikim,* 5, n. 2.

physical confrontations.[66] He also maintained that the rabbis had destroyed priestly genealogical records in order to undercut claims of priestly privilege. In this case he historicizes the succession of the rabbinic sages to leadership in Israel.[67] This polemic is doubly effective for it not only vilifies the rabbis, but also explains the absence of the priesthood from a position of leadership in contemporary Judaism. One might not expect such an argument from a scripturalist perspective wherein the priesthood would be acknowledged and sought after in the present. In effect, the rabbis are discredited for a central tenet of their historical view, that even as they are the inheritors of Moses and the prophets they are the successors, albeit through usurpation, of the priesthood.

Other tenth- and eleventh-century Karaites evidence a lack of historical consistency similar to Salmon. Sahl ben Maṣliaḥ, who flourished in Jerusalem during the later half of the tenth century, claimed that Karaism goes back to the time of the Second Temple without referring to any specific schism or event.[68] Elsewhere he bases the division of Israel into two sects on a reading of Zechariah, chapter 11, where he expresses a positive attitude toward the Four Kingdoms, who have permitted Israel to survive and follow its religion. The villains of this scenario are the rabbis and their two academies in Iraq.[69] Sahl articulates a principle that is used consistently by later Karaite historians, that the truth has always been held by a small minority in Israel. Often observing the true religion in secret, this small group is aided by God, in the same way He aided Jeremiah and Baruch.[70]

Finally, Karaite writers varyingly accepted or rejected the rabbinic accusation that they were in fact an offshoot of the Second Temple Sadducees, a sect that, like the Karaites, rejected the Oral Law.[71] On the Rabbanite side, Saadia Gaon claimed that the remnants of Zadok and Boethos had joined Anan in his schism,[72] while in the eleventh century Abraham Ibn Daud and Abraham

66. Poznanski, "Karaite Literary Opponents," 144; and Mann, *Texts and Studies, 2: Karaitica,* 21–22.

67. *Sefer Dinim,* cited by Samuel b. Moses al-Maghribī, *Kitāb al-Murshid,* xi, 1 (Arab.), 11ff. (Germ.).

68. Pinsker, *Likkute Kadmoniyyot,* 2:35; and Revel, "Karaite Halakah," 5, n. 4.

69. Pinsker, *Likkute Kadmoniyyot,* 2:42. The two academies are named Sura and Anbār (Pumbeditha), represented by the two women in Zechariah 5:9, the bearers of wickedness into the land of Shinar, which is Babylonia, or Iraq.

70. Poznanski, "Karaite Literary Opponents," 17, where he cites Pinsker, *Likkute Kadmoniyot,* 2:35. Cf. Jacob ben Reuben, a Byzantine Karaite biblical commentator, *Sefer ha-ʿOsher* on Cant., 11c–d, "Most of Israel is on [the side] of the lie." Cited in Ankori, *Karaites in Byzantium,* 331–32, n. 82, where the recycling of antirabbinic polemics is described.

71. See Yoram Erder, "The Karaites' Sadducee Dilemma."

72. Pinsker, *Likkute Kadmoniyyot,* 2:103; cited by Revel, "Karaite Halakah," 7. It is assumed by Revel that Saadia is the author of the historical account by Anan in

Ibn Ezra maintained that they *were* Sadducees.[73] Even Maimonides, who held relatively tolerant attitudes toward the Karaites said, "In Egypt they are called Karaites, while in the Talmud they are named Sadducees and Boethusians."[74] Among the Karaites Yefet ben ʿElī ha-Levi, a contemporary of Sahl's, called the Sadducees "contemptible,"[75] while Yūsuf al-Baṣīr, of the early eleventh century, is claimed to have identified the Karaites with the Sadducees.[76]

The thin representation of the past among the early Karaites is partially explained in two ways. One is the ahistorical worldview shared with the rabbis. That is, Karaites were more concerned with halakhic and biblical perspectives on Judaism than with constructing a picture of the past. Secondly, and more importantly, early Karaism was messianic and millennial in character.[77] The immediacy of millennial messianism in itself obviates a need for representing the past, except to the extent that it serves the purposes of the imminent and ultimate future. On a practical level, the pietistic quasi-ascetic ideology of the Mourners for Zion supported Palestino-centrism, which in turn generated the call for immigration to the Land of Israel and the concomitant negation of the exile.[78] The immediacy of pietistic rigor in conjunction with forward-looking messianic millennialism left little room for rumination on post-biblical history or use of the non-biblical past.

This review of medieval Islamicate Karaite historical notions is, by no means, a complete survey. The current state of research in Karaite studies requires the continued identification, publication, and translation of texts.[79] Karaism inherited the history of the Bible. Like the rabbis the incorporation of historical time from the sanctioned distant biblical past into the ritual calendar and biblical interpretation was more influential than a focus on the recent past and Jewish history. In addition, the polemic against the rabbinic

---

the twelfth century *Ḥilluk ha-Kara'im veha-Rabbanim.* On Anan in this text, see below, this chapter, esp. n. 87. On the text's Byzantine provenance, see chapter 3.

73. See Cohen, *Sefer ha-Qabbalah,* xxxviiiff.; and Ibn Ezra's introduction to the commentary on the Bible, Lev. 3:9; 23:17, 40; cited in Revel, "Karaite Halakah," 7, n. 10.

74. Commentary on Abot 1:3, *Mishnah ʿim perush rabbenu Mosheh ben Maimon,* Joseph David Kafah, ed., 410. See also Revel, "Karaite Halakah," 8.

75. Poznanski, "Anan et ses Écrits," 171–72. Revel, "Karaite Halakah," 8, n. 13.

76. Supposedly in the *Kitāb al-Istibṣār* in Harkavy, *Zikhron la-Rishonim,* 5:47; cited by Revel, "Karaite Halakah," 8, n. 13. The problem of the reliability of older scholarship is indicated in this citation.

77. See Frank, "The *Shoshanim* of Tenth-century Jerusalem."

78. Ankori, *Karaites in Byzantium,* s.v. "Palestino-centric" and "Palestino-centrism" in the index. Although methodology connecting Karaism to the Dead Sea Scrolls is awkward, see Erder, "The Negation of the Exile"; and Astren "The Dead Sea Scrolls."

79. See Daniel Frank, "The Study of Medieval Karaism, 1959–1989: A Bibliographical Essay."

chain of tradition supported a posture that eschewed historical research and writing. For the purposes of this study, it is clear that classical Karaism of the late ninth through eleventh centuries lacked a consensus on matters historical.

Salmon ben Yeruḥim and the Karaite Past. It seems the lack of a consistent historical ideology among Karaites did not divorce Salmon ben Yeruḥim entirely from a historical outlook. As pointed out by Salo Baron, Salmon indicates four stages of Karaite development in his commentary on Psalm 69:1. They are represented first by Anan ben David, and then Benjamin al-Nahawendī, a ninth-century jurisprudent who differed with some of Anan's teachings. The third stage is designated as that of the *bene mikra*, the "people of Scripture," and the fourth is that of the "men of the East and West." Salmon locates the four stages of Karaite history in a global context by using the Four Kingdoms from the Book of Daniel, a common exegetical topos in both Rabbanite, Karaite, and Christian writings. In this case the Fourth Kingdom represents the Caliphate. Karaism is thereby embedded in the divine plan for the unfolding of history, being the true form for Judaism under the Fourth Kingdom.[80] The transformation through the four stages from the personal ideologies of Anan and Benjamin to a group designation, the *bene mikra*, and then to a wide geographical dispersion, is Salmon's exegesis of the past, whose purpose is to contextualize Karaism in history. Historical growth is acknowledged, multiple origins are implied, and Islam provides a backdrop.[81]

The historical consciousness evident in Salmon's periodization begs further comment. Salmon is not merely constructing a literary nicety, but demonstrates the encounter with memory. By the beginning of the tenth century, the non-rabbinic and anti-rabbinic Judaisms that came together to form Karaism brought with them their separate pasts. Anan had lived 200 years earlier! By this time, immediacy and ahistoricity could no longer be considered intellectually honest. We know that Karaite religious ideology is scripturally based, and at the same time is fundamentally opposed to the historicizations of the

80. Cited in Baron, *Social and Religious History*, 5:232. Arabic text in Lawrence Marwick, ed., *The Arabic Commentary of Salmon ben Yeruham the Karaite on the Book of Psalms, Chapters 42–72*, 97–98. Hebrew translation in Pinsker, *Likkute Kadmoniyyot*, 1:21f. The ninth-century writer Daniel al-Qūmisī mentions the Muslim role in connection with the Karaite presence in Jerusalem. See his letter in Mann, "Tract by an Early Karaite Settler." Extracts are translated in Gil, *History of Palestine*, 787: "The kingdom of Ishmael . . . always helps the Karaites to keep [the precepts] as in the Torah of Moses, therefore we have to say benedictions for them"; "they love those who guard [the custom of] fixing the months according to the moon; why therefore, should you fear the Rabbanites?" See Ben-Shammai, "Attitude." Cf. Sahl ben Maṣliaḥ, n. 68, above.

81. Many Karaites credited the benevolence of Muslim sovereignty as a support for Karaism. See Gil, *History of Palestine*, 607; and Ben-Shammai, "Attitude."

rabbis. Such an ideology might logically eschew any historical postulation and seek identity and self explanation through its relationship to and interpretation of the divine text. Yet, in the text at hand Salmon understands that there exists an evolutionary character to Karaism. The homogeneous and easily identifiable movement characterized by the "Golden Age" of Karaism in the tenth and eleventh centuries veils a complex past. In fact, many Karaites of that period and subsequent centuries did recognize a founder for their movement, the eighth-century Anan ben David. This view was inherited and incorporated into modern scholarly understanding of early Karaism, and has only recently been subject to critical review and reevaluation. It must be remembered that due to the paucity of sources and the problems associated with their interpretation "we will never know the whole story" behind Anan and early Karaism.[82]

Karaism must be viewed *within* history. By seeking to avoid biases of interpretation that could result in a characterization of the movement that is monolithic or reductionist, it becomes difficult to maintain a view that in the medieval period Karaism's essential character was ahistorical and scripturalist. Significantly, the ahistorical scripturalism that *is* present in the tenth and eleventh centuries has been accepted by many modern scholars as an essential element in all periods and manifestations of what has been traditionally recognized as Karaism. Recent more sophisticated analyses of Anan ben David and early Karaism would indicate that the somewhat homogeneous and easily identifiable movement of the tenth and eleventh centuries evolved from several original socio-religious groups and movements, which in the eighth and ninth centuries are distinct and separate. It cannot be said of the Karaites that "they had no historical ideas because they had no history," as if the movement was some kind of medieval intellectual reformation movement that spontaneously came to life in the mind of an individual or at the hands of a few colleagues. These groups and ideologies have histories of their own, some of which had a history of coming together to form Karaism. Salmon is witness to this historical process. Using Salmon's four stages, comment can be made on important aspects of early Karaism and its precursors.

Anan ben David. What is known about Anan comes from four sources that date from the late ninth to the middle of the twelfth century.[83] The first two present an incomplete picture.[84] The locus classicus for Anan's story is an

82. Daniel J. Lasker, "Rabbanism and Karaism: The Contest for Supremacy," 48.

83. Summarized by Leon Nemoy in "Anan ben David: A Reappraisal of the Historical Data."

84. These are:

1. *Siddur Rav 'Amram Ga'on,* attributed to Natronai Gaon, c. 880. Anan is barely mentioned in a text that originated in the same Babylonian milieu from which he is supposed to have emerged. Nemoy cites the edition by Frumkin, 2:206–7, which reads (based upon Nemoy's trans.): "These men are heretics and scoffers who hold in contempt the words

anti-Rabbanite Byzantine Karaite work of the twelfth century attributed to Elijah ben Abraham, which oddly enough clearly replicates an anti-Karaite rabbinic version of Anan's story.[85] Daniel J. Lasker summarizes it as follows:

> Anan, who lived in the second half of the eighth century, was in line to become the exilarch, or chief civil authority, of all Babylonian Jewry. Since, however, he was accused of lawlessness and lack of piety, his learned but humble brother Hananiah was chosen for this prestigious and powerful position. Out of jealousy, Anan gathered around him remnants of those sectarian groups which had flourished at the time of the Second Temple, namely Sadducees and Boethusians, and organized his own group with himself as exilarch.
>
> This affair was discovered by the Muslim authorities, and Anan was put in prison and sentenced to death. In jail with him was a Muslim scholar, identified by other sources as Abū Hanīfah al-Nuʿmān ibn Thābit, who likewise was sentenced to death. The Muslim suggested that Anan bribe the viceroy into permitting him an

---

of scholars, may they be blessed, and who are disciples of Anan, may his name rot, the grandfather of Daniel . . . who said to those who strayed and were seduced to follow him, 'Forsake ye the words of the Mishnah and of the Talmud, and I will compose for you a Talmud of my own!' To this day they remain in error, and have become a people unto themselves, while he fabricated an evil and wicked Talmud for himself. My master Eleazar Alluf has seen this abominable book of his, which they call *Sefer Miṣvot;* it contains many (heretical) tricks." Nemoy points out that "the text of the *Siddur* has undergone considerable modifications in the course of time, and that the account of Anan contained in it may have been somewhat different originally." Nemoy, "Anan ben David," 309–11.

2. al-Qirqisānī, *KA* 1:2.14 (Lockwood, 103). The text reads (adapted from Lockwood's trans.): After Yudghān, came ʿĀnān who was exilarch in the days of Abū Ja'far al-Manṣūr. He was the first to reveal some of the truth about the laws. He was learned in the teachings of the Rabbanites, none of whom could impugn his learning. It is said that Hai, the head of the Academy, and his father, while translating a book by ʿĀnān from Aramaic to Hebrew, found nothing among his doctrines whose source they could not attribute to the Rabbanites, save only his teaching on the first-born, and the difference between what is planted in Israel and what is planted among the Gentiles: they knew of no source for this, until they found it in the songs of Yannai. The Rabbanites attempted to murder him, but God did not allow him to fall into their hands." al-Qirqisānī also discusses Anan's halakhah, *KA* 1:13. On this, see below.

85. The text is *Ḥilluk ha-Kara'im veha-Rabbanim,* published in Pinsker, *Likkute Kadmoniyyot,* 2:97–106. See also Nemoy, "Elijah ben Abraham and His Tract." This text will be dealt with more directly in chapter 3, below.

> audience with the caliph. At that meeting Anan could persuade the ruler that he did not claim to be the head of Judaism but was the leader of a different religion. Therefore, since he was not contesting his brother, whom the caliph had appointed exilarch, he was not, in effect, challenging the authority of the caliph. If Anan could entice his followers to support this assertion that they had their own religion, Abu Hanifah told him, his life would be spared. He was able to convince his supporters by claiming a vision from the prophet Elijah.
>
> When he was received by the caliph, Anan is reported to have said: "The religion of my brother employs a calendar based upon calculation of the time of the new moon and intercalation of leap years by cycles, whereas mine depends upon actual observation of the new moon and intercalation regulated by the ripening of new grain." Since the caliph's religion likewise declared the new moon on the basis of astronomical observation, Anan gained his favor and good will. Thus, Karaism was founded.[86]

Later, to escape the continued machinations of the rabbis, who sought to have him killed, he and his followers migrated to Jerusalem, where he established the synagogue that subsequently bears his name. The polemical intent of the narrative is obvious. It is to Anan's personal discredit that he was motivated by jealousy in his endeavor and utilized both trickery and manipulation to gain the support of the non-Jewish Muslim ruler to achieve his goals. Furthermore, it is to his doctrinal and theological discredit that he engaged remnants of the Second Temple period heresies for support and furthermore aligned some of his doctrines to that of Islam. In this way both he and his teaching are contextualized beyond the pale of rabbinic orthodoxy. It is significant in the cultural translation of Karaism from the Middle East to twelfth-century Byzantium that the absence of any Karaite consensus on the past permitted such a negative characterization of Anan to be accepted, and even "internalized," reinterpreted, and used, in order to supply Karaism with a foundation myth.

The fourth medieval source on Anan, Ibn Daud's *Sefer ha-Kabbalah,* is largely based upon Elijah ben Abraham.[87] Together these versions tell us very

86. Lasker, "Rabbanism and Karaism," 48–49.

87. The text reads: "In his days (Jehudai Gaon) there lived Anan and his son Saul, may the name of the wicked rot. Although this Anan was a descendant of the house of David, and, at first, a scholar as well, some blemish was detected in him, and he was, accordingly, not appointed gaon; nor was he vouchsafed divine assistance to become exilarch. Because of the sordid envy in his heart, he revolted and set out to seduce Jews away from the tradition of the sages, which the latter had taken over from the prophets—[all of them] trusty witnesses, as we have set forth

little about Anan and his movement. By adding to the analysis a consideration of what is known regarding Anan's halakhah and doctrines, we can postulate only a few certain or highly probable generalizations: (1) Anan's halakhah embodies (from a rabbinic point of view) non-normative practices, offering alternatives to ritual and practical provisions of rabbinic law. He was the first to put an anti-rabbinic ideology into writing and the first Jewish author since Hellenistic antiquity to pen a work under his own name.[88] (2) Anan was not a scripturalist, but used hermeneutical interpretation to develop his halakhah. In accord with the stories about him, he was probably a member of the rabbinic class, if not of the exilarchic family. His *Sefer ha-Miṣvot* was written in Aramaic, the language of the Talmud and rabbinic usage. No later Karaite would consider writing in Aramaic.[89] So although Anan was a revolutionary for writing a book in an era when rabbinic texts were primarily oral in character, attaching his name to it when rabbinic authorship was corporate, and in it compiled a definitive list of halakhot when rabbinic halakhah was not yet to be found in codes of law, he still adhered to the traditional language of rabbinic discourse.

To continue the generalizations: (3) Anan was Babylonian, in contrast to the "Palestino-centric" character of Karaism in the tenth and eleventh centuries. (4) Although discounted by Nemoy for lack of substantive proof, he was likely of the exilarchic line. His descendants and successors considered him a

---

in this book. Thus he became an elder who rebels against the decision of the court 'in disregarding' the judges. He composed books, set up disciples, and fabricated 'statutes that were not good, and ordinances whereby they should not live.' Alas, after the destruction of the Temple the heretics had dwindled until Anan came and gave them strength." Cohen, *Sefer ha-Qabbalah,* 49–50. Hebrew pagination, 37–38. In addition, Anan is mentioned in *'Iggeret Rav Sherira Ga'on,* in a brief citation that helps date him to the time of R. Yehudai. See Rabinovich, op. cit., 132. On this last point, see Gil, *History of Palestine,* 777–78.

88. See Poznanski, "Anan"; and Martin A. Cohen, "Anan ben David and Karaite Origins."

89. Portions of Anan's code have appeared in several publications: Poznanski, "Anan"; Abraham Harkavy, *Zikhron la-Rishonim,* vol. 8, who compiled a large fragment of the original work with Hebrew translations and citations from later Rabbanite and Karaite works; Solomon Schechter, *Documents of Jewish Sectaries,* 2: *Fragments of the Book of the Commandments by Anan;* Jacob Mann, "Anan's Liturgy and his Half-yearly Cycle of the Reading of the Law"; M. N. Sokolov in *Izvestia* (Bulletin), USSR Academy of Sciences, Class of Humanities, 7th ser. (1928), 243–53, cited in Baron, *Social and Religious History,* 5:389, n. 3; and J. N. Epstein, "New Fragments from Anan's Book of Laws." That Anan was educated within the rabbinic milieu is supported by Ibn Daud's report. See note 87, above. See also H. H. Ben-Sasson, "The First Karaites: The Trend of Their Social Conceptions."

nasi, or exilarch, and he was recognized as the founder of a line of Karaite patriarchs in the tenth and eleventh centuries.[90] (5) It should be kept in mind that Anan's alternative to rabbinic orthopraxy was proffered at a time of other non-rabbinic movements, such as that of Abū ʿĪsā al-Isfahānī and his follower Yudghān. Little is known about these movements, but they were primarily of a messianic character. Concurrently, the Islamic milieu was suffering dislocation and disorder from the eruption of quasi-messianic movements claiming spiritual and political authority for their leaders. Anan's image of Judaism must be contextualized into its era, and perhaps his career should be considered within the context of messianism.[91]

Benjamin al-Nahawendī. Benjamin ben Moses al-Nahawendī, who lived about a century after Anan (c. 830–60), hailed from Nahavand, in Persia. His known work, *Sefer Dinim,* reveals a more systematic method to jurisprudential interpretation than Anan. Writing in Hebrew, he differed with Anan on many points, but also cannot be regarded as a true scripturalist. His pragmatic approach to legal problems suggests that he acted as a judge in some capacity.[92] Mirroring a position among many Muslim jurisprudents in the host environment, he relied on independent investigation of Scripture for decision making. Just as Muslim lawyers had not yet achieved a consensus of systematization as this time, so Benjamin's individualistic methodology reflects a similar state of affairs in non-rabbinic Jewish circles.[93] He was the first to use

90. Nemoy, "Anan ben David," 318. On the Karaite *nesi'im,* see below, this chapter. See also Gil, *History of Palestine,* 782f., 790–94.

91. The primary source for many of these Jewish movements is al-Qirqisānī's account of sectarianism in Judaism, discussed below. *KA,* 11–19, vol. 1, 1–64. See also Steven M. Wasserstrom, "Who Were the Jewish Sectarians under Early Islam?". There is an extensive literature on the contemporary upheavals in Islam. See Ignaz Goldziher, *Introduction to Islamic Theology and Law,* esp. "The Sects," 167–229; W. Montgomery Watt, "Shiʿism under the Umayyads"; idem, "Khārijite Thought in the Umayyad Period"; idem, *The Formative Period of Islamic Thought;* Marshall G. S. Hodgson, "How Did the Early Shīʿa Become Sectarian?"; idem, *Venture of Islam,* 1: *The Classical Age of Islam,* esp. "The Islamic Opposition, 692–750," 241–79; and John Wansbrough, *The Sectarian Milieu, Content and Composition of Islamic Salvation History.* On the Islamic context of Karaism, see Ben-Shammai, "Attitude"; M. A. Cook, "Anan and Islam: the Origins of Karaite Scripturalism"; and Daniel J. Lasker, "Islamic Influences on Karaite Origins." The proposal for a messianic-based examination of Anan and the Ananites comes from Prof. Aryeh Grabois of Haifa University in private conversations of June 9, 1992 in Berkeley, California. He suggested that Rabbanite anti-Karaite polemic which typifies Anan as a messianic figure might have some basis in history.

92. The incomplete text as it is known today was published by the Karaite community as *Sefer Dinim, Mas'at Binyamin.* This is based on the Karaite edition of Eupatoria, 1836.

93. On *ra'y,* see conclusion to part 1, below.

the term *bene mikra* ("People of Scripture," the term later used by the Karaites to designate themselves) in reference to some proto-Karaite scripturalists. He also wrote biblical commentary and a "Book of Precepts," but they have survived only in brief quotations within other works.

Bene mikra. Whether in this chronology these can be called the Karaites or not is an open question. If we accept that Karaism of the tenth and eleventh centuries resulted from a coalescence of non-rabbinic groups and views, we still do not know who is represented by this designation in the ninth century. Both Benjamin and Salmon could have been referring very specifically to a scripturalist movement or perspective on jurisprudence that represents only one element that would contribute to the evolution of tenth and eleventh century Karaism.[94]

"A scripturalist religion which sets great store in tradition invites scripturalist dissidence."[95] Besides being an alternative logic for an anti-traditional stance in a religion focused on a divinely revealed text, proto-Karaites and Karaite scripturalists would have found parallel developments taking place in the Islamic milieu. Dialectical theologians and sectarian Khārijites offer the closest comparisons. Michael Cook has catalogued Islamic anti-tradition positions and discussed some particular issues that may have influenced proto-Karaism. Although Cook's presentation is useful to help contextualize Jewish scripturalism against its Islamic background, he has erroneously accepted the view that Anan was the author of Karaite scripturalism. This is a modern scholarly echo, along the lines of early Karaite scholars Harkavy and Mahler, of an understanding of Anan that is traditional to both Karaites and Rabbanites.[96] The *bene mikra* are undoubtedly only one of the groups that later become subsumed under the appellation "Karaite."

Salmon's statement contextualizes the *bene mikra* in a historical and developmental scheme. It must be understood as a backward projection of an essentialist understanding of Karaism from the perspective of the "Golden Age." Salmon posits a unified movement that began with Anan, and was then followed by Benjamin and the *bene mikra.* This would serve the purposes of tenth-century self explanation, providing a historical scheme for contextualizing Karaism against the backdrop of rabbinic and Islamic history, embracing Anan as the forebear, and incorporating the essential scripturalist element into one story.

94. The earliest explicit attestation of scripturalism is found in the denunciation of Ben Baboi in the early ninth century. See Louis Ginzberg, *Genizah Studies,* 2: *Geonic and Early Karaitic Halakah,* "Pirkoi Ben Baboi," 501–73, esp. 571.

95. M.A. Cook, "Anan and Islam: the Origins of Karaite Scripturalism."

96. Harkavy's view is summarized in his article, "Karaites" in *JE* 7:438–46. Mahler's perspective was Marxist, and he endowed the movement with a stronger essentialist character, see R. Mahler, *The Karaites: a Medieval Jewish Movement for Deliverance.* This is a translation from the original Yiddish (New York, 1947). See also idem, "National and Social Foundations of 'Anan's Religion.'"

"Men of the East and West." Salmon's designation for a more fully developed Karaite movement is explicit in its geographic context. The name indicates a proliferation and wide distribution for Karaite thinkers. These men more likely are to be recognized as Karaites, a movement bound together by certain ideas, and in which Salmon understood that he himself had a place. The "Eastern" aspect of the Jewish sectarianism of the day is witnessed by al-Qirqisānī, who identifies "Persians, like the men of Tustar," who are "said to be Karaites."[97] Indeed, the list of sects in al-Qirqisānī's heresiography include many individuals and movements from the Eastern Caliphate.[98] Perhaps we can understand this designation, "Men of the East and West," by looking at the next known Karaite scholar of importance. The career of Daniel ben Moses al-Qūmisī, (fl. late ninth century), about which little is known, encompasses this geographic range. Otherwise known as al-Damaghānī, he moved from Iran to Palestine, perhaps playing a leading role in the early Karaite movement in Palestine.[99] Ankori credits him with signal influence in the "Palestinization" of tenth-century Karaism.[100] His halakhah differed significantly from both Anan and Benjamin. Showing the influence of the host culture, he wrote in Arabic and was the first to utilize the scholastic terminology of Muslim jurisprudents and "rationalist" theologians without embracing its attendant philosophies.[101]

By the beginning of the tenth century a new center arose in Palestine, probably in Jerusalem, and probably under the aegis of Daniel and his followers. As early as the first half of the ninth century the burgeoning Karaite presence in Jerusalem dovetailed with the pan-Jewish movement of the Mourners for Zion.[102] These characteristics correspond to the self-abnegatory elements in Anan's teachings and to other more specific halakhic features of Benjamin and Daniel. In a way, the Palestinization of Karaism led to some unification in purpose and thinking. With a new center in Jerusalem a call could go out to anti-rabbinic constituencies throughout the Jewish world, and in response immigration would build up the Karaite center. This laid the foundations for the highly sophisticated Karaite intellectual life of the later tenth and eleventh centuries.[103]

97. *KA*, 1:1.2 (Lockwood, 93).

98. See note 127, below.

99. Ben-Shammai, "Fragments of Daniel al-Qūmisī's Commentary."

100. *Karaites in Byzantium,* 22, 217, 299, 310ff., 320, and 368. See Mann, "Tract by an Early Karaite Settler," 257–98.

101. See Ben-Shammai, "Fragments of Daniel al-Qūmisī's Commentary." See also Mann, *Texts and Studies,* 2: *Karaitica,* 8–18 and 74–81.

102. See note 23, above. See also Avraham Grossman, "Aliya in the Seventh and Eighth Centuries."

103. This is Zucker's thesis: "Responses," 378ff. [Heb.]. Gil says, regarding Daniel, that he "rendered Karaism the character it assumed from then onward, which can be summed up in three principles: the utter exclusion of all Rabbanite

The Karaite Exilarchs. We return to Salmon ben Yeruḥim in order to add a final ingredient to this historiographical stew. In his commentary on Psalm 119:176, Salmon denied the historic claims of the *nasi,* or Exilarch, the head of the Jewish community in Iraq whose position was based upon Davidic descent.[104] In so doing Salmon opened up the possibility of the counterclaims of Karaite *nesi'im,* descendants of Anan ben David. In seeking to create a model for the origins of Karaism in the eighth through tenth centuries, it needs to be understood that the Ananites were but one of the groups that would later be a constituent element of Karaism.[105] In the Rabbanite context, descendants of Anan appear as heads of the rabbinic Palestinian academy in the eighth and ninth centuries, and one is known as a candidate for the exilarchate in the early ninth century.[106] Lists of Karaite *nesi'im* have survived, and their presence is corroborated by other sources.[107] Perhaps followers of the eighth-century scion of the princely exilarchic house, would have maintained their allegiance to a "ruling" family and figurehead while adhering to halakhah rooted in the teachings of their founder, Anan. On the other hand,

---

teachings, the actual return to Palestine, and accepting ways of asceticism and mourning." *A History of Palestine, 634–1099,* 785.

104. Commentary on Psalm 119:176. Cited in Baron, *Social and Religious History,* 5:236. It is not clear whether his statement was intended for the specific context of an early tenth-century contest for the Babylonian exilarchate, or more generally for the *nasi,* in reference to the head of the medieval Palestinian Rabbanite academy.

105. al-Masʿūdī differentiates between the Ananites and Karaites (cited in note 122, below), as does al-Shahrastānī, the Muslim heresiographer, in the first half of the twelfth century. See Muḥammad ʿAbd al-Karīm al-Shahrastānī, *Kitāb al-milāl wal-nihāl.* The continued survival of Ananism is explicit in *Siddur Rav 'Amram Ga'on,* vol. 2, 206–7: "To this day they remain in error, and have become a people unto themselves." It is also implied by al-Qirqisānī, *KA* 1:13 (Lockwood, 145–47). See Ben-Shammai, "Between Ananites and Karaites," which also discusses the presence of Karaism in later medieval Spain in the form of Ananism. See also Cohen, *Sefer ha-Qabbalah,* xlvi–l.

106. These are, respectively, Jehoshaphat and Semah, sons of Josiah ben Saul ben Anan, and Daniel ben Saul ben Anan. Daniel's contest for the exilarchate is mentioned in *'Iggeret Rav Sherira Ga'on.* See Rabinovich, op. cit., 138–39. See Gil, *History of Palestine,* 782; and idem, "The Exilarchate."

107. Poznanski supplies a list of Karaite *nesi'im* in *Babylonische Geonim im nachgaonäischen Zeitalter* (Berlin, 1914), 128ff., cited in Gil, *History of Palestine,* 791, which is part of a summary of the problem, including a genealogical table of the Ananids, 790–94. See also Pinsker, *Likkute Kadmoniyyot,* 2:53, for the list of Solomon the Nasi; and Mann, *Texts and Studies,* 2: *Karaitica,* 2:43–49, 2:120–55. See al-Masʿūdī, cited in note 122, below. Muḥammad ibn Aḥmad al-Bīrūnī (c. 1000) provides Anan's lineage back to the Muslim conquest: Anan ben Daniel ben Saul ben Anan ben David ben Hasdai ben Kafnai ben Bustanai. See E. Sachau, ed., *al-Āthār al-bāqiyyah ʿan al-qurūn al-khāliyyah.*

all references to the "sons of Anan" in the ninth century indicate no connection to the Karaites, or any other proto-Karaitic phenomenon.[108] Only in the late ninth century does there seem to be a joining of this branch of the exilarchic family with that dissident movement in Judaism that rejected Rabbanism and focused itself in Jerusalem in accordance with principles of the Mourners for Zion and its attendant Palestino-centrism. Whether Anan's exilarchic branch actually had a following in the period between Anan and Daniel al-Qūmisī is unknown.

The co-optation of the princely family and its followers into the dissident movement provided the Karaites with an extant historical sense. As Davidids the exilarchic family was linked to biblical history and its historical continuity was attested to in such works as *Seder ʿOlam Zuta.* The presence of a Karaite prince may have provided a kind of historical buttress for the Karaite presence within the community of Israel, obviating other complicated ideologies for establishing continuity with the past, and supplying just enough historical rootedness for self-explanation within a milieu that was fully Jewish but millennial and scripturalist. In the newly crystallized formation of the Karaites—Salmon's "men of the East and the West"—several proto-Karaitic pasts were gathered together resulting in conflicting senses of continuity with preceding centuries. The consensus that may have developed concerning an Ananite dynastic claim created a nexus to link otherwise differing and unconnnected pasts. Salmon's historicization made them sequential and cumulative in development. But this was simply a projection of contemporary conditions into the past. Even Muslim historians and ethnographers refer to the Karaites as *aṣḥāb ʿAnān wa-Binyāmīn* (the people of Anan and Benjamin), connecting the two names together in one sect.[109]

In practicality, the Karaite *nesiʾim* had little legislative function, although they proclaimed the new moon each month. Although W. Montgomery Watt's model for a community organized around charismatic leadership does not fit to the reality of the Karaite *nesiʾim,* the presence of a Karaite Davidid prince may have provided enough symbolic claim to history to support the otherwise seemingly ahistorical psychology of Karaism.[110] On the other hand, Karaite intellectuals are often characterized by their adherence to speculative rationalism, an intellectual method that would certainly conflict with historical foundations based upon princely leadership. As significant as the Karaite *nesiʾim* were in tenth and eleventh century Palestine and Egypt, they were not perceived as bearers and expositors of a divine truth.[111]

108. Gil, *History of Palestine,* 791.

109. Nemoy, in *Encyclopedia of Islam,* 3:603–8, s.v. "Karaites"; and Georges Vajda, ibid., 1:481, s.v. "Ananiyya."

110. Watt, *The Formative Period of Islamic Thought.*

111. Gil, *History of Palestine,* 790–94. For a parallel example in Shīʿite Islam of tension between rationalist interpretation and divinely inspired leadership, see Josef van Ess, "The Logical Structure of Islamic Theology," 21–50, esp. 44f.

The office of the Exilarch (*nasi*) may have been thought of along lines of charismatic leadership by some Jewish constituencies. The co-optation of Ananism and the Ananite princely line by Karaism could provide those with messianic outlooks a charismatic leadership to hold in high regard. That is, those who had followed messianic charismatic leaders in the eighth and early ninth century could have found an understandable form of community by virtue of the presence of a Davidid prince among their milieu. The evidence does not support such a belief in regard to the Ananite *nesiʾim,*[112] and speaks more strongly to the success of Karaite ideology from the late ninth century onward, wherein charismatic leadership was subsumed into non-specific teachings regarding a messiah to come, especially in the context of Palestino-centrism. Charismatic leadership would be inconsistent with the principle of Anan's dictum, ". . . and do not rely on my opinion." Activistic charismatic leadership was remembered in connection with earlier messianic claimants, but was relegated to the past as Karaites moved toward a quietistic sense of leadership. Karaites turned away from notions of charismatic leadership, not considering a strategy similar to that adopted by some Shīʿites (and the ʿĪsāw-ites!)—that the legitimate but eclipsed Ananite leadership of the entire Jewish people had gone into hiding (*ghaybah*) in order to await return at a more auspicious time to be determined by God. Karaism after the late ninth century—millenarian, Palestino-centric, quasi-ascetic, and putatively scripturalist—gave meaning through the notion of being a charismatic community rather than through following a charismatic leader.[113] Karaite attitudes with regard to leadership were redirected in society toward scholars, whose charisma was anything but activistic, and in the mythical sphere toward an unknown messiah of the future.

In this regard, Karaite use of a term known from the Dead Sea Scrolls, *moreh ṣedek* (Righteous Teacher), may suggest a notion of charismatic leadership as it is used in the Scrolls, but more likely refers to an awaited messiah who in the eschatological future would resolve the halakhic dilemmas of the people. It also echoes the function of the *doresh* in the Dead Sea Scrolls, who inquires in the Law, much like the *mujtahid* in Islam and the practitioner of *ḥippus* in Karaism.[114]

However, the story of Anan presents itself in a "Shīʿite" manner. The ideology of Anan as a legitimate but rejected and threatened spiritual and communal leader replicates the ideology of Shīʿism, wherein ʿAlī and his family are continually rejected and even oppressed by the established Muslim powers. Beyond mere narrative parallels is the quasi-ascetic character of both Karaism and Shīʿism. Karaites and other *abelei ṣiyyon* mourn the suffering

112. Gil, *History of Palestine,* 790–94; Ben-Shammai, "The Karaites." Cf. Gil, "The Exilarchate," 33–65.

113. Watt, *Formative Period of Islamic Thought,* 36.

114. See the conclusion to part 1, below.

and humiliation that is concomitant with the Exile and loss of the Temple, while Shīʿites mourn the suffering, humiliation, and oppression of the true leaders of Islam, the family of Muḥammad, their *imāms.* Shīʿite rigorism evolved from a political narrative of early Islam that critiqued imperial pragmatism, and the questionable Muslim character of the early caliphate. In comparison, Karaite rigorism emanated from old Jewish sources, but at the same time, critiqued rabbinic Jewish elites of the early centuries of Islam. Karaite rigor and ideologies of mourning represent ritual and lifestyle alternatives to the commercial success of segments of Mediterranean and Middle Eastern Jewish society which mostly supported and intermarried with the rabbinic class. More powerfully, ideologies of mourning coupled with Palestinocentrism reflect Karaite rejection of the rabbinic diasporic orientation.

Proto-Karaitic Phenomena, Karaism, and History. Can an understandable picture emerge regarding the history of proto-Karaitic phenomena in the eighth and ninth centuries? The question is more complicated than can be summarized here, and solutions to its problems may never be worked out. Whatever conclusions are reached at this time can only be preliminary.

If we look at the halakhic and theological character of the writers in question, it is clear that they share little that can be called essential, and diverge widely in method and thinking. It is best to reject out of hand a traditional view that Anan and his followers were Karaites, and that the movement produced its essential intellectual elements under the aegis of its founder. Such a traditional view, embraced by Karaites and Rabbanites alike, was defended by eminent scholars, including Harkavy in the early part of the century, and Mahler, who saw Karaism as a movement of social dissidence.[115] A more sober analysis by Baron characterized Anan's ideology by three points: diaspora nationalism, self-abnegation, and individualism. He saw Anan as the leader of an elite-oriented intellectualist movement that adopted a pietist and ascetic perspective.[116] Others have remained more reserved regarding Anan and Karaism.

Anan's halakhah had many elements that were peculiar to him. He taught that circumcision should be performed with a scissors and by someone who himself had been circumcised in this manner. He eliminated several rabbinic prescriptions, among which are the minima for contamination, phylacteries, Sabbath candles, the prohibition against mixing meat and milk, and he substituted psalms for the traditional rabbinic liturgy. Other aspects of his teaching are shared with Karaism in general: the new moon should be determined by direct observation, intercalation should be based on the barley harvest, Shavuot must fall on a Sunday (based on a literal reading of Leviticus 23:15), rigorous rules regarding consanguinity, prayers are to take place twice a day,

115. See note 96, above.

116. Baron, *Social and Religious History,* 5:210–22.

and the entire Hebrew Bible can be used for jurisprudential reasoning. The aspect of self-abnegation described by Baron is indicated in several points: Purim should be a day of fasting instead of rejoicing, the eating of meat is prohibited in the diaspora, and Jews should engage in a seventy-day fast from Nisan 13 to Sivan 23.[117] Anan's fairly elaborate system was not supported by either anti-rabbinic polemic or historical self-explanation. Nothing in Anan's known work indicates an acknowledged relationship to the Second Temple period Sadducees, with whom Anan is later associated. In addition, Anan does not engage in speculative theology or adopt strategies characteristic of the rationalists of his day, or of later Karaism.

Benjamin is closer to Rabbanism in his halakhah than Anan. He is credited with the anti-tradition statement, "Do not take lesson from his sayings," referring to himself.[118] Whereas Anan prohibited using the scalpel for circumcision, Benjamin requires it. Whereas Anan's self-abnegatory aspect led to prohibiting sex on the Sabbath, Benjamin permits it. Differences appear regarding other laws, including inheritance, the levirate, the Paschal sacrifice, and the calendar. Like Anan, Benjamin does not resort to historical argument. However, he is credited with the use of allegorical interpretation, and he engaged in speculative theology regarding angels. He posited a system of intermediaries between God and the world to dispel problems of anthropomorphism. The acts of creation recounted in Genesis were performed by a creating angel, based upon an interpretation of Exodus 3:2–6.[119] The differences between these two "fathers" of Karaism are diverse enough to suggest that there was no unified Karaite movement in these early centuries. At best, it can be said that there were shared elements in Jewish sectarianism of the day. From al-Qirqisānī's descriptions we know that other sectaries show a similar latitude in their halakhah.

Daniel al-Qūmisī's famous remarks about Anan support a view that early Karaism was halakhically non-essentialist, that is, there is no single essential element that is characteristic and identifying in its halakhah. At first he designated Anan as *rosh ha-maskilim* (chief of the wise), but later relented and in a play on words declared him *rosh ha-kesilim* (chief of the fools).[120] Daniel opposed individual reasoning as a method for deducing the Law, and opposed secular knowledge as well.[121] Whereas the Karaites of the tenth and eleventh centuries are often characterized as "rationalists" in their adherence to *kalām*

117. Baron provides an adequate review of Anan's halakhah, ibid.

118. In the commentary on Daniel 11:36, cited both in Jacob Mann, "Early Karaite Bible Commentaries," esp. 519; and Ankori, *Karaites in Byzantium*, 211, n. 14.

119. See Harry Austryn Wolfson, "The Pre-Existent Angel of the Magharians and al-Nahāwandī"; Baron, *Social and Religious History*, 223–26; and Poznanski, in *Encyclopedia of Religion and Ethics*, 664, s.v. "Karaites."

120. *KA* 1:1.3 (Lockwood, 94–95).

121. *KA* 1:18.1 (Lockwood, 151–52).

(speech) and their opposition to anthropomorphic interpretation, Daniel, and later, Salmon were staunchly opposed to such approaches.[122] In spite of his quadri-partite historicization, Salmon also finds Anan's halakhah in error, describing it as the "path of the Rabbanites."[123]

Contemporaneous to Salmon, al-Qirqisānī polemicizes throughout his great work against the halakhah of all three of his predecessors. In his description of Jewish sects al-Qirqisānī treats each one of them as a separate sect.[124] The lack of unity among Karaites in the tenth century suggests a corresponding lack of uniform homogeneous development as a movement. The situation is attested to by al-Qirqisānī as he laments, "Of those present-day Karaites who are not members of the schools which we have mentioned, scarce two of them are to be found who agree on anything, but this one will disagree with the other in one matter, and this one will disagree with that on various matters."[125] Nonetheless, a sense of group cohesiveness is present as he worries, ". . . the matter is daily growing worse. It may be that some of our co-religionists will blame me for having mentioned them, since some of the Rabbanites may use them to attack us."[126]

al-Qirqisānī not only witnesses the fragmentation among groups that could be identified with the Karaites, but also recounts a number of other

122. al-Masʿūdī, the tenth-century Muslim historian, geographer, and philosopher declares that the Ananites "believe in justice and unity," code for the doctrines of the Muʿtāzilite *kalām,* referring respectively to free will in God's relations to human affairs and the denial of attributes and anthropomorphism. See *al-Tanbīh wal-ishrāf,* 112.18–113.1 (159). The report is repeated by Aḥmad ibn ʿAlī al-Maqrīzī in the fifteenth century in *al-Mawāʿiz wal-iʿtibār bi-dhikr al-khiṭaṭ wal-āthār,* 3:370ff., 375. These are cited in Gil, *History of Palestine,* 780–81. See Harry Austryn Wolfson, *The Philosophy of the Kalam;* and an accompanying volume, *Repercussions of the Kalam in Jewish Philosophy.* Salmon ben Yeruḥim, commenting on Eccl. 7:16, decries "one who is roaming through towns and fairs in search of secular writings, such as the books on philosophy and the volumes of Ibn al-Rawāndī and Ibn Suwayd, that seduce unto the denial of God, prophets and scripture. May God chasten him and his ilk, for these are doomed to hellfire for ever and ever." Cited and translated by Moshe Perlmann, "The Medieval Polemics Between Islam and Judaism."

123. Also in the commentary on Psalm 69:1, cited in Gil, *History of Palestine,* 782.

124. *KA* 1:18.2 (Lockwood, 152), near the conclusion of the description of Jewish sects: "These are all the doctrines of the sectarians who have arisen up to the present day, so far as we have information."

125. *KA* 1:2.21 (Lockwood, 104–5). Elsewhere (1:1.4; Lockwood, 95) he says, "Furthermore one of the greatest calamities that afflict some of our fellows is this very internecine warfare, the ill-will and hatred they bear each other, to which they are moved for the most part by jealousy and eagerness for mastery." He devotes an entire chapter of part 1 (1.19) to halakhic differences among the Karaites.

126. *KA* 1:19.6 (Lockwood, 156).

medieval Jewish sects that would otherwise have been forgotten. These include the followers of Abū ʿĪsā al-Isfahānī and his disciple, Yudghān, both of whom claimed to be prophets, Ismāʿīl al-ʿUkbarī, Abū ʿImrān al-Tiflīsī, Mālik al-Ramlī, and Mīshawayh al-ʿUkbarī.[127] The followers of the latter were of some threat to the Karaites of Byzantium, against whom polemical attacks were devised.[128] al-Qirqisānī's heresiography, the subject of the following section of this study, gathered together known Jewish religious groups and individual thinkers into a historical exegesis that differs from Salmon's. That the proto-Karaitic groups were simply a constellation of elements within the larger sectarian milieu is supported by the title of the concluding sub-chapter of al-Qirqisānī's description of sects, "Account of the disagreements of the Karaites at the present time and formerly, *who do not belong to any of the sects already mentioned*" (my italics).[129] al-Qirqisānī recognizes the wide distribution of the roots of contemporary Karaism. Nonetheless, this is not what Zvi Ankori calls a "non-normative *Weltanschauung*," as if to say that non-normative Judaic groups and movements came together into some kind of Karaitic consensus. On the contrary, such coming together occurred among only *some* non-rabbinic Judaic groups and movements. Karaism may have emerged as the most successful non-rabbinic (and therefore non-normative) Jewish movement of the Middle Ages, but it never represented or co-opted the entire spectrum of non-rabbinic Judaisms.[130]

Karaism, then, is a religio-social configuration that crystallized under the leadership of a Palestinian element in the late ninth and early tenth centuries.[131] In its classical form it is characterized by anti-Rabbanism, something of an ascetic orientation akin to the Mourners for Zion, and scripturalism, that is, the recognition of only the Bible for deciding halakhah. These three fundamentals worked together to support millennial and Palestino-centric ideologies. Another characteristic usually associated with the intellectuals of this movement is dialectical rationalism, to be discussed in the next section

127. *KA* 1:1.2; and sections appropriate to individual sectarians: 1:11 (Abū ʿĪsā al-Isfahānī); 1:12 (Yudghān); 1:15 (Ismāʿīl al-ʿUkbarī); 1:16 (Abū ʿImrān al-Tiflīsī); and 1:17 (Mīshawayh al-ʿUkbarī). Note that many of these sects arose in the East. One could suggest that elements originating among them or in the East were later incorporated into tenth- and eleventh-century Karaism, highlighting al-Qūmisī's designation "men of the East and the West."

128. See Ankori, *Karaites in Byzantium*, s.v. "Mishawayh," "Mishawism, Mishawite Creed, Mishawite Sect, Mishawites," and "Mishawite activists" in the index.

129. *KA* 1:19 (Lockwood, 152).

130. Ankori, *Karaites in Byzantium*, 368.

131. In an echo of the traditional linear serial view of Karaite development, Zvi Ankori calls this phenomenon "tenth-century revisionism": *Karaites in Byzantium*, 216ff., which he characterizes by (1) the bankruptcy of Ananism, (2) Palestino-centrism, and (3) the adoption of the ideology of individual interpretation, which he equates with rationalism.

of this chapter. In the end, scripturalism placed the focus of attention for most Karaite writers on their relationship with the divinely revealed text to the exclusion of a relationship to the past. Self-definition found expression in legal and pietistic activity, obviating history as a means of understanding the community. Reflecting their own personal Rabbanite backgrounds, Poznanski and Revel, among others, subjected parenthetic historical statements of medieval Karaite literature to denigration and ridicule. In their view such a poor historical consciousness could not compare to the rich multifaceted aggadic and historical literature of the rabbis. For the Karaites themselves, this was not a deficiency, for although historicization was an important weapon in their polemical arsenal, their gaze was focused on the coming fullness of time in the days of the messiah.

Yaʿqūb al-Qirqisānī: Heresiography and Rationalism in a Karaite Construction of History

Heresiography, History, and Rationalism in Karaite Thought. Heresiography, common in Christian and Muslim writing, is a literary form almost entirely absent in rabbinic literature.[132] Rabbanite Jews tended to write heresiology embedded within the literature of law, biblical commentary, and, of course, the chain of tradition. In contradistinction to this attitude, and to the lack of historical ideology among fellow Karaites, is the aforementioned Yaʿqūb al-Qirqisānī, and his *Kitāb al-anwār wal-marāqib,* written in 937. This massive work of law, philosophy, exegesis, and other ancillary topics begins with a major section (*maqālah*) of nineteen chapters (each called a *bāb*) describing and sometimes refuting a number of Jewish sects or sectarian thinkers. The chapter titles of this section follow:[133]

1:1. [Introduction] (4 sub-chapters in fragmentary condition).
1:2. A chronological account of the Jewish sects (21 sub-chapters).
1:3. On the doctrines which distinguish the Rabbanites from all other Jewish sects, except for the few who follow them in this: things in which they contradict Scripture, and the inconsistency of their doctrines (50 sub-chapters).
1:4. Account of these things (18 sub-chapters).
1:5. An account of the doctrines of the Samaritans which differ from those of all the rest of the people (1 sub-chapter).

132. The following section, "Yaʿqūb al-Qirqisānī: Heresiography and Rationalism in a Karaite Construction of History," was published as "History or Philosophy? The Construction of the Past in Medieval Karaite Judaism." Only minor revisions have been made.

133. For full bibliographical information, see notes 36 and 37, above. The titles are from Lockwood's translation. Sections are designated by a numeral preceding the colon. After the colon, numerals are chapters. Sub-chapters follow the period. Thus 1:2.3 for section 1, chapter 2, sub-chapter 3.

1:6. An account of the doctrines of the Sadducees, which are as follows (1 sub-chapter).
1:7. An account of the doctrines of the Maghārians (1 sub-chapter).
1:8. An account of Jesus and the doctrines of the Christians, together with what Dā'ūd al-Muqammiṣ relates of the origin of their teachings (7 sub-chapters).
1:9. Account of the Qarāʿians (1 sub-chapter).
1:10. Account of the differences between the Rabbanites of Syria and of Iraq (9 sub-chapters).
1:11. Account of Abūʿ Īsā, also called Obadiah al-Isfahānī (2 sub-chapters).
1:12. An account of the doctrine of Yudghān, called "the Shepherd" (1 sub-chapter).
1:13. Account of the distinctive teaching of Anan the Exilarch and his followers (3 sub-chapters).
1:14. Account of the distinctive teaching of Benjamin al-Nahawendī (2 sub-chapters).
1:15. Account of the ill-deeds of Ismāʿīl al-ʿUkbarī (2 sub-chapters).
1:16. Account of Abū ʿImrān al-Tiflīsī and Mālik al-Ramlī (1 sub-chapter).
1:17. Account of the distinctive teachings of Mīshawayh (1 sub-chapter).
1:18. Account of the distinctive doctrines of Daniel al-Damaghānī (2 sub-chapters).
1:19. Account of the disagreements of the Karaites at the present time and formerly, who do not belong to any of the sects already mentioned (6 sub-chapters).

The introduction (1:1) contains remarks about the use of rational speculation in religion, but the context is not entirely clear because the beginning is missing. It does bear witness both to the variety of opinion on this topic, and to the "internecine warfare" found among contemporary Karaites. The second chapter, "A chronological account of the Jewish sects," is a kind of précis of the section as a whole. With the exception of the opening discussion on Jeroboam, the successor to Solomon in the northern kingdom of Israel (I:2.1–4), its 21 sub-chapters provide brief notices for the sects and sectarians that are discussed more fully in the subsequent eighteen chapters.

This portion of *Kitāb al-anwār wal-marāqib* was first published and discussed by Abraham Harkavy in 1894 in the Transactions of the Imperial Russian Archaeological Society.[134] Harkavy's introduction provides an erudite summary and analysis of the material. He was interested in extracting useful

134. (St. Petersburg), vol. 8, 247–78 ("Abū Yūsuf Yaʿqūb al-Qirqisānī on the Jewish Sects"), and 279–319 (Arabic text). The introductory article is translated from the Russian by Wilfrid Lockwood in Bruno Chiesa and Lockwood, *Yaʿqūb al-Qirqisānī on Jewish Sects and Christianity*, 49–90; henceforth, the English version will be cited.

historical and chronological information from the descriptions of sects. From him we learn such things as the works of al-Qirqisānī that did not survive, that some of al-Qirqisānī's remarks on particular topics can or cannot be corroborated with other known Jewish literature, that some material likely resulted from the author's personal experience, perhaps his travels to Persia and India, and that he had probably read Saadia Gaon. We also are provided with Harkavy's speculation regarding the true identity of some of the sects that are mentioned. Ultimately, he sees the description of sects only as a historical work. "These notices are remarkable as coming from a Karaite author, since, in general, the Karaites are the most indifferent of men with regard to history, and in all the rich Karaite literature, both in Arabic and in Hebrew, there is extremely little historical information, even concerning the Karaites themselves, and as such as there is, is usually unreliable or confused."[135] The pioneer of al-Qirqisānī studies was concerned only with what the text could supply in modern terms of what history means, but he never asked what this material meant to Yaʿqūb al-Qirqisānī.

Shortly after this publication, Wilhelm Bacher offered an appreciation of Harkavy's work, also contributing an analysis of the material, but he asked the same kind of questions.[136] As indicated above, Samuel Poznanski's attitudes toward Karaite historiography, and his expectations of historiography in general, led him to dismiss al-Qirqisānī's heresiography because it did not answer the questions that he thought were important. Poznanski sought to establish *continuity* between past religio-historical phenomena and medieval Karaism as described by al-Qirqisānī.[137] Bruno Chiesa has correctly pointed out that Poznanski's view represents a narrow perspective found among many early scholars of Karaism, who would regard the heresiography as merely an introductory section to a larger encyclopedic "Book of Precepts," or *Sefer Miṣvot.* Failing to see the purpose of the heresiography, Poznanski only recognizes it as a repository of "disconnected historical information."[138]

Chiesa has gone beyond these older views to demonstrate important parallels in structure and content shared by al-Qirqisānī and the eighth-century

135. Ibid., 77.

136. Bacher, "Qirqisani, the Qaraite, and His Work on Jewish Sects."

137. His introduction to *Zekher Ṣaddikim,* "An Introduction to the Karaites' Manner of Writing Their own History," 13ff. [Heb.].

138. Ibid., 14. See also Bruno Chiesa, "A Note on Early Karaite Historiography," 56–65, esp. 58f. Many Karaite scholars of later centuries wrote "Books of Precepts," compendia of *halakhah.* The ubiquity of this literary form led modern scholars to assume that a work containing so much *halakhah,* like al-Qiriqisānī's, must be of that genre. Bacher begins to approach the problem, but misses the mark, in "Qirqisani, the Qaraite, and His Work on Jewish Sects," 261–62. Other early scholars made similar erroneous assumptions having seen only portions of the work, not the form of the whole.

Melkite Christian theologian, John of Damascus. His work, *The Fount of Knowledge,* is the first of the *summae,* a literary form characterized by a systematic attempt at comprehensive rational organization.[139] Like the *Kitāb al-anwār wal-marāqib,* it also contains a long heresiographical section. Through parallels in structure and content evident in John of Damascus the *Kitāb al-anwār wal-marāqib* can now be understood as a *summa theologiae Karaitica.*[140]

Much Karaite thinking in the tenth and eleventh centuries can be characterized as rationalist, to the point that it is sometimes regarded as an identifying characteristic.[141] Rationalism, of course, offered a reasonable and consistent position from which to critique the traditionism of the rabbis and to understand the Scriptures, in a manner that parallels developments in Islam. In the second and third centuries after the initial Arab conquests, Muslim legal scholars began to articulate precise methodologies for interpreting

139. John W. Baldwin, *The Scholastic Culture of the Middle Ages, 1000–1300,* 85. The *summa* form was adopted by medieval European jurisprudents in their efforts toward a rational systematization of Roman law, ibid., 74–76. Theologians followed this approach, most notably, Thomas Aquinas in his *Summa Theologica.* See also Charles Homer Haskins, *The Renaissance of the Twelfth Century,* "The Revival of Philosophy."

140. Chiesa argues that *KA* be seen in the larger context as the first part of "a comprehensive commentary on Pentateuch." It was intended to precede the commentary on the nonlegislative portions of the Torah, *Kitāb al-riyāḍ wal-ḥadā'iq.* See "A Note on Early Karaite Historiography," 59. Such literary and conceptual dependence need not be taken at face value. Although *KA* is indeed integral to al-Qirqisānī's overall intellectual project, it needs to be understood and contextualized on its own terms within the cultural, religious, and intellectual environments of the day. See also, Bruno Chiesa and Wilfrid Lockwood, "al-Qirqisānī's Newly-found Commentary on the Pentateuch: The Commentary on *Gen.* 12."

141. On Karaite rationalism, see Isaac Husik, *A History of Mediaeval Jewish Philosophy,* for chapters on Yūsuf al-Baṣīr and Yeshuah ben Yehudah (11th c.), 48–58, and Aaron ben Elijah of Nicomedia (14th c.), 362–87. See Yūsuf al-Baṣīr (Georges Vajda, trans. and comm.); David R. Blumenthal, ed., *al-Kitāb al-Muḥtawī de Yusuf al-Basir;* and David E. Sklare, "Yūsuf al-Baṣīr: Theological Aspects of his Halakhic Works." Husik's section on Yeshuah ben Yehudah is based on the important work by Martin Schreiner, *Studien über Jeschuʿa ben Jehuda.* See also Ben-Shammai on Jeshua ben Judah in *Peʿamim,* 32 (1987). On Karaite philosophy in general, see Harry Austryn Wolfson, *Repercussions of the Kalam in Jewish Philosophy,* for sections on al-Qirqisānī, Yūsuf al-Baṣīr, Jeshua ben Judah, and Judah Hadassi; Ben-Shammai, *The Doctrines of Religious Thought of Abū Yūsuf Yaʿqūb al-Qirqisānī and Yefet ben ʿElī;* idem, "Studies in Karaite Atomism"; and many articles by Daniel J. Lasker, including "The Philosophy of Judah Hadassi the Karaite"; "Nature and Science in the Philosophy of Aaron b. Elijah the Karaite"; and "The Destiny of Man in Karaite Philosophy." On Aaron ben Elijah, see his philosophical work (Morris Charner, trans.), *The Tree of Life,* which is a translation chapters 1–78 of that work.

the Qurʾān and *ḥadīth* literature. At the same time cultural influences from the conquered populations began to be felt. In this period rationalism is "associated in the minds of occidental scholars with the study of Greek philosophy in the Islamic world and its partial acceptance by theologians," but is also rooted in rational methods of Islamic jurisprudence.[142] In contemporary Islam those who rejected the traditions as sources for jurisprudence were understood to be either fundamentalist scripturalists or Muʿtāzilites, adherents of "rationalism."[143] Similarly, in the literary arena "foreign" influences were contested in the *shuʿūbiyyah,* a *Kulturkampf* pitting Arabism against Persianate culture. In the sciences Greek medicine and astronomy took hold. But in the religious sciences it was Greek philosophy that presented a challenge.[144]

In the late antique evolution of Christian philosophy resulting from the marriage of Greek thought to Christian doctrines such as Creation, the preexistent Christ, Incarnation, and the Trinity, new ways of theological expression created new intellectual problems.[145] After the Arab conquests, Muslim theology engaged Greek rationalism with the keen gaze of the church fathers in the background. Among the Christian populations of the Arab empire were scholars, some of whom may have become Muslim, whose knowledge represented the philosophical traditions of Christianity. With the evolving interaction of Muslims with Christians and Jews, both in everyday life and in academic engagement, the tenets of Islam were subject to fairly sophisticated attack from representatives of the more established and more confident older religions. "The contacts between Muslims and non-Muslims led to polemical arguments, and these were a stimulus to rational thinking in Islamic theology."[146] This type of theological discussion, whether polemical or otherwise,

142. Watt, *Formative Period of Islamic Thought,* 180.

143. See Schacht, *Origins of Muhammadan Jurisprudence,* 40–41, and 258–59. They are often referred to as *ahl al-kalām,* "the people of rational speculation," among other designations. See note 141, above.

144. See Majid Fakhry, "The Legacy of Greece, Alexandria, and the Orient," in *A History of Islamic Philosophy,* 1–36. See also A. Badawi, *La transmission de la philosophie grecque au monde arabe;* and Louis Gardet, "Philosophie et religion en Islam avant l'an 330 de l'hegire."

145. The standard work is Harry Austryn Wolfson, *The Philosophy of the Church Fathers,* vol. 1, *Faith, Trinity, Incarnation.* On the results of Christian philosophy, see ibid., 575ff.: "How the rise of Christian philosophy led to the discovery of inherent difficulties in the catholic belief with regard to the relation of the preëxistent Christ to God and with regard to the relation of the born Christ to God."

146. Watt, *Formative Period of Islamic Thought,* 184. See also M. Cook, "The Origins of *Kalām*; and compare C. H. Becker, "Christliche Polemik und islamische Dogmenbildung."

came to be known in the Islamic milieu as *kalām*.[147] As defined by Ibn Khaldūn in the fourteenth century, "this is a science that involves arguing with logical proofs in defense of the articles of faith and refuting innovators who deviate in their dogmas from the early Muslims and Muslim orthodoxy."[148]

al-Qirqisānī was not isolated from the general movement of the day toward philosophy and rationalism. His work shows dependence on and affinities with the Muslim philosophers.[149] Thus we have a *summa theologiae Karaitica* based upon Christian philosophical antecedents, and contemporary Muslim philosophy, which was itself indebted to Christian philosophy.[150] In this context, the heresiography of the opening section is understood to be a foundation for the dialectical method, whereby an exposition of theological principles must start with opposing positions that need first be identified and then refuted.[151] Appositely, the second section is a presentation of "the validity of the application of rational investigation for theology and jurisprudence."[152] Only after establishing historical and methodological foundations does the

147. Kalām, or *Speech*, may be taken figuratively to mean disputation, or argumentation, but the technical meaning of the term is "rational or speculative theology." Practitioners of the *kalām* method are called *mutakallimūn*. See Watt, *Formative Period of Islamic Thought*, 182. The standard work is Wolfson, *Philosophy of the Kalam*. See also Louis Gardet, "Quelques réflexions sur la place du *ʿilm al-kalām* dans les 'sciences religieuses' musulmanes." See also Fakhry, "The Rise of Islamic Scholasticism *(Kalām)*," in *History of Islamic Philosophy*, 42–65.

148. Ibn Khaldun (Franz Rosenthal, trans.), *The Muqaddimah: An Introduction to History*, 3:34; often cited, including Chiesa, "Yaʿqūb al-Qirqisānī come fonte storiografica," 26.

149. al-Qirqisānī cites al-Wāqidī (*KA*, 301.15), Abū al-Hudhayl al-ʿAllāf (*KA*, 248.7; 304.7), and discusses two Muslim sects, the Mannāniyya (*KA*, 71.8, 11; 323.13), and the Dahriyya (*KA*, 71.8,11; 78.13; 559.2). His source on interpretive principles was derived from Mutahhar ibn Ṭāhir al-Maqdisī, *Kitāb al-badʾ wal-taʾrīkh*, dated 964. On this, see Georges Vajda, "Etudes sur Qirqisânî, 5: Les règles de la controverse dialectique"; idem, "La contribution de quelques textes judéo-arabes à la connaissance du mouvement d'idées dans l'Islam du III–IXe siècle," 87–97, esp. 96–97. al-Qiriqisānī also shared a source with Ibn ʿAqīl (d. 1111), see George Makdisi, "Dialectic and Disputation: The Relation between the Texts of Qirqisani and Ibn ʿAqīl."

150. See Shlomo Pines, "Some Traits of Christian Theological Writing in Relation to Moslem *Kalām* and to Jewish Thought."

151. Chiesa, "Yaʿqūb al-Qirqisānī come fonte storiografica," 26; and idem, "A Note on Early Karaite Historiography," 59. On the dialectical method in Islam, see van Ess, "The Logical Structure of Islamic Theology," 42f.; and Louis Gardet and M. M. Anawati, *Introduction* à *la théologie musulmane: essai de théologie comparée*, 205ff.

152. *KA*, 64–179. This section is discussed, with translations, in Vajda, "Etudes sur Qirqisânî, 2: Les fondements speculatifs de la legislation religieuse."

third section, on the refutation of heretical beliefs, appear. It is important to note that the chapters of this third section do not have a direct correspondence to the enumeration of Jewish sects from the first section. This is a dialectical theological description and refutation of beliefs, not a heresiography. Here we find such topics as the Christian Trinity, creation, transmigration of souls, angelology, the primordiality of the logos, resurrection of the dead, reward and punishment, and prophecy.[153] Only inasmuch as a given sect adheres to such doctrines are they alluded to in this section. The heresiological function is secondary, embedded within the larger topical conceptual structure. If part of the problematic in section 1 is historical, the argument in section 3 is not, and can be more appropriately compared to the near contemporary *Tamhīd* of al-Baqillānī,[154] to Saadia Gaon's list of wrong opinions,[155] or to the ninth-century *Summa Theologiae Arabica* of the Melkite, Stephen of Ramlah.[156] The fourth section then concludes the introductory portion of the larger work, being a statement on the proper methods for interpreting the Law; that is the application to the Torah of the rational principles from section 2, in accordance with the doctrinal principles established in sections 1 and 3.[157] The remaining nine sections of the *Kitāb al-anwār wal-marāqib* are on the Decalogue and the remainder of the laws in the Torah, and do not constitute a "Book of Precepts" per se, but a dialectical interpretation of the Law.[158]

153. A part of 3:16 was translated by Nemoy in "al-Qirqisānī's Account of the Jewish Sects and Christianity," 369–76. Since he did not yet have the complete form of the text and the content of the material was related to a refutation of Christian principles, Nemoy placed this part of the third section into his translation of section 1.

154. al-Baqillānī (R. J. McCarthy, ed.), *Kitāb al-tamhīd;* also (Maḥmūd Muḥammad al-Khuḍayrī and Muḥammad ʿAbd al-Hādī Abū Riḍā, eds.), *Tamhīd.*

155. In the introductory treatise of *Kitāb al-amānāt wa'l-iʿtiqādāt,* which is edited and translated by Y. Kafih under the title *Sefer ha-Nibhar ba-'Emunot uba-Deʿot (ha-'Emunot veha-Deʿot) le-Rabbenu Seʿadyah ben Yosef Fayyumi.* See the English translation, Samuel Rosenblatt, *Saadia Gaon: The Book of Beliefs and Opinions,* 3–37.

156. See Sidney H. Griffith, "The First *Summa Theologiae* in Arabic: Christian Kalam in Ninth-century Palestine"; and idem, "A Ninth Century Summa Theologiae Arabica," esp. its bibliography.

157. "On the means by which knowledge of duties is arrived at," *KA,* 343–494.

158. The remaining sections are

5. On circumcision and the Sabbath [the first of the Ten Commandments]
6. An explanation of the nine duties of the Ten Commandments
7. On the times of the New Moon and the *Abib* [time of ripening of the grain harvest]
8. On the Feast of Shavuot and of the time between the evenings
9. On the other festivals
10. On Levitical uncleanness in animals and men

al-Qirqisānī Reading Christian History. al-Qirqisānī had contacts with Christian scholars, and no doubt used literary sources of Christian provenance. In the relatively tolerant and increasingly homogeneous culture of the Islamicate world of the Middle Ages contacts between Jews, Christians, and Muslims were neither unusual nor without cultural significance. Jews found daily contact with non-Jews in the marketplace, the domicile, through communal activities, and in the political arena. Business partnerships with members of the other religions were not uncommon.[159] It has been argued that Jews, Christians, and Muslims found "common need," going beyond the necessities of daily life to incorporate shared concerns in such areas as medicine, architecture, lexicography, philosophy, literature, grammar, and the important medieval enterprise of translating texts. Such concerns then led to both deeper analysis of religious writing, that is, to religious disputation, rational speculation, and *kalām.*[160] Actual disputations between Jews and non-Jews in the Islamic world are less well known than the polemical literature that such encounters spawned, but the Karaite Ḥasan ben Mashiaḥ disputed with a Christian physician, Abū ʿAlī ʿĪsā ibn Zarʿa.[161] al-Qirqisānī reports on his own conversation with Yasūʿ Sekhā, the bishop of ʿUkbarā,[162] and cites Cyprian[163]

---

11. On incest and marriage with the widow of a childless brother
12. On what is forbidden to eat, wear, or plant, and on the fringes on the edge of garments
13. On inheritances

The organization of material reveals that the four introductory sections and the discussions of the laws in Sections 7 through 13 frame the central discussion of the Decalogue in Sections 5–6, the heart of the work. See Chiesa, "Yaʿqūb al-Qirqisānī come fonte storiografica," 27f. This is the first example of a characteristic form of organization for the commandments based upon the Decalogue that was adopted by the Karaites.

159. See Goitein, *A Mediterranean Society,* 1: *Economic Foundations,* 254; and 2: *The Community,* 273–311, esp. 289–99. This openness was described by Goitein to lead to a Jewish-Muslim symbiosis, an idea interrogated by Wasserstrom in *Between Muslim and Jew.*

160. Wasserstrom, "Species of Misbelief," 38ff.

161. Ibn Zarʿa wrote an anti-Jewish polemical work in 997 after the disputation. See Poznanski, "Karaite Literary Opponents," 145; and Baron, *Social and Religious History,* 5:263, and 410, n. 63. Ibn Zarʿa is undoubtedly Abū ʿAlī ʿĪsā ibn Isḥāq ibn Zurʿah ibn Mūrqus ibn Zurʿah ibn Yuḥannā (b. 942/43). Cf. Bayard Dodge, ed. and trans., *The Fihrist of al-Nadīm: A Tenth Century Survey of Muslim Culture,* 2:632. For an overview, see David E. Sklare, "Responses to Islamic Polemics by Jewish Mutakallimun in the Tenth Century."

162. *KA,* 3:6.16 (220.8). See Chiesa, "Yaʿqūb al-Qirqisānī come fonte storiografica," 44, n. 81.

163. *KA* 1:4.16. Cyprian is credited with claiming Syriac as "the primaeval language."

as well as the Jacobite philosopher, Yaḥyā al-Nāhwī.[164] His awareness of pre-Christian philosophical sources may have come via Christian works. He cites Porphyry, Alexander of Aphrodisias, the Sophists, and the "logicians," a reference to Aristotelians.[165]

More significant as a source for al-Qirqisānī on Christianity is Dā'ūd al-Muqammiṣ, who is cited several times. Often referred to as the "first Jewish *mutakallim*," much of what we know about him comes from al-Qirqisānī.

> Dā'ūd ibn Marwān al-Raqqī, known as al-Muqammiṣ, was a philosopher. At first he was a Jew, then he converted to Christianity in Nisibis by a man named Nānā. This Nānā was a great man among the Christians because he was a perfect philosopher; his profession was medicine. Dā'ūd al-Muqammiṣ was his pupil for many years and he learned the principles of Christianity and its secrets and became skillful in philosophy. He wrote two books about the Christians in which he criticizes them. The books are well-known. He also translated from among the books of the Christians and their commentaries a commentary on Genesis, which he called "The Book of Creation," and also a commentary on Ecclesiastes.[166]

Nānā has been identified as the Jacobite Nonnus of Nisibis, who was last reported to be alive in 862.[167] This places al-Muqammiṣ squarely at the beginnings of *kalām* in the ninth century. In an introduction to his philosophical work, *ʿIshrūn Maqāla,* Sarah Stroumsa points out the resemblances to other early *kalām* works. It is based on themes similar to those found in those works which comment on various Aristotelian concepts, and it uses common *kalām* techniques.[168] "Analysis of the *ʿIshrūn Maqāla* confirms al-Qirqisānī's testimony concerning al-Muqammiṣ's Christian connection. Both the form and the content of this treatise reflect Christian teaching." Stroumsa goes on to suggest that al-Muqammiṣ derived his work from a Syriac *Summa Theologica,* of which many are supposed to have existed although none are

164. *KA,* 223.12. See Bayard Dodge, *The Fihrist of al-Nadīm,* 2:612–13, who identifies Yaḥyā as Joannes Alexandrinus Grammaticus, a bishop of Alexandria in the seventh century, also called Philoponus.

165. See *KA,* 223.12 (Porphyry and Alexander of Aphrodisias); 69.6, 78.1 (Sophists); 82.14, 322.6 ("logicians" [*manṭiqiyyun*]); and 43.18, 618.16 (Christian philosophers).

166. *KA* 1:8.5 (Lockwood, 137); but see also ibid., s.v. "Dā'ūd ibn Marwān al-Muqammiṣ" in the index.

167. See Vajda, "La finalité de la création de l'homme selon un théologian juif du IXe siècle," 61–85, n. 1; cited in Sarah Stroumsa, *Dāwūd ibn Marwān al-Muqammiṣ's* Twenty Chapters ("Ishrūn Maqāla"), 16.

168. Ibid., 23–33. Stroumsa indicates parallels with such Muslim writers as al-Māturidī, ʿAbd al-Jabbār, al-Ashʿarī, al-Shahrastānī, and others.

extant.[169] The influence of Christian theology on al-Qirqisānī can be fully established through al-Muqammiṣ as well as other minor channels.[170]

Chiesa's contribution demonstrates the important elements of form shared by al-Qirqisānī and John of Damascus. "The most striking parallel to al-Qirqisānī's *Kitāb al-anwār wal-marāqib* is precisely Damascenus' *Fount of Knowledge,* the latest patristic example of a theological handbook introduced by a heresiological compendium. Here too one finds a theoretical (*Capita philosophica,* or *Dialectica*), and historical (*De haeresibus*) part preceding the *Expositio de fide orthodoxa.*"[171] That is to say, the elements of *The Fount of Knowledge* are: 1) the philosophical chapters by which the principles of speculation are established; 2) the heresiography, which presents the collected positions to be refuted; and 3) the Exposition of the Orthodox Faith, three books which use the method and historico-doctrinal basis of the preceding two parts to construct a comprehensive theological presentation.[172]

If al-Qirqisānī, as an advocate of the dialectical method, adopted the philosophical imperative and method from the Muslim rationalist milieu of the day and the *summa* form from Christian antecedents, then from whence his heresiography? Steven Wasserstrom has commented on the cultural transmission from Christianity to Islam and demonstrated that al-Qirqisānī utilized some Christian heresiological motifs.[173] He has shown that "at least five characterizations of the Samaritans were taken over from the Christian texts."[174]

169. Ibid., 34–35.

170. Sarah Stroumsa, "On Jewish Intellectuals Who Converted in the Early Middle Ages."

171. Chiesa, "A Note on Early Karaite Historiography" 62.

172. See Frederic H. Chase, ed. and trans., *Saint John of Damascus: Writings,* xxv–xxxv (intro.). See also J. Nasrallah, *Saint Jean de Damas: Son époque, sa vie, son oeuvre;* G. Richter, *Die Dialektik des Johannes van Damaskos: Eine Untersuchung des Textes nach seinen Quellen und seiner Bedeutung.*

173. Wasserstrom, "Species of Misbelief," 50–51. Wasserstrom has shown that the accepted belief among scholars that Muslim heresiographers received their anti-Jewish material from the Karaites is false. Even as Muslims and Jews were the recipients of a philosophical culture originating in the Christian world, so they received the heresiological culture of Christianity. If the older view were true, one might ask in the face of scholarly consensus regarding the transmission of philosophy and speculative reason to the Muslims whether the Karaites were also the transmitters of those cultural traditions. Needless to say, such a view has not held credence. With this important dissertation, the Karaites are absolved from an undeserved privilege of acting as transmitters of heresiology and are correctly contextualized into the larger general flow of cultural materials in the early Islamic centuries.

174. *KA* 1:5 (Lockwood, 133): "The Samaritans acknowledge no prophet but Moses and Joshua, and believe in no book of prophecy except the Torah and the Book of Joshua. They do not recognize the Temple and their prayer is toward Shiloh. They still offer sacrifices. They have a priest who does not mix with them or

Three of these, the denial of resurrection, the observance of stringent ritual purity, and the rejection of post-Mosaic prophecy, are literary topoi recognized from such sources as John of Damascus and Photius, Patriarch of Constantinople (d. 891).[175] We find these topoi repeated in later Muslim heresiographies,[176] but more importantly, they originate in the heresiographical tradition that includes the sources of John of Damascus.

Early Christian concern for the Samaritans focused on Dositheus and Simon as figures in early gnosticism, and not as leaders of Samaritan sects per se.[177] As early as Hippolytus (d. 235 or 236) a heresiological scheme for dealing with the Samaritans had been worked out,[178] and in Epiphanius of Salamis of the fifth century it received the form in which it would be taken over by John.[179] In this tradition the Judaic origins of Samaritanism could be acknowledged, but the group was recontextualized as a form of "Hellenism." This formulation is based on a taxonomy used for the schematization of world religion, history, and culture derived from a statement of Paul (Col. 3:11 and Gal. 3:28): "In Christ Jesus there is neither Barbarian, Scythian, Hellene nor Jew." In proto-orthodox Christianity's early struggle with gnosticism, Samaritanism was understood to be a source for gnostic error and was thereby categorized as a Christian heresy. Samaritanism was both important enough and

---

intermarry with them, according to what we have been told. They do not mix with or approach anyone else, and if they do approach one who is not of their number, they purify themselves by washing." The Samaritans are dealt with in several other places in *KA*; s.v. "Samaritans" in the index, and 2:1 for a refutation of some of their beliefs.

175. Wasserstrom, "Species of Misbelief," 50–51. See Chase, *Saint John of Damascus,* 114: "They hold everything that the Jews do, except that they hold the Gentiles in abomination, avoid contact with certain things, deny the resurrection of the dead, and reject the post-Mosaic prophecies." See also Photius (R. Henry, ed. and trans.), *Bibliothèque,* 5:60–64, cited by Wasserstrom, "Species of Misbelief," n. 42, 75.

176. Ibid., 51, who cites al-Masʿūdī, Shahrastānī, and al-Balādhurī.

177. For an early treatment, see Origen (Henry Chadwick, ed. and trans.), *Origen: Contra Celsum,* 52, 312, and 325. For the doctrinal bases of gnostic Simonianism as transmitted by Justin Martyr, Irenaeus, Hippolytus, pseudo-Tertullian, Epiphanius, and Theodoret, see also Wolfson, *Philosophy of the Church Fathers,* "Simon," 512–20.

178. Hippolytus (P. Wendland, ed.), *Hippolytus Werke,* Bd. 3, *Refutatio omnium haeresium* 6:7–20; 10:12; cited in Wolfson, *Philosophy of the Church Fathers,* 513.

179. Frank Williams, trans., *The Panarion of Epiphanius of Salamis, Book 1 (Sects 1–46),* 1:9, 1, p. 10: "All their opinions are the same as the Jews', except that they detest gentiles and will not touch certain persons, and that they deny the resurrection of the dead and the other prophecies, the ones after Moses." Early Christian material on the Samaritans is collected in S. Isser, *The Dositheans*; cited in Wasserstrom, "Species of Misbelief," n. 40, p. 75.

adequately threatening to Christian doctrine to be added as an additional fifth category to the quadri-partite taxonomy, but its source was recognized in Hellenism.[180] It is ultimately portrayed as a corrupt blend of Judaism and Hellenism.

Although al-Qirqisānī transmitted these elements of Christian heresiological data regarding the Samaritans, as we shall see, he contextualizes them, and all of history, very differently. I would add another example of a heresiographical topos of Christian origin which is found in al-Qirqisānī. In the section on Christianity he repeats a Christian polemic against Judaism: "Present-day Christian philosophers assert that the laws of the Torah were presented to the Children of Israel in wrath, and that they have chosen them for themselves, because of their resemblance to the laws of the Sabians. This was because they had become accustomed to the practices of the Egyptians when they lived among them, and these latter are of the same type as the practices of the Sabians."[181] This statement reiterates the Christian heresiographical contextualization that the Egyptians, like the Samaritans, are adherents of Hellenism, the source for all error. The motif is found in Epiphanius and by duplication in John of Damascus.[182] What is revealing is that this ethnographic notice lifted from the Christian context for a history of culture appears only as a parenthetic entry in al-Qirqisānī's section on Christian belief, and has no part in the overall historical argument. In this case, although he had been exposed to Christian heresiological material, al-Qirqisānī did not find it useful for his own historical argument. In addition, al-Qirqisānī refers to the Sabians on several other occasions, and in his chapter

180. In this historicization, Hellenism was founded by Nimrod, the builder of the Tower of Babel (Gen. 11:1–9), who is equated with Zoroaster. At this time "every transgression in the world was disseminated," "idolatry and Hellenism began," and "the human reason originated its own evil and invented transgression instead of goodness with its freedom, reason, and intellect." Epiphanius, *Panarion,* 1:3, 3–4 (Williams, 17); see also ibid., "Anacephaleosis" 1:3, 1–8, 1 (Williams, 9–10); the whole section on Hellenism is 1:3, 1–12 (Williams, 16–18). Hellenism is credited with idolatry, astrology, and magic, which led to despotism. Thus the source for these universal evils is both rooted in the Bible through the connection to Nimrod, but is externalized from the tradition of truth by identifying Hellenism as a foreign phenomenon.

181. *KA* 1:8.4 (Lockwood, 136).

182. "Hellenism originated with Egyptians, Babylonians and Phrygians, and it now confused men's ways. After that historians and chroniclers borrowed from the imposture of the Egyptians' heathen mythology and conveyed it to the other nations, thus giving rise to sorcery and witchcraft. But from the time of Cecrops these things were brought to Greece." Epiphanius, *Panarion,* 1:3, 11 (Williams, 17–18). See also "Anacephaleosis" 1:3,4 (in epitome, Williams, 8–9), which is repeated in John of Damascus, heresy no. 3 (Chase, 111–13). Thus Egypt is the mother of Greece, and Hellenism is the father of heretical philosophy.

on astronomy even cites the Sabian astronomer, mathematician, and philosopher, al-Thābit ibn Qurra.[183]

Keeping in mind the early Christian historical contextualization of peoples and religion, and al-Qirqisānī's Christian connections, we can investigate further the resemblance suggested by Chiesa between al-Qirqisānī and John of Damascus. By means of a broader comparison of patristic heresiography and early Christian attitudes toward history, it is possible to understand in both historical and dialectical contexts the heresiography of section 1 of the *Kitāb al-anwār wal-marāqib.* Judaism and Islam defined a relationship to the pre-monotheistic and non-ethnically-specific past by respectively repudiating the "idolatry" and "ignorance" of their predecessors.[184] Christianity, on the other hand, was based explicitly on its own Jewish heritage, and through theological development, on its inheritance from Greek thought. In an early Christian historicization, the teachings of Homer, Pythagoras, Socrates, or Plato, to name a few, were understood to have been derived from Moses and the Bible.[185] Creative history of this type permitted an interpretation of continuity between various pasts and Christianity. In an example from the *Stromata,* or *Tapestries,* of Clement of Alexandria (d. before 215), the sanctioned past of Judaism is credited with the authorship of the philosophical heritage of the Greek past, whose sanctity would otherwise be considered questionable. In this way the Old Testament, by no means a systematic or rational document, is endowed with reason, while at the same time the character of the heathen Greek past is enhanced through its transmission and development of philosophical knowledge. Clement develops a complete categorization and contextualization embracing biblical elements, Jews, Greeks, barbarians, and philosophers in a world historical format.[186] In like manner, al-Qirqisānī

183. *KA,* 591.17, 21. On the Sabians, see, D. Chwolson, *Die Ssabier und der Ssabismus;* Tamara M. Green, *The City of the Moon God: Religious Traditions of Harran;* and Şinasi Gündüz, *The Knowledge of Life, The Origins and Early History of the Mandaeans and their Relations to the Sabians of the Qur'ān and to the Harranians.*

184. See Fred Astren, "De-Paganizing Death: Aspects of Mourning in Judaism and Islam." Cf. Hawting, *Idea of Idolatry and the Emergence of Islam.*

185. It is interesting that this historicization predates Christianity, coming from the efforts of Hellenistic Jews to harmonize their past with the knowledge and history of cosmopolitan Greek culture. See Targum 2 to Esther 1:2; Josephus, *Contra Apionem,* 2:4. See also Husik, *History of Mediaeval Jewish Philosophy,* xvif. For a discussion of the Christian historicizations, see Harry Austryn Wolfson, *Philo: Foundations of Religious Philosophy in Judaism, Christianity, and Islam,* 161ff. The idea appears as early as Justin Martyr, and it is recycled much later by the Muslims.

186. Clement of Alexandria, *Stromata,* see esp. 1:13–29; 2:5, 18, 21–22; and 5:14. For a discussion of the problem, see Pelikan, *The Christian Tradition,* 1:27–41. In a parallel example, Clement co-opts the term *gnostic* for orthodox Christianity. The non-Christian and Greek philosophical elements of gnosticism that are dangerous

embraces a similar view, that the Greeks received philosophy from Solomon.[187] But al-Qirqisānī's historical ideology goes beyond this co-optation of the non-Jewish philosophical past.

The *Elenchos* of Hippolytus of Rome offers another parallel to al-Qirqisānī's *Kitāb al-anwār wal-marāqib.* The first book of this magnum opus, known separately as the *Philosophoumena,* is a heresiography. Hippolytus' treatment of Greek thought contextualizes what is true and what is false according to an idea of "succession," or *diadoche.* Thus the "various traditions of Greek philosophy had . . . been arranged and rearranged as successions and schools of thought."[188] In the historical-polemical context, for example, the gnostics are presented as the recipients of a tradition that is "parasitical,"

---

to orthodox Christianity are not acknowledged by the church, while useful elements are adopted. *Stromata,* 4:21–23; 6:9–10, 12; 7:1; 8:8, 11–15. See Wolfson, *Philosophy of the Church Fathers,* 495–520, and 575ff. Clement uses a historicization to support this philosophical ideology, wherein the gnostic Valentinus is understood to have been a disciple of Theudas, the false messiah. *Stromata,* 7:17. See also E. F. Osborn, *The Philosophy of Clement of Alexandria;* S. R. C. Lilla, *Clement of Alexandria: A Study in Christian Platonism and Gnosticism;* and G. Apostolopoulou, *Die Dialektik bei Klemens von Alexandria: Ein Beitrag zur Geschichte der philosophischen Methoden.* Historicization that connects heresy to an unsanctioned past was a common weapon in the battle against gnosticism. Irenaeus and Hippolytus credit various forms of gnosticism with such antecedents as Greek mythology, philosophy, the mysteries of the Assyrians, Chaldaeans, and Egyptians, among others, "magical arts and Pythagorean numbers," and so forth. A full list of these examples is given in Wolfson, *Philosophy of the Church Fathers,* 559–61.

187. *KA,* 2:7.4. See Hartwig Hirschfeld, *Qirqisani Studies,* 19–20. In the Middle Ages such historicizations were maintained by other Jewish philosophers. See the twelfth-century philosopher Judah Halevi *Kitab al-Khazari,* Hartwig Hirschfeld, trans., 1:63, p. 53:

> Being Grecians, science and religion did not come to them as inheritances. They belong to the descendants of Japheth, who inhabited the north, whilst that knowledge coming from Adam, and supported by the divine influence, is only to be found among the progeny of Shem, who represented the successors of Noah and constituted, as it were, his essence. This knowledge has always been connected with this essence, and will always remain so. The Greeks only received it when they had become powerful, from Persia. The Persians had it from the Chaldaeans. It was only then that the famous [Greek] Philosophers arose, but as soon as Rome assumed political leadership they produced no philosopher worthy of the name.

A large corpus of pseudo-Solomonic works appeared in the Middle Ages, some claiming his name for the source of rational speculation. See Max Seligsohn, in *JE* 11:446–48, s.v. "Solomon."

188. Mansfeld, *Heresiography in Context,* xv.

because it "apes" the genuine teaching of the legitimate *diadoche* of Greek philosophy.[189] Like al-Qirqisānī Hippolytus uses a form of the dialectical method to collect all relevant views, but then selects out those views that require refutation. A strong historical argument is present, but doctrinal considerations are paramount. Like the chain of tradition of the rabbis, a linear idea of history and the transmission of knowledge is utilized in order to explain what portions of Greek philosophy are appropriate in Christian thought, and more importantly, what accounts for heresy.[190] The historical concerns of Clement are combined with dialectical method in order to comment upon the creators of that dialectical method, the philosophers.

Heresiography, then, is history inasmuch as it bears information that supports the purpose of the author's presentation. It is only incidentally history of the Herodotean, or one might say in the context of this study, the Poznanskian type. Nonetheless, heresiographers such as Hippolytus and al-Qirqisānī will use important historical data to further their doctrinal and polemical purposes. As the early scholars of al-Qirqisānī extracted the parts from the whole, thus failing to recognize the overall form and intent, so the *Philosophoumena* has been subject to the same kind of violence by modern scholars. Hermann Diels's source criticism of the Presocratic materials found in the text led subsequent scholars to isolate portions of the text as "Presocratic fragments," devoting themselves to these to the exclusion of the text as a whole. Such an approach led to a failure to acknowledge that some of the historical information was not genuinely Presocratic, but had been "doctored" by Hippolytus in order to further his aims.[191]

With the above comparisons in mind, a closer examination of historical contextualization in the heresiography of John of Damascus evinces a better

189. Ibid. For example, among the fathers of gnosticism Simon Magus is credited with having been inspired by Pythagoras, Heraclitus, and Empedocles, whereas Valentinus developed his doctrines from Pythagoras, Empedocles, and others. Ibid., 172–77. This kind of historicization follows Clement and, particularly, Irenaeus. Ibid., 52–53, and 166–72.

190. Ibid., xvi. It should be noted that Eusebius (d. 339 or 340) attaches great importance to the lines of bishops in the various bishoprics of the empire. The "lines of succession from the holy apostles" is named explicitly as one of the "chief matters to be dealt with" in *The History of the Church.* See the translation by G. A. Williamson, 31. See also the appendices in this edition, including "Emperors and bishops," "bishoprics," "martyrs," "heretics," 415ff. In Eusebius's eyes, one of the foundations for the authority of the church was the apostolic succession, which in earliest Christianity guaranteed the "authority of a normative body or writings," but later supported the institutional organization and power of the church. See Pelikan, *The Christian Tradition,* 1:108–20, esp. 112ff.

191. Ibid., xiiiff., and 1–19. See Diels, *Doxographi Graeci;* and Diels and W. Kranz, eds., *Die Fragmente der Vorsokratiker.* These are cited in Mansfeld, *Heresiography in Context;* see his bibliography.

understanding of al-Qirqisānī. The full title of John's heresiography is *Heresies in Epitome: How They Began and Whence They Drew Their Origin.*[192] Of the 103 heresies that are listed, the first 80 are taken verbatim from summaries or epitomes of sects in the *Panarion* of Epiphanius of Salamis, who died in 402 or 403.[193] Heresies 81 to 100 are from another unknown source, and only 101–103 are original to John.[194] In the *Panarion* the epitomized headings are expanded upon and refutations are proffered in later corresponding sections. As discussed above regarding the Samaritans and Sabians, the purpose of this literary form is not only refutation, but following Clement, Irenaeus, and Hippolytus, contextualization. All religious sects are derived from the five ethno-religious categories, Barbarism, Scythianism, Hellenism, Judaism, and Samaritanism, in order to establish the causes and the nature of the transmission of error in human history.[195] Using this construction Epiphanius provides a developmental history of knowledge on a world scale reflecting universalist tendencies of Christianity. In contrast, the heresiographical data of Epiphanius has been transferred into *The Fount of Knowledge* only in the form of the epitomized headings in order to fulfill the dialectical methodological purpose. John's heresiographical intentions were quite limited, and accordingly he was able to borrow the skeleton of the heresiographical basis of the dialectical argument without constructing a carefully integrated argument structure of his own. Unlike Epiphanius, in John there is no direct correspondence between the enumeration of sects and later refutations and theological promulgations. So, although the bulk of this heresiography fulfills its purpose as a dialectical point of departure, the information and structure was derived from a different literary and religio-historical setting. John's only original contributions are found in heresies 101–103, which are respectively, the Ishmaelites (Muslims), the Christianocategori (Iconoclasts), and Aposchistae, a

192. See Chase, *Saint John of Damascus,* xxix. The Greek text is found in Migne, *Patrologia graeca,* 94.521–1228; the heresiography begins at 94.677.780.

193. Williams, trans., *The Panarion,* op. cit. Williams offers a complete translation of the first of three books in the *Panarion,* whereas another translation offers an abridgment of the complete work, focusing on the historical aspect of the text and leaving out refutatory material; see Philip R. Amidon, trans., *The* Panarion *of St. Epiphanius, Bishop of Salamis: Selected Passages.*

194. Chase, *Saint John of Damascus,* xxix–xxxii. See also Bonifatius Kotter, *Die Schriften des Johannes von Damaskos,* 4: *Liber de haeresibus. Opera polemica,* 1–67, which includes a critical edition of the Greek text; but see esp. 7–10, introductory remarks on John's sources.

195. Epiphanius, *Panarion,* Proem 1 and Anacephalaeosis 1 (Williams, 3–11), epitomes, and the corresponding expanded sections, 1:1, 1–20,3,4 (Williams, 13–50). See note 180, above on Col. 3:11 and Gal. 3:28: "In Christ Jesus there is neither Barbarian, Scythian, Hellene nor Jew." See also J. H. Waszink, "Some Observations on the Appreciation of the 'Philosophy of the Barbarians' in Early Christian Literature."

sect known only from this source.[196] Islam is given a significant treatment including a refutation placed within the heresiography, whereas John's opposition to Iconoclasm appears elsewhere.[197] With these entries John not only brings his material "up to date," but engages two, if not three, of the most significant challenges to Christian orthodoxy of his day. The philosophical bases for "arguing Christianity" had been worked out over centuries. John was able to provide for the heresiographical foundation of his dialectical presentation by borrowing from extant sources. His few original contributions were necessary only to the extent that intellectual honesty required some comment on Islam and Iconoclasm, important contemporary phenomena.[198]

Reading al-Qirqisānī. By taking into account the historical and dialectical contexts by which Christian heresiography is understood, we can then ask what is al-Qirqisānī's scheme for contextualization? It is clear that the history of error begins with Jeroboam. "The first to propagate dissension in religion and to sow rebellion in the family of Israel, was Jeroboam."[199] Like Hippolytus or Epiphanius, al-Qirqisānī has placed the origin of error and the beginning of the differentiation of sects into the most remote past. Significantly, he differs with the plain sense of the Bible when he goes out of his way to deny that Jeroboam was an idolator. "For Jeroboam did not deny or disbelieve in the Creator . . . , nor did he worship idols, as some imagine."[200] By limiting Jeroboam's error to "changes and alterations which he made to the religious law," it is kept within the fold of religion.[201] al-Qirqisānī re-creates him as the ancestor of all error. "From that time, from the time when Jeroboam did what he did, there grew dissension among the Children of Israel and those practices were planted among them, and were handed down to those who followed

196. Chase, *Saint John of Damascus,* 153–63.

197. Ibid., 370–73, in the exposition of the faith. See also P. Khoury, "Jean Damascène et l'Islam."

198. John's polemic against Iconoclasm is found in separate works: *Apologetic Discourses against the Attackers of the Holy Images,* in Migne, *Patrologia graeca,* 94.1231–420; cited in Chase, *Saint John of Damascus,* xviii.

199. *KA* 1:2.1 (Lockwood, 95).

200. *KA* 1:2.2 (Lockwood, 97). al-Qirqisānī offers two proofs for his statement: (1) He only changed the laws for his own purposes. "Had he renounced religion altogether, he would have abandoned, caused to vanish, and thrown away the law entirely, and would have not have needed to substitute for them" (ibid.). (2) One of Jeroboam's successors, Jehu, is credited with destroying the idols and slaying their worshippers, while subsequently he followed the way of Jeroboam (ibid., citing 2 Kings 10:28–29). Thus idolatry and the sins of Jeroboam are not to be equated. The better part of two subchapters are devoted to further proofs for this position (*KA* 1:2.2–3).

201. *KA* 1:2.2 (Lockwood, 96–97).

them."[202] "Thus all went into exile persisting in these practices and were scattered through the world and were confined in this way of life which has been transmitted from generation to generation until our own day."[203] al-Qirqisānī is in accord with both Christian and Muʿtāzilite heresiographers who identify a single source as the origin of all heresy.[204]

In contrast to al-Qirqisānī's reading of the past, Christian heresiographers followed the intent of the Bible's contextualization of idolatry in their understanding of the origins of error, by attributing it to *external* influences. The errors of the manifold Christian heresies were the result of influences that emanated from most ancient sources. These were cultures that were outside of divinely sanctioned prophecy and history recorded in the Bible, such as the Barbarians, Scythians, Hellenes, and their offspring, Egyptians, Chaldaeans, Phrygians, Sabians, Stoics, Platonists, Pythagoreans, Epicureans, and others. For al-Qirqisānī the history of error is encompassed completely *within* the history of Israel.

The Christian theory of history is more explicit than al-Qirqisānī's. In Epiphanius, and by duplication in John, the four archaic cultures represent a developmental scheme of history and religion that also explains why error exists. Under Barbarism, "there was no difference of opinion yet, no people that was at all different, no name for a sect, and no idolatry either."[205] "The people of that time had no leader or common agreement. Everyone followed his own lead instead and served as a law for himself."[206] This era represents unfettered individualism without either religious and societal limits on behavior, or a social contract for societal organization. After the Flood came the period of Scythianism, which replicated the previous era for "there was nothing on earth yet, no sect, no divided opinion. There were only 'men,' 'of one speech and one language.' There were only ungodliness and godliness, the natural law and the natural error, not learned from teaching or books, of each

202. *KA* 1:2.4 (Lockwood, 99).

203. *KA* 1:2.4 (Lockwood, 100).

204. Among the Muʿtāzilites are al-Nāshī' al-Akbar (d. 906) and al-Ashʿarī (d. mid-tenth c.). See Josef van Ess, *Frühe muʿtazilitische Häresiographie,* 25, who characterizes the origins of heresy as the "trauma of history." Cited in Chiesa, "Yaʿqūb al-Qirqisānī come fonte storiografica," n. 101, 47. At this point it is interesting to compare Ibn Daud, who is focused on the idea of transmission. He certainly has a contextualization for the history of error, which originates with the Samaritans, but he is without a theory of error. See chapter 1, above. See also Cohen, *Sefer ha-Qabbalah,* lix, n. 73, which cites Lactantius, Eusebius, and refers to Maimonides, who does develop a theory of error in the *Mishneh Torah,* "Hilkhot avodah zarah ve-ḥukot ha-goyim," 1, on idolatry and laws of the gentiles.

205. Epiphanius, *Panarion,* 1,9 (Williams, 14).

206. Epiphanius, *Panarion,* Anacephalaeosis 1:1,1 (Williams, 8); John of Damascus, *The Fount of Knowledge: On Heresies,* 1 (Chase, 111).

individual's will."[207] In the Scythian period concepts of natural law and religion began to penetrate human consciousness, but there was no differentiation in regard to religion and peoples. The building of the Tower of Babel which was the result of the first societal organization and its ungodly intention, ended this era. The third period, of Hellenism, witnessed the dispersion and differentiation of religion and ethnicity in the wake of the debacle at Babel. "This began in Serug's time with idolatry and submission to it by the people of the era—each in accordance with some superstition—for the sake of a higher civilization and fixed customs and laws."[208] In this time idolatry was introduced, the result of the use of human reason without the benefit of natural law and religion. "Egyptians, together with Babylonians, Phrygians, and Phoenicians, were the first to introduce this religion, which consisted of image-manufacture and mystery rites."[209] These three eras in biblical and human history correspond to levels of experience as the human mind moves toward true religion and rational apprehension. The approach of the philosophers was historicized and superimposed upon both the biblical narrative and the ethnographic map of Late Antiquity within the matrix provided by Galatians 3:28 (and Colossians 3:11).

"But a type of worship of God existed together with the natural law, and was customary from the time of these peoples. It set itself apart from the foundation of the world, and existed during the period of Barbarism, Scythianism, and Hellenism, till it was combined with Abraham's worship of God."[210] So Judaism (as a proto-Christianity) became the form of true religion because "God made choice of Abraham,"[211] thereby granting to mankind guidance to take them beyond the limitations of natural law and human reason. With this all the components were in place for religion to *use* reason and natural law, but to have divine guidance to keep it from erring. The only missing element was Christ, who would appear later. Error is explained as the result of the improper use of human reason or the failure to recognize God's natural law.

In al-Qirqisānī's heresiography there is no developmental scheme of error in history. Error is connected to the course of archaic biblical history only through the deviations of Jeroboam and his successors. "The only reason for

207. Epiphanius, *Panarion,* 2,3 (Williams, 15). The quotes are from Gen. 11:1, and 1:26, respectively.

208. Epiphanius, *Panarion,* Anacephalaeosis 1:3,1 (Williams, 8). Cf. John of Damascus, *The Fount of Knowledge,* 2 (Chase, 111).

209. Epiphanius, *Panarion,* Anacephalaeosis 1:3,2 (Williams, 8). See ibid., 3,8 (Williams, 9): "But afterwards, at a later period, Hellenism was made into sects—I mean Pythagoreans, Stoics, Platonists, Epicureans and the rest." See also John of Damascus, *The Fount of Knowledge,* 3 (Chase, 112).

210. Epiphanius, *Panarion,* Anacephalaeosis 1:3,9 (Williams, 9).

211. Epiphanius, *Panarion,* 1:4.1,1 (Williams, 18). Cf. John of Damascus, *The Fount of Knowledge,* 4 (Chase, 113).

his alterations and changes was the fear of losing the kingdom."[212] His religious innovations were motivated by a sense of realpolitik, by his "desire to strengthen and prolong the rebellion and by [a fear that] the people [might] long for their king who was of the children of David."[213] For al-Qirqisānī political power was the foundation for religious differentiation and sectarianism. Correspondingly, the rabbis resort to murder and expulsion when their hegemony is threatened, even within their own ranks.[214] And even Karaite internecine conflict is attributed to "jealousy and eagerness for mastery."[215] For al-Qirqisānī the roots of error are motivationally based, whereas the Christian heresiographers looked to human capability and the lack thereof to construct a philosophically-based scheme.

al-Qirqisānī mirrors another significant aspect of form in Christian heresiography. The relatively lengthy discussion of Jeroboam is part of 1:2, described above as a kind of précis of section 1 as a whole. This section for the most part corresponds to the heresiography of Epiphanius, wherein the epitomized headings for lists of heresies precede the individual treatments of each heresy in its own chapter. Even the epitomes have their own epitomes in a preliminary listing known as "Anacephalaeosis," or Preface, of which their are three. In copying only the epitomized "headings" of Epiphanius, John of Damascus nonetheless transmitted an important element of contextualization that is reflected in al-Qirqisānī's construction of 1:2. It is only in the first Preface that the quadri-partite contextualization of archaic history is most explicit, presenting most broadly and most cogently the differentiation of Barbarians, Scythians, Hellenes, and Jews. The later chapters on individual heresies deal with specific aspects of history, doctrine, and refutation. So too, al-Qirqisānī places the account of Jeroboam in the "epitomized heading," not in a chapter of its own. "It may be that a reader of this section may object to its length, since my aim in this chapter is only to give account of the sects, not to report the reason for the change in laws. Let such a one know that I do so only for a reason which will not be hidden from him who is earnest in examining the matter."[216] He is saying that Jeroboam's error is fundamental,

212. *KA* 1:2.2 (Lockwood, 96).

213. Ibid.

214. In regard to Jesus: "The Rabbanites plotted against him and eventually killed and crucified him." *KA* 1:2.9 (Lockwood, 102); and "The Rabbanites conspired against him and killed him just as they sought to kill ʿĀnān also, but without success. This is their way with all who would oppose them." *KA* 1:8.1 (Lockwood, 135). In regard to Anan: "The Rabbanites attempted to murder him, but God did not allow him to fall into their hands." *KA* 1:2.14 (Lockwood, 103). On Rabbanite internecine violence: "The break between the schools of Hillel and Shammai took place on the third of Adar, when several of either party were killed." *KA* 1:2.11 (Lockwood, 102).

215. *KA* 1:1.4 (Lockwood, 95).

216. *KA* 1:2.4 (Lockwood, 100).

as fundamental as the differences between Barbarians, Scythians, Hellenes, and Jews are in the Christian history of culture.[217]

al-Qirqisānī is explicit in the fact that he is offering "a chronological account of Jewish sects," which is the title of 1:2. As one would then expect, the Samaritans are the first sect to be dealt with in a sub-chapter under the "headings," because their dissociation from the Jews is recorded in the Hebrew Bible (1:2.5). Then the Rabbanites are mentioned, who "led the majority only because they followed the practices and the license inherited from Jeroboam, that is, they established and built them up, argued for them and codified them in the Mishnah and other works."[218] The order of the sects in their respective sub-chapters in 1:2 is not replicated in the subsequent chapters. Significantly, the first chapter devoted to an individual sect (1:3) is given over to the Rabbanites, the longest in section 1 (fifty sub-chapters). "We begin with these because we have said that the laws in which they differ from Scripture are inherited from Jeroboam."[219] This and the following chapter (1:4, eighteen sub-chapters) then go on to cover many halakhic and theological points over which al-Qirqisānī differs with the Rabbanites. Only after the primary polemic is established against Rabbanism does the author return to his chronological scheme. In 1:5 the Samaritans are described, using the above-mentioned Christian heresiographical topoi. They are further discredited with having introduced alterations into the text of the Torah, and "it is said that they fix the beginning of months by their own system of intercalation, which is said to be the system of intercalation of Jeroboam."[220] Thus both historical deviations from true religion, Rabbanism and Samaritanism, are connected to Jeroboam.

217. It is interesting to note that there is no refutation in the Christian heresiographies of Judaism in general, as compared to Barbarism, Scythianism, and Hellenism and its subsects. Since Judaism is conceived of as a kind of proto-Christianity, the form of God's true religion before Christianity, only where it deviates from this norm is it described and refuted. Forms of Judaism that did not culminate in and become part of Christianity, which identified itself as the New Israel, were therefore considered sectarian (that is, those that survive Christianity). These are Sadducees, Scribes, Pharisees, Hemerobaptists, Nasaraeans, Ossaeans, and Herodians. See Epiphanius, *Panarion,* Proem 1:3,5 (Williams, 4); Anacephalaeosis 1:14,1–20,1 (Williams, 10–11); and 1: 14.1,1–20.3,4 (Williams, 36–50). See also John of Damascus, *The Fount of Knowledge,* 14–20 (Chase, 115–16). Note also that the Essenes are considered a Samaritan heresy. See Epiphanius, *Panarion,* Proem 1:3,4 (Williams, 4); Anacephalaeosis 1:12,1 (Williams, 10); and 1, 10.1,1–1,5 (Williams, 34). See also John of Damascus, *The Fount of Knowledge,* 12 (Chase, 114).

218. *KA* 1:2.6 (Lockwood, 101).

219. *KA* 1:3.1 (Lockwood, 105).

220. *KA* 1:5 (Lockwood, 133). The Samaritans themselves speak of their method of intercalation as the "Hebrew calculation." See also 3:1, for a refutation of some Samaritan principles.

The next sect to be dealt with is the Sadducees (1:6), whose place in al-Qirqisānī's theory of history appears in the headings. There it is described that Zadok and Boethos broke from the Rabbanites, and "it was Zadok who first exposed the Rabbanites and openly disagreed with them. *He had learned something of the truth.*"[221] This statement not only acknowledges affinities between Sadducean and Karaite halakhah, but begins a new thread in the narrative. The first thread establishes the origins of error in Israel, and connects the heretical Rabbanites and Samaritans to Jeroboam. The second thread tells the reader that in spite of the obfuscations of heretics, apprehension of the truth is possible. Zadok is the first to realize this possibility.

The narrative then continues chronologically according to al-Qirqisānī's understanding, describing the Maghārians (1:7)[222] and the Christians (1:8). The section on Christianity is substantial and probably represents some of the material of Dāwūd al-Muqammiṣ. al-Qirqisānī only half-heartedly draws Christianity into his theory of history. "*Some* of the Karaites say that Jesus was a good man and that his way was the way of Zadok, Anan and others; and that the Rabbanites conspired against him and killed him just as they sought to kill Anan also, without success. This is their way with all who oppose them."[223] Thus Christianity is not explicitly connected to Jeroboam's errors, and is only given questionable connection to those who had learned something of the truth. Later, we find mention of al-Muqammiṣ's testimony of Sadducean and Qarāʿian origins for Christianity parenthetically added to the section on the Qarāʿians. al-Qirqisānī is explicit in telling us that this information is included only for chronological reasons: ". . . which shows that the Qarāʿians existed before Christianity."[224]

Lest there be any suggestion of pro-Christian sympathy on the part of al-Qirqisānī, the strong refutation of Christianity that fills the chapter testifies to his antipathy.[225] This underscores a secondary level of contextualization

221. My italics. *KA* 1:2.7 (Lockwood, 101).

222. See Fred Astren, "The Dead Sea Scrolls and Medieval Jewish Studies: Methods and Problems"; and idem, *Encyclopedia of the Dead Sea Scrolls,* s.v. "Magharians." See also Jarl Fossum, "The Magharians: A Pre-Christian Jewish Sect and Its Significance for the Study of Gnosticism and Christianity"; Norman Golb, "Who Were the Maġārīya?"; and Steven M. Wasserstrom, "Šahrastānī on the Maġāriyya."

223. My italics. *KA* 1:8.1 (Lockwood, 135). It should be noted that this view is echoed in al-Shahrastānī, who maintained that the Karaites believed Jesus was a righteous man, but not a prophet, and that the Gospels were not divinely revealed but were compiled by Jesus and his disciples. al-Maqrīzī claims that Anan spoke well of Jesus and recognized Muḥammad as a prophet. Cited in Gil, *History of Palestine,* 780–81.

224. *KA* 1:9 (Lockwood, 140).

225. Other refutations of elements of Christian doctrine are found in *KA*, 3:2–6; 3:12.5; and 3:16.

being constructed in the heresiography. When a sect cannot be easily placed into the theory of history either chronologically or in connection with the dual threads of the perpetuation of error or the apprehension of the truth, then that sect's halakhic agreements and divergences form a matrix for understanding its relationship to other groups. "Jesus forbade divorce, just as the Sadducees forbade it."[226] To cite another example: "The Sadducees said that the glorious Creator has a body and interpret literally those Scriptural passages which affirm that he has. The opposite is true of the Maghārians, i.e. they do not teach anthropomorphism and at the same time do not deprive these descriptions of their literal meaning, for they assert these are descriptions of an angel, who created the world. We shall mention later a similar doctrine held by Benjamin al-Nahawendī."[227] In this way the many recent and contemporary sects that al-Qirqisānī could not overlook for lack of completeness are contextualized, even though they are not integral to his theory of history.

The "thread of error" is continued in the narrative by returning to the rabbinic milieu in order to indicate further differentiation and dissension within that community. "Then the Rabbanites split into two groups: the school of Hillel and the school of Shammai."[228] In the headings these two scholars are recognized to be the disciples of Shemaiah and Abtalion, a direct allusion to the chain of tradition of the rabbis. The two scholars are understood to be the sources for the distinction between rabbinic custom in Babylonia and Palestine even in al-Qirqisānī's time. "The people of Iraq followed the school of Hillel, while those of Palestine followed the school of Shammai."[229] The corresponding later chapter of section 1 (1:10) is a lengthy list of the halakhic differences that separate these two rabbinic traditions. Harkavy failed to understand the meaning of the heresiography, for he says: "This chapter is placed out of the proper order, since the author is concerned with polemic against the Rabbanites in the 3rd and 4th chapters."[230] Not only are Hillel and Shammai chronologically appropriate in a position within the narrative adjacent to Christianity, but as a separate chapter the material adds another important dimension to the "thread of error." Chapters 1:4 and 1:5 are direct

226. *KA*, 1:8.1 (Lockwood, 135).

227. *KA*, 1:7 (Lockwood, 134–35). See Wolfson, "Pre-Existent Angel."

228. *KA* 1:2.11 (Lockwood, 102).

229. Ibid. The polemic against Shammai and Hillel is found in other Karaite literature. See Yūsuf al-Baṣīr, *Sefer Miṣvot,* cited in Harkavy, *Zikhron la-Rishonim,* vol. 4, 394; and Yashar ben Ḥesed, *Sefer ha-Miṣvot,* cited in Poznanski, *Zekher Ṣaddikim,* 5, n. 2.

230. Harkavy, "Abū Yūsuf Yaʿqūb al-Qirqisānī on the Jewish Sects," 66. Harkavy also reveals his own bias as a Rabbanite Jew, perceiving rabbinic halakhah as a kind of organic whole that should be dealt with in a single context. He simply could not see history as al-Qirqisānī had presented it.

refutations and critiques of specific points of rabbinic halakhah, whereas 1:10 is an argument proving the inconsistencies of an Oral Law that the rabbis maintain is divinely given and transmitted, and therefore without error. In Gerson Cohen's four points of Karaite polemic against rabbinism cited at the beginning of this chapter, the contents of 1:4 and 1:5 are the material for the second complaint, and 1:10 corresponds to the third.

After this, two chapters deal with the messianic-prophetic movement of Abū ʿĪsā al-Isfahānī and his successor, Yudghān (1:11 and 1:12). They are not tied to the theory of history, but are contextualized halakhically and theologically. "He forbade divorce just as the Sadducees and the Christians forbid it." "He extolled and magnified the Rabbanites, to the extent of giving them a position like that of prophets. He claimed that God had told him to recite the eighteen benedictions and the Shema-prayer, just as the Rabbanites say." "For that reason the Rabbanites and the community do not exclude the ʿĪsūniyya and do not regard them in the same way they regard the Ananites and Karaites."[231] "Abū ʿĪsā acknowledged the claim to prophecy of Jesus the son of Mary, and similarly to the master of the Muslims."[232]

Returning to the second thread, the narrative turns to Anan. The entry in the headings (1:2.15), and especially the chapter that deals with him (1:13) are primarily devoted to halakhic discussion. Interestingly, there is no halakhic contextualization drawing comparison to other sects, as mentioned above. Only one statement brings Anan into al-Qirqisānī's theory of history. "He was the first to reveal *much* of the truth about the laws."[233] Lockwood has translated: "He was the first to reveal the whole truth about the laws," and Nemoy has translated: "He was the first to explain the whole truth about the laws." The Arabic *jumlah,* while usually meaning "the sum, whole, or total" or "all," cannot have that meaning here. It often has a relative meaning corresponding literally to "a sum of something," but meaning "a large amount of something."[234] al-Qirqisānī could not have meant to say that Anan perceived the whole of the truth about the laws, because he simply did not believe it. Much of the halakhic polemic in *Kitāb al-anwār wal-marāqib* is directed against the teachings of Anan and the Ananites,[235] who are constantly juxtaposed with, and distinguished from, the Karaites. The discrepancies between Anan's halakhah and that of other Karaites, including al-Qirqisānī himself, would not allow Anan to be credited with such apprehension and authority.

231. *KA* 1:11.1 (Lockwood, 144).

232. *KA* 1:11.2 (Lockwood, 145).

233. *KA* 1:2.14. The translation is mine. See note 84, above, for the full text.

234. Lockwood, 103; and Nemoy, "al-Qirqisānī's Account," 328 [12]. See E. W. Lane, *Arabic–English Lexicon,* 1:460. I am indebted to Michael Cook for suggesting this reading.

235. *KA*, s.v. "Anan" and "Ananites" in the index.

Anan is followed by Benjamin al-Nahawendī and Daniel al-Qūmisī,[236] who, along with other medieval sectarians, adhere to different systems of belief and practice, and are contextualized in the halakhic manner accordingly.

With the historical contextualization laid out before us, what then are we to conclude from this heresiography? Poznanski wanted al-Qirqisānī to tell us what happened between Zadok and Anan, and what the reason was for the rise of Anan.[237] Such questions of historical influence and continuity within the Karaite milieu do not interest al-Qirqisānī. Another of Poznanski's questions is, if Anan revealed all of the truth, how is it that later some arose among his followers to differ with him?[238] Although Poznanski may be excused for mistranslating the Arabic *jumlah* in 1:2.14, he ends up asking exactly the wrong question. Because Poznanski did not understand the true nature of the *Kitāb al-anwār wal-marāqib,* he could not see that the answer to that question is an underlying principle for the entire work.

For al-Qirqisānī, divine knowledge left in the hands of human beings results in disorder and division. No one possesses the truth, and the truth has no history. Neither charismatic community nor charismatic leadership offers an escape from this dilemma. Some groups are worse than others, but the only sure medicine to alleviate the illness of differences in apprehending and interpreting the divine word is through rational speculation. Neither Zadok nor Anan, Benjamin al-Nahawendī nor Daniel al-Qūmisī were rationalists, and therefore none of them possessed the tools for a full appreciation of the Law. Only someone like al-Qirqisānī himself was prepared for the task. He was equipped with the tools of rational speculation, and could benefit from the correct and incorrect conclusions and methods of his predecessors.

The argument departs from the historical, without recourse to either messianic ontology or the evocation of a pristine past that may have existed before the usurpation of Jeroboam after the death of Solomon. The truth is to be found in a direct methodological approach to Scripture. Like Hippolytus, there is a strong chronological element in the presentation, but the only idea of succession or transmission is where error is concerned. Since the truth had not been apprehended, it could not be transmitted. Nor is transmission a reliable technique. Only direct intellection of Scripture could lead one to the truth. With this philosophy al-Qirqisānī could not be utopian about Karaite belief and practice, so that he was bound to expose elements of differentiation and historical development evident within the Karaite milieu in order to support his thesis. Like Epiphanius, al-Qirqisānī adopts a wide contextualization, but the result is not a world history of ethnicity and heresy, but a theory

236. On Benjamin, see *KA* 1:2.16, and 1:14 (Lockwood, 104, and 147–49). On Daniel, see 1:2.20, and 1:18 (Lockwood, 104, and 151–52).

237. Poznanski, *Zekher Ṣaddikim,* 16f.

238. Ibid.

of knowledge and error firmly grounded in biblical and doctrinal formulations, thereby resulting in a wholly "Jewish" history.

In postscript it should be noted that although al-Qirqisānī offered a historical perspective which could potentially replace the lack of historical self-definition evident among his contemporaries, it is not clear that he was at all influential among Karaites in the Islamic world.[239] Although by the last decades of the twelfth century alternative forms of historical self definition were promulgated within the Karaite community (see chapter three, below), al-Qirqisānī's heresiographical notices maintained some significance by being transmitted to the Byzantine Karaite milieu, appearing in a somewhat confused Hebrew translation in the twelfth-century encyclopedic compendium of Judah Hadassi, *'Eshkol ha-kofer.*[240] Like Epiphanius, al-Qirqisānī's heresiography was divorced from its original conceptual setting and became a realization of Poznanski's flawed understanding of the original material, becoming "disconnected historical information."

239. al-Qirqisānī was occasionally cited by other Karaites, but seems to have had limited recognition. See Samuel al-Maghribī, *Murshid,* cited in Adolf Neubauer, ed., *Aus der Petersburger Bibliothek,* 114; and Ankori, *Karaites in Byzantium,* 207, n. 7. A recent edition is Samuel ben Moses al-Maghribī, *Sefer ha-Miṣvot (Kitāb al-murshid),* Yosef ben 'Ovadyah Algamil, ed. By the twelfth century, al-Qirqisānī was sometimes confused and conflated with Yūsuf al-Baṣīr, an important philosopher and jurisprudent of the early eleventh century. See the chain of Yefet ben Ṣa'ir in chapter 4, below.

240. See chapter 3, below.

~3

Confronting the Past: Karaite Historical Thought in the Byzantine Empire, Twelfth through Thirteenth Centuries

By the end of the eleventh century the center of Karaite influence and activity had shifted from the Middle East to the Byzantine Empire. From that time onward Karaism would produce more notable scholars under the sovereignty of Orthodox Christian emperors than in Muslim lands. The Crusader destruction of Jerusalem signaled a decline that had already begun for Islamicate Karaism in conjunction with a general decline for Jews of the Middle East in the eleventh century under the Saljūqs, and continuing in the twelfth and thirteenth centuries under their successors, the ʿAyyūbids, Mamlukes, and Mongols. The Karaite experience in the Byzantine Empire is marked by a florescence in the eleventh and twelfth centuries accompanying the general security and prosperity of strong rulers of the dynasties of the later Macedonians, the Ducas, and the Comneni. Important scholars of this period, such as Judah Hadassi and Jacob ben Reuben, wrote works of lasting importance to later Karaite thought. A period of decline followed which corresponded to the Crusader conquest of the capital in 1204 and the disruption of Greek cultural continuity by the establishment of the Latin Empire of Constantinople, which lasted until 1261. Karaite scholarship reemerged in the fourteenth century advancing toward a new age of creativity and literary production in the fifteenth century.

The growth of Karaite scholarship in the Byzantine Empire of the eleventh and twelfth centuries resulted in new objectives and literary forms that were designed to meet particular needs of the new Karaite immigrant community and cultural conditions in which it found itself. The failure of messianism to revolutionarily reform Middle Eastern Jewry led Karaites to a new appreciation of their minority sectarian status, while the cultural translation of Karaism from the Arabo-Islamic world to Greek-Christian Byzantium led to changes in its relationship with rabbinic thought and literature and in its own conception of the Law. A specifically Byzantine Karaite view on the past appears in a text that accounts for the origins and character of the division between the Karaites and Rabbanites, the *Ḥilluk ha-Kara'im veha-Rabbanim.*

Early Byzantine Karaism: Tobias ben Moses and the Karaite Hebrew Literary Project

Zvi Ankori's magnum opus, *The Karaites in Byzantium,* describes the beginnings of Byzantine Karaism, showing that the growth of the previously nonexistent Karaite community was a result of the empire's successful military policies of the tenth century which expanded the borders of the Empire.[1] Jews, both Karaite and Rabbanite, were attracted by security and economic opportunity in the reinvigorated Byzantine Empire and chose to settle there: in the mercantile cities of Asia Minor, in the maritime ports of the Aegean coast, in Constantinople, and in European Byzantium, too.[2] Whereas these regions had indigenous Rabbanite Jewish communities, some with roots in antiquity, the Karaites represented a new socioreligious group introduced into these territories from Islamic lands.

Byzantine Karaite Scholarship. The Karaites of Byzantium turned from the Arabic language of their cultural ancestry to Hebrew for writing and scholarship. In the Middle East, Arabic was a koine through which Jews, Christians, and Muslims alike communicated and engaged in intellectual discourse. In the Byzantine Empire, Greek was the identifying language of government, the Church, and culture at large. Whereas the Jews were excluded from government and excluded themselves from the Church, they sought to participate in society at large, specifically in the economy. For the Karaites in particular, the adoption of Greek became an important cultural marker for their brand of Judaism, imbuing them with local authenticity.[3] As a result, the first generations of Karaite settlers may have lost facility in both Hebrew and Arabic, being concerned less with scholarship and more with business and the affairs of day to day life.[4] Only after three generations or so did Byzantine

1. Ankori, *Karaites in Byzantium,* 87–92ff.

2. The foundation for these developments was the reversal by Constantine VII (913–59) of the previously restrictive Byzantine Jewish policy, thus permitting a relative degree of tolerance for the empire's Jews. Subsequently, the conquests in the east by Nicephoras II Phocas (963–69) and John I Tzimisces (969–76) introduced large Islamicate Jewish communities to Byzantine sovereignty. In addition, in the early eleventh century, Byzantium afforded refuge to Jews fleeing the persecutions of the Egyptian Fāṭimid Caliph al-Ḥākim. For a general summary, see Andrew Sharf, *Byzantine Jewry from Justinian to the Fourth Crusade,* 107–27. Much of this chapter is dependent on Ankori, *Karaites in Byzantium,* esp. 87–168, where the material pertaining to early Byzantine Karaism is dealt with.

3. On Byzantine Jewish Grecization, see Ankori, 193–94.

4. Ibid., 189–93. The general tenor of Jewish intellectual life in Byzantium prior to this period is described as "mediocre" by Joshua Starr in *The Jews in the Byzantine Empire, 641–1204,* 50.

Karaite scholarship emerge in its own right in the early eleventh century. As a language for theological and halakhic discourse Arabic was no longer practical in the new environment and might be subject to suspicion on the part of imperial and ecclesiastical officials. Alternately, Greek was too closely associated with Christianity and the government. So, with the growth of Byzantine Karaite scholarship the traditional and "international" language of the Jews, Hebrew, was adopted as the language of discourse.[5]

In addition, it must be emphasized that the adoption of Hebrew was requisite for the Byzantine Karaite engagement with Rabbanite polemic. The content of much Karaite literary production was directed against rabbinic anti-Karaite writings, exemplified by Tobias ben Eliezer, a Byzantine Rabbanite, whose biblical commentary, *Lekaḥ Ṭov,* put forth new denunciations against Karaism. In the Byzantine context of the day, they were accused of being foreign,[6] of being novices who lacked in scholarship,[7] and were often equated with other sects, including the Sadducees and Boethusians of the Second Temple period, and the contemporary Mishawites.[8] Two generations before Ibn Daud would write his exposition of rabbinic orthodoxy based upon the chain of transmission, Tobias ben Eliezer offered an evolutionary theory of the development of rabbinic halakhah that combined the historical idea of transmission with the immediacy of continual reinterpretation by the authorized rabbinic authorities of any given generation.[9] In contrast, he portrayed the Karaites as novices, intellectual failures, and arbitrary innovators. To counter the accusation of being foreign the Karaites sought to define themselves as "native," often inserting Greek glosses in their texts.[10] In order to

5. Ankori, *Karaites in Byzantium,* 200–203. Elsewhere he speaks of a "trilingual amalgam." Ibid., 424.

6. Ibid., 362–66. Ankori cites *Lekaḥ Ṭov* on Leviticus, 69 [35a], 19b: "These fools who have come and introduced new doctrines—why, they have come just recently!" The scholarly edition of Tobias ben Eliezer, *Midrash Lekaḥ Ṭov ha-mekhuneh Pesikta Zutrata,* was edited in three parts: Genesis-Exodus, by S. Buber; Leviticus-Numbers-Deuteronomy, by A. M. Padowa; and Canticles, by A. W. Greenup. The commentary on the Torah was reprinted in Jerusalem, 1959.

7. Ankori, *Karaites in Byzantium,* 360–62.

8. Ankori goes into detail on Tiflisite and Mishawite challenges to Karaism. See *Karaites in Byzantium,* 366–415.

9. Ibid., 358–62.

10. Ibid., 194, n. 94 and 95. See also Starr, *Jews in the Byzantine Empire,* 50, 243–44. See references in Ankori and Starr on early studies by Frankl and Bacher on this topic. See also Starr, "A Fragment of a Greek Mishnaic Glossary." Ankori notes that Jacob ben Reuben's biblical commentary of the late eleventh or early twelfth century, *Sefer ha-ʿOsher,* contains an estimated five hundred Greek words and phrases. See Ankori, *Karaites in Byzantium,* 198. Of course, these glosses were not simply ideological insertions into a text but parts of a necessary linguistic apparatus for the Byzantine Karaite reader.

avoid identification with other sects the Karaites became vehement in their battles against the Mishawites, a medieval sect mentioned by al-Qirqisānī that was still found in the Byzantine Empire of the day. By seeking to outdo the Rabbanites in the struggle against "sectarian error," Karaites tried to position themselves within the bounds of a kind of orthodoxy that included Rabbanites, but excluded Mishawites. Finally, the Karaites attempted to prove "to the Rabbanite neighbors that there did exist a coherent, scholarly system of Karaite exposition of Mosaic Law and not just a made-up jumble of willful anti-talmudic excesses."[11] Such a program is a far cry from the tenth-century Karaism of al-Qirqisānī, wherein no one possessed the whole truth and there was little consensus even among Karaites!

The translation of the Middle Eastern Karaite Arabic heritage into Hebrew mirrored the transmission and translation from Arabic into Hebrew of philosophical and scientific knowledge among the Jews in general. This great communal project is exemplified in the career of Tobias ben Moses, known as *ha-maʿatik*, or "the translator."[12] Tobias studied in the Karaite academy of Jerusalem in the first half of the eleventh century, and is credited with personally transmitting its teachings to the Karaites of Constantinople.

In Karaite legend Tobias ben Moses is declared to have been the student of Jeshua ben Judah, the last of the Jerusalemite Karaite scholars, who flourished in the latter half of the eleventh century. According to Elijah Bashyachi, the great fifteenth-century codifier of Karaite law, Byzantine Karaism began "at the time that Rav Tobias ha-Maʿatik went and studied with Rabbi Yeshuah, and translated his books from the Arabic language to the Holy Language, and brought them to Constantinople."[13] In fact Tobias and Yeshua were contemporaries, both having studied under the renowned philosopher and legalist, Yūsuf al-Baṣīr.[14] Such a chronological error, which places this important figure one generation later than he actually lived, might be explained by the so-called poor historical outlook of the Karaites, or by the difficult times which disrupted historical traditions in the thirteenth century. On the other hand, such a legend provides an uncomplicated construct for the transmission of Karaism to Byzantium. Echoing rabbinic notions of tradition, the first of the Byzantine Karaites "received" from the last of the Jerusalemites, creating a direct transmission of Karaite learning coincidental with

11. Ibid., 365.

12. On Tobias, ibid., s.v. "Tobias ben Moses" in the index. See also n. 16, below.

13. Elijah Bashyachi, *ʾAdderet ʾEliyahu,* in the unpaginated introduction of the edition of Gozlow, 1835 (reprinted by the Karaite community, Israel, 1966). On Bashyachi's historical thinking, see below, chapter 5.

14. See Zvi Ankori, "The Correspondence of Tobias ben Moses, the Karaite, of Constantinople," 1–38. The chronology of Tobias is further corroborated in idem, "Ibn al-Hītī and the Chronology of Joseph al-Baṣīr the Karaite." On Yūsuf al-Bāṣīr, see David Sklare, "Yūsuf al-Baṣīr: Theological Aspects of his Halakhic Works."

the historical caesura marking the end of the Jerusalem school. Furthermore, in the context of a Karaite reading of a rabbinic text, the legend has been shown to be dependent upon an entry in Ibn Daud that specifies Jeshua ben Judah as the teacher of Ibn al-Taras, who imported Karaism to eleventh-century Spain.[15] In this way Jeshua ben Judah is represented as a transmitter of Karaite knowledge to Karaites, and a reporter of Karaite knowledge to Rabbanites. Thus, the psychological needs of later Constantinopolitan Karaites were harmonized with textual-historical knowledge as it was known to Bashyachi in the fifteenth century.

Tobias ben Moses initiated what Ankori calls the Byzantine Karaite "Hebrew literary project," an extended effort on the part of the Karaite communal leadership and its scholars to compile and translate their Islamicate literary heritage into Hebrew.[16] Tobias himself was personally responsible for compilations from the Arabic into Hebrew of materials from the Jerusalem Karaite school. His philosophical treatise, *Meshivat Nefesh,* and his halakhic commentary, *Sefer ʾOṣar Neḥmad le-Vayikra,* fall under this category.[17] The Hebrew exegetical compilation, *ʾOṣar Neḥmad,* is based primarily on the Arabic works of the tenth-century Yefet ben ʿElī and the late tenth to early eleventh-century David ben Boaz, a Karaite patriarch. Tobias also translated several of the works of his teacher, Yūsuf al-Baṣīr.[18] Thus the characterization of the larger Karaite literary project as compilation and translation is already evident in Tobias' output.

These trends of compilation and translation continued so that a series of works representing the Islamicate Karaite heritage was made available in the Byzantine environs. The earliest works, in the 1040s or 1050s were probably the private notebooks compiled by Karaite students who had studied in Jerusalem and returned to Constantinople.[19] We know of another Byzantine Karaite, Jacob ben Simon, who studied in Jerusalem in the generation after

15. See Ibn Daud, *Sefer ha-Qabbalah,* 94–96, where he is Abu'l Taras. The problem is analyzed by Zvi Ankori in "Elijah Bashyachi: An Inquiry into His Traditions Concerning the Beginnings of Karaism in Byzantium."

16. Ankori speaks of "the eleventh-century Hebrew Literary Project of the empire's Karaites." *Karaites in Byzantium,* 415ff. For a complete discussion of the Karaite literary project, see also, ibid., 417–52.

17. See the article in *EJ* 15:1182–83, "Tobias ben Moses ha-Avel," attributed to the editors of the encyclopedia, but actually written by Ankori. See also Georges Vajda, *Al-Kitāb al-Muḥtawī de Yūsuf al-Baṣīr,* ed. David Blumenthal, esp. 1–31. The text is extant in MS no. 290 in the Bodleian Library, Oxford.

18. These include *Sefer Neʿimot,* a translation of *Kitāb al-Muḥtawī; Sefer Maḥkimat Peti,* a translation of *Kitāb al-Tamyīz,* also known as *Kitāb al-Manṣūrī; Sefer ha-Moladim,* a translation of a portion of *Kitāb al-Istibṣār.* See David Sklare, "Yūsuf al-Baṣīr: Theological Aspects of his Halakhic Works."

19. Ankori, *Karaites in Byzantium,* 426–31.

Tobias.[20] Subsequently, complete translations of Arabic works and sections of larger works were produced.[21] In the middle of the twelfth century Judah Hadassi refers to some of his predecessors as "compilers" (*ba'ale 'asuppot*),[22] and mentions numerous Hebrew Karaite works that he used as sources.[23] Eventually the use of Hebrew had become a linguistic necessity, having been established by the ideological program of the literary project, but becoming the language of Karaite intellectual discourse.[24] For Byzantine Karaites the literary canon was in Hebrew—in the Bible itself, and for the articulation of biblical commentary, philosophy, and halakhah.

The engagement with Rabbanite halakhic polemics forced Karaite attention on Leviticus, which is mostly legal in nature. The Rabbanite Tobias ben Eliezer framed most of his anti-Karaite utterances in the Leviticus portion of his biblical commentary.[25] In juxtaposition, it is important to note that several Karaite works of the eleventh and twelfth centuries focus in part or wholly on Leviticus and the Priestly Code: Tobias ben Moses' *'Oṣar Neḥmad,* the anonymous commentary on Exodus-Leviticus,[26] and Jacob ben Reuben's *Sefer ha-'Osher.*[27] When the determination of truth is based upon halakhah, as in the Rabbanite-Karaite struggle, then the legal code of Leviticus becomes an

20. He is credited with translating a treatise of Yeshuah ben Yehudah's on incest, *Sefer ha-Yashar*, known in Arabic as *Kitāb al-'Arayoth.* Ankori, *Karaites in Byzantium,* 188, n. 74; and 446.

21. Ibid., 443–49. In addition to the aforementioned translations of Tobias ben Moses, there exists a Hebrew translation of Levi ben Yefet Halevi, *Sefer ha-Miṣvot* (Book of Precepts), MS Warner no. 22 in the Bibliotheek der Rijksuniversiteit Leiden.

22. *Eshkol ha-Kofer,* alphabet 226, 87a, cited in Ankori, *Karaites in Byzantium,* 439, n. 216. The term is derived from Eccl. 12:11.

23. In the heresiographical section of *'Eshkol ha-Ko,* alphabet 98, 42a, Hadassi mentions *Sefer Ne'imot al-Muḥtavi, Sefer Me'irat 'Enayim, Sefer Maḥkimat Peti, Sefer ha-Datot, Sefer 'Oṣar Neḥmad, Sefer Ḥokhmat Gevulim, Sefer Maṭok la-Nefesh,* and *Sefer Marpe le-'Eṣem.* Some of these titles are unknown today. Other titles appear in alphabet 33, 21c; and alphabet 258, 98c–d. See Ankori, *Karaites in Byzantium,* 438, n. 215, where some of these texts are reproduced. See also the seventeenth-century Karaite Simhah Isaac Lutzki, *'Oraḥ Ṣadikkim,* 101–15, where these titles can be referenced in his alphabetical bibliography of Karaite texts.

24. Ankori, *Karaites in Byzantium,* 448.

25. Ibid., 432–33.

26. *Perush li-Shemot va-Yikra,* MS Warner no. 3 in the Bibliotheek der Rijksuniversiteit Leiden. This work was composed in 1088. See Ankori, *Karaites in Byzantium,* 448, n. 233.

27. MS Warner no. 8 in the Bibliotheek der Rijksuniversiteit Leiden. The portion of this work on Jeremiah-Chronicles, excluding Psalms, was published with the commentary of the fourteenth-century Byzantine Karaite Aaron ben Joseph, *Mivḥar Yesharim,* in a Karaite imprint (Gozlow, 1834).

appropriate field of battle. The construction of a Hebrew cultural heritage for Byzantine Karaites was determined in part by Rabbanite attacks, and in part by the inappropriateness of other languages.

Encyclopedism and Judah Hadassi

A secondary, but no less important, characteristic of the Karaite literary project is what Ankori calls its "encyclopedic objectives."[28] In conjunction with the impulse to represent a systematic exposition of Mosaic law, many works of the new Hebrew canon of the Byzantine Karaites were compilations and compendia of law and commentary. Tobias' *ʾOṣar Neḥmad,* which translates as "Precious Treasure," can be conceived as an early enchiridion for Karaite controversialists and scholars. In his colophon Tobias saw his work as part of a larger collection, which he called *Kuppat ha-Rokhelim,* "The Peddlers' Bag." Whereas the title, *ʾOṣar Neḥmad,* derives from a biblical expression, *Kuppat ha-Rokhelim* is of talmudic derivation in praise of scholarship with the connotation of amassed knowledge.[29] The adoption of rabbinic talmudic terminology speaks to the aim of an inter-sectarian dialogue for the literary project and a Karaite familiarity with rabbinic texts, which will be discussed below. Working some decades later, Jacob ben Reuben had many Hebrew translations available to use as sources. His *Sefer ha-ʿOsher* (The book of riches) has been described as the "sum total of eleventh-century exegetical knowledge in Karaism," "a veritable mine of information."[30]

The acme of encyclopedic composition is Judah Hadassi's *ʾEshkol ha-Kofer,* written in 1148.[31] The title, which translates as "A Cluster of Henna," is a biblical allusion referring to encyclopedic knowledge.[32] This work has

28. Ankori, *Karaites in Byzantium,* 440–43.

29. For *ʾOṣar Neḥmad,* see Prov. 21:20: "Precious treasure and oil are in the house of the wise man, and a fool of a man will run through them." For *Kuppat ha-Rokhelim,* see BT Git. 67a, which precedes another definition of scholarship as "a bag of spices," *kuppah shel besamim.*

30. Ankori, *Karaites in Byzantium,* 196–98, esp. n. 105 on Jacob's method and sources.

31. On Judah Hadassi, see *JE* 6:132–33; *EJ* 7:1046–47; and Skoss's article in the German *Encyclopaedia Judaica,* which is the best available. *ʾEshkol ha-Kofer* remains without a critical edition, a scholarly desideratum noted by Ankori in *Karaites in Byzantium,* 28, n. 5 and 6. The current edition is a 1971 reprint of Gozlow (Eupatoria), 1836, supplemented with recovered material that was previously censored. This edition also contains *Naḥal ʾEshkol,* an index written in 1497 by Caleb ben Elijah Afendopolo. *Naḥal ʾEshkol* exists in manuscript in the Library of the Jewish Theological Seminary of America, JTS Mic. 3428 (MS Adler no. 14).

32. The verse is from Cant. 1:14: "My beloved to me is a spray of henna blooms, from the vineyards of En-gedi." See Cant. Rabbah, 1, 61, 12b (Vilna, 1887): "Rabbi Berkhaya says . . . 'A Cluster of Henna.' What is a cluster? A man who possesses

been described as "the vast sea into which all the rivulets of Karaite lore emptied themselves."[33] This great encyclopedia of twelfth-century Karaite knowledge stands in marked contrast to al-Qirqisānī's voluminous exposition of philosophy and law written two centuries before. Although both works were intended to present complete expositions of biblical law, al-Qirqisānī was able to organize his work by employing the principles of speculative dialectical rationalism, whereas Hadassi lacked a sound philosophical method. In an effort at complete exposition Hadassi adopted a system of organization based upon the idea that all the commandments are epitomized by and can be categorized under the Ten Commandments. This artificial construct resists rational deductive organization, often leading to forced interpretations of the material.[34] Eschewing other methods associated with the rabbis for enumerating and categorizing the commandments, the Karaites often turned to this somewhat logical, but non-comprehensive and awkward organizational technique.[35]

---

everything—Scripture, Mishnah, Talmud, Toseftot, and Aggadot. [What is] Henna? That which will atone for the sins of Israel." The pericope plays on the Hebrew word *eshkol,* so that "a man who possesses everything" is *ish sheha-kol bo.* Thus, encyclopedic knowledge brings redemption for Israel. I am indebted to Ronald Kiener, of Trinity College, Hartford, Connecticut, for this citation. See also Ankori, *Karaites in Byzantium,* 442.

33. Poznanski, "Karaite Literary Opponents," 198, who cites J. M. Jost, *Geschichte des Judenthums und seiner Sekten,* 2:352: "Alle diese Bäche ergossen sich endlich in das grosse Meer der Karäischen Wissenschaft."

34. Philo, in *De Decologo* and *De Specialibus Legibus,* uses this principle to present the Mosaic law. Recognizing that the epitome concept cannot be used exhaustively in order to incorporate all commandments into categories, he introduces additional principles for categorization based on the classic virtues. Justice, courage, and humanity are used as "heads" for commandments in the latter chapters of *De Specialibus Legibus.* Elsewhere he invokes temperance, wisdom (identified with prudence), and piety.

35. The actual identification and enumeration of individual precepts and their categorization under rational and philosophical systems of organization follows three main systems among the rabbinic halakhists: the system of *Halakhot Gedolot,* that of Ḥefeṣ b. Yaṣliaḥ's *Kitāb al-Sharīʿah,* and that of Maimonides in *Sefer ha-Miṣvot,* which postdates Hadassi by some decades. Following Maimonides is *Sefer Miṣvot Gadol* by R. Moses b. Jacob of Coucy and *Sefer ha-Ḥinnukh* attributed to R. Aaron ha-Levi of Barcelona, both of the thirteenth century. *Halakhot Gedolot,* probably dating from the eighth century, is the first rabbinic work to include an introduction, which may have been intended as a polemic against the Karaites. The first edition is Venice, 1548, but a second recension was published in Berlin, 1888–92, by E. Hildesheimer. See also B. Halper, *A Volume of the Book of Precepts by Hefes B. Yasliah;* G. Appel, *A Philosophy of Mizvot;* and I. Twersky, *Introduction to the Code*

'Eshkol ha-Kofer is divided into ten chapters, each corresponding to one of the Ten Commandments.[36] The vast amount of material readily reveals inconsistencies and repetitions. Under the heading of the first commandment are incorporated broad concepts of God, His nature and existence, and the character of His relationship with His creatures. This includes discussions on prayer, repentance, and resurrection. However, by extension, Hadassi uses this chapter to deal with astronomy, physics, natural history, geography, folklore, and religious philosophy.[37]

The second chapter is used by Hadassi as a vehicle for heresiography. "You shall have no other Gods besides Me. You shall not make for yourself a sculptured image, or any likeness of what is in the heavens above, or on the earth below, or in the waters under the earth. You shall not bow down to them or serve them. For I the Lord your God am an impassioned God . . ."[38] Under this heading, the second commandment, Hadassi places his descriptions and refutations of sects, Jewish and otherwise, including Christianity[39] and Islam. The material depends heavily on al-Qirqisānī, yet its treatment and that of other sources indicates that the author did not always understand the material he was preserving.[40] The over-arching context of al-Qirqisānī described in the previous chapter is nowhere evident in this section of *'Eshkol ha-Kofer.* The enumeration of sects begins with some groups from Greek and

---

of Maimonides (Mishneh Torah). This method of enumeration of the commandments has rabbinic origins, most notably in the *'azharot* liturgical poems.

36. These chapters consist of varying numbers of sections of rhymed prose, usually ending with the rhyme *-kha.* The verses begin with a letter of the alphabet, forming alternately the acrostics *Tashrak* or *Abagad,* although others are occasionally used. There are 379 of these "alphabets," which are used in addition to the pagination of the Gozlow edition to cite references from the text.

37. Like Philo and Nissī ben Nūḥ, a tenth-century Karaite whose work may have utilized the same organizational principle, the first heading provides a rubric under which several small essays are incorporated. On Nissī, see Pinsker, *Likkute Kadmoniyyot,* 2:1–13; and Nemoy, "Nissi ben Noah's Quasi-Commentary," 307–48.

38. Ex. 20:3–5.

39. Sections on Christianity (alphabets 98, in part, 99, and 100, in part) were removed from the text by the Karaites or through Byzantine censorship. When Afendopolo wrote his index to *'Eshkol ha-Kofer* at the end of the fifteenth century, these sections were already missing. They were recovered from manuscripts by Bacher, "Inedited Chapters of Jehudah Hadassi's 'Eshkol Hakkofer.'" Other missing pericopae were recovered by Alexander Scheiber, "Manuscript Material Relating to the Literary Activity of Judah Hadassi." Both articles are reproduced in the 1971 reprint edition of *'Eshkol ha-Kofer.*

40. Material in *'Eshkol ha-Kofer* taken from al-Qirqisānī includes sections on philosophy, grammar, interpretation of the law, liturgy, and others. The study of Hadassi's sources remains a scholarly desideratum.

Islamic contexts[41] and then proceeds to utilize most of al-Qirqisānī's entries. The Hebrew translation is often confused and the names of sects and individuals are often garbled. Hadassi was clearly reproducing texts without fully understanding them. The claim by the Karaite Mordecai ben Nisan in the seventeenth century that Hadassi knew Arabic is not evident in this material.[42]

It should not be surprising that this haphazard collection of religious and doctrinal descriptions bears no overall historical argument. Even as Epiphanius's compositional intent was lost in John of Damascus, so Hadassi did violence to al-Qirqisānī's heresiography. There is no heresiology to Hadassi's heresiography. That is, it lacks a context which unites the material to create an argument, nor does it necessarily marry itself to the larger text. Neither does the encyclopedic character of *'Eshkol ha-Kofer* lend itself to a systematic argument. In another feature similar to John, Hadassi included an "updated" section on Islam that was lacking in al-Qirqisānī.

But we must ask what elements of historicity or historical treatments are to be found in *'Eshkol ha-Kofer?* Ankori has shown that Hadassi's treatment of the Tiflisites and Mishawites, two Jewish groups that continued to exist into the twelfth century, reflects the concerns of the times, as opposed to the received text of al-Qirqisānī. Hadassi adds his own evaluation of Tiflisite beliefs, censuring their deviations from Karaite halakhah and praising their parallels.[43] The Mishawites are treated similarly, but since they offered a real threat to the Karaites in the Byzantine Empire, one finds more solid condemnation in their description.[44] Originating in the East, they had entered the empire at the same time and under the same circumstances as the Karaites. To deflect the Rabbanite accusation that conflated or equated the two groups, the Karaites engaged in acrimonious battle with the Mishawites. The Karaites sought to be the sole representatives of nonrabbinic Judaism. In a sense, they began in the Byzantine Empire to postulate a kind of Karaite orthodoxy for Jewish heterodoxy.

Drawing upon the Karaite Arabic literary heritage by means of the Hebrew compositions of the Karaite literary project of the eleventh and

41. These include from alphabet 96, 41a–c, the Philosophers, the *Sofsayah* (Sophists), the *Mujabbira* (those who deny free will), and the *Hashisha'i* (Assassins), among others also found in subsequent alphabets.

42. Mordecai ben Nisan, *Dod Mordekhai* (Israel, 1966; reprint of Vienna, 1830), 69. Of course, there is no reason to believe that Hadassi used anything other than Hebrew translations and compilations created in the previous century.

43. *'Eshkol ha-Kofer,* alphabet 98, 41d. See Ankori, *Karaites in Byzantium,* 369–72, esp. n. 38 and 39, where he presents parallel readings from al-Qirqisānī and Hadassi.

44. *'Eshkol ha-Kofer,* alphabet 98, 42a. Cf. Ankori's aforementioned analysis of Mishawite doctrine and the threat it presented to the Byzantine Karaites, *Karaites in Byzantium,* 372–415.

twelfth centuries, Hadassi replicates the general lack of historical outlook of his Islamicate predecessors. Elements of Jewish history and legend are derived from Yosippon, a medieval narrative loosely based upon the work of Josephus, and the legendary tale of Eldad ha-Dani.[45] In the heresiographical chapter, Hadassi's treatment of prophecy moves to the Book of Daniel, which requires comment upon prophecies of the four kingdoms and the seventy weeks.[46] This leads Hadassi to a discussion of biblical chronology and the different eras used by Jews for dating the years.[47] Although one might have hoped for some remarks on the continuation of history beyond the biblical era, only chronology is dealt with.

In another instance, Hadassi tantalizingly suggests a theory of law in his discussion of the laws of inheritance. The law is an expression of the *bet din*, or court of law. The first was lead by Moses and Aaron, followed by Joshua and Phinehas. Mirroring the initial portion of what could be a Rabbanite exposition of the chain of tradition, Hadassi is unwilling to historicize and avoids any discussion of continuity from antiquity into the future.[48] Hadassi resolutely maintains the classical Karaite stance against developing historical contextualization. The vastness of this encyclopedia remains almost devoid of any history of the Karaites or of the Jews of latter days.

Byzantine Greek Scholarship. Whereas Ankori has indicated a concurrent trend shared by the Karaite Hebrew revival and the Byzantine Greek revival of the twelfth century, he failed to see the shared tendency toward encyclopedism.[49] The reigns of the tenth-century military emperors whose conquests created favorable conditions for the immigration of Jews, Karaite and Rabbanite, also brought about a decline in education.[50] But subsequently, in the eleventh century there arose in Byzantine society both institutions of higher learning, imperial and ecclesiastical, and an intellectual class associated with the ruling class.[51] Like the Byzantine Karaites, Byzantine society at large

45. See Scheiber, "Eléments fabuleaux dans l' Eshkôl Hakôfer de Juda Hadasi."

46. *'Eshkol ha-Kofer,* alphabet 125, 46b–d. This includes a discussion of the chronology of the patriarchs and the years of slavery in Egypt.

47. Ibid., alphabets 126, 127, and 128, 46d–48a. The discussion concludes with more remarks on prophecy.

48. Ibid., alphabet 258, 98c–d.

49. Ankori, *Karaites in Byzantium,* 193–96. The term *encyclopedism* was introduced "to replace the less precise 'Macedonian Renaissance' as a characterization of Byzantine culture of the ninth through the beginning of the eleventh century." A. P. Kazhdan, in *The Oxford Dictionary of Byzantium,* 1:696, s.v. "Encyclopedism." See also P. Lemerle, *Le premier humanisme byzantin,* 121–346.

50. Georgina Buckler, "Byzantine Education," 217.

51. A. P. Kazhdan and A. W. Epstein, *Change in Byzantine Culture in the Eleventh and Twelfth Centuries,* 121–33, and 158; and N. G. Wilson, *Scholars of Byzantium,* 148–50. Wilson's view suggests more continuity in Byzantine institutional and intellectual life than is currently acknowledged by scholars. It seems specious

experienced the growth of intellectual life and the enlargement of scholarly cadres from negligible beginnings in the late tenth century.

Byzantine intellectual culture had always been more engaged with the literary and intellectual inheritance of classical Greece than was the case in the West. It was established in Late Antiquity that the classic authors were to be used as school texts. Although they were reinterpreted and sometimes censored in light of the tenets of Christian doctrine, the ancient Greek texts remained part and parcel of the literary canon.[52] With a reemergence of intellectual life in the ninth century after the period of iconoclastic emperors of the Isaurian and Amorian dynasties, classical disciplines such as rhetoric, philosophy, grammar, mathematics, and other sciences became the subjects of occupation for some individuals.[53]

The works of Photius (died circa 893), one of the giants of Byzantine culture, represent the emerging intellectual trends of the day.[54] The *Bibliotheca* is "a record of Photius' reading of Greek literature over a period of many years. He says in the dedicatory letter that it covers the books read when his brother was not present," having been sent to Baghdad on a diplomatic mission.[55] The work consists of 280 chapters, each representing a classical, late antique, or early Byzantine Greek work, comprising in toto sixteen hundred pages in the modern critical edition.[56] This encyclopedic compilation is supplemented by another work, the *Amphilocia,* comprising 300 chapters on various short topics, more theological than the *Bibliotheca,* and including a wider representation of philosophical reading.[57] Earlier in his career, he wrote his *Lexicon,* a dictionary of classical and patristic Greek.[58] Contemporaneous to Daniel al-Qūmisī's activity in Jerusalem, the career of Photius augurs both

---

to ascribe some kind of monolithic continuity to the course of a thousand-year empire and its culture. In Jewish history, such views are being revised all the time. See H. G. Beck, "Bildung und Theologie im frühmittelalterlichen Byzanc." For the older view, see Buckler, "Byzantine Education."

52. Wilson, *Scholars of Byzantium,* 1–27. "Education in Byzantium was based on two contradictory principles: Greco-Roman tradition and Christian faith," from Gary Vikan, in *Oxford Dictionary of Byzantium,* 1:677, s.v. "Education."

53. Such a range of interest characterized the career of Leo the Mathematician (d.c. 869), one of the early personalities in the reappearance of Byzantine scholarship. See Wilson, *Scholars of Byzantium,* 79–84. The imperial school was reorganized by Caesar Bardas in the mid-ninth century. See ibid., 678.

54. "Photios conféra au mouvement intellectuel de Byzance, tant par sa personnalité que par son action, des traits dominants." Basile Tatakis, *La Philosophie Byzantine,* fascicule supplémentaire no. 2 de Émile Bréhier, *Histoire de la Philosophie,* 131.

55. Wilson, *Scholars of Byzantium,* 95.

56. Ibid., 93–111.

57. Ibid., 114–19.

58. Ibid., 90. On the *Lexicon* in general, see ibid., 90–93.

the encyclopedic trend that will follow in Byzantine literature and the effort at classical revival.

The tenth century then witnessed a flurry of book production.[59] This was accompanied by a paleolinguistic transformation beginning in the preceding century, wherein uncial manuscripts were transliterated into the new minuscule script. This process entailed the eventual copying of the entire literary canon, resulting in errors of transmission in the texts.[60] During the interrupted reign of Constantine VII Porphyrogenitus (913–59), an emperor with literary ambitions of his own, there was some institutional growth in higher learning, although there were no personalities of the stature of a Photius to impel progress. Constantine's own works were compilatory and encyclopedic, seeking to "describe" the empire.[61] He envisaged a massive project of fifty-three sections on all aspects of human activity. Whether this encyclopedia was completed is not known, but the literary projects for which he was responsible, either personally or by commission, have preserved many works that would have otherwise been lost to humanity.

After the conquests of the general-emperors that facilitated Jewish immigration to the Empire at the end of the tenth century, a second period of intellectual stagnation set in. At this time, another Byzantine encyclopedia-dictionary was compiled. Described as a "compilation of compilations,"[62] the *Souda* "justly claims preeminence" in the genre of encyclopedias.[63] It contains thirty thousand entries derived from ancient and medieval texts, commenting primarily on ancient and biblical topics.[64] Only decades before the Karaites

59. Ibid., 148. Many of the oldest manuscripts of classical texts extant today are results of the activity of the copyists of this period.

60. A. P. Kazhdan and Ihor Ševčenko, in *Oxford Dictionary of Byzantium,* 3:2108, s.v. "Transliteration of Texts." Compilations from this period include treatises on taxation, on bureaucracy *(taktika),* on military matters *(strategika),* the *Anthology* of Kephalas, a collection of fragments from John Chrysostom by Daphnopates, and the *Geoponika,* an agricultural manual. See Kazhdan, in *Oxford Dictionary of Byzantium,* s.v. "Encyclopedism."

61. Wilson notes in *Scholars of Byzantium,* "It is the attempt to compile encyclopedias which makes Constantine most interesting to historians" (143). In this genre he wrote *De ceremoniis, De administrando imperio,* and *De thematibus.* See the general introduction to Gy. Moravcsik, ed., and R. J. H. Jenkins, trans., Constantine Porphyrogenitus, *De Administrando Imperio,* 7–14. He also wrote a biography of his grandfather, Basil I, now known as book 5 of Theophanes Continuatus.

62. Lemerle, *Le premier humanisme byzantin,* 345.

63. E. A. Hanawalt, in *Dictionary of the Middle Ages,* 11:501, s.v. "Suda." The *Souda* was conceived on less of a grand scale than the encyclopedia of Constantine, but has maintained more lasting importance in Byzantine and classical studies.

64. See also Kazhdan, in *Oxford Dictionary of Byzantium,* 3:1930–31, s.v. "Souda"; and Wilson, *Scholars of Byzantium,* 145–47. The standard edition is Ada Adler, ed., *Suida lexicon* (Leipzig, 1928–38; reprinted 1967–71).

embarked on their great literary project, the Byzantine Greek scholarly milieu produced a monumental document that exhibited methods and objectives similar to those of the Byzantine Karaites of one or two generations later.

Similar parallels can be cited in the field of law. "In the ninth and tenth centuries official or semi-official legal compilations were produced that imposed an order on the inherited corpus of Roman law."[65] Compilations include the *Ecloga* (eighth century), the *Epanagoge* (late ninth century), and the *Prochiron* (early tenth century).[66] The *Basilika* of the emperor Leo VI (886–912), which arranged the content of Justinian's legal works according to subject, "remained the major source of law for the following centuries; it was constantly studied and commented upon."[67] By the eleventh century, the study of canon law had also submitted to the hand of epitomization and compilation, producing the *Nomocanon in Fourteen Chapters* and the *Rules of the Apostles.*[68] By the era of Karaite *Sifre Miṣvot* in Jerusalem and the beginnings of Byzantine Karaite halakhic compilation, Byzantine Greek legal encyclopedism was in full swing.

In the eleventh century, the Greeks began to move away from the encyclopedism and compilation of the tenth century toward commentary and intellectual discourse.[69] In addition, the growth of the imperial and patriarchal schools institutionalized scholarship far more than had been the case in previous centuries.[70] The intellectual life of the period was dominated by the work and personality of Michael Psellos, more even than the ninth century had been imprinted with the personality of Photius. Psellos, who died some time in the last decades of the century, left an enormous amount of written material. In his most famous work, the *Chronographia,* a history of the era, he

65. Kazhdan and Epstein, *Change in Byzantine Culture,* 145.

66. Kazhdan, in *Oxford Dictionary of Byzantium,* 2:1191–93, s.v. "Law." See also Andreas Schminck, ibid., 3:1725, s.v. "Prochiron." The legal codes had already been paraphrased in an earlier era by the antecessors of the law schools in Constantinople and Beirut of the sixth century. See Schminck, in *Oxford Dictionary of Byzantium,* 1:109, s.v. "Antecessors." The term is reminiscent of the Hebrew *rishonim,* "the first ones," or "predecessors."

67. Kazhdan, in *Oxford Dictionary of Byzantium,* 2:1191–93, s.v. "Law." This led to a subject index, the *Tipoukeitos,* a *Great Synopsis of the Basilika,* and *The Practical Synopsis* in the eleventh century. See Kazhdan and Epstein, *Change in Byzantine Culture,* 145–47. In addition, compendia of tenth and eleventh century legislation were drawn up.

68. Ibid., 148.

69. "The corpus of classical literature was gathered and transcribed in the ninth and tenth centuries; in the eleventh and twelfth centuries, the process of assimilation and reflection began." Ibid., 136.

70. Ibid., 120–33; Wilson, *Scholars of Byzantium,* 148–53; and Tatakis, *La Philosophie Byzantine,* 138. See also Vikan, in *Oxford Dictionary of Byzantium,* 1:678, s.v. "Education."

portrays himself in a position of personal power behind the throne.[71] The works of Psellos and his near-contemporaries John Mauropous, John Italos, and John Xiphilinus were dependent upon the compilations and anthologies of the previous centuries to the exclusion of the primary texts themselves. Psellos's arrogant claims to intimate knowledge of the ancient writers has been shown in many cases to be false—he knew them only through the filter of the products of encyclopedism.[72]

It must be asked why this culture was so heavily invested in a struggle with the past. And why did the reading of antiquity take the form of encyclopedism and epitomization? The answers suggested by scholars are varied. This focus of attention on antiquity has been explained as reaction to the enforced political philosophy of the empire, as the doctrinaire orthodoxy of the church, and as being due to the unstable conditions of day-to-day life.[73] From the standpoint of the church, the complicated historical constructions of the church fathers were inherited and elaborated upon.[74] The ambivalent attitudes toward pre-Christian and non-Christian history were internalized in the Byzantine milieu. On the other hand, the empire represented a cultural and institutional continuity that transcended any precise knowledge of the past that was available at the time. The emperors sat on the throne of the caesars. In this way, antiquity was never lost sight of in the identity and daily operations of the empire and society. The thought of ancient Greece provided psychological security through established continuity with a "solid" past.

The works of Photius, the many reference works, lexicons, and florilegia of these centuries, and the vast output of Psellos were engaged with a cultural problematic that sought to deal with the relationship of contemporary life to classical Greek antiquity. Commentary on the significant problems of the day

71. Wilson, *Scholars of Byzantium,* 156. The *Chronographia* is published as E. R. A. Sewter, trans., *Fourteen Byzantine Rulers, the "Chronographia" of Michael Psellus.* See the introduction for a brief survey of the life of Psellos.

72. On his knowledge of the classics, see Wilson, *Scholars of Byzantium,* 159–66, 172–79. "Psellos is always open to the suspicion that he is making a great display of knowledge when his acquaintance with the primary source material is less extensive than he would like his readers to believe." Ibid., 159. "Apart from the Chaldaean Oracles and some Neoplatonic writings Psellos knew little more of Greek literature than we do." Ibid., 163.

73. Kazhdan and Epstein, *Change in Byzantine Culture,* 138–41, wherein are cited the works of H. C. Beck, *Byzantinistik heute;* and Cyril Mango, *Byzantine Literature as a Distorting Mirror.* Hanawalt, in *Dictionary of the Middle Ages,* 11:501, s.v. "Suda," states: "The Byzantines inherited the Hellenistic passion for epitomizing and organizing ancient learning, history, and literature."

74. For a summary, see Cyril Mango, *Byzantium: The Empire of New Rome,* 189–201.

was encoded within classical allusions using "antiquated vocabulary and traditional subjects."[75] From the standpoint of the church, the literary remnants of ancient Greek culture might provide pedagogic materials, but truth was to be found in the Bible and the writings of the church fathers.[76] The ancient pagan literary canon was much less threatening to the church than the Greek philosophical heritage, especially some of the beliefs of Plato. For such ideas, John Italos, a disciple of Psellos's, would be condemned and anathematized.[77] Like the kalām philosophy of the Karaites, Psellos's outlook embraced rationalism in opposition to some of the superstition and mystical theology of the day.[78] Notwithstanding the doctrinal stance of the church, the elites of the Byzantine Empire learned classical Greek and exhibited some knowledge of its literature.[79] In the tenth century, Constantine Porphyrogenitus apologizes to his son, for whom the *De administrando imperio* was written, for his weak literary style,[80] while the works of Plutarch were very popular among the literary classes of the eleventh century.[81]

All this having been said regarding the encyclopedic and revivalist character of Byzantine Greek intellectual life, there is little evidence that permits identifying any direct influence or interaction between the Karaites and scholars of the host culture. The aforementioned Greek glosses found in both Rabbanite and Karaite texts may represent a vague hint of such a relationship. The glosses found in Karaite texts often use the philosophical terminology of the academy, whereas the Rabbanite glosses more usually represent colloquial expressions.[82] Although the most that can be said is that the Karaite literary project participated in the scholarly spirit of the time, the parallel development is highly suggestive. Whereas the Greeks were working out their relationship with the distant past, the Karaites were trying to preserve a more recent, albeit foreign, past, at the same time remaining secure in the ahistorical exegetical and doctrinal mindset inherited from Islamicate Karaism and rabbinic Judaism in general. Both cultures, however, were determined to attain their objective of preservation, whether of the ancient Greek heritage or the Islamicate Karaite.

75. Kazhdan and Epstein, *Change in Byzantine Culture,* 140.

76. Psellos wrote a short piece in answer to the question "Which Christian writers deserve to be compared for their literary merits to Lysias and Demosthenes?" See Wilson, *Scholars of Byzantium,* 168–69.

77. Ibid., 153–56. See also Lowell Clucas, *The Trial of John Italos and the Crisis of Intellectual Values in Byzantium in the Eleventh Century.*

78. Psellos's philosophy is discussed in some detail in Tatakis, *La Philosophie Byzantine,* 161–210.

79. Kazhdan and Epstein, *Change in Byzantine Culture,* 138.

80. Constantine Porphyrogenitus, *De Administrando Imperio,* ch. 1, 49.

81. Wilson, *Scholars of Byzantium,* 151.

82. See note 10, above.

Karaite Encyclopedism and the Past. The Karaites of Byzantium in the eleventh and twelfth centuries were engaged in a massive act of translation encompassing both language and culture. The compilatory character of this movement was intrinsic to the Byzantine environment as a result of the need for the newcomers to engage their Rabbanite adversaries with a systematic exposition of Karaite belief and practice and to provide a Hebrew language canon of halakhah and exegesis based upon Arabic Karaite sources. In fact, the roots of compilation can be identified in the Islamic environment, where growing social consolidation among Karaites had begun to impel similar trends.[83] But in Byzantium, the process took on specific characteristics, specifically the use of Hebrew and the inclusion of Greek glosses.

The salient characteristic of this process was encyclopedism, most pronounced in Judah Hadassi's *'Eshkol ha-Kofer.* The Karaites shared with the host Greek culture this academic tendency. Although we can say that the Karaites participated in the spirit of the times, it is extremely difficult to indicate direct influences. The only exception to this condition are the Greek glosses in Karaite texts, but they are yet to be fully examined in the light of modern scholarship.

However, the Greco-Karaite cultural parallel does lend itself to enlightened questioning. The cultural discourse of the Byzantine Greeks sought to answer the question, How are we to remain rooted in our classical past, while at the same time remaining true to our Christian heritage, a heritage that opposes many aspects of the classical worldview? With the twin inheritances of classical Greek and patristic literature, the Byzantine effort passed through preservation, compilation, encyclopedism, and eventually to a new age of analysis and creative thought. For the Karaites, the question was not dissimilar: How are we to remain true to our relationship to Scripture while at the same time acknowledging a past of our own, a past of social and religio-legal dimensions specific to our group and its transformations in the lands of Islam and Orthodox Christianity? Exhibiting impulses toward preservation through translation and compilation, the Karaite cultural discourse reached a stage of encyclopedism. But due to the cultural disruption in the Byzantine world that resulted from the establishment of the Latin Empire at Constantinople in 1204, it would not be until the fourteenth and fifteenth centuries that a period of new Karaite creativity would emerge.

Existing as a minority within the larger Jewish religious tradition, the Karaites worked out these problems under the influence of their relationship with Rabbanites and rabbinic Judaism. The engagement with Rabbanism led

83. See Mann, *Texts and Studies,* 2: *Karaitica,* 41–42, on the career of ʿAlī ibn Sulaymān, who composed digests from previous Karaite works at the end of the eleventh century. Some of these compilations were based upon existing digests and summaries of original works, indicating a compilatory process that had been going on for at least a generation.

to a literary and legal accommodation that would be a major characteristic of the creativity of the fourteenth and fifteenth centuries. In the meantime, the use of rabbinic texts became the norm, and conceptualization in the theory of Karaite law moved toward rabbinic construction. The Karaite jurisprudential idea of tradition that came to be known as *haʿtakah* would eventually lead to new Karaite approaches to Jewish history. New ways of Karaite historical expression and the accommodation to rabbinic halakhah will be dealt with in sections of this chapter below.

On the opposite side of the relationship with Rabbanism was the ongoing polemic and refutation of sibling rivals. The redirection of some of the Karaite polemic toward the sectarian Mishawites must be understood in light of the rabbinic relationship. The Karaites sought more than to be the only expression of non-rabbinic—that is, non-normative—Judaism. More importantly, strong opposition to the threat of Mishawite competition enabled the Karaites to position themselves closer to Rabbanism. We might confer with a pillar of Byzantine Christian culture to offer us a reading on this development. Basil the Great distinguishes between heresy and schism. Heretics are "men who were altogether broken off and alienated in matters relating to the actual faith." In distinction, schismatics are "men who had separated for some ecclesiastical reasons and questions capable of mutual solution."[84] The Rabbanites may have defined the Karaites as heretics, using the talmudic model for Samaritans, Sadducees, and Boethusians. But to an observer of little partiality, it was clear that the Karaites by and large believed in the same fundamental principles as the rabbis.[85] The Karaites themselves, while never articulating their sectarian status, had conceded the doctrine of consensus, thereby admitting their minority position in the community of Israel. Understanding themselves as clearly *not* being heretics, the Karaites could only gain advantage in the eyes of the Byzantine authorities and the rabbis if they could identify true heresy (Mishawism) and, at the same time, be able to submit an implicit argument in a Basilian mode for the "schismatic" nature of their differences with the Rabbanites.

Ḥilluk ha-Karaʾim veha-Rabbanim: A Byzantine Karaite Claim to History

The *Ḥilluk ha-Karaʾim veha-Rabbanim* (The division of the Karaites and Rabbanites) was published by Pinsker in *Likkute Kadmoniyyot* based upon two

84. Basil of Caesarea, *Letters and Selected Works,* Letter no. 188.1, 223f. Basil (4th c.) also has a third category, unlawful congregations *(parasynagogoi)*—"gatherings held by disorderly presbyters or bishops or by uninstructed laymen." Ibid.

85. For a medieval analysis of some equanimity by a Rabbanite, see Leon Nemoy, "Ibn Kammūnah's Treatise on the Differences between the Rabbanites and the Karaites."

manuscripts.[86] The text is attributed to Elijah ben Abraham, a Karaite of the eleventh century.[87] Little is known of Elijah; nor are other works of his known. But this tract, which circulated among Karaites, provides an elementary historical explanation for the schism in Jewish history that led to Karaism and Rabbanism and for some specific historical and doctrinal characteristics of Karaism. Many elements of the narrative illustrate the Byzantine context of the document's provenance and exemplify aspects of Karaite halakhah, exegesis, and polemic. The *Ḥilluk* is also one of the four primary sources of the account of Anan ben David as it has come down to us.[88] In addition, included is a list of Karaite personalities and scholars, providing valuable factographic data, but also hinting at the idea of a linear historical progression of Karaite activity through time.

The text begins with an invocation and dedication to the author's patron.[89] The narration commences with remarks regarding the origins of dissent in Israel. "From the time that the Temple was destroyed, when the tiara and crown, the Holy Spirit, the Ark of the Covenant, the Glory, and true prophecy had come to an end in Israel, from then until now beliefs were divided, this view and that view. And we became like the blind feeling the walls." "For this reason we were forgotten all these years."[90] These statements

86. Pages 97–106; the actual text begins on 99 and will henceforth be designated as *Ḥilluk*, with pagination referring to Pinsker's text. One manuscript belonged to Firkovitch and the other was owned by a R. Masri. Portions were previously published by Jacob Trigland, *Diatribe de Secta Karaeorum: Trium Scriptorum Illustrium de Tribus Judaeorm Sectis Syntagma*, 2; and was subsequently abridged in German in several installments as "Abhandlung über die Sekte der Karäer." On Trigland, see chapter 6, below. An article by Nemoy provides invaluable notes and a synopsized translation in "Elijah ben Abraham and His Tract." It is not known whether the title is Elijah's or was attached to the text by later copyists.

87. Dating Elijah is difficult. Poznanski places him before Hadassi because (1) Hadassi is not mentioned in the list of scholars near the end of the document; and (2) Hadassi discusses neither the Karaites as a sect nor Anan and his situation other than relying on the text of al-Qirqisānī. See *Zekher Ṣadikkim*, 19, n. 1. There is mention of an otherwise unidentified Judah at the end of Elijah's list of scholars in a position where Hadassi might be placed. *Ḥilluk*, 106. See also Poznanski, "Karaite Literary Opponents," 202–4. Cf. Nemoy, "Elijah ben Abraham and His Tract," 82, esp. n. 95 and 96.

88. See chapter 2, above, esp. Lasker's summary of the Anan narrative found in *Ḥilluk*, 103.

89. See Nemoy, "Elijah ben Abraham and His Tract," 65–66, 68.

90. *Ḥilluk*, 100. The translations are mine. However, they are based upon Nemoy's synopsis and esp. the suggested corrections and emendations to Pinsker's Hebrew text listed in "Elijah ben Abraham and His Tract," 83–87. Unfortunately, Nemoy did not translate the complete text.

refer to the First Temple, for the text later states, "And this was the circumstance also for the people of the Second Temple."[91] In addition, a covenantal moral construct is evoked to explain this loss in terms of divine chastisement, "because Rome exiled us from our land, and to this day they hold us in servitude."[92] If the scholars of the Second Temple "were deceived in matters of Torah," remaining confused in regard to the truth, "how can we receive [*nekabbel*] from them a transmission [*haʿtakah*] or tradition [*kabbalah*] or anything?"[93]

One might be surprised to learn that Elijah dates the origins of confusion—the necessary condition for dissent in Israel—to the destruction of the First Temple. Similarly, the rabbinic *shalshelet ha-kabbalah* locates a critical narrative element in the time of the cessation of prophecy following the destruction of the First Temple and followed by the process of reconsolidation and rebuilding of the Second Temple that is associated with Ezra and the Great Assembly. Elijah's analysis invokes the first great caesura in Jewish history to explain the confused state of divine knowledge among the Jews, going for the jugular of the rabbinic chain of tradition. Using the technical terms *haʿtakah* and *kabbalah,* his argument is hardly veiled. In regard to the destruction of the Second Temple, the argument also signifies exile as a condition for ignorance, an idea that al-Qirqisānī would not employ but that echoes the role in rabbinic historical thought regarding Rome and Christianity, and, by extension, Islam.

"From then and to this day fourteen sects have arisen in succession, but today in our time there are only four: Rabbanites, Karaites, Tiflisites, and Mishawites."[94] This is important corroboration for the existence of the latter two sects in the eleventh century. Moreover, the fourteen is not an arbitrary number. It suggests that Elijah knew the text of al-Qirqisānī, which lists fourteen sects in section 1, including those of Anan and Benjamin, but excluding the Karaites themselves.[95]

91. *Ḥilluk,* 100.

92. Ibid.

93. Ibid.

94. Ibid.

95. See chapter 2, above. Such enumerations can become fixed in religious traditions. Islam provides an example of an arbitrary enumeration for the number of sects. "ʿAbdullāh ibn ʿAmr reported God's messenger as saying: 'My people will experience what the Children of Israel experienced. . . . The Children of Israel were divided into seventy-two sects, but my people will be divided into seventy-three, all of which but one will go to Hell.' On being asked which it was, he replied, 'It is the one to which I and my companions belong.'" *Mishkat al-masābiḥ,* book 1, part 6, 2, p. 45. Later heresiographers went out of their way to make sure they had a complete listing. Cf. John of Damascus, who "borrowed" one hundred sects from

The exilic theory is not allowed to stand alone, and in acknowledgment of al-Qirqisānī's text, Jeroboam's innovations are listed.[96] He is designated as the originator of "the new Torah called the Oral Torah" in which "the Karaites do not believe."[97] Jeroboam and those who subsequently followed his teaching "denied the belief in the Sender, in the messenger, in the divine message, and in the House of Prayer."[98] Whereas al-Qirqisānī made a point of keeping Jeroboam's deviations within the Jewish fold, Elijah credits him with nothing less than apostasy. Elijah uses al-Qirqisānī for his own purposes, denouncing rabbinic error as a greater perversion of true religion than al-Qirqisānī's philosophical purpose permitted.

A basic question of historical continuity emerges in this text, which al-Qirqisānī seemingly addressed but failed to answer. Once one has posited Jeroboam as the originator of the schism in Israel, a historical question emerges. What happened in the intervening centuries that explains the current existence of Karaites and Rabbanites? al-Qirqisānī holds Jeroboam responsible for only one schism in Jewish history, albeit the one that has caused the most damage and led to the evolution of other sects. His argument, veiled in a chronological listing of the sects, appears as a history, but, as shown above, it was more of a philosophical argument. He had no need to provide arguments for historical continuity other than rooting rabbinic practice in Jeroboam's teaching.[99] Elijah addresses the same lack of historical continuity that Poznanski decried.

Elijah presents a new twist to an old theme from Jewish literature, stating that from the time of Jeroboam those among the ten northern tribes who feared God's word "separated themselves from their brethren in Israel and went off beyond the rivers of Cush. On account of them, it says, 'We have a little sister.' (Canticles 8:8)."[100] Echoing legends of remote Jewish lands found

---

Epiphanius and another source and then added three entries of his own. See chapter 2, above.

96. *Ḥilluk,* 101.

97. Ibid., 100.

98. Ibid.: *ve-hikkhish meha-yom ha-hu va-hal'ah darkhe ha-emunah la-sholeaḥ vela-shaliaḥ veli-sheliḥut ule-vet ha-tefilah.* The wordplay on the root *sh-l-ḥ* indicates God (the Sender), Moses (the messenger), and the divine message, which is annotated by Pinsker to mean the Tree of Life. Is Elijah saying that the Rabbanites deny the Torah? Yes, in the sense that they have created their own Oral Torah which makes genuine toraitic observance impossible. Pinsker supplied an explanation (the Tree of Life) that both suited his own rabbinic background and generally accepted knowledge that the Rabbanites do not deny the Torah. He could not read Elijah properly.

99. As well as indicating the Samaritan connection to Jeroboam, and rabbinic roots for the Sadducees, Boethusians, and Anan.

100. Ibid., 101.

in the account of Eldad ha-Dani or based upon accounts of the Khazar kingdom, Elijah describes a world where a large but unknown Karaite majority might exist.[101] Such a legend offers psychological reassurance to a community for whom the idea of consensus has failed. Clearly, a projection of the minority status of the Karaites among Jews at large can be detected in this historicized explanation.

The narrative continues, explaining that a few of the faithful remained in Jerusalem because they were afraid to leave the holy city devoid of true believers. "They are the ones who are called 'they that sigh and cry.' (Ezekiel 9:4)."[102] In this instance, the minority character of Karaism is given image but also imbued with the qualities of the Mourners for Zion. Near the end of the text are arguments for the possibility that "the few to perceive the truth [are] better than the many."[103] Job, even though a gentile, attained better knowledge of God than his four companions. Caleb and Joshua perceived the truth "better than their ten fellow-spies."[104]

"And they, too, were exiled along with the rest of the people, the 'good figs,'[105] the 'craftsmen and the smiths,'[106] Daniel, and Hananiah, Mishael, and Azariah, and those like them, Jeshua ben Jehozadak, Zerubbabel ben Shealtiel, Ezra the Scribe, Nehemiah ben Hacaliah, the prophets, and their brothers. Their faith is our faith, and their path is our path."[107] In this passage, a sanctioned Karaite past is derived from the Bible. The list cites men from the

101. For Eldad ha-Dani, see A. Epstein, ed., *Eldad ha-Dani;* and an abridged English translation in Elkan Nathan Adler, *Jewish Travellers in the Middle Ages.* Similar legends often appear in messianic context (cf. *The Fourth Book of Ezra,* otherwise designated *Esdras II,* 13:39), wherein the Jews of far-off unknown lands, usually the remnants of the exiled Ten Tribes, appear in Jerusalem with the ingathering of exiles. In the seventeenth century, these Jewish masses were reported to have arrived in the Middle East as a powerful army in support of the messiahship of Sabbatai Ṣevi. See Gershom Scholem, *Sabbatai Ṣevi, the Mystical Messiah, 1626–1676,* 332–54. Around the same time, John Dury, an English millenarian Puritan, imagined the Karaites leading the Ten Lost Tribes from the East. See Richard H. Popkin, "The Lost Tribes, the Caraites and the English Millenarians." On the early modern perception of a Karaite-Protestant interface, see chapter 6, below.

102. *Ḥilluk,* 101. This reading was first used by ʿAlī ibn Sulaymān (fl. c. 1100) in his commentary on the Torah, Gen. 18:24. See Poznanski, *Zekher Ṣadikkim,* 20, n. 1. For other names, cf. Frank, "The *Shoshanim* of Tenth-century Jerusalem."

103. *Ḥilluk,* 104.

104. Ibid.

105. Jer. 24:1–10. The "good figs" are the Judean exiles whom God will return to the land, while the "bad figs" are those who will be punished for not heeding the words of Jeremiah and supporting a pro-Egyptian foreign policy.

106. Jer. 24:1, a category of exiles brought to Babylon by Nebuchadnezzar.

107. *Ḥilluk,* 101. See also ibid., 104, where the list includes Ezekiel, Daniel, Hananiah, Mishael, Azariah, and Ezra, "with his companions, Haggai, Zechariah,

period of the Exile and the Return, including Jeshua and Zerubbabel, representatives of the priestly and Davidic lines, respectively. In addition, Ezra and Nehemiah are included, important figures both in the Hebrew Bible and the rabbinic *shalshelet ha-kabbalah.* Also, near the end of the text are lists of the legislation derived from the later prophets, Ezekiel, Daniel, and his companions, and the people of the Second Commonwealth.[108] These halakhic precedents from the prophets and writings of the Hebrew Bible stand in marked contrast to rabbinic law, which recognizes the Torah only as a source for halakhah. Lacking an equivalent of the rabbis' Oral Law, the Karaites required the broadest possible base for developing laws.

In direct reference to the rabbinic theory of transmission, Elijah later states, "And as for the Rabbanites who say that [their tradition goes back to] Haggai, Zechariah, and Malachi, we are willing to accept from them what was heard from the mouths of those men. But if it contradicts the Torah, we cannot accept it from them. Perhaps they misheard it."[109] One might take this statement as representative of the Karaite accommodation to rabbinic tradition, but at that early stage such explicit statements are unknown. It does not fit into the logic of Elijah's arguments, whereby a notion of tradition can be accepted, but only if corroborated by Torah itself. It should be seen as a stated willingness to recognize rabbinic traditions that are clearly in accordance with the Torah—which is to say, with the Karaite understanding of the Law. Correspondingly, Elijah demonstrates familiarity with rabbinic literature. He quotes the *Halakhot Gedolot* and refers to both Talmuds, the Babylonian (B.M. 59b, Ber. 29a, Yeb. 76b, B.K. 82a, and Kid. 15a) and Palestinian (Meg. 4:1), Sifre on Deuteronomy, and Mekhilta.[110]

"In the Second Temple they [the true believers] did not revert to folly. Neither were they identified with the corrupters of the masses in [matters of] Torah, nor were they deceived in [matters of] Torah, on account of whom [the corrupters] the Second Temple was again destroyed."[111] Pinsker's second manuscript is more explicit, "They [the true believers] were the reason that

---

and Malachi." The latter, of course, represent the last of the prophets and part of the critical link in the rabbinic chain of tradition following the destruction of the First Temple, the Great Assembly. Such a strategy is similar to that of early Christianity, wherein the Old Testament prophets are transformed into proto-Christians, while the rebellious Israelites represent the ancestry of latter-day Jews. See Rosemary Radford Ruether, "The *Adversus Judaeos* Tradition in the Church Fathers: The Exegesis of Christian Anti-Judaism," 27–50.

108. *Ḥilluk,* 104–5.

109. Ibid.

110. See Nemoy's notes in "Elijah ben Abraham and His Tract." These references usually appear in connection to specific halakhic points.

111. *Ḥilluk,* 101.

they [the corrupters] invented a new Torah, which they were not commanded."[112] In regard to the true believers, "They, too, were exiled by the kings of Edom. Still with them were 'they that sigh and cry,' who settled with them in Babylonia and other lands. As a result, they are few to this day"[113]—the second manuscript adding, "because those who know *(maskilim)* are always few in comparison to most of the people. They feared the word of God."[114] The masses abolished observation of the new moon and observation of the fields in the spring, "following the faith of Edom and [Ishmael]" and introduced mathematical calendation.[115]

The exilic theory suggested here establishes the background against which Elijah further defines the Karaites in history. The transgression worthy of punishment is the corruption of the masses by the followers of Jeroboam's teaching, while the agent of divine punishment is Edom (Rome). The nature of this punishment, exile, is even more onerous on the followers of the truth, who can maintain only a minority status in Israel. The Jewish masses become subject to the religious innovations of the proto-Rabbanites, who learned them from the masters of the Exile. Questions of cause and effect are addressed, and aspects of historical continuity are provided, especially the location of archaic proto-Karaites in Babylonia. This is the first Karaite text to provide a fully historicized explanation for the division of Israel into two camps—followers of the truth and followers of corruption.

"And the children of they that sigh and cry hid themselves from them [the corrupters] and from the treachery of the exile."[116] This statement provides for a secret history of the truth, whereby the followers of the truth are understood to have existed outside of events as they might otherwise be remembered. Thus, any reading of rabbinic or even Christian history can be reformulated to incorporate the presence or even central importance of a kind of archaic proto-Karaism. This will become a useful tool for later Karaite historians. "And this continued in the days of the Hasmoneans, who were responsible for most of the sins of impurity that were incorporated into the community." "And God stirred up the spirit of the foreigners so they were again enemies of Israel."[117] The failure of the Second Commonwealth is attributed to the sins of the proto-Rabbanites, whose misinterpretation of the laws of purity is laid at the feet of the Hasmoneans.

112. Ibid.
113. Ibid.
114. Ibid.
115. Ibid.
116. Ibid.
117. Ibid. The text here continues with reference to the defiling of women at the hands of the foreigners. The Herodians, "their servants," in reference to the Hasmoneans, are implicated. Karaite concern with laws of purity are reflected here.

"The Rabbanites themselves have even recorded the occurrences between the priests of the Second Temple and the Palestinian sages, between the school of Shammai and the school of Hillel, between Zadok and Boethos, and among all the sages themselves. This one says thus, and that one says otherwise."[118] One of the principle Karaite polemics against rabbinic practice is alluded to here. How could a tradition that claims to be based upon the transmission of divine knowledge be so full of internal inconsistencies?[119] "Since the time of Ashi and Ravina the teachings of those who fear [God][120] were established in one school.[121] That is the *haʿtakah* of the Karaite faith which we possess. We came before them![122] It is by us that they are designated as Jerusalemites, Shammaites, Sadducees, and Boethusians. Their arguments come from our words."[123] What we would today describe as the medieval dominance of rabbinism is represented in the two redactors of the Babylonian Talmud, Ashi and Ravina, who are historically contextualized against the rise of a single, nonrabbinic movement. Reflecting the anti-Mishawite polemic of Hadassi and other contemporary Karaites, Karaism is portrayed as the only true nonrabbinic Judaism. This historicization reflects Karaite memory, narrativizing conditions of Islamicate society that nurtured both the international dominance of rabbinism among Jews and the growth of dissidence.[124]

More significant in this pericope is the assertion that, as Nemoy renders it, "we are more ancient than they."[125] The cryptohistorical esotericism of a small group of true believers who somehow survive the crises of history permits a claim of Karaite chronological antecedence and the corresponding claim that rabbinic pronouncements are derivations of archaic, proto-Karaite teaching. The assertion needs also to be understood in the context of the Byzantine environment, where the Karaites were considered immigrant newcomers, whose pedigree was highly questionable. The intellectual discourse in the Islamic environs in previous centuries was such that a claim to historical anteriority was of negligible value. Islam clearly was dominant, yet was historically recent. The Islamic religio-legal discourse became focused on the relationship to the text and, historically, to the life of the Prophet, to the exclusion

118. Ibid.

119. See chapter 2, above, for Gerson Cohen's description of Karaite antirabbinic polemic; and in reference to al-Qirqisānī, *KA* 1:3 ("and the inconsistency of their doctrines."), and 1:10 ("Account of the Differences between the Rabbanites of Syria and of Iraq").

120. *ha-meravim.* Nemoy states that the text may be corrupt here. "Elijah ben Abraham and His Tract," 85. I have selected one of his suggestions, *ha-ḥaredim.*

121. Nemoy renders *be-maʿamad eḥad* as "in one setting." Ibid., 69.

122. *Rishonim anaḥnu mehem.*

123. *Ḥilluk*, 101.

124. See chapter 1, above.

125. "Elijah ben Abraham and His Tract," 69–70.

of other currents of thought that sought roots for Islam in pre-Islamic antiquity.[126] In Byzantium, the Karaites looked for new arguments in support of legitimacy, and the claim to historical priority was one of the strongest, especially in the context of the Byzantine reliance on ancient Greek and patristic literature for their theories of history and culture.

Going beyond the self-imposed limitations of al-Qirqisānī's argument, which defines heresy without defining orthodoxy, Elijah establishes Karaism as orthodoxy. Such an assertion suggests that a sufficiently developed level of consolidation had been achieved in Byzantine Karaite law and society to be expressed as a kind of orthodoxy. Reference to an idea of tradition *(haʿtakah)* foretells the consolidation of legal principles and method that would influence historical thinking. More on this below.

The historical development of Karaite halakhah is the subject next addressed by Elijah. Anticipating a weakness in the argument that connects his historical theories to Anan ben David, the author lists objections that could be directed against Anan: (1) he erred concerning the Torah; (2) later Karaites do not rely on most of his teaching; and (3) if his teaching was part of the tradition originating with "they that sigh and cry," then why were his words not relied upon for later halakhah?[127]

Elijah affirms that Anan is relied upon by the Karaites. In spite of later Karaism's halakhic differences from Anan's halakhah, Anan is centralized in the historical discussion and is represented as the inheritor of the small community of true believers in Israel. The halakhic divergences are to be accounted for by three refutations of the aforementioned objections: (1) Anan and the followers of the truth were not prophets and were therefore not free from error in their tradition;[128] in fact, in some matters they observed greater strictness than required; (2) it is possible that Anan and his generation made errors; and (3) the Karaites admit that some traditions have been forgotten: "Look at Israel, even when they had every advantage, they erred, as it is said, 'And when you shall err.' (Numbers 15:22). They were sometimes [even] puzzled about [scriptural] *miṣvot,* as it is said, 'If there arise a matter too

126. The popularity and later intermediate status of the *Isrāʿīliyyāt* ("Israelite stories"), otherwise known as *qiṣaṣ al-ʾanbiyāʾ* ("tales of the prophets"), engages the more mainstream Islamic doctrine of an ancient chain of prophecy that culminated with Muḥammad, "the seal of the prophets." However, these pre-Islamic tales had no legal legislative standing. See William M. Brinner, "Prophets and Prophecy in the Islamic and Jewish Traditions," 63–82; and now Brinner's translation and annotation of Abū Isḥaq Aḥmad ibn Muḥammad ibn Ibrāhīm al-Thaʿlabī's "tales of the prophets," idem, *ʿArāʾis al-majālis fī qiṣaṣ al-ʾanbiyāʾ, or "Lives of the Prophets."* Cf. Gordon D. Newby, *The Making of the Last Prophet: A Reconstruction of the Earliest Biography of Muhammad.*

127. *Ḥilluk,* 101. "To him who says, 'But look at Anan . . .' "

128. *Kabbalatam,* "their *kabbalah.*" Ibid.

puzzling for you in judgment.' (Deuteronomy 17:8)."[129] How much more so might Israel err in the postbiblical exile lacking priests and prophets to guide them?

With this technique, Karaite halakhah is rooted in the ancient true beliefs, and Anan is forged as the central link in a linear progression that leads to later Karaism. The social and halakhic developments of the Islamicate period, whereby Anan and the Ananites were incorporated as one element of the nascent Palestino-centric, quasi-ascetic scripturalist movement are canonized in this historicized expression of legal history. The halakhic facts are little obstacle to the historicized magnification of Anan. Nonetheless, he is not made out to be infallible, nor does the argument go as far as the rabbinic chain of tradition to suggest that the Karaite tradition has been maintained without error over the centuries.

The argument appears in a different guise later in the text. "If you will see that from the time when 'they that inhabit those waste places' (Ezekiel 33:24) were exiled to the first year of Cyrus only forty-nine years had passed, yet the returnees from Tel Melah and Tel Harsha 'could not tell their father's houses, nor their seed, whether they were of Israel.' (Nehemiah 7:63). They had forgotten their genealogy. Even the priests, 'the children of Habaiah' (Nehemiah 7:63) and their like, had forgotten their genealogy. If they had forgotten their genealogy in forty-nine years, how much more so [must they have forgotten] the interpretation of the Torah!"[130]

Of course, this theory of error that derives from the exigencies of external conditions faced by Israel in history applies equally to both Karaites and Rabbanites, even though the latter are already the bearers of false traditions originating with Jeroboam that were exacerbated by Roman and Muslim influence. Elijah quotes the eighth-century rabbinic halakhic collection *Halakhot Gedolot* to demonstrate that the rabbis acknowledged their own confusion and internal divisions. "Similarly, see that between the House of Shammai and the House of Hillel they could not satisfy all their [halakhic] needs from their [the rabbinic] interpretation, and fell into controversy. On this the Rabbanites say that on the ninth of Adar they have decreed a fast [to commemorate] that the House of Shammai and the House of Hillel separated themselves one from the other. And this day was as grievous for them as the affair of the Golden Calf."[131] The text continues by asking how it is that the Rabbanite "braggarts" were not able to admit the same fundamental break in regard to the disagreements between the Houses of Shammai and Hillel and the sages of Jerusalem and Babylonia? Why did they not condemn Zadok and Boethos? Why did they take recourse in a Heavenly Voice? Why did Eliezer ben Hyrcanus resort

129. Ibid., 101.

130. Ibid., 102.

131. Ibid., 101. Cf. *Halakhot Gedolot* (Warsaw, 1874), 40aa, cited by Nemoy in "Elijah ben Abraham and His Tract," 70.

to miraculous proofs for his halakhic arguments?[132] And so, the text returns to a more developed attack on the inconsistencies of rabbinic tradition.

"But let us put aside [for the moment] the tradition [*ha'takah*] that we possess, and that we were the predecessors, and let us learn from the *miṣvot* [themselves] who was first. We say that he who possesses innovated *miṣvot* is the latter. Behold! They possess innovated *miṣvot,* like . . ."[133] The narrative proceeds to list examples of Rabbanite halakhic innovations; that is, practices that the Karaites believe have no scriptural basis.[134] "Hence he who possesses the *miṣvot* of the Torah alone is the first."[135]

In a dramatic departure from the historical and halakhic argument for Karaite historical anteriority, Elijah continues, "Even if it were according to their words that Karaism became known only since the time of Anan, what harm is there in this to our community?"[136] Although the author seemingly disavows the historical argument in favor of a greater truth, he cannot escape historicization. "One could say that when those who fear God [the proto-Karaites] saw the disagreements that took place . . . [among the Rabbanites], they said, 'Surely tradition has fallen into doubt.' But it is not hidden from us. So those who fear God were compelled to research and examine closely in order to find rest for their souls in the word of God. Even if they [the Karaites] were the latter ones, what harm would this do to them, and what would it avail being the first?"[137] A historicized setting is hereby established for the beginnings of scripturalist attention to the Hebrew Bible, with allusion to such academic approaches as *ḥippus* (investigation) and grammatical study *(le-dakdek).* Method supersedes history.

The author returns to a covenantal moral construct, evoking the sins of Israel to explain the reason for the exile. "Concerning the shepherds of our exile, it says, 'My anger is kindled against the shepherds,'' in reference to the rabbis who govern the Jews in exile. "Had our shepherds pastured us towards the dwelling places of our Torah, why would the Lord's anger have been kindled against them?" "There is only one explanation for this—our own continuing transgressions, and above all, the persistent iniquities of the evil shepherds,"[138] Expanding the classic covenantal explanation for the exile, Elijah puts the blame squarely on the heads of the rabbis. In comparison with previous exiles, "that is why our situation is different from that of our forefathers

132. *Ḥilluk,* 101.

133. Ibid., 102.

134. The innovations are calendrical calculation, the postponement of holidays, celebration of New Moons and holidays for two days each, introduction of the celebration of Hanukkah, introduction of the afternoon prayer, and liturgical innovations.

135. Ibid.

136. Ibid.

137. Ibid.

138. Ibid.

in Egypt and Babylon, for whom the duration of their exile was defined precisely as 400 and 70 years, respectively, in round figures."[139] The author goes on to discuss disagreements among the masoretes to support his image of confusion.

Reading Anan ben David in the Ḥilluk. Much of the rest of the tract involves the Rabbanite account of Anan ben David (summarized earlier in chapter 2) and its refutation by Elijah.[140] The primary premise is that "the account proves the opposite of what the Rabbanites had intended."[141] By taking up the Rabbanite account on a point-by-point basis, Elijah sought to harmonize Anan's story with contemporary Karaite doctrine and the historical construction of the tract.

Some of the arguments are summarized as follows. Anan could not have begun his career as a freethinker, as is claimed, because the Karaite teaching "is ancient and antedates Anan."[142] The fact that Anan was inspired by a dream in which Elijah the prophet exhorts him to observe the written Torah was not a ruse used to convince his followers to accept his religious innovations, but a genuine dream-vision. The use of a bribe to influence the vizier must not be true, for the Rabbanites, who represent the Jewish majority, could easily have outbid the Karaite price. Important details regarding Anan originate with this account and become accepted facts in what is emerging as a Karaite historical metanarrative.

A closer examination of the narrative is revealing. The association of Anan with Abū Hanīfah as cellmates is problematic, but revealing. The best dating for Anan locates him in the middle of the eighth century, while the dates for Abū Hanīfah are given by scholars as 700–767. Indeed, Abū Hanīfah was imprisoned late in his life, probably as a result of his support for a Zaydī Shīʿite rebellion. Even if the historicity of this element of the narrative is doubtful, the function of Abū Hanīfah, as the founder of one of the orthodox Muslim law schools, is as a narrative element that makes the Muslim host culture culpable for the birth of Karaism. The narrative takes refuge in Islamic constitutional notions that explain and acquiesce to the presence of non-Muslims as *dhimmīs* in the domain of Islam *(dār al-Islām).*

Abū Hanīfah's advice to Anan is to persuade the caliph that Anan is the head of a separate community from that of his brother, the (rabbinic) exilarch. This narrative element more properly mirrors a later time, when in the

139. Ibid.

140. See chapter 2, above. The narrative has been attributed to Saadia Gaon, perhaps coming from his *Kitāb al-radd ʿalā ʿAnān,* "The Book of Refutation against Anan," which is no longer extant. This view was put forth by Pinsker and accepted by Poznanski. See Nemoy, "Anan ben David," 313ff., who prefers to describe the account as "pseudo-Saadian"; see idem, "Elijah ben Abraham and His Tract," 74.

141. Ibid., 74.

142. *Ḥilluk,* 104.

ninth century under Caliph al-Maʾmūn it is recorded that the caliphate might recognize a group as a separate religion with as few as ten adherents. This historical tidbit is recorded by the Christian Michael the Syrian, in the context of a Jewish exilarchic contest of that century.[143] The rabbinic Jewish story seems to conflate a later genuine controversy with the episode of Anan ben David.

Anan's law regarding observation of the new moon also requires comment. By asserting to the caliph that months are to be declared by observation of the new moon and not by means of calendrical calculation, Anan established a halakhah that was also recognized in Muslim *sharʿīah.* The presence of this feature in the narrative tells us that a perceived Islamic (and therefore foreign) character of Karaism is identified by the anti-Karaite rabbinic author of the story. Later Karaites would also consider this historical datum to be true and useful, and accordingly they preserved it in the narrative.

Although the narrative has little factual veracity, its mood and context are instructive. Such a truculent etiology for the birth of Karaism could only represent a rabbinic standpoint. That is, Karaism is portrayed as a sect whose very existence is the fault of the non-Jewish Muslim host culture.[144]

When we move to the period of the narrative's textual origin, the twelfth century, other readings emerge. In the translation of Karaism from Islamic environs to Byzantium, the absence of any Karaite consensus on the past and lack of historical data emanating from the eleventh-century Islamicate milieu permitted, even required, that this otherwise negative characterization of Anan be appropriated. Such a story was needed, whether historically true or otherwise. Of course, it was reinterpreted, and was eventually internalized, to become the foundation myth of the later movement.

The Karaites of Byzantium fully embraced the notion that they constituted a sect by retaining the rabbinic accusation embedded in the narrative that their ancestors included the Second Temple heresies of Zadok and Boethos.

143. Michael the Syrian, *La chronique de Michel le Syrien,* 517. The fact is repeated by Bar Hebraeus.

144. This is a literary-historical trope that can be found in other cultures. See James C. Scott, *Domination and the Arts of Resistance: Hidden Transcripts.* A parallel is found in the tenth-century *Fihrist* of Ibn al-Nadīm, where it is reported that in the eighth century the polytheistic inhabitants of Ḥarrān in upper Mesopotamia were able to justify their existence in the face of antipolytheistic Muslim assumptions of collectivity by means of a ruse using "inside knowledge" of the Muslim host culture. See *The Fihrist of al-Nadīm,* 751–53. The main sources on the Sabians are D. Chwolson, *Die Ssabier und der Ssabismus,* 2 vols.; Tamara M. Green, *The City of the Moon God: Religious Traditions of Harran;* Şinasi Gündüz, *The Knowledge of Life, The Origins and Early History of the Mandaeans and their Relations to the Sabians of the Qurʾān and to the Harranians.* For another example of this trope, see the Gibeonite story in Joshua 9. See Fred Astren, "The Gibeonite Gambit: Sabians and Karaite Jews on the Margins of Medieval Islamic Society" (forthcoming).

It is argued in the story that Anan gathered "all manner of evil and worthless men from among the remnants of Zadok and Boethos, and set up a dissident sect."[145] The text refutes this by asking why, if these two had taught heresy, were they not excommunicated or even executed by the rabbis? Similarly, why was John Hyrcanus not executed as a heretic, seeing that he served as high priest but ended up as a Sadducee? Evidently these men were not heretics but were zealous religious teachers. Instead of rejecting these historic figures whose beliefs were, in fact, contrary to Karaism,[146] the text says inclusion in the narrative accepted as predecessors. By doing so, the text says both that these ancient sectarians were not as deviant as the rabbis considered and that the Karaites themselves were relinquishing claim to being the sole possessors of the ancient heritage of Israel by imagining a past with a great deal of legitimate Judaic variety.

When one looks at the Byzantine environment of the twelfth century, one notes the presence of several Jewish sects. The narrative implies that the Karaites sought to portray to the rabbis and to the Byzantine authorities a spectrum of Jewish heresy in which the Karaites represented themselves as a minor aberration from the rabbinically self-identified and Christian-recognized mainstream. This effort at social positioning is more pronounced in other Byzantine Karaite works, as mentioned above. What we witness is a strategy by which a marginalized minority group seeks to situate itself close to the "center" by further marginalizing other competing minority groups. In this way, the Karaites sought a place for themselves in relation both to medieval Greek society, by representing themselves as a Jewish sect with sanctioned historical roots in the Islamic past, and to Rabbanites, by emphasizing that there were other Jewish groups with whom the rabbis had greater disagreement.

We still need to ask: Why, in Christendom, use an Islamic story? The two obvious explanations do not go far enough to answer the question: that (1) the Karaites were, in fact, Islamicate in culture; and (2) they had no other narrative to seize upon. The best explanation is derived from identifying transformations of meaning in the story. In the earlier, anti-Karaite rabbinic reading of the story, Anan's legitimacy is clearly not based on the original "Jewish" question of Davidic descent but is informed by narrative setting and leverage of the host culture. The caliph was able to offer recognition to the nascent Karaite community because the problem of Anan and the rabbis corresponded to Muslim jurisprudential notions, whereby a *madhhab* (law school) can coexist with other, equally orthodox schools of methodological legal interpretation. In this version, Anan is the epistemological progenitor of a

145. Ibid., 103.

146. Zadok and Boethos are reported to have denied the fundamental Jewish beliefs of divine reward and punishment and of the afterlife.

jurisprudential school worthy of recognition in the eyes of the Muslims, mirrored by the image of his cellmate Abū Hanīfah. The caliph could easily understand Anan's legally defined position.

In Byzantium, the same story is read differently, actually accommodating itself to the Christian environment. Having discarded the ahistorical immediacy of pure scripturalism and millenarianism, the Karaites were able to present themselves in their new diaspora as a heretical sect connected with Zadokites and Boethusians. *Heresy* is a word that Byzantine Christians could understand, and Byzantine rabbinic Jews would hardly disagree with such an obviously negative characterization of the Karaites. Byzantines might turn to the authoritative heresiographies of the church fathers, which usually identified seven or eight Jewish heresies but recognized no correct contemporary version of Judaism.[147] In terms of Christian theology, the true descendants of Israel were its spiritual descendants, the Christians. From this point of view, twelfth-century Karaites might merely be continuators of ancient Jewish heresies or simply another of the sects of Judaism, all of which were equally erroneous in terms of true religion.

The history of the Anan narrative may be absurd at first glance, but it is brilliant in its illumination of the complexity of sectarian identity in terms of historical consciousness and the complex relations that prevailed with the host cultures. Karaite self-definition in regard to history appears to us to be protean and dynamic. The transformation of the Anan story from rabbinic to Karaite historical consciousness indicates plasticity on the edges of medieval Jewish textuality. Appositely, the transformation from ahistorical scripturalism to embracing a notion of the past reflects both internal Karaite developments and a changing external environment. Even as Karaite identity was constructed from within, it was simultaneously constructed externally. In the first instance, the rabbinic story emanating from the eighth century offers explanation for the presence of an anomalous nonrabbinic group within the Jewish community that challenged rabbinic assumptions of collectivity. The narrative demonstrates knowledge of the host culture in order to describe a hoax perpetrated on the Muslims, thereby arrogating to that host culture responsibility for the existence of Karaism. In the second instance, four hundred years later, the Karaites adopted the same story, preserving the original purpose of the narrative, which offered an explanation for Karaite existence but with Islam no longer blamed as an agent that interfered with the Jewish community; Islam here is an acknowledger and sanctioner of an ancient and separate Judaism inscribed in the image of Christian heresy.

Elijah's treatment of the Rabbanite account leaves the general outline and many details intact. In fact, this strategy works as a mechanism for the internalization of this historical narrative by the Karaites. Being without traditions concerning the "founding father," the Karaites found it eminently more

147. These are Sadducees, Scribes, Pharisees, Hemerobaptists, Nasaraeans, Ossaeans, and Herodians. See chapter 2, n. 217, above.

useful to "correct" the known version of Anan's history. The predilection to avoid history in earlier centuries had left a historical gap that needed filling, and the Rabbanite narrative performed that function. The image of the past was adopted from the enemy.

As a footnote, it must be stated that the Karaites appended a small, elaborative feature to the narrative, stating that after the successful denouement of this affair, Anan had to depart Iraq, and he made his way to Jerusalem, where he became a founder of the Mourners for Zion and set up a synagogue.[148] Again, there is no historical evidence to support this element of the story, but it does provide a foundation myth for the Jerusalem center of the tenth and eleventh centuries, thereby homogenizing into a single historical narrative what are likely to have been unrelated historical phenomena.

The Ḥilluk *in Karaite Historical Thought.* Before the text concludes there is a list of Karaite worthies and scholars: "I shall mention some of our teachers, whose names I saw mentioned in books." The list supplies an image of continuity from the time of Anan to that of the author in the Byzantine environment. No claim for transmission is implied, but the vaguely chronological arrangement of names implies history and approaches the idea of a chain of tradition. The list has fifty-two entries, including Anan and eight of his lineal descendants, as well as important scholars, such as Benjamin al-Nahawendī, Daniel al-Qūmisī, Sahl ben Maṣliaḥ, Yefet ben ʿElī ha-Levi, Joseph ha-Roʾeh (Yūsuf al-Baṣīr), Nissi ben Nuḥ, Salmon ben Yeruḥim, Tobias, "the expert" (ben Moses), and Yeshuah, "the great master" (Yeshua ben Judah).[149] The list begs the question of Elijah's sources. Only a few have been identified; a conclusive analysis of his historical vision cannot answer the question of whether he created something new or adapted materials from other sources.[150]

Lists of scholars, a kind of bibliographic image of history, reappear in Karaite literature. Most notable is a small description in Judeo-Arabic of Karaite scholars and their works by the fifteenth-century David ben Saʿadʾel Ibn al-Hītī. This important little work offers corroboration for identification of names that appear in the *Ḥilluk* and in later Karaite versions of the chain of tradition. It also has important information on the Jerusalem academy under the leadership of Joseph ben Noah in the eleventh century.[151]

The tract ends with an affirmation of Jewish unity. "Most of these have said that the Rabbanites, even though they err in [regard to] most of the *miṣvot,* are nevertheless our brethren and co-religionists, and therefore our

148. One can visit today the Synagogue of Anan ben David in the Jewish Quarter of the Old City in Jerusalem.

149. Ibid., 106.

150. See Poznanski, *Zekher Ṣadikkim,* 21–22, n. 2.

151. G. Margoliouth, "Ibn al-Hītī's Arabic Chronicle of Karaite Doctors." In the eighteenth century, Simhah Isaac Lutzki included a complete bibliography and listing of scholars in two of his works. See chapter 6, below.

souls are grieving over their error." "There is still hope that a seed of truth will come forth from them."[152]

Unlike any earlier Karaite work that is currently known, the *Ḥilluk* presents a rich tapestry of historical narrative and explanation. Although some of the polemical and exegetical elements are derived from earlier Karaite literature,[153] the author has constructed a *true* historical narrative. In this regard, questions of historical continuity are addressed, and several historical theories are postulated to explain questions relating to the minority status of those who believe in the truth and the abuse of power on the part of the majority Rabbanites. The question of continuity eschewed by al-Qirqisānī's heresiography is answered: What happened in the intervening centuries after Jeroboam created a schism in religious tradition?

The text is exemplary of many trends in Byzantine Karaism of the eleventh and twelfth centuries, including the interlinear reading of rabbinic texts and the contemporary state of Karaite halakhah. The narrative anticipates changes in Karaite law that permitted a Karaite idea of tradition to evolve and laid the foundation for the construction of a new history of the truth. The need to assert Karaite anteriority in relation to the Rabbanites is characteristically Byzantine, postulated as a response to accusations that the Karaites were newcomers and innovators. In fact, the *Ḥilluk* responds reflexively, recreating the rabbis as the innovators.

Two most important features of the work should be noted. The first is the incorporation of the Rabbanite, anti-Karaite description of Anan into the Karaite tradition. The narrative is transformed and co-opted to become the canonized version of their "founder's" history. The second is the incorporation of a list of Karaite scholars and notables. This completes a construction of historical continuity, filling in the years from Anan to the time of the author. That is, an *archaic* history is supplied that reworks the biblical and late antique historical data from Jeroboam to Anan; and a list of names represents the *contemporary* history of Karaism. This is a true historical supplement to the vast literature of Karaite law, biblical exegesis, and polemic, whose creation required several centuries and a complete change in cultural venue to be articulated.

152. *Ḥilluk,* 106. This is followed by a short section confirming that Israel remains the chosen people. At the end is an addendum on the prohibition against sexual intercourse on the Sabbath, which is probably a late addition to the text.

153. The text is thickly interwoven with biblical citations used to support most of the author's statements. A study of the selection and use of these verses by a scholar of medieval Jewish biblical exegesis would be a desired project.

Conclusion to Part One

Karaite Legal Theory, Notions of Tradition, and the Reading of Rabbinic Literature

Halakhah and History. Questions concerning the origins and evolution of Karaite halakhah are not readily answered, yet the unfolding of Karaite legal history suggests models for understanding Karaite relationships with the past in the early Islamic and Byzantine periods. Changes in Karaite law are difficult to understand for several reasons. Islamicate Karaism before the twelfth century was focused on the immediacy of scripturalism, whereby all that was needed to fulfill divine requirements was a relationship to the text. In a sense, this emphasis on sanctification echoes the rabbinic problematic of the Mishnah. Second, Karaites were additionally focused on millennial immediacy, looking toward the future to the exclusion of the past, even their own halakhic past. Thus, Karaites again mirrored the rabbis of Late Antiquity by mobilizing ideologies of salvation and the End with which to give meaning and purpose to sanctification. Thirdly, later Karaites tried to project uniformity on their movement's mixed past. The problem of understanding early Karaite halakhah is further exacerbated by modern scholarship on Karaism, which has tended to see Karaite halakhah from a rabbinic point of view, as a kind "anti-halakhah."

In spite of Karaism's declared scripturalist doctrine, Karaite Judaism would never represent a pure Jewish scripturalism. The Hebrew Bible, with its extensive legal content, simply does not provide enough legislation with which to govern a complex society. Where the Torah provides specific laws, it may not indicate the manner in which those laws are to be observed. Alternately, the Torah may offer vague formulations whose required execution can only be guessed at.[1] The voluminous rabbinic legal corpus was generated in

1. For example, the Torah specifies that the Sabbath is a day of rest (Ex. 31:15) upon which "you shall not do any work" (Deut. 5:14). It does not define work in a precise way. The rabbinic ideology is expressed in a modern orthodox handbook on the Sabbath, I. Grunfeld, *The Sabbath: A Guide to Its Understanding and Observance,* 13: "What is really meant by 'work' in the Biblical injunction . . . can be ascertained only by careful study of the oral tradition." The rabbis defined work as

response to the Torah's incompleteness, built upon the historical structure of a theory of tradition that was eventually articulated in the idea of the chain of tradition. In a different way, Karaites would offer their own solutions to the problems embedded in this gigantic toraitic desideratum, at first struggling to avoid notions of tradition and then creating their own chains of tradition.

It has already been indicated that the origins of Karaism are obscure and complicated. Indeed, due to the legal orientation of Judaism and the predominance of textual evidence as source material, the story of Karaism is, in large part, the story of Karaite law. And consequently, the construction of a Karaite Judaic past also is connected to law. By the tenth century and the dominance of the Jerusalem school, there were two conditions present in the law among Karaites that required explanation:

1. There existed an actual history of law, in the sense that it was generations ago that Benjamin and Anan had promulgated halakhah that now was considered part of, or prototypical to, Karaite halakhah (in the case of Benjamin, almost one hundred years had passed since the promulgation; in the case of Anan, two hundred years). With the incorporation of the Ananite house and its followers and other proto-Karaitic legal cultures into what was to become classical Islamicate Karaism, the components of a real history of law were inherited by the nascent movement. Almost as a halakhic echo of the quadripartite historicization of Salmon ben Yeruḥim, intellectual honesty required of Karaism an encounter with legal memory. Time had passed.
2. This passage of time also represented a history of law that was characterized by the accumulation of widely differing customs and many mutually incompatible interpretations of the Torah. The halakhah of Anan was different from that of Benjamin, and both differed substantially from that of Daniel al-Qūmisī and the first Karaites of the ninth century. Distinction and difference would demand a response, and the desire for consistency would become felt.

---

any of thirty-nine tasks that were necessary for the construction of the Tabernacle in the wilderness, which are listed in M Shab. 7:2. Grunfeld comments: "The written law thus gives the outline of the Sabbath legislation. The oral tradition has only to fill in the details, by defining terms, and by applying the given principles to all the practical questions which arise in everyday life." Ibid, 15. The Karaites do not observe these thirty-nine categories. See Aaron ben Elijah, *Keter Torah,* 22c–37b; and Bashyachi, *'Adderet 'Eliyahu,* 40c–56d. Another example is the rabbinic dietary restriction separating milk and meat, which is based upon three verses that state, "You shall not boil a kid in its mother's milk." (Ex. 23:19, 34:26; Deut. 14:21). The Karaites take this prohibition literally and thus do not construct dietary laws that separate all milk products from all meat products. Aaron ben Elijah, *Keter Torah,* 2:79a–b; and Bashyachi, *'Adderet 'Eliyahu,* 114d–15a.

Eschewing both a theological judgment on Jewish orthodoxy and a historical judgment on normative medieval Judaism, Karaism and rabbinic Judaism share basic elements. The rabbis viewed the sectarianism that they perceived in Karaism in the same way that classical rabbinic literature understood sects, primarily the Samaritans and the Sadducees.[2] The ahistorical limitations of the rabbinic view had limited the rabbis' ability to deal with heterodoxy, forcing their interpretation of Karaism to be based upon their own sanctioned, textually known past. However, it was clear to reasonable observers that both groups shared basic theological values, among them belief in the unity of God, reward and punishment, the world to come, and prophecy.[3] It must also be remembered that they shared the text of the Hebrew Bible.[4] The arena of contention was on how to interpret the Law; that is, what form Judaism should take in day-to-day life in the postbiblical world.

Social Origins of Karaite Halakhah. As mentioned above, the unification of Jewry under Islam brought distinct, and previously independent, Jewish communities into contact with each other.[5] In the lands of the Byzantine

2. The Sadducee polemic is exemplified in J. D. Eisenstein, *Oṣar Dinim u-Minhagim,* 366, a comprehensive digest of the *miṣvot:* "Karaites: An Israelite sect whose followers moved to schism over the [issue of the] Oral Law in the time of the geonim. . . . They are like the Sadducees in the time of the Talmud." Cf. Erder, "The Karaites' Sadducee Dilemma," 195–226.

3. Judah Hadassi articulated ten principles of Jewish belief, antedating Maimonides' thirteen principles by several decades. See *Eshkol ha-Kofer,* alphabet 33, 21c–d. The principles are listed by Daniel J. Lasker in "The Philosophy of Judah Hadassi the Karaite," 477–92 [Heb. with Engl. summary]: (1) the existence of a Creator; (2) the eternity and unity of the Creator; (3) Creation; (4) the prophecy of Moses and the other prophets; (5) the truth of the Torah; (6) the obligation to know Hebrew; (7) the Temple being the habitation of God's glory and Presence; (8) resurrection of the dead; (9) divine judgement; and (10) reward and punishment. Intermarriage between Rabbanites and Karaites in the Middle Ages indicates both sides acknowledged shared fundamental principles. Some rabbinic halakhists, such as Maimonides and, later, David ben Solomon ibn Abī Zimra sought to uphold a definition of Karaites that included them within the community of Israel, even though they might observe unaccepted halakhot. See Fred Astren, "Some Notes on Intermarriage among Rabbanites and Karaites in the Middle Ages, and Its Subsequent Prohibition," 45–54.

4. The Karaites were active along with Rabbanites in the masoretic movement. One historical theory credits the Karaites with initiating the masoretic movement as a result of their scripturalism. This view also holds Karaite polemical attack to be the impetus for the resurgence of medieval rabbinic study of the Bible. This view was held by Pinsker, Graetz, and Fürst, but was refuted by Steinschneider, *Magasin für Wissenschaft des Judenthums,* 20, 236. Now see Drory, *Emergence of Jewish-Arabic Literary Contacts,* 126–57.

5. In the tenth century, al-Qirqisānī testifies to differing Karaite practices from such eastern localities as Baghdad, Ṭusṭār, Baṣra, Fars, Syria, Khurāsān, and Jibāl. al-Qirqisānī, *KA* 1:19 (Lockwood, 152–56).

Empire, local autonomy developed in the wake of the disappearance of central rabbinic authority marked by the empire's dissolution of the patriarchate. Nonrabbinic Jewries likely existed in the Byzantine cultural sphere, either surviving remnants of late antique Hellenistic Judaism or other regional variations on ancient Judaisms.[6] A variety of local practices evolved, none more orthodox or "less Jewish" than the next. To the east, such Jewish communities as those of Iran, Transcaucasia, and Central Asia had long been isolated from the academic authority of the academies and exilarchate in Babylonia.[7] The world of Jewish practice and observance in the seventh and eighth centuries was likely much more variegated than we will ever know. Local traditions may also have emerged when whole communities entered into treaty-like relations with the Arabs during the seventh-century conquests. We are at a disadvantage to appreciate fully this variety in Middle Eastern Judaism: the majority of evidence for the period comes down to us by way of rabbinic literature, which presents its Judaism as normative and correct. Yet, even rabbinic literature indicates a great deal of halakhic variety, some of which resulted from the exigencies of local custom.[8]

6. The problem of pre-Islamic Jewish influences and antecedents for medieval Karaism engages questions regarding connections and continuity between Jewish sects of the Second Temple period and proto-Karaitic phenomena. A ninth-century letter of the Nestorian Catholicos of Baghdad, Timotheus, reports that a bedouin had discovered a chamber in the Judean desert filled with ancient books and that the Jews of Jerusalem came to the find seeking copies of the Bible and other Hebrew books. It appears that these books were at that time acknowledged to be heretical and, subsequently, may have influenced early Jerusalemite Karaites. Concepts and terminology known from the Dead Sea Scrolls are indeed found in Karaite literature. On Timotheus's letter, see O. Braun, "Ein Brief des Katholikos Timotheos I über biblische Studien des 9. Jahrhunderts." On Karaism and the Dead Sea Scrolls, see Fred Astren, "The Dead Sea Scrolls and Medieval Jewish Studies"; idem, in Lawrence H. Schiffman and James C. VanderKam, eds., *Encyclopedia of the Dead Sea Scrolls,* s.v. "Karaites" and "Magharians"; Naphtali Wieder, *The Judean Scrolls and Karaism;* and A. Paul, *Écrits de Qumran et sectes juives aux premiers siècles de l'Islam.* Even before the discovery of the Dead Sea Scrolls, Abraham Harkavy asserted on the testimony of al-Qirqisānī that the ninth-century Karaites had in their possession Sadducean texts. See Harkavy in "Abū Yūsuf al-Qirqisānī on the Jewish Sects" (1984), 49–90, esp. 57. He also cites a Karaite commentary on Exodus from the manuscripts in the Russian National Library in St. Petersburg that acknowledges the same. See ibid., 83, n. 29. This text is also quoted in Harkavy, *Zikhron la-Rishonim* (St. Petersburg, 1891), vol. 5, 225. See the bibliographical notes in Gil, *A History of Palestine,* 785–86. See now the works of Yoram Erder, esp. "When Did the Karaites?" Cf. Ben-Shammai's response, 69–86.

7. Karaism as a reaction to Iranian influence in rabbinic Judaism was suggested in Zvi Cahn, *The Rise of the Karaite Sect.*

8. Libson, "Halakhah and Reality in the Gaonic Period."

Tension was no doubt high in the struggle between the centripetal impulse of the rabbis toward uniformity and the centrifugal pull of localities toward maintaining their time-honored customs. Such tension was evident in the differences that separated the newly reunited Palestinian and Babylonian varieties of rabbinic Judaism, a point that later Karaites emphasized for polemical purposes.[9] Differences in halakhah by and large remained academic. Why was the Karaite-Rabbanite difference not confined to the academy? Why did the Karaite-Rabbanite halakhic difference not generate a medieval Jewish world inhabited by two distinct but mutually recognized orthodoxies, as in Islam?[10]

Academic answers to these questions were developed by rabbis and Karaites and were written into their literatures in the late ninth and tenth centuries. Now, by examining the earlier eras of proto-Karaitic phenomena and the origins of Karaism from a sociological perspective, one can speculate on how difference was manifest in the social world of real Jews. To put the question in a different way, what might be so important that some localities would refuse to accept rabbinic practice?

It was proposed by Aryeh Grabois that the very fabric of social identity in nonrabbinic Jewish communities was threatened by Rabbanism.[11] Suggested in his model for the beginnings of proto-Karaitic resistance to rabbinic practice are two fundamental elements: (1) existing differences among Jewish communities in the manner of effecting marriage; and (2) whether Jewish identity is transmitted through the male or female line.

First, local communities in the early Islamic period are likely to have practiced marriage differently than the rabbis. The rabbis defined the manner by which betrothal was effected through three modes: *ketubbah,* or *shetar; kesef;* and *bi'ah* (a written instrument; the exchange of money or something of value; and sexual consummation). In regard to *bi'ah,* a rabbinic writer of one hundred years ago states that "this rather too primitive mode of contracting marriage was already in ancient times declared morally objectionable, and even punishable."[12] An attitude such as that writer's would be resented and

9. A medieval text lists halakhic differences between these communities. See B. M. Lewin, *Oṣar ḥilluf minhagim;* and M. Margaliot, *ha-Ḥillukim she-ben 'anshe mizraḥ 'u-vne ereṣ yisra'el.* For a Karaite list, see al-Qirqisānī, *KA* 1:10 (Lockwood, 140–44). For another example, the controversy between Saadia and the head of the Palestinian academy, Aaron Ben Meir, see H. Malter, *Saadia Gaon: His Life and Works,* 69–88.

10. In contemporary Sunnī Islam, there are four mutually recognized "orthodox" schools *(madhāhib)* of law. They are the Ḥanāfī, Ḥanbalī, Mālikī, and Shāfi'ī.

11. These two suggestions developed from private conversations that took place with Professor Grabois in Berkeley, California, in the summer of 1992.

12. M. Mielziner, *The Jewish Law of Marriage and Divorce in Ancient and*

rejected by Jewish communities for whom *bi'ah* had always been the fundamental method of effecting marriage. In addition, such a practice may have been normative in local host-culture environments. This practice may have been found among far-flung Jewish communities whose contact with the rabbinic centers of Late Antiquity had been limited.[13]

A second point of departure from rabbinic ways of marriage may have been significant. Such isolated communities would not necessarily have adopted the *ketubbah* contract as a formal written instrument. The final form of the *ketubbah* developed under Byzantine dominance in Palestine, where the document was submitted to the authorities so that the government could acknowledge the validity of Jewish contracts and law.[14] Its form is known as *Ketubbat Kushta,* "The *Ketubbah* of Constantinople," reflecting in its name the orbit of Byzantine political power.[15] Even in its beginnings, rabbinic matrimonial law was used as a measure to establish and enforce uniformity. An early form of the *ketubbah* suggests that Hillel adopted it as a safeguard against the matrimonial irregularities of Alexandrian Jews.[16] Further support for wide variety in Jewish marriage practice is found in the Talmud, which testifies to locales where the *ketubbah* document was not used even though rabbinic matrimonial regulations were held to be obligatory.[17] Correspondingly, proliferation of the *ketubbah* cannot be well established for the early Muslim era.[18] Also, whether the practice of polygamy was an additional issue that separated Jewish communities in this era is worthy of investigation.[19]

Grabois' second suggestion is that many non-Rabbanized communities had traditionally defined Jewish identity patrilineally, in contradiction to rabbinic definitions of matrilineal descent. Shaye Cohen indicates that matrilineal

---

Modern Times, 77f., which also cites BT Kid. 12, and Maimonides, *Mishneh Torah,* "Issurei Bi'ah," 21, 14.

13. It is interesting that the traditional rabbinic marriage ritual includes all three modes for betrothal: a formal signing of the *ketubbah,* an exchange of rings as tokens of value, and the withdrawal of the wedding couple to a private room for a short time after the ceremony *(yiḥud),* a ritual representation of *bi'ah,* the physical consummation of the marriage.

14. The Talmud credits Simeon ben Shetah with originating or regulating use of the *ketubbah* (BT Ket. 82b; and Shab. 14). See also BT Ket. 10a.

15. BT Ket. 16b.

16. Quoted in Tos. Ket. 9:9, and BT Bab. M. 104a

17. BT Ket. 16b.

18. On the other hand, for later periods, see Judith Olszowy-Schlanger, *Karaite Marriage Documents from the Cairo Geniza: Legal Tradition and Community Life in Mediaeval Egypt and Palestine;* and M. A. Friedman, *Jewish Marriage in Palestine: A Cairo Genizah Study.*

19. In a late-eleventh/early-twelfth-century Torah commentary, *Lekaḥ Tov,*

Jewish identity was unknown in Second Temple times.[20] Also, patrilineal identity corresponds to Islamic law and mores, which originated in pre-Islamic tribal Arabia, whereby Islam is inherited from a Muslim father. The relationship between Judaic (proto-Karaitic or other) and Muslim patrilineality might be characterized either as influence or as mere validation from the emerging host culture. It is also possible that such a view was ancient in origin and would come to be understood by its adherents in a scripturalist or (later) "Karaitic" way, supported by notions of patrilineal descent—tribal, priestly, and Davidic—as evidenced in biblical law and narrative.

Taken together, differences in matrimonial practice and the definition of who is a Jew would likely lead to whole communities and families being split in the encounter with the process of Rabbanization. People on the street in their everyday lives would have recourse to refer to their cultural opponents as "bastards." The issue becomes even more complex when we recognize that the ongoing process of Islamization would create intermediate and hybrid Judeo-Muslim identities that would also divide communities and families.[21] In addition, the rise of messianic-charismatic movements could capitalize upon or introduce nonrabbinic formulations into communities of marginal Rabbanization.[22] As early as Benjamin al-Nahawendī, the offspring of a gentile mother and a Jewish father were understood to be a Jew,[23] and subsequently Hadassi repeated this halakhic point.[24] Karaite halakhah developed other responses to these matrimonial and descent issues, redefining personal relationships within the Jewish community through strict laws of consanguinity, some of which contradicted and undermined normative rabbinic practices, such as niece marriage.[25]

Tobias ben Eliezer charged Karaites as polygamists. See Ankori, *Karaites in Byzantium*, 289–90.

20. Shaye J. D. Cohen, "The Matrilineal Principle," in *The Beginnings of Jewishness*, 263–307. On Jewish matrilineal identity, see also references cited there, including Lawrence Schiffman, *Who Was a Jew*, 9–17.

21. See chapter 1, above. Cp. Shaye J. D. Cohen, "Israelite Mothers, Israelite Fathers: Matrilineal Descent and the Inequality of the Convert," in *The Beginnings of Jewishness: Boundaries, Varieties, Uncertainties*, 308–40.

22. Note that Abū ʿĪsā al-Isfahānī, an eighth-century messianic claimant, proclaimed a chain of prophecy that included the previous prophets, including Jesus and Muḥammad, and that culminated with himself. He also forbade divorce, a tenet that would immediately identify any child of a second marriage as illegitimate. See al-Qirqisānī, *KA* 1:11 (Lockwood, 144–45).

23. See Benjamin al-Nahawendī, *Sefer Dinim, Mas'at Binyamin* (1978), 39.

24. Judah Hadassi, *Eshkol ha-Kofer*, alphabet 366, 141d, and alphabet 365, 140b. See also Revel, "Karaite Halakah," 68.

25. A. Harkavy, *Anan's Book of Commandments*, 8:93; Daniel al-Qūmisī, in Nemoy, *Karaite Anthology*, 40, and in Mann, *Texts and Studies*, 2: *Karaitica*, 81. Cf. Revel, "Karaite Halakah," 70, n. 101.

On the rabbinic side, the *takkanah* attributed to Gershom of Mainz (950–1028), which prohibited polygamy and introduced female consent into divorce proceedings, made those who observed nonrabbinic matrimonial practice even more unacceptable to the rabbinically dominated mainstream.[26] Correspondingly, Karaites could be defined as *mamzerim* as a result of their nonconformity to rabbinic halakhic matrimonial and divorce practices.[27] In addition, by the late Middle Ages a complete schedule of Karaite deviations from rabbinic halakhah had evolved, so that these issues were less fundamental, having been subsumed under the larger rabbinic anti-Karaite agenda.

This model suggests that a break between communities, both of which defined themselves as Jewish, could have real sociological roots, resulting from more than halakhic-academic promulgations. Such an approach to early Karaism deserves more concentrated examination.

Halakhah and Sharīʿah. As suggested, Karaite halakhah is improperly understood to be a kind of antihalakhah. It is better understood as a social force active in Karaite society that developed in a reflexive relationship to the scholastic-academic activities of scholarly writers. The association of sociological reality and academic development is also apparent in the evolution of Islam in this period and bears comparing with Karaism.

Halakhic matters lie at the heart of Karaite distinctiveness in its classical period and can help outline the coalescence of proto-Karaitic phenomena into the Karaite movement of the late ninth and the tenth centuries. Perhaps more importantly, while the complex of Karaite scripturalism, Palestinocentrism, millenarianism, and messianism before the twelfth century mark a fundamentally different response to the world than that of the rabbis, contention with rabbinic Judaism afterward became mostly legalistic and ritualistic, with less fundamental disagreement.[28]

26. This would especially be true if Karaites, found primarily in the east, practiced polygamy. See note 19, above.

27. Karaites did not use the *get* document to validate divorce. One of the primary rabbinic accusations against the Karaites, and other nonrabbinic Jews, is that over the course of time nonrabbinically recognized divorces followed by remarriage and the birth of children within their communities could lead to the communal "infection" of *mamzerut.* See Michael Corinaldi, *The Personal Status of the Karaites,* 34–100 [Heb.].

28. Wilson, *Magic and the Millennium,* esp. 1–69. Wilson developed a taxonomy of sects, describing seven types, each according to a *response to the world* incorporating its approach to theodicy, the problem of divine or holy power, and the presence of evil: conversionist, revolutionist, introversionist, manipulationist, thaumaturgical, reformist, and utopian. After the decline of the Jerusalem center, the Karaite theoditic perspective changed from utopian and reformist to an eighth supplemental type of sect described as *ritualistic,* one that distinguishes itself from a larger group only through practice, not by way of fundamental belief.

Some elements of Karaite halakhah are similar to sharīʿah. For example, direct observation of the moon for calendrical purposes could "appear Muslim," as it is represented in the medieval story of Anan, whose Muslim calendrical method is viewed favorably by the caliph.[29] Other similarities are listed by Moshe Zucker: prayers that are composed of blessings without supplication or personal requests, impurity of a corpse not effective in the diaspora, prohibition against drinking alcohol, and other parallels in laws of incest, inheritance, and other areas.[30] Notwithstanding such specific legal parallels, the definition of the sources of law in Islam and Karaism is strikingly similar. Muslims came to consider the sources of law to be four: the Qurʾān (scripture), the custom *(sunnah)* of the Prophet Muḥammad, consensus *(ijmāʿ)*, and analogy *(qiyyās)*. Many Karaites would supplement the first source of law, the Hebrew Bible (scripture) with the two latter sources used by Muslims: consensus (*kibbuṣ* or *ʿedah*, "community") and analogy *(hekkesh)*.[31]

In terms of law, the new "cultural stew" that resulted from the interaction of a wide variety of Jewish practice in the eighth and ninth centuries posed serious challenges for the rabbis as they sought to consolidate their own system, but it also explains the emergence of proto-Karaitic Judaisms. Identified by later Karaites as a founding figure, Anan ben David (fl. ca. 760) is portrayed as a failed aspirant for the exilarchate whose candidacy precipitated a schism within rabbinic ranks.[32] His *Sefer ha-Miṣvot* represents an alternative to rabbinic halakhic norms, even though it is, by and large, based upon the Talmud. Anan's halakhah emphasized religious rigorism and a separation from non-Jews,[33] an ideology that would defend against the inroads of Islamization and the uncertainties of hybridity. Rather than look at Anan as the first Karaite, it is more appropriate to see his halakhot as variants from within the talmudic discourse. Among these are embedded antecedents for Karaite halakhic method appropriated from rabbinic tradition, the use of *hekkesh* and *ḥippus*. al-Qirqisānī states that Anan established the principle of *ḥippus*,[34] which represented a new, revolutionary reading of Scripture whereby individuals use reasoning to interpret divine writ. *Ḥippus*, investigation of scripture on the part of the halakhic researcher, became associated with scripturalism, one of Karaism's primary professed doctrines. Focus on scripture implies a

29. See chapter 3, above, and Astren, "The Gibeonite Gambit."

30. Zucker, *Rav Saadya Gaon's Translation of the Torah*, 144ff., cited in Gil, *History of Palestine*, 779.

31. For a different treatment of Muslim and Karaite Jewish sources of law, see Lasker, "Islamic Influences," 23–47.

32. Poznanski, "Anan"; and Martin Cohen, "Anan ben David and Karaite Origins."

33. Salo W. Baron, "Karaite Schism," in *Social and Religious History*, 5:209–85.

34. al-Qirqisānī, *KA*, 2:9.2. Cf. Vajda, "Études sur Qirqisânî, II," 67.

denial of the Oral Law, the foundation of rabbinic traditionalism, and parallels Khārijite and other Muslim scripturalist strategies that antedate Anan.[35] Cognate to *ḥippus* in Islam is *ijtihād*, which requires careful analysis of Scripture and other texts to develop legal opinions and yield *sharīʿah* rulings. Other reading strategies would have emerged in Jewish societies in this period as Jews began to translate the Bible and other texts to the new lingua franca, Arabic. Translation traditions, oral and otherwise, would have generated particularity and additional variety in an already variegated Judaism.[36]

In the first centuries A.H., the diversity of Jewish communities across a very large empire often led rabbinic leaders of remote areas to pragmatic decision making without recourse to the orthodox guidance of the academies. The world of the rabbis had enlarged, and the exigencies of communication and transportation in this premodern world, coupled with the disruptions in political and social life in the ninth and tenth centuries, often left the isolated rabbi to his own means, to resort to individual interpretation in solving halakhic and societal problems. For nonrabbinic Jewish communities, judges and leaders would have been accustomed to ruling on law and local custom under similar non-catholic circumstances.

In the unstable social and political environment of the ninth century, Benjamin al-Nahawendī (ca. 830–60) is acknowledged by Karaites as the next great figure, but is better understood as proto-Karaite. Benjamin likely functioned as *dayyan*, or judge, as suggested by what is extant of his work.[37] As a result of the wide-ranging autonomy granted to the Jews under Islam, he likely had quasi-official responsibilities to the Islamic government in the form of census taking and tax collection, as well as involvement in local intercommunal relations. He developed a halakhah with some nonrabbinic features, often differing with Anan, but for the most part he did not deviate widely from the talmudic discourse.[38] He was the first to use the term *bene mikra* (People of Scripture), the term later used by the Karaites to designate themselves, in reference to proto-Karaite scripturalism. He also wrote biblical commentary and a "Book of Commandments," but they have survived only as brief quotations within other works.[39] Benjamin's Muslim judicial

35. Michael A. Cook, "Anan and Islam: The Origins of Karaite Scripturalism."

36. Meira Polliack, *The Karaite Tradition of Arabic Bible Translation: A Linguistic and Exegetical Study of Karaite Translations of the Pentateuch from the Tenth and Eleventh Centuries* C.E.

37. Benjamin al-Nahawendī, *Sefer Dinim, Masʾat Binyamin.*

38. Small sections of Benjamin's *Sefer Dinim* correspond to sections of *Halakhot Pesukot.* See Neil Danzig, *Introduction to Halakhot Pesuqot with a Supplement to Halakhot Pesuqot,* 272–74 [Heb.].

39. For example, see Zucker, *Rav Saadya Gaon's Translation of the Torah,* 160–65.

contemporary, the *qāḍī*, offers a striking parallel to illuminate historical circumstances. In Islam the legal situation was confused by the momentous conquests of the seventh century, whereby Muslims found themselves as rulers of the Middle East only a few years after having received the jurisprudentially incomplete divine revelation of the Qur'ān. In this situation judges who were posted to the provinces had little legal precedent of a specifically Islamic nature with which to work, and no authoritative legal codes. By necessity, unwritten local law had standing, as well as Arab traditional law and legal precedents of Byzantine and Persian origin. Lacking systematized Muslim administrative or religious law, the *qāḍī* resorted to pragmatic decision making known as *ra'y* for the governance of day-to-day affairs. Decision making by a *qāḍī* would have been understood to be based upon the Qur'ān, whether it was effectively true or not. Such an effort *(ijtihād)* later came to denote the utilization of systematic methodology for the evaluation of legal tradition.[40] In the increasingly unstable social and political environment of the mid-ninth century, Benjamin al-Nahawendī, a local *dayyan*, would have no recourse other than to make decisions as necessity required; that is, to engage in a Jewish analogue of *ra'y* in combination with the Hebrew Bible and some transmitted Jewish legal materials. He states:

> I have composed this book of laws only for your benefit, so that you, O Men of Scripture (*ba'ale mikra*), may pass judgements on your brothers and friends. For every law, I have referred to its source in scripture. If for some other legal cases adjudicated among, and recorded by Rabbanites, I was unable to supply the scriptural authority, I have nevertheless decided to write them down here so that you may, if you desire, apply then in your judgments.[41]

It is difficult to locate Benjamin among the halakhic possibilities. Was he a *dayyan* with scripturalist leanings and no particular animus against rabbinic halakhah? Was he a *dayyan* working in a partially rabbinized setting? Or was he a proponent of a distinct, nonrabbinic or antirabbinic Judaism?

A comparison of Anan's and Benjamin's halakhah clearly reveals great differences, discouraging the view that they were members of a single movement.[42] If they are understood to be participants in the rabbinic Judaism of

40. On the use of personal opinion (*ra'y*, and in its earliest designation, *ijtihād*) in Islamic jurisprudence, see Louis Milliot, *Introduction a l'étude du droit musulman*, 10, 12; Schacht, *Origins of Muhammadan Jurisprudence*, 99, 105f., 115, 130; idem, *An Introduction to Muslim Law*, 26, 37, 46, 53, 60, 70; Coulson, *History of Islamic Law*, 30, 39f., 60, 95ff.; and Watt, *Formative Period of Islamic Thought*, 180–82. See chapter 1, above.

41. Benjamin al-Nahawendī, *Sefer Dinim*, 6b; adapted from Baron's translation, "Karaite Schism," 225; also in Ankori, *Karaites in Byzantium*, 215.

42. Ben-Shammai, "Between Ananites and Karaites."

the day, then clearly they considered the Babylonian Talmud to be an open scripture, which could be expanded upon. By focusing on Anan and Benjamin's deviations from rabbinic norms, scholars have overlooked their location within talmudic discourse, thereby perpetuating both inherited simplistic rabbinic notions of sectarianism and Karaite notions of the past, neither of which address the complexity of early Islam. This complexity reveals a Jewish halakhic world of great variety, many of whose monuments are embedded in the heterogeneity of Karaite halakhah, which preserved individualistic and particularistic halakhot in accord with the principle of *ḥippus.* Later Karaites would struggle with contradiction and inconsistency in dealing with the many halakhic variations that survived in later centuries.[43]

As early as the ʿUmayyad period (before 750), the many differences in Muslim law congealed into several foci of general accord known as the "ancient schools," which were distinguished one from another by geographical distribution more than by essential differences in doctrine, methodology, or allegiance to a particular scholar. These schools are the Medinan or Hijāzī, Syrian, and Iraqi.[44] As the methods for evaluating Muslim legal traditions came to be subjected to critical analysis and systematization, the proponents of the ancient schools found themselves at a loss. Lacking a methodologically systematic legal practice, they claimed that their religious law, or *sharīʿah,* was supported by a concept of *ijmāʿ*. This was interpreted to be either the consensus of the Muslims in general regarding main principles and duties about which there could be no doubt or the consensus of religious scholars on details.[45] In a sense, consensus provided an idea of internal consistency and community-wide homogeneity when such conditions were not actually present.

In tenth-century Judaism, centripetal forces compelled some nonrabbinic groups to begin to unify proto-Karaitic phenomena in reaction to rabbinic halakhic dominance, the extremism of charismatic messianic Jewish movements, and the success of Islamization. This is not merely a "non-normative *Weltanschauung,*" as Zvi Ankori has described it,[46] for, indeed, many nonrabbinic Judaisms were not part of this phenomenon. In particular, however, certain legal features became characteristic among many proto-Karaitic groups. Some examples include the dating of Shavuot, the determination of the new moon, calendrical intercalation, and forbidden fats, among others.[47]

43. One need only refer to *ʾAdderet ʾEliyahu,* the fifteenth-century legal compendium of Elijah ben Moses Bashyachi, to observe Karaite halakhic diversity.

44. See Schacht, *Origins of Muhammadan Jurisprudence,* 6–10.

45. Ibid., 82–97; and Kamali, *Principles of Islamic Jurisprudence,* 168–94. This distinction is also present in rabbinic halakhah. See Libson, "Halakhah and Reality in the Gaonic Period," 96.

46. Ankori, *Karaites in Byzantium,* 368.

47. These halakhic issues are repeated and amplified in later Karaite "Books of

By virtue of its varied antecedents, the new movement was faced with a proliferation of halakhic configurations analogous to the Muslim "ancient schools."

Daniel al-Qūmisī laments on disagreements among the *baʿale mikra,* prescribing study of the Torah "so that they may know which way is true."[48] al-Qirqisānī devotes an entire chapter of his *Kitāb al-anwār waʾl-marāqib* to halakhic differences among the Karaites.[49] He testifies to both a coming together of those who would identify themselves as Karaite and the divisions within this identity:

> Of those present-day Karaites who are not members of the schools which we have mentioned, scarce two of them are to be found who agree on anything, but this one will disagree with the other in one matter, and this one will disagree with that on various matters.[50]

> Furthermore one of the great calamities that afflict some of our fellows is this internecine warfare, the ill-will and hatred they bear each other, to which they are moved for the most part by jealousy and eagerness for mastery.[51]

By the late ninth and the tenth century, the coalescence of proto-Karaitic phenomena into a nascent Karaism suggests a taxonomy of known and possible antecedents that originated from the great variety of Judaisms of the preceding era: (1) the party of Anan representing rigorous and scripturalist tendencies characterized by the use of *ḥippus,* with a ready-made exilarchic dynastic ideology; (2) the variegated customs and outlooks of Jewish communities that had had little contact with rabbinic Judaism in recent times; (3) those with Judeo–Muslim and other hybrid identities, for whom neither Islam nor rabbinic Judaism was attractive or beneficial; (4) antitraditionalist—that is, antirabbinic—scripturalists (first attested to in the early-ninth-century denunciation of Pirkoi Ben Baboi, perhaps better known as *bene mikra*);[52] (5) messianists, remnants from the activist phase of the ʿĪsāwiyyah and other failed messianic movements; and (6) those with rigorist and semi-ascetic tendencies, shared both by the Ananites and the pan-Jewish Palestino-centric movement of the Mourners for Zion.

The process that brought these groups together necessitated that some internal contradictions be addressed, even if they might not be worked out. These included rejection of portions of Anan's and Benjamin's halakhah, the place of a patriarch in a scripturalist movement that had no scriptural basis

---

Precepts"—that is, compendia of halakhah. Many halakhic issues are summarized in Nemoy, "Mourad Farag." See also Revel, "Karaite Halakah."

48. Mann, "Tract by an Early Karaite Settler," 280.

49. al-Qirqisānī, *KA* 1:19 (Lockwood, 152–56).

50. al-Qirqisānī, *KA* 1:2.21 (Lockwood, 104–5).

51. al-Qirqisānī, *KA* 1:1.4 (Lockwood, 95).

52. See Ginzberg, *Genizah Studies,* 2: *Geonic and Early Karaitic Halakah,* "Pirkoi Ben Baboi," 504–73.

for such an office, and the role of speculative reason in the movement. By the eleventh century, the Karaites, led by their Palestinian cohorts, had an organized movement of their own. A portion of the wide spectrum of nonrabbinic activity, some of which is evidenced in al-Qirqisānī's heresiography, had come together under the leadership of the Karaite Jerusalem school.

This consolidation led eleventh-century Karaite scholars to begin to construct a legal interpretation of Judaism expressed in a literary genre known as Books of Precepts *(sifre miṣvot).* These compositions are halakhic handbooks that list the laws, their proper observance, and their interpretations. They often take as their point of departure fixed sectarian custom and then worked to establish scriptural support for the halakhah.[53] Works of this type were produced by Karaite luminaries such as Levi ben Yefet ha-Levi (written in 1006),[54] Yusūf al-Baṣīr (written 1036–37),[55] and Jeshua ben Judah.[56] As Karaite scholars were composing their own personal halakhic compilations, they were impelling movement toward consolidation. Whereas much of the tenth-century literary production had been exegetical, the eleventh century witnessed these legal compilations. It was now an acceptable exercise to list and detail the commandments as one saw them. The individualism of scripturalism seemed to maintain itself in the production of these books by individuals, while the gathering of halakhic interpretation began to exhibit consensus among those scholars, most of whom had studied in the same scholarly environment.

Karaism was becoming the dominant nonrabbinic Judaism and so began to move toward an internal legal consistency of its own. The lack of legal consistency testified to by al-Qirqisānī, which was supported by scripturalist tendencies and individual speculation, was subject to legal anarchy and gave way to an increasingly recognized Karaite legal interpretation of Judaism—that is, a Karaite halakhah. Unlike Islam, wherein different schools of law were later recognized to be equally orthodox, this "school of law" would not come to be acknowledged by the older and more developed rabbinic "school."

53. Ankori, *Karaites in Byzantium*, 210.

54. His *Sefer ha-Miṣvot* was only known until recently in its Hebrew translation. See chapter 3, note 21, above.

55. *Kitāb al-istibṣār* is dated by the early-fifteenth-century Ibn al-Hītī. See Margoliouth, "Ibn al-Hītī's Arabic Chronicle," 434. One fragment of the *Kitāb al-Istibṣār* is dated to 1019. See Poznanski, "Karaite Literary Opponents," 176.

56. His Book of Precepts may have gone by the title of *Sefer ha-Yashar.* A portion is extant in Hebrew translation as *Sefer ha-ʿArayot,* MS Warner 4116 in the Bibliotheek der Rijksuniversiteit Leiden, and in the Russian National Library in St. Petersburg. See Poznanski, "Karaite Literary Opponents," 182. Other Karaite *sifre miṣvot* are known, including one by Israel ben Daniel (written in 1062). See ibid., 190–91. It is important to remember that al-Qirqisānī's *Kitāb al-anwār* is not a Book of Precepts per se, but a speculative philosophical exposition of the Law.

Concurrently, rabbinic halakhah was faced with a similar problem as new challenges that arose from custom *(minhag)* were incorporated into law by using consensus.[57]

As among the Muslims, an idea of consensus, identified by Karaites as *ʿedah* or *kibbuṣ*, was found to be useful and was superimposed on a wide range of this nonrabbinic halakhah in order to supply an idea of consistency. Indeed, some commonality of laws did exist to support this view, and in turn it supported further consolidation of particular halakhic principles that become identified with Karaism in its various stages. To quote Ankori, "deviationist usages and observances were the practical expression of a general consensus of opinion in areas in which their adherents lived in compact groups and which had been only slightly affected by normative geonic legislation. To them the practices based on *ʿedah* or *kibbuṣ* were no less valid than precepts clearly formulated by the biblical Lawmaker."[58]

Needless to say, such a legal rationale did not provide real consistency, and it was ultimately reconsidered in both Islam and Karaism. The doctrine of consensus is an argument for majority and is a two-edged sword for a minority within a minority. The Karaites might argue that rabbinic halakhah was without authority because consensus was lacking on the transmissional basis of Rabbanite rulings among the whole community of Israel (meaning both Rabbanites and Karaites).[59] On the other hand, when the Karaites sought to utilize consensus as a legal methodological foundation for their own nonrabbinic halakhah, they, too, were then vulnerable to the same criticism. They could not maintain lack of consensus as a condition for disregarding law when their own law was clearly adhered to by a minority within Israel.[60] In Islam, the architect of systematic law, Muḥammad ibn Idrīs al-Shāfiʿī (767–820), developed a legal methodology that proved to be the undoing of the ancient schools, leading to the diminution and redefinition of consensus as a legal principle. al-Shāfiʿī revolutionized *sharīʿah* by reducing dependence on local law and establishing a "scientific" method for evaluating traditions emanating from the prophet Muḥammad in preference to other traditions that had been used to support the ancient schools.[61] In support of a pure methodological approach, al-Shāfiʿī also counseled against accepting anyone's opinion.

57. Libson, "Halakhah and Reality in the Gaonic Period," 92–98.

58. For his discussion of consensus, see *Karaites in Byzantium*, 208–9. Cf. n. 10, where the Hebrew *ʿedah* is compared with the Arabic *ʿādah*, "local custom." On consensus in rabbinic halakhah, see Chajes, *Student's Guide*, 96–102.

59. Cohen, *Sefer ha-Qabbalah*, xliv.

60. The supremacy of Medinan consensus over other sources of Muslim law was attacked on similar grounds. See Kamali, *Principles of Islamic Jurisprudence*, 186–87.

61. The first third of Schacht's *Origins of Muhammadan Jurisprudence* (pp. 1–137) is a close examination of al-Shāfiʿī's law in comparison to the ancient schools. Cf.

Anan, as an emblem of *hekkesh* and *ḥippus,* would be credited by the tenth-century Karaite, Yefet ben ʿEli ha-Levi, with the saying, "Search thoroughly in the Torah, and do not rely on my opinion."[62] The first part of this Karaite halakhic dictum is a precise prescription of legal exegetical methodology. *Search* is translated from the Aramaic *ḥapisu,* the cognate of *ḥippus,* which corresponds to the Muslim *ijtihād.* In another way, Karaites would find a factualistic methodological approach to halakhah that was akin to al-Shāfiʿī's in the masoretic movement, which supported scripturalism by widening interpretive possibilities through deeper knowledge of grammar, syntax, and the biblical lexicon.

al-Shāfiʿī also expanded upon the generally accepted sources for Muslim law, the Qur'ān, the *sunnah* (custom of Muḥammad), and the inclusive *ijmāʿ*, by adding *qiyyās,* or analogic reasoning, which remained necessarily vague and widely applicable in the later Muslim schools of law.[63] Similarly, the Karaites adopted analogic reasoning *(hekkesh)* as a method for harmonizing consensus with biblical foundations of the law. In rabbinic terminology, *hekkesh* has a narrow specific meaning, being one of many carefully defined hermeneutical principles. But, *hekkesh* in Karaite halakhah is broadly conceived, and could be as vague and wide-ranging as *qiyyās* in Islam. Although, the adoption of *hekkesh* also acted as a response to rabbinic halakhah, it worked primarily as a device for inner-Karaite halakhic development. *Hekkesh* offered the Karaites a way to bring together notions of individual interpretation of the law associated with the idea of *ḥippus* and its corollary, scripturalism, with new types of legal thinking connected to the use of rational speculation.

In the second and third centuries A.H., as *sharʿīah*-minded Muslim legal scholars began to articulate reasoned methodologies for interpreting the Qur'ān and *ḥadīth* literature, their opponents rejected tradition as a source of law. These antitraditionists were understood to fall into two categories, scripturalists or Muʿtāzilites, who were the adherents of *kalām* and are often referred to as "rationalists."[64] Using Islamic Aristotelianism and *kalām,* Karaites were able to construct a reasoned and consistent critique of rabbinic traditionism while rationalizing *ḥippus* and *hekkesh.*[65] In this context, *hekkesh* could be understood as the methodology of *kalām.* Unfettered individualism in the interpretation of Scripture had to be limited, while a systematic and

al-Imām Muḥammad ibn Idris al-Shāfiʿī (Majid Khadduri, trans.), *al-Risāla fī uṣūl al-fiqh: Treatise on the Foundations of Islamic Jurisprudence.*

62. Commentary on Zechariah 5:8, cited in Poznanski, "Anan," 184.

63. Schacht, *Origins of Muhammadan Jurisprudence,* 98–102; and Kamali, *Principles of Islamic Jurisprudence,* 197–226.

64. See Schacht, *Origins of Muhammadan Jurisprudence,* 40–41, and 258–59. They are often referred to as *ahl al-kalām,* "the people of rational speculation," among other designations.

65. al-Qirqisānī, *KA,* 4:30–32. Cf. Makdisi, "Dialectic and Disputation."

demonstrable method was needed if the movement could offer intellectual competition to the centuries-old tradition of rabbinic Judaism. Karaites became so identified with *kalām* that they are referred to by Muslim writers as "the people of justice and unity," a Muʿtazilite designation.[66] Although Aristotelian and Muʿtazilite philosophy had become antiquated among the rabbis by the thirteenth century, the Karaites remained distinctive by championing that approach for centuries longer.[67]

While scripturalism was coming to be acknowledged as a central Karaite principle in the tenth century, *hekkesh* permitted seemingly nonsystematized halakhic rulings of earlier centuries (Karaite *ra'y*) to be provided with a justification, which in turn permitted the appropriation and reinterpretation of Anan and Benjamin on the part of later Karaites. Indeed, as early as 937, al-Qirqisānī reports that some Ananites and Karaites regard the sources of law as three: the text, analogical deduction, and consensus.[68]

Built into this configuration of sources of law is an inherent contradiction between *ḥippus* and *kibbuṣ*. Karaite evocations of scripturalism supported individualism in the interpretation of law that could lead to anarchy. Consensus was mobilized to limit unbridled individualism, but was limited by vagueness and inconsistency. *Hekkesh* was mobilized to methodologize *ḥippus* and *kibbuṣ*. But both were limited by scripturalism. Both al-Shāfiʿī and the Karaites were concerned with the danger of "innovation" in law, but the Muslim jurist was working within a traditionist system wherein the recovery of a useful pristine juridical past was seemingly possible. The only juridical past available to Karaites, as antitraditionists, was embedded in Scripture. They lacked a flexible font of law that could supplement Scripture, something like Muslim *ḥadīth*, or the rabbinic Oral Law. The circle of *ḥippus-kibbuṣ-hekkesh* could not generate the variety and depth of law necessary, and it failed both to limit individual interpretation and to create a comprehensive legal system. Working toward a solution led to the transformation of consensus into a Karaite concept of tradition and vision of the past, known as *haʿtakah* (later, known as *sevel ha-yerushah*).[69]

66. al-Masʿūdī, *al-Tanbīh wa'l-ishraf,* 112f., 219. Cp. al-Maqrīzī, *al-Mawāʿi wa'l-iʿtibār bi-dhikr al-khiṭaṭ wa'l-āthār,* 3:326, cited in Gil, *History of Palestine,* 779–81.

67. Wolfson, *Philosophy of the Kalam,* 82–111; and idem, *Repercussions of the Kalam,* passim. See also Collette Sirat, *A History of Jewish Philosophy in the Middle Ages,* 37–56.

68. *KA*, 2:12.1, beginning at 141.9. Here, analogical deduction, the tool of *ḥippus,* is *hekkesh,* which corresponds to the Arabic *qiyyās.* In regard to Scripture, al-Qirqisānī regarded *naql* as the "sound transmission" of the Prophets and Writings. See *KA*, 2:14.1, beginning at 148.1. Cf. Ankori, *Karaites in Byzantium,* 229–30, n. 48. See also *KA* 2:18. and Vajda, "Études sur Qirqisânî, II," 92–98.

69. See next section, below.

Whether Muslim sources of law were developed from rabbinic Jewish antecedents is not fully known, and even if it were this would not be useful for determining whether the origins of Karaite sources of law are to be found only in rabbinic halakhah or by way of Muslim influence.[70]

A Need for Tradition. As, centuries earlier, the rabbis had discovered a strong need for the existence of the Oral Law, so, by the twelfth century, Karaites were faced with similar problems: (1) As experienced by the rabbis of Late Antiquity, the written Torah alone was insufficient for governing a real society; (2) Karaite law and the Karaite movement had existed long enough to possess communal and legal memory; (3) Karaite legal history had generated wide diversity in halakhah resulting in an unwieldy and noncoherent legal corpus characterized by some internal inconsistencies; (4) Theories of *kibbuṣ* and *hekkesh* were insufficient to deal with halakhic problems; and (5) Rabbinic halakhah was more developed in its application and more consistent in its theoretical formulations, thereby presenting a formidable challenge to Karaism. These factors would plague Karaite scholars as they sought to maintain scripturalism, while at the same time coming to grips with their own history and creating a systematic consistent halakhah.

Lacking an inherited scheme for the systematization of halakhah and trying to avoid recourse to rabbinic law, the Karaite trend of personal investigation *(ḥippus)* became influenced by the speculative rationalism of the day, as described above. But through the centuries, problems emerged in Karaite legal discourse that had been worked out eminently well in rabbinic halakhah centuries earlier. In fact, the intrinsic logic of some rabbinic halakhah was overwhelming, and Karaism gradually had to face this fact as a phenomenological reality. The decline of consensus was "an inevitable adjustment to the ruling (Rabbanite) majority."[71] And similarly, efforts at systematizing Karaite halakhah proceeded in the shadow of the well-established more systematic halakhah of the rabbis. In the Byzantine period, we see a clear trend toward accommodation to rabbinic law and method that had already commenced in the later Islamic period.

"Having lost its original source of strength, the *ʿedah* increasingly absorbed the features of another principle with which it was integrally connected, although the sect was for a long time reluctant to admit it and had no specific name for it. That other principle was 'tradition.' "[72] The accumulation of Karaite practice and interpretation over centuries had created a kind of corpus of nonrabbinic halakhah that could be conceived of as tradition. The passing of time itself created a kind of tradition. At the same time that the idea of consensus lost its technical legal validity, it began to be associated with

70. For another view, see Judith Romney Wegner, "Islamic and Talmudic Jurisprudence: The Four Roots of Islamic Law and Their Talmudic Counterparts."

71. Ankori, *Karaites in Byzantium,* 223.

72. Ibid.

an inchoate idea of tradition; that is, the vaguely defined corpus of Karaite halakhah, especially its nonbiblically supported elements, came to be seen as something preserved from, and sanctioned by, antecedent Karaism. Although Islamicate Karaite scholars of the tenth and eleventh centuries may have conceived of their halakhah with an implicit concept of tradition, such an idea was not articulated until Tobias ben Moses translated it into legal usage.[73]

Tobias's appellation, *ha-maʿtik* (the translator), is in fact a double entendre. Tobias's introduction of a concept of tradition appears in the guise of a legal application designated as *haʿtakah.* Although the word *haʿtakah* can be rendered as *translation,* its halakhic context implies an idea of tradition. Accordingly, it is to be translated as *transmission,* paralleled by the Rabbanite *kabbalah.*[74] At first, the term was used by Karaites in two ways. It could refer either to rabbinic ideas of transmission or, in a Karaite context, to the Prophets and Writings in the Hebrew Bible. In this latter usage, Karaites understood that these texts were distinguished from Moses' divine revelation by being the transmitted material of the priests and prophets.[75] Ankori indicates that in the Byzantine Karaite environment, *haʿtakah* became associated with, and eventually synonymous with, *consensus.* In the effort at articulating legal theory, it was a short semantic leap from the increasingly outmoded idea of consensus to an explicit idea of transmission.[76]

One hundred years after Tobias, Hadassi categorically declares that "*ʿedah* and *sevel, kabbalah* and *haʿtakah* . . . have one and the same content."[77] Karaite

73. Ibid., 224.

74. The term was not coined by Tobias, having appeared in geonic circles in the tenth century. See R. Elhanan's question addressed to Hai Gaon, published by Harkavy in *Studien und Mitteilungen,* 4:24, responsum no. 47; and Hai's responsum no. 119 in *Temim Deʿim* in *Tummat Yesharim* (Venice, 1622), 22d. Cited in Ankori, *Karaites in Byzantium,* 224, n. 41. On Abraham ibn Ezra and others' use of the term, see ibid., 224–25, and 228, n. 47. Ankori proposes that the term is a Hebrew translation of the Arabic *al-naql,* which originated in Saadia's writings.

75. Ankori cites the tenth-century Sahl ben Maṣliaḥ who defines *haʿtakah* in this manner in distinct opposition to rabbinic formulations of tradition "and this, indeed, is the transmission *(haʿtakah)* which all recognize [as true]. Now, if someone should argue that the 'footsteps of the flock' (Cant. 1:8) alludes to the ways of the many [i.e., of the Rabbanite majority], and that the 'shepherds' tents' refers to the pronouncements of the [talmudic] sages under all circumstances—his argument is not valid"; ibid., 227, translated from Simhah Pinsker, *Likkute Kadmoniyot,* 34.

76. Tobias and Hadassi even used the term *kabbalah,* but it did not catch on in Karaite writing because it was too closely associated with the appellative used to describe the Rabbanites, *baʿale ha-kabbalah,* "possessors of tradition" or "traditionists": Ankori, *Karaites in Byzantium,* 228–29.

77. *Eshkol ha-Kofer,* alphabet 169, 64d. *Sevel* (yoke) underwent a semantic transformation similar to *haʿtakah.* However, it was not given explicit halakhic usage

law, now seemingly liberated from consensus, became able to evoke the new idea of tradition in support of its halakhah. However, the Karaite idea of tradition was qualified in order to avoid either the appearance or reality of arbitrary acceptance of rabbinic tradition. Under Tobias's lead, *haʿtakah* was acceptable only when two conditions were met: (1) that there was a unanimous consensus of *all* Israel on the matter; and (2) that the matter in question was based upon positive support from the Bible. The concept of consensus would remain useful by positioning Karaite *haʿtakah* in juxtaposition to that of the Rabbanites, whose *kabbalah* was a simple doctrine of the majority, not of all Israel.[78] Similarly, scripturalism was maintained in essence by the need for biblical textual proofs.

The new concept of tradition provided Karaite legal exegetes with a tool to continue their efforts at justifying and systematizing existing Karaite halakhah, while maintaining a degree of flexibility for adaptation. Law originating in the early period and supported by conservative scripturalism could be changed by means of the new idea of tradition.[79] In addition, Byzantine Karaite scholars would need a new tool in order to find precedent for practices that were not known to have existed in the Islamicate environment. Tobias represents this position, as quoted by the fourteenth-century scholar Aaron

---

until the fourteenth or fifteenth century. See Ankori, *Karaites in Byzantium,* 230–31, n. 50. Later Karaites would use the term *sevel ha-yerushah* (the yoke of inheritance) to refer to transmission, or tradition. *Yerushah* is found in rabbinic literature (M Ber. 2:2; and M Abot 3:5), and gains acceptance among Islamicate Karaites with meanings along the lines of *haʿtakah.*

78. Ankori, *Karaites in Byzantium,* 232. The convergence of the new idea of tradition with the old idea of consensus elegantly mirrors the old idea of *haʿtakah,* for indeed, all of Israel would agree on the veracity of the Prophets and Writings.

79. One of the primary examples of a sea change in Karaite law concerns the laws of incest. The accepted norm in early Karaism was based upon an analogical expansion of the biblical verse, "man . . . shall cleave to his wife, and they shall be one flesh" (Gen. 2:24). In this interpretation, after marriage a spouse's relatives become as closely related to the one spouse as to the other. Then, in the case of divorce or remarriage after the death of a spouse, all of one's relatives—blood relatives and the former spouse's relatives—are subject to the laws of consanguinity. By extension to the fourth degree, larger and larger groups comprise forbidden marriage partners. Such a theory of forbidden marriage wrought social havoc on small communities and, eventually, on the minority Karaite community as a whole. See Astren, "Notes on Intermarriage among Rabbanites and Karaites." By the eleventh century, Yūsuf al-Baṣīr and his students Jeshua ben Judah and Tobias ben Moses developed ways to circumvent the so-called catenary theory. See Nemoy, *Karaite Anthology,* 124ff. The best example for the Rabbanization of Karaite halakhah comes from the fifteenth-century struggle over the use of Sabbath candles. By that time, the accommodation with Rabbanism was more pronounced. See chapter 5, below, on Elijah Bashyachi.

ben Elijah: "And the meaning of this verse according to all the Karaite scholars is that any *haʿtakah* that has no support in Scripture is void. Yet, those who would say that one can rely on the *haʿtakah* alone without support from Scripture, behold, the scholar R. Tobias says in his comment on the verse that this [condition] does not exist other than on account of the shortness of the arm of their reason to find strength from the law of the Torah."[80] Aaron's statement, a conservative defense of scripturalism and statement of resistance to liberal notions of *haʿtakah,* is testimony to movement within Karaite halakhah toward accommodation to an idea of tradition.

Reading Rabbinic Texts. The seeming reconciliation to something that resembled the rabbinic idea of tradition was accompanied by a new attitude toward rabbinic literature. As in the Islamic world, the attitude of Karaite scholars toward rabbinic literature was characterized by both repulsion and attraction. From the early days of Karaism, there was an acknowledged interest in rabbinic writing, if only for refutation. Such an approach locates Karaism in a sectarian relationship to rabbinic Judaism, developing in close intellectual proximity to the rabbis and their literature. Ankori states it expressively: "Had not ʿAnan ben David been a Rabbinic scholar of the first rank? Was not Karaism's very existence inseparably intertwined with the Talmud? For, after all, the sect was born in the heat of battle against talmudic institutions and their legislation. It breathed the air of the Talmud from the very inception of its independent history, and, though claiming to be choked by it, it was incapable of living without it."[81]

Although *rejection* and *refutation* are bywords for Karaite attitudes toward Rabbanism, there was always an element of interplay with rabbinic literature, a distinguishing feature of the sectarian relationship. Although Anan does not cite rabbinic sources as prooftexts, his *Sefer Miṣvot* was written in Aramaic, the language of rabbinic discourse, and his formulations are less divergent from rabbinic practice than those of later Karaites. al-Qirqisānī confirms this impression, maintaining that Anan's halakhah was not "un-rabbinic."[82] Anan's Judaism was rabbinic in formulation, if not in result.

80. *Gan ʿEden,* 8b–c. Aaron was a conservative who sought to limit *haʿtakah.* Tobias's principle is used repeatedly by Elijah Bashyachi in the fifteenth century in his effort to justify a more flexible halakhah. See *ʾAdderet ʾEliyahu,* 9d, 48c, and 82b; cited in Ankori, *Karaites in Byzantium,* 233, and 237.

81. Ibid., 240.

82. *KA* 1:2.14 (Lockwood, 103): "He was learned in the teachings of the Rabbanites, none of whom could impugn his learning. It is said that Hai, the head of the Academy, and his father, while translating a book by Anan from Aramaic to Hebrew, found nothing among his doctrines whose source they could not attribute to the Rabbanites, save only his teaching on the first-born, and the difference between what is planted in Israel and what is planted among the Gentiles: they knew of no source for this, until they found it in the songs of Yannai." Yannai was

In relation to polemic and apology, it is obvious that knowledge of rabbinic texts would be extremely useful. Commenting on inconsistencies in rabbinic thought, al-Qirqisānī observes, "Our co-religionists neglect their words because they are careless and have not noticed them. If they were to examine them, they would be able to dispense with speculation and dialectics in their arguments with them. However, some have recently studied them, and these absurdities and contradictions have been revealed to me."[83] In fact, al-Qirqisānī shows more than a little familiarity with rabbinic texts. He refers to both the Mishnah and the Babylonian Talmud throughout the *Kitāb al-anwār wal-marāqib,* especially in 1:3 and 1:4, where he refutes rabbinic laws and beliefs.[84] In 1:4.18 he discusses the rabbinic attitude toward the Aramaic translation of the Torah, Targum Onkelos.[85] Other rabbinic works cited include the *Tosefta,* the *Alphabet of Rabbi Akiva, Massekhet Yir'at Ḥet* (which is actually *Derekh 'Ereṣ Zuta*), *Halakhot Gedolot,* the *Book of Ishmael* (which is the mystical work *Hekhalot de-Rabbi Yishm''ael*), *Mekhilta de-Rabbi Yishma''el, Midrash Leviticus Rabbah,* the *Midrash on Psalms,* among others that are lesser known or of questionable rabbinic provenance.[86] In addition, al-Qirqisānī refers to a Rabbanite work on the differences between Palestinian and Babylonian Rabbanite traditions, *Kitāb fī ikhtilāfāt rabbāniyyī al-shām wa-rabbāniyyī al-ʿirāq:* "All that we have reported about them we had from themselves and learned from themselves and is to be found recorded in their own books. One of them has collected it together in summary form, from which we took it and learned it and so you need not pay attention to their blustering denials."[87]

Indeed, other scholars of the early Islamic period encouraged Karaite acquaintance with rabbinic literature. In the tenth century, Salmon ben Yeruḥim reveals knowledge in the last four chapters of his *Sefer Milḥamot Adonai* of such rabbinic texts as the Babylonian Talmud, the *hekhalot* literature, the *Alphabet of Rabbi Akiva,* and *Sefer Raziʿel,* among others.[88] Around the same time, Sahl ben Maṣliaḥ defends the Karaites, who, unlike the Rabbanites, do

a Palestinian *payyeṭan,* or liturgical poet, of the sixth or seventh century, whose work often bears halakhic meaning.

83. *KA* 1:3.46 (Lockwood, 121). Bacher states that this passage refers to rabbinic midrash, in "Qirqisani, the Karaite, and His Work on Jewish Sects," 264.

84. Many of the tractates of M and BT are referred to in his discussions of rabbinic halakhah and beliefs. See the citation index (A) in Chiesa and Lockwood, *Yaʿqūb al-Qirqisānī on Jewish Sects and Christianity,* 191–92.

85. Lockwood, 132–33.

86. See Chiesa and Lockwood, *Yaʿqūb al-Qirqisānī on Jewish Sects and Christianity,* 192. al-Qirqisānī's sources were given tentative discussion by Bacher in "Qirqisani, the Karaite, and His Work on Jewish Sects," 269ff.

87. Referred to in *KA* 1:10.9 (Lockwood, 144).

88. Davidson, ed., *The Book of the Wars of the Lord,* 108–32. N.B. the marginal notes accompanying the text.

not seek to lead the nation with self-interest as motivation. "Rather they search and investigate in the Law of Moses and in the books of the Prophets, and they even look into the words of the Rabbanite forerunners."[89] Sahl verifies the sectarian outlook by pointing to the integral conceptual linkage that connected Rabbanite and Karaite Judaisms. Explicitly, he is saying that even though the rabbis are in error, their writings may be useful for searching the Torah. More importantly, the implicit message that would be taken up later in Karaite history is that rabbinic writings might contain some truth and were not merely guides to help searching for the truth in the Torah.

Later in the tenth century, Yefet ben ʿElī ha-Levi's historicized remark in his commentary on Deuteronomy is revealing. He sought to prove that Jewish scholars of the mishnaic period engaged in rational study and research of the principles of law "in the manner of Anan and Benjamin [al-Nahawendī] and all the opponents of the Rabbanites who composed Books of Precepts. And each of them said what he thought and documented it by evidence . . . , and his opinion may or may not be in agreement with the actual truth."[90] This example of Karaite reading of rabbinic literature projects Karaite legal philosophy and literary form of the day back into history, indeed directly engaging rabbinic history, in order to justify the halakhic form of the "Book of Precepts" genre and to "Karaize" the rabbinic process. Of course, these antique, rabbinic Books of Precepts were lost when Judah ha-Nasi compiled his Book of Precepts, the Mishnah, and suppressed the others. This Karaite historical theory does, if in a backhanded way, acknowledge the existence of other mishnah compilations that were in part incorporated into or rejected for use in Judah's Mishnah and that are mentioned in rabbinic literature.[91]

Nissī ben Nūḥ, who probably lived some time in the eleventh century, describes the necessary qualifications for a scholar in the following oft-quoted statement. In addition to his diligence, use of analogy, ability to question, among other qualifications, a scholar "must be well-versed in Mishnah, in Talmud, and in the Rabbinic enactments *(halakhot),* as well as in the supplementary rules *(tosefot)* and the Aggadic tales *(ve-haggadot).*"[92] In the same period, Levi ben Yefet ha-Levi states in his Book of Precepts, "Know that the

89. *Divre ha-rishonim,* "words of the predecessors," which refers to the rabbinic sages. Sahl's epistle is published in Pinsker, *Likkute Kadmoniyyot,* 2:34. The passage is translated by Nemoy in *Karaite Anthology,* 119.

90. The Arabic text (British Library, MS Or. 2479, 124r) with a French translation is reproduced in Poznanski, "Anan," 184. On this text and the previous one by Sahl ben Maṣliaḥ, see Ankori, *Karaites in Byzantium,* 216–17, n. 24.

91. Cf. BT San. 86a, where R. Yohanan reports that the Mishnah derives from earlier mishnahs of R. Akiva and R. Meir, and the Tosefta from R. Nehemiah, one of Akiva's disciples. See Moore, *Judaism,* 150–60.

92. Nemoy, "Nissi ben Noah's Quasi-Commentary," 341. The text is published in Pinsker, *Likkute Kadmoniyyot,* 1:13.

scholars and researchers have assembled many statements that are found in the Mishnah and the Talmud."[93]

Jeshua ben Judah, the last great scholar of the Jerusalem school of the eleventh century, also made thorough use of rabbinic sources. His commentary on Leviticus was described as "extensive for understanding the words [*kalām*] of learned men [*ʿulamāʾ*] and authors, both the earlier and later ones, from among a number of the Rabbanites and Karaites."[94] Jeshua cites in his works Mishnah, *Mekhilta, Sifra, Halakhot Gedolot, Halakhot Keṣuvot,* Samuel ben Ḥofni's Introduction to the Talmud, and Saadia's refutation of sectarian calendation, and he refers to a digest of both Talmuds.[95] He was the first Jewish scholar to cite the second recension of Avot de-Rabbi Natan.[96] The fourteenth-century Karaite Aaron ben Joseph states, "I will mention in the midst of my explanation words of the Mishnah, and I have evoked in my view of this principle the distinguished R. Yeshua, may he rest in Eden."[97]

Karaites of the Byzantine period continued the engagement with Rabbanite sources. We have already seen how language used to describe encyclopedic knowledge was culled from rabbinic literature. Tobias ben Moses adopted aspects of exegesis from rabbinic sources and showed great familiarity with rabbinic texts in *ʾOṣar Neḥmad.*[98] The anonymous commentary on Exodus-Leviticus makes a point "to say that we should read the words of the Rabbanites."[99]

Reference has been made to Judah Hadassi's use of some rabbinic sources for legendary material in *ʾEshkol ha-Kofer.* In addition, he utilized the *Maʿaseh Bereshit* of Rabbi Ishmael *(Hekhalot de-Rabbi Yishmaʾʿel), Baraita de-Rabbi Shemuʾel,* grammatical material from both Judah Ḥayyūj and Jonah Ibn

93. *Sefer ha-Miṣvot,* Leiden MS Warner no. 22, 15a, cited by Ankori in *Karaites in Byzantium,* 241, n. 80.

94. From his introduction to a shortened version of the pentateuchal commentary. The Arabic text (formerly cataloged as MS Firkovitch 2, no. 3204, now in the Russian National Library, St. Petersburg) is reproduced in Mann, *Texts and Studies,* 2: *Karaitica,* 34–35. Apparently the scholarly citations on Leviticus were so extensive that he was asked by a wealthy patron to write a shorter version. Jeshua's writings are yet to be edited and published, a desideratum of Karaite studies.

95. Ibid., 36, n. 65; and ibid., 38.

96. Ibid., 36.

97. *Sefer ha-Mivḥar,* cited in Ankori in *Karaites in Byzantium,* 241, n. 80, where the folio is designated as 9b, referring to MS Warner no. 2 in the Bibliotheek der Rijksuniversiteit Leiden. Aaron also refers to Nissī ben Nūḥ's dictum to study Mishnah and Talmud.

98. See Ankori, *Karaites in Byzantium,* 245; idem, "The Correspondence of Tobias ben Moses, the Karaite, of Constantinople," 14, n. 24; and Poznanski, in *Oṣar Yisraʾel,* 5:13b, s.v. "Tobias ben Moses ha-Maʿtik" [Heb.].

99. *Perush li-Shemot uva-Yikra,* 13b. Cited in Ankori, *Karaites in Byzantium,* 241, n. 80. Cf. chapter 3, note 26, above.

Janāḥ, also citing the thirteen hermeneutical rules of R. Ishmael and the thirty-two rules of R. Eliezer ben Yose the Galilean. Significantly, Hadassi incorporates a fairly large section of Abraham Ibn Ezra's *Moznayim* in his grammatical discussions.[100] This work was written in Spain in 1140, only eight years before Hadassi began *'Eshkol ha-Kofer.* One could surmise that Karaites were necessarily not isolated from rabbinic literary circles. By the same token, Ibn Ezra mentions Jeshua ben Judah[101] and knew the work of the Byzantine Rabbanite Tobias ben Eliezer.[102] The world of Jewish books in the twelfth century was cosmopolitan. Information traveled relatively quickly, even to and from Karaites.

The conclusion of this trend of the Karaite reading of rabbinic texts is exemplified in another statement of Aaron ben Joseph. "I do not deny most of the *miṣvot* from the words of the Mishnah that I do not mention in the midst of my explanation . . . and most of the scholars of our exile do thusly . . . and this is no crown for the traditionists [*ba'ale ha-kabbalah*] because most of the sayings are the sayings of our forefathers."[103] Whereas the rabbinic process had been Karaized by Yefet ben 'Elī ha-Levi, as mentioned above, now the very pronouncements of the rabbis were accorded sanction. The stage was set for what Ankori calls a Karaite "interlinear reading" of rabbinic texts.[104]

100. Max Seligsohn, in *JE* 6:132, s.v. "Hadassi, Judah ben Elijah ha-Abel."

101. Poznanski, "Karaite Literary Opponents," 178.

102. Starr, *Jews in the Byzantine Empire,* 63; and 215ff. (text no. 164). Another Byzantine Rabbanite, Hillel ben Eliakim, knew the work of an older contemporary, the tosafist Samuel ben Meir of northern France (RaSHBaM); ibid., 62; and 227f. (text no. 179).

103. *Sefer Mivḥar,* cited in Ankori, *Karaites in Byzantium,* 241, n. 79, where the folio is designated as 9a. See note 97, above.

104. The term seems to have been coined by Ankori in *Karaites in Byzantium,* 32, n. 14; 236; and 425.

Part Two

~ 4

The Problem of a Karaite Chain of Tradition

The creation of a chain of tradition by scripturalist Jews is astonishing. As the rabbis had complemented their otherwise mostly ahistorical ideology with this linear historical construction, so the Karaites created their own version of the same ideological tool, notwithstanding their fundamental opposition to the idea of tradition. Before examining the historical and halakhic implications of this development, and the text itself, we begin by trying to identify the author who is credited with composing the "authorized version" of the Karaite chain of tradition.

Three Yefets: The Problem of Authorship

"Three Karaite authors are known to me by the name of Yefet," says Pinsker.[1] The first of these is easily identified, the well-known tenth-century exegete Yefet ben ʿElī ha-Levi. And the third is also known, Yefet ben Ṣaʿir, of the fourteenth century, portions of whose Book of Precepts have survived.[2] But the second, Yefet ben Saʿīd, is barely known. The Karaites variously attribute to Yefet ben Saʿīd or Yefet ben Ṣaʿir a composition entitled *Shalshelet ha-kabbalah ve-haʿtakat ha-Torah* (The chain of tradition and the transmission[3] of the Torah). Described as a "shadowy figure" by Daniel Frank,[4] Yefet ben Saʿīd is mentioned in the traditional Karaite prayer book in a memorial list, standing between Jeshua ben Judah (second half of the eleventh century) and

1. *Likkute Kadmoniyyot,* 181.

2. Ibid., 188–91. His name appears in a medieval Karaite memorial list published by Mann in *Texts and Studies,* 2: *Karaitica,* 282; see n. 76. He was a physician and scholar in Cairo, a student of Israel ha-Maʿaravi (d. before 1354). Parts 5 through 9 of his *Sefer ha-Miṣvot* are extant, cited in Steinschneider, *Die arabische Literatur der Juden,* 244.

3. The Hebrew root, *ʿayin-taf-kuf,* bears the core meaning of something that is moved, shifted, or displaced, including the meaning of translating from one language to another. See chapter 3 and the conclusion to part 1, above.

4. Personal conversation, December 14–15, 1992, in Boston, Mass.

Judah Hadassi (middle of the twelfth century).[5] The question of properly identifying and dating this Yefet is thorny at best.[6] The text itself is ensconced in Karaite literary tradition as part of Moses Bashyachi's *Mateh Elohim* in the sixteenth century, extant until recently only in manuscript,[7] from which it is quoted by later Karaite authors.[8] No necessarily datable earlier source for this text is known, but it exists in two versions published by Pinsker (henceforth, designated as P^1 and P^2),[9] and in several fragments, all but one in the Russian National Library in Saint Petersburg.[10]

P^2 attributes the text to Yefet ben Saʿīd. Internal evidence in one part of the text suggests that Yefet lived at approximately the time indicated in the Karaite prayer book. He states: (1) 413 years had elapsed since the division of the Karaites and Rabbanites; that is, Anan's schism; (2) 1075 years had passed since the destruction of the Second Temple; and (3) 662 years had separated

5. *Siddur ha-Tefillot ke-Minhag ha-Yehudim ha-Kara'im,* 1:400.

6. Poznanski, *Zekher Ṣaddikim,* 24.

7. I have used MS Mic. 9828 from the Jewish Theological Seminary of America in New York. It is a seventeenth- or eighteenth-century manuscript (henceforth, designated *Matteh 'Elohim*) from the Ottoman Empire. The Karaite chain of tradition appears on 6v–8r. Another manuscript is known, MS Warner no. 54, in the Bibliotheek der Rijksuniversiteit Leiden. See the recent edition published by the Karaite community of Israel: Moses ben Elijah Bashyachi (Yosef ben ʿOvadyah Algamil, ed.), *Matteh 'Elohim* (Ramlah, Israel: Tiferet Yosef, 5761 [2000 or 2001]) (henceforth, *Matteh 'Elohim*–Ramlah). This edition likely represents a late manuscript, including many post-Bashyachi interpolations. On Moses Bashyachi, see chapter 5, below.

8. *Matteh 'Elohim*–Ramlah, 27–34. It appears in Mordecai ben Nisan, *Dod Mordekhai,* 58–61; and Simhah Isaac Lutzki, *'Oraḥ Ṣaddikim,* 95–97.

9. P^1 in *Der Orient* 12 (1851): 737–43 from a manuscript epitome of Bahya Ibn Pakuda's *Ḥovot ha-Levavot,* dated 1682, that was owned by the eighteenth-century Karaite Simhah Isaac Lutzki. For a translation, see appendix 2. P^2 in *Likkute Kadmoniyyot,* 185–87, n. 3. This version, from an Arabic manuscript of Firkovich's is published only in part, lacking a complete text. The chain used by Lutzki in *'Oraḥ Ṣaddikim* (Jerusalem, 1966, based on Vienna, 1830), 94–97, is attributed to Yefet ben Saʿīd and is probably derived from Bashyachi. On Lutzki, see chapter 6, below.

10. These are in the Firkovich Collections: RNL (Russian National Library) Evr. I,741 (6 fols., dated 1573 or 1578); RNL Evr.-Arab. I,1242 (1 fol.); RNL Evr.-Arab. I,1279 (2 fols.); RNL Evr.-Arab. I,2994.1 (6 fols., copied by Abraham ha-Levi, possibly of late-eighteenth- or early-nineteenth-century Cairo); RNL Evr.-Arab. II,1012 (2 fols.); and RNL Evr.-Arab. II,3296 (1 fol.). My thanks to David Sklare, of the Manuscript Department of the Jewish National and University Library in Jerusalem for bringing these to my attention. In addition, there is an otherwise unknown Arabic chain of tradition extant in the collection of the Jewish Theological Seminary of America in New York, MS ENA 1275, attributed to Yefet ben Saʿīd. My thanks to Shaul Shaked of the Hebrew University, Jerusalem, for this reference.

the destruction of the Temple from the division of the Karaites and Rabbanites.[11] One should not use modern chronology, which places the destruction of the Temple in 70 C.E., but should use the accepted medieval Jewish date of 68.[12] Nevertheless, when the arithmetic is done to find the dates, we arrive at: (1) 730 C.E. for Anan; and (2) 1143 C.E. for Yefet. Whether this is acceptable is complicated by the fact that Yefet places Anan's career in the caliphate of al-Manṣūr, whose reign was 754–75 C.E. Yefet's error is further complicated by his use of a date accepted by Jews for al-Manṣūr: 4400 A.M., corresponding to 640 C.E.[13] He also cites the year 136 A.H. for al-Manṣūr, which is 753–54 C.E.[14] Furthermore, another Karaite tradition, cited in the eighteenth century, places Yefet at the beginning of the sixth millennium A.M., which began in 1240 C.E.[15] Needless to say, the chronological elements are impenetrable. What, then, to do?

The solutions to this problem suggested by scholars are all unsatisfactory. Poznanski offers an emendation to Yefet's text in P². He bases his terminus a quo on a literary borrowing in Yefet's text derived from Judah Halevi's *Kuzari,* which was written in the late 1130s.[16] For a terminus ad quem, he chooses the fourteenth-century Yefet ben Ṣaʿir, who mentions Yefet ben Saʿīd.[17] Poznanski suggests: (1) 513 years from the division of the Karaites and Rabbanites; that is, Anan's schism; and (2) 1198 years from the destruction of the Second Temple to the time of Yefet. For Anan's date he uses 753 C.E., the first year of the caliphate of al-Manṣūr, cited by Yefet as 136 A.H., and thereby arrives at 1266 C.E. as the date for Yefet. He corroborates this chronology with the

11. Poznanski, *Zekher Ṣaddikim,* 24. It is significant that these dates are found only in Pinsker's incomplete text in *Likkute Kadmoniyot,* 186, and are lacking in the Bashyachi MS.

12. This date is based upon *Seder ʿOlam Rabbah* and BT A.Z. 9b, which places the destruction of the Second Temple in 3828 A.M. Although by convention it has become understood that this represents 68 C.E., in fact the rabbis were using a different calculation for A.M. and did correctly calculate the corresponding date for 70 C.E. See Edgar Frank, *Talmudic and Rabbinical Chronology: The System of Counting Years in Jewish Literature,* 11–24.

13. See Moses Bashyachi, *Matteh ʾElohim,* 7b (*Matteh ʾElohim*–Ramlah, 30). In reference to Anan it says: "And this was in the time of Abu Ja'far the King in the year four thousand and four hundred from the creation of the world."

14. This date is also found in RNL Evr.-Arab. II,1012.

15. See Lutzki, *ʾOraḥ Ṣaddikim,* 97: "And this is Rabbenu Yefet who wrote this Sefer Shalshelet ha-kabbalah ve-haʿtakat ha-Torah. And he lived at the end of the fifth and beginning of the sixth millennium."

16. See below in this chapter.

17. In his *Sefer Miṣvot,* currently in the Russian National Library, MS no. 613, cited in Poznanski, *Zekher Ṣaddikim,* 31, n. 2. See also Pinsker, *Likkute Kadmoniyot,* 185, n. 3; and 191.

corresponding year of 5026 A.M. to bring the emended calculations in line with the aforementioned Karaite tradition.[18] It is conspicuous that Poznanski does not mention Yefet's third corollary, which in the emendation would be 685 years from the destruction of the Temple to the break between Karaites and Rabbanites. The first number 413 can easily represent an error that is corrected to 513, but transforming the second figure from 1075 to 1198 seems far-fetched. Perhaps he wanted to avoid suggesting a second improbable emendation for the third corollary. Not only are the calculations incomplete, but reliance on a tradition that is cited only in the eighteenth century is problematic.

Harkavy and Steinschneider both suggested that the name Yefet ben Saʿīd is either forged from or mistaken for Yefet ben Ṣaʿir.[19] Indeed, some scholars have conflated the two, adding to the confusion.[20] The case for mistaken identity can be based upon the similarity of names of these two Yefets, which could easily be confused one for the other.[21] If the text of the Karaite chain of tradition is the work of Yefet ben Ṣaʿir, then we would have a text that originated two hundred years before it is attested to by Bashyachi, with provenance in the Islamic world. Indeed, in the version in *Matteh ʾElohim* the text is attributed to him, and he appears as a tradent near the end of the chain. On the other hand, in P[1] there is no attribution of authorship, but the chain includes Yefet ben Ṣaʿir, with no mention of Yefet ben Saʿīd.

18. Poznanski, *Zekher Ṣaddikim,* 31–32.

19. Ibid., 27. Harkavy suspects the text is a nineteenth-century forgery by Abraham Firkovich, who was not above such an act in his support of Karaite causes. See Harkavy, "Notes and Additions to the Fourth Section of Graetz's *History of the Jews,*" 50 (rpt., Jerusalem, 1970, 158), and "Notes and Additions to the Fifth Section of Graetz's *History of the Jews,*" 29 (rpt., Jerusalem, 1970, 227). The existence of the manuscript in the former Adler Collection at the Jewish Theological Seminary of New York (MS ENA 1229) was unknown to Harkavy. Since Adler's Geniza fragments were collected decades after Firkovich visited Cairo, MS ENA 1229 indicates the existence of old Karaite manuscripts that are independent of Firkovich. It is highly unlikely that Firkovich corrupted Genizah materials *in Cairo* in anticipation of later scholars discovering them. Indeed, we can begin to see that in spite of Firkovich's known forgeries, it is prudent not to dismiss manuscripts from his collections, which were the result of years of collecting among both Karaite and Rabbanite Jews of the Middle East. I wish to thank Shaul Shaked not only for the reference but also the inference based upon it.

20. Including Firkovich. See Poznanski, *Zekher Ṣaddikim,* 31, n. 2.

21. The final *dalet* of *Saʿīd* could be mistaken for the *resh* of *Ṣaʿir,* which is written in Arabic as *Saghīr.* The Hebrew letters resemble each other, and both words take the *paʿīl* form. Once this orthographic error had been recorded, a hypercorrection might then transform the beginning *samekh* into what was thought to be the appropriate *ṣadeh.* The process could also operate in reverse, thus mistaking *Yefet ben Ṣaʿir* for *Yefet ben Saʿīd.*

The argument for Islamicate authorship for the text may be supported by the historical setting. The approach of Gerson Cohen to Ibn Daud's *Sefer ha-Kabbalah* bears directly on such an examination, helping to explain a Karaite chain of tradition in light of both Islamic concepts of tradition and the rabbinic chain of tradition. If the author is the later Yefet ben Ṣaʿir, then halakhic issues emanating from the circle of his teacher in Egypt, Israel ha-Maʿaravi, need to be addressed for full historical and halakhic contextualization.[22] Israel and Yefet are associated with the final defeat of the catenary theory of consanguinity. It is possible that they used a chain of tradition to support their "new" halakhah, but until the appropriate halakhic studies are undertaken this can be only speculation. Indeed, one would seek to know whether halakhic transformations, similar to those that occurred among Byzantine Karaites, had taken place to support such a concrete construction of tradition.[23] It is also unknown whether there was a significant halakhic influence from the Karaite center in Byzantium. It could be argued that Egyptian Karaites of the fourteenth century utilized the backward historical projection of a chain of tradition as an expression of both cultural and religious transmission from and continuity with the Palestinian center (before 1099).[24]

The argument for Islamicate origins for the Karaite chain of tradition depends upon a greater understanding of the fourteenth- and fifteenth-century Karaite milieu in Egypt, the most active Karaite community in the Islamic world. If this conclusion is embraced, then Yefet ben Ṣaʿir is much preferred to the little-known Yefet ben Saʿīd, whose date is suspiciously early.

Alternatively, we have already seen that in the Byzantine environment a need for linking the Islamicate past to the present was important. As with the chronology ascribed to Tobias ben Moses by the Karaites, it would be in the interests of Byzantine proponents of a Karaite chain of tradition to project its

22. On Israel ha-Maʿaravi, see Pinsker, *Likkute Kadmoniyyot,* 174–78; and Poznanski, "Karaite Literary Opponents." 208.

23. Texts that might help answer questions of halakhah and history relating to fourteenth-century Egyptian Karaism remain in manuscript, as yet unpublished. Especially important is the Book of Precepts by the fifteenth-century Samuel ben Moses al-Maghribī, recently published in an uncritical edition by the Karaite community in Israel. See Samuel ben Moses al-Maghribī, *Sefer ha-Miṣvot (Kitāb al-murshid),* Yosef ben ʿOvadyah Algamil, ed. Cf. Poznanski, "Karaite Literary Opponents," 211–12.

24. The Karaite community that continued to exist in Egypt after 1099 was much more integrated into Egyptian society in general than their coreligionists in Byzantium. Of course, the medieval Islamicate environment in general offered more opportunities for cultural participation, even in the declining conditions of the Mamluke period to which we are referring. In addition, the generally nonhostile, if not good, relations between Egyptian Rabbanites and Karaites also suggest that an urge toward historical self-definition might have emerged as a result of Rabbanite influence.

roots, or at least its definitive expression, back in time to the classical Islamicate period. As changes in the concept of *haʿtakah* in Karaite halakhah permitted jurisprudential recourse to tradition, it was logical that questions of continuity would arise, even as the rabbis of the third century faced similar challenges from mishnaic law. Such a halakhically based explanation fits with cultural requisites of the Byzantine environment, where the Karaites looked for historical roots to explain both their teaching and presence. A historicized strategy whereby the author of the Karaite chain of tradition is dated to the late eleventh century, only a few historical moments away from the end of the Jerusalem center, is pregnant with the possibilities for cultural transmission to Byzantium. Whether the chain is a Byzantine or Islamicate creation, it would have been the Byzantine Karaites who much needed the earlier Yefet to be the author of their chain of tradition. A text adopted from Yefet ben Ṣaʿir, but attributed to Yefet ben Saʿīd, would easily lend itself to antedating its authorship two and a half centuries.

Although no satisfactory solution can be offered, I would like to refine the considerations for looking at this problem. In light of halakhic conditions requisite for a Karaite chain of tradition, a later date is preferred. Islamicate origins—that is, authorship by Yefet ben Ṣaʿir—depend upon halakhic matters that are as yet not fully understood. Internal evidence in the text in all Hebrew versions seems to support Islamicate origins. Many names are clearly Hebraized from the Arabic, and P[1] even uses the characteristically Islamic technical term *silsilah* for *chain.* Close examination of the chain of tradition itself reveals confusion in regard to names and chronology, as will be seen below, supporting the conclusion that the text is a late forgery—perhaps preferably called creative history.[25] However, since the copies in our hands are very late in relation to the text's attribution of authorship, it is possible that Arabic and Islamic features represent Islamicate accretions to a text that was taken over from its original Byzantine environment.

If Byzantine origins are to be accepted, the halakhic conditions in support of *haʿtakah* as an independent jurisprudential source are placed at the earliest in the last half of the fifteenth century.[26] In addition, there is no testimony for a Karaite chain of tradition by Karaite authors of the late fourteenth and early fifteenth centuries, such as Elijah Bashyachi, Caleb Afendopolo, and Joseph Beghi.[27] Nor does Ibn al-Hītī's list of Karaite scholars suggest an idea of tradition or transmission. One might suppose that the elder Bashyachi would certainly have welcomed a Karaite chain of tradition to support his theory of the Law.

25. The term *creative history* is taken from D. Mendels, "'Creative History' in the Hellenistic Near East."

26. See chapter 5, below, on Elijah Bashyachi and the use of tradition in Karaite halakhah.

27. On these authors, see ibid.

Little can be said with confidence about the textual history of the documents. It seems that P^1 and P^2 may represent earlier versions. P^2 may be the earliest, because in following Judah Halevi it attributes the break between the Karaites and Rabbanites to the time of Simeon ben Shetah and Judah ben Tabbai without specifying who is the leader of each faction. P^1 clearly represents a later development that became standard in Karaite tradition by identifying and vilifying Simeon as the proto-rabbi.[28] Whereas P^1 and the fragments list a line of transmission through the Babylonian exilarchs of the talmudic period, the version in *Matteh ʾElohim* interweaves a dual chain of both exilarchs and priests. However, the exilarchic list in P^1 includes names that appear as priests in *Matteh ʾElohim.* P^1 has far fewer Karaite scholars in the chain after Anan ben David than are in *Matteh ʾElohim.* If the level of complexity speaks to posteriority, then P^2 is the oldest, followed by P^1, and then *Matteh ʾElohim.* This is neither satisfactory textual criticism nor necessarily based on true assumptions. The disorder of P^1 might have been derived from an attempt to simplify a version congruent to that in *Matteh ʾElohim.* Also, the documentary evidence is not helpful, since P^1 and *Matteh ʾElohim* are from the same late period, and the date for P^2 is unknown.[29]

In regard to the name Yefet ben Saʿīd, it is possible that whoever created this history sought to evoke a name from an early Karaite past that bore some significance. A very well-known scholar such as Yefet ben ʿElī could not be named as the author of the *Haʿtakat ha-Torah* because his work was too well known, and the chain would have been vulnerable to charges of forgery. But the name Yefet ben Saʿīd could have been chosen to associate the Karaite chain of tradition to the earlier Yefet's family. The first Yefet was the father of Levi ben Yefet ha-Levi, who composed a Book of Precepts in 1006–7. Levi ben Yefet is also known as Abū Saʿīd, suggesting that he had a son named Saʿīd.[30] It was not uncommon in medieval Jewish families for names to be recycled through the generations.[31] It could then be presumed, or even based

28. See below, this chapter. P^1 is translated in appendix 2, but with only basic annotations.

29. As mentioned, *Matteh ʾElohim* is from the seventeenth or eighteenth century, and P^1 is dated 1682. See Pinsker in *Der Orient,* 737.

30. See Poznanski, "Karaite Literary Opponents," 172–76.

31. In a Karaite memorial list from the Cairo Genizah, a family of Levites reused the names Yefet and Saʿīd in several generations. See Mann, *Texts and Studies, 2: Karaitica,* 257ff., esp. 263. In tenth-century Spain, the rabbinate's break with Babylonian authority is marked by the appointment of Moses ben Ḥanokh to the rabbinical seat of Cordoba by Ḥasdai ibn Shaprut. His son was Ḥanokh ben Moses, whose son was Moses ben Ḥanokh. With several generations so named, the historian becomes unable to adequately identify individuals within such a family without corroborating data. See Ibn Daud, *Sefer ha-Qabbalah,* Cohen, ed., 63ff., and s.v. "Moses" and "Hanok" in the index. See also the Kalonymus family that flourished in the Rhineland in the ninth century through the thirteenth. In a text on family

upon a fact that is no longer able to be corroborated, that Saʿīd ben Levi had a son named Yefet ben Saʿīd. Thus, the "new" Karaite chain of tradition would have originated from most noble beginnings.

Ultimately, no answer can be positively demonstrated. While reviewing the problem, I have resorted to arguments from silence and speculation. Unless new textual evidence becomes available, most likely from the Cairo Genizah or the Firkovich collections, it is best to consider Yefet ben Saʿīd's *Shalshelet ha-kabbalah ve-haʿtakat ha-Torah* as a later creation—that is, more likely of Islamicate rather than Byzantine-Turkish origins.

Killing the Scholars: Judah Halevi and the Origins of Karaism

The twelfth-century Spanish Rabbanite poet and philosopher Judah Halevi places the break between the Karaites and rabbinic tradition in the time of Simeon ben Shetah and Judah ben Tabbai.[32] This historical explanation, adopted by the Karaites, became a central feature of their later historiography. The following brief remarks on the text's history and development will shed some light on both rabbinic historical thinking and the Karaite reading of rabbinic texts.

In Halevi's brief description of tradition, which introduces a discussion of the early rabbis, he elaborates on Mishnah Avot, chapter 1. The following excerpt begins immediately after mention of Nittai the Arbelite:[33]

> After him came Judah ben Tabbai and Simeon ben Shetah, with the friends of both. At this period arose the doctrine of the Karaites in consequence of an incident between the Sages and King Jannai who was a priest. His mother was under suspicion of being a "profane" woman. One of the Sages alluded to this, saying to him: "Be satisfied, O king Jannai, with the royal crown, but leave the priestly crown to the seed of Aaron." His friends prejudiced him against the Sages, advising him to browbeat, expel, scatter and kill them. He replied: "If I destroy the Sages what will become of the law?" "There is always the written law," they replied, "whoever wishes to study it may come and do so; take no heed of the oral law." He followed their advice

traditions (Paris BN MS Heb. 772, 60a) it is recorded: "I, Eleazar ha-Katan, received the true version of the prayers from my father and teacher, Rabbi Judah, son of Rabbi Kalonymus, son of Moses, son of Rabbi Judah, son of Rabbi Kalonymus, son of Judah." Cited in Joseph Dan, *EJ* 10:719, s.v. "Kalonymus."

32. *Kuzari,* 3:65. The standard scholarly edition is David H. Baneth, ed., *Kitāb al-radd wal-dalīl fil-dīn al-dalīl* (*Al-Kitāb al-Khazarī*) (Jerusalem, 1977).

33. The English translation of Hartwig Hirschfeld, *Judah Hallevi's Kitab al Khazari,* 187ff. The late Lawrence V. Berman of Stanford University was working on a new translation of the *Kitāb al-Khazarī* when he died. A copy of his uncompleted, unpublished manuscript, currently in my possession, had not yet included part 3.

> and expelled the Sages and among them was Simon ben Shetah, his son-in-law. Rabbanism was laid low for sometime. The other party tried to establish a law built on their own conception, but failed, till Simon ben Shetah returned with his disciples from Alexandria, and restored tradition to its former condition. Karaism had, however, taken root among people who rejected the oral law, and called all kinds of proofs to their aid, as we see to-day.

In a surprisingly fair appraisal of Karaism, Halevi departed from the standard rabbinic understanding of Karaism. Most medieval Rabbanite scholars would have described Karaism as a movement that began in the eighth century with Anan, understood to be a disappointed candidate for the exilarchate who was able to mobilize the remnants of the Sadducees in support of his schism. Halevi clearly identifies the Karaites as scripturalists who capitalized on the expulsion of the rabbinic sages. Although this narrative is embedded within a recapitulation of Mishnah Avot, chapter 1, the source for the story is found in the Babylonian Talmud, Kiddushin 66a:[34]

> It once happened that King Jannai[35] went to Kohalith in the wilderness and conquered sixty towns there. On his return he rejoiced exceedingly and invited all the Sages of Israel. Said he to them, "Our forefathers ate mallows when they were engaged on the building of the [Second] Temple; let us too eat mallows in memory of our forefathers." So mallows were served on golden tables, and they ate.[36] Now, there was a man there, frivolous, evil-hearted and worthless, named Eleazar son of Poʿirah, who said to King Jannai, "O King Jannai, the hearts of the Pharisees are against thee." "Then what shall I do?" "Test them by the plate between thine eyes."[37] So he tested them by the plate between his eyes. Now, an elder, named Judah son of Gedidiah, was present there. Said he to King Jannai, "O King Jannai! let the royal crown suffice thee, and leave the priestly crown to the seed of Aaron." (For it was rumoured that his mother had been taken captive in Modiʿim.)[38] Accordingly, the charge was investigated, but not sustained, and the Sages of Israel departed in anger.

34. Translated by H. Friedman, *The Babylonian Talmud: Seder Nashim, Tractate Kiddushin,* 332–34. The short annotations accompanying this translation are in part adapted from Friedman's notes.

35. The Hasmonean Alexander Jannaeus, son of John Hyrcanus, who ruled in 103–76 B.C.E.

36. A food of the poor, related to both cotton and okra.

37. The high priest wore an inscribed golden plate or frontlet suspended from his headdress by a cord over his forehead. See Ex. 28:36–38.

38. During the persecution of Antiochus Epiphanes, 168–165 B.C.E. The law assumes that a woman who had been a captive has been sexually compromised, making her son ineligible for the priesthood.

> Then said Eleazar b. Poʿirah to King Jannai: "O King Jannai! That is the law even for the most humble man in Israel, and thou, a King and a High Priest, shall that be thy law [too]!"[39] "Then what shall I do?" "If thou wilt take my advice, trample them down." "But what shall happen with the Torah?" "Behold, it is rolled up and lying in the corner: whoever wishes to study, let him go and study!"
>
> Said R. Nahman b. Isaac: Immediately a spirit of heresy was instilled into him, for he should have replied, "That is well for the Written Law, but what of the Oral Law?" Straightway, the evil burst forth through Eleazar son of Poʿirah, all of the Sages of Israel were massacred, and the world was desolate until Simeon b. Shetah came and restored the Torah to its pristine [glory].[40]

The talmudic tale corresponds to a version recounted by Josephus in the *Antiquities of the Jews*,[41] which begins with the relationship between the Hasmonean king, in this case identified as Hyrcanus, and the Pharisees, who

> have so great a power over the multitude, that when they say any thing against the king, or against the high priest, they are presently believed. Now Hyrcanus was a disciple of theirs, and greatly beloved by them. And when he once invited them to a feast, and entertained them very kindly, when he saw them in a good humour, he began to say to them, that "they knew he was desirous to be a righteous man, and to do all the things whereby he might please God, which was the profession of the Pharisees also. However, he desired, that if they observed him offending in any point, and going out of the right way, they would call him back and correct him." On which occasion they attested to his being entirely virtuous; with which commendation he was well pleased. But still there was one of his guests there, whose name was Eleazar, a man of an ill temper, and delighting in seditious practices. This man said, "Since thou desirest to know the truth, if thou wilt be righteous in earnest, lay down the high priesthood, and

39. Perhaps a lacuna in the text, which can be filled in by Josephus's narrative, below.

40. In the days of Queen Salome Alexandra (76–67 B.C.E.). The rabbis refer to other aspects of the history of these times. The dominance of the Sadducees under John Hyrcanus and Alexander Jannaeus is confirmed in BT Ber. 29a. Later reconciliation between the monarchy and the Pharisees occurred through the mediation of Salome Alexandra, while Jannaeus was still king, thus permitting the exiled scholars to return to Judah, including Judah ben Tabbai (PT Hag., 2:2, 77d; cp. BT Sot. 47a in the uncensored version). The deposition of the Sadducees from power is commemorated in a festival on Tevet 28 (Meg. Taʿan. 10; cp. ibid., 1, 4, and 5).

41. The translation is from William Whiston, trans., *The Works of Flavius Josephus,* 13:10, §5, 453–54.

> content thyself with the civil government of the people." And when he desired to know for what cause he ought to lay down the high priesthood? the other replied, "We have heard it from old men, that thy mother had been a captive under the reign of Antiochus Epiphanes." The story was false, and Hyrcanus was provoked against him; and all the Pharisees had a very great indignation against him.
>
> [6] Now there was one Jonathan, a very great friend of Hyrcanus's, but of the sect of the Sadducees, whose notions are quite contrary to those of the Pharisees. He told Hyrcanus, that "Eleazar had cast such a reproach upon him according to the common sentiments of all the Pharisees; and that this would be made manifest if he would but ask them the question, what punishment they thought this man deserved? for that he might depend upon it, that the reproach was not laid on him with their approbation; if they were for punishing him as his crime deserved." So the Pharisee made answer, that "he deserves stripes and bonds, but that it did not seem right to punish reproaches with death." And indeed the Pharisees, even upon other occasions, are not apt to be severe in punishments. At this gentle sentence Hyrcanus was very angry, and thought that this man reproached him by their approbation. It was this Jonathan who chiefly irritated him, and influenced him so far that he made him leave the party of the Pharisees, and abolish the decrees they had imposed on the people, and to punish those that observed them. From this source arose that hatred which he and his sons met with from the multitude.

These three texts provide us with a model with which to examine Jewish historiography, and at the same time they provide a historiographical motif that becomes central for the Karaite chain of tradition and subsequent interpretations of history. Needless to say, each of these accounts represents a literary strategy particular to its text. The most complete and earliest version, from Josephus, tells of the break between the ruling Hasmonean house and the Pharisees. The king's two antagonists are a Pharisee and a Sadducee, representing the struggle for power over contemporary Judean society and establishing the overall context of the narrative. As part of a Hellenistic history of the Jews, Josephus constructed narrative in the "Herodotean" style, providing cause and effect in order to apologize for Jewish particularity in the wake of the Jewish revolt of 66–70 C.E., in which the author played a central role. Josephus sought to show that "the state of affairs moved the Jews to envy Hyrcanus, but they that were the worst disposed to him were the Pharisees,"[42] who were extremely powerful. The tale ends without any reference to an incident of "killing the scholars."

42. Ibid.

Although we cannot accept Josephus's version as a "true account," it is reasonable for it to serve as a foundation for this portion of our study. When we examine the talmudic version, we are dealing with a text that was edited in its literary form some seven centuries after the event. We have already seen how the rabbis use historical accounts and bits of historical data for their own purposes, and this text serves as an excellent example. The rabbis had clearly maintained a tradition that embodied some of the original character of the events. However, the story is contextualized against the question of whether the king's mother had been sexually compromised while in captivity at Modi'im. The narrative's function is as supporting material for a talmudic discussion that seeks some conclusion regarding the number and character of witnesses who may have testified for or against her sexual condition. This intriguing and illustrative incident from the first century B.C.E. is, to the rabbis, merely material for an academic exercise in the laws of forbidden sexual relations.

The rabbis not only misidentified the king, substituting Alexander Jannaeus for his father, Hyrcanus, but removed the event completely from its setting amid the struggle between the Pharisees and Sadducees. By the time the talmudic discourse was being worked out, the Sadducees were no longer in existence, and the story was of more value in terms of matrimonial law than as an example of rabbinic antipathy toward the Sadducees.[43] Nonetheless, the very development of the narrative clearly indicates that its preservation was once linked to the battle over the authority of the Oral Law. The "spirit of heresy" is never actually named, but the "killing of the scholars" is explicitly situated as the denouement of the narrative.

As historiographically confused as the rabbinic text appears, it preserves in a veiled manner the flavor of the Sadducee-Pharisee battle. The "killing of the scholars" is not simply a concocted ending to this story. Josephus tells us that such a massacre did take place. The rabbis' confusion of John Hyrcanus and Alexander Jannaeus may stem from a conflation of the narrative in Kiddushin 66a with the following episode:[44]

> As to Alexander [Jannaeus], his own people were seditious against him, for at a festival which they celebrated, when he stood upon the altar, and was going to sacrifice, the nation rose upon him, and pelted him with citrons, [which they then had in their hands, because] the law of the Jews required, that at the feast of Tabernacles every one should have branches of the palm-tree and citron-tree; which thing we have elsewhere related. They also reviled him as derived

43. In a different setting, Hyrcanus's conversion to Sadduceeism is the result of the king succumbing to his evil impulse. See *Pesikta de-Rab Kahana,* Piska 11.1.

44. Josephus, *Antiquities of the Jews,* 13:13, §5, 461.

> from a captive, and so unworthy of his dignity and of sacrificing. At this he was in a rage, and slew of them about six thousand.

The stories are all linked by the issue of matrimonial eligibility, for Jannaeus is accused of the same defect as the son of Hyrcanus. Unmentioned is any reference to the Sadducee-Pharisee struggle. Undoubtedly the people's antipathy is sparked by Jannaeus's Sadducean methods of sacrifice.[45] Elsewhere, Josephus also credits him with killing ten thousand Jews who rebelled against him at Gaza.[46] Later, following political and military setbacks, "he fled to Jerusalem, where, besides his other ill success, the nation insulted him, and he fought against them for six years, and slew no fewer than fifty thousand of them."[47] The echo of the killing stemming from these inter-Jewish conflicts is plainly heard in the rabbinic account, in spite of the fact that the rabbis recorded it solely for halakhic purposes that are completely unrelated to the recording of history.

In terms of the internal relationships between rabbinic texts, the talmudic version serves another purpose. Almost as a footnote, Simeon ben Shetah's restoration of the law is appended to the narrative. The historicization provides concretized support to the hyperbolic statement "Simeon b. Shetah came and restored the Torah to its pristine [glory]." Even as the chain of tradition historicized the legal expression "Law of Moses from Sinai," so this pericope creates the narrative and historicized setting for Simeon's restoration of the Law. A similar statement appears in the Babylonian Talmud, Sukkah 20a. In a discussion whose legal outcome seeks support for authority in Palestine that is Babylonian in origin, it is stated, "At first the Torah was forgotten in Israel and Ezra came up[48] from Babylonia and [re]established it. Again it was forgotten and Hillel the Babylonian [re]established it. Again it was forgotten and Rav Ḥiyya and his sons came up and [re]established it."[49] Such hyperbole lent itself to legendary historicization associated with Ḥiyya's name in later rabbinic texts.[50] This literary construction, based upon an idea of restoration, or of the recovery of lost teaching, has roots in rabbinic literature, but will come to play an important role in later Karaite historical explanations.

45. On other points of conflict between Sadducee and Pharisee Temple ritual, see M Par. 3:3, 7;

46. Josephus, *Antiquities of the Jews,* 13:13, §3, 459–60.

47. Ibid., 13:13, §5, 461. Other conflicts of his led to the killing of Jews, including the crucifixion of the men who had opposed him at Bethome, and the killing of their wives and children before their eyes while they still lived. Ibid. 13:14, §2, 461–62.

48. *'Alah* (to go up) means to immigrate into the land of Israel.

49. My translation. The halakhic question regards the ritual purity of a mat that might be used for the roof of a *sukkah* (booth).

50. See BT M.K. 28a for legends about his death.

Judah Halevi devotes a good portion of the *Kuzari* to anti-Karaite argumentation.[51] In fact, in a letter written by Halevi, extant in an autograph from the Cairo Genizah, he indicates the original intent for writing this work was to combat Karaism in Christian Spain.[52] What is Halevi's strategy in selecting this talmudic pericope as a historical explanation for the origins of Karaism? The answer is found immediately preceding mention of the Karaites, embedded within the recapitulation of Mishnah Avot, chapter 1:[53]

> The next generation[54] was that of the High Priest Simon the Just and his disciples and friends. He was followed by Antigonus of Socho of great fame. His disciples were Sadok and Boethos who were the originators of the sects called after them Saddocaeans and Boethosians.

The text continues to follow Avot, but derives the origins of the Sadducees and Boethusians from the alternative and expanded version found in Avot de-Rabbi Natan, chapter 5.[55] After mention of Jose ben Joezer and Jose ben Johanan, the narrative continues:[56]

> He was followed by Joshua ben Perahyah whose history is known. Among his disciples was Jesus the Nazarene,[57] and Nittai of Arbela was his contemporary.

This portion of the *Kuzari* functions as heresiography, succinctly contextualizing the Sadducees, Boethusians, Christians, and Karaites into rabbinic history and clearly establishing distinct origins for each. Immediately after the pericope directly relating to the beginnings of Karaism stands a synopsis that further indicates Halevi's intent:[58]

> As regards the Saddocaeans and Boethosians, they are the sectarians who are anathematized in our prayer.[59] The followers of Jesus are the Baptists who adopted the doctrine of baptism, being baptized in the

51. Particularly *Kuzari,* 3:22–63, although all of part 3 can be read as an anti-Karaite argument.

52. See S. D. Goitein, "Autographs of Yehuda Hallevi"; idem, "The Biography of Rabbi Judah Ha-Levi in Light of the Cairo Geniza Documents"; and David H. Baneth, "Some Remarks on the Autographs of Yehudah Hallevi and the Genesis of the *Kuzari.*"

53. *Kuzari,* 3:65 (Hirschfeld, 187).

54. After the Great Assembly.

55. See chapter 1, above.

56. *Kuzari,* 3:65 (Hirschfeld, 187).

57. Jesus is identified as a contemporary of Joshua ben Perahiah in BT Ber. 17b and San. 103a.

58. *Kuzari,* 3:65 (Hirschfeld, 188).

59. In the Amidah prayer.

> Jordan. The Karaites turned their attention to the fundamental principles, deducing the special laws from them by means of arguments. The damage often extended to the roots, through their ignorance rather than intention.

In our pericope, Halevi intimates recognition of the rational deductive basis of the Karaite approach to halakhah, but elsewhere in the *Kuzari* he is more precise in this identification.[60] Daniel J. Lasker has carefully analyzed Halevi's treatment of the Karaites, indicating that Halevi's attacks on philosophy, particularly in its Aristotelian form, and his polemic against Karaism are part of the same argument against reliance on human reason to the exclusion of tradition.[61] In this way, Halevi categorically understands that *ḥippus* is part and parcel of the Karaite approach to halakhah, even though such thinking will lead to heresy.[62] He also specifies that the primary Karaite error is in regard to the "special laws," referring to details and particulars derived from more general pronouncements of the Torah. Although the Karaite error sometimes extends "to the roots" of the law—that is, elemental toraitic halakhah—Halevi seems to distinguish such a type of error from more fundamental heresies, such as denial of life after death or resurrection, which are primary religious principles. Further softening his denunciation of the Karaites, Halevi even suggests that they act through ignorance and not through evil intention.[63]

Why would the Karaites adopt a historical reading from a Rabbanite whose views opposed theirs? Lasker has shown that there are several areas where the Karaites might have seen correlations between their beliefs and Halevi's views.[64] Whatever conceptual correspondences to their own beliefs

60. Cf. *Kuzari,* 3:22 (Hirschfeld, 161); and 3:50 (Hirschfeld, 179–80).

61. Daniel J. Lasker, in "Judah Halevi and Karaism."

62. *Minut.* Cf. *Kuzari,* 3:49 (Hirschfeld, 176–79), where Halevi gives hypothetical examples of how deductive reasoning in halakhah can lead to error.

63. In the history of Rabbanite halakhah regarding the Karaites, the less extreme view often uses this rationale. Cf. Maimonides responsa on the Karaites in *Teshuvot ha-Rambam*, vol. 2, no. 263, 495–99, where he states that the Karaites are not heretics *(minim);* and vol. 2, no. 449, 729–32, where it is stated that one should ask about their health, even entering their homes, circumcise their sons, and bury their dead—because they are acting in error according to customs they have received, not because they are intentionally heretical. Cf. Maimonides' other responsa concerning the Karaites: ibid., vol. 2, no. 242, 434–44; no. 265, 502ff.; no. 351, 628f., extant only in Hebrew; and no. 365, p. 639.

64. "Judah Halevi and Karaism," 115–17. These include the fact that section 1 of the *Kuzari* is based solely on biblical texts without recourse to rabbinic literature, In addition, Halevi's ideas about divine glory *(kavod),* his Palestino-centric orientation, and some remarks on the role of reason for understanding the commandments could be received congenially by Karaites.

the Karaites might have seen in the *Kuzari*, the evolving trend toward reading rabbinic texts supported the Karaites seizing upon this portion of narrative for their own purposes. We have already seen how the Rabbanite narrative devised as a polemic against Anan was incorporated into Karaite historical thinking. Elijah ben Abraham followed his recounting of the Anan narrative with refutations of its anti-Karaitic polemical elements, thereby Karaizing the content. The Karaite utilization of Judah Halevi's material also transformed the narrative's shape. Karaite use of this text goes beyond the mere adoption and reexplanation of rabbinic material, but exemplifies an *interlinear* reading of rabbinic literature. In addition, by grasping the basic elements of Mishnah Avot, chapter 1, the Karaites were able to borrow a solution to the tricky problem of explaining the transition from biblical to postbiblical authority in Israel. The Great Assembly serves the Karaites as it did the rabbis. This type of interlinear reading, as we will see, represents a foundation in Karaite historical expression upon which a structure of literary accretion is built.

This literary construction requires several points with which to link Karaite historical ideas. The rabbinic versions grasp upon Simeon ben Shetah as a central figure,[65] although Halevi does not indicate whether the Karaites have a leader. It is a small leap for the Karaites to postulate that Judah ben Tabbai was the proto-Karaite. In doing so, they set up an opposition between their newly recognized founder and one of the most important of rabbinic figures. Consonant with the pronouncements of al-Qirqisānī and many Karaites of the classical Islamicate period, innovations and deviations in religion in their later rabbinic form can be laid at the feet of this rabbinic personality. The prestige of Simeon ben Shetah in rabbinic thought becomes mirrored in his vilification by the Karaites.

The significance of what may seem like merely a literary borrowing of obvious meaning should not be understated. In rabbinic literature, Simeon is credited with instituting the written *ketubbah,* or rabbinic marriage contract, and as such, would be considered by Karaites as especially culpable in an area where Rabbanite and Karaite halakhah differed greatly.[66] The scenario suggested above, in the conclusion to part 1, offers explanation for the break with Rabbanism on the part of local and regional Jewries in the early Islamic period based upon matrimonial practices. The embrace of Judah ben Tabbai can represent the ongoing Karaite hostility to Rabbanite laws of marriage and

65. Elsewhere in rabbinic literature, Simeon is variously identified as the president of the Sanhedrin, or head of the court *(av bet din)* (Tos., Hag. 2:8). BT records a harvest of miraculous dimensions following his death (Ta῾an. 23a). He is also credited with refining judicial procedure (Tos., San. 8:3. Cf. Tos., San. 6:6, where Judah ben Tabbai decides always to defer to Simeon's legal judgment).

66. Tos. Ket. 12:1. Other legal enactments credited to him are the institution of childhood education (PT Ket. 8:11, 32c) and declaring that glass and metal vessels are capable of carrying ritual impurity (PT, ibid., BT Shab. 14b).

consanguinity that could be used to exclude and degrade Karaites. Such Karaite acknowledgment of aspects of rabbinic teaching indicates a more than passing familiarity with rabbinic literature, which paradoxically provides a kind of validation to the new Karaite historical expression. This is a good example of the use of rabbinic texts to support Karaite historical formulations and controversialist objectives. Thus it could be demonstrated that a Rabbanite as prestigious as Judah Halevi clearly distinguishes between Sadducees and Boethusians, on the one hand, and Karaites, on the other, recognizing that the latter are not heretics who deny fundamental principles. Avot de-Rabbi Natan could also be invoked in support of this distinction. Thus, numerous points of contact between rabbinic text and Karaite ideology permitted the Karaites to elaborate on their history through the use of this Rabbanite narrative.

The Chain of Tradition in the *Matteh 'Elohim* of Moses Bashyachi[67]

The Karaite chain of tradition presents an alternative vision to that of the rabbis and incorporates the historical assumptions derived from Judah Halevi. The language of transmission is purposefully distinct in contrast to rabbinic versions. Whereas the rabbis tended to use the Hebrew verb *kibbel* (to receive), this text utilizes two different verbal forms. The first, *masar* (to pass on, or transmit), is used for the transmission from Moses to Anan, while from Anan onward it uses *he'etik,* which shares its root with *ha'takah.* In this way, Karaite halakhah is explicitly specified to the time from Anan to the present, even if it is the continuation of earlier tradition. Karaite tradition *(ha'takah),* which is substantively different from rabbinic tradition, is thus imagined to be historically distinct from rabbinic *kabbalah.*

The text is indebted to the rabbinic chain of tradition by virtue of its form as well as through the use of rabbinic content. This text exemplifies the trend among Karaite scholars to read and rework materials from rabbinic literature. Minor references are built into the text, such as the inclusion of Boaz from the Book of Ruth into the period of the judges, or mention of the High Priest Eliho'eini, who is known from the Mishnah. Of greater import is the treatment of the Great Assembly, which mirrors rabbinic concerns. The transmission from that time follows Mishnah Avot, chapter 1, but presents a completely Karaitic reading that rewrites the text using material derived from Judah Halevi. Finally, the treatment of Anan reflects the Rabbanite narrative that had become part of Karaite tradition since the *Ḥilluk.*

A complete translation of this text follows. In the first section, the handing down of tradition begins with Moses and is passed to the judges, with

67. *Matteh 'Elohim.* See note 7, above. The text begins in the first column of fol. 6b (*Matteh 'Elohim*–Ramlah, 27).

only slight reference to the priesthood.[68] The names are mostly taken from the Book of Judges and therefore require no comment. Note the reference to courts of law (in the singular, *bet din*) presided over by Gideon and Samson, a literary device that projects an image of the medieval legal system back into biblical antiquity.

> Rabbenu[69] Yefet ben Ṣaʿir, may he rest in Eden, said, and these are his words: This is the Order of the Transmission of the Torah[70] that is, the faith of the Karaites,[71] which preserved the true evidence and proofs[72] of all the miṣvot that our master the Messenger Moses ben Amram, peace be upon him, received,[73] [which is] Torah from Sinai. And he transmitted it[74] to the priests, the elders, and his disciple, Joshua ben Nun, peace be upon him.[75] As it says, "Moses wrote down this Teaching and gave it to the priests, etc."[76] He transmitted it to Phinehas and the elders who outlived Joshua, whom had seen what God had done for Israel. And the elders taught it to the judges. The first of the judges was Othniel ben Kenaz. And Othniel [transmitted it] to Ehud ben Gera; and Ehud to Shamgar ben Anath; and Shamgar ben Anath to Deborah and Barak; and Deborah and Barak to Gideon ben Joash; and Gideon ben Joash to Abimelech his son and to his court of law, the Ṣaddikim;[77] and Abimelech to Tola ben Puah; and Tola ben Puah to Jair the Gileadite; and Jair the Gileadite to Jephthah; and Jephthah to Ibzan of Bethlehem who is Boaz,[78] and Boaz

68. In comparison, neither Ibn Daud nor Maimonides describes the chain of transmission of this period with reference to individual names, simply stating that Moses passed the tradition on to Joshua, the elders, and the judges. Ibn Daud does list the judges, but for chronological purposes only. Ibn Daud, *Sefer ha-Qabbalah,* 3 [Heb.], 6 [Eng.]; and 5 [Heb.], 9 [Eng.]. Cf. Maimonides, *Mishneh Torah,* introduction, 3b; and *Mishnah ʿim perush rabbenu Mosheh ben Maimon,* 14–15.

69. Translated henceforth as "our master."

70. *Seder Haʿtakat Torah.*

71. *dat Bene Mikra.*

72. *ha-raʾayot ha-amitiyot veha-moftim.*

73. *kibbel.*

74. *mesarah.* Although Moses "receives" (described by the "rabbinic verb" *kibbel),* here he "transmits" *(masar),* as do all other tradents.

75. Unlike the rabbis, in whose interest it was to delete any reference to priestly claims to authority, Bashyachi's version includes them in their chain. They are not included consistently in the fragments, wherein only an occasional priestly tradent is indicated.

76. Deut. 31:9.

77. *ule-vet dino ha-ṣaddikim.*

78. The inclusion of Boaz in this list of judges incorporates the Book of Ruth into the biblical chronology. The association is based upon Bethlehem, which was Boaz's residence. This interpretive strategy is rabbinic in origin. Cf. BT B.B. 91a.

to Elon the Zebulunite; and Elon the Zebulunite to Abdon ben Hillel; and Abdon ben Hillel to Manoah; and Manoah to Samson his son and to his court of law, the *Ḥasidim;*[79] and Samson ben Manoah, used to judge at Dan.[80]

The next section continues by indicating those priests and prophets who transmitted tradition through the time of the Babylonian Exile. The list includes major prophets as well as lesser-known names taken from references within the biblical narrative.[81]

And Phinehas used to sit with the elders and the priests. And Phinehas and Samson transmitted it to Eli the Priest, who was the last of the judges. Eli transmitted it to Samuel the Prophet, who was the first of the prophets and a judge. Samuel transmitted it to King David, Nathan the Prophet, Gad the Seer, Shemaiah, man of God,[82] and Iddo the Prophet.[83] They transmitted it to Ahijah of Shiloh[84] and Jehu ben Hanani.[85] Ahijah and Jehu transmitted it to Elijah the Prophet; and Elijah the Prophet to Elisha ben Shaphat, Micah ben Imlah,[86] Obadiah the Prophet, Jonah ben Amittai, and Eliezer ben Dodayahu.[87] Elisha transmitted it to Jehoiada the Priest[88] and Habakkuk the Prophet. They transmitted it to Zechariah the Prophet and Priest;[89] and Zechariah to Hosea ben Beeri; and Hosea ben Beeri to

79. *ule-vet dino ha-ḥasidim.*

80. See 1 Sam. 12:11 and 1 Chron. 7:17. The rabbis refer to him as *ben Dan,* "son of Dan." Cf. Tos. R.H. ii, 3 [1]. Rashi and David Kimhi agree. In this text, *be-Dan* is "at Dan," not *ben Dan.*

81. Some annotations are supplied in reference to lesser-known biblical names. Maimonides' list in *Mishneh Torah,* introduction, 3b, differs in sequence.

82. 1 Kgs. 12:22. Cf. 2 Chron. 12:15.

83. 2 Chron. 12:15; 13:22.

84. 1 Kgs. 11:29; 14:1–18. Cf. 2 Chron. 19:29. There is a rabbinic tradition that Ahijah lived for an extremely long time, from the time of Amram, Moses' father, or even earlier. As a result, he could be placed almost anywhere in this portion of the chain. He was active in the time of Jeroboam and is credited with having written the history of Solomon's reign. Maimonides alludes to this in his version of the chain of tradition, but is opposed by Abraham ben David. See *Mishneh Torah,* 3b.

85. 1 Kgs. 16:1, 7; and 2 Chron. 19:2, 3; 16:7; 20:34.

86. Micaiah ben Imlah: see 1 Kgs. 22:8–9; and 2 Chron. 18:7–8.

87. Eliezer ben Dodavahu: see 2 Chron. 20:37.

88. High priest in the ninth century B.C.E. who opposed Baal worship. He is also named in versions of the rabbinic chain of tradition. Cf. Maimonides, *Mishneh Torah,* 3b.

89. The appellation confuses the prophet with others named Zechariah. For example, see 1 Chron. 15:18, 20; 24:25; and 26:11; 2 Chron. 20:24; and 29:15. See esp. Zechariah, the son of Jehoiada, in 2 Chron. 24.

> Amos; and Amos the Prophet to Micah the Morashtite. Micah the Morashtite transmitted it to Joel ben Pethuel. Joel ben Pethuel transmitted it to Nahum the Elkoshite; and Nahum to Zephaniah the Prophet. Zephaniah transmitted it to Jeremiah the Prophet. Jeremiah the Prophet transmitted it to Baruch ben Neriah and Ezekiel the Priest.

In the section that follows, the narrative focuses on the Great Assembly, mirroring rabbinic traditions regarding its membership.[90] It concludes with the transmission to Simeon the Just, a direct reference to Mishnah Avot.

> Baruch transmitted it to Ezra the Priest, the Leader, the Scribe,[91] skilled in the Torah of Moses, a man of the living God,[92] and to his court of law, who are called the Great Assembly. They are Haggai, Zechariah, Malachi, Daniel, Hananiah, Azariah,[93] and twelve prophets, who are Ezra the Priest, Nehemiah ben Hacaliah, Mordecai, Zerubbabel, Jeshua, Seraiah, Reelaiah, Bilshan, Mispar, Bigvai, Rehum, Baanah,[94] and many wise men with them up to the complement of one hundred and twenty elders.[95] Ezra and his court of law taught it to Simeon the Just, the High Priest, who held office after Ezra, peace be upon him.

Beginning with Simeon the chain is based upon Mishnah Avot, chapter 1. Given the Karaite reading of rabbinic texts, it is not surprising to find

90. The rabbis consider Haggai, Zechariah, and Malachi to be members of the Great Assembly, in BT Meg. 17b. Although not mentioned in M Avot 1, it is explicit in Avot de-Rabbi Natan, 1.3, 16b. See the translation by Elie Cashdan in *'Aboth d'Rabbi Nathan,* 3. See also chapter 1, above.

91. *ha-rosh ha-sofer.* This could be an error, to be corrected to "first of the scribes," echoing Othniel as "first of the judges" and Samuel as "first of the prophets." Cf. RNL Evr.-Arab. 1,2994.

92. *'ish ha-elohim ḥayyim.*

93. Daniel's third companion, Mishael, is absent. His name usually appears in the middle of the other two, as it does in some of the manuscript fragments. See Dan. 2:17ff. Cf. Maimonides, *Mishneh Torah,* introduction 3b.

94. The latter eleven men are those who led the returnees from Babylon to Jerusalem and Judah in Ezra 2:2. The change in sequence here apparently represents the perceived importance of the individuals. Ezra has been added at the head of the list. Cf. Ibn Daud, *Sefer ha-Qabbalah,* 5–6 [Heb.], 9 [Eng.].

95. This is the exact wording in Maimonides' chain of tradition in *Mishneh Torah,* intro., 3b: *ve-harbeh ḥakhamim 'immahem tashlum me'ah ve-'esrim zekenim.* The number 120 is derived from BT Meg. 17b, which states, with reference to the Great Assembly, that the academy *(metivta)* at Yavneh (first century C.E.) had that many members.

the rabbinic chain of tradition replicated and changed to suit Karaite needs. Ironically, the very textual foundation of rabbinic tradition is utilized to create a new tradition.

It is important to note that the chain's progression is briefly interrupted with a description of Zadok and Boethus. Since the Karaites were constantly accused of being Sadducees and Boethusians, the text provides a clear chronological and conceptual differentiation between them and the "archaic" Karaites. Unlike the Karaites, these heretics denied fundamental principles, which were considered to be part and parcel of the Torah itself. In addition, their break with the community took place two generations before the definitive division between Rabbanites and Karaites.[96] A clear distinction is made between these early heretics and those who are accused of being their progeny. The chain follows Judah Halevi by ascribing Rabbanism to Simeon ben Shetah, but goes beyond Elijah Bashyachi to expand the reading by attributing the birth of Karaism to Judah ben Tabbai. Simeon, as the proto-Rabbanite, is portrayed banning the written text, intimating that the rabbis observe their Oral Law to the exclusion of Scripture.

> Simeon transmitted it to Antigonus of Socho, who had two students, one named Zadok and the other Boethos. They denied the truth, one man grasping the hands of his friend, and they became heretics,[97] denying reward and punishment, and similarly, [denying] the resurrection of the dead and the foundation[98] of the Torah of Moses our master, peace be upon him. [fol. 7a] Antigonus transmitted it to Joseph ben Yoezer of Zeredah and Joseph ben Yohanan of Jerusalem. They transmitted it to Nittai the Arbelite and Joshua ben Perahiah. Nittai and Joshua ben Perahiah transmitted it to Judah ben Tabbai and Simeon ben Shetah. In their time Simeon ben Shetah sought to ban the true written text.[99] Woe![100] Judah ben Tabbai, who stood in the breach, made clear[101] the true faith, the faith of the Karaites, may the Rock of Ages protect them. He made strong and preserved His truth,[102] as it had been since ancient days [supported by] clear proofs. [Thus] Rabbi Judah ben Tabbai caused the truth to be strengthened. He compelled them with his method[103] and answers to them, and he returned the truth to its place.

96. Based upon the entry in Avot de-Rabbi Natan, ch. 5.
97. *ve-yaṣʾu le-minut,* literally "they went out to heresy."
98. Or *essence, ʿikkar.*
99. *ha-rashum bi-khtav emet.*
100. *she-alelai.*
101. *nitbarer,* not usually transitive, could also mean "purified."
102. *amituto.*
103. *be-ʿiyyuno.*

The text is corrupt in the section that follows. As a result of the break between Simeon and Judah, two distinct chains of transmission should be indicated. The "pairs" of transmitters from Avot are now differentiated one from another, one a Karaite and the other a Rabbanite. In this way, Shammai is transformed into a Karaite transmitter and hero, in contrast to Hillel, who is a central figure in rabbinic thought and the founder of the rabbinic patriarchal house in Palestine.

> Judah transmitted it to Shemaiah; and Shemaiah[104] to Abtalion. Shemaiah[105] transmitted it to Rav Hillel. Rav Hillel transmitted it to the traditionists,[106] who received [it] from their master, Simeon ben Shetah and Shemaiah.[107] Shemaiah transmitted it to Rav Shammai. Rav Shammai, the Elder, the Honorable, the Righteous,[108] transmitted it to the Karaites, may the Rock of Ages protect them, and be their aid, destroying their enemies, those who hate them, and the students of their faith. Amen.[109]

The narrative continues with two interwoven chains of transmission, one priestly and the other of the exilarchs, extending into the early Islamic period. The priestly transmission is completely hypothetical since it is unlikely that a priestly tradition survived for long after the destruction of the Temple in 70 C.E.[110] The names are all names of priests and Levites from the Bible, especially from the Books of Ezra, Nehemiah, and 1 and 2 Chronicles. By postulating a priestly transmission, the Karaite chain would claim that an important precept of the Bible had been maintained, the establishment of priests as leaders

104. This is an error. In the Karaite version, it is Simeon ben Shetah who transmits the false tradition to Abtalion, who transmits it to Hillel. Read: *Simeon.*

105. This is an error. Abtalion is credited in the Karaite version with the transmission from Simeon ben Shetah to Hillel. In this way two distinct chains of transmission are postulated, the Rabbanite and Karaite. Read: *Abtalion.*

106. *baʿale ha-kabbalah,* the Rabbanites.

107. This is an error. Read: *Abtalion.* The entire pericope should read: "Judah transmitted it to Shemaiah; and Simeon to Abtalion. Abtalion transmitted it to Rav Hillel. Rav Hillel transmitted it to the traditionists, who received [it] from their master, Simeon ben Shetah and Abtalion. Shemaiah transmitted it to Rav Shammai." However, compare *Matteh ʾElohim*–Ramlah, 29: "Judah transmitted it to Shemaiah; and Simeon to Abtalion. And Shemaiah transmitted it to Rav Hillel. Rav Hillel transmitted it to the traditionists, who received [it] from ha-Rav Simeon ben Shetah. And Rav Shammai, the Elder, the Honorable, the Righteous, transmitted it to the *baʿale ha-mikra.*"

108. *ha-zaken ha-nikhbad vehe-ḥasid.*

109. A pause is indicated here in the manuscript. See *Matteh ʾElohim*–Ramlah, 29.

110. However, at the 2001 annual meeting of the Society of Biblical Literature and American Academy of Religion (Denver, Colo.), Jodi Magness and Paul Flesher presented work suggesting that priestly leadership may have survived into later centuries.

of the people. The second line of transmission is that of the exilarchs of Babylonia, descendants of David and the kings of Judah, thus representing the second pillar of Jewish authority established in the Bible.[111] These chains of tradition are hereby established with doubled authenticity in contrast to the claims of transmission professed by the rabbis.

It is difficult to harmonize the exilarchic line in this text with that of *Seder ʿOlam Zuta* or the accepted chronologies of modern scholarship. However, there is a medieval Rabbanite document that describes the ninth-century controversy between David ben Zakkai and Saadia Gaon and that is preceded by a list of the "generations of the world in short from Adam to David ben Zakkai."[112] The list appears to be a genealogy tracing a line from Adam, through Abraham, Judah, David, and Jehoiachin, to the exilarchs. The differences between this list and the Karaite chain of tradition are minor. Because it seems that the Karaite author utilized this lesser-known Rabbanite genealogical list of Babylonian exilarchs, we need not criticize the text from a modern historiographical point of view on account of its confused chronology and prosopography. The Karaite author's sources were completely satisfactory for their time.

Note that Yohanan ben Zakkai, a key figure in rabbinic historical thinking, is designated as a "Karaite" tradent.

> Rav Shammai transmitted it to Rav Kahana the Priest ben Eloni,[113] who prepared the water of the heifer in the Second Temple, ben Abithar ben Jedaiah the Priest, and to Rav Yohanan ben ʿIkuv ha-Zakkai[114] the Prince and his court of law. There were many sages

111. For the exilarchs, see the chronology established by Felix Lazarus in "Die Häupter der Vertriebenen." For a more recent view, see Neusner, *A History of the Jews in Babylonia,* 5:45–69, 124–27, and 248–59.

112. Published in part by Neubauer in *Mediaeval Jewish Chronicles,* 77–88 (henceforth, *Dorot ha-ʿOlam,* 77). The text was used in an article in *MGWJ* 24 (1875): 43, 90, and is identified only as a manuscript "now in the possession of my learned friend Herr A. Epstein." *Mediaeval Jewish Chronicles,* vii and x.

113. Corruption of Elihoʿeini, who is ben Hakkof (or ha-Kayyaf, which corresponds to Caiaphas), in M. Par. 3:5 (Eliehoenai in Danby's translation, *The Mishnah*), or Elonaeus son of Cantheras (or Cithaerus) in Josephus, *Ant.*, 19:342. Cf. Edna Elazary, s.v. "Elionaeus, Son of Cantheras," in *EJ* 6:663.

114. Yohanan ben Zakkai (first century C.E.) in the rabbinic tradition is the only head of the Palestinian rabbinic academy who was not a Hillelite. Whether he was actually considered a *nasi* (prince) is questionable. He did arrogate to himself some princely legislative prerogatives. Yohanan is mentioned in *Dorot ha-ʿOlam,* 77. The reference could also be derived from the exilarchic name Mar Yuhna, associated with Rava and Abbaye (early fourth century). See BT Hul. 133a, and A.Z. 16b. Cf. Neusner, *A History of the Jews in Babylonia,* 5:249–50, with reference to some exilarchic names also found in *ʾIggeret Rav Sherira Gaʾon.*

with them. Rav Kahana transmitted it to Rav Shimʿi,[115] his son. Rav Yohanan ben ʿIkuv ha-Zakkai transmitted it to Rav Shafat,[116] his son. Rav Shimʿi the Priest transmitted it to Rav Yohanan, his son. Rav Shafat the Prince transmitted it to Rav Anan,[117] his son. Rav Yohanan the Priest transmitted it to[118] Rav Nathan Rezuzita,[119] his son. Rav Zadok[120] the Priest transmitted it to Rav Ezekiel. Rav Nathan the Prince transmitted it to our Rav Nehemiah,[121] his son. Rav Nathan Ezekiel[122] the Priest transmitted it to Rav Ahituv,[123] his son. Rav Nehemiah the Prince transmitted it to Rav ʿUkba,[124] his son. Rav Ahituv

115. A priestly family mentioned in many places in the Bible. For examples, see Num. 3:21; Zech. 12:31; Ezra 10:23; 2 Chron. 31:12–13.

116. The name appears in the list in *Dorot ha-ʿOlam,* 77. In the Bible, a member of the Davidic family of Zerubbabel, in 1 Chron. 3:22.

117. In the Bible, one of the "heads of the people" in Neh. 10:27, while other names in this list are found in the eleven leaders of Ezra 2:2. In this entry, Anan may refer to the first of the Babylonian exilarchs., who is known to the Rabbanites as Nathan ʿUkban, but was probably Naḥum (140–70 C.E.). Cf. *Dorot ha-ʿOlam,* 77; and *Seder ʿOlam Zuta,* 71.

118. There is a gap in the text. This and the following sentence should read: "Rav Yohanan the Priest transmitted it to Rav Zadok his son. Rav Anan transmitted it to Rav Nathan Rezuzita his son." See *Matteh ʾElohim*–Ramlah, 30.

119. This should read Nathan de-Zuzita, which appears in *Dorot ha-ʿOlam,* 77, as "Nathan de-Zuzita (Huna)." He is erroneously identified in BT Shab. 56b as ʿUkban bar Nehemiah (Mar Ukba II, 317–37 C.E.), but in *Seder ʿOlam Zuta,* 71, two different exilarchs have this name, Nathan ʿUkban (Nathan de-Zuzita), who is probably Nathan I (260–70 C.E.), and Mar ʿUkban de-Zuzita, who is probably Mar Ukba II. Cf. BT San. 31b, which refers to Nathan Masukba, an obvious corruption of Mar Ukba. See David Joseph Bornstein, *EJ* 12:860–61, s.v. "Nathan de-Zuzita Resh Galuta."

120. In the Bible, the priest of David, founder of a line of high priests.

121. This is probably the exilarch Nehemiah (270–313 C.E.). Cf. *Dorot ha-ʿOlam,* 77; and *Seder ʿOlam Zuta,* 72.

122. The text is corrupt. The name Nathan should be omitted. Also in *Matteh ʾElohim*–Ramlah, 30.

123. In the Bible, a priestly name, either the father of Ahimelech the priest (1 Sam. 22:9, 11–12, 20), or the father of Saul's priest, Ahijah (1 Sam. 14:3), or of Zadok the Priest (2 Sam. 8:17). The latter reference, although probably an error, led to a tradition associating Ahituv with Zadok the high priest that is repeated in 1 Chron., Ezra, and the extracanonical books of 1 and 2 Esdras. He is also the father or grandfather of a later priest named Zadok (1 Chron. 6:12; 9:11). See R. W. Corney, IDB 1:71, s.v. "Ahitub."

124. Probably the exilarch Mar Ukba II (313–37 C.E.). See *Dorot ha-ʿOlam,* 77, which has ʿUkba. Cf. *Seder ʿOlam Zuta,* 72, where he is identified as Akaviah. See *Matteh ʾElohim*–Ramlah, 30, where ʿUkba is named Akiva.

the Priest transmitted it to Rav Jeshua,[125] his son. Rav ʿUkba the Prince transmitted it to Rav Abuʾamar,[126] his son. Rav Yeshua the Priest transmitted it to Rav Nathaniel,[127] his son. Rav Abuʾamar the Prince transmitted it to Rav Huna,[128] his son. Rav Nathaniel the Priest transmitted it to Heman,[129] his son. Rav Huna the Prince transmitted it to Rav Nathan,[130] his son. Rav Heman the Priest transmitted it to Rav Unni,[131] his son. Rav Nathan the Prince transmitted it to Rav Kahana,[132] his son. Rav Unni the Priest transmitted it to Rav Zephaniah,[133] his son. Rav Kahana the Prince taught

125. In the Bible, Jeshua ben Jozedek was the high priest at the time of Zerubbabel and Ezra (Ezra and Neh., passim). Another priest in the time of Hezekiah bore this name (2 Chron. 31:15).

126. Probably the exilarch Huna Mar I, also known as Huna III (337–50 C.E.). Ukba was actually his brother. The name in the chain is clearly an Arabicization of an otherwise no-longer-identifiable name. In *Dorot ha-ʿOlam*, 77, the entry following Ukba is "Abba Bar Huna." Whether this is one name or should be read as Abba followed by Bar Huna is unknown. Abba was probably the nephew of Huna Mar. The text is clearly corrupt here. Cf. *Seder ʿOlam Zuta*, 72.

127. In the Bible, this name was born by priests in the time of David (1 Chron. 15:24; 21:4; 24:6).

128. Alluding to either of the exilarchs, Huna IV (415–42 C.E.), which appears much too late, or to Huna Mar I, who was already listed. Since this name occupies an intermediate position between Huna Mar I and Nathan, it is likely to be Abba (350–70 C.E.). Cf. *Dorot ha-ʿOlam*, 77, which has no Huna here; and *Seder ʿOlam Zuta*, 72. Others named Huna appear later in both *Dorot ha-ʿOlam* and *Seder ʿOlam Zuta*, but not in this Karaite list.

129. In the Bible, one of the wise men to whom Solomon is compared (1 Kgs. 5:11), but the priestly association is with singers in the Tabernacle in the time of David (1 Chron. 15:17, 19; 25:1, 4).

130. Probably the exilarch Nathan II (370–400 C.E.), son of Abba. Cf. *Dorot ha-ʿOlam*, 77.

131. In the Bible, a priestly name, either of the time of David or of Zerubbabel (1 Chron. 15:18, 20; Neh. 12:9). Or perhaps another corruption of Elihoʿeini. See note 113, above. Not to be confused with four priests of Second Temple times known as Onias, whose Hebrew equivalent is Ḥonyo, or Ḥoni.

132. Probably the exilarch Kahana I (400–15 C.E.), who was the brother of Nathan II. Cf. *Dorot ha-ʿOlam*, 77; and *Seder ʿOlam Zuta*, 72. Not to be confused with Kahana II (455–65).

133. In the Bible, besides the prophet for whom the book is named, there is also a priest who appears in the Book of Jeremiah (Jer. 21:1; 29:25, 29; 37:3; 52:45; and 2 Kgs. 25:18), and a name that is part of the levitical descent of Heman from Kohath (1 Chron. 6:20). Priestly identity is often conferred upon the prophet Zephaniah as a result of these biblical references, as in the text of the Karaite chain of tradition.

> Zutra,[134] his son. Rav Mar Zutra the Prince transmitted it to Rav Hunamar,[135] his son. Rav Hunamar the Prince transmitted it to Rav Kafnai,[136] his son. Rav Zephaniah the Priest transmitted it to Rav Shemariah,[137] his son. Rav Kafnai the Prince transmitted it to Rav Haninai[138] [fol. 7b], his son. Rav Haninai the Prince transmitted it to Rav Bustanai,[139] his son. Rav Bustanai the Prince transmitted it to Rav Hisdai,[140] his son. Rav Shemariah the Priest transmitted it to Rav Zuta,[141] his son. Rav Hisdai the Prince transmitted it to our master[142] David the Prince,[143] his son.

The two lines of transmission, exilarchic and priestly, then come together with Anan, who is cast as a second Judah ben Tabbai. Note that al-Qirqisānī was able to foreshadow Anan with Zadok, but now that the Karaites found themselves repeatedly defending themselves against accusations of Sadducee-ism, such a historical foundation would only act as a polemical liability. The

134. The exilarch Mar Zutra I (442–55 C.E.), the son of Kahana I. Cf. *Dorot ha-ʿOlam,* 77; and *Seder ʿOlam Zuta,* 72.

135. More likely the exilarch Huna V (465–70 C.E.), the son of Mar Zutra I, rather than Huna VI (484–508 C.E.), his grandson. Both Kahana I and Kahana II were succeeded by sons named Huna, hence the possibility of confusion. Cp. *Dorot ha-ʿOlam,* 77, which has "Huna Mar"; *Seder ʿOlam Zuta,* 72. *ʾIggeret Rav Sherira Gaʾon,* 118–19, has references to both Huna bar Mar Zutra (Huna V) and Huna the Exilarch (Huna VI). See also Ibn Daud, *Sefer ha-Qabbalah,* 31 [Heb.], and 41–42 [Eng.], for Huna V, who is identified as Huna Mar.

136. Probably the exilarch Hofnai (560–80 C.E.). Several generations have been skipped at this point of the chain. Cf. *Dorot ha-ʿOlam,* 77.

137. In the Bible, the minor name Shemariah has no priestly connotations but might have originally appeared in the chain as Shemaiah. A scribal error replacing an *ʿayin* with a *resh* would explain this entry. Of the twenty-eight different individuals who bore the name Shemaiah in the Bible, nineteen have levitical and priestly associations. The prophet Shemaiah, who was not a priest, is mentioned in the chain above as having received the tradition from Samuel.

138. The exilarch Haninai (580–90 C.E.). Perhaps mentioned in *Seder ʿOlam Zuta,* 72.

139. The exilarch Bustanai (d. 670 C.E.), who ruled at the time of the Muslim conquest. Cf. *Dorot ha-ʿOlam,* 77. See also Ibn Daud, *Sefer ha-Qabbalah,* 34–35 [Heb.], and 44–45 [Eng.].

140. Bustanai had a son Ḥisdai, who succeeded him. See *Dorot ha-ʿOlam,* 77. There was also a Ḥisdai II ben Bar Adai ben Bustanai.

141. An early Karaite scholar is identified as Ben Zuta or Zita, but he probably lived in the tenth century, with no known association to the exilarchic house. See Poznanski, "Karaite Literary Opponents," 134.

142. *adonenu.*

143. Perhaps a brother to Solomon ben Ḥisdai II (c. 733–59), who is mentioned in *Dorot ha-ʿOlam,* 77.

text shows some debt to the *Ḥilluk,* especially the erroneous chronology for the ʿAbbāsid Caliph al-Manṣūr.

> Rav Zuta the Priest and Rav David the Prince transmitted it to Rav Anan the Prince, peace be upon him. It was he who explained the true faith for the second time after it had disappeared. And he explained and revealed it with clear true proofs and strong teachings [text is corrupt], even exposing himself to danger. This was in the time of Abu Ja'far, the King in the year four thousand and four hundred years according to the creation of the world.[144] He was the exilarch for all of the house of Israel in Babylon. He answered the disciples of Rav Hillel and those who walk in their tracks. A great nation repented with him from among our brethren because he explained to them the truth, and in his tracks traveled all those who possessed the fear of God.

In the final section, the chain of tradition becomes completely Karaitic, in the sense that there is no direct borrowing from rabbinic texts and, except for reference to Saadia Gaon, no rabbinic references are found. Indeed, true to Poznanski's image of the Karaite concern for history, the chronology is convoluted, as are the identifications. Resembling more the list of scholars near the end of the *Ḥilluk* or of Ibn al-Hītī than the chain of tradition of the rabbis, such a lack of historical exactitude demonstrates that the text supports the general claim being made by the profession of a chain of tradition rather than being the record of an ongoing historical tradition. While the rabbis actually had some halakhic-methodological purpose in maintaining their chains of tradition, the Karaitic approach to halakhah required no such thing. The anteriority or posteriority of any Karaite scholar had little bearing on the manner in which his halakhah was accepted by later readers.

A few points should be noted. Many of the identifications are so confused that a chronological sequence is only partially discernible. Only a few Karaite *nesiʾim* are included, at the beginning and end of the list.[145] We also find Yefet ben Ṣaʿir near the end. Finally, the common strategy of recreating a rabbinic scholar as the student of a notable Karaite is seen here, whereby Saadia Gaon is made into the student of Salmon ben Yeruḥim.[146]

144. RNL Evr.-Arab. II,1012 states in Arabic: "This was the time of Abū Ja'far al-Manṣūr the Caliph in the year 136 according to the [counting of] the Little Horn." Little Horn is a biblical reference to the Fourth Kingdom in Daniel's prophecy (Dan. 7:8); often a reference to Islam.

145. For other lists of Karaite *nesiʾim,* see Mann, *Texts and Studies,* 2: *Karaitica,* 128–55; and Gil, *History of Palestine,* 790–94.

146. Annotations are supplied in order to identify lesser-known names.

> To our master Rav Saul[147] his son [it] was transmitted[148] to him from him [Anan]. Rav Saul transmitted it[149] to Rav Josiah[150] the Prince, his son; and he to Rav Benjamin al-Nahavendi; and he transmitted it to Rav Daniel al-Qumisi, Rav Isaac ha-Basri,[151] and Rav David ha-Mukammis, a sincere convert. They transmitted it to Rav Noah.[152] He transmitted it to Rav Salmon ben Yeruḥim, Rav Joseph ben Noah,[153] Rav Jacob ben Isaac ha-Kirkisani, Rav Hasun ben Mashiaḥ,[154] and Rav Abraham ben Isaac ha-Basri.[155] In their time lived Saadia Gaon the Pithomite, who was a disciple of Rav Salmon ben Yeruḥim. Rav Joseph ha-Ro'eh[156] was [Salmon's] second [disciple], who existed[157] together in the same time. Rav Joseph asked him [Saadia] difficult questions,[158] compelling him with his arguments, as is mentioned in his book *Sefer ha-Ma'or ha-Gadol,* written in the year four thousand, six hundred and seventy according to Creation.[159]

147. Generally acknowledged as Anan's son and successor. Cf. *Ḥilluk,* 106. See Poznanski, *Babylonische Geonim im nachgaonäischen Zeitalter nach handschriften und gedruckten Quellen,* 125–34.

148. *ne'tak.*

149. *he'etikah.* From this point on, the verb for *to transmit* is changed, in allusion to the typically Karaite designation of tradition as *ha'takah.* In this way, the existing Karaite tradition is closely associated with the teaching of Anan and its continuation.

150. Josiah is also generally acknowledged in the succession. See *Ḥilluk,* 106; and Poznanski, *Babylonische Geonim im nachgaonäischen Zeitalter,* 125–34.

151. Probably Isaac ben Bahlūl, identified by Nemoy in the *Ḥilluk,* 106, in "Elijah ben Abraham and His Tract against the Rabbanites," 79, n. 60.

152. This Rav Noah is otherwise unknown, but probably is inserted in order to create a link to the well-known Joseph ben Noah, who would then be understood to be this Noah's son.

153. Head of the Jerusalem Karaite academy in the late tenth and early eleventh century. Also known as Abū Ya'qūb. Cf. *Ḥilluk,* 106; and Nemoy, "Elijah ben Abraham and His Tract," 84, n. 78. See also Ibn al-Hītī in Margoliouth, "Ibn al-Hītī's Arabic Chronicle," passim, which includes much information.

154. He is Ḥasan or Ḥusayn. The text is probably a corruption of the latter, with a *vav* replacing a *yud.* Cf. Poznanski, "Karaite Literary Opponents," 145–46.

155. Otherwise unknown. Ibn al-Hītī mentions an Abū Yiṣhāk (Isḥāq) Abraham ben al-Isfahānī. See Margoliouth, "Ibn al-Hītī's Arabic Chronicle," 438.

156. Yūsuf al-Baṣīr.

157. Lit., "were found."

158. *hikshah.*

159. Translated as the "Book of the Great Light," this probably refers to a Hebrew translation or, more likely, an epitome of al-Qirqisānī's *Kitāb al-anwār wal-marāqib* ("Book of Lights and Watchtowers"). The confusion often found in later Karaite texts of al-Qirqisānī and Yūsuf al-Baṣīr is evident here. 4670 A.M. corresponds to 910 C.E.; however, al-Qirqisānī states that he wrote his work in 937. (Some scholars

They transmitted it to Rav David ben Boaz ben Jehoshafat ben Josiah the Prince,[160] Rav Abu Ali,[161] Rav Amram and Rav Saadia bnei Rav Abraham ha-Basri, Rav Jacob ben Rav Joseph ben Rav Abraham ha-Basri,[162] and Rav Joseph ha-Ro'eh Rav Jacob ha-Qirqisani,[163] who wrote *Sefer Miṣvot Gadol* on all the details and grammar, [a] very fine [work].[164] He transmitted it to Rav Aaron Abu al-Faraj,[165] Rav Abraham ha-Varzalani ha-Bavli,[166] Rav Joseph ha-Bavli, Rav Zedakah ben Shomron ha-Bavli, Rav Abraham ben Ilan ha-Bavli,[167] Rav Ezra ben Bakhuyah,[168] and Rav Jacob ben Abraham ben G-L-M.[169] They transmitted it to Rav Jeshua ben ʿEli, who explained[170] all of the Torah, Prophets, and Writings, and made the *Sefer ha-Yashar* on all the miṣvot.[171] And to Rav Yefet ha-Levi, who

---

prefer the year 927.) On this date, see Margoliouth, "Ibn al-Hītī's Arabic Chronicle," 437, n. 1.

160. Probably of the late tenth or early eleventh century. Tobias ben Moses, *'Oṣar Neḥmad,* is in part based upon David's Torah commentary. See chapter 3, above. See also Gil, *History of Palestine,* 790–94. David appears in the *Ḥilluk,* 106. Cf. Nemoy, "Elijah ben Abraham and His Tract," 79, n. 63. David also is mentioned by Ibn al-Hītī. See Margoliouth, "Ibn al-Hītī's Arabic Chronicle," 437–38.

161. Possibly Yefet ben ʿElī ha-Levi. See ibid., 439.

162. I cannot identify these five names.

163. Again the confusion of names regarding al-Qirqisānī and Yūsuf al-Baṣīr.

164. If Yūsuf al-Baṣīr is intended, then this might indicate his Book of Precepts, *Kitāb al-istibṣār fil-farā'iḍ,* written in 1036/37. It is usually not designated by the title *Sefer Miṣvot Gadol,* which could be a second mistaken reference to al-Qirqisānī's *Kitāb al-anwār wal-marāqib.* See Yūsuf al-Baṣīr, *al-Kitāb al-Muḥtāwī de Yūsuf al-Basir.*

165. Abū al-Faraj Hārūn ibn al-Faraj, grammarian and exegete of the early eleventh century. Cf. Nemoy, "Elijah ben Abraham and His Tract," 81, n. 79.

166. Mentioned in Ibn al-Hītī. See Margoliouth, "Ibn al-Hītī's Arabic Chronicle," 441.

167. Mentioned in Ibn al-Hītī. See Margoliouth, "Ibn al-Hītī's Arabic Chronicle," 439. Perhaps confused with Judah ben ʿIlān ha-Tabarānī, indicated in the *Ḥilluk,* 106. Cf. Nemoy, "Elijah ben Abraham and His Tract," 81, n. 80.

168. I cannot identify this name. Bakhuya may correspond to the Arabic Baḥya.

169. Vocalization is unclear. Ibn al-Hītī mentions the Sheikh Abū Yaʿqūb ben Abraham ben Jils, who is perhaps identical with al-Baṣīr. Margoliouth, "Ibn al-Hītī's Arabic Chronicle," 439. A Jacob ben Abraham al-Jazzar is mentioned in some poetry, but he does not seem to have been a scholar. See Mann, *Texts and Studies, 2: Karaitica,* 212, 249. See *Texts and Studies,* 1:532, for a Jacob of Gh-L-A or J-L-A, an unknown location from a Kurdistani Jewish document.

170. *be'er.*

171. Yefet ben ʿElī ha-Levi, again. This is the Hebrew title of his Bible commentary, although he wrote in Arabic. See Poznanski, "Karaite Literary Opponents," 150ff.

> commented[172] on the Torah and made the *Sefer Miṣvot.*[173] And to Rav Israel ben Daniel,[174] Rav Abusurri, who explained the entire Torah,[175] Rav Bayzani ha-Bavli,[176] Rav Isaac ben Ali ben Rav Isaac,[177] and Rav Yashar ben Mansuri.[178] They transmitted it to our master Abu Said ben [text is corrupt][179] and our master Levi ben Rav Yefet ha-Levi, blessed be his memory.[180] They transmitted it to our master Hisdai ben Solomon the Prince[181] and our master Abu al-Faraj ben Hesed.[182] They transmitted it [fol. 8a] to our master Aaron ha-Hiti[183] and our master Yefet ben Ṣaʿir. They transmitted it to David ben Boaz ha-Damishi[184] and Rabbi Boaz ben Solomon the Prince ben David ben Rav Hisdai the Prince, peace be upon him.[185]

The text concludes with an epilogue, the last sentence of which appears to have been written by Moses Bashyachi. Note the explicit polemical intent that is indicated.

172. *peresh.*

173. Levi ben Yefet ha-Levi, who did write a *Sefer Miṣvot.* See ibid., 172ff.

174. Wrote a Book of Precepts in 1062, according to Firkovich. Quoted by Elijah Bashyachi. See Poznanski, "Karaite Literary Opponents," 190f.

175. Abu al-Surrī, who is Sahl ben Maṣliaḥ. See ibid., 160ff.

176. I cannot identify this name.

177. ʿAbū ʿAnān Isḥāq ben ʿAlī ben Isḥāq. See ibid., 146; and Ibn al-Hītī. See Margoliouth, "Ibn al-Hītī's Arabic Chronicle," 435, 439.

178. Perhaps Yashar ben Ḥesed, who is Sahl ibn Faḍl al-Tustarī. See Poznanski, "Karaite Literary Opponents," 183f.

179. Probably not Levi ben Yefet ha-Levi, also known as Abū Saʿīd Levi, the teacher of Yeshua ben Yehudah, but Abū Saʿīd David ben Boaz. See note 160, above.

180. Probably Levi ben Yefet ha-Levi. Ibn al-Hītī mentions that Jeshua ben Judah was his student. See Margoliouth, "Ibn al-Hītī's Arabic Chronicle," 440.

181. Hezekiah ben Solomon ben David ben Boaz, Karaite *nasi* of the eleventh century. See Mann, *Texts and Studies,* 2: *Karaitica,* 135–37. Mentioned in the *Ḥilluk,* 106, and identified by Nemoy, "Elijah ben Abraham and His Tract," 79, n. 65.

182. Jeshua ben Judah, who is Abū al-Faraj Furqān ibn ʾAsad, early eleventh century.

183. Perhaps a predecessor of Ibn al-Hītī, who is David ben Saʿadʾel ibn al-Hītī. Cf. Poznanski, "Karaite Literary Opponents," 212.

184. David ben Ḥisdai, Karaite *nasi* in the early twelfth century. The appellation ha-Damishi could mean "the Damascene" since one branch of the Karaite princely family settled there because they were no longer able to reside in Crusader Palestine. Or, it is an orthographic corruption of the Arabic *al-rayyis* (head, or prince). See Mann, *Texts and Studies,* 2: *Karaitica,* 138–40.

185. On the Karaite nasi Solomon ben David ben Ḥisdai, see ibid., 140–42. After Solomon, it is difficult to ascertain the family lines. Ibid., 142ff.

> To this point God has helped us, and we have found the true *ha*ʿ*takah*, which is the splendid chain[186] of the true faith which was transmitted from man to man since the time of our master Moses, peace be upon him. It is the true support which gouges the eyes of those who say that the faith of the Karaites is new. For this [reason] I was compelled to make clear the truth from the midst of books of the sages written in their hands, written close to three hundred years [ago], which I found [in the possession of][187] our master Samuel the Prince, may his memory grow, ben (ben) Rav our master Solomon the Prince,[188] may he rest in Eden.

With this text, the Karaites transformed rabbinic historical assumptions in order to serve their own purposes. The artificiality of the text is revealed in the obvious borrowing of biblical names to use in the priestly line that follows the transmission adapted from Mishnah Avot, chapter 1. The last section represents an effort at constructing a linear scheme for transmission among the Karaites themselves, using known names, but its inconsistencies and misidentifications indicate its contrived nature. In fact, the artificial character of the text reflects the lack of historical tradition available to its author, and, perhaps more importantly, that the idea itself is intrinsically alien to Karaite thought. Nonetheless, this ideological device became integral to most later Karaite expressions of history and tradition. Its existence represents enough of a historical expression to accompany Karaite halakhic theories of tradition.

When the manuscript fragments from the Russian National Library are taken into account, conclusions in regard to the text's origins are only slightly modified. They indicate that there was an Arabic version of the chain, but its origin remains unknown. The fragments use Muslim *sharī*ʿ*ah* terminology, which most likely indicates an Arabic-speaking environment rather than a Greek or Turkish one.[189] One fragment even uses the "rabbinic verb" *kibbel.*[190] There are considerable minor variants in the prosopographic elements of the chain, but the more significant textual variations suggest an earlier recension of the material than the versions of P[1], P[2], and *Matteh ʾElohim.* For example, the line of tradents in its beginnings follows Avot, chapter 1, closely without bifurcating into two transmissional lineages in order to delineate proto-Rabbanite and proto-Karaite lines.[191] The pairs *(zugot)* of Avot are not mobilized

186. *shalshelet atekat.*

187. *maṣati ʾotam be-mizeihem le-yad.*

188. Cairene *nasi* and contemporary of Moses Bashyachi, who died in 1572.

189. Five of the six Firkovich fragments are in Judeo-Arabic and use such terms as *madhhab* for the equivalent of "school of law," in reference to a distinct Karaite law, and *sharī*ʿ*ah* for the equivalent of halakhah.

190. JTS MS ENA 1275, 2a.

191. RNL Evr. I,741; RNL Evr.-Arab. I,1242; and RNL Evr.-Arab. I,2994.1.

in order to create an archaic Karaite past but are preserved in their "rabbinic form." However, there is no interweaving of a priestly line of transmission into the chain after the destruction of the Temple.[192]

Most importantly, Halevi and the *Kuzari* are cited explicitly in two fragments, suggesting possible textual dependence on Elijah Bashyachi (d. 1490), who named Judah Halevi as a source for identifying Simeon ben Shetah as the founder of the Rabbanites.[193] However, in the fragmentary chains of tradition, the Simeon ben Shetah-Judah ben Tabbai narrative can be located in the beginning of the narrative and/or in the section on Anan, and not where one might expect it to be in the chronology of the transmissional scheme.[194]

The fragments point to the existence of an Arabic version of the Karaite chain of tradition in which Halevi is used but not mentioned, and Avot is followed closely. Moses Bashyachi may have borrowed and supplemented it for his chain of tradition in *Matteh 'Elohim.* Although the evidence remains inconclusive, the manuscript fragments offer tenuous additional support for Islamicate origins of the Karaite *haʿtakah ha-mishtalshelet.* Alternatively, they also suggest the influence of Elijah Bashyachi, unless Bashyachi knew these texts but chose not to use a Karaite chain of tradition. That is to say, the Karaite chain of tradition may indeed come from Arabic-speaking Karaites, but its date of origin remains unknown.

192. Except in JTS MS ENA 1275, which is a late recension and follows Moses Bashyachi's *Matteh 'Elohim.* However, see RNL Evr. I,741. Many priestly and prophetic names are absent in RNL Evr.-Arab. I,2994.1.

193. RNL Evr.-Arab. I,2994.1. On Elijah Bashyachi's historical thought, see chapter 5, below. JTS MS ENA 1275 can also be cited here, but it seems to follow Moses Bashyachi's *Matteh 'Elohim* since it distinguishes between the Judah-Shemaiah-Shammai and Simeon-Abtalion-Hillel lines and includes lines of priestly transmission after the destruction of the Temple.

194. RNL Evr.-Arab. I,2994.1

~5

Mobilizing the Past: Later Byzantino-Turkish Karaism, Fifteenth and Sixteenth Centuries

This era of Byzantino-Turkish Karaism was preceded by a period of severe disruption in the thirteenth century, followed by recovery and a new florescence among fifteenth-century scholars. The Karaite authors of this period remain of central importance to later Karaism, having especially shaped the character of the movement in its newer environments in the Crimea, Poland, and Lithuania. In this period, various strands of Karaite historical expression were brought together in an effort toward creating a unified conception of Jewish history that both explained the schism that separated Karaite believers of the truth from the misguided Rabbanites and posited a continuity with the past incorporating elements drawn from biblical, rabbinic, and Karaite history. In this period, the increasing use of Rabbanite literary sources for halakhic purposes is mirrored in the Rabbanization of Karaite historical expression.

Prelude to Reflorescence: Thirteenth through Fifteenth Centuries

The disruption of the thirteenth century, a result of the Crusader conquest of Constantinople in 1204, completely dislocated Byzantine society. Political life survived in a series of Greek successor states, some of which exhibited strong anti-Jewish proclivities.[1] On the other hand, the Palaeologan state that would

1. For a summary of these events in connection to the Jews, see Steven B. Bowman, *The Jews of Byzantium, 1204–1453,* 9–48. For general history of these centuries, see George Ostrogorsky, *History of the Byzantine State,* 418–572. See also J. W. Barker, *Manuel II Palaeologus, 1391–1425: A Study in Late Byzantine Statesmanship;* and Deno Geanakoplos, "Byzantium and the Crusades, 1261–1354," and idem, "Byzantium and the Crusades, 1354–1453," including a useful bibliography.

eventually supersede the others and expel the Latins adopted a fairly pro-Jewish policy, as a counterweight to the influence of the church and in opposition to its neighbors.[2] Under these conditions, the Karaites were recognized by the Greek authorities, establishing a precedent for later Turkish recognition.[3] Unfortunately, there is no evidence for Karaite scholarship in this period, with the exception of a bill of sale in 1288 for a philosophical work sold to an otherwise unknown Karaite.[4] It should be noted that the work, *Midrash ha-Ḥokhmah,* is an encyclopedic scientific treatise written in the 1240s by a Rabbanite.[5] The Karaite purchaser displays interest in current intellectual trends and, as a Karaite, was not cut off from contact with the general Jewish literary milieu.

The reemergence of Karaite scholarship toward the end of the thirteenth century is associated with Aaron ben Joseph, whose known work indicates that, compared with the earlier period, there was increased accommodation and adaptation to rabbinic thought.[6] A century earlier, Judah Hadassi's *Eshkol ha-Kofer* summarized, in part, most of classical Karaite thought from the Islamicate and early Byzantine period, whereas Aaron's philosophy and exegetical methods show a great deal of borrowing from Rabbanites, including Maimonides. This transformation represented in Aaron's approach was characterized by the adoption of some Aristotelian philosophical propositions to the abandonment of kalamic thinking, which had dominated earlier Karaite philosophy.[7] In addition, Aaron is credited with arranging the Karaite liturgy,

2. Bowman, *Jews of Byzantium,* 19. By way of comparison, see Bernard S. Bachrach, *Early Medieval Jewish Policy in Western Europe,* for an analysis of medieval Jewish policies and their role in foreign affairs in an earlier period.

3. Ibid., 108–9.

4. Ibid., 139–40, with the text of the bill itself translated (no. 26*) on pages 232–33.

5. On this work and its author, see Colette Sirat, "Judah b. Solomon ha-Cohen, philosophe, astronome et peut-être kabbaliste de la première moitié du XIIIe siècle."

6. Little is known about Aaron ben Joseph, although he supposedly visited the Crimea, perhaps even originating there. His Bible commentaries were published in Gozlow (1834–35) under the titles *Sefer ha-Mivḥar* (on the Torah, written in 1292–93) and *Mivḥar Yesharim* (on Joshua through Isaiah 59, which represents the extant text available to Abraham Firkovich, the publisher). See Poznanski, "Karaite Literary Opponents," 206–8, and the older treatment in Julius Fürst, *Geschichte des Karäerthums,* 238–50, which summarizes much of what is known of Aaron.

7. This is discussed by Daniel J. Lasker in "Aaron ben Joseph and the Transformation of Karaite Thought." Lasker posits a more revolutionary turn by Karaites toward rabbinic philosophy in this period than is presented in this dissertation. I prefer to understand the foundations of "Rabbanization" in Karaism to have been established earlier through the increased use of rabbinic texts and the emergence of *haʿtakah.* The deeper changes exemplified by Aaron ben Joseph and those who

which included the use of rabbinic *piyyutim.*[8] In regard to law, Aaron was better versed in rabbinic halakhah than any previous Karaite, and he suggested a reevaluation of the past that permitted a closer examination of rabbinic literature. Thus he regarded the rabbinic tradition as *Jewish* tradition, worthy of halakhic use as long as it did not conflict with primary Karaite principles.[9] In this way, Aaron is more explicit than Yefet ben ʿEli ha-Levi in appropriating rabbinic terms and halakhic sources. In fact, in a significant break with a central Karaite tenet, he authorized observance according to the Rabbanite calendar, thus obviating direct springtime observation of the fields in Palestine in order to determine intercalation.[10] Aaron, however, does not directly address historiographical issues or make explicit historical claims.

The other significant Karaite author of this period is Aaron ben Elijah (d. 1369), who carries the appellation "the Nicomedian," indicating his provenance or place of domicile, but is referred to by the Karaites as Aaron the Younger, to distinguish him from the earlier Aaron.[11] This Aaron is one of the most important of Karaite thinkers. His three major works form a complete presentation of Karaite thought: the philosophical work *ʿEṣ Ḥayyim* (1346); his code of Karaite law, *Gan ʿEden* (1354); and the Torah commentary *Keter Torah* (1362).[12] In reaction to the Rabbanization of Aaron the Elder, Daniel J.

---

follow are the ultimate implications of principles that were accepted earlier. In another article, Lasker casts his net more widely, demonstrating the significant impact of Maimonides on later Karaism in general. See Daniel J. Lasker, "Maimonides' Influence on Karaite Theories of Prophecy and Law," 99–115. See also Daniel Frank, "Ibn Ezra and the Karaite Exegetes Aaron ben Joseph and Aaron ben Elijah," 99–107.

8. Among the Rabbanite poets whose works appear in the Karaite prayer book are Solomon Ibn Gabirol, Judah Halevi, and Abraham Ibn Ezra. Aaron also composed some verse of his own. See Bowman, *Jews of Byzantium,* 141. The Karaite prayer book is *Siddur Tefillot ke-Minhag ha-Karaʾim* (Ramlah, Israel: ʿAdat ha-Yehudim ha-Karaʾim be-Yisrael, 1971), 4 vols.

9. See the conclusion to part 1, above, note 97. See also, Ankori, *Karaites in Byzantium,* 232, n. 53, also cited in Bowman, *Jews of Byzantium,* 140.

10. He states that the rabbinic calculations are "correct." Ibid., 141. The text (*Mivḥar,* Exodus 15b) is excerpted and translated by Bowman, *Jews of Byzantium,* no. 28, 233.

11. Like Aaron the Elder, little is known about Aaron ben Elijah. See Poznanski, "Karaite Literary Opponents," 209–11.

12. *ʿEṣ Ḥayyim* (edited by Delitzsch and Steinschneider, Leipzig, 1841; and Gozlow, 1847, with a commentary by Simhah Isaac Lutzki); *Gan ʿEden* (Gozlow, 1866, reprinted Israel, 1972); and *Keter Torah* (Gozlow, 1866–67, reprinted Ramlah, Israel, 1972). There is also an English translation and introduction to chapters 1–78 of *ʿEṣ Ḥayyim* by Morris Charner, *The Tree of Life by Aaron ben Elijah of Nicomedia.* One is tempted to seek comparisons with contemporary Byzantine scholarship in this period, a topic worthy of closer examination. Aaron's *Gan ʿEden* is the first

Lasker states, "Aaron ben Elijah's literary project was intended to restore Karaite faith in the accomplishments and intellectual honesty of the great Karaite scholars of the earlier era, to the extent that their views were still tenable."[13] Fully aware of the inroads that rabbinic thought and literature had made within the Karaite milieu, Aaron nonetheless continued the trend of interlinear reading of rabbinic texts, including quotations from contemporaries,[14] and in his philosophy he tried to find a balance between the *kalām* and Aristotelianism.[15] Like his namesake, this Aaron does not address historiographical concerns explicitly. In contrast however, aspects of his thinking become influential in later Karaite historical formulations.[16]

The Karaite community under Greek suzerainty declined seriously in the latter half of the fourteenth century. Plague depopulated the region, and the conquests of the Turks brought whole sectors of the Jewish population under their rule. The vast cultural movement that was transforming lands and populations in Anatolia and southeastern Europe from Christianity to Islam also had implications for the Karaites.[17] Aaron the Younger was the last personality of Byzantine Karaism, perhaps having left Nicomedia before the Ottoman conquest in 1337 in order to reside in Constantinople.[18] Not long afterward, in 1361, the Turks conquered Adrianople and established their European capital there. Within a generation, the Karaite community there began to prosper, and scholarship developed.[19] Nonetheless, the dislocation of the

---

code of Karaite halakhah, not merely a *sefer miṣvot,* and is roughly contemporaneous with the height of Byzantine legal codification, marked by the *Syntagma* of Matthew Blasteres, completed in 1335. See Bowman, *Jews of Byzantium,* 30–31, and translated excerpts of Blasteres, 264–68, doc. no. 57. See also Alexander Kazhdan, *Oxford Dictionary of Byzantium,* 1:295, s.v. "Blasteres, Matthew."

13. Lasker, "Aaron ben Joseph and the Transformation of Karaite Thought," 121.

14. In *Keter Torah,* Aaron quotes many rabbinic sources: Judah Hayyūj, Abū Walīd ibn Janāḥ, Moses Ibn Gikatilla, Rashi, Abraham Ibn Ezra, Maimonides, Nahmanides, David Kimḥi, Judah ben Solomon ibn Matqa of Toledo, and Shemaryah Ikriti, a contemporary of Aaron's. For specific references, see Poznanski, "Karaite Literary Opponents," 211, n. 1.

15. See Lasker, "Nature and Science According to Aaron ben Elijah, the Karaite"; and idem, "Maimonides' Influence on Karaite Theories," passim. For a somewhat outdated view, see the chapter on Aaron in Husik, *History of Medieval Jewish Philosophy,* 362–87.

16. See chapter 6, below.

17. This is the subject of the important study by Speros Vryonis Jr., *The Decline of Medieval Hellenism in Asia Minor and the Process of Islamization from the Eleventh through the Fifteenth Century,* s.v. "Jew" and "Jewish" in the index.

18. Suggested by Bowman in *Jews of Byzantium,* 142, based upon the chronological speculation of Ankori in *Karaites in Byzantium,* 133–34, n. 176.

19. The Karaite school at Adrianople may have preceded the Ottoman conquest. See Abraham Danon, "The Karaites in European Turkey," 296–98. For a history of

previous decades left its mark, to the extent that Karaite texts and traditions were lost to the community. Hadassi's *'Eshkol ha-Kofer* was completely unknown until it was revived in the late fifteenth century.[20] A witness as early as Aaron ben Joseph decries the poor quality of Karaite Hebrew texts, indicating that of those that existed, the Hebrew style was almost impenetrable.[21] It would seem that Turkish Karaism was cut off to a great extent from its literary heritage, a condition that persevered for at least a century, even after the community reestablished itself in Constantinople following the city's conquest by the Turks in 1453.[22]

One of the reactions to the sorry state of Karaite intellectual affairs is that Karaite students increasingly studied with Rabbanite teachers.[23] The fact that Rabbanite teachers would accept students from among those whom they considered sectarian adversaries suggests that Karaism was no longer vying for the hearts and minds of world Jewry. Certainly, the depressed state of the Karaite community presented a picture of a struggling minority within a minority. It no longer represented a threat to Rabbanism as it once had, and,

---

the Jews in the early Ottoman Empire, see Salomon Rosanes, *Divre Yeme Yisra'el be-Togarmah* (History of the Jews in Turkey), vol. 1, which covers the years 1300 to 1520. See also Mark A. Epstein, *The Ottoman Jewish Communities and Their Role in the Fifteenth and Sixteenth Centuries;* idem, "The Leadership of the Ottoman Jews in the Fifteenth and Sixteenth Centuries"; Joseph Hacker, "Ottoman Policy toward Jews and Jewish Attitudes toward the Ottomans during the Fifteenth Century"; and idem, "The Intellectual Activity of the Jews of the Ottoman Empire during the Sixteenth and Seventeenth Centuries." There is a considerable amount of published material on the Jews of the Ottoman Empire. The more recent contribution by Stanford J. Shaw, *The Jews of the Ottoman Empire and Turkish Republic,* is considered by some scholars to be overly apologetic in terms of Turkish nationalist sensibilities.

20. The text was reintroduced into Karaite circles by Shabbetai ben Elijah Pravado in 1482. See Bowman, *Jews of Byzantium,* 143, and the translated text, no. 148, 323–24.

21. Cited by Lasker in "Aaron ben Joseph and the Transformation of Karaite Thought," 125; and idem, "Maimonides' Influence on Karaite Theories," 100, n. 2.

22. Shabbetai Pravado's text (see n. 20, above) begins: "Because of this, our exile has been lengthened due to our sins and Torah has been forgotten because there is no longer any prophet and Torah has been lost to the *kohen*—all Israelites as is known are called *kohanim.* And we, the Assembly of the Karaites (*'adat ha-Kara'im*), have become few in number, and the books which lit up the eyes of our brethren have disappeared from among us."

23. Shabbetai's text (ibid.) continues: "We are taught by the Rabbanites among whom we live in Constantinople; we are accustomed to their books which we hear continuously and their commentaries. . . . Some agree with them completely, and hesitantly say that they are correct in saying that our sect broke away from them because of our great evil and lack of understanding in the interpretation of the Torah."

accordingly, Karaite students might be tolerated or even drawn into the fold of rabbinic Judaism.

Greater Jewish cultural movements of the day also contributed to the increased interaction, if not participation, of Karaites within the larger Jewish community. Rabbinic Judaism in Constantinople in the tenth through the fourteenth century was, by and large, indigenous, identifying itself by the name Romaniote.[24] These Jews spoke Greek, perhaps claiming an ancestry that extended into classical antiquity. Their intellectual world in the Middle Ages evidenced more interest in Bible commentary and aggadah than in talmudic studies. In addition, much of their halakhah was based upon Palestinian models, rather than Babylonian ones, and their liturgy had many distinct features.[25] However, the homogeneity of Romaniote rabbinic Jewish culture was challenged by the influx of Sephardic Jews at the end of the fourteenth century, following the riots and massacres in Spain in 1391 and 1415. The immigrant Sephardic community, which continued to receive newcomers through the fifteenth century, brought its own particular talmudic and philosophical tradition, which at first influenced and later eventually dominated the Romaniotes and other Jewries of North Africa and many parts of the Ottoman Empire.[26] The encounter with Sephardic Jews generated increased diversity in Jewish social settings. We have already framed earlier Karaite antagonism to the Mishawites in terms of positioning the Karaite community in a more favorable relationship to rabbinic Judaism, but now the Karaites found themselves in an environment that permitted defining Karaism more easily as one type of Judaism among many.

The forced baptisms of fourteenth- and fifteenth-century Spain also created a class of ethnic Jews who had little or no Jewish background—who in fact would have had exposure to the Bible through Spanish Christianity and who carried with them cultural and religious assumptions of a Christian rather than Jewish character.[27] These religious refugees often sought out their

24. On Romaniote Jewry, see Starr, *Jews of the Byzantine Empire;* idem, *Romania: The Jewries of the Levant after the Fourth Crusade;* Rosanes, *Divre Yeme Yisra'el bi-Togarmah,* passim, and esp. 133–44; and the many works of Abraham Galante published in Istanbul in the 1930s and 1940s, esp. *Les Juifs de Constantinople sous Byzance.*

25. On the Romaniote liturgy, see Daniel Goldschmidt, "On the *Maḥzor Romania,*" 205–36.

26. See Avigdor Levy, *The Sephardim in the Ottoman Empire,* 1–70.

27. See José Faur, *In the Shadow of History, Jews and* Conversos *at the Dawn of Modernity.* Some scholars use the term *Marrano theology* to characterize a religious outlook bearing Christian theological assumptions, perhaps philosophized or imbued with elements of skepticism or humanism. For example, see Richard H. Popkin, "The Marrano Theology of Isaac La Peyrère." See also Yirmiyahu Yovel, *Spinoza and Other Heretics: The Marrano of Reason* and its sequel *Spinoza and Other Heretics: The Adventures of Immanence.*

Jewish roots after emigrating from Spain. Rabbinic consensus recognized the need to bring these marginal Jews into the fold of Judaism through education and the inculcation of rabbinic culture.[28] Could the Karaites be considered in a different light? Were they not, like their Christianized and "philosophized" Spanish brethren, simply ignorant and in need of correct instruction? The rabbinic educators in this multicultural environment, which also included

---

The connection in this period between Karaites and Sephardic Jews is a topic that requires closer examination. Sephardim, whose "Marrano" outlook might lead them to consider rabbinic Judaism as a kind of deviation from biblical religion, would have found Karaism attractive. The Karaites in Egypt have preserved a text that describes the arrival of some "European Jews" in Cairo in 1465. The practices of these Jews, based upon the Bible, without support from rabbinic tradition, seemed more in accordance with Karaism. A public controversy arose with the rabbinic establishment over the affiliation of these newcomers so that the matter ended up in the hands of the Muslim religious authorities, whose rulings are recorded in the text. The subsequent involvement of Egyptian governmental authorities led to arrests and confiscations, and in the end the Karaites enjoyed a victory over their Rabbanite adversaries. The Europeans were permitted to "convert" to Karaism without hindrance from the rabbinic authorities. See William M. Brinner, "A Fifteenth-century Karaite-Rabbanite Dispute in Cairo." The text is translated by Hartwig Hirschfeld in "A Karaite Conversion Story," from British Library MS Or. 2538, fols. 73–83. Other copies are found in the Jewish Theological Seminary of America in New York under the title *Sippur ʿAravi* (An Arabic story), Mic. 3328; and in the Blumenthal Rare Book and Manuscript Library of the Judah L. Magnes Museum in Berkeley, California, in an uncataloged manuscript in the Karaite collection.

In another incident, in eighteenth-century Amsterdam, members of the Spanish-Portuguese community were excommunicated for being "Karaites." These heterodox Sephardim had been exposed to the idea of Karaism by way of the literature of Christian Hebraism, rather than through contact with real Karaites. The problem is analyzed by Yosef Kaplan in "The 'Karaites' of Amsterdam in the Early Eighteenth Century: An Unknown Chapter in the Fermentation of Ideas in the Sephardic Community"; revised and published in English as " 'Karaites' in Early Eighteenth-century Amsterdam." On the interface between Christian Hebraism and Karaism in the early modern period, see chapter 6, below.

Fifteenth-century Adrianople became a center for Sephardic immigration, suggesting avenues for future scholarly inquiry regarding Karaite-Sephardic interaction in that period. In regard to fifteenth- and sixteenth-century Constantinople, Ankori remarks on Elijah Bashyachi's predilection toward matters Sephardic found throughout his code of law, *ʾAdderet ʾEliyahu,* including Spanish cantillation of the Torah. See *Karaites in Byzantium,* 196, n. 100. Ankori also mentions Caleb Afendopolo's contact with Sephardim, which is reported in Afendopolo's *Patshegen Ketav ha-Dat,* 138–39, cited by Ankori from the excerpts in Abraham Danon, "Documents Relating to the History of the Karaite of European Turkey," 172–73.

28. An example can be found in the career of the Rabbanite Jacob Sasportas (d. 1698), whose anti-Sabbatean career was built upon the foundation of anti-Marrano

Ashkenazi and Italian Jews, among others,[29] embraced a religious-intellectual rationale that supported such teaching and, at the same time, found means for their own financial support through the diverse student population to which they catered.[30]

The outstanding Rabbanite scholar of late-fifteenth-century Constantinople was Mordecai Comtino (or Komatiano).[31] Although Comtino's exegetical work is thoroughly and specifically anti-Karaite in orientation,[32] he numbered among his students many important Karaites, including Elijah Bashyachi, Judah Gibbor, Caleb Afendopolo, Judah Maruli, and Joseph Revitzi, whom Comtino held in some esteem.[33] Although it was normal for Karaites to study under Rabbanite teachers in Constantinople in this period, the situation was not without detractors who strongly opposed imparting rabbinic teaching to Karaite pupils. Among the leaders of the opposition was Moses Capuzato ha-Yevani, whose anti-Karaite polemics were answered by Bashyachi, Afendopolo, and even the Rabbanite Comtino.[34] The obstructionists met in the synagogue and declared those who taught the Karaites (who taught them even secular sciences) to be excommunicated. Moses Capsali, the leader

---

activism. See Elisheva Carlebach, *The Pursuit of Heresy: Rabbi Moses Hagiz and the Sabbatian Controversies,* 5f. On Hagiz's philosophy regarding the Marranos, see ibid., 22–23.

29. See Rosanes, *Divre Yeme Yisra'el bi-Togarmah,* where appendices are found on the Jewish communities of the Romaniotes, France, Hungary, Italy, the Ashkenazi, the Moldau–Wallachia, the lands of Islam, Navarre and Provence, North Africa, Spain, and Portugal. See also S. Spitzer, "The Ashkenazim in the Ottoman Empire from the Middle of the Fifteenth Century until the Middle of the Sixteenth Century"; and L. Bornstein, "The Ashkenazim in the Ottoman Empire in the Sixteenth and Seventeenth Centuries."

30. Karaite pupils were sometimes required to take an oath promising not to defame rabbinic teachers. This is mentioned in a seventeenth-century exposition of the chain of tradition by the Rabbanite David Conforte, *Kore ha-Dorot,* 31a–b: "And they used to teach the Oral Law to the Karaites, by receiving [promise] from them that they would not violate the sacred holidays of God, and they would not make light of the sages, whether living or dead, peace be upon them." The translation is mine. The text is cited by Bowman in *Jews of Byzantium,* 143, n. 50.

31. This is the Greek form. On this name, see Bowman, 149, n. 68.

32. See Jean-Christophe Attias, *Le commentaire biblique: Mordekhai Komtino ou l'herméneutique du dialogue.*

33. Danon, "Karaites in European Turkey," 311. See also Jean-Christophe Attias, "Intellectual Leadership: Rabbanite-Karaite Relations in Constantinople as Seen through the Works and Activity of Mordekhai Comtino in the Fifteenth Century." On Bashyachi and Afendopolo's historical expression, see below, this chapter.

34. See Bowman, *Jews of Byzantium,* 149–50. The appellation *ha-Yevani* means "the Greek."

of the Romaniotes, issued a formal ban.[35] A meeting of less-intolerant Rabbanites, including the teachers whose livelihood was threatened, was arranged to annul the excommunication, but it was broken up by armed thugs acting in support of the ban. Teaching continued, and the issue was resolved by a responsum of Elijah Mizraḥi, whose more tolerant position was based upon Hai Gaon and Maimonides. He maintained that, contrary to banning such teaching, it was obligatory to impart the rabbinic tradition to Karaites in hopes of changing their ways.[36] The entire episode is recounted by Joseph ben Moses Beghi, a contemporary Karaite.[37]

Increased contact and interaction between the Rabbanite and Karaite communities certainly fueled the reaction of the obstructionists. Economic factors were contributory. Wealthier Karaites lent money to the Rabbanite community at the usual usurious rates of the era. They also were known to engage poorer Rabbanites as servants, whose religious orthodoxy might be compromised in such a situation.[38] The course of Karaite-Rabbanite social relations can be gauged against a situation about which it was recorded that in the thirteenth century Rabbanite men would leave the Sabbath services early in order to go to the Karaite prayers to hear sermons from the renowned scholars of that community, so that disputation over the correct interpretation of the text became interminable. The situation led to adjustments in the annual reading of the Torah, whereby the Karaites began the cycle in the month of Nisan, while the Rabbanites maintained their long-standing tradition of beginning in Tishre.[39] By the fifteenth century, the changes being promulgated in Karaite halakhah brought about a reinstitution of the Tishre beginning for the Torah cycle, among other significant, if not revolutionary, changes.

35. See Meir Benayahu, *Rabbi Eliyahu Kapsali of Candia,* 42–45 [Heb.].

36. For a summary of the affair, see Danon, "Karaites in European Turkey," 318–22. See also A. Ovadiah, "Rabbi Eliyahu Mizraḥi." The responsa of Mizraḥi are published in *Sefer She'elot u-Teshuvot R. Eliyahu Mizraḥi;* and *Sefer Mayyim Amukim* (Book of deep waters). The issue is addressed in responsum number 57. Interestingly, responsum number 58 intimates approval of Rabbanite-Karaite intermarriage. Mainstream rabbinic interpreters have constructed apologetic explanations for Mizraḥi's apparent pro-Karaite attitudes, denying that he ever approved of such marriages. For an apology in a modern popular context, see Rabbi Hersh Goldwurm, ed., *The Early Acharonim,* 50–51. Mizraḥi eventually succeeded Capsali as head of Constantinopolitan Jewry.

37. *'Iggeret Kiryah Ne'emanah* (Letter of the faithful city), which exists in a unique manuscript, MS Warner no. 30/2 in the Bibliotheek der Rijksuniversiteit Leiden, fols. 190a–203b. Excerpts and an introduction are published in Mann, *Texts and Studies,* 2: *Karaitica,* 294–315.

38. See ibid., 295; and Danon, "Karaites in European Turkey," 319, esp. n. 149.

39. In Caleb Afendopolo, *Patshegen Ketav ha-Dat,* 13–14, excerpted in part in Danon, "Documents," 168–69. The text is translated in Bowman, *Jews of Byzantium,* 324–25, doc. no. 149.

These halakhic changes, to a great extent, represent a more complete accommodation to rabbinic tradition and method than before. Earlier Karaite textuality can be characterized in a rabbinic context, perhaps in terms of both polemic as well as adaptation. In a quantum leap, elements of the Adrianople Karaite community of the early fifteenth century adopted halakhic reforms that were directly correspondent to rabbinic halakhah. Under the leadership of Menaḥem ben Joseph Bashyachi, the initial elements of these reforms were imparted to students who came to Adrianople from Constantinople (which was still in the hands of the last of the Byzantines). Bashyachi's reforms are marked by a halakhic decree *(takkanah)* of 1440, wherein he reversed the long-standing Karaite prohibition against Sabbath candles lit before sundown and used to usher in the Sabbath on Friday evening.[40] This radical reinterpretation of halakhah was opposed by conservatives in the Karaite community, but eventually became the norm for Ottoman Karaites, as well as those in Poland, Lithuania, and the Crimea.[41] The new ruling not only contradicted a scripturalist halakhic interpretation of the prohibition against using fire on the Sabbath but represents a fundamental psychological departure from the ascetic, mournful character of early Karaism, which tended to oppose the rabbinic view of the Sabbath as a time for joy.[42]

In addition to the annual Torah reading cycle and the use of Sabbath candles, calendar reform was an area of significant movement toward rabbinic practice.[43] Other areas of innovation, some of which succeeded while others

40. See Ankori, "House of Bashyachi and Its Reforms," an introduction to the recent Karaite edition of Elijah Bashyachi's *'Adderet 'Eliyahu.* On Sabbath candles, see 2f. See also idem, "Elijah Bashyachi."

41. Conservative elements opposed the reforms for centuries. The Karaites were divided into the "friends of light" and the "enemies of light" in regard to the Sabbath candle controversy. The aforementioned rehabilitation of Hadassi's *Eshkol ha-Kofer* was the result of the "orthodox" party seeking support for its opposition to reform. See also Danon, "Karaites in European Turkey," 312, where Danon states that Crimean and Russian Karaites were resistant to the reforms.

42. See Elijah Bashyachi, *'Adderet 'Eliyahu,* 52d, in a section (xvi) that begins: "Concerning matters that are forbidden based upon *ha'takah.*" The historical-traditional basis of the Bashyachi reforms are supported by *ha'takah.* See the next section, xvii, 53a–c, for Bashyachi's ruling on Sabbath candles. Cf. Aaron ben Elijah, *Gan 'Eden,* 22–36, for an earlier conservative view.

43. The Karaites had steadfastly opposed the Rabbanite precalculated calendar, but now abandoned direct observation of the fields *(aviv)* in Palestine in the spring in order to declare an intercalary year. Under the Bashyachis, Karaites outside the land of Israel could use a precalculated calendar. See Bashyachi, *'Adderet 'Eliyahu,* 39a–b, translated in Bowman, *Jews of Byzantium,* 321–22, doc. no. 147. The Karaite accommodation to the rabbinic calendar is corroborated by the fact that few instances of holidays being celebrated by the two communities on different days are recorded in this period. See ibid., 145–46, with reference to some of the translated documents.

did not, include the eating of meat adjacent to the sciatic nerve,[44] the introduction of Sephardic Rabbanite Torah cantillation, inclusion of rabbinic liturgical elements in fixing the Karaite prayers, introduction of fringes on the prayer shawl in accordance with Rabbanite models, and increased use of blessings in conformity with rabbinic formulations.[45] It should also be noted that the Karaites of this period continued to abandon the long-obsolete philosophy of the *kalām* in favor of Aristotelian formulations, perhaps under the influence of Maimonides' writings.[46]

The fifteenth and sixteenth centuries witnessed a consolidation of the Anatolian and Balkan Karaite communities within the burgeoning Ottoman Empire. At the same time, Karaism no longer posed a fundamental threat to Rabbanism, having lost some of the attractiveness to wide audiences that it had exhibited in the Islamic period. The Karaites remained a small minority, but were able to move toward a kind of social rapprochement with the majority Rabbanites. These conditions contributed to the Rabbanization that had already characterized much of Karaite textuality and halakhah from the eleventh century onward. Paradoxically, these conditions also led to a kind of Karaite renaissance, wherein scholars wrote important new works of biblical commentary, halakhah, and philosophy, as well as secular science. The concurrent trends of intellectual florescence and Rabbanization resulted from the tolerant domestic policies of the Ottomans, whose Islamic culture seemed to influence the Karaites as little as did the moribund Byzantine culture.[47] Karaism is best understood in this period in the context of engagement within the

---

The calendrical reform also indicates a Karaite acknowledgment of the precision of astronomical calculation, a field of science that was quite popular among Jewish scholars of the day, both Rabbanite and Karaite. The penetration of secular science into the Karaite milieu of the day is a topic worthy of further investigation. Caleb Afendopolo was known as an astronomer. See ibid., 152. See also Poznanski, "Karaite Literary Opponents," 213. On Afendopolo's historical ideas, see this chapter, below.

44. Elijah Bashyachi disputed with Moses Capsali over this problem. See Bashyachi's *ʾIggeret Gid ha-Nasheh* (Epistle concerning the sciatic nerve) in the unpaginated introduction to the Gozlow, 1835, edition of *ʾAdderet ʾEliyahu.* Later, Elijah Mizraḥi commented on the problem at the beginning of his supercommentary on Rashi, *Sefer ha-Mizraḥi.* See also Danon, "Karaites in European Turkey," 313. On another dietary distinction between Karaites and Rabbanites, see the description of the "fish scale controversy," ibid., 314.

45. On these other reforms, see Ankori, *Karaites in Byzantium,* 252, n. 104.

46. See Lasker, "Maimonides' Influence on Karaite Theories"; and idem, "Maimonides' Influence on the Philosophy of Elijah Bashyatchi the Karaite."

47. The last hundred years of Byzantine scholarship were of little significance in comparison with previous accomplishments. See Wilson, *Scholars of Byzantium,* 265–72. The influence of Renaissance Italy completely overshadowed the epigoni of the Greek academy. See the works of Deno John Geanakoplos, including *Constanti-*

multicultural Jewish environment provided by the new Islamic society of the Ottoman Empire.

Halakhah and the Past: Elijah Bashyachi

The most important codification of Karaite halakhah is the *'Adderet 'Eliyahu* by Elijah ben Moses Bashyachi (d. 1490).[48] Although it never fully supplanted Aaron ben Elijah's *Gan 'Eden,* the halakhah of *'Adderet 'Eliyahu* represents the full elaboration of *ha'takah* as an independent source of law. Correspondingly, it represents the reforms and accommodation to rabbinic halakhah begun by the author's grandfather in Adrianople and continued under the grandson. It is beyond the scope of this study to discuss the full import of the halakhic innovations; however, as the very nature of such a source of law forced the rabbis of the Mishnah into creating the chain of tradition of Avot, so Bashyachi was compelled to address historical issues in his introduction. The final portion of his introduction is entitled "The Division of the Karaites from the Rabbanites."[49] Even in its title, Rabbanism is privileged by being designated as the mother culture. The process of Rabbanization in Karaite thought had proceeded to such an extent that issues of legitimacy were no longer necessarily completely couched in discussions of historical anteriority.

Bashyachi begins by addressing the reason for the "secession" of the Karaites: "I searched the books of the sages and could not find one of them who spoke about this. However the traditionists say that we broke away in the time of Zadok and Boethos, as it is said. . . ."[50] Here Bashyachi turns to the traditional rabbinic account of the breaking away of Zadok and Boethos from Rabbanism found in *'Avot de-Rabbi Natan,* but he quotes only the proverb of Antigonus that prefaces the brief narrative.[51] Bashyachi goes on to state that the Rabbanites use the foundation story of the Sadducees and Boethusians to explain the origins of Karaism. Two points are immediately to be observed here. One, citing the text as any good rabbi would, Bashyachi quotes

---

nople and the West: Essays on the Late Byzantine (Palaeologan) and Italian Renaissances.

48. Elijah Bashyachi, *'Adderet 'Eliyahu* (Ramlah, Israel, 1966); reprint of Odessa, 1870.

49. The text appears in the most recent edition (Ramlah, Israel, 1966) on the fifth and sixth pages of the unpaginated introduction.

50. Ibid.

51. *'Avot de-Rabbi Natan* is traditionally found in the Babylonian Talmud at the end of the Order of Nezikin among the minor tractates, in the Vilna edition, 25b–47b. The section on the transmission of tradition from Antigonus of Socho, and the failure of Zadok and Boethos to comprehend it, is in chapter 5 on 30a–b. The text is translated by Eli Cashdan in *'Aboth d'Rabbi Nathan,* 42: "Be not like servants who serve the master for the sake of receiving a reward, but be like servants who serve the master without the expectation of receiving a reward." Cf. M Avot 1:3.

only the introductory passage, under the assumption that readers are familiar with the rabbinic canon and are able to supply the complete pericope for their own use. Bashyachi's style is completely rabbanized.

The second point is of greater significance. The absence of Karaite historical knowledge is explicitly affirmed. Bashyachi's remark has been central to the historiographical views of Poznanski and Harkavy. Nonetheless, it is clear that Bashyachi did not have a version of the Karaite chain of tradition before him. Had he had one, it would have provided him with the perfect historical explanation for the *haʿtakah* as utilized by himself and his grandfather. What is more, we can be sure that al-Qirqisānī's text was unknown to late-fifteenth-century Karaites and that its heresiographical contents were known only through the jumbled section on Jewish sects in Hadassi's *ʾEshkol ha-Kofer.* However, since Hadassi's text was revived by the conservative faction that opposed the Bashyachi reforms, it is possible that the author chose not to use it because he feared being perceived as acknowledging his opponents.

Bashyachi disposes of the Sadducean accusation by rhetorically asking how would it be possible that the founders and heads of a nation[52] would not be acknowledged or mentioned anywhere in the literature of that nation.[53] That, in effect, was to point out that the Karaites did not claim Zadok and Boethos as founders.

Bashyachi's search for a reason to explain the separation of Karaites and Rabbanites then leads him to none other than Judah Halevi and Babylonian Talmud (BT) Kiddushin 66a, citing them both by name. He quotes Halevi's account of the affair with King Yannai, followed by a recapitulation of the narrative in Bashyachi's own words:[54]

> It is to be seen that because Simeon ben Shetah remained alive, and came and told them the Oral Law, that Israel was split into two sects.[55] Because all the sages were killed and only he remained alive, because he was the brother-in-law of King Jannai, he concocted[56] a different faith according to his own opinion and departed from Scripture. Indeed, if all the sages who lived in that generation had lived, they would not have suffered the burden of all the precautionary measures [that existed] between the Torah of Moses and the Oral Law that Simeon ben Shetah had concocted according to his own opinion. Surely their words were explanations of the Torah, not divisions based upon it. And who knows whether, if they all had lived, we would be one nation, or if Simeon ben Shetah had been killed when the other sages were killed, we would all be one nation.

52. *Umah.*
53. *ʾAdderet ʾEliyahu,* fifth and sixth pages of the unpaginated introduction.
54. Ibid.
55. *Kittot.* The king is Alexander Jannaeus.
56. *Ḥiddesh.*

The rhetorical purpose of the recapitulation is to lay blame for the deviation from religious truth squarely with Simeon ben Shetah. As we have seen in al-Qirqisānī and the *Ḥilluk,* the earliest Karaite historical notions followed a standard literary-historical motif used by sectarian and deviant movements throughout history, that the sect represents the core of truth from which the mainstream is a deviation. Thus, the sect preserves and maintains an original religious knowledge and truth that has been lost to the mainstream. Bashyachi is no different from his Karaite predecessors, embracing this truth through an inverted reading of Judah Halevi. Like the approach of the Karaite chain of tradition, Simeon ben Shetah is represented as the deviant, while Judah ben Tabbai is simply privileged as the bearer of the truth. Thus, both Bashyachi and the Karaite chain of tradition provide the requisite function of establishing lines of continuity and deviation. But Bashyachi is not interested in long lines of historical continuity—only in establishing a historical basis for his halakhah. The interpretation that privileges Judah ben Tabbai fulfills no purpose for him and is not utilized. Bashyachi is more properly concerned with a history that both explains the separation of Karaism from Rabbanism (perceived as the deviation of Rabbanism from the truth) and a historical basis for a pan-Jewish halakhah that permits the selective use and rejection of individual elements of rabbinic law. This historical view is neither Karaite nor Rabbanite, but halakhic.

This position is creatively expressed by means of a kind of sociological interpretation of the times of Simeon ben Shetah that intimates a theory of tradition. Bashyachi begins with a primary assumption that tradition cannot be wholly encompassed within the mind of any individual. In fact, it requires many tradents to preserve and transmit the numerous halakhot that comprise tradition. Unfortunately, at the time of catastrophe when all the sages were killed, only Simeon ben Shetah remained. Thus, all of rabbinic tradition is founded upon tradition as transmitted from one individual, which by virtue of such a circumstance could only be incomplete. Correspondingly, the Talmud indicates the many disagreements that arose among subsequent sages. Echoing centuries-old Karaite polemics, Bashyachi argues that rabbinic tradition is inconsistent and therefore not a true tradition, as it claims to be. What is more, if such disagreements existed among the sages in the time of Simeon ben Shetah—that is, if there existed contemporaneous and competing true and false traditions—there is no doubt that many of the true traditions would have been lost as a consequence of the killing of the scholars.[57] One can see that, with this argument, it is inconceivable that Bashyachi would embrace a chain of tradition that privileged a "counter-Rabbanite," as Judah ben Tabbai was understood to be in the Karaite chain of tradition. The same problem would have existed for that tradent, too.

57. *ʾAdderet ʾEliyahu,* fifth and sixth pages of the unpaginated introduction.

If all that Bashyachi says is true, then, one might ask, how was it that this account had not been known until now? Anticipating the question, Bashyachi provides a weak, historicized answer. He states that Judah Halevi was the first to tell this story in its truth because he feared for his life before the Khazar king;[58] throughout the previous centuries, the rabbis had kept the story secret. This is the weakest part of Bashyachi's historical presentation, since his argument can be devastated by the same logic he used earlier to refute the rabbinic claim that Zadok and Boethos were the founders of Karaism.

Bashyachi's historical exercise seems to draw to a conclusion by reiterating that Halevi clearly distinguishes Sadducees and Boethusians from Karaites and that the Karaites do not differ from the Rabbanites in terms of fundamentals. Following a strategy similar to that employed centuries earlier whereby the excesses of the Mishawites were decried in order to position the Karaites closer to Rabbanism and within the fold of Israel, Bashyachi reminds the reader that the rabbis are wrong when they claim that the Karaites differ with them on fundamentals. Reflecting the Rabbanite-Karaite rapprochement of the times and the Rabbanization of Karaite halakhah, Bashyachi reminds the reader that the Karaites are Jews. The difference between them and the Rabbanites is only a matter of interpretation, not fundamental belief.[59]

Although the historical character of Bashyachi's introduction is played out at this point, the discussion goes on to show that "those who say there is a second law are in error."[60] The text repeats many classic Karaite arguments against the rabbis and engages Saadia, with support from Abraham Ibn Ezra, to prove that God wrote the entire Torah, not simply the Ten Commandments, leaving the writing of the text to Moses. The implications revolve around arguments supporting the Oral Law. These arguments need not concern us here.[61]

Although the absence of a chain of tradition as part of the introduction to the new code of Karaite halakhah calls into question the origins of the Karaite chain of tradition, we have shown that such a historical scheme would not have served Bashyachi's purposes. Bashyachi's historical reading presents us with other alternatives to the thorny question of Karaism's understanding of its own origins. Like the chain of tradition, it relies on Judah Halevi, but alternatively uses the *Kuzari* to prepare a foundation for *ha'takah* based upon as wide a foundation as possible for sources of halakhic exegesis. Thus, Bashyachi offers a theory to explain the confused condition of rabbinic law, which

58. Ibid. Bashyachi places Halevi himself in the court of the Khazar king, a curious misreading of Halevi's text! It is clear in the first paragraph of the *Kuzari* (1:1) that the events being portrayed took place some four hundred years before the time of Halevi. See Judah Halevi, *Judah Hallevi's Kitab al Khazari,* 35.

59. *'Adderet 'Eliyahu,* fifth and sixth pages of the unpaginated introduction.

60. Ibid.

61. See Caleb Afendopolo, *Patshegen Ketav ha-Dat,* for a discussion of this and other issues relating to the writing of the Torah.

would necessitate careful selection if it was to be used halakhically by Karaites. Unlike the chain of tradition, it does not identify the Karaites as the sole interpreters of Jewish law. The Karaite accommodation to the Mishnah and Talmud is clearly permitted in this historicization. The Karaite chain of tradition represents a more complicated historical presentation. Although it is constructed by using rabbinic texts and historical assumptions inherited from the rabbis, it does not take into consideration the relationship of Karaite halakhah to rabbinic halakhah. In this regard, Bashyachi's presentation is much more elegant and functional and does not require a claim for Karaite historical continuity going back to Moses.

Pieces of a Metanarrative: Caleb Afendopolo

Bashyachi's son-in-law and student Caleb Afendopolo (d. 1509) is described by Poznanski as a polyhistor.[62] Although the majority of his extensive literary output remains in manuscript, his work covers such diverse areas as halakhah, allegorical homilies, introductions to biblical books, philosophical commentary, mathematics, astronomy, and even some hymns. He inherited Bashyachi's incomplete *ʾAdderet ʾEliyahu* and worked toward its completion, without finishing the task.[63] He also wrote a work that summarized Karaite belief entitled *Sefer ʿAsarah Maʾamarot* (Ten discourses). Until recently, this work was extant only in manuscript, and although it is often cited by scholars of Karaism, their remarks were usually only the repetition of statements from Steinschneider and the quotations from this text found in the published work of the seventeenth-century Karaite Mordecai ben Nisan.[64] The ten essays in *ʿAsarah Maʾamarot* cover a variety of theological and philosophical topics and include some historical ideas.[65]

62. Poznanski, "Karaite Literary Opponents," 213.

63. Afendopolo's works are discussed by Kaufmann Kohler and Richard Gottheil in *JE* 1:222–23, s.v. "Afendopolo, Caleb b. Elijah b. Judah."

64. See Steinschneider, "Kaleb Afendopolo." On Mordecai ben Nisan, see chapter 6, below. I have used a copy found in the Library of the Jewish Theological Seminary of America. *Sefer ʿAsarah Maʾamarot,* JTS Mic. 3327, 275 fols. This manuscript probably dates from the 18th century. Other copies are found in the Bibliotheek der Rijksuniversiteit Leiden and the Bodleian Library, Oxford. These are: Leiden MS Warn. 52/10 (Cod. or. 4790), fols. 68r–80r (intro.); Leiden MS Warn. 30/4 (Cod. or. 4768), fols. 210r–261r (pts. 1–2); Oxford-Bodleian 2386/1 (Opp. Add. 4* 121), fols. 4r–122r Kaffa; and Oxford-Bodleian 2392, 2, Commentary on Psalm 119. The published edition is Caleb ben Elijah Afendopolo, *Sefer ʿAsarah Maʾamarot* (Ramlah, Israel: Makhon Tiferet Yosef, le-Ḥeker ha-Yahadut ha-Karait, 1999) (henceforth, *ʿAsarah Maʾamarot*–Ramlah).

65. The essays are summarized in *ʿAsarah Maʾamarot,* 2a–12b. Their topics are (1) God, philosophical propositions, metempsychosis, good and evil, and creation; (2) a homily on the Song of Songs with a philosophical orientation; (3) eternity of the world, perfection of the Torah, and the *miṣvot;* (4) on the types of *miṣvot;* (5)

Concerns for history appear in two places in *ʿAsarah Maʾamarot.* First, the introduction offers a sketch of Jewish history that goes toward explaining the Karaite-Rabbanite schism. Second, in the fourth essay, which deals with the different kinds of *miṣvot,* is found a more detailed appraisal and refutation of the rabbinic claim that the Karaites are actually Sadducees and Boethusians.

The beginning of the general introduction[66] indicates a series of historical topics to be covered. The derivative character of this work in general is indicated in Afendopolo's assertion that "all that I will relate has previously been related by the sages, from whose books I have gathered it."[67] Without further historical elaboration, he relates:[68]

> In our words in this general introduction, we have related the reasons for the division that [exists] between us and our brethren the Rabbanites. And, that their tradition is not true according to human reason. And, why our forefathers, "the good figs,"[69] peace be upon them, did not accept it. It tells of the era in which the Karaites and Rabbanites separated. It makes known with convincing proofs that to the time of Ezra and somewhat beyond, all of Israel listened only to the written Torah of Moses, not to any other, and they had no teaching of tradition.[70] And it tells how [1b] Alexander of Macedon unintentionally . . . to Jerusalem. It tells somewhat of the Jewish sects that went out from the community of Israel, and how they built another temple on the Mount of Olives.[71] It begins with the matter of the story of Antigonus of Socho, and the saying he told to his disciples, Zadok and Boethos. And it tells some of the story of Jesus the Christian and his twelve emissaries, how they went out from the community [to form] the first sects. It tells . . . the house of the Hasmoneans, the Priests and their courage. And the reason for the . . . [killing?] of the sages. And it relates the matter of Jannai the King,[72] and except for . . . the hate of the sages. And the reason for their hate of him . . . in the story of Simeon ben Shetah, peace be

happiness and fear, the world to come; (6) resurrection of the dead; (7) the soul; (8) human nature and God, Moses' prophethood; (9) against astrology, free will; (10) the giving of the Torah, Shavuot, secrets of the tablets, the cherubim, on prophecy.

66. *petiḥah ha-kolelet.*

67. *ʿAsarah Maʾamarot,* 1a; *ʿAsarah Maʾamarot*–Ramlah, 10–11.

68. Ibid. The text in the JTS manuscript is smeared and has several lacunae on this folio.

69. Jer. 24. See chapter 3, above.

70. *torat ha-kabbalah.*

71. This is probably a manuscript error, and should read, "Mount Gerizim," in reference to the Samaritans.

72. Alexander Jannaeus.

> upon him. And it relates [with] clear [proofs] that the Rabbanites went out from the community of Israel, [not] the Karaites. And that we went along [the path] that the [prophets?] and the Great Sanhedrin followed, not [deviating?] to the right or the left. And it tells the reason that . . . our sages, peace be upon them, the "chosen figs," teach . . .

The text continues to describe several specifics of Karaite ritual and doctrine.

Later in the introduction, Caleb tells the reader that he wrote the work to demonstrate the rationality of the *miṣvot,* and that this approach originated with the "good figs."[73] As we have seen in the introductory remarks reproduced above, this reading from Jeremiah, which is borrowed from the *Ḥilluk,* becomes an important interpretive device. The good figs represent a pristine and rationalist understanding of the Torah as held in biblical times, becoming a font for later Karaism in Afendopolo's reading of history.[74] Although the author lays blame at the feet of Jeroboam for antirationalistic error on the part of interpreters of the Torah (which is, of course, the error of the Rabbanites), he does not incorporate Jeroboam into his historical reconstruction.[75]

One can see from the introductory remarks that the narrative follows Judah Halevi's account of the affair with Alexander Jannaeus and Simeon ben Shetah, but Afendopolo adds a new, additional, feature by including Alexander the Great. In order to consider Afendopolo's narrative historically, we turn to the expanded historical narrative of the general introduction, which is missing from the JTS manuscript, but is published in Mordecai ben Nisan's *Dod Mordekhai.*[76] Afendopolo begins with a refutatory discourse on three interpretive reasons to explain why Israel is divided into two: (1) against the rabbinic doctrine of the chain of tradition; (2) against the rabbinic contention that when the Torah is in need of interpretation or expansion, such a task can

73. *ʿAsarah Maʾamarot,* 16a–b.

74. Cp. *ʿAsarah Maʾamarot,* 21b: "Our *haʿtakah* is proven by perception and reason. And this is the path which is stronger than that which came before."

75. *ʿAsarah Maʾamarot,* 16b. Afendopolo was familiar with Hadassi, and therefore was acquainted with al-Qirqisānī's portrayal of Jeroboam from that source. It is unlikely that Afendopolo knew Arabic or had access to al-Qirqisānī. See Steinschneider, "Kaleb Afendopolo."

76. Mordecai ben Nisan's, *Dod Mordekhai,* 42–51. See page 42, where Mordecai states, in reference to *Sefer ʿAsarah Maʾamarot,* "I will transcribe from that introduction several pages letter by letter, word for word." Either Afendopolo wrote different versions of *ʿAsarah Maʾamarot,* with and without the historical material, or the manuscript of the Jewish Theological Seminary is defective. I suspect the former is true, because the introduction in the manuscript appears complete unto itself, with no indications of editing or omissions. A scholarly edition of this work is a desideratum in Karaite Studies. See the uncritical edition, *ʿAsarah Maʾamarot–*Ramlah, 13–15.

only be done by means of their tradition; and (3) against the rabbinic claim that the Torah sanctions addition and subtraction of its principles based upon the consensus of the sages of a generation.[77] Afendopolo then defines tradition in terms of Karaite rationalism, "called by our sages,[78] peace be upon them, the yoke of inheritance or the transmitted tradition.[79] That which is explained by it, all of Israel agrees upon together as one, if it has a foundation in the written text."[80] With a clear understanding of rabbinic halakhah, Afendopolo continues by attacking the doctrine of "Law of Moses from Sinai."

Beginning his historical narrative, the author writes, "The era in which the Karaites and Rabbanites separated was in the time of the Second Temple, when Mattathias ha-Kohen ben Yoḥanan the High Priest and his sons prevailed, and killed Pollopus [Phillipus], captain of the army of Antiochus, King of Greece. For after Cyrus ruled, even though Israel was in exile, they were all as one, without any schism among them."[81] Afendopolo introduces new details to the Karaite historical narrative that come from the medieval Hebrew chronicle Josippon.[82] Josippon was "reintroduced" to Jewish scholarship in the middle of the fourteenth century by the Byzantine Rabbanite, Judah ibn Moskoni. Discovering the text while traveling in search of manuscripts of Ibn Ezra's commentaries, he was so impressed with its contents that he edited existing versions of the text and added an introduction.[83] A century later,

77. *ʿAsarah Maʾamarot*–Ramlah, 13–14; *Dod Mordekhai*, 42–43.

78. *maskilim.*

79. *sevel ha-yerushah ve-haʿtakah mishtalshelet.*

80. *ʿAsarah Maʾamarot*–Ramlah, 15, and *Dod Mordekhai*, 43, where he goes on to cite Tobias ben Moses, stating that the *haʿtakah* always has a hint in the written text. Elsewhere (*ʿAsarah Maʾamarot*, 21b) he states, "The yoke of inheritance is ours from our holy forefathers, transmitted one generation after another. There is not found in any nation one who can diminish it."

81. *ʿAsarah Maʾamarot*–Ramlah, 16; *Dod Mordekhai*, 44.

82. The standard text is David Flusser, ed., *Sefer Yosippon* (Jerusalem, 1981), 2 vols. Volume 1 is the edited text; volume 2 is an introduction and notes. Subsequent references to Josippon will be from this edition. Josippon is a tenth-century chronicle of ancient Jewish history derived from Josephus, but less reliable historically. The Jews did not possess a version of Josephus, which was preserved in Greek and Latin within the Christian milieu. Flusser has shown that the text was based upon the Latin translation of Josephus and edited in southern Italy in the tenth century. Josippon was considered historically authoritative by the Jews, who attributed its authorship to Joseph ben Gorion ha-Kohen (understood incorrectly to be the proper name of Josephus).

83. The standard scholarly edition of Flusser's, representing an Italian and northern French version, is about a third shorter than the version edited by Judah ibn Moskoni, which represents a Byzantine manuscript tradition that was embellished with material from the Apocrypha and from Jewish legends. Judah's text was first printed in Constantinople in 1510 by Jacob Tam ibn Yahya, and has been

Afendopolo became the first Karaite to follow Judah's lead and use Josippon as an authoritative historical source.[84] As a result, the affair of Jannaeus is embellished with new detail not found in Halevi or other rabbinic sources. Afendopolo goes further, even writing dialogue for the characters. In this way, more rabbinic sources are integrated into a Karaite version of history, creating a kind of metanarrative.

This metanarrative, or metatext of Karaite history, is composed of any and all historical pericopae and data that might be used for Karaite purposes. The materials of this metatext became increasingly accepted within Karaite circles, representing a consensus in regard to historical ideas. The foundations of the metanarrative were extracted from rabbinic literature as well as from Hadassi (a filter for al-Qirqisānī), the *Ḥilluk,* and Elijah Bashyachi (a link with Judah Halevi), but in the hands of Afendopolo and with the aid of Josippon it begins to resemble a true literary narrative. Karaite history could now be expressed in vague similarity with the emerging Jewish historiography of the day, exhibiting some of the influence of Renaissance thinking and scholarship. Even as Judah ibn Moskoni's career reflects that of a typical wandering Latin scholar who would be found later in the same century, so Afendopolo's wide scholarship and careful scrutiny of Karaite sources parallels the intellectual ferment experienced as much in Constantinople of the day as in Italy and the rest of Europe.[85]

Jewish history according to Afendopolo is summarized as follows: All Israel followed one pristine Torah, even under Cyrus and Alexander, because there still existed prophets and authoritative elders. Among these prophets were Haggai, Zechariah, Malachi, Ezra, Daniel, Mordecai (who is the same as Bilshan), and others "to the complement of one hundred and twenty" who comprised the membership of the Great Assembly.[86] As we saw in the Karaite version of the chain of tradition, rabbinic history is appropriated into the

---

edited in a modern edition by H. Huminer (Jerusalem, 1957). On Judah ibn Moskoni and his scholarship, see Bowman, *Jews of Byzantium,* 133–37, esp. the notes on 135.

84. Judah ibn Moskoni explicitly intended that his version establish Josippon as an authoritative historical work. He recognized it could be an inspiration for Jews to read about their ancestors' glorious exploits in contrast to contemporary conditions of exile. In addition, but no less important, it would remind the reader of their fathers' sins and the reasons for the exile. In this way, rabbinic moral notions and covenantal theology are expressed to maintain the historiosophy of the rabbis, and to apologize for the very enterprise of historical research. See ibid., 136. Most of the early historiographers would include such apologies in their introductions. See Yerushalmi, *Zakhor,* 62, and 66.

85. See Bowman, *Jews of Byzantium,* 137, esp. n. 22. On Afendopolo's Renaissance literary side, see Michal Saraf, "The 'Discussion between Wine and the Poet' by Kaleb Afendopolo the Karaite."

86. *'Asarah Ma'amarot*–Ramlah, 16; *Dod Mordekhai,* 44.

narrative. The critical juncture between biblical and postbiblical history is contextualized around the rabbinic conception of the Great Assembly. Afendopolo goes to great lengths to describe how all Israel followed the teachings of the biblically authoritative teachers, the priests, judges, and prophets. He cites Scripture to reiterate that no addition or subtraction to the Law was ever initiated and that there was complete unanimity of purpose and observance in Israel through these times.[87]

The next section summarizes chronological information derived from rabbinic sources[88] and continues with an account, taken from Josippon, of Alexander the Great's conquest of the Middle East and his legendary visit to Jerusalem.[89] The conflict between the Samaritans and the Jews forms the background for Alexander's eventual visit to Jerusalem, which results in the granting of privileges to the Jews, including power over the Samaritans.[90] Echoing the rabbis, Afendopolo describes the Samaritan schism as the first division in Israel. "And Israel was divided at that time into halves, half of the people followed Sanballat and his sons-in-law, the priests, and half the people followed Simeon the Just and his comrades who testified to the words of Ezra and the prophets according to what was written in the Torah of God."[91] The narrative is compressed chronologically to bring the events described in the biblical Book of Ezra into proximity with the beginning of the Hellenistic era. Thus, the relations between the Jews and the Samaritans ascribed to the time of Alexander, and conflated with the time of the Hasmoneans, are understood as part of the emergence of this first schism in Israel. Afendopolo ignores the claims of Hadassi and al-Qirqisānī' that Jeroboam is the culprit.

The narrative immediately moves on to describe the schism of Zadok and Boethos, who are also linked to the Samaritans. Perhaps Afendopolo was

87. *'Asarah Ma'amarot*–Ramlah, 17; *Dod Mordekhai,* 44–45, which uses Dt. 13:1. For anecdotal proof, Afendopolo includes and comments upon the celebration of Sukkot recounted in Neh. 8 and 9, when Ezra reads the Torah to the assembled people.

88. He differs with Ibn Daud's chronology in many respects, following other sources, including *Seder 'Olam Rabbah.* See Cohen, *Sefer ha-Qabbalah,* 14–15.

89. *'Asarah Ma'amarot*–Ramlah, 18–19. See *Sefer Yosippon,* 1:54–60. The version in Josippon brings together elements of the Latin Josephus, rabbinic legends regarding Alexander, and the medieval romances of Alexander, known as the *Gests of Alexander.* See ibid., 2:216–56, for Flusser's important essay on this portion of the text. There is an extensive literature on the Alexander romances. See the bibliography in Minoo S. Southgate, trans., *Iskandarnamah, A Medieval Alexander-Romance,* 225–28. Cf. Albert Mugrdich Wolohojian (trans. with intro.), *The Romance of Alexander the Great by Pseudo-Callisthenes,* which is based on the Armenian text. Other versions have been translated from Ethiopic, Syriac, Latin, and even Old English.

90. *'Asarah Ma'amarot*–Ramlah, 19; *Dod Mordekhai,* 46–47.

91. Ibid., 46.

familiar with Ibn Daud's historical contextualization of heresy. Although Afendopolo recognizes that Zadok and Boethos did not accept all the teachings of the Samaritans, nonetheless he portrays heresy as a species unto itself.[92] This strategy represents an intermediate position between Ibn Daud, who would ascribe all heresy to the Samaritans, and Judah Halevi, who clearly differentiates between sects. He goes on to describe the Sadducean and Boethusian teaching, characterizing it as a rejection of the doctrine of reward and punishment. The text follows Bashyachi's introduction to *ʾAdderet Eliyahu* and also cites Mishnah Avot, chapter 1.

Afendopolo also deals with the problem of Zadok and Boethos elsewhere in *Asarah Maʾamarot,* in the fourth discourse, which categorizes and discusses the different kinds of *miṣvot.* In the context of *taʿame ha-miṣvot* (reasons for the commandments), these heresies are understood as "the beginning of one wrong way of thinking."[93] The text here also follows Bashyachi and Avot, but then develops differently.[94] He acknowledges that the Karaites agree with the Rabbanites, in that the Sadducees and Boethusians are *minim* and *apikorsim* (literally, heretics and Epicureans). He then quotes Hadassi (whose work he had provided with an index-like summary), also citing Dāʾūd al-Muqammiṣ, to provide descriptive details of the teachings of these sects.[95] He notes that they were not in total error, for their interpretation of the dating of Shavuot was correct, but using rabbinic terminology concludes, "Whoever says that the Karaites are Sadducees and Boethusians is not speaking the truth, because in our belief they are *minim* and *apikorsim.*"[96]

By acknowledging that there is a halakhic similarity between the Karaites and the Sadducees and Boethusians, Afendopolo provides two reasons for the rabbinic error of not distinguishing between these groups: (1) both groups deny the rabbinic *kabbalah;* and (2) both groups follow the same calendation

92. Ibid., 46–47.

93. *ʿAsarah Maʾamarot,* 106r; *ʿAsarah Maʾamarot*–Ramlah, 154ff.

94. Cf. *ʿAsarah Maʾamarot,* 106r–107r; and *ʿAsarah Maʾamarot*–Ramlah, 154–55.

95. *ʿAsarah Maʾamarot,* 107v; *ʿAsarah Maʾamarot*–Ramlah, 155. He states that the Sadducees and Boethusians follow deceptive thinking, seeking proof in opposites. They forbade divorce, utilized a thirty-day month, and did not consider Passover and Shemini ʿAṣeret to be holidays on the level of a Sabbath.

96. Ibid. The Karaite defense against the accusation of Sadduceeism was also taken up by Joseph ben Moses Beghi (fl. 1511), a member of the conservative element of Karaite scholars. His letter *ʾIggeret Kiryah Neʾemanah* takes up much of the same arguments as Afendopolo. In addition, it includes a valuable account of the controversy regarding Rabbanites teaching Karaite students. See Mann, *Texts and Studies,* 2: *Karaitica,* 294–315, which includes excerpts from the text, 302–15. The text comes from a unique manuscript in the Bibliotheek der Rijksuniversiteit Leiden, MS Warner 30/2, fols. 190r–203v.

for Shavuot.[97] In a way, he apologizes for the rabbinic polemic, but distances the Karaites from the heretics. Elsewhere he says that the Sadducees and Boethusians differ in interpreting the written text, but both do so without either of them possessing a tradition or using a methodological foundation for interpretation.[98]

Although it appears that the author has concluded his argument, he returns to the Samaritans, who only follow the books of the Torah and Joshua, make sacrifices without a Temple, and "follow the innovations of Jeroboam."[99] He thus returns to Hadassi and al-Qirqisānī as sources, stating, "we cannot discuss all the others who have left the paths of the Torah."[100] Nonetheless, he does list some of them by name,[101] and then recapitulates Bashyachi's argument against the Sadducees and Boethusians and Halevi's contextualization of Jewish sects.[102] In reference to the details of Halevi's narrative, he explicitly credits Josippon: "We have already related this story of Joseph ben Gorion ha-Kohen in his book, *Milḥamot ha-Shem,* in its fourth book, as we have written in the general introduction."[103]

Returning to the historical material in the introduction, the narrative depends heavily upon Josippon to describe the rise of the Hasmoneans, their struggle with Antiochus, and then on to relate the affairs of John Hyrcanus and Alexander Jannaeus—how they killed the scholars, creating a vacuum of teaching into which Simeon ben Shetah injected his own halakhic fabrications, thus initiating Rabbanism.[104] Since Josippon is derived from Josephus, many of the details of these affairs discussed in chapter 4 became available and are included in Afendopolo's text, becoming part of the Karaite metanarrative. In this way, the outrages against the scholars, "the killing of the scholars," are enhanced, adding to the ideology of persecution that is built into the narrative.

Unlike the chain of tradition attributed to Yefet ben Ṣaʿir, Judah ben Tabbai is not privileged as the proto-Karaite in opposition to Simeon ben Shetah. The idea of a Karaite chain of tradition, articulated in complete detail, is not part of Afendopolo's presentation. For him, tradition is still expressed in terms of a relationship to Scripture, even though *haʿtakah* was now functioning as an independent source for the Law. Appositely, the origin of error

97. *ʿAsarah Maʾamarot,* 108r; *ʿAsarah Maʾamarot*–Ramlah, 156.

98. *ʿAsarah Maʾamarot,* 110r; *ʿAsarah Maʾamarot*–Ramlah, 158–59.

99. *ʿAsarah Maʾamarot,* 108r; *ʿAsarah Maʾamarot*–Ramlah, 156.

100. *ʿAsarah Maʾamarot,* 108r; *ʿAsarah Maʾamarot*–Ramlah, 156.

101. *ʿAsarah Maʾamarot,* 108r–v; *ʿAsarah Maʾamarot*–Ramlah, 156. He mentions in somewhat corrupted form the Gariah [Jabariyyah?], the Qaraʿians, Obadiah ha-Isfahani, Ishmael al-Ukbari, Moses al-zafarani, and Meshwi ha-Ukbari. Again, he notes there are others without naming them.

102. *ʿAsarah Maʾamarot,* 108v–109r; *ʿAsarah Maʾamarot*–Ramlah, 157.

103. *ʿAsarah Maʾamarot,* 109r; *ʿAsarah Maʾamarot*–Ramlah, 157–58.

104. *ʿAsarah Maʾamarot*–Ramlah, 23–24; *Dod Mordekhai,* 47–51.

is not developed from Jeroboam, even though he is credited with wrong thinking. Afendopolo's history is not a complete historical contextualization like al-Qirqisānī's, but is concerned specifically with the error of the rabbis, not the course of religion through time. He is not concerned with retelling biblical history.

In a sense, Caleb Afendopolo's historical presentation is a response to his teacher, Elijah Bashyachi. In direct contradiction to Bashyachi's statement in regard to the writing of history by Karaites, that he "could not find one of them who spoke about this," Afendopolo supplies a compilation based upon Karaite and rabbinic texts, representing an accumulation of materials that comprise a Karaite historical metanarrative, culled from various disconnected sources, but unified by antirabbinic sentiment and the thematic development of particular elements.

First Attempts at Narrative History: Moses Bashyachi

The great-grandson of Elijah, Moses Bashyachi (d. 1572), seems to have been something of a prodigy. Unlike the other Karaite worthies of Constantinople in the fifteenth and sixteenth centuries, Moses Bashyachi traveled throughout the Middle East, and probably knew Arabic.[105] We have already examined the Karaite chain of tradition found in the younger Bashyachi's *Matteh ʾElohim,* which is framed within a wider construction of Karaite history.[106]

Moses Bashyachi's history is claimed to be derived, in part, from the historical construction of Yefet ben Ṣaʿir's Karaite chain of tradition. The greatest deviation from the Karaite metanarrative is the position of Shammai and his followers in this version of Jewish history. The author goes to great lengths to show that the record of Shammai and the House of Shammai in the Mishnah and Talmud are the record of early Karaites.[107] Previously, the Karaites mentioned Shammai only in connection to his disagreements with Hillel, in order to prove that the rabbinic tradition was characterized by dissension and fraught with inconsistencies.[108] In the past, if a Karaite studied

105. It is recorded that he died at the age of eighteen, but his chronology has not been fully established. See *Dod Mordekhai,* 52. On Moses Bashyachi, see Poznanski, "Karaite Literary Opponents," 214–15.

106. I have used MS Mic. 9828 from the Jewish Theological Seminary of America in New York. On this manuscript, see chapter 4, note 7, above. Most of the historical portion of *Matteh ʾElohim* is reproduced in *Dod Mordekhai,* 53–64, which also includes Yefet ben Ṣaʿir's chain of tradition, 58–62 (6r–8r in *Matteh ʾElohim*). Now see the recent edition published by the Karaite community of Israel: Moses ben Elijah Bashyachi (Yosef ben ʿOvadyah Algamil, ed.), *Matteh ʾElohim* (Ramlah, Israel: Tiferet Yosef, 5761 [2000 or 2001]), designated in the notes as *Matteh ʾElohim*–Ramlah.

107. *Matteh ʾElohim,* 5r–v (*Matteh ʾElohim*–Ramlah, 27–29).

108. See chapter 2, above.

rabbinic texts regarding Shammai and Hillel, it would be for an antirabbinic polemical purpose. Moses Bashyachi's knowledge of rabbinic texts is used in a new way to penetrate and appropriate the Shammai-Hillel controversy. Discussions from the Mishnah and Talmud are quoted at length in order to prove that the preponderance of the truth lies at the feet of Shammai. Many rabbinic pericopae lacking any direct connection to Shammai and Hillel are read in terms of the opposition of these two halakhic schools. Thus, rabbinic texts, which were classically used by Karaites to denounce Rabbanite practice, are utilized to enhance the position of Shammai and those who are reputed to be his followers and to degrade and condemn the Hillelites. In this way, examples of halakhic dissension from the early rabbinic period are magnified as examples of the Karaite-Rabbanite schism. The Karaite chain of tradition properly contextualizes this fragment of the larger narrative into its schematization of the transmission of the truth from antiquity. Moses Bashyachi supplemented this construction by mining the Mishnah and Talmud in an effort to produce a record of this halakhic and, therefore, historical schism in the Jewish past.[109]

The second significant development derived from the Karaite chain of tradition parallels the aggrandizement of Shammai: it tells of the appropriation of Judah ben Tabbai, the "partner" of Simeon ben Shetah as portrayed in Mishnah Avot, and his transformation into a founder of Karaism. Although the primary sources that describe the events and stand as background to Judah Halevi's influential account of the affair do not implicate Judah ben Tabbai—nor is he included in Josippon—Moses Bashyachi has magnified his importance. If Simeon ben Shetah is the archvillain and proto-Rabbanite, then Judah is correspondingly transformed into the pious hero who preserved the true teachings and who is responsible for the true transmission of knowledge to Karaite posterity. In this scheme, Judah ben Tabbai is linked through intermediaries to Shammai, creating the earliest links in the Karaite chain of tradition.

If Moses Bashyachi came upon Yefet's chain of tradition in his travels in the Islamic Middle East, one could explain his innovations in Karaite historical expression as an effort at harmonizing elements of the chain with both the existing metanarrative, based largely on Halevi's narrative, and rabbinic literature. The task could have been accomplished without recourse to the latter, but his confident use of rabbinic texts indicates the seriousness with which he approached the problem. It was important that evidential traces of the new historical theory be derived from rabbinic literature because one could not find support for such assertions in existing Karaite texts. The new claim that Judah ben Tabbai and Shammai were proto-Karaites could best be maintained with the support of the rabbis themselves.

The classical Karaite representation that utilized dissension and inconsistency in the Mishnah, Talmud, and Aggadah as proofs of the falseness of

109. *Matteh 'Elohim.* 8r–10v (*Matteh 'Elohim*–Ramlah, 33–34).

rabbinic tradition was now mobilized to support the existence of an early archaic Karaism, whose traces, strewn throughout rabbinic literature, only needed to be identified and demonstrated. Mirroring the ongoing Rabbanization of Karaite thought, rabbinic texts were now becoming the "possession" of the Karaites, to be used to support historical expression, even as it was being used for halakhic considerations. If, in fact, the late antique rabbinic tradition was really a *Jewish* tradition, then the Karaites might find their own past and legal system embedded in the canon.

Before concluding, one must mention an account of historical "field research" conducted on Moses Bashyachi's travels. He states:[110]

> In my travels I went to Egypt, traveling to the city of Alexandria, where I stayed some days. One day I was in the market with a certain Rabbanite, and before us stood a Muslim house of prayer.[111] It was very large, and its construction was mighty and awe-inspiring, and very beautiful. This Rabbanite unintentionally said that this had been a synagogue of ours, which the Muslims had taken from us many years ago. It was from ancient times, built by Simeon ben Shetah in which to pray when he fled here on account of King Jannai. And, there is an altar inside upon which they used to offer burnt-offerings and sacrifices at that time. I said that it is not possible for a man such as he to do that, and he assured me that it was true. I was compelled to know if his words were true. I investigated and studied, and the truth was made known to me that thus it had occurred. I questioned and investigated among the Muslims regarding the matter of the altar, and they answered that it was true. They said that they did not honor it at all. I returned to the Rabbanites and said to them, "How could a man do thusly, to build an altar and offer burnt-offerings in other than the chosen place [Jerusalem]?"

This tantalizing account of Moses Bashyachi's visit to Alexandria introduces a halakhic discourse on the offering of sacrifices and on laws pertaining specifically to the Land of Israel. The purpose of the author's inclusion of this story is to argue against Simeon ben Shetah by claiming that he had acted in direct opposition to the injunctions of the Torah against offering sacrifices anywhere other then at Jerusalem. This is a prototypical sin, which plagues Israel and Judah in the time of their kings and is characteristic of the Samaritans, who sacrifice on Mount Gerizim.[112] Thus, further arguments were brought to bear against the progenitor of the rabbis.

110. Ibid., 6r; *Dod Mordekhai,* 56–57; *Matteh 'Elohim*–Ramlah, 25.

111. *bet tefilah shel ha-Yishme' 'elim.*

112. *Dod Mordekhai,* 56–57; *Matteh 'Elohim*–Ramlah, 25. Bashyachi utilizes the Bible and rabbinic literature in support of his argument.

Matteh ʾElohim is the first attempt since al-Qirqisānī at an all-inclusive historical presentation on the part of a Karaite. Whereas others addressed particular historical questions, Moses Bashyachi brought together three elements to fully embrace the metanarrative that had been developing for centuries and thus create a new Karaite history: (1) the anti-Sadducean apology; (2) the historiographical narrative derived from Judah Halevi and Josippon, incorporating the affair of Simeon ben Shetah (the aggrandizement of Shammai is simply an extension of this by way of a Karaite reading of Avot); and (3) the Karaite chain of tradition, which creates a superstructure upon which existing historical and halakhic considerations could be welded.

Poznanski had categorized this stage of Karaite historical expression simply, placing it under the rubric of Judah Halevi's influence. Only by way of description did he differentiate between the "Yefet problem," Elijah Bashyachi's introduction to *ʾAdderet ʾEliyahu,* Afendopolo's historical arguments, and the younger Bashyachi's synthesis. Such an approach restricts analysis and does not ask questions concerning the evolution of these "versions," their authors' individual purposes, and the cumulative result. The analysis provided in this chapter contributes to a more complex appreciation of these literary and historical phenomena.

Whereas Karaite historical expression in the Islamic period exhibited influence from both Muslim and Christian thought, in the Byzantino-Turkish environment historical thought was engaged more exclusively with rabbinic thought and halakhah.

~6

The Narrative Past: Karaite Apologetic Historiography in Eastern Europe, Seventeenth and Eighteenth Centuries

The status of being a minority within a minority was to be the fate relegated to Karaism. Even the florescence of Karaite scholarship in fifteenth- and sixteenth-century Constantinople was the result of its close sectarian relationship to Rabbanism. Karaism no longer represented a threat to mainstream rabbinic Judaism. Sectarian threats in the seventeenth and eighteenth centuries would emanate from communities driven by mystical and charismatic teachings. Consolidation within Karaite scholarship became emblematic, with little original or influential writing added to the Karaite literary canon.

The general decline of Karaism is marked by the weakness of scholarship coming from Constantinople.[1] In fact, the epigones of Karaite thought were to be found, by and large, among the Karaites of the Crimea and eastern Europe. The Crimea had had a Karaite presence for centuries, being part of the Byzantine sphere of influence. The thirteenth-century Aaron ben Joseph, as already indicated, had visited or even originated there.[2] From there, Karaites along

1. See Danon, "Karaites in European Turkey," 333–60, which covers a period through the nineteenth century.

2. See chapter 5, above. On the Karaites of the Crimea, see Mann's sparse remarks in *Texts and Studies,* 2: *Karaitica,* 287–93, and several later (18th c.) texts pertaining to the Karaites of the Crimea which he has reproduced, ibid., 437–550. See also Simon Szyszman, *Les Karaïtes d'Europe,* 30–33. With the Mongol conquest of the early thirteenth century and the subsequent Islamization of Mongol domains, the Karaites of the Crimea became themselves culturally Islamicate. Some of the work of Abraham Firkovich on the early settlement of the Karaites in the Crimea was later shown to have been based upon forged evidence. As a result good archaeological and textual data was lost or damaged to an extent that reconstruction is problematic. See Albert Harkavi (Abraham Elijah), *Altjüdische Denkmäler aus der Krim mitgetheilt von Abraham Firkowitsch 1839–1872,* and "Po voprosu o iudeyskikh

with other Jews had penetrated the interior of eastern Europe, following the trade routes of the rivers Don, Donets, and Dnieper. Problematic claims of historicity for Karaite settlement in such places as Troki go back to the thirteenth century, but one can be fairly secure in placing Karaites in Lithuania and Poland in the fifteenth century. Certainly, there was a burst of new Karaite settlement activity in the sixteenth and seventeenth centuries.[3]

In this chapter the development of what can now be recognized as Karaite literary historiography is examined; that is, among a few Karaite writers a genuine concern for history found expression in concerns for sources and narrative. The historical work of these authors will be described in terms of (1) the inheritance of extant Karaite literary sources and the effort on the part of these scholars to harmonize the content; (2) a culmination in Rabbanization that, in conjunction with Karaite-Rabbanite relations in eastern Europe, led to a new anti-Rabbanism; and (3) the influence of the Christian host culture, which shaped the literary results of these authors.

Declining Social Conditions and the Christian Renaissance-Reformation Discourse

From the sixteenth century onward, Karaite scholars of early modern Poland and Lithuania found themselves living in an intellectual environment that was charged with the fallout of the Renaissance and the Reformation. The religious and intellectual discourse of the day led the Karaites to become the objects of curiosity and academic interest on the part of Christian rulers and, most notably, Protestant scholars. By the same token, Karaite scholars were to avail themselves of opportunities for expression by engaging with this intellectual discourse.

We can begin to gauge the character of the eastern European Karaite environment by examining the world of Isaac ben Abraham Troki (d. 1594), whose work does not embrace historiography but does gives us insight into the eastern European environment. In his famous defense against Christianity, *Ḥizzuk ʾEmunah*, he reports on contacts with the clergy and aristocracy of sixteenth-century Poland.[4] The princes of Poland ruled over a large empire

---

drevnostyakh naydennykh Firkovichem v Krymu" (On Jewish antiquities found by Firkovich in Crimea). See also H. Strack, "Abraham Firkowitsch und der Wert seiner Entdeckungen."

3. For a somewhat outdated, but extensive introduction to the Karaites of Lithuania and Poland, see Mann, *Texts and Studies,* 2: *Karaitica,* 553–756. See also Szyszman, *Les Karaïtes d'Europe,* 24–68. It should be noted that Szyszman, a Karaite, occasionally indulges in historical speculation that supports his political agenda, which magnifies the importance of the Karaites. He is a staunch supporter of the Khazar theory. Cf. Omeljan Pritsak, "The Role of the Bosporus Kingdom and Late Hellenism as the Basis for the Medieval Cultures North of the Black Sea."

4. Possibly first published in Hebrew in 1593, where such claims are made throughout. See Isaac Troki, *Faith Strengthened, The Jewish Answer to Christianity.*

that stretched from the Baltic to near the Black Sea, encompassing numerous ethnic and religious groups. Under their dominion were Christians of both the Roman Catholic and Eastern rites, as well as lesser sects, including an important Armenian community. From its beginnings, Protestantism made headway in the east. In addition, there were Muslims in the Black Sea region. The Jews were represented by the Rabbanites and Karaites. It can be said that the sixteenth-century princes of Poland-Lithuania ruled over a society of such ethnic and religious diversity that order could be maintained only through a careful balance of state policy and a relative degree of tolerance.[5] This relative tolerance broke down many of the obstacles that had isolated Jews in other parts of Europe. Troki's education reflected this state of social openness. He knew Hebrew, Tatar, Polish, and perhaps a little Latin. The multicultural milieu provided a suitable environment in which to write his Jewish commentary on Christian theology.

By looking beyond sixteenth-century Polish pluralism to Christian intellectual concerns of the day one can more fully understand Troki's historical context. The intellectual setting for Troki's work was shaped to a great degree by the publication in 1564 of a Polish edition of Justin Martyr's *Dialogue with Trypho,* which became the source for Polish-Lithuanian antitrinitarian arguments of the day.[6] The Polish version of this discussion is part of a larger religious discourse that began with the growth of Christian-Hebraica in the

---

The generally acknowledged first edition was edited by Johann Christoff Wagenseil, *Tela ignea Satanae. Hoc est: Arcani, et horribiles Judaeorum adversus Christum Deum, et Christianam Religionem Libri Anekdotoi.* A more modern edition is found in David Deutsch, ed., *Rabbi Iizchak, Sohn Abrahams Sefer Chizzug Emunah: Befestigung im Glauben.* There have been many traditional Hebrew editions over the years of this important polemical work. The Karaite community of Israel has published an edition of *Ḥizzuk 'Emunah* (Ashdod, 1972) based upon the edition of New York, 1932. The textual transmission of *Ḥizzuk 'Emunah* is quite confused, and there is no identifiable "Karaite version."

5. See Janusz Tazbir, *A State Without Stakes, Polish Religious Toleration in the Sixteenth and Seventeenth Centuries.* For discussions of Polish religious toleration in the context of the Reformation, see Jean Bérenger, "The Spread of the Reformation in Eastern and Northern Europe"; and William J. Rose, *The Protestant Churches in Poland,* 1–33.

6. Translated by Simon Budny and published by Wawrzyniec Krzyszkowski *The Dispute of St. Justin, the Philosopher and Martyr, with Trypho the Jew* [Pol.]. Simon Budny was a leading antitrinitarian contemporary of Troki's. See David A. Frick, "The Biblical Philology of Szymon Budny: Between East and West," an introduction to a new edition to Simon Budny's Polish Bible (1572). I am grateful to David Frick, of the University of California, Berkeley, for allowing me to use this work in its prepublication manuscript form, now published in *Biblia, to jest Ksiegi Starego i Nowego Przymierza: In der Übersetzung des Simon Budny, herausgegeben von Hans Rothe und Frederich Scholz (1572).*

fifteenth and sixteenth centuries.[7] This European academic phenomenon, whose primary concern was the text of the Hebrew Bible, opened the door for the influence of Jewish thought on Christian scholars.[8] Indeed, scholars have postulated Jewish influences on the Reformation in general.[9] The result of academic engagement on the part of Christians with Jewish thought was a fear of "judaization," a theological error that originated in the earliest days of Christianity as the church sought to differentiate itself from Judaism and the Jewish people. "Such widespread popularity of Jewish opinion evinced fears that this renaissance age would witness the rebirth of the Jewish religion through its influence in Christian scholarly circles."[10] These fears helped create an intra-Christian debate regarding the Old Testament, the Law, and Jewish beliefs.[11] The Jews themselves sometimes became participants in these discussions, both by choice and through coercion.

Justin Martyr's dialogue became an important source for antitrinitarian Christians, whose views emerged in the context of the Reformation and with whose works Troki was familiar.[12] He reflects this by classifying Christians according to their views on the unity of God.[13] He also cites several Christian sources that were written in Polish and Latin, including works by Marcin

7. See Jerome Friedman, *The Most Ancient Testimony: Sixteenth-Century Christian-Hebraica in the Age of Renaissance Nostalgia.* Friedman coined the term *Christian-Hebraica,* indicating a diverse intellectual trend, to replace the older *Christian-Hebraism,* which could be misunderstood as a kind of movement with a particular ideological bent. See ibid., 7. See also William McKane, *Selected Christian Hebraists;* Hans Joachim Schoeps, *Philosemitismus im Barock;* and Charles Berlin and Aaron L. Katchen, *Christian Hebraism: The Study of Jewish Culture by Christian Scholars in Medieval and Early Modern Times.*

8. See Aaron L. Katchen, *Christian Hebraists and Dutch Rabbis: Seventeenth Century Apologetics and the Study of Maimonides'* Mishneh Torah.

9. See Louis I. Newman, *Jewish Influence on Christian Reform Movements,* for sections on Zwingli (454–510) and Martin Luther (617–30). Other important works on the Jews and the Reformation include Hayim Hillel Ben-Sasson, "The Reformation in Contemporary Jewish Eyes"; Jerome Friedman, "Sixteenth-Century European Jewry: Theologies of Crisis in Crisis"; idem, "Sixteenth-Century Christian-Hebraica: Scripture and the Renaissance Myth of the Past"; and idem, "The Reformation in Alien Eyes: Jewish Perceptions of Christian Troubles."

10. Jerome Friedman, "The Reformation and Jewish Antichristian Polemics," 83.

11. For an overview, see the first half of Frank E. Manuel, *The Broken Staff, Judaism through Christian Eyes.*

12. For an analysis of Troki's familiarity with contemporary Christian sectarian thought, see Robert Dán, "Isaac Troky and his 'Antitrinitarian' Sources." Cf. J. M. Rosenthal, "Marcin Czechowic and Jacob Belzice: Arian-Jewish Encounters in Sixteenth-century Poland."

13. He describes the contemporary Ebionites, Servetians, and Arians as believers in the "unity of God," as opposed to Catholics and Lutherans, who were trinitarian

Czechowic, Nicolò Paruta, the Cracow Bible, and the Brest Bible.[14] But, most importantly, Troki mentions at least twenty-six times the Budny Bible of 1572, to which he seems to have been responding directly.[15] Various arguments of Troki are in corresponding agreement or disagreement with specific exegetical discussions of contemporary Christian Poland. Consequently, the context for understanding *Ḥizzuk 'Emunah,* which as yet is not fully understood, goes beyond merely contextualizing it within the centuries-old medieval and early-modern genre of Jewish anti-Christian polemic.[16] Jewish engagement with Christian intellectual culture, as exemplified by Troki, also characterizes Karaite historiographers of the following centuries.

In a parallel manner, Christian Hebraists became interested in what was a previously unknown Jewish sect. Guillaume Postel's visit to Constantinople in 1538 introduced the European intellectual scene to Karaism, first exposing Christian scholars to the idea that there existed contemporary, nonrabbinic varieties of Judaism.[17] The idea of the Karaites became useful in the intrareligious debates in Christendom, so that the division between Protestants and Roman Catholics was projected onto the division between Karaites and Rabbanites. Academic interest in the Karaites began in religious and historical discussions concerned with Second Temple groups such as the Hasideans, Pharisees, Sadducees, and Essenes, about whom knowledge was newly proliferating from the academic study of the texts of Josephus and Josippon. The

---

in their beliefs. See the section on Troki in Frick's introduction to *Biblia.* On Michael Servetus's debt to Jewish thought, see Newman, *Jewish Influence on Christian Reform Movements,* 511–609; and Jerome Friedman, *Michael Servetus: A Case Study in Total Heresy.*

14. His references to Saint Ambrose and Martin Luther probably came from Czechowic and Budny. See Frick, introduction to *Biblia;* and Dán, "Isaac Troky and his 'Antitrinitarian' Sources," passim. The Cracow Bible is the Leopolita Bible published in 1561, 1575, and 1577, while the Brest Bible was published in 1563. See ibid., 32.

15. In the Wagenseil edition. See ibid., 75.

16. For an analysis of many of Troki's arguments, see Friedman, "The Reformation and Jewish Antichristian Polemics." It is unfortunate that Friedman used only the nineteenth-century English translation of *Ḥizzuk 'Emunah* (London, 1850), now published as *Faith Strengthened: The Jewish Answer to Christianity,* trans. Moses Mocatta, because the majority of Troki's critique of Christianity and specific details regarding the Lithuanian Christian scene, which are found in the Hebrew, were not included in the translation.

17. Described in his *Linguarum duodecim characteribus differentium alphabetum introductio,* 2:100. Postel described the Karaites as "Lecturarii," coining a phrase to indicate the scripturalist character of their beliefs. On Postel and the Karaites, see Marion Leathers Kuntz, *Guillaume Postel, Prophet of the Restitution of All Things: His Life and Thought,* 95f. See also William J. Bowsma, *Concordia Mundi: The Career and Thought of Guillaume Postel.* Postel also reported on Samaritans in Constantinople.

manner in which any of these groups might be portrayed was usually an overtly formulated polemic. The Karaites were introduced into the debate in 1604, when the Jesuit Nicolaus Serarius, a professor at the University of Mainz, claimed that there existed in his own time followers of Sadduceeism, known as Karaites.[18] In the following year, even the famous Joseph Justus Scaliger took a position on the Karaites, mirroring the Catholic-Protestant debate: "Just as the zealots of today hate those who are better then they themselves are, so are the Karaites hated by the rabbinic Jews because of the integrity of their life as well as their neglect of the traditions."[19]

J. van der Berg states, "With Protestant theologians, the Karaites remained in favour, though initially their knowledge of the Karaites was not as great as the sympathy they evinced for them."[20] Over time, Protestant academic interest in the Karaites led to research on Karaite texts and contact with contemporary Karaite scholars and communities.[21] The Reformed Dutch and the Lutheran Swedes in particular became interested in a sect that could be understood as reformist.[22] Even as the Protestants sought to recover the Christian past and repudiate the apostolic succession of Rome, so were they sometimes perceived and denounced as "Karaites" in Catholic polemical writing.[23]

18. See J. van den Berg, "Proto-Protestants? The Image of the Karaites as a Mirror of the Catholic-Protestant Controversy in the Seventeenth Century."

19. Translated in ibid., 36.

20. Ibid., 37.

21. Scaliger reports that he gained information from a certain Philippus Ferdinandus, a Christian convert from Judaism who visited the Karaites in Constantinople. See H.F. Wijnman, "Philippus Ferdinandus, Professor in het Arabisch aan de Leidse Universiteit . . . ," 558–80. For another contemporary report on the Karaites, see J. van den Berg, "John Covel's Letter on the Karaites (1677)."

22. On Dutch academic interest in the Karaites, see Yosef Kaplan, "The 'Karaites' of Amsterdam in the Early Eighteenth Century: An Unknown Chapter in the History of the Fermentation of Ideas in the Sephardi Community" [Heb.], now in English: " 'Karaites' in Early Eighteenth-century Amsterdam"; and E. G. E. van der Wall, "Johann Stephan Rittangel's Stay in the Dutch Republic, 1641–1642." On Dutch Christian-Hebraica, see the other studies in van den Berg and van der Wall, *Jewish-Christian Relations in the Seventeenth Century,* and Peter T. van Rooden, *Theology, Biblical Scholarship and Rabbinical Studies in the Seventeenth Century: Constantijn L'Empereur, 1591–1648, Professor of Hebrew and Theology at Leiden.*

On Swedish academic interest in the Karaites, see Simon Szyszman, "Gustaf Peringers Mission bei en Karäern," 215–28; idem, *Les Karaïtes d'Europe;* and Schoeps, *Philosemitismus im Barock,* passim. For a survey of the contemporary Swedish intellectual scene, see Susanna K. Åkerman, *Queen Christina and Her Circle: The Transformation of a Seventeenth-century Philosophical Libertine.*

23. The Catholic Richard Simon used the term, "Karaite," perhaps jocularly, when addressing Protestant correspondents. See Heinrich Graetz, *History of the Jews,* V, 181. On Richard Simon and the Karaites, see William McKane, *Selected*

Correspondingly, Protestants might think that study of this Jewish sect could serve their purposes in the struggle with Rome.[24]

Considerations beyond the Reformation discourse influenced the examination of the past in seventeenth-century eastern Europe.[25] The struggle between Protestant and Catholic remained unresolved, and a new statism emerged that undermined Polish unity from within and strengthened the governments and armies of Poland's neighbors. Beginning with the sixteenth century, the uncertainty of political and social life in the present, and the seeming uprooting of conceptual foundations based in the past led European intellectuals to seek to redefine the place of church or nation in their understanding of the world.[26] In Poland, an ideology emerged based in creative history that reclaimed a non-Christian past from church-bound historical ideology, and in the context of the Renaissance recovery of antiquity, rehabilitated and claimed as ancestors for the Polish aristocracy the ancient Sarmatians, masters of the great eastern European plain. Sarmatism, used in the fifteenth and sixteenth centuries to justify war and expansion, by the seventeenth century stood as an underpinning to the decline of Poland, supporting the dominance of the feudal nobility in the kingdom.[27]

Christian Hebraists, 143ff.; Richard Popkin, "Les Caraïtes et l'Émancipation des Juifs," and idem, "Lost Tribes." On Reformation historiography in general, see also Heinz Scheible, *Die Anfänge der Reformatorischen Geschichtesschreibung: Melanchton, Sleidan, Facius, und die Magdeburger Zenturien.*

24. The connections between early modern Christian scholarship and the Karaites were discussed by Elisheva Carlebach in "Christian Hebraism and Jewish Sectarianism: The Polemical Uses of Jewish Heresy," presented at the annual meeting of the Association for Jewish Studies, Boston, 1987. The best review is van den Berg, "Proto-Protestants?"

25. See Anthony Grafton, *Bring Out Your Dead: The Past as Revelation;* and idem, *Defenders of the Text: Traditions of Scholarship in an Age of Science, 1450–1800.*

26. See Eric Cochrane, *Historians and Historiography in the Italian Renaissance,* 457f. From 1559 to 1574, the so-called *Magdeburg Centuries* were published by Matthias Flacius Illyricus as a "major historical manifesto of the radical Lutherans." The Roman Catholic response came in the form of the *Annales Ecclesiasticae* (first folio published in 1588). See Scheible, *Die Angange der Reformatorischen Geschichtesschreibung: Melanchton, Sleidan, Facius, und die Magdeburger Zenturien.* On pan-Slavic ideologies in the Counter Reformation, see Frances Dubrovnik, *The Slavs in European History and Civilization,* 426–30. For a recent review, see Patrick J. Geary, *The Myth of Nations: The Medieval Origins of Europe.*

27. See S. Cynarski, "The Shape of Sarmatian Ideology in Poland." A contemporary English work deals with Sarmatism: Hartmann Schedel (1440–1514), *Sarmatia: The Early Polish Kingdom: From the Original Nuremburg Chronicle.* In contrast, the Lithuanian and Ruthenian nobles adopted an ideology that claimed the Trojans as ancestors. See Antoni Maczak, "Poland," 188; and Harold B. Segel, *Renaissance*

In the seventeenth and early eighteenth centuries, during which three Karaite historians were active, the situation in Poland-Lithuania was extremely unsettled. The military campaigns that crisscrossed the great plains of northeastern Europe in the seventeenth and eighteenth centuries heralded the decline into impotence of Poland, the growth of Brandenburg-Prussia, and the eventual failure of Sweden to position itself as a great power.[28] Beginning with the Chmielnicki massacres of 1648, these upheavals meant Jews, Rabbanite and Karaite alike, would face death, economic disruption, intermittent famine, and rapacious conduct on the part of foreign troops.[29] Shortly thereafter, the rise and collapse of the Sabbatean messianic movement and the

---

Culture in Poland: The Rise of Humanism, 1470–1543. Compare Gothicism in Sweden as an important parallel. See Kurt Johannesson, *The Renaissance of the Goths in Sixteenth-century Sweden: Johannes and Olaus Magnus as Politicians and Historians.* For a general discussion of Renaissance historicization, see Peter Burke, "The Uses of Italy." Early modern ethnographies were commented upon by Elisheva Carlebach in "Jewish Unbelief in the Seventeenth Century: The Case of Friedrich Christiani," presented at the annual meeting of the Association for Jewish Studies, Boston, Mass., 1992. For other approaches to Renaissance historical thinking, see Cochrane, *Historians and Historiography in the Italian Renaissance;* Stephen A. McKnight, *The Modern Age and the Recovery of Ancient Wisdom: A Reconsideration of Historical Consciousness, 1450–1650.* Cf. D. P. Walter, *The Ancient Theology: Studies in Christian Platonism from the Fifteenth to the Eighteenth Century.*

28. On the decline of Poland, see A. Kaminski, "The Eclipse of Poland," 681–715; Jill Lisk, *The Struggle for Supremacy in the Baltic: 1600–1725;* and Robert I. Frost, *After the Deluge: Poland-Lithuania and the Second Northern War, 1655–60.* On the Jews in this period, see Bernard D. Weinryb, *The Jews of Poland: A Social and Economic History of the Jewish Community in Poland from 1100–1800,* 179–205; M. J. Rosman, *The Lord's Jews: Magnate–Jewish Relations in the Polish–Lithuanian Commonwealth during the Eighteenth Century,* 1–7. The hardships of the era are emphasized by Mann in his description of the Karaite communities of eastern Europe in this period. See *Texts and Studies,* 2: *Karaitica,* 553–766.

29. The impact upon the Karaites of the Chmielnicki massacres and the subsequent decades of war in eastern Europe has not been the special subject of an article or monograph. In *Texts and Studies,* 2: *Karaitica,* Mann provides some information on the important Karaite centers of Troki and Lutzk (especially the Karaite suburb of Lutzk, Derazhne, which was destroyed in 1648). See 565ff., 584–87 and s.v. "Chmielnicki" in the index. Now see Mikhail Nosonovskii, "The Karaite Community in Derazhnia and Its Destruction."

A few particulars are known beyond Troki and Lutzk regarding the Karaites at this time. Karaites were massacred at Krasnoye, and survivors were transferred to Lutzk by General Kalinovski (see Yehuda Slutsky, *EJ* 10:1242, s.v. "Krasnoye"). There is no reason to believe that Karaites were excluded from anti-Jewish activity in the period 1648–55. Forced baptism was a principal element in these actions, and the Karaites would have been considered to be as much in need of Christian redemption as other Jews. One major characteristic of the events of 1648 was the

subsequent Jewish "witchhunt" for crypto-Sabbateans strained the Jewish world.[30] The great-grandfather of one of the later Karaite historiographers, Jeshua ben Simhah, had been killed in the Chmielnicki massacres.[31] Four generations later, the great-grandson, Simḥah Isaac Lutzki, was able to escape the continuing troubles in Poland-Lithuania by emigrating to the Crimea, where a larger, more secure Karaite community lived under the Muslim rule of Tatar khans. Nonetheless, the traumas and questions of eastern Europe impelled him, as it had his predecessors and Christian contemporaries, toward self-explanation through historical writing. Indeed, the idea of crisis and response is used as an interpretive device by Lutzki.

Invitation to Historiography: Solomon ben Aaron Troki and Mordecai ben Nisan

In the seventeenth and eighteenth centuries, some eastern European Karaite scholars were provided with an impetus toward self-explanation and creative history by direct queries originating from the Christian milieu. One of these writers, Solomon ben Aaron Troki, wrote *ʾAppiryon ʿAsah Lo* to inform the reader of "the reason for the division of the House of Israel into two, Karaites

---

gathering of refugee Jews into the larger fortified cities, where they might either be massacred or find protection. Undoubtedly, Karaites were among these refugees. If one of the main reasons that Jews were the objects of resentment was their role as arendars and lessees of the Polish nobility in the Ukraine, then the Karaites, fulfilling the same functions, would also be victims. For a general discussion of the Jews and the Chmielnicki massacres, see Weinryb, *The Jews of Poland,* 181–203.

In the subsequent period, it is reported that around 1690 Jan Sobieski relocated many Karaites from the communities of Lutzk, Troki, and Halicz to his royal estates in Galicia and elsewhere. See Heinrich Graetz, *History of the Jews,* 5:182; and Mann *Texts and Studies,* 2: *Karaitica,* 568. The general economic decline further contributed to the emigration of Karaites from towns to country locations. See Mann, ibid., 565. See also Roman Freund, *Karaites and Dejudaization: A Historical Review of an Endogamous and Exogenous Paradigm,* which states without citing a source that the Swedish invasion and plague of 1710 was commemorated by the Karaites of eastern Europe. This work needs to be used with care.

30. Very little is known about the Karaites and Sabbateanism. There is an anti-Sabbatean poem written by Daniel ben Moses Melamed of Damascus in 1669. See Samuel Poznanski, "Zweiter Nachtrag zur Karäischen Familie Firuz," 149–52. According to one source, Sabbetai Ṣevi numbered Karaites among his followers, and that he had a favorable attitude toward them. See Scholem, *Sabbatai Ṣevi, the Mystical Messiah, 1626–1676,* 775; and idem, "Sabbatian Documents Concerning Nathan of Gaza from the Archives of R. Mahallalel Halleluyah of Ancona," 225–41, esp. 233 [Heb.], which describes conversations between Nathan and R. Mahallalel Halleluyah and mentions the Karaites.

31. See Fürst, *Geschichte des Karäerthums,* 3:107.

and Rabbanites, and also to explain . . . the foundations of the faith of Karaism."[32] As attested to in its introduction, this small work was written sometime around 1696 in response to the scholarly interest of Johann Puffendorff, head of the Swedish Royal Academy in Riga, who arranged for Troki to lecture there.[33] Troki also wrote a large compendium of Karaite law and lore under the same title, similar to the Books of Precepts written in earlier centuries. This is extant only in manuscript.[34]

In the introduction to the shorter version of *ʾAppiryon ʿAsah Lo,* Troki briefly summarizes Karaite history. He begins by repeating the concerns of his Christian interrogator, stating that "the Rabbanites are known in all places, [beyond] remote lands and faraway seas. Whereas the name of the Karaites is only mentioned in books of scholars, like the books of Buxtorf and other transmitters of sacred books."[35] Puffendorff goes on to ask whether Rabbanite claims regarding Karaite history are correct, citing Ibn Daud, Judah Halevi, Maimonides, and three early modern Rabbanites whose chronology and descriptions of the age of Antigonus of Socho and Simeon ben Shetah are not in full agreement. These are Isaac ben Judah Abarbanel, Abraham Zacuto, and David Gans.[36]

Troki responds by stating that the Rabbanites who claim the Karaites are descended from Zadok and Boethos are lying and confused regarding history, with the exception of Judah Halevi.[37] As suggested by this beginning of his

32. Solomon b. Aaron Troki, *ʾAppiryon ʿAsah Lo* (shorter version), published by Neubauer in *Aus der Petersburger Bibliothek* (Leipzig, 1866), 1–29 [Heb.]; see 4 [Heb.]. Karaite editions were published in Israel in 1965 and 1999/2000 (see bibliography).

33. *ʾAppiryon ʿAsah Lo* (shorter version), 4. Troki visited the Academy in Riga in 1696 or 1697.

34. I have used a copy in the collection of the Jewish Theological Seminary of America in New York, JTS Mic. 3325 (246 fols.). They also possess another copy, JTS Mic. 3427 (251 fols.). Ten copies are known to exist, found in Vienna, Cincinnati, Oxford, New Haven, Paris, and in the Montefiore collection. On Troki, see Mann, *Texts and Studies,* 2: *Karaitica,* 740–45. Three selections were excerpted from MS Appiryon 2 of the Klau Library of the Hebrew Union College in Cincinnati and published by Mann, ibid., 1444–51.

35. *ʾAppiryon ʿAsah Lo* (shorter version), 4. There were two famous Buxtorfs, father (1564–1629) and son (1599–1664), both named Johannes and both Christian Hebraists at the University of Basel, one succeeding the other. The elder Buxtorf's Hebrew grammar and lexicons were quite influential among Christian scholars. It is not clear as to which Buxtorf Puffendorff is referring. See E. F. Kautzsch, *Johannes Buxtorf der Aeltere.*

36. *ʾAppiryon ʿAsah Lo* (shorter version), 4. Puffendorff is clearly conversant with contemporary Jewish historiography.

37. Ibid.

historical discussion, Troki's answer to the question is dependent upon the Karaite materials inherited from Constantinople. The metanarrative of Karaite history had by this time gained wide acceptance. The new consensus for Karaite historical expression was built upon Caleb Afendopolo's *ʿAsarah Maʾamarot* and Yefet ben Ṣaʿir's chain of tradition, both of which are cited by Troki.[38] Repeating and outlining the narrative, Troki places the division between Rabbanites and Karaites in the time of Simeon ben Shetah and Judah ben Tabbai, offering little of new interest. He does, however, indulge in a bit of chronological speculation, dating events from the Seleucid Antiochus and the rise of the Hasmoneans to the time of Simeon and Judah, claiming that Zadok and Boethos lived an astonishing 254 years before them.[39]

Troki's discussions on halakhah, which comprise the larger part of the longer version, show a great familiarity with rabbinic literature and law, yet his chronological speculation is almost ridiculous when compared with Mishnah Avot and the chronological exercises of Rabbanite historians. Nonetheless, the derivative character of Troki's historical expression (and halakhah) is representative of the compilatory character of the work in general. The larger version repeats the historical arguments in greater detail, but they are buried within the encyclopedic volume of the work.[40] His primary contribution to Karaite historiography is the inclusion of Karaite notables and scholars from Poland–Lithuania[41] and careful and extensive exegesis of rabbinic literature of all periods used to support the Karaite historical metanarrative.[42]

38. Ibid., 5.

39. Ibid., 5–6. The events as described follow Josippon.

40. *ʾAppiryon ʿAsah Lo* (long version) is divided into two large sections. Following a general introduction the first is entitled "Rehoboam ben Solomon" and follows the Book of Precepts genre. The second section, entitled "Jeroboam ben Nebat," engages rabbinic Judaism in matters of halakhah, exegesis, and history. Chapter 1 of "Rehoboam" contains the Karaite chain of tradition and material extracted from the *Ḥilluk,* as well as the names of later Karaite scholars (9r–13r). The introduction to the second section, "Jeroboam" (61r–96v), also reviews elements of the Karaite historical metanarrative, and chapter 41 in "Jeroboam" deals with "the difference between the Karaites and Sadducees according to the words of the author," reviewing responses to that accusation (217v–220r). Although there are several sections on Judah Halevi (in "Jeroboam," chapters 36–38, 199r–210v; and chapter 40, 214r–218r), these are focused on philosophical concerns, not history.

41. These are found following the chain of tradition in chapter 1 of "Rehoboam," 12v–13r. They were published by Mann in *Texts and Studies,* 2: *Karaitica,* 1446–48.

42. In the introduction to the second section (61r–96v, Troki cites rabbinic works extensively, using the literature to create textual support for the formulations of the Karaite historical metanarrative. Importantly, he cites works by their printed editions. A desideratum in Karaite studies is a careful examination of this work.

About the same time, the discussion of historiographical issues was taken up by Mordecai ben Nisan of Kokizow, who wrote two works presenting different versions of Jewish history. The first is his tract on Karaite history and belief, *Dod Mordekhai,* written in 1699. It is framed as a series of replies to questions from the Dutch scholar Jacob Trigland, of the University of Leiden.[43] The second work, *Levush Malkhut,* is a small handbook of Karaite law written in reply to more general questions from Charles XII, king of Sweden, who was interested in the Karaites as a result of his invasion of Poland in 1702.[44]

The circumstances that led to Trigland's inquiry can help us further understand the historical setting for a Christian-Karaite relationship in this period. In his letter, the text of which is included in the preface to *Dod Mordekhai,* Trigland states that he was informed of the presence of Karaites in Poland by a Jacob Thomson, a scholar and the son of a great Dutch merchant in Poland. Through the agency of Thomson, Trigland's letter of inquiry was sent to the east.[45] Mordecai recounts that the community of Lutzk had received a letter from an unknown Christian scholar, but since their community leader *(ḥazzan)* had died,[46] there was no one of scholarly ability to be found there. The letter was given to Mordecai when he was visiting Lutzk. He then made this inquiry known to all the Karaite scholars in the Kingdom of Poland and the Duchy of Lithuania, traveling "from scholar to scholar to 'ask of the mouths' [look at the sources] of their books."[47] Apologizing for his limited scholarship and effort, Mordecai explains that he wrote *Dod Mordekhai* and sent it via Zechariah ben Nisan, a Karaite merchant, who gave it to Jan Farhir of Danzig, while they were both in Lemberg.[48]

Although Karaites lived in the age of print, they rarely participated in the publication of printed materials. Troki's work will give some indication of the kind of library he had at his disposal and his exposure to printed Jewish (Rabbanite) texts.

43. Mordecai ben Nisan, *Dod Mordekhai,* first published with a Latin translation by Johann Christophorus Wolfius in *Notitia Karaeorum.* This work was later published under its own title together with three other small Karaite works (Vienna, 1830). Trigland was a colleague of Constantijn L'Empereur, a noted Hebraist and scholar of Judaism. See van Rooden, *Theology, Biblical Scholarship, and Rabbinical Studies.*

44. *Levush Malkhut* was published by Neubauer in *Aus der Petersburger Bibliothek,* 30–66 [Heb.].

45. *Dod Mordekhai,* 8. Trigland instructs whoever will answer his letter to send their reply to either Wilhelm Thomson in Lublin or Jan Farhir̊ [?] in Danzig, either of whom will forward the letter to Leiden. Ibid., 9.

46. David ha-Ḥazzan ben Shalom ha-Ḥazzan. See ibid., 10, in a footnote, which may or may not be a part of the original text.

47. Ibid.

48. Ibid., 11. This transaction is dated to the Hebrew month of Shevat (i.e., around January in the common calendar), 5460, which corresponds to the year 1700.

It is interesting to note that a second letter reached Mordecai before Trigland had received the text of *Dod Mordekhai.* In his second letter, Trigland indicates that he will write to R. Lev ben Lazarus in Zolkiew, a place of Karaite inhabitation. R. Lev's son resided in Leiden and offered to act as an interlocutor for these discussions. In this letter, Trigland sought to acquire Karaite texts.[49] Mordecai's response to the second letter gives us another glimpse of Karaite scholarship of the day. He says that "most of the books of our sages are in manuscript and on account of this only two or three copies are found in the hands of a select few. And they are comparatively expensive."[50] He is also deterred from sending such books to the Netherlands for fear of their falling into the hands of the Rabbanites; so he proposes to have such books copied and sent by way of a trusted Karaite. Most significantly, he adds, "or, you may desire, my lord, to have them printed."[51] Since Rabbanite printers would generally and necessarily avoid printing any Karaite text, in this correspondence Mordecai saw an opportunity for publication. In fact, Trigland did publish this and other Karaite texts in his *Diatribe de Secta Karaeorum.*[52]

Thus we have an account of the search by a Christian academic for contacts with eastern European Karaites. His interests are outlined in four questions that he posed in his letter, the first having the most historical content:[53]

I. The first question, divided into four parts:

1. Are those Karaites who are found today to be included in the time of the Second Temple among the sect of the Sadducees, who denied the resurrection of the dead, as is maintained by some Christian scholars, and who only in the end, on account

49. Ibid. It should be noted that Trigland is excessively complimentary and fawning in tone.

50. Ibid., 12. He goes on to describe the reluctance with which the owners of these manuscripts might accede to having them copied, and what it might cost in terms of both Polish and Prussian currencies.

51. Ibid.

52. Leiden, 1703. In the post-Sabbatean era, the publication of a book often required permission *(reshut)* and an imprimatur *(haskamah)* from community and rabbinic authorites to assure the orthodoxy of a book's contents. See Carlebach, *Pursuit of Heresy,* passim.

53. Ibid., 8–9, in the preface and repeated in the first chapter, 18–19. The second question is concerned with a purported correspondence between a certain R. Menaḥem, a Karaite, and Aqilas. Trigland wants to know whether this is Aquila, who translated the Torah into Greek, or Onkelos, who translated the Torah into Aramaic. The third seeks to identify a Karaite text belonging to Trigland. The fourth concerns the masoretic text of the Bible: Do the Rabbanites and Karaites share the same text? Secondly, did the vocalization originate with Moses, Ezra, or the scholars of Tiberias?

of shame, so they would not be considered heretics, admitted to the resurrection of the dead?

2. Or, were the Karaites in the time of the Second Temple a sect unto themselves?
3. Or, is it according to the belief of the scholars of the Talmud that they began in the days of Rav Anan, who disagreed regarding the exilarchate, and wanted to become exilarch, and because they did not want to appoint him as exilarch, he "went out" to an evil teaching and denied the Oral Law, and many people were attracted to him, and from them emerged the Karaites, this happening after the redaction of the Talmud?
4. And if you wish to say that they were in the time of the Second Temple a sect unto themselves, it is my desire to know the truth of the matter with clear proofs, and with wisdom and knowledge, from stories of events, whether it is true.

Mordecai, like his contemporary Solomon ben Aaron, used a compilatory approach to answer these historical questions. What emerges is a kind of handbook on Karaite history derived entirely from existing texts. Of the twelve chapters, ten are concerned with the first question. Whole chapters are comprised of lengthy extracts from Elijah Bashyachi, Afendopolo, Moses Bashyachi (and, thereby, Yefet ben Ṣaʿir), and from Rabbanite authors.[54]

Mordecai's primary contribution to the Karaite historical metanarrative is the inclusion of material taken from Azariah de' Rossi (d.c. 1578), an Italian Rabbanite who first utilized critical methods for examining rabbinic historical material.[55] With this slight innovation, Mordecai introduced the influence of the Italian Renaissance into Karaite historiography. According to de' Rossi, the *Panarion* of Epiphanius of Salamis indicates that the Rabbanites conflated

54. Chapter 2 (ibid., 20–22), which begins the response, follows Solomon ben Aaron Troki by engaging Ibn Daud, David Gans, Abraham Zacuto, and others in order to establish a chronology for the period of the Second Temple and to set the foundations for the discussion of Simeon ben Shetah and Judah ben Tabbai, which is based upon Judah Halevi and the Karaites who follow him. Chapter 6 (32–37) reproduces the chain of tradition attributed to Yefet ben Ṣaʿir, and chapter 8 (41–51) is taken from both Elijah Bashyachi's *ʾAdderet ʾEliyahu* and Afendopolo's *ʿAsarah Maʾamarot.* Chapter 9 (52–66) reproduces the historical sections of Moses Bashyachi's *Matteh ʾElohim,* with a short conclusion by Mordecai.

55. On de' Rossi, see Salo W. Baron, "Azariah de' Rossi: A Biographical Sketch," in *History and Jewish Historians: Essays and Addresses;* idem, "Azariah de' Rossi's Attitude to Life"; idem, "Azariah de' Rossi's Historical Method"; and Lester A. Segal, *Historical Consciousness and Religious Tradition in Azariah de' Rossi's* Me'or ʿEinayim. The translated text is Azariah de' Rossi, *Light of the Eyes,* trans. Joanna Weinberg.

two groups under the name Sadducee.[56] One group indeed followed Zadok and could be considered *minim* (heretics) and *apikorsim* (heretics or Epicureans). The other was a group that "sought after justice," *rodfe ṣedek,* and thus were known as *Ṣeddukim.* With the change of a vowel, Mordecai transformed these *Ṣeddukim* (Sadducees) into *Ṣaddikim* (righteous ones), thus differentiating archaic proto-Karaites from the heretical Sadducees, but answering in the positive to Trigland's question that the Karaites were a separate sect in the time of the Second Temple. In this way, Mordecai could co-opt those characteristics of the ancient Sadducees that were appropriate to his history (Sadducean opposition to the rabbis), while dissociating the Karaites from their "heretical" characteristics (denial of the resurrection of the dead).

Mordecai's other work, *Levush Malkhut,* begins with a short section on history. When Charles XII invaded Poland and Lithuania in 1702, he asked regarding his new subjects, "From what nation are they? What is their belief? What is the difference between the Talmudists and them?"[57] In this version of history, Mordecai departed from the Karaite metanarrative. He begins with Jeroboam's deviation from religion, but does not use this division to assign origins to the break between the Rabbanites and Karaites, but only to say that in Judah the true traditions were maintained. The false teachings of Jeroboam passed away with the disappearance beyond the River Sambatyon of the ten tribes of Israel who had been exiled by the Assyrians. Mordecai goes on to say that these tribes exist to this day, and, having repented of their error, possess a pristine copy of the Torah, with which they observe the Law without recourse to an extracanonical tradition.[58] In this way, Mordecai utilized the myth of the Ten Lost Tribes, which was quite popular in both Jewish and Christian circles of the day, often used for millennial and eschatological purposes.[59] Perhaps more importantly, he imagines a truly scripturalist Jewry possessing unimpeachable historical credentials. This imaginary Judaism casts a veil over the practice of the less-than-fully-scripturalist Karaites, while at the same time offers hopeful possibility in the historical representation of a people who erred but repented.

Mordecai goes on to say that the Torah was lost to the Jews in the days of Antiochus and was subsequently recovered by the Hasmoneans by using the Ptolemaic copy in Egypt.[60] This is loosely based on a reading of Josippon, where it says that Philip, a Macedonian captain, "killed many from the community of the righteous."[61] Josippon supplies the reason why the Torah was

56. See Azariah de' Rossi, *Me'or 'Enayim, 'Imre Binah*, ed. Cassel, section 3, 90–97. On Epiphanius (d. 402), see chapter 2, above.

57. *Levush Malkhut,* 30.

58. Ibid., 31.

59. See Popkin, "Lost Tribes."

60. *Levush Malkhut,* 33.

61. *Sefer Yosippon,* Flusser, ed., 68.

lost. Its recovery is derived by appropriating the account of the translation of the Septuagint to explain the recovery of the Torah from Egypt. The purpose of this convoluted historical narrative is to establish a condition wherein disagreements began to emerge among the scholars of antiquity in the absence of the written Torah. The stage is thereby set for the division of the Karaites and Rabbanites.

The narrative goes on to review the affairs of John Hyrcanus and Alexander Jannaeus and the now well-accepted Karaite version of Simeon ben Shetah and Judah ben Tabbai. The Sadducees and Boethusians, as well as Judah ha-Nasi and Anan, are mentioned in passing.[62] The focus of this narrative is the "archaic history" of the Karaites; that is, the period preceding Anan and historically identifiable medieval Karaism.

These two Karaites, Solomon ben Aaron Troki and Mordecai ben Nisan, were the first to draft fully articulated versions of Karaite history based upon Karaite and rabbinic historiographical notions. Their contacts with Christian scholars left a self-conscious mark on their writing and were used as literary framing devices within the historical narratives themselves.[63]

The Creative History of Simhah Isaac Lutzki

The most complete construction of Karaite historical expression is found in the works of Simhah Isaac ben Moses of Lutzk (d. 1766), known as Lutzki. Lutzki's view of Jewish history is found in two of his works. One is a small work on the differences between the Karaites and Rabbanites, entitled *ʾOraḥ Ṣaddikim* (Way of the righteous), written in 1757.[64] The other, a large volume from which the smaller one is derived, is *Meʾirat ʿEnayim,* a major compilation of law, commentary, and theology.[65] Although *ʾOraḥ Ṣaddikim* has

62. *Levush Malkhut,* 36.

63. On other Christian contacts with Karaite scholars, see Szyszman, *Les Karaïtes d'Europe,* passim, but esp. 49–52.

64. Published in *Dod Mordekhai,* fols. 16r–27v. This volume, which includes three other small Karaite works, was reprinted by the Karaite community in Israel, 1966. *Oraḥ Ṣaddikim* is found on 77–119. On Lutzki in general, see Isaac Broydé in *JE* 8:219–20, s.v. "Luzki, Simhah Isaac." In addition, some of his correspondence is found in Jacob Mann, *Texts and Studies,* 2: *Karaitica;* see index.

65. For this study I have used JTS MS Mic. 5448 (180 fols.) from the collection of the Jewish Theological Seminary of America in New York. *Meʾirat ʿEnayim,* comprises folios 1r–157v. Like Solomon ben Aaron's long version of *ʾAppiryon ʿAsah Lo,* the text is divided into two main sections. The first, *Ner Miṣvah* (1r–100r), is a compilation and commentary on the commandments arranged according to the Decalogue. The second section, *Ner Ṣaddikim* (101r–157v), describes the differences between the Karaites and Rabbanites, including sections on Karaite genealogy and bibliography. For the historical sections, see 101r–134r. Other known manuscripts of *ME* are at Yale University (Heb. 131, 76 fols.) and at the Klau Library of the Hebrew Union College in Cincinnati (849/2 = MS Fränkel, no. 170, fols. 91r–242r). On the latter manuscript, see Mann, *Texts and Studies,* 2: *Karaitica,* 1409ff.

received some scholarly attention, especially its section on Karaite bibliography, *Me'irat 'Enayim,* extant only in manuscript, has largely been ignored.

Lutzki provides a complete reading of the Karaite historical metanarrative. That is to say, he seeks to utilize as much of the material as possible, harmonizing any contradictory elements, to create a single narrative text. In addition, it can be defined as "creative history," a kind of historicized thinking that utilizes available traditional sources and, in the realm of rhetorical and doctrinal probability, fictionalizes upon them with the purpose of maintaining particular theological, legal, and polemical agendas.[66] In this context, it establishes the historico-conceptual bases for a Karaite chain of tradition,[67] which proceeds forward in time from Anan[68] by way of two constructs: genealogical stemmae of both high priests and Karaite patriarchs, and chronological bibliographical lists of Karaite scholars and literature.[69] Lutzki's "creative history" fulfills the need for narrative and historical continuity by "filling in" the period between Moses and Anan. It supplements the skeletal chain of tradition by narrating what we may call an "archaic history of religion."

Lutzki's history in its broader outlines conforms with that of the rabbis, beginning with Moses and the revelation at Sinai. Astonishingly (from a scripturalist point of view), but in accordance with the texts we have reviewed, it assumes the existence of an extrabiblical tradition, an idea the Karaites had come to embrace, as has been shown, in order to explain their particular legal interpretations of the Hebrew Bible. In addition, Lutzki describes the Karaite chain of tradition, with all of its accompanying historical implications. If the Karaites were willing to posit an extrabiblical legal tradition, then it was only a logical step to describe the origins and history of such a tradition. Additionally, one cannot describe such a history without creating an origin and history for the Rabbanites, for one would want to know how the majority of Jews came to hold false beliefs. By addressing these concerns, Lutzki's narrative becomes an heresiographical essay in Jewish history. He portrays a Judaism that differs from that of the rabbis without going so far as to claim that the Karaites are a different Israel.

66. The term *creative history* is taken from D. Mendels, "'Creative History' in the Hellenistic Near East." On historical thinking in antiquity that is similar, see Isaiah M. Gafni, "'Pre-Histories' of Jerusalem in Hellenistic, Jewish, and Christian Literature."

67. See *OṢ,* 79: "How each man received [tradition] from the mouth of another from the time of Moses to the time of our latter sages."

68. For Lutzki's Karaism, Anan's career represents the point where the schism between the Rabbanites and Karaites is finalized. See *ME,* 124v; *OṢ,* 89.

69. For the lists of patriarchs, high priests, and scholars who comprise the Karaite chain of tradition, see *ME,* 131v–134r and *OṢ,* 94–101. For the important bio-bibliographical lists, see *ME,* 134r–157r; and *OṢ,* 101–17.

Lutzki's conclusion to what can be called a Karaite historical project is found in writings that represent the most comprehensive Karaite reading of the Jewish past. Lutzki constructed his work using multiple sources, Karaite and rabbinic, interweaving many different versions of the past that had resulted from Karaite struggles with history. But he went beyond other Karaite writers by mobilizing the content of the Karaite historical "metatext" in an effort to create as seamless and consistent a narrative as possible.

Torah and Truth. In the smaller work, *ʾOraḥ Ṣaddikim,* Lutzki holds that there was no division in Israel until the death of Solomon, when Jeroboam, a member of the Great Assembly, fabricated false teachings in order to support a separate northern kingdom. Lutzki credits Jeroboam with the introduction of halakhot that would later be part of rabbinic law. These include the determination of the new moon by reckoning, the nineteen-year calendrical cycle, the worship of intermediaries, such as angels and spirits, the use of talismans and astrology, and that sacrifices be offered at a place other than Jerusalem, leading to the proliferation of unsanctioned altars and false prophets.[70] The heresiographical intent of the narrative follows the material of al-Qirqisānī as it was transmitted by Judah Hadassi. The emphasis on points of halakhic difference between the Karaites and Rabbanites, which are ascribed to Jeroboam, provides historicized setting for the origins of these practices. The division of Israel after the death of King Solomon had became an event of symbolic importance to the Karaites. Accordingly, Solomon ben Aaron Troki had named the two main sections of *ʾAppiryon ʿAsah Lo* after King Solomon's successors, Rehoboam ben Solomon and Jeroboam ben Nebat.[71]

In the larger, more scholarly systematic work, *Meʾirat ʿEnayim,* Lutzki fails to credit Jeroboam with the first *maḥloket* (schism), but does hold to First Temple origins for the beginnings of division in Israel.[72] In this he concurs with the important fourteenth-century Karaite philosopher, legalist, and commentator Aaron ben Elijah, but disagrees with him regarding the nature of this division. For Aaron, there was no disagreement in Israel regarding divine teachings until the *galut,* or exile, when the response to crisis would lead to the dissemination of and adherence to false teachings.[73] Lutzki adopts this theme in part, but develops a theory based on social hierarchy to explain the maintenance and conveyance of knowledge in ancient Israel based on a philosophical explanation of prophecy and human knowledge lifted from a different part of Aaron ben Elijah's work.[74]

70. *OṢ,* 82–83.

71. See note 40, above.

72. In fact, he reviews three opinions regarding the origins of the Karaites (i.e., in the period of the Hasmoneans, at the time of Antiochus's persecution, and in the period of the First Temple). See *ME,* 103v–107r.

73. Aaron ben Elijah, Morris Charner, trans., *ʿEṣ Ḥayyim,* chap. 1, 6–8.

74. Aaron ben Elijah, *Keter Torah,* Beshallaḥ, sec. 14, 75f.

According to Lutzki, Moses made a single transcription of the Torah, containing no errors, which was kept concealed in the side of the Ark of the Covenant, and could be viewed only by the high priest. From this "master," copies were made, such as the *mishneh Torah* for the king and for a very few others such as prophets, elders, judges, members of the Sanhedrin, and priests of the upper echelons. In this way, the text of the Torah was kept to an elite few and no error or change crept into the text. In the same way, the oral teaching, the *perush* that was given to Moses, was transmitted among this elite.[75] Although the high priests and members of the *bet din ha-gadol,* or high court, taught the tradition to only a select few, there would always be men with evil intentions. Those who were lacking in wisdom and rationality or those who had perhaps received a divine message but did not have the capability to understand it properly began to teach secret matters, utilizing astrology and magic, and saying whatever was necessary to influence the masses. These are the *nevi'e ha-sheker,* or "false prophets."[76]

In a centuries-old, parallel development, the warnings of the prophets had been transformed by some of the church fathers into the accusations of proto-Christians against a sinful erring Israel.[77] But for Lutzki, they became the warnings of good prophets and the *bet din ha-gadol* against the evil *nevi'e ha-sheker.* When the condition of exile is added to these circumstances—that is, after Israelites began to live outside of the Land of Israel—they lost the natural basis of community leadership and were more likely to be misled by false prophets.[78]

Lutzki contrasts such conditions to his own time, when "every man has a Sefer Torah."[79] The imagined societal construction in which the elite, the priests and prophets, protect and restrict the dissemination of religious knowledge works at three levels. First, it recalls medieval Karaite accusations directed against the rabbis, who as "shepherds of the exile" held positions of power over all Israel. By taking hold of the Torah, Karaite scripturalists had hoped to break the dominance of the rabbinic elite. Second, there is an embedded subtle suggestion that associates the elites of ancient Israel, a noble minority in biblical (sanctioned) time, with the Karaites, a minority in the time of the author. The equation suggests that if the two minorities can be identified one with the other, then the nobility of the biblical elite can be

75. *ME,* 108v–109v.

76. Lit., "prophets of the lie." *ME,* 110v–111r. In *OṢ*, the origin of the *nevi'e ha-sheker* is simply located in the period following Jeroboam (83). Those lacking in wisdom or rationality is an idea derived from Aaron ben Elijah's account of prophecy. Compare to Maimonides, *Guide for the Perplexed,* part 2, chapters 32–47, esp. chapter 36, entitled by M. Friedländer in his translation as "On the Mental, Physical, and Moral Faculties of the Prophets."

77. See Ruether, "The *Adversus Judaeos* Tradition," 27–50.

78. *ME,* 111r.

79. *ME,* 109v.

transferred to the latter-day minority, which can now see itself as an elite. Third, it echoes some of the debates of Lutzki's lifetime. In the age of printing, especially after Sabbetai Ṣevi, who mobilized mass messianic activism using kabbalistic ideology, it was argued that esoteric knowledge could be dangerous if available to the masses.[80] Lutzki's historical thinking also reflects conditions within the small, scattered eastern European Karaite communities, whose scholarly class was attenuated and whose general population was hard-pressed. To note a historical irony, the religious and legal anarchy that the elites of ancient Israel sought to contain (as portrayed by Lutzki) echoes the very conditions within the medieval Karaite community to which al-Qirqisānī testifies in the tenth century, before a common Karaite belief and tradition had crystallized.[81]

In *Me'irat ʿEnayim,* Lutzki describes another feature of tradition. He distinguishes between two types of interpretation of the Law given to Moses by God: the material or physical *(perush ha-gashmi),* and the spiritual *(perush ha-ruḥani).* He states that the physical teachings are found in the Mishnah, Talmud, Midrashim, the collections of the Yalkutim, and the works of the geonim.[82] As the following historical narrative will show, although rabbinic texts contain some genuine traditions, the true physical teachings were forgotten and reworked, and as a result are full of error.[83] This somewhat apologetic theme is typical in later Karaism, embodying a denunciation of rabbinic texts while at the same time permitting some accommodation between Karaite jurisprudence and rabbinic halakhah. In contrast, the spiritual *perushim* are true and ancient, and can be found in the Zohar, Cordovero's *Pardes Rimmonim,* and the works of Isaac Luria. Although Karaism has traditionally rejected mysticism, in clear opposition to kabbalah, Lutzki in fact reveals himself to be a kabbalist. Idiosyncratically, Lutzki confirms the necessary rootedness of kabbalistic teaching in the idea of tradition, but separates those teachings from the defective halakhic and aggadic literature of Rabbanism.[84]

"Killing the Scholars." With the destruction of the First Temple, Lutzki uses a theory of crisis and response, while harmonizing his narrative with

80. See Carlebach, *Pursuit of Heresy,* passim, but esp. 137ff.

81. See chapter 2, above. Regarding the Karaites, al-Qirqisānī laments that "scarce two of them are to be found who agree on anything, but this one will agree with the other in one matter, and this one will disagree with that on various matters." *Kitāb al-anwār wal-marāqib,* trans. Lockwood, 1:2.21, 104. See also ibid., 1:18, 151–52, for a lengthy list of Karaite halakhic variations.

82. *ME,* 107r–v.

83. *ME,* 108r, *OṢ,* 94.

84. *ME,* ibid., also 114v. Lutzki's mystical works include *Kevod 'Elohim,* a commentary on Joseph ben Mordecai Malinovski Troki's mystical prayer "Ha-'Elef Lekha"; *Sefer Bereshit,* a mystic explanation of the Creation; *Rekhev 'Elohim,* on the *ma'aseh merkavah; Kevod Mal'akhim,* a mystical explanation of the letters of the Hebrew alphabet; *Sefer ha-Tappuaḥ,* on the Creation and the *maʿaseh merkavah*

elements from the works of the fourteenth-century Aaron ben Elijah. In both books, Lutzki establishes a historical principle that will be used four times. He models four historical waves of crisis and response that led to deepening explanations for the Karaite–Rabbanite rift. The Babylonian conquest of Judah and Jerusalem led to the killing of the prophets, priests, Levites, and members of the *bet din ha-gadol,* all of whom were the guardians of an unsullied transmission of text and teaching from the time of Moses. These leaders were the first victims of the conquering armies, and as a result more false prophets than true ones survived. "Killing the scholars" becomes a motif to explain the decline of true learning in Israel—"because this is the nature of the world."[85] When the elites are killed, then leadership is lost and foolishness in the form of Rabbanism prevails.[86]

The idea that the Law suffered or was lost as a result of crisis is not unique to Karaism. Parallels in rabbinic literature indicate the appropriation of a rabbinic theme that parallels other examples of the interlinear reading of

---

according to Lurianic kabbalah; and *Livnat ha-Sappir,* on the ten *sephirot.* None of these have been published. Cf. Isaac Broydé's article in *JE:*

> Luzki was a strong believer in Cabala, which he defends in his "Or ha-Hayyim," "Libnat ha-Sappir," and "Sefer ha-Tappuah." He asserts that the Zohar was composed before the Mishnah, although it became known only at the time of Joseph Gikatilla. Had Maimonides, he says, known of this divine book he would not have spent his time on the futilities of philosophy; and when Luzki criticizes the Cabala, it is only the practical and not the speculative Cabala. Luzki cites the great rabbinical authorities who believed in the authenticity of the Zohar, from Abravanel down to Joseph Delmedigo. According to him there were cabalists even among the Karaites.

'Or ha-Ḥayyim is a commentary on Aaron ben Elijah's philosophical work, *'Eṣ Ḥayyim.* See Daniel J. Lasker, "Simhah Isaac Lutzki: An Eighteenth-century Karaite Kabbalist" [Heb.].

85. *OṢ,* 84. The full citation reads: "Because it is the nature of the world that when great trouble and evil comes to a particular nation and kingdom then the leaders who are great and faithful and superior are lost, while the small and deficient remain. Thus it was also during the destruction of the Temple."

86. Compare Christian interpretations of the killing of the prophets, a historicizing device used to explain the evils committed by Israel against God's chosen messengers. See Matt. 23:37; Luke 13:34; Justin, *Dialogue with Trypho* 120, 5; and Origen's letter to Julius Africanus. For other examples, see Ruether, "The *Adversus Judaeos* Tradition."

For parenthetic historicizations that portray the killing of the prophets in rabbinic literature, see Sifre Zuta, Num. 15:23; Ex. Rab. 31:16; Tanhuma, Tazria, 9; Pes. Rabbati 129a. On King Manasseh killing Isaiah, see BT Yeb. 49b; PT Sanhedrin 10, 2 (28b); BT San. 103b; Lev. Rab. 10, 2; and also the pseudepigraphic *Ascension of Isaiah.* On the murder of Zechariah, see PT Taan. 4, 8 (69a); Pes. R. Kahana on Lamentations. On the killing of Jeremiah, see *Midrash Aggadah,* Num., 157–58.

rabbinic literature that characterizes aspects of later Karaite legal and exegetical thought. To cite one instance, the Rabbanite David Kimḥi (d.c. 1235) uses this theme in the introduction to his commentary on Joshua to explain the differences between the *ketiv* and *kere* readings of the Torah in a similar manner, "In the course of the first exile the books were lost, the scholars dispersed and the students of the Torah dead, so that the men of the Great Assembly who restored the Torah to its previous status" were required to develop masoretic methodology.[87]

Me'irat ʿEnayim continues describing the historical procession of knowledge. At the time of the destruction of the First Temple, the prophet Jeremiah hid Moses' *editio princeps* of the Torah, never to be seen again, and wrote down in a book all the true *perushim;* that is, a true (read, Karaite) version of tradition. He gave this book to his scribe, Baruch ben Neriah, who continued to teach the complete true tradition in Babylon. Baruch's foremost pupil was Ezra, whose foremost pupil was his own nephew, Simeon the Just, the first tradent in the rabbinic chain of tradition in Mishnah Avot, chapter 1. Following the strictures of the period, the true teachings were reserved for the few, not for the masses. Only Ezra and Simeon were taught all of the teachings, whereas other students received portions of the law or individual halakhot. Ezra and Simeon are portrayed in the image of Moses and Eleazar, uncle and nephew, prophet and priest, together inaugurating a new Temple.[88] Mirroring

87. See Baker and Nicholson, eds., *The Commentary of Rabbi David Kimhi on Psalms CXX–CL,* xxiv. Similarly, the ninth-tenth-century Muslim historian al-Ṭabarī claims the Torah was lost in the Babylonian destruction and credits Ezra with its recovery by way of an angelic revelation. See al-Ṭabarī, *The History of al-Ṭabarī (Ta'rīkh al-rusūl wa'l-mulūk),* vol. 4: *The Ancient Kingdoms,* 65–66. The Renaissance Jewish historian, Azariah de' Rossi quotes Origen and Rhodiginus to similar effect—that Moses did receive the Oral Ḷaw, which was forgotten by the Jews but restored by Ezra. See *Maṣref la-Kesef,* ch. 29, n. 26.

88. *ME,* 112r–113r. It is interesting that other creative histories have focused on Jeremiah and Baruch, or Ezra, to explain the nature of the transmission of divine knowledge. In the creative history of the Anglo-Israelites, Jeremiah and Baruch embark on a journey to Ireland, accompanied by a daughter of King Zedekiah. There they establish God's true teaching, while the daughter, the seed of David of the tribe of Judah, is wed into the Irish royal house, descendants of the tribe of Ephraim. For an example from this wide-ranging literature, see Joseph Wild, *The Ten Lost Tribes.* This creative history was outlined in great detail by the television evangelist Dr. Gene Scott in his broadcast of the week of March 3, 1991, on the "Inter-Varsity Network." See also my forthcoming article "What Has Anglia to Do with Jerusalem? A Biblical Explanation for Anglo–Saxon Ethnogenesis."

Among some early church fathers, and especially in Islam, Ezra is accused of altering and forging the divine text, sullying the procession of revealed knowledge to humankind. See Mahmoud Ayoub, "'ʿUzayr in the Qur'an and Muslim Tradition"; and "Ezra-ʿUzayr: The Metamorphosis of a Polemical Motif," in Hava Lazarus-Yafeh, *Intertwined Worlds: Medieval Islam and Bible Criticism,* ch. 3, 50–74.

the "pairs" of Avot 1, *Me'irat 'Enayim* stipulates that from the time of Moses and Aaron until the destruction of the Second Temple there were always two heads of the *bet din ha-gadol*—a high priest and either a king, prophet, or judge.[89] For most of this time, they were the bearers of a complete and uncorrupted tradition. In this span of history, Lutzki uses both themes of crisis and response and preservation of the truth by social elites.

'Oraḥ Ṣaddikim presents a different treatment of the transmission of knowledge from the First Temple to the Second Temple. The few who followed true teachings and true prophets survived by following Jeremiah to Egypt. Those who adhered to lies and the teachings of false prophets flourished in the Land of Israel. In the shorter work, Lutzki follows the *Ḥilluk*, utilizing a reading from Jeremiah, chapter 24, to depict Israel after the rebuilding of the Temple. He divides Israel between the "good figs," who represent the later prophets, and the "bad figs," a sect of evildoers. These are also identified as "destroyers of the covenant," who took Ammonite and Moabite wives, divorced their Hebrew wives, and offered sacrifices in states of impurity.[90] However, some of the "bad figs" escaped the Babylonian conquest by going to Egypt. Shortly thereafter, what had now become the false sect postulated a second Torah, at the time of *ḥatimat ha-ḥazon*, the end of prophecy.[91] Lutzki clearly understands the rabbinic connection between halakhah and prophecy. The transition created problems for the rabbis, forcing them to seek explanations to resist appearances of prophecy in their own times. In the rabbinic theory of transmission, the prophets become sages, standing in the chain of tradition as tradents and scholars. The members of the Great Assembly, the transitional nexus of prophetic-rabbinic succession, is made up of both prophets and sages, including such colleagues as Ezra, Malachi, Zechariah, and Haggai, as well as Simeon the Just.[92] Lutzki's accusation is a distorted reflection of the rabbis' own historical ideology.

The theme of crisis and response reappears in both texts in the time of Mattathias and Antiochus. Citing Josippon, Lutzki states that the Sanhedrin and the sages were killed by the Greeks.[93] As before, only a few survivors

89. *ME*, 110v.

90. "As with these good figs, so will I single out for good the Judean exiles" (Jer. 24:5). "And like the bad figs . . . I will make them a horror—an evil—to all the kingdoms of the earth, a disgrace and a proverb, a byword and a curse in all the places to which I banish them" (Jer. 24:8–9). Compare the transgressions of the evildoers to the illegal innovations ascribed to Jeroboam, above.

91. *OṢ*, 84.

92. See chapter 1, above. The rabbinic discourse eschewed an explicit acknowledgment of innovation and sought an eternal basis for the Law. The rabbinic idea of transmission barely conceals an idea of the succession of the rabbis to the priests and prophets.

93. *Sefer Yosippon*, 68.

bearing portions of the true tradition remained alive by hiding in the wilderness. As a result of this second instance of "killing the scholars," all written materials were destroyed, marking an end to an unsullied transmission of the complete true tradition that started with Moses. Great confusion proliferated, and the division between what was now two sects increased.[94] In *Me'irat ʿEnayim,* the effects of the crisis are described more fully. The loss required that knowledge be recovered, so human agency and rational speculation became necessary to deduce the correct interpretation of the divine text. This beginning of halakhic research led to the origins of *hekkesh,* the characteristic Karaite exegetical tool. Through human effort different interpretations of the Law now proliferated, leading to two types of problem: teachings that either deviated from the intention of the Torah and those that added to or subtracted from the specifics of the Law.[95] Lutzki uses this explanation as a device to present a list of differences between Karaite and Rabbanite halakhah.[96]

The third instance of the "killing the scholars" takes place in the time of the Hasmoneans, based upon Halevi and the accounts that appear in BT Kiddushin 66a and Josephus. The Sanhedrin and the sages were killed when offense was taken by the king, identified by Lutzki as both Yannai (Alexander Jannaeus) and Yohanan (John Hyrcanus).[97] There are only two survivors. The first is Judah ben Tabbai, who is saved by God; the other is Simeon ben Shetah, brother of the queen and founder of the protorabbinic Pharisees.[98]

With this episode, Lutzki follows the well-accepted Karaite metanarrative, reflecting a more direct engagement with the rabbinic historiographic tradition. Like Simeon the Just, who had been grounded in Lutzki's Karaite reading of history through his relationship to Ezra, so the later pair of Simeon ben Shetah and Judah ben Tabbai are found in the primary rabbinic source for the chain of tradition in Mishnah Avot. This example of the interlinear reading of rabbinic literature recognizes the centrality of this mishnaic text to rabbinic notions of history and tradition. In further accordance with the version of BT Kiddushin, Simeon escapes Jannai's anger by going to Egypt. But in the context of Karaite polemic, the hubris of Jeroboam is recalled, as Simeon aggrandizes personal power among the Jews of Egypt. He builds a temple and an

94. *OṢ,* 85.

95. *ME,* 113v–115r. On *hekkesh* in Karaism, see chapter 2, and the conclusion to part 1, above. Cf. Ankori, *Karaites in Byzantium,* 217–18, esp. notes.

96. *ME,* 115r–116r. These laws include the use of a blue thread in the *ṣiṣit,* the use of a ram's horn on Rosh ha-Shanah, regulations regarding incest, Sabbath prohibitions, the determination of the New Moon, methods of calendation, fixing the date of Shavuot, methods of slaughtering, rules regarding the eating of milk and meat, the eating of certain fats, and issues of purity.

97. Whether the king was actually Alexander Jannaeus or his father, John Hyrcanus, is immaterial to the Karaite reading. Lutzki's confusion reflects the problem within rabbinic literature. See chapter 4, above.

98. *ME,* 116v–118v, *OṢ,* 85.

altar and offers unsanctioned sacrifices. He "concocted strange interpretations" of the Law, and by claiming that they were "laws of Moses from Sinai" he established the false chain of tradition of the rabbis.[99] In accordance with the narrative in *'Oraḥ Ṣaddikim,* Simeon studied false teachings with descendants of the "bad figs," who survived in Egypt after the destruction of the First Temple, thus becoming a follower of the *torah* (teaching) of Jeroboam.[100]

In BT Kiddushin, it is emphasized that Simeon ben Shetah "restored the traditional Law."[101] To the Karaites, such a restoration was a crime. Although the idea of restoration is not central to rabbinic ideology, it is nevertheless not unknown. To cite one example, in BT Sukkah 20a it is recorded "that when Torah began to be forgotten in Israel, Ezra came up from Babylon and restored it, again it was forgotten and Hillel came up from Babylon and restored it, again it was forgotten and Rabbi Hiyya and his sons came up from Babylon and restored it." Such remarks can appear, as in this case, as support for the prominence of Babylonian rabbinic scholarship and the high standing of its rabbis. However, such a transformation of law into narrative becomes part of a larger historical ideology. Several other instances of this type of didactic device can be noted, including that of Kimḥi, cited above.[102] For Karaite historical ideology, the necessity of recovering a lost or hidden Law became paradigmatic. Such an explanation creates a context for Karaism's need to "seek diligently in the Law" in order to recover the truth in the face of the defective majority consensus within Israel represented by the Rabbanites.[103] It also historicizes the suitability of rabbinic law and texts for the Karaite occupation of "searching diligently," since rabbinic tradition may have inadvertently preserved ancient truths.

99. The language used in *ME,* 117r, is the same used to describe Jeroboam in *OṢ,* 82. The reference to "laws of Moses from Sinai" uses the language of the rabbis (*ME,* 117v) and is repeated throughout the remaining narrative as a denunciation of the rabbis. According to the Karaites, no one could know what the halakhot were at Sinai.

100. *ME,* 116v–118r; *OṢ,* 85–86.

101. Lutzki adapts the phrase to refer to both Simeon and Judah, using what may be a kabbalistic reference to God's teaching, the "diadem": "And he restored the diadem as of old." *ME,* 115r, 118r.

102. For another example, see BT Temurah 16a: "In the days of mourning for Moses 300,000 halakhot were lost due to grief. Joshua forgot 300 as a punishment for his self-sufficiency. Neither he, nor the priests or prophets were able to restore them. Many hundreds of others were lost, but were recovered by the acumen of Othniel."

103. The rabbinic historical ideology exemplified in the chain of tradition works in a particular way by supporting the authority of the whole class of rabbis, not just individuals and their halakhot. The rabbinic Jewish paradigm is not of the recovery of a pristine past, but is a discourse on revealing what is always present in the Law.

As has been discussed, the origin for the central role played by the pair Judah ben Tabbai and Simeon ben Shetah is derived from Judah Halevi's *Kuzari* and first appears in Karaite literature in the introduction by Elijah Bashyachi to his *ʾAdderet ʾEliyahu.* Whatever Halevi's reasons may have been for placing the origins of Karaism at the time of Judah and Simeon, the story serves Karaite apologetics well.[104] If it is a story of origins, as Bashyachi took it, then the Karaites are to be endowed with roots in antiquity, a position that refutes the accusation that the Karaites were an eighth-century heretical innovation and thereby supports Karaite claims in the Byzantine Empire that they are legitimate members of the Jewish community. On the other hand, by using rabbinic literature as a basis for historical knowledge, the origins of the Sadducees are found in Avot de-Rabbi Natan, chapter 5, where Zadok and Boethos are portrayed as the erring students of Antigonus of Socho. In such a chronology, that separation from the rabbinical mainstream took place three generations *before* Judah and Simeon. This story remained ensconced in the Karaite historical metanarrative, endowing the Karaites with a historical position that is both ancient yet free of Sadducean accusations.[105]

Taking a stand against Elijah Bashyachi, but following Afendopolo and the younger Bashyachi, Lutzki maintains that the Judah-Simeon episode is only a link in the historical progression, not a story of origins. The episode in Judah Halevi was a fabrication for the Khazar king. When the sun was concealed in the afternoon, the king was convinced of the statement's falsity.[106] Neither did Lutzki follow his more immediate predecessor Mordecai ben Nisan in a complicated explanation for the divisions of Israel in the time of the Second Temple, but he did borrow the idea that Mordecai took from Azariah de' Rossi, which distinguished two groups designated as Sadducees.

It should be noted as an important distinction between the idea of transmission in rabbinic Judaism as opposed to Lutzki's Karaite Judaism and Islam. The *isnād* of Islamic *ḥadīth* literature is not a *shalshelet ha-kabbalah.* In Islam, the historical and legal paradigm was established in the life and leadership of Muḥammad, which needed to be recalled and incorporated into the law.

104. Although recognizing the difference between Karaites and Sadducees, Halevi's story places Karaite origins in the early rabbinic period. It can be interpreted as a rabbinic heresiological *derash,* contextualizing the Karaites as one heresy among many.

105. According to Solomon ben Aaron Troki, either 133 or 254 years passed from the time of Antigonus, the teacher of Zadok and Boethos, to the time of Simeon ben Shetah and Judah ben Tabbai, while Mordecai ben Nisan followed the chronology of David Gans and Ibn Daud, maintaining that it was 121 years. It is interesting that Zadok and Boethos are not referred to in Lutzki's narrative.

106. *ME,* 103v. This problem is not addressed in *OṢ.* See Bashyachi, *ʾAdderet ʾEliyahu,* fifth and sixth pages of the unpaginated introduction, which state that Halevi himself was afraid of the Khazar king and therefore told the truth.

One group indeed followed Zadok, while the other archaic, proto-Karaitic group was actually the *Ṣaddikim,* whose name was similar to that of the Sadducees, or *Ṣaddukim.* The so-called founder of the newly designated proto-Karaites was Judah ben Tabbai.[107] From this episode in the narrative we can understand the wordplay in the title of Lutzki's small work *'Oraḥ Ṣaddikim.*

Completely ignored in *'Oraḥ Ṣaddikim* is the transmission of knowledge from Judah ben Tabbai until the time of Judah ha-Nasi. In *Me'irat ʿEnayim,* the pairs of tradents from Mishnah Avot, chapter 1, are incorporated into a dual line of transmission following Yefet ben Ṣaʿir and Moses Bashyachi. The true teachings were transmitted from Judah ben Tabbai to Shemaiah, and then to Shammai. The false teachings pass through the line of Simeon ben Shetah-Abtalion-Hillel.[108] The final break between these two sects came on Adar 9, a day of fasting. Although we are not told what occurred, it is stated that "it was as grievous as the incident of the Golden Calf."[109] Based upon this dual transmission, Lutzki then explains the disagreements between R. Eliezer the Great and R. Joshua in BT Baba Mezia 59b and between R. Gamaliel I and R. Joshua in M Rosh ha-Shanah 2:5–9. Following Moses Bashyachi and Mordecai ben Nisan, the House of Shammai is incorporated into the Karaite chain of tradition.[110]

The fourth incident of "killing the scholars" occurs following the destruction of the Second Temple. Most of the upper class of *Ṣaddikim,* consisting of the Sanhedrin, administration, and warriors, were killed by Titus and, as a result, true teaching declined. The Pharisees were cowards, not caring if the Temple survived. They fled to Titus and found favor with him and all subsequent caesars.[111] Here rabbinic history is mirrored in two ways. First, the diasporic orientation of the rabbis is parodied in their disregard for the Temple. Second, the flight to Titus alludes to the rabbinic story of Yoḥanan ben Zakkai, who left Jerusalem during its investment by the Roman legions and made accommodation with the Roman authorities. In rabbinic historiography, Yoḥanan is a hero for having saved Pharisaic teaching from destruction, realizing that the transmission of divinely appointed knowledge transcended the immediate earthly concerns of the war for national independence.[112] In a larger context, the Karaites remained throughout the centuries engaged to a notion of mourning for Zion and the Temple, whereas the rabbis made a vital transition to religious life centered on the home and community.[113]

107. *ME,* 116v–119v; *OṢ,* 85–86. See Poznanski, *Zekher Ṣaddikim,* 39–42.

108. *ME,* 120r.

109. Ibid., 120v.

110. Ibid., 121r. See *Dod Mordekhai,* 44–66.

111. *ME,* 121v–122r; *OṢ,* 86–87.

112. See Avot de-Rabbi Natan, version 1, 4, 22–24; ibid., version 2, 6, 19; Lam. Rab. 1:5, no. 31; and BT Git. 56a–b.

113. This should not be understated. The postdestruction Karaite chain of

At this point in the narrative, Lutzki returns to the exilic theme. In the wake of destruction and loss, Judah ha-Nasi saw that those in the exile had come to exceed in numbers the population in the land, and he decided to create a compilation of teachings so that the Torah would not be forgotten. This compilation, the Mishnah, includes some good and much bad tradition, collected without distinction. The fairly benign treatment given to Judah ha-Nasi on the part of Lutzki allows for the accommodation to rabbinic halakhah that characterizes later Karaite law. Lutzki maintains that as early as the Islamic period, Nissi ben Nūh taught that the Karaites should study the Mishnah and Talmud because they contain some truth.[114]

After Judah ha-Nasi, Ashi and Ravina, who wrote respectively the Jerusalem and Babylonian Talmuds, increased the division and hatred in Israel. The Pharisees turned their backs on the Torah, making it subordinate to the Oral Law. A transgression against the Torah merited stripes, whereas a transgression against the *divre ḥakhamim*, "words of the sages," meant death.[115]

This Karaite "archaic history" concludes with Anan ben David, the most eminent of the sages and seed of David. Lutzki's account of Anan conforms to much in the standard versions that came down from the Middle Ages and became part of the Karaite historical metanarrative,[116] except that he is now understood to be one of the *Ṣaddikim*. Due to the continuing division in Israel and the attacks he suffered at the hands of his opponents, he proclaimed that the *Ṣaddikim* should withdraw completely from the Pharisees in order to keep the Torah from being forgotten altogether.[117] Although there existed only one Israel, there now were two Judaisms. He renamed the *Ṣaddikim* and Pharisees as Karaites and Rabbanites, respectively, and continued to teach

tradition incorporates high priests into the transmission of divine knowledge. *ME*, 132r, *OṢ*, 95–96. Cf. chapter 4, above. On medieval Karaites as *Avele Ṣiyyon*, see chapter 2, above. Cf. Ankori, *Karaites in Byzantium*, passim, but also s.v. "Mourners" in the index.

114. *ME*, 108r, which also cites other Karaite writers who support this position. See chapter 5, above.

115. *ME*, 122v; *OṢ*, 87–88.

116. *ME*, 123r–v; *OṢ*, 88–89: He was chosen as *av bet din* and *resh galutha* and confirmed by the king of Ishmaelites. After his accession, he "donned the garment of zealotry" and began to teach against the Mishnah and Talmud. The Pharisees conspired to denounce him to the king and have him killed, but the king had mercy on him. The Pharisees managed to have him exiled to Jerusalem, accompanied by family, disciples, and friends, where he built a synagogue ("a small temple"). There he wept, prayed, and made confession. See chapter 3, above.

117. *ME*, 123r–v; *OṢ*, 88–89. He sanctioned a prohibition against eating with Pharisees, or their food, because they do not observe all forms of purity, and they eat carcasses and forbidden fats. He also prohibited intermarriage with Pharisees because they transgress prohibitions subject to *karet* (excommunication), and have "strange offspring."

in accordance with the "good figs" and the good prophets of the days of the kingdom.[118]

Lutzki's History. The feeling of crisis that permeated the European Karaite communities provided an impetus and context for self-explanation through the use of "creative history." The imminence and implication of danger and loss are mirrored in the narrative motifs of the "killing the scholars," the response to crisis, and the effects of exile. In comparison, it should be noted that Gerson Cohen has presented Ibn Daud and the production of *Sefer ha-Kabbalah* in the context of the Almohad invasions of Spain in the twelfth century.[119]

The era of crisis also created contacts between the Karaites and Christian intellectuals. Two Karaite authors of apologetic history in this era, Solomon ben Aaron Troki and Mordecai ben Nisan, were responding directly in their work to Christian inquiries. Not only did such contacts provide an external stimulus to their creative histories, but were also used as a framing device within these narratives. Lutzki also evokes the support of non-Jews, stating that Jacob Trigland and others "who studied the books of our sages honor and praise us."[120] As Europeans investigated the religions and cultures of other peoples, they also created new histories and ethnographies for themselves. Similarly, the Karaites found opportunity to create a fully articulated historical narrative to explain their place in the world.

The construction of Lutzki's narrative, however, reveals a more than cursory understanding of rabbinic principles and texts, characteristic of the Karaite historical metanarrative. Lutzki's narrative is a multilayered historical exercise with allusions to most types of Jewish literature, both Karaite and Rabbanite. The most developed Karaite interlinear reading of rabbinic texts permitted clever historical formulations for the presentation of polemical and apologetic material, which were derived from parenthetic historical information embedded in rabbinic texts. In rabbinic literature, the literary transformation of early forms of genealogy and chronicle into historical narrative takes place in discrete segments, scattered across a vast literature.[121] However, if it can be imagined that such materials could be gathered together, then a "metatext" emerges. For medieval and early modern Jews, Karaite or Rabbanite, this metatext is the sourcebook for the components of creative historical

118. Lutzki's history then goes on the reproduce the chain of tradition from Yefet ben Ṣaʿir. See *ME,* 131v–133r; *OṢ,* 94–101, which includes names of later Karaites. In addition, a bio-bibliographical list represents another sequential link to the past. See *ME,* 134r–157r, also published in part by Mann from another manuscript, in *Texts and Studies,* 2: *Karaitica,* 1409–43; and *OṢ,* 101–17.

119. *Sefer ha-Qabbalah,* xxvif.

120. *OṢ,* 91.

121. See Hayden White, "The Value of Narrativity in the Representation of Reality."

narrative. It can be argued that all facts in this "text" are equally valid, a characteristic of disconnected medieval chronicles, whose textual elements are uncollated and have not been arranged into a narrative that imparts meaning to its contents. Equally, because these "facts" derive from a divinely inspired literature, they must be true. In this way the inherited protonarrative canon of rabbinic historical material lends itself to reformulation. The Karaites, having already accommodated themselves to much of rabbinic jurisprudence and the use of rabbinic legal texts, capitalized on the plasticity of the historical inheritance to create their own metanarrative, upon which Lutzki based his own textual narrative.

Lutzki's history provides conceptual foundations for the existence of a Karaite chain of tradition, which is designated variously as *sevel ha-yerushah* (yoke of inheritance), *haʿtakat ha-Torah* (tradition of the Torah), and *haʿtakah ha-mishtalshelet* (transmitted tradition). Lutzki's narrative not only offers "Karaized" explanations for events in the Jewish past but presents historicized settings for particular deviations of rabbinic law from the true teachings of Karaism. The legal and ritual distinctions that separate Karaites and Rabbanites are thus contextualized into the unfolding of the divine plan. Rabbinic accusations are deflected or refuted. The rabbis contention that Karaism is a Second Temple innovation is reversed, so that Rabbanism is presented as a First Temple deviation. Moreover, the subtleties of the Karaite-Rabbanite relationship are explored, recognizing the rapprochement between the two religio-legal systems that had prevailed at times. Rabbanism before the time of Anan ben David is not represented as a static lifeless phenomenon, but as a dynamic, albeit misguided, movement. Later Karaites, exhibiting an ambivalent attitude toward Rabbanism, might have said, "We don't deny the whole Mishnah and Talmud. In fact, they contain *some* true teaching." Lutzki went further to explain the how and why of it, while at the same time he argued in a sectarian voice that categorically, Karaism *is* Judaism.

Conclusion to Part Two

The Meaning of Karaite Historical Narrative

Simhah Isaac Lutzki represents the apogee of "Jewish" Karaite historiography. After the final partition of Poland in 1795, the majority of eastern European Jews, Rabbanite and Karaite, were subject to both Russian imperial rule and anti-Jewish attitudes of the Russian Orthodox Church. The social context changed to such an extent that eastern European Karaites sought to disassociate themselves from Rabbanite Jews, and from Judaism, in an effort to avoid the harsh policies of church and state.[1] New forms of self-definition led to a new historical explanation for the Karaite presence in eastern Europe known as the "Khazar theory." This new historiography offered a connection to ancient Israel by way of the Ten Lost Tribes, understood to have been the ancestors of the medieval Turkic Khazars, who occupied the southern Russian steppes in the early Middle Ages.[2] According to historical sources, the Khazars had converted to Judaism in the eighth century,[3] and in the nineteenth century eastern European Karaites claimed them as descendants.[4] This new Karaite identity maintained roots in the biblical past while separating ethnically

1. On the mission to petition the czarina for Karaite exemptions and privileges, see Philip E. Miller, *Karaite Separatism in Nineteenth-century Russia: Joseph Solomon Lutski's "Epistle of Israel's Deliverance."*

2. On the Khazars, see D. M. Dunlop, *The History of the Jewish Khazars;* Norman Golb and Omeljan Pritsak, *Khazarian Hebrew Documents of the Tenth Century;* and Peter B. Golden, *Khazar Studies; An Historical-Philological Inquiry into the Origins of the Khazars.*

3. On the Khazar conversion to Judaism, see Peter B. Golden, "Khazaria and Judaism"; Omeljan Pritsak, "The Khazar Kingdom's Conversion to Judaism"; Simon Szyszman, "Le Roi Bulan et le probléme de la conversion des Khazars"; and George Vernadsky, "Byzantium and Southern Russia: Two Notes. 1: The Eparchy of Gothia. 2: The Date of the Conversion of the Khazars to Judaism," esp. 76–86.

4. The Khazar theory was presented by the last great Karaite scholar, Abraham Firkovich (1786–1874), in *Avnei Zikkaron.* On the Khazar theory used to explain Karaite and eastern European Jewish origins, see Simon Szyszman, "Die Karäer in Ost-Mitteleuropa"; idem, "Les Khazares: Problèmes et controverses"; A.

and doctrinally from the majority Rabbanite Jews, thus deflecting the church's primary theological argument against the Jews—the accusation of ancient deicide. If eastern European Karaites were actually Khazars, then they obviously were not participants in events as described in the Gospels that took place in Roman Judea in the first century C.E. The strategy of "dejudaization" by and large succeeded, leading to the exemption of Karaites from forced conversion and the onerous military service required of male Rabbanites, as well as the acquisition of other privileges.[5] After more than a century of czarist rule followed by Soviet Communism, eastern European Karaites today are few in number and have little culture or identity that can be characterized as Judaic or Jewish.[6]

The Khazar theory represents a partial repudiation of the traditional Karaite historical metatext, which claims that the Karaites are *the* Jews. This theory is more of a kind of ethnogenesis that characterized early modern ethnographies and histories than an engagement with Jewish thought. Until czarist reality necessitated accommodation, the Karaites maintained their relationship to mainstream rabbinic Judaism, never renouncing membership in the people of Israel. The Khazar theory requires a separate study that would reveal its intellectual roots in early modernity, but, in a fashion following this study, would contextualize it against the cultural and historical conditions of the day.

In the Middle East, small Karaite populations persisted into modernity, especially in Egypt. In the Islamic world, Karaites maintained the sectarian relationship with Rabbanite Jews—they recognized each other as coreligionists. Also, since the Muslim host society had traditionally grouped different types of Jews together under the concept of *dhimmah*, Karaites felt neither any extra-Judaic compulsion to distance themselves from the dominant Rabbanite Jews[7] nor a need for radical reinterpretations of the past. With the rise of Arab and Egyptian nationalism in the twentieth century, Egyptian Karaites

---

Zajaczkowski, *Ze Studiów nad Zagadnieniem Chazarskim;* and idem, "Khazarian Culture and Its Inheritors." The Khazar theory is widely held by scholars to be ahistorical. On its refutation, see Zvi Ankori, *The Karaites in Byzantium,* 58–86; and Bernard Weinryb, "The Beginnings of East-European Jewry in Legend and Historiography." For outlandish speculation based upon the Khazar theory, see Arthur Koestler, *The Thirteenth Tribe;* and A. Posselt, *Geschichte des chazarisch-jüdischen Staates.*

5. One scholar speaks of a "complete deracination of the Eastern European Karaites." See Freund, *Karaites and Dejudaization.* This work needs to be used with care.

6. See Emanuela Trevisan Semi, "A Brief Survey of Present-day Karaite Communities in Europe."

7. The different historical profiles of European and Middle Eastern Karaites is outlined in William M. Brinner, "Karaites of Christendom-Karaites of Islam."

would try to define themselves as indigenous Jewish Egyptians, in contradistinction to Zionists and Israeli Jews, but without a strongly nonconformist reading of the past.[8] By the latter half of the twentieth century, nationalist pressures in Egypt and in other Middle Eastern countries would have led Karaites to choose emigration, mostly to Israel.[9] In recent decades, Karaites in Israel have manipulated the Karaite historical "metanarrative" to engage the process of "creative history" anew by claiming the sectarianism of the Dead Sea Scrolls as their heritage.[10] In so doing, they have claimed for themselves an important piece of the archaeological and historically sanctioned past that is part and parcel of the Israeli grand historical narrative. In addition, they have connected themselves to an arena of academic inquiry that is sometimes volatile and enjoys wide popularity. Thereby, the marginalization of this small, nonrabbinic (and therefore culturally disadvantaged) group is transcended to centralize its story into the story of the land, of Judaism, and of the Jewish people.

Simple estimates of the development and emergence of historical thought and historical ideology in Karaite Judaism are not sufficient for a proper understanding of the Karaite contribution to the development of historical thinking in Jewish culture and in religious culture in general. The Karaite texts must first be grasped on their own terms. Whereas the approach of the first modern scholars of Karaitica in the early part of the twentieth century reflects a great deal of the bias of their times, we now have the advantage of hindsight in formulating more interesting and less judgmental questions for examining the materials. Scholars such as Harkavy, Bacher, and Poznanski remained true to their roots in the "Wissenschaft des Judenthums" by mirroring methodologies that were current at the time.[11] They looked for fact and falsity and sought to identify historical and literary elements that exhibited continuity with phenomena of antecedent significance. In addition, they often replicated their own personal rabbinic orientation through less than fair evaluations of Karaite literature.

Much of the material examined in this study falls under the rubric of sacred history. In two major works on historiography, Barnes and Collingwood reduced sacred history to a kind of *preparatio historiographica*, which

8. In seeking to establish indigeneity, Egyptian Karaites have claimed that they were present at the time of the Arab conquests in the seventh century or that they established themselves in Egypt at the time of Anan ben David in the eighth century. See Joel Beinin, *The Dispersion of Egyptian Jewry: Culture, Politics, and the Formation of a Modern Diaspora*, 39–40.

9. Ibid., esp. 39–44, 181–84.

10. Daniel J. Lasker, "The Dead Sea Scrolls in the Historiography and Self-image of Contemporary Karaites."

11. For a wide-ranging view, see Ismar Schorsch, *From Text to Context: The Turn to History in Modern Judaism.*

preceded the evolution of the modern scientific study of history. Barnes connected literary form in sacred history to particular periods, and Collingwood identified the presence in these histories of a divine plan with an attendant form of periodization.[12] Collingwood establishes one primary premise of sacred history by indicating the presence of a divine plan. Indeed, sacred histories must correspond to theological assumptions. That is, the course of events as they are portrayed must not deviate from notions of divine creation and revelation, the impact of revelation on humanity, and mechanisms by which humanity achieves salvation. In this regard, sacred histories embody substantive characteristics of the belief systems from which they are derived.

Sacred histories, however, are not simply mythic histories that fulfill only doctrinal and theological functions. They are not merely fictions. These narratives and their attendant ideologies are also functional representations of sacred communities and religious classes. Although they are not necessarily *rational* histories in the modern critical sense of the word, they do include accounts of real events and people. The early scholars of modern Karaite studies tried to extract historical realia from the fabric of Karaite and rabbinic historical narratives. The results of these literary and historical exercises comprise the foundations of modern Karaite scholarship, but lack a complete understanding of sacred history.

What the early scholars of Karaism did not recognize was the real character of sacred history, which must blend elements of what is occasionally fictive or mythic with "real" history. Events on the ground needed to be harmonized with doctrinal and theological assumptions in order to represent a consistent and meaningful whole. It must also be remembered that generally recognized facts and postulates in the premodern world were conceived of in a very different light than we understand them today. The task of writing history in a sacred context could be daunting, and it certainly required a great deal of creativity.

With these considerations in mind, it must be acknowledged that expressions of sacred history can and will be representative of the times in which they were written. Although this is a well-accepted assumption among modern historians, it is not often applied in the analysis of sacred history. By unpacking the narratives and examining the historical and religious contexts of the authors, the immediacy and creativity of the material is available to the modern observer. Thus, Karaite sacred histories and historical formulations do not exist independent of doctrinal and halakhic developments in the community. Neither are they generated from a world that is wholly Jewish. The exigencies of Jewish diasporic life were compounded for this minority within a minority. In the end, Karaite historical expression offers avenues of inquiry into Karaite thought and history that connect with numerous facets of the life

12. See Harry Elmer Barnes, *A History of Historical Writing;* and R. G. Collingwood, *The Idea of History.*

of the community, including the evolution of halakhah, the engagement with medieval speculative rationalism, the development of particular literary forms and genres, relationships to the non-Jewish host cultures, and, significantly, the sectarian relationship to the dominant Jewish culture. It may not be history as we recognize it in the modern academy, but it represented for Karaites a reflection of their own pragmatic concerns and realities.

On a visit to Jerusalem in 1987, I was walking in the Jewish Quarter of the Old City near the alleyway that leads to the Karaite house of prayer, the Synagogue of Anan ben David. I overheard a tour guide explaining to his group that the Karaites "are just like the Reform Jews" who had renounced the Talmud. This modern analogy, which does violence to both the Karaites and Reform Judaism, is not far removed from the reductionist definitions of Karaism found in rabbinic literature. The rabbis understood the Karaites in the context of their own sacred history, and lacking the need or ability to engage a dynamic or realistic form of definition, knew the Karaites to be latter-day Sadducees. A more complicated, "dehistoricized" definition of Karaism might result in a list of halakhic and doctrinal deviations by which the Karaites distinguish themselves from Rabbanite Jews. Both of these portrayals of Karaism result in a static representation of the multifaceted relationship that has existed between the dominant culture and a sectarian group.

What emerges from the studies in this book is a dynamic and complex model for Karaite sectarianism in Judaism. The slender historical notions of the rabbis, rooted in the Hellenistic and early Christian worlds and nourished under Islam, form a backdrop. Divorced from imperial ideologies, perhaps the Jews had little use for the history of great men and their deeds. The ahistorical construct of sanctification as exemplified in the Mishnah gave way to an implicit idea of sacred history that embodied a covenantal moral construct of reward and punishment. In addition, the doctrine of the messiah offered a teleological framework that originated with God's creation and moved through his revelation to Israel. Supplementing this vague historical formulation was the central idea of the chain of tradition. This genealogy of knowledge was a schematic matrix superimposed upon history that sought to establish functional support for both the rabbis, as interpreters of the Law and leaders of the community, and the Talmud, the "constitution" of the community.

Later Karaites claimed as their "founder" Anan ben David, whose position was based in part upon Davidid ancestry. The early followers of Anan, only one element among proto-Karaites, would have had recourse to an existing historical ideology based upon exilarchic genealogy. Subsequent Ananites might turn to the family line of *their* princes for a link with the past, including implicit connections to existing rabbinic historical notions.

Other elements of proto-Karaitic Judaism came together under the influence of the Muslim host culture in the ninth and tenth centuries. The emergence of antitraditionist scripturalism among the Jews replicated similar contemporary phenomena among Muslims and was established in conscious opposition to the tradition and historical assumptions of the rabbis. Even as the sectarian Khārijites of the day rejected the nascent traditionism of Islam, so Jewish scripturalists eschewed any type of historical ideology, preferring a direct relationship with the sacred text of the Hebrew Bible. The Khārijites incorporated mythic time into their lives, for example, by replicating the *hijrah* of Muḥammad in their "pilgrimage" to Khārijite camps, while among Jews the Mourners for Zion awaited the rebuilding of the Temple with ascetic discipline, calling the faithful to Jerusalem.

At the same time, nonrabbinic Jewish law developed from a variety of diverse origins, perhaps even incorporating halakhic elements from the messianic movements of the day. Transcending Anan's formulations, which exhibit many similarities to rabbinic halakhah, a kind of non-normative legal consensus was established among some antirabbinic Jews. As the proliferation of an unsystematic law in Islam required the reforms of al-Shāfiʿī, so non-normative Jewish law sought the means to systematize itself in response to uncontrolled organic growth and in answer to attacks from the rabbis. The early Karaites turned to speculative rationalism, particularly in its Muʿtazilite form, as a means toward consistent and logical legal formulation. Such an intellectual position permitted the central principle of scripturalism to be enunciated, while at the same time different types of hermeneutical approaches were tried regarding various aspects of halakhah.

These elements all came together, centered in Jerusalem in the tenth century, to coalesce into Karaism. Whereas the general consensus among Karaite scholars maintained an ahistorical attitude, al-Qirqisānī wrote a highly articulated heresiographical presentation with a strong historical argument. His "chronological account of Jewish sects" rejects any notion of tradition and its transmission, while supporting no particular brand of Karaism. This heresiography, brilliantly modeled upon Christian antecedents, details heresy without advocating any type of orthodoxy. The only correct position advocated by al-Qirqisānī is that of rational methodology. Nonetheless, his halakhah remains cloaked in the garb of scripturalism. It is difficult to ascertain whether al-Qirqisānī was sui generis or he had currency among his contemporaries. Whatever the case, he "created facts" that gained credence among the Karaites and later became "canonized" in the twelfth-century encyclopedia of Judah Hadassi.

With the passage of time, even an ahistorical scripturalist movement will acquire a history of its own. This is reflected in the comment of the tenth-century Salmon ben Yeruḥim on Psalm 69:1 and later became a matter of some importance among the Byzantine Karaites, who sought to establish legitimacy in the Byzantine environment. Hadassi's reconfiguration of al-Qirqisānī's data sought to define the sectarian Mishawites as truly heretical Jews, while positioning the Karaites merely as schismatics. Such a contextualization reifies rabbinic Judaism as a kind of norm, even though Hadassi on the whole is quite vehemently antirabbinic. This historical and heresiographical repositioning begs other questions. Concurrently, the possibilities for interpretation in Karaite halakhah had become depleted and solutions to legal problems were often borrowed from the rabbis. As Karaite halakhah gradually moved closer to some of the legal formulations of the rabbis and Karaites began to read rabbinic texts for purposes other than the polemical, so historical representation changed.

The passage of time and the exigencies of the Byzantine environment created conditions for the writing of the *Ḥilluk ha-Kara'im veha-Rabbanim,* which marks history by incorporating some rabbinic legends and a list of Karaite scholars. It is a short conceptual jump from a list of scholars to a chain of tradition. When Karaite halakhah arrived at a point where it required support from its own tradition—that is, when allegiance to scripturalism and rational interpretation did not fulfill the needs of jurisprudence and gave way to legal assertions based upon Karaite antecedents—then a Karaite genealogy of knowledge was introduced. Modeled on the rabbinic chain of tradition, the new Karaite chain reinterpreted elements of the Mishnah and other rabbinic works, fictionalized an intermediary period between the Mishnah and Anan with the presence of a priestly line that existed subsequent to the destruction of the Temple, and then rewrote the Karaite list of scholars into a garbled chain that sought to represent linear transmission.

Once this historical expression had gained acceptance, Karaites began to introduce historical details into the chain. Narrative elements were added to answer historical questions implicit in the chain, resulting in more fully developed narrative texts and, eventually, works, or portions of works, of explicit historiographical content. The Karaite writers of early modern eastern Europe represent the fullest development of this process, which culminated in the eighteenth century with Simhah Isaac Lutzki's detailed history of Judaism.

This "history of a history" offers a gauge for estimating the character of Karaism's relationship to mainstream rabbinic Judaism. The larger outline of historical and historiographical development is detailed in this study by the examination of particular problems that are specific to time and place. The oppositional self-definition of the early period is, in itself, an expression of a relationship to the rabbis and the Talmud. As Karaite halakhah moved closer to rabbinic legal formulations, historical expression began to take form. The Karaite practice of an interlinear reading of rabbinic texts emerged. Forms of Karaite historical expression were not only the result of the dynamic relationship of the Karaites to the Rabbanites but were profoundly influenced by the environment of the host culture. The sectarian relationship became defined through the encounter with Islam and various forms of Christianity. The speculative rationalism of medieval Islam was embraced as a halakhic method that offered consistency and systematization in the face of the cogency of rabbinic law. The encyclopedism of the Byzantines was mirrored in literary forms that evolved in that environment, and the reappearance of Islam into the Constantinopolitan world of the fifteenth century invigorated Karaism through a new rapprochement with rabbinic Judaism and the encounter with Sephardic Jews. Later, Karaism would be engaged at a high level with the host culture through its participation in the Renaissance-Reformation discourse in sixteenth- and seventeenth-century eastern Europe.

The model that emerges for the sectarian relationship and for the complex interactions of a minority with its host culture goes well beyond simple formulations of belief and law. Indeed, in the case of the Karaites, aspects of belief and especially law experienced change and transformation as a result of the sectarian relationship and interplay with the host environment. The very human activity of recording the past as a way of defining the present cannot take place in a historical vacuum. Although theological and legal issues provide the core for expressions of sacred history, the passage of time and the impact of events cannot be overlooked by the authors of these historical writings, nor by modern observers. As participants in a living religious tradition, their worldviews are simultaneously reshaped by the exigencies of fact and the reinterpretation of belief and practice. Whereas modern historians might believe that they are looking for a truth whose existence need only be uncovered, sacred historians seek an existence whose greater truths are known, but whose outward manifestations need be interpreted and conceived. Notwithstanding the theological and doctrinal requirements of the religious community, these histories cannot be mere fiction. A mythic fictive history does not permit explanation and discussion of events as they have transpired, and is usually only functional with regard to the most distant past. The blending of "creative history" with realities dictated by events allows these sacred historians to engage their own creativity to make sense of the world and their beliefs all at once.

Appendix

The Chains of Tradition Published by Pinsker in Der Orient

The chain is interpolated into the text of an epitome of *Ḥovot ha-Levavot* (Duties of the heart), by the eleventh-century Spanish Rabbanite philosopher Baḥya Ibn Pakuda. The manuscript, of 102 pages, according to its colophon was completed in 1682. The name of a previous owner appears on the covers: Daniel ben Moses, known as a buyer of Arabic and Hebrew manuscripts. When Pinsker examined it, the manuscript was in the possession of Abraham Firkovich. The text appears on two pages in the epitome of the seventh chapter of the third section (*sha'ar* in Hebrew; *bāb* in Arabic), which is concerned with the worship of God. Pinsker notes that the interpolation was penciled in, probably by Daniel ben Moses, but clearly could not have been forged at that time.[1] Following the chains of tradition is the only version of a *bakkashah* attributed to Baḥya.[2]

The revelation to the people who inherited the Law[3] from the prophets, peace be upon them, all of their meanings,[4] and all of their understanding,[5] and all of their elaborations,[6] and their principles.[7] They are the men of the Great Assembly, and here is their lineage:

Moses received the Torah from Sinai, and transmitted[8] it to Joshua, and Joshua to the elders, and the elders to the prophets. The prophets transmitted it to the men of the Great Assembly, and the men of the Great Assembly to Simeon

From *Der Orient* 12 (1851): 737–43, v. 12, 737–43, designated in chapter 4 as P[1].

1. Ibid., 739.
2. Ibid., 743–49.
3. *sharī'ah.*
4. *ma'nah.*
5. Arabic root is from *f-q-h.*
6. *furū'iha.* Cf. Hans Wehr, *A Dictionary of Modern Written Arabic,* 707: "*ilm al-furu,*" "the doctrine of branches" (i.e., applied *fiqh,* applied ethics—consisting of the systematic elaboration of canonical law in Islam).
7. *'usul,* could also be translated as roots, or sources.
8. *ve-mesarah.*

the Just, and Simeon the Just to Antigonus, and Antigonus to Joseph ben Yohanan, and Joseph ben Yohanan of Jerusalem to Joshua ben Perahiah and Nittai the Arbelite. They transmitted it to Judah ben Tabbai and Simeon ben Shetah. And in their time Simeon ben Shetah sought to destroy the true written record, but Judah ben Tabbai stood in the breach, and explained the true faith, the faith of the Karaites, may the Creator of the created watch over them. Judah transmitted it to Shemaiah, and Shemaiah to Abtalion and Rav Hillel, and Rav Hillel transmitted to the traditionists[9] as he had received it from his master Simeon ben Shetah.

Rav Shammai the Elder, the Honored, the Pious, transmitted it to the Karaites,[10] may the Rock of Ages watch over them and come to their aid, and cause their enemies and oppressors[11] to perish, and intend evil for them. Amen. Rav Shammai transmitted it to Rav Kahana and Rav Yohanan ben ʿIkuv ha-Nasi and his court and the many sages among them. Rav Kahana transmitted it to his son Shimʿi. Rav Shimʿi transmitted it to his son Yohanan. Rav Yohanan transmitted it to his son Rav Zadok. Rav Zadok to his son Ezekiel, and R. Ezekiel to Rav Nehemiah ha-Nasi, and R. Nehemiah to R. ʿUkba, and Rav ʿUkba to Rav Abu Amar and R. Abu Amar to R. Jeshua, and R. Jeshua to R. Nathaniel, and R. Nathaniel to R. Abu Amar ha-Nasi, and R. Abu Amar to R. Huna, and R. Huna to R. Nathan, and R. Nathan to R. Heman, and R. Heman to R. ʿUnni, and R. ʿUnni to R. Zephaniah, and R. Zephaniah to R. Kahana, and R. Kahana to R. Zutra, and R. Zutra to R. Hunamar, and R. Hunamar to R. Kafnai, and R. Kafnai to R. Zephaniah ha-Kohen, and R. Zephaniah to R. Shemariah, and R. Shemariah to R. Kafnai ha-Nasi, and R. Kafnai to R. Haninai, and R. Haninai to R. Bustanai, and R. Bustanai to R. Hasdai, and R. Hasdai to R. Shemariah ha-Kohen, and R. Shemariah to R. Zuta, and R. Zuta to R. Hisdai, and R. Hisdai to R. David, and R. David to R. Zuta ha-Kohen, and R. Zuta to R. Anan the Prince.

This is our lord[12] Anan, who explained and revealed the true faith for the second time, revealing it with clear true proofs, and numerous teachings, risking his life. This was in the time of Abu Jaʿfar the king in the year 4 thousand and 4 hundred according to the creation of the world. He was the exilarch of all of the people of Israel in Babylonia, answering the disciples of Rav Hillel and those who walk in their tracks. A great nation repented with him from among our brethren, because he explained the truth for them, and in his tracks traveled all those who possessed the fear of God.

And he transmitted it to his son Rav Saul, and Rav Saul to R. Josiah, and R. Josiah to R. Benjamin ha-Nahavendi, and R. Benjamin to R. Daniel ha-Qumisi and R. Isaac ha-Boṣri and R. David Ger Zedek, and R. David to R. Noah, and R. Noah to R. Salmon ben Yeruhim and R. Joseph and R. Jacob ha-Qirqisani and R. Hassun and R. Abraham ha-Boṣri. And in their time was Rav Saadia Gaon, peace

9. *baʿale ha-kabbalah.*
10. *baʿale mikra.*
11. Heb.: flagellators.
12. *adonenu.*

be upon his memory, the Pithomite, who was a disciple of R. Salmon ben Yeruhim, peace be upon his memory. And he transmitted it to R. David ben Boaz and R. Abu Ali and R. Amram and R. Saadia and R. Abraham and R. Jacob and R. Joseph ha-Qirqisani,[13] who composed a very fine Book of Precepts. And he transmitted it to R. Aaron Abu al-Faraj and R. Abraham and R. Joseph and R. Zedakah and R. Abraham and R. Ezra, and R. Jacob, and R. Jeshua, who explained all of the Torah, Prophets and Writings and made the *Sefer ha-Yashar* on all the commandments, and to Rav Yefet ha-Levi, who commented on the Torah and made a Book of Precepts, and to R. Israel ben Daniel, and R. Abu Zuri, who explained all the Torah, and to R. Ali, and R. Bayzani, and R. Isaac, and R. Israel ben Mansuri, and R. Abu Saʿid, and R. Levi ben Yefet ha-Levi, and R. Hasdai, and R. F.[14] al-Faraj, and R. Aaron, and R. Yefet ben Ṣaʿir, and R. David ben Susan, and R. Boaz the Prince, peace be upon them. Up to here God has helped us. And this is the true *haʿtakah*, and it is the *silsilah* of the true faith, transmitted[15] from man to man, a true support.

Moses our master received the Torah at Sinai by divine command from God in Heaven, and transmitted it[16] to Joshua ben Nun, and Joshua to Phinehas, to Eli the priest, to Samuel the prophet, to King David, to Ahijah the Shilonite, to Elijah the prophet, to Elisha the prophet, to Jehoiada the priest, to Zechariah the priest, to Hosea the prophet, to Amos the prophet, to Isaiah the prophet, to Micah the Morashtite, to Joel the prophet, to Nahum the prophet, to Zephaniah the prophet, to Jeremiah the prophet, to Baruch ben Neriah, to Ezra the scribe, to R. Simon, to R. Antigonus, to R. Joseph, to R. Nittai the Arbelite. to R. Judah ben Tabbai, to R. Shemaiah, to R. Shammai the Pious, to R. Yohanan ben ʿIkuv, to R. Kahana, to R. Shimʿi, to R. Yohanan, to R. Zadok, to R. Ezekiel, to R. Ahituv, to R. Jeshua, to R. Nathaniel, to R. Heman, to R. Unni, to R. Zephaniah, to R. Shemariah, to R. Zuta, to R. David the Prince, to our lord Anan the Prince, to R. Saul the Prince, to R. Josiah the Prince, to R. Benjamin ha-Nahavandi, to R. Noah ha-Basri, to R. Salmon ben Yeruhim, to R. Joseph ha-Ro'eh, to R. Solomon the Prince, to R. Levi, to R. Hisdai the Prince, to R. Yefet ben Ṣaʿir, to R. Boaz.

These are the people who confirmed the Law[17] and all those who adhere[18] to reward and punishment in the two abodes.[19] And they were aroused from heedlessness and they corrected the rest of them, and they understand with the vision of their hearts the duties of God Almighty that are incumbent upon them because of the greatness of his benefit.

13. Note the conflation with Yaʿqūb al-Qirqisānī, a few lines above.

14. Furqan.

15. *neʿetkah.*

16. *ve-heʿetikah.*

17. *sharīʿah.*

18. I have emended the *waw* that precedes *lazimahum* to a *yay,* thus rendering *yalzamuhum.* Thanks to Ariel Bloch of the University of California, Berkeley, for this suggestion.

19. Heaven and hell or, less likely, this world and the world-to-come. I have emended the *samekh-yud* prefix of this word to *fe-yud,* for the Arabic *fī* ("in"). For this emendation, my thanks again to Ariel Bloch.

Bibliography

Aaron ben Elijah. *'Eṣ Ḥayyim.* Edited by F. Delitzsch and M. Steinschneider. Leipzig, 1841.

———. *'Eṣ Ḥayyim.* Gozlow, 1847.

———. *Gan 'Eden.* Jerusalem, 1972. Reprint of Gozlow, 1864.

———. *Keter Torah.* Ramlah, Israel, 1972. Reprint of Gozlow, 1866–67.

———. "The Tree of Life." Trans. Morris Charner. Ph.D. diss., Columbia University, New York, 1949.

Aaron ben Joseph. *Mivḥar Yesharim.* Gozlow, 1836.

———. *Sefer ha-Mivḥar.* Gozlow, 1835.

A'ot de Rabbi Natan. Edited by Solomon Schechter. Vienna: N.p. 1887.

'Aboth d'Rabbi Nathan. Trans. Elie Cashdan. In A. Cohen, ed., *The Minor Tractates of the Talmud,* 1–210. London: Soncino Press, 1965.

Abraham ben Isaac of Narbonne. *Sefer ha-'Eshkol.* Edited by B. H. Auerbach. Halberstadt: N.p., 1867/68 or 1868/69.

———. *Sefer ha-'Eshkol.* Edited by Shalom Albeck and Hanokh Albeck. Jerusalem: R. Mass, 1934/35–1938.

Abraham ben Solomon of Torrutiel [Ardutiel]. *Sefer ha-Kabbalah.* In Adolf Neubauer, ed., *Medieval Jewish Chronicles.* Oxford: Clarendon Press, 1895, 1:101–14.

Abramson, Shraga. "Le-Mavo ha-Talmud le-Rav Shemu'el ben Ḥofni." *Tarbiṣ* 26 (1956–57): 421–23.

———. *Rab Nissim Ga'on.* Jerusalem, 1965.

———. "Min ha-perek ha-Ḥamishi shel mevo ha-Talmud la-Rav Shemu'el ben Ḥofni." *Sinai* 88 (1981): 193–218.

———. "Milon ha-Talmud la-Rav Shemu'el ben Ḥofni." In *Sefer Abraham Even Shushan,* 13–66. Jerusalem, 1985.

———. *Ha-Rav Shemu'el ben Ḥofni (Geon Sura), Perakim min Sefer 'Mevo ha-Talmud'.* Jerusalem: Mekiṣe Nirdamim, 1990.

Ackroyd, Peter. "The Jewish Community in Palestine in the Persian Period." In *The Cambridge History of Judaism,* vol. 1: *Introduction: The Persian Period,* 130–61. Cambridge: Cambridge University Press, 1984.

Adler, Ada, ed. *Suida lexicon.* Leipzig, 1967–71. Reprint of 1928–38 edition.

Adler, Elkan Nathan. *Jewish Travellers in the Middle Ages.* New York: Dover, 1987. Reprint of London, 1930.

Afendopolo, Caleb ben Elijah. *Naḥal 'Eshkol.* JTS Mic. 3428 (MS Adler No. 14), Jewish Theological Seminary of America, New York.

———. *Patshegen Ketav ha-Dat.* Ramlah, Israel: ha-Moʿaṣah ha-arṣit, 1977.

———. *Sefer ʿAsarah Maʾamarot.* JTS MS Mic. 3327, Jewish Theological Seminary of America, New York.

———. *Sefer ʿAsarah Maʾamarot.* Ramlah, Israel: Mekhon Tifʾeret Yosef le-Ḥeker ha-Yahadut ha-Karaʾit, 5760 [1999].

Ahroni, Reuben. *Yemenite Jewry: Origins, Culture, and Literature.* Bloomington: Indiana University Press, 1986.

Åkerman, Susanna K. *Queen Christina and Her Circle: The Transformation of a Seventeenth-century Philosophical Libertine.* Leiden: E. J. Brill, 1991.

Alon, Gedaliah. *Toldot ha-Yehudim be-ereṣ Yisrael bi-tekufat ha-Mishnah veha-Talmud.* 2 vols. Jerusalem: Hoṣaʾat ha-Kibbuṣ ha-Meʾuḥad, 1980 and 1984.

———. *The Jews in Their Land in the Talmudic Age, 70–640* C.E.. Cambridge: Harvard University Press, 1989.

Anan ben David. *ha-Sarid veha-Palit mi-Sifre ha-Miṣvot ha-Rishonim li-Bene ha-Mikra* (Anan's book of commandments). Edited by Abraham Harkavy. In *Zikharon la-Rishonim (Studien und Mittheilungen),* vol. 8. Jerusalem: Makor, 1969. Reprint of St. Petersburg, 1903.

Anderson, Benedict. *Imagined Communities: Reflections on the Origin and Spread of Nationalism.* London: Verso, 1983.

Ankori, Zvi. "Elijah Bashyachi: An Inquiry into His Traditions Concerning the Beginnings of Karaism in Byzantium." *Tarbiṣ,* 25, no. 1 (1955): 44–65; ibid. 25, no. 2 (1956): 183–201 [Heb. with Eng. summary].

———. "Ibn al-Hītī and the Chronology of Joseph al-Baṣīr the Karaite." *JJS* 8 (1957): 71–81.

———. "The Correspondence of Tobias ben Moses, the Karaite, of Constantinople." In J. Blau et al., eds., *Essays on Jewish Life and Thought Presented in Honor of Salo Wittmayer Baron,* 1–38. New York: Columbia University Press, 1959.

———. *Karaites in Byzantium: The Formative Years, 970–1100.* New York: Columbia University Press, 1959.

———. "House of Bashyachi and Its Reforms." In Elijah Bashyachi, *ʾAdderet ʾEliyahu,* 1–16. Ramlah, Israel, 1966.

Apostolopoulou, G. *Die Dialektik bei Klemens von Alexandria: Ein Beitrag zur Geschichte der philosophischen Methoden.* Frankfurt am Main: Peter Lang, 1977.

Appel, Gersion. *A Philosophy of Mizvot: The Religious-Ethical Concepts of Judaism, Their Roots in Biblical Law, and the Oral Tradition.* New York: Ktav, 1975.

Aristeas. "Letter." Edited and translated by J. H. Shutt. In James H. Charlesworth, ed., *The Old Testament Pseudepigrapha,* vol. 2: *Expansions of the "Old Testament" and Legends, Wisdom and Philosophical Literature, Prayers, Psalms, and Odes: Fragments of Lost Judeo-Hellenistic Works,* 7–34. Garden City, N.Y.: Doubleday, 1985.

Assaf, Simha. *Be-ohole Yaʿakov: Perakim me-Ḥaye ha-Tarbut shel ha-Yehudim bi-Yeme ha-Benayim.* Jerusalem: Mosad ha-Rav Kook, 1943.

———. *Tekufat ha-Geʾonim ve-Sifrutah: Harṣaʾot ve-Shiʾurim.* Edited by M. Margaliot. Jerusalem: Mosad ha-Rav Kook, 1955.

Astren, Fred. "Some Notes on Intermarriage among Rabbanites and Karaites in the Middle Ages, and Its Subsequent Prohibition." *Journal of the Association of Graduates in Near Eastern Studies* 1, no. 1 (1990): 45–54.

———. "History or Philosophy? The Construction of the Past in Medieval Karaite Judaism." *Medieval Encounters* 1, no. 1 (1995): 114–43.

———. "De-Paganizing Death: Aspects of Mourning in Judaism and Islam." [San Francisco State University] *Magazine* 17, no. 1 (1999): 89–105.

———. "Karaite Approaches to History in Medieval Islam." In Benjamin H. Hary, John L. Hayes, and Fred Astren, eds., *Judaism and Islam: Boundaries, Communication, and Interaction: Essays in Honor of William Brinner*, 321–34. Leiden: E. J. Brill, 2000.

———. "Karaites" and "Magharians." In Lawrence H. Schiffman and James C. VanderKam, eds., *Encyclopedia of the Dead Sea Scrolls,* s.v. "Karaites" and s.v. "Magharians." Oxford: Oxford University Press, 2000.

———. "The Dead Sea Scrolls and Medieval Jewish Studies: Methods and Problems." *Dead Sea Discoveries* 8, no. 2 (2001): 105–23.

———. "The Gibeonite Gambit: Sabians and Karaite Jews on the Margins of Medieval Islamic Society." Forthcoming.

———. "What Has Anglia to Do with Jerusalem? A Biblical Explanation for Anglo-Saxon Ethnogenesis." Forthcoming.

Attias, Jean-Christophe. *Le Commentaire Biblique: Mordekhai Komtino ou l'herméneutique du dialogue.* Paris: Cerf, 1991.

———. "Intellectual Leadership: Rabbanite-Karaite Relations in Constantinople as Seen through the Works and Activity of Mordekhai Comtino in the Fifteenth Century." In Aron Rodrigue, ed., *Ottoman and Turkish Jewry, Community and Leadership*, 67–86. Bloomington: Indiana University Press, 1992.

Attridge, H. W. "Historiography." In Michael E. Stone, ed., *Jewish Writings of the Second Temple Period: Apocrypha, Pseudepigrapha, Qumran Sectarian Writings, Philo, Josephus,* 157–84. Assen, The Netherlands: Van Gorcum, 1984.

———. "Josephus and His Works." In Michael E. Stone, ed., *Jewish Writings of the Second Temple Period: Apocrypha, Pseudepigrapha, Qumran Sectarian Writings, Philo, Josephus,* 185–232. Assen, The Netherlands: Van Gorcum, 1984.

Augustine. *Concerning the City of God against the Pagans.* Trans. Henry Bettenson. London: Penguin Books, 1984.

Avi-Yonah, M. *The Jews of Palestine: A Political History from the Bar Kokhba War to the Arab Conquest.* New York: Schocken Books, 1976.

Avnery, Zvi. S.v. "Avelei Zion." In *EJ* 3:945–46.

Ayoub, Mahmoud. "'Uzayr in the Qur'an and Muslim Tradition." In William M. Brinner and Stephen D. Rick, eds., *Studies in Islamic and Judaic Traditions I*, 3–18. Atlanta, Georgia: Scholars Press, 1986.

The Babylonian Talmud: Seder Nashim, *Tractate Kiddushin.* Trans. H. Friedman. London: Soncino Press, 1934–39.

Bacharach, Jere L. "Palestine in the Policies of Tulunid and Ikhshidid Governors of Egypt (A.H. 254–358/868–969 A.D.)." In Amnon Cohen and Gabriel Baer, eds., *Egypt and Palestine: A Millennium of Association*, 51–65. Jerusalem: Ben Zvi Institute for the Study of Jewish Communities in the East, 1984.

Bacher, Wilhelm. "Qirqisani, the Qaraite, and His Work on Jewish Sects." *JQR*, o.s., 7 (1895). Reprinted in P. Birnbaum, ed., *Karaite Studies*, 259–82. New York: Hermon Press, 1971.

———. "Inedited Chapters of Jehudah Hadassi's 'Eshkol Hakkofer.'" *JQR*, o.s., 8 (1896): 431–44.

———. "Satzung von Sinai." In *Studies in Jewish Literature Issued in Honor of Professor Kaufmann Kohler*, 56–70. 1913.

Bachrach, Bernard S. *Early Medieval Jewish Policy in Western Europe*. Minneapolis: University of Minnesota Press, 1977.

Badawi, ʿAbd al-Rahman. *La transmission de la philosophie grecque au monde arabe*. Paris: J. Vrin, 1968.

Bainbridge, William Sims. *The Sociology of Religious Movements*. New York: Routledge, 1997.

Baldwin, John W. *The Scholastic Culture of the Middle Ages, 1000–1300*. Lexington, Mass.: D. C. Heath, 1971.

Baneth, David H. "Some Remarks on the Autographs of Yehudah Hallevi and the Genesis of the *Kuzari*." *Tarbiṣ* 26 (1956–57): 297–303 [Heb.].

al-Baqillānī, Muḥammad ibn al-Tayyib. *al-Tamhīd fi al-radd ʿalā al-mulhidah al-muʿattilah wa-al-rāfiḍah wa-al-khawārij wa-al-muʾtazilah*. Edited by Maḥmūd Muḥammad al-Khuḍayrī and Muḥammad ʿAbd al-Hādī Riḍā. Cairo: Maṭbaʿat Lajnat al-Taʾlif wa-al-Tarjamah wa-al-Nashr, 1947.

———. *Kitāb al-Tamhīd*. Edited by Richard Joseph McCarthy. Beirut: al-Maktabah al-Sharqiyah, 1957.

Barker, J. W. *Manuel II Palaeologus (1391–1425): A Study in Late Byzantine Statesmanship*. New Brunswick, N.J.: Rutgers University Press, 1969.

Bar-Kochva, Bezalel. *Pseudo-Hecataeus, "On the Jews": Legitimizing the Jewish Diaspora*. Berkeley: University of California Press, 1996.

Barnabas, Epistle of. In J. B. Lightfoot, ed., *The Apostolic Fathers*, 133–58. London, 1891.

Barnes, Harry Elmer. *A History of Historical Writing*. 1937. Rev. ed., New York: Dover, 1963.

Baron, Salo W. "Saadia's Communal Activities." In *Saadia Anniversary Volume*, 9–74. New York: American Academy of Jewish Research, 1943.

———. *A Social and Religious History of the Jews*. 19 vols. New York: Columbia University Press, 1952–83.

———. "Azariah de' Rossi's Attitude to Life." In *History and Jewish Historians: Essays and Addresses*, 174–204. Philadelphia, Pa.: Jewish Publication Society of America, 1964.

———. "Azariah de' Rossi's Historical Method." In *History and Jewish Historians: Essays and Addresses*, 205–39.

———. "Azariah de' Rossi: A Biographical Sketch." In *History and Jewish Historians: Essays and Addresses*, 167–73.

Bashyachi, Elijah. "'Iggeret Gid ha-Nasheh" (Epistle concerning the sciatic nerve). In unpaginated introduction to *'Adderet 'Eliyahu*, Gozlow, 1835.

———. *'Adderet 'Eliyahu*. Israel, 1966. Reprint of Gozlow, 1835.

Bashyachi, Moses ben Elijah. *Matteh ʾElohim.* JTS MS Mic. 9828, fols. 1a-29a, Jewish Theological Seminary of America, New York.

———. *Matteh ʾElohim.* Edited by Yosef ben ʿOvaydah Elgamil. Ramlah, Israel: Tifʾeret Yosef, 5761 [2000 or 2001].

Basil of Caesarea. *Letters and Selected Works.* Trans. Blomfield Jackson. In *The Nicene and Post-Nicene Fathers,* vol. 8. Grand Rapids, Mich.: Wm. B. Eerdmans, 1983.

Bat Ye'or. *The Dhimmi: Jews and Christians under Islam.* Rutherford, N.J.: Fairleigh Dickinson University Press, 1985.

Beck, Hans Georg. "Bildung und Theologie im frühmittelalterlichen Byzanc." In Peter Wirth, ed., *Polychronion. Festschrift Franz Dölger zum 75. Geburstag,* 69–81. Heidelberg: C. Winter, 1966.

———. *Byzantinistik heute.* Berlin: de Gruyter, 1977.

Becker, C. H. "Christliche Polemik und islamische Dogmenbildung." *Zeitschrift für Assyriologie* 26 (1911): 179–95.

Beghi, Joseph ben Moses. "ʾIggeret Qiryah Neʾemanah." Leiden MS Warner 30/2, fols. 190a–203b, in Bibliotheek der Rijksuniversiteit Leiden, The Netherlands.

Beinin, Joel. *The Dispersion of Egyptian Jewry: Culture, Politics, and the Formation of a Modern Diaspora.* Berkeley: University of California Press, 1998.

Bell, Richard. "Muhammad and Previous Messengers." *Moslem World* 24 (1934): 330–40.

Benayahu, Meir. *Rabbi ʾEliyahu Kapsali, ʾish Kandi'ah: Rav, Manhig ve-Historyon* ("Rabbi Eliyahu Kapsali of Candia'). Tel-Aviv: ha-Makhon le-Ḥeker ha-Tefuṣot, Tel-Aviv University, 1983 [Heb.].

Benjamin al-Nahawendī. *Sefer Dinim, Mas'at Binyamin.* Eupatoria, 1836.

———. *Sefer Dinim, Mas'at Binyamin.* Ramlah, Israel: ha-Yehudim ha-Kara'im be-Yisra'el, 1978. Based on Eupatoria, 1836.

Benjamin of Tudela. *The Itinerary of Benjamin of Tudela.* Edited and translated by Marcus Nathan Adler. New York: Philipp Feldheim, n.d. Reprint of 1907 ed.

Ben Shemesh, A. *Taxation in Islam.* 2 vols. Leiden: E. J. Brill, 1967.

Ben-Sasson, Haim Hillel. "The First Karaites—the Trend of Their Social Conceptions." *Ṣiyyon* 15 (1950): 42–56 [Heb., with Eng. summary].

———. "The Reformation in Contemporary Jewish Eyes." *Proceedings of the Israel Academy of Sciences and Humanities* 4, no. 12 (1970): 239–326.

———. "The Karaite Community of Jerusalem in the Tenth–Eleventh Centuries." *Shalem* 2 (1976): 1–18 [Heb.].

Ben-Sasson, Menahem. "Varieties of Inter-Communal Relations in the Geonic Period." In Daniel Frank, ed., *The Jews of Medieval Islam: Community, Society, and Identity,* 17–31. Leiden, E. J. Brill: 1995.

Ben-Shammai, Haggai. "The Doctrines of Religious Thought of Abū Yūsuf Yaʿqūb al-Qirqisānī and Yefet ben ʿElī." Ph.D. diss., Hebrew University, Jerusalem, 1977 [Heb.]

———. "Rabbanite and Karaite Attitudes toward Aliya." In Lee I. Levine, ed., *The Jerusalem Cathedra,* vol. 3. 190–91. Jerusalem: Yad Izhak Ben-Zvi: 1983.

———. "The Attitude of Some Early Karaites towards Islam." In I. Twersky, ed., *Studies in Medieval Jewish History and Literature*, 2:3–40. Cambridge: Harvard University Press, 1984.

———. "Studies in Karaite Atomism." *Jerusalem Studies in Arabic and Islam* 6 (1985): 243–98.

———. "Yeshuah ben Yehudah: The Figure of an Eleventh-Century Karaite Scholar in Jerusalem." *Pe'amim* 32 (1987): 3–20 [Heb., with Eng. summary].

———. "Fragments of Daniel al-Qūmisī's Commentary on the Book of Daniel as a Historical Source." *Henoch* 13, no. 3 (1991): 259–81.

———. "Between Ananites and Karaites: Observations on Early Medieval Jewish Sectarianism." *Studies in Muslim-Jewish Relations* 1 (1993): 19–31.

———. "Return to the Scriptures in Ancient and Medieval Jewish Sectarianism and in Early Islam." In E. Patlagean and A. LeBoulluec, eds., *Les Retours aux écritures: fondamentalismes présents et passés*, 319–39. Louvain-Paris: Peeters, 1993.

———. "Poetic Works and Lamentations of Qaraite 'Mourners of Zion'—Structure and Contents." In Shulamit Elizur, et al., eds., *Knesset Ezra: Literature and Life in the Synagogue: Studies Presented to Ezra Fleischer*, 191–234. Jerusalem: Yad Yiṣḥak Ben-Ṣevi u-Mekhon Ben-Ṣevi le-Ḥeker Kehilot Yisra'el ba-Mizraḥ, 1994 [Heb.].

———. "The Karaites." In Joshua Prawer and Haggai Ben-Shammai, eds., *The History of Jerusalem: The Early Muslim Period, 638–1099*, 201–24. Jerusalem: Yad Izhak Ben-Zvi, 1996.

Ben Shemesh, A. *Taxation in Islam*. 2 vols. Leiden: E. J. Brill, 1967.

Bérenger, Jean. "The Spread of the Reformation in Eastern and Northern Europe." In Pierre Chaunu, ed., *The Reformation*, 223–30. New York: St. Martin's Press, 1986.

Berg, J. van den. "John Covel's Letter on the Karaites (1677)." In van den Berg and van der Wall, *Jewish-Christian Relations in the Seventeenth Century*, 135–43.

———. "Proto-Protestants? The Image of the Karaites as a Mirror of the Catholic-Protestant Controversy in the Seventeenth Century." In van den Berg and van der Wall, *Jewish-Christian Relations in the Seventeenth Century*, 33–49.

Berg, J. van den, and E. G. E. van der Wall, eds. *Jewish-Christian Relations in the Seventeenth Century: Studies and Documents*. Dordrecht, 1988.

Berger, Michael S. *Rabbinic Authority*. New York: Oxford University Press, 1998.

Berger, Peter L., and Thomas Luckmann. *The Social Construction of Reality: A Treatise in the Sociology of Knowledge*. Garden City, N.Y.: Doubleday, 1966.

Berlin, Charles, and Aaron L. Katchen. *Christian Hebraism: The Study of Jewish Culture by Christian Scholars in Medieval and Early Modern Times*. Cambridge: Harvard University Press, 1988.

Bianquis, Thierry. "Autonomous Egypt from Ibn Ṭūlūn to Kāfūr, 868–969." In Carl F. Petry, ed., *The Cambridge History of Egypt*, vol. 1: *Islamic Egypt, 640–1517*, 86–119. Cambridge: Cambridge University Press, 1998.

Bickerman, Elias. "La chaine de la tradition pharisienne." *Revue biblique* 59, no. 1 (1952): 44–54.

Birnbaum, Philip, ed. *Karaite Studies.* New York: Hermon Press, 1971.

al-Bīrūnī, Muḥammad ibn Aḥmad. *al-Āthār al-bāqiyyah ʿan al-qurūn al-khāliyyah.* Edited by C. Edward Sachau. Leipzig: Brockhaus, 1878.

Bornstein, David Joseph. "Nathan de-Zuzita Resh Galuta." In *EJ* 12:860–61.

Bornstein, L. "The Ashkenazim in the Ottoman Empire in the Sixteenth and Seventeenth Centuries." in H. Z. (J. W.) Hirschberg, ed., *Mi-Mizraḥ umi-Maʿarav,* 81–104. Ramat-Gan, Israel, 1974 [Heb.].

Bowersock, G. W. *Hellenism in Late Antiquity.* Ann Arbor: University of Michigan Press, 1990.

Bowman, Steven B. *The Jews of Byzantium, 1204–1453.* University: University of Alabama Press, 1985.

Bowsma, William J. *Concordia Mundi: The Career and Thought of Guillaume Postel.* Cambridge, Mass.: Harvard University Press, 1957.

Boyarin, Daniel. *Dying for God: Martyrdom and the Making of Christianity and Judaism.* Stanford, Calif.: Stanford University Press, 1999.

Braudel, Fernand. *The Mediterranean and the Mediterranean World in the Age of Philip II.* New York: Harper & Row, 1972.

Braun, O. "Ein Brief des Katholikos Timotheos I über biblische Studien des 9. Jahrhunderts." *Oriens Christianus* 1 (1901): 299–313.

Brinner, William M. "Prophets and Prophecy in the Islamic and Jewish Traditions." In Brinner and Stephen D. Ricks, eds., *Studies in Islamic and Judaic Traditions,* 63–82. Vol. 2. Atlanta, Ga.: Scholars Press, 1989.

———. "Karaites of Christendom—Karaites of Islam." In C. E. Bosworth, Charles Issawi, Roger Savory, and A. L. Udovitch, eds., *The Islamic World, From Classical to Modern Times: Essays in Honor of Bernard Lewis,* 55–73. Princeton, N.J.: Princeton University Press, 1989.

———. "A Fifteenth-century Karaite-Rabbanite Dispute in Cairo." In Hava Lazarus-Yafeh, et al., eds., *The Majlis: Interreligious Encounters in Medieval Islam,* 184–96. Wiesbaden: Harrassowitz, 1999.

Brody, Robert. *The Geonim of Babylonia.* New Haven, Conn.: Yale University Press, 1998.

Brown, Peter. "The Rise and Function of the Holy Man in Late Antiquity." *Journal of Roman Studies* 61 (1971): 80–101.

———. *The Cult of the Saints: Its Rise and Function in Latin Christianity.* Chicago: University of Chicago Press, 1981.

Brownlee, William H. *The Midrash Pesher of Habakkuk.* Missoula, Mont.: Scholars Press, 1979.

Broydé, Isaac. S.v. "Luzki, Simhah Isaac." In *JE,* 8:219–20.

Buckler, Georgina. "Byzantine Education." In N. H. Baynes and H. St. L. B. Moss, eds., *Byzantium: An Introduction to East Roman Civilization,* 200–220. Oxford: Clarendon Press, 1948.

Bulliet, Richard W. *Conversion to Islam in the Medieval Period: An Essay in Quantitative History.* Cambridge: Harvard University Press, 1979.

———. "Conversion to Islam and the Emergence of a Muslim Society in Iran." In Levtzion, ed., *Conversion to Islam,* 30–51. New York: Holmes & Meier, 1979.

Burke, Peter. "The Uses of Italy." In Roy Porter and Mikulás Teich, eds., *The Renaissance in National Context*, 6–20. Cambridge: Cambridge University Press, 1991.

Cahn, Zvi. *The Rise of the Karaite Sect: A New Light on the Halakah and Origin of the Karaites*. New York: M. Tausner, 1937.

Carlebach, Elisheva. "Christian Hebraism and Jewish Sectarianism: The Polemical Uses of Jewish Heresy." Presented at the annual meeting of the Association for Jewish Studies, Boston, 1987.

———. *The Pursuit of Heresy: Rabbi Moses Hagiz and the Sabbatian Controversies*. New York: Columbia University Press, 1990.

———. "Jewish Unbelief in the Seventeenth Century: The Case of Friedrich Christiani." Presented at the annual meeting of the Association for Jewish Studies, Boston, 1992.

Carlebach, Elisheva, John M. Efron, and David N. Myers, eds. *Jewish History and Jewish Memory: Essays in Honor of Yosef Hayim Yerushalmi*. Hanover, N.H.: Brandeis University Press, 1998.

Chajes, Z. H. *The Student's Guide Through the Talmud*. New York: Philipp Feldheim, 1960.

Charlesworth, James H., ed. *The Old Testament Pseudepigrapha*, vol. 2: *Expansions of the "Old Testament" and Legends, Wisdom and Philosophical Literature, Prayers, Psalms, and Odes: Fragments of Lost Judeo-Hellenistic Works*. Garden City, N.Y.: Doubleday, 1985.

Chestnut, Glenn F. *The First Christian Historians: Eusebius, Socrates, Sozomen, Theodoret, and Evagrius*. 2d ed., Macon, Ga.: Mercer University Press, 1986.

Chiesa, Bruno. "Yaʿqūb al-Qirqisānī come fonte storiografica." In Bruneo Chiesa and Wilfrid Lockwood, *Yaʿqūb al-Qirqisānī on Jewish Sects and Christianity: A Translation of "Kitāb al-anwār."* Book 1, with two introductory essays, 15–47. Frankfurt am Main: Verlag Peter Lang, 1984.

———. "A Note on Early Karaite Historiography." In Ada Rapaport-Albert, ed., *Essays in Jewish Historiography*, 56–65. Middletown, Conn.: Wesleyan University, 1988.

Chiesa, Bruno, and Wilfrid Lockwood. *Yaʿqūb al-Qirqisānī on Jewish Sects and Christianity: A Translation of "Kitāb al-anwār."* Book 1, with two introductory essays. Frankfurt am Main: Verlag Peter Lang, 1984.

———. "al-Qirqisānī's Newly-Found Commentary on the Pentateuch: The Commentary on *Gen*, 12." *Henoch* 14 (1992): 153–80.

Chill, Abraham. *Abrabanel on Pirke Avot: A Digest of Rabbi Isaac Abrabanel's "Nahalat avot" with Selections from Other Classical Commentaries on Pirkei avot*. New York: Sepher-Hermon Press, 1991.

Chwolson, D. *Die Ssabier und der Ssabismus*. 2 vols. St. Petersburg: Der Kaiserlichen Akademie der Wissenschaften, 1856.

Clement of Alexandria. *Stromata* in *The Anti-Nicene Fathers*. Vol. 2. Grand Rapids, Michigan: Wm. B. Eerdmans, 1975.

Clucas, Lowell. *The Trial of John Italos and the Crisis of Intellectual Values in Byzantium in the Eleventh Century*. Munich: Institut für Byzantinistik, Neugriechische Philologie und Byzantinische Kunstgeschichte der Universität, 1981.

Cochrane, Charles Norris. *Christianity and Classical Culture: A Study of Thought and Action from Augustus to Augustine.* New York: Galaxy, 1957.

Cochrane, Eric. *Historians and Historiography in the Italian Renaissance.* Chicago: University of Chicago Press, 1981.

Cohen, Gerson D. "Esau as Symbol in Early Medieval Thought." In Alexander Altmann, ed., *Jewish Medieval and Renaissance Studies,* 19–48. Cambridge: Harvard University Press, 1967.

Cohen, Mark R. *Jewish Self-government in Medieval Egypt.* Princeton, N.J.: Princeton University Press, 1980.

———. *Under Crescent and Cross: The Jews in the Middle Ages.* Princeton, N.J.: Princeton University Press, 1994.

Cohen, Martin A. "Anan ben David and Karaite Origins." *JQR,* n.s. 68, no. 3 (1978): 129–45; 68, no. 4 (1978): 224–34.

Cohen, Shaye J. D. *From the Maccabees to the Mishnah.* Philadelphia, Pa.: Westminster Press, 1987.

———. *The Beginnings of Jewishness: Boundaries, Varieties, Uncertainties.* Berkeley: University of California Press, 1999.

Collingwood, R. G. *The Idea of History.* London: Oxford University Press, 1946.

Conforte, David. *Kore ha-Dorot.* Edited by David Cassel. Berlin: Abraham ben Asher, 1846.

Cook, M. A. "The Origins of *Kalām.*" *Bulletin of the School of Oriental and African Studies* 43 (1980): 32–43.

———. "Anan and Islam: the Origins of Karaite Scripturalism." *Jewish Studies in Arabic and Islam* 9 (1987): 174–75.

Corinaldi, Michael. *The Personal Status of the Karaites.* Jerusalem: Reuven Mas, 1984 [Heb.].

Corney, R. W. S.v. "Ahitub." In *The Interpreter's Dictionary of the Bible,* George Arthur Buttrick et al., eds., 1:71. New York: Abingdon Press, 1962.

Coulson, N. J. *A History of Islamic Law.* Edinburgh: Edinburgh University Press, 1964.

Courbage, Youssef, and Philippe Fargues. *Christians and Jews under Islam.* London: I. B. Tauris, 1998.

Cronon, William. "A Place for Stories: Nature, History, and Narrative." *Journal of American History* 78, no. 4 (March 1992): 1347–76.

Cynarski, S. "The Shape of Sarmatian Ideology in Poland." *Acta Poloniae Historica* 19 (1968): 5–17.

Dan, Joseph. S.v. "Kalonymus." In *EJ* 10:719.

Dán, Robert. "Isaac Troky and his 'Antitrinitarian' Sources." In Robert Dán, ed., *Occident and Orient: A Tribute to the Memory of A. Scheiber,* 69–82. Budapest: Akadémiai Kiadó, 1988.

Danby, Herbert, trans. *The Mishnah: Translated from the Hebrew, with Introduction and Brief Explanatory Notes.* Oxford: Clarendon Press, 1933.

Danon, Abraham. "The Karaites in European Turkey." *JQR,* n.s., 15, no. 3 (1925): 285–360.

———. "Documents Relating to the History of the Karaites of European Turkey." *JQR,* n.s., 17 (1926–27): 165–98, 239–322.

Danzig, Neil. *Introduction to Halakhot Pesuqot, with a Supplement to Halakhot Pesuqot.* New York: Jewish Theological Seminary of America, 1993 [Heb.].

David, Avraham. "Mif'alo ha-historyografi shel Gedalyah Ibn Yahya ba'al Shalshelet ha-Kabbalah" ("The historiographical work of Gedaliah Ibn Yahya, author of *Shalshelet ha-Kabbalah*"). Ph.D. diss., Hebrew University, Jerusalem, 1976.

Diels, Hermann. *Doxographi Graeci.* Berlin: G. Reimer, 1879.

Diels, Hermann, and W. Kranz, eds. *Die Fragmente der Vorsokratiker, griechisch und deutsch.* 3 vols. Berlin: Weidmann, 1952–56. Reprint of 1903.

Dippie, Brian W. "The Winning of the West Reconsidered." *Wilson Quarterly* 14, no. 3 (summer 1990), 70–84.

Drory, Rina. *The Emergence of Jewish-Arabic Literary Contacts at the Beginning of the Tenth Century.* Tel-Aviv: ha-Kibbuts ha-me'uhad, 1988 [Heb.].

———. *Models and Contacts: Arabic Literature and Its Impact on Medieval Jewish Culture.* Leiden: E. J. Brill, 2000.

Dubrovnik, Frances. *The Slavs in European History and Civilization.* New Brunswick, N.J.: Rutgers University Press, 1962.

Dunlop, D. M. *The History of the Jewish Khazars.* Princeton, N.J.: Princeton Univesity Press, 1954.

Eisenstein, J. D. *Oṣar Dinim u-Minhagim.* New York: N.p., 1917.

Elazary, Edna. S.v. "Elionaeus, Son of Cantheras." In *EJ* 6:663.

Eldad ha-Dani: Sippurav ve-Hilkhotav. Edited by A. Epstein. Pressburg: Abraham Alkalai, 1891.

Ephrathi, Jacob E. *The Savoraic Period and Its Literature in Babylonia and the Land of Israel.* Petah Tikvah, Israel: Hotṣa'at 'Agudat bene 'Asher, 1973. [Heb.].

Epiphanius of Salamis. *The Panarion of Epiphanius of Salamis, Book I (Sects 1–46).* Trans. Frank Williams. Leiden: E. J. Brill, 1987.

———. *The "Panarion" of St. Epiphanius, Bishop of Salamis: Selected Passages.* Trans. Philip R. Amidon. New York: Oxford University Press, 1990.

Epstein, Isidore, ed. *The Babylonian Talmud: Shabbat.* London: Soncino Press, 1938.

Epstein, J. N. "New Fragments from Anan's Book of Laws." *Tarbiṣ* 5 (1935): 283–90 [Heb.].

Epstein, Mark A. *The Ottoman Jewish Communities and Their Role in the Fifteenth and Sixteenth Centuries.* Freiburg: K. Schwarz, 1980.

———. "The Leadership of the Ottoman Jews in the Fifteenth and Sixteenth Centuries." In Benjamin Braude and Bernard Lewis, ed., *Christians and Jews in the Ottoman Empire: The Functioning of a Plural Society,* 101–16. 2 vols. New York, 1982.

Erder, Yoram. "When Did the Karaites First Encounter Apocryphic Literature Akin to the Dead Sea Scrolls?" *Katedrah be-toldot 'ereṣ-yisra'el ve-yishuvah* 42 (1987): 54–68, followed by comments by Haggai Ben-Shammai.

———. "The Origin of the Name Idrīs in the Qur'ān: A Study of the Influence of Qumran Literature on Early Islam." *Journal of Near Eastern Studies* 49 (1990): 339–50.

———. "The Karaites' Sadducee Dilemma." *Israel Oriental Studies* 14 (1994): 195–226.

Ess, Josef van. "The Logical Structure of Islamic Theology." In G. E. von Grunebaum, ed., *Logic in Classical Islamic Culture,* 21–50. Wiesbaden, 1970.

———. *Frühe muʿtazilitische Häresiographie: zwei Werke des Nasiʾ al-Akbar, gest. 293 H.* Beirut: In Kommission bei F. Steiner, Wiesbaden, 1971.

Eusebius. *The History of the Church.* Trans. G. A. Williamson. Baltimore, Md.: Penguin Books, 1965.

Fakhry, Majid. *A History of Islamic Philosophy.* New York: Columbia University Press, 1983.

Faragher, John Mack. "The Frontier Trail: Rethinking Turner and Reimagining the American West." *American Historical Review* 98, no. 1 (1992): 106–17.

Faur, José. *In the Shadow of History: Jews and "Conversos" at the Dawn of Modernity.* Albany, N.Y.: State University of New York Press, 1992.

Fenton, Paul. *A Handlist of Judeo-Arabic Manuscripts in Leningrad.* Jerusalem: Ben Zvi Institute, Hebrew University, 1991 [Heb.].

Finkelstein, Louis. *Mavo le-Massekhtot ʾAvot ve-ʾAvot dʾRabbi Natan* (Introduction to the treatises of Abot and Abot of Rabbi Nathan). New York: Jewish Theological Seminary of America, 1950 [Heb., with Eng. summary].

Firkovich, Abraham. *Avnei Zikkaron.* Vilna, 1872.

Fossum, Jarl. "The Magharians: A Pre-Christian Jewish Sect and Its Significance for the Study of Gnosticism and Christianity." *Henoch* 9 (1987): 303–44.

Fowden, Garth. "The Pagan Holy Man in Late Antique Society." *Journal of Hellenic Studies* 102 (1982): 33–59.

———. *Empire to Commonwealth: Consequences of Monotheism in Late Antiquity.* Princeton, N.J.: Princeton University Press, 1993.

Frank, Daniel. "Ibn Ezra and the Karaite Exegetes Aaron ben Joseph and Aaron ben Elijah." In Fernando Díaz Esteban, ed., *Abraham Ibn Ezra and His Age: Proceedings of the International Symposium,* 99–107. Madrid: Asociación Española de Orientalistas, 1990.

———. "The Study of Medieval Karaism, 1959–1989: A Bibliographical Essay." *Bulletin of Judaeo-Greek Studies* 6 (summer 1990): 15–23.

———. "The *Shoshanim* of Tenth-century Jerusalem: Karaite Exegesis, Prayer, and Communal Identity." In Daniel Frank, ed., *The Jews of Medieval Islam: Community, Society, and Identity,* 199–245. Leiden: E. J. Brill, 1995.

Frank, Edgar. *Talmudic and Rabbinical Chronology: The System of Counting Years in Jewish Literature.* New York: P. Feldheim, 1956.

Frerichs, Ernest S., and Jacob Neusner, eds. *"To See Ourselves as Others See Us": Christians, Jews, "Others" in Late Antiquity.* Chico, Calif.: Scholars Press, 1985.

Freund, Roman. *Karaites and Dejudaization: A Historical Review of an Endogamous and Exogenous Paradigm.* Stockholm: Almquist & Wiksell, 1991.

Frick, David A. "The Biblical Philology of Szymon Budny: Between East and West." In *Biblia, to jest Ksiegi Starego i Nowego Przymierza/in der Übersetzung des Simon Budny: Herausgegeben von Hans Rothe und Friedrich Scholz, 1572.* Paderborn: F. Schoningh, 1994.

Friedman, H. trans. *Midrash Rabbah.* London: Soncino Press, 1983.

Friedman, Jerome. *Michael Servetus: A Case Study in Total Heresy.* Geneva: Droz, 1978.

———. "Sixteenth-century European Jewry: Theologies of Crisis in Crisis." In M. Chrisman and O. Gründler, eds., *Social Groups and Religious Ideas in the Sixteenth Century*, 102–12. Kalamazoo, Mich.: Medieval Institute, Western Michigan University, 1978.

———. "The Reformation and Jewish Antichristian Polemics." *Bibliothèque d'Humanisme et Renaissance* 41 (1979): 83–97.

———. "Sixteenth-century Christian-Hebraica: Scripture and the Renaissance Myth of the Past." *Sixteenth Century Journal* 11, no. 4 (1980): 67–85.

———. *The Most Ancient Testimony: Sixteenth-century Christian-Hebraica in the Age of Renaissance Nostalgia*. Athens: Ohio University Press, 1983.

———. "The Reformation in Alien Eyes: Jewish Perceptions of Christian Troubles." *Sixteenth Century Journal* 16, no. 1 (1983): 23–40.

Friedman, Mordechai Akiva. *Jewish Marriage in Palestine: A Cairo Genizah Study*. 2 vols. Tel-Aviv: Tel-Aviv University, Chaim Rosenberg School of Jewish Studies, 1980.

Frost, Robert I. *After the Deluge: Poland-Lithuania and the Second Northern War, 1655–60*. Cambridge: Cambridge University Press, 1993.

Fueck, J. "The Role of Traditionalism in Islam." In Merlin L. Swartz, trans. and ed., *Studies on Islam*, 99–122. Oxford: Oxford University Press, 1981. Reprint of 1939.

Fürst, Julius. *Geschichte des Karäerthums*. 3 vols. Leipzig: Ries'sche Buchdruckerei, 1862–69.

Gafni, Isaiah M. "'Pre-Histories' of Jerusalem in Hellenistic, Jewish, and Christian Literature." *Journal for the Study of Pseudepigrapha* 1 (1987): 5–22.

Galante, Abraham. *Les Juifs de Constantinople sous Byzance*. Istanbul, 1940.

Gardet, Louis. "Philosophie et religion en Islam avant l'an 330 del'hegire." In *L'élaboration de l'Islam: Colloque de Strasbourg, 12–14 juin 1959*, 39–60. Paris: Presses universitaires de France, 1961.

———. "Quelques réflexions sur la place du *ʿilm al-kalām* dans les 'sciences religieuses' musulmanes." In *Arabic and Islamic Studies in Honor of H.A.R. Gibb*, 258–69. Leiden: E. J. Brill, 1965.

Gardet, Louis, and M. M. Anawati. *Introduction à la théologie musulmane: essai de théologie comparée*. Paris: J. Vrin, 1948.

Gätje, Helmut. *The Qurʾān and Its Exegesis: Selected Texts with Classical and Modern Muslim Interpretations*. Berkeley: University of California Press, 1976.

Geanakoplos, Deno. "Byzantium and the Crusades, 1261–1354." In Harry W. Hazard, ed., *A History of the Crusades*, vol. 3: *The Fourteenth and Fifteenth Centuries*, 27–68. Madison: University of Wisconsin Press, 1975.

———. "Byzantium and the Crusades, 1354–1453." In *A History of the Crusades*, vol. 3: *The Fourteenth and Fifteenth Centuries*, 69–103.

———. *Constantinople and the West: Essays on the Late Byzantine (Palaeologan) and Italian Renaissances*. Madison: University of Wisconsin Press, 1989.

Geary, Patrick J. *The Myth of Nations: The Medieval Origins of Europe*. Princeton, N.J.: Princeton University Press, 2002.

Gervers, Michael, and Ramzi Jibran Bikhazi, eds. *Conversion and Continuity:*

Indigenous Christian Communities in Islamic Lands, Eighth to Eighteenth Centuries. Toronto: Pontifical Institute of Mediaeval Studies, 1990.

Gil, Moshe. "Karaite Antiquities." *Teʿudah* 15 (1999): 71–107. [Heb.].

———. "Aliya and Pilgrimage in the Early Arab Period, 634–1009." In Lee I. Levine, ed., *The Jerusalem Cathedra,* vol. 3, 163–73. Jerusalem: Yad Izhak Ben-Zvi, 1983.

———. *Palestine during the First Muslim Period, 634–1099.* 3 vols. Tel Aviv: Tel-Aviv University, 1983 [Heb.].

———. *A History of Palestine, 634–1099.* Cambridge: Cambridge University Press, 1992.

———. *In the Kingdom of Ishmael in the Era of the Geonim,* 4 vols. Tel-Aviv: Tel-Aviv University, 1997. [Heb.].

———. "More about Palestine during the First Muslim Period." *Cathedra* 70 (1993): 29–58 [Heb.].

———. "The Exilarchate." In Daniel Frank, ed., *The Jews of Medieval Islam: Community, Society, and Identity.* Leiden: E. J. Brill, 1995, 33–65.

Ginzberg, Louis. *Genizah Studies in Memory of Doctor Solomon Schechter,* 2: *Geonic and Early Karaitic Halakah.* New York: Jewish Theological Seminary of America, 1929.

Glatzer, Nahum. "The Tannaim and History." In Neusner, ed., *The Christian and Judaic Invention of History,* 125–42. Atlanta, Ga.: Scholars Press, 1990.

———, ed. *The Passover Haggadah.* New York: Schocken Books, 1979.

Goitein, S. D. "Autographs of Yehuda Hallevi." *Tarbiṣ* 25 (1955–56): 393–412 [Heb.].

———. *Jews and Arabs: Their Contacts through the Ages.* 3rd ed. New York: Schocken Books, 1974.

———. "The Biography of Rabbi Judah Ha-Levi in Light of the Cairo Geniza Documents." *PAAJR* 28 (1959): 41–56.

———. *A Mediterranean Society: The Jewish Communities of the Arab World as Portrayed in the Documents of the Cairo Geniza,* vol. 1: *Economic Foundations.* Berkeley: University of California Press. 1967; 2, *The Community.* Berkeley: University of California Press, 1971.

———. "Jewish Society and Institutions under Islam." *Cahiers d'histoire mondiale* 11 (1968): 170–84.

Golb, Norman. "Who Were the Maġārīya?" *Journal of the American Oriental Society* 80 (1960): 347–59.

Golb, Norman, and Omeljan Pritsak. *Khazarian Hebrew Documents of the Tenth Century.* Ithaca, N.Y.: Cornell University Press, 1982.

Golden, Peter B. *Khazar Studies: An Historical-Philological Inquiry into the Origins of the Khazars.* 2 vols. Budapest: Akadémiai Kiadó, 1980.

———. "Khazaria and Judaism." *Archivum Eurasiae Medii Aevi* 3 (1983): 127–56.

Goldin, Judah. *The Living Talmud: The Wisdom of the Fathers.* New Haven, Conn.: Yale University Press, 1955.

———. S.v. "Avot de-Rabbi Natan." In *EJ* 2:984–85.

Goldschmidt, Daniel. "On the *Maḥzor Romania,*" *Sefunot* 8 (1964): 205–36 [Heb.].

Goldwurm, Hersh, ed. *The Early Acharonim*. Brooklyn, N.Y.: Mesorah, 1989.

Goldziher, Ignaz. *Muslim Studies*. London: George Allen & Unwin, 1966. English trans. of *Muhammedanische Studien*, 1889–90.

———. *Introduction to Islamic Theology and Law*. Princeton, N.J.: Princeton University Press, 1981. Trans. of German 1910 ed.

Graetz, Heinrich. *History of the Jews*. 5 vols. Philadelphia, Pa.: Jewish Publication Society of America, 1949.

Grafton, Anthony. *Defenders of the Text: Traditions of Scholarship in an Age of Science, 1450–1800*. Cambridge: Harvard University Press, 1991.

———. *Bring Out Your Dead: The Past as Revelation*. Cambridge: Harvard University Press, 2001.

Green, Tamara M. *The City of the Moon God: Religious Traditions of Harran*. Leiden: E. J. Brill, 1992.

Griffith, Sidney H. "A Ninth Century Summa Theologiae Arabica." In Khalil Samir, ed., *Actes du Deuxième Congrès International d'Études Arabes Chrétiennes*, 123–41. Rome: Pont. Institutum Studiorum Orientalium, 1986.

———. "The First *Summa Theologiae* in Arabic: Christian Kalam in Ninth-century Palestine." In Gervers and Bikhazi, eds., *Conversion and Continuity: Indigenous Christian Communities in Islamic Lands, Eighth to Eighteenth Centuries*, 15–32. Toronto: Pontifical Institute of Mediaeval Studies, 1990.

Grossman, Avraham. "Aliya in the Seventh and Eighth Centuries." In Lee I. Levine, ed., *The Jerusalem Cathedra*, vol. 3, 174–87. Jerusalem: Yad Izhak Ben-Zvi, 1983.

———. "Jerusalem in Jewish Apocalyptic Literature." In Joshua Prawer and Haggai Ben-Shammai, eds., *The History of Jerusalem: The Early Muslim Period, 638–1099*, 295–310. Jerusalem: Yad Izhak Ben-Zvi, 1996.

Gruen, Erich S. *Heritage and Hellenism: The Reinvention of Jewish Tradition*. Berkeley: University of California Press, 1998.

Grunfeld, I. *The Sabbath: A Guide to Its Understanding and Observance*. Jerusalem: Philipp Feldheim, 1972.

Gündüz, Şinasi. *The Knowledge of Life: The Origins and Early History of the Mandaeans and Their Relations to the Sabians of the Qur'ān and to the Harranians*. Oxford: Oxford University Press, 1994.

Hacker, Joseph. "Ottoman Policy toward Jews and Jewish Attitudes toward the Ottomans during the Fifteenth Century." In Benjamin Braude and Bernard Lewis, eds., *Christians and Jews in the Ottoman Empire. The Functioning of a Plural Society*, 117–26. 2 vols. New York: Holmes & Meier, 1982.

———. "The Intellectual Activity of the Jews of the Ottoman Empire during the Sixteenth and Seventeenth Centuries." In Isadore Twersky and Bernard Septimus, eds., *Jewish Thought in the Seventeenth Century*, 99–135. Cambridge: Harvard University Press, 1987.

Hadassi, Judah. *Eshkol ha-Kofer*. Westmead: Gregg, 1971. Reprint of Gozlow, 1836.

Halakhot Gedolot. Venice, 1548.

Halakhot Gedolot. Edited by Azriel Hildesheimer. Berlin: N.p., 1888–92.

(Sefer) Halakhot Gedolot: Meḥubbar u-Meyussad la-Halakhot ke-fi Seder Shita Sidre Talmud ha-Bavli. Warsaw: Yitshak Goldman, 1874.

Halakhot Pesukot. Edited by Soliman Sassoon. Jerusalem: Mekiṣe Nirdamim, 1950.

Halper, B. *A Volume of the Book of Precepts by Hefes B. Yasliah.* Philadelphia, Pa.: N.p., 1915.

Hanawalt, E. A. "Suda." In J. R. Strayer, ed., *Dictionary of the Middle Ages,* s.v. "Suda." New York: Scribner, 1982.

Harkavy, Abraham (Garkavi, Albert). *Altjüdische Denkmäler aus der Krim mitgetheilt von Abraham Firkowitsch, 1839–1872,* 1876. Reprinted Wiesbaden: M. Sändig, 1969.

———. "Po voprosu o iudeyskikh drevnostyakh naydennykh Firkovichem v Krymu" (On Jewish antiquities found by Firkovich in the Crimea). In *Zhurnal Ministerstva narodnago prosveshcheniya.* 1877.

———, ed. *Zikhron la-Rishonim (Studien und Mittheilungen),* vol. 4. *Zikhron kamah go'enim: uve-yihud Rav Sherira ve-Rav Hai beno veha-Rav R. Yiṣḥak Alfasi.* Berlin: Bi-defus Ittskovski, 1886–87. Reprint Jerusalem, 1965–66.

———, ed. *Zikhron la-Rishonim (Studien und Mittheilungen),* vol. 5. Saadia Gaon, *ha-Sarid veha-palit mi-sefer ha-egron ve-sefer ha-galui.* St. Petersburg, 1891.

———. "Abū Yūsuf Yaʿqūb al-Qirqisānī on the Jewish Sects." *Transactions of the Imperial Russian Archaeological Society,* 8:247–78. St. Petersburg, 1894. [Rus.]

———, "Notes and Additions to the Fourth Section of Graetz's *History of the Jews*" in *Ḥadashim Gam Yeshanim,* no. 7 (Berlin, 1895–96), 3–60. Reprint Jerusalem: Karmiel, 1970, 109–68.

———, "Notes and Additions to the Fifth Section of Graetz's *History of the Jews*" in *Ḥadashim Gam Yeshanim,* no. 10 (Berlin, 1896), 3–52. Reprint Jerusalem: Karmiel, 1970, 199–250.

———. *Zikhron la-Rishonim (Studien und Mittheilungen),* vol. 8. Anan ben David, *ha-Sarid veha-palit mi-sifre ha-miṣvot ha-rishonim li-vene ha-Mikra* (Anan's book of commandments). St. Petersburg, 1903. Reprint Jerusalem: Makor, 1969.

———. "Abū Yūsuf Yaʿqūb al-Qirqisānī on the Jewish Sects." In Chiesa and Lockwood, *Yaʿqūb al-Qirqisānī on Jewish Sects and Christianity,* 49–90.

Haskins, Charles Homer. *The Renaissance of the Twelfth Century.* Cambridge: Harvard University Press, 1927.

Hawting, G. R. *The Idea of Idolatry and the Emergence of Islam: From Polemic to History.* Cambridge: Cambridge University Press, 1999.

Heilprin, Jehiel. *Seder ha-Dorot.* Karlsruhe: Stern, 1768.

Heinemann, Isaak. *Taʿame ha-Miṣvot be-Sifrut Yisra'el* (The reasons for the commandments in the literature of Israel). Jerusalem: ha-Mador ha-Dati ba-Maḥlakah le-ʿInyene ha-Noʿar vehe-Ḥaluṣ shel Hanhalat ha-Histadrut ha-Ṣiyyonit, 1953/54 [Heb.].

———. *Three Jewish Philosophers.* New York: Atheneum, 1969.

Henderson, John B. *The Construction of Orthodoxy and Heresy: Neo-Confucian, Islamic, Jewish, and Early Christian Patterns.* Albany, N.Y.: State University of New York Press, 1998.

Herodotus. *The Histories.* Trans. Aubrey de Sélincourt. Baltimore, Md.: Penguin Books, 1954.

Hippolytus. *Hippolytus Werke,* Bd. 3: *Refutatio omnium haeresium.* Edited by P. Wendland. Hildesheim, 1977. Reprint of Leipzig: J. C. Hinrichs, 1897.

Hirschfeld, Hartwig. "A Karaite Conversion Story." In *Jews College Jubilee Volume.* London: Luzac, 1906.

———. *Qirqisani Studies.* London: Jews College, 1918.

Hitti, Philip K. *History of the Arabs,* 9th ed. London: Macmillan, 1967.

Hodgson, Marshall G. S. "How Did the Early Shīʿa Become Sectarian?" *Journal of the American Oriental Society* 75 (1955): 1–13.

———. *The Venture of Islam.* 3 vols. Chicago, Ill.: University of Chicago Press, 1974.

Holladay, Carl. *Fragments from Hellenistic Jewish Authors,* vol. 1: *Historians.* Chico, Calif.: Scholars Press, 1983.

Hourani, A. H., and S. M. Stern, eds. *The Islamic City.* Philadelphia: University of Pennsylvania Press, 1970.

Humphreys, R. Stephen. *Islamic History: A Framework for Inquiry.* Princeton, N.J.: Princeton University Press, 1991.

Husik, Isaac. *A History of Mediaeval Jewish Philosophy.* New York: Meridian Books, 1958.

Ibn Aknin, Judah ben Jacob. *Mavo la-Talmud* translated and published as *Einleitung in den Talmud.* In H. Graetz, ed., *Festschrift . . . Zacharias Frankel.* 1967. Reprint of Breslau, 1871.

Ibn Daud, Abraham. *Sefer ha-Qabbalah: The Book of Tradition by Abraham Ibn Daud: A Critical Edition with a Translation and Notes,* by Gerson D. Cohen. Philadelphia, Pa.: Jewish Publication Society of America, 1967.

———. *The Exalted Faith.* Trans. Norbert M. Samuelson. Rutherford, N.J.: Fairleigh Dickinson University Press, 1986.

Ibn Khaldun. *The Muqaddimah: An Introduction to History.* Trans. Franz Rosenthal. 3 vols. Princeton, N.J.: Princeton University Press, 1958.

Ibn al-Nadīm. *The Fihrist of al-Nadīm: A Tenth Century Survey of Muslim Culture.* Edited and translated by Bayard Dodge. 2 vols. New York: Columbia University Press, 1970.

Ibn Shahin, Nissim ben Jacob. *Sefer ha-Mafteaḥ shel Manʿule ha-Talmud.* Edited by Jacob Goldenthal. Vienna: N.p., 1847.

Ibn Yahya, Gedaliah. *Shalshelet ha-Kabbalah.* Venice, 1587.

Ibn Zerah, Menahem ben Aaron. *Ṣedah la-Derekh.* Warsaw: H. Kelter, 1880.

ʾIggeret Rav Sherira Gaʾon. Edited by Aaron Hyman. London: N.p., 1910/11.

———. Edited by Benjamin Menasseh Lewin. Jerusalem, 1972. Reprint of Haifa: Godah-Itskovski, 1921, with addenda and corrections.

———. Edited and translated by Nosson Dovid Rabinowich. Jerusalem: Rabbi Jacob Joseph Jewish School—Ahavath Torah Institute, 1988.

Innis, Harold A. *Empire and Communications.* Toronto: University of Toronto Press, 1972.

Iskander, John. "Islamization in Medieval Egypt: The Coptic-Arabic 'Apocalypse of Samuel' as a Source for the Social and Religious History of Medieval Copts." *Medieval Encounters* 4, no.3 (1998): 219–27.

Isser, S. *The Dositheans.* Leiden: E. J. Brill, 1976.

Jeffery, Arthur. *A Reader on Islam: Passages from Standard Arabic Writings Illustrative of the Beliefs and Practices of Muslims.* The Hague: Mouton, 1962.

Jeshua ben Joseph ha-Levi of Tlemcen. *Halikhot 'Olam.* Lisbon(?), 1490.

Johannesson, Kurt. *The Renaissance of the Goths in Sixteenth-century Sweden: Johannes and Olaus Magnus as Politicians and Historians.* Berkeley: University of California Press, 1991.

John of Damascus. *Saint John of Damascus: Writings.* Edited and translated by Frederic H. Chase. New York: Fathers of the Church, 1958.

Johnson, Marshall D. *The Purpose of Biblical Genealogies with Special Reference to the Setting of the Genealogies of Jesus.* 2nd. ed. Cambridge: Cambridge University Press, 1988.

Josephus. *The Works of Flavius Josephus.* Trans. William Whiston. Philadelphia, Pa.: J. B. Lippincott, 1869.

Josippon. *Sefer Yosippon.* Edited by David Flusser. 2 vols. Jerusalem: Bialik Institute, 1981.

———. *Sefer Yosippon.* Edited by H. Huminer. Jerusalem: Huminer, 1967.

Jost, J. M. *Geschichte des Judenthums und seiner Sekten.* 3 vols. Leipzig: Dörffling & Franke, 1857–59.

Judah Halevi. *Judah Hallevi's Kitab al Khazari.* Trans. Hartwig Hirschfeld. London: G. Routledge, 1905.

———. *Kitāb al-radd wal-dalīl fil-dīn al-dalīl (Al-Kitābal-Khazarī).* Edited by David H. Baneth. Jerusalem: Magnes Press, 1977.

Justin Martyr. *The dispute of St. Justin, the philosopher and martyr, with Trypho the Jew.* Nieświez, Poland: 1564. Trans. Simon Budny and Wawrzyniec Krzyszkowski. [Pol.]

Kahle, P. E. *The Cairo Genizah.* New York: Praeger, 1960.

Kamali, Mohammad Hashim. *Principles of Islamic Jurisprudence.* Cambridge: Islamic Texts Society, 1991.

Kaminski, A. "The Eclipse of Poland." In J. S. Bromley. ed. *The New Cambridge Modern History,* 6:681–715. Cambridge: Cambridge University Press, 1970.

Kaplan, Yosef. "The 'Karaites' of Amsterdam in the Early Eighteenth Century: An Unknown Chapter in the Fermentation of Ideas in the Sephardic Community." *Ṣiyon* 52, no. 3 (1987): 279–314 [Heb., with Eng. summary].

———. "'Karaites' in Early Eighteenth-century Amsterdam." In David S. Katz and Jonathan I. Israel, eds., *Sceptics, Millenarians, and Jews,* 196–236. Leiden: E. J. Brill, 1990.

Katchen, Aaron L. *Christian Hebraists and Dutch Rabbis: Seventeenth Century Apologetics and the Study of Maimonides.* Mishneh Torah. Cambridge: Harvard University Press, 1984.

Kautzsch, E. F. *Johannes Buxtorf der Aeltere.* Basel, 1879.

Kazhdan, A. P. S.v. "Matthew Blasteres." In *Oxford Dictionary of Byzantium.*

———. S.v. "Encyclopedism." In *Oxford Dictionary of Byzantium.*

———. S.v. "Law." In *Oxford Dictionary of Byzantium.*

———. S.v. "Souda." In *Oxford Dictionary of Byzantium.*

Kazhdan, A. P., and A. W. Epstein. *Change in Byzantine Culture in the Eleventh and Twelfth Centuries.* Berkeley: University of California Press, 1985.

Kazhdan, A. P., and Ihor Ševčenko. "Transliteration of Texts." In *Oxford Dictionary of Byzantium.*

Kennedy, Hugh. *The Prophet and the Age of the Caliphates.* London: Longman, 1986.

Khoury, P. "Jean Damascène et l'Islam." *Proche-Orient chrétienne* 7 (1957): 44–63; 8 (1958): 313–39.

Kimhi, David. *The Commentary of Rabbi David Kimhi on Psalms CXX–CL.* Edited by J. Baker and E. W. Nicholson. Cambridge: Cambridge University Press, 1973.

Klassen, William. "Anti-Judaism in Early Christianity: The State of the Question." In Peter Richardson. ed., *Anti-Judaism in Early Christianity,* vol. 1: *Paul and the Gospels,* 1–20. Waterloo, Ont., 1986.

Klausner, Joseph. *The Messianic Idea in Israel, from Its Beginning to the Completion of the Mishnah.* New York: Macmillan, 1955.

Koch, K. "Ezra and the Origins of Judaism." *JJS* 19 (1974): 173–97.

Koehler, Kaufmann. "Karaites and Karaism." In *JE,* 7:438–47.

Koehler, Kaufmann, and Richard Gottheil. S.v. "Afendopolo, Caleb b. Elijah b. Judah." *JE,* 1:222–23.

Koestler, Arthur. *The Thirteenth Tribe.* New York: Popular Library, 1976.

Kotter, Bonifatius. *Die Schriften des Johannes von Damaskos,* vol. 4: *Liber de haeresibus: Opera polemica.* Berlin: de Gruyter, 1981.

Krauss, Samuel. *Paras ve-Romi ba-Talmud uva-Midrashim* (Persia and Rome in the Talmud and Midrash). Jerusalem: Mosad ha-Rav Kook, 1947–48.

Kuntz, Marion Leathers. *Guillaume Postel, Prophet of the Restitution of All Things: His Life and Thought.* The Hague: Nijhoff, 1981.

Labourt, J. *Le Christianisme dans l'Empire Perse sous la Dynastie Sassanide, 224–632.* Paris: V. Lecoffre, 1904.

Lane, E. W. *Arabic-English Lexicon.* 2 vols. Cambridge, 1984. Reprint of 1863 ed.

Lasker, Daniel J. *Jewish Philosophical Polemics against Christianity in the Middle Ages.* New York: Ktav, 1977.

———. "Rabbanism and Karaism: The Contest for Supremacy." In R. Jospe and S. W. Wagner, eds., *Great Schisms in Jewish History,* 47–72. New York: Ktav, 1981.

———. "Maimonides' Influence on the Philosophy of Elijah Bashyatchi the Karaite." *Jerusalem Studies in Jewish Thought* 3 (1983–84): 405–25 [Heb.].

———. "The Destiny of Man in Karaite Philosophy." *Da'at,* 12 (1984): 5–13.

———. "Nature and Science in the Philosophy of Aaron b. Elijah the Karaite." *Da'at,* 17 (1986): 33–42 [Heb.].

———. "The Philosophy of Judah Hadassi the Karaite." In *Shlomo Pines Jubilee Volume,* 1:477–92. Jerusalem, 1988 [Heb.].

———. "The Philosophy of Judah Hadassi the Karaite." *Shlomo Pines Jubilee*

Volume, part 1, *Jerusalem Studies in Jewish Thought,* 7:477–92. Jerusalem, 1988 [Heb., with Eng. summary].

———. "Islamic Influences on Karaite Origins." In W. Brinner and S. Ricks, eds., *Studies in Islamic and Judaic Traditions II,* 23–47. Atlanta: Scholars Press, 1989.

———. "Judah Halevi and Karaism." In Jacob Neusner, Ernest S. Frerichs, and Nahum M. Sarna, eds., *From Ancient Israel to Modern Judaism: Intellect in Quest of Understanding: Essays in Honor of Marvin Fox,* 3:111–25. 4 vols. Atlanta, Ga.: Scholars Press, 1989.

———. "Maimonides' Influence on Karaite Theories of Prophecy and Law." In Arthur Hyman, ed., *Maimonidean Studies,* 1:99–115. New York: Michael Scharf Publication Trust of Yeshiva University Press, 1990.

———. "Aaron ben Joseph and the Transformation of Karaite Thought." In Ruth Link-Salinger, ed., *Torah and Wisdom Studies in Jewish Philosophy, Kabbalah, and Halacha: Essays in Honor of Arthur Hyman,* 121–28. New York: Shengold, 1992.

———. "The Dead Sea Scrolls in the Historiography and Self-image of Contemporary Karaites." *Dead Sea Discoveries* 9, no. 3 (2002): 1–14.

———. "Simhah Isaac Lutzki, an Eighteenth-century Karaite Kabbalist." In Z. Gries, H. Kreisel, B. Huss, ed. *Shefa Tal: Studies in Jewish Thought and Culture, Presented to Bracha Sack,* 171–89. Beer Sheva, Israel: Ben-Gurion University Press, 2004.

Layton, Robert, ed. *Who Needs the Past? Indigenous Values and Archaeology.* London: Routledge, 1994.

Lazarus, Felix. "Die Häupter der Vertriebenen." *Jahrbücher für jüdische Geschichte und Literatur* 10 (1890): 1–181.

Lazarus-Yafeh, Hava. *Intertwined Worlds: Medieval Islam and Bible Criticism.* Princeton, N.J.: Princeton University Press, 1992.

Lemerle, P. *Le premier humanisme byzantin.* Paris: Presses universitaires de France, 1971.

Lerner, M. B. "The Tractate Avot." In Samuel Safrai, ed., *The Literature of the Sages,* 263–81. Maastricht: Van Gorcum, 1987.

Levy, Avigdor. *The Sephardim in the Ottoman Empire.* Princeton, N.J.: Darwin Press, 1992.

Levtzion, Nehemia, ed. *Conversion to Islam.* New York: Holmes & Meier, 1979.

Lewin, B. M. *Oṣar ḥilluf minhagim ven Bene Ereṣ Yisra'el u-ven Bene Bavel.* Jerusalem: Mosad ha-Rav Kook she-'al yad ha-Mizraḥi ha-'Olami, 1942.

Lewis, Bernard. *The Jews of Islam.* Princeton, N.J.: Princeton University Press, 1984.

Libson, Gideon. "Halakhah and Reality in the Gaonic Period: Taqqanah, Minhag, Tradition, and Consensus: Some Observations." In Daniel Frank, ed., *The Jews of Medieval Islam: Community, Society, and Identity,* 67–99. Leiden, New York, and Köln: E. J. Brill, 1995.

———. "Halakhah and Law in the Period of the Geonim." In N. S. Hecht et al., eds., *An Introduction to the History and Sources of Jewish Law,* 197–250. Oxford: Clarendon Press, 1996.

Lilla, S. R. C. *Clement of Alexandria: A Study in Christian Platonism and Gnosticism.* Oxford: Oxford University Press, 1971.

Limerick, Patricia Nelson. *The Legacy of Conquests: The Unbroken Past of the American West.* New York: W. W. Norton & Company, 1988.

Lisk, Jill. *The Struggle for Supremacy in the Baltic: 1600–1725.* London: Minerva Press, 1967.

Lowenthal, David. *The Past Is a Foreign Country.* Cambridge: Cambridge University Press, 1985.

———. *Possessed by the Past: The Heritage Crusade and the Spoils of History.* New York: Free Press, 1996.

Lutzki, Simhah Isaac ben Moses. *Me'irat 'Enayim,* JTS MS Mic. 5448, Jewish Theological Seminary of America, New York.

———. *Oraḥ Ṣaddikim.* In Mordecai ben Nisan, *Dod Mordekhai,* 77–119. Israel: Haṣlaḥah li-vene mikra, 1966.

———. *Or ha-Ḥayyim.* Gozlow, 1835.

———. *Tore Zahav 'im Nikudat ha-Kesef.* Ramlah: ha-Mo'aṣah ha-Arṣit, 1978.

Machsor Vitry. Edited by S. Hurwitz. Berlin: Itzkowski, 1893.

Maczak, Antoni. "Poland." In Roy Porter and Mikulás Teich, eds., *The Renaissance in National Context,* 180–96. Cambridge: Cambridge University Press, 1991.

Madelung, Wilferd. *Religious Trends in Early Islamic Iran.* Albany, N.Y.: Bibliotheca Persica, 1988.

Mahler, Raphael. "National and Social Foundations of 'Anan's Religion.'" *YIVO Bleter* 9 (1936): 31–62.

———. *The Karaites: A Medieval Jewish Movement for Deliverance.* Merḥaviah, Israel, 1949 [Heb.; trans. from Yiddish ed., New York, 1947].

Maimonides. *Le Guide des égarés.* Edited by S. Munk. 3 vols. Paris: A. Franck, 1856–66.

———. *The Guide for the Perplexed.* Trans. M. Friedländer. New York: Dover, 1956. Revised reprint of London, 1904.

———. *Dalālat al-ḥā'irīn.* Edited by Issachar Joel. Jerusalem: Y. Yunovitz, 1930/31.

———. *Mishnah 'im perush rabbenu Moshe ben Maimon.* Edited by Joseph David Kafah. Jerusalem: Mosad ha-Rav Kook, 1963–68.

———. *The Guide of the Perplexed.* Trans. Shlomo Pines. 2 vols. Chicago: University of Chicago Press, 1963.

———. *Mishneh Torah.* Jerusalem: Orekh Merav Kook, 1964.

———. *A Maimonides Reader.* Edited by Isadore Twersky. New York: Behrman, 1972.

———. *Teshuvot ha-Rambam.* Edited by Jehoshua Blau. 2 vols. Jerusalem: Mekiṣe Nirdamim, R. Mas, 1986.

———. *Maimonides' Introduction to the Talmud.* Trans. Zvi Lampel. Rev. ed., New York: Judaica Press, 1987.

———. *Moses Maimonides' Commentary on the Mishnah: Introduction to Seder Zeraim and Commentary on Tractate Berachoth.* Trans. Fred Rosner. Northvale, N.J.: Jason Aronson, 1995.

Makdisi, George. "Dialectic and Disputation: The Relation between the Texts of Qirqisani and Ibn ʿAqīl." In Pierre Salmon, ed., *Mélanges d'islamologie: Volume dédié à la mémoire de Armand Abel par ses collègues, ses élèves et ses amis*, 201–6. Leiden: E. J. Brill, 1974.

Malinowski, Bronislaw. *Magic, Science, and Religion*. Garden City, N.Y.: Doubleday, 1948.

Malter, H. "Saadia Studies." *JQR* n.s., no. 3 (1912–13).

———. *Saadia Gaon: His Life and Works*. Philadelphia, Pa.: Jewish Publication Society of America, 1942.

Mango, Cyril. *Byzantine Literature as a Distorting Mirror*. Oxford: Clarendon Press, 1975.

———. *Byzantium: the Empire of New Rome*. New York: Charles Scribner's Sons, 1980.

Mann, Jacob. "Anan's Liturgy and His Half-yearly Cycle of the Reading of the Law." *Journal of Jewish Lore and Philosophy* 1 (1919): 329–53. Reprinted in *The Collected Articles of Jacob Mann*, 1–25. Gedera, Israel: M. Shalom, 1971.

———. "The Responsa of the Babylonian Geonim as a Source for Jewish History." *JQR*, n.s., no. 7 (1916–17): 457–90; 8 (1917–18): 339–66; 9 (1918–19): 139–79; 10 (1919–20): 121–51, 309–65.

———. "A Tract by an Early Karaite Settler in Jerusalem." *JQR*, n.s., 12 (1922): 257–98.

———. "Early Karaite Bible Commentaries." *JQR*, n.s., 12 (1921–22): 435–526; 15 (1924): 361–88.

———. *The Jews in Egypt and in Palestine under the Fatimid Caliphs*. New York: Ktav, 1970. Reprint of New York, 1920 and 1922.

———. *Texts and Studies in Jewish History and Literature, 2: Karaitica*. New York: Ktav, 1972. Reprint of New York, 1931.

———. *The Collected Articles of Jacob Mann*. 3 vols. Gedera, Israel: M. Shalom, 1971.

Mansfeld, Jaap. *Heresiography in Context: Hippolytus'* Elenchos *as a Source for Greek Philosophy*. Leiden: E. J. Brill, 1992.

Manuel, Frank E. *The Broken Staff: Judaism through Christian Eyes*. Cambridge: Harvard University Press, 1992.

al-Maqrīzī, Ahmad ibn ʿAlī. *al-Mawāʿiz wal-iʿtibār bi-dhikr al-khiṭaṭ wal-āthār*. Beirut, n.d.

Margaliot, M. *ha-Ḥillukim she-ben ʾAnshe Mizraḥ ʾu-vene Ereṣ Yisraʾel*. Jerusalem, 1938.

Margoliouth, G. "Ibn al-Hītī's Arabic Chronicle of Karaite Doctors." *JQR*, n.s., 9 (1896–97): 426–43.

Markus, R. A. *The End of Ancient Christianity*. Cambridge: Cambridge University Press, 1990.

Marmorstein, A. "Daniel al-Qūmisī's Homilies." *Ṣiyyon* 3 (1929): 26–42. [Heb.].

———. *The Doctrine of Merits in Old Rabbinic Literature*. New York: Ktav, 1968. Reprint of 1920.

al-Masʿūdī, ʿAlī ibn Ḥusayn. *al-Tanbīh wal-ishrāf*. Edited by M. J. de Goeje. Leiden, 1894.

McKane, William. *Selected Christian Hebraists.* Cambridge: Cambridge University Press, 1989.

McKnight, Stephen A. *The Modern Age and the Recovery of Ancient Wisdom: A Reconsideration of Historical Consciousness, 1450–1650.* Columbia: University of Missouri Press, 1991.

Meeks, Wayne A. "Breaking Away: Three New Testament Pictures of Christianity's Separation from the Jewish Communities." In Jacob Neusner and Ernest S. Frerichs, eds., *"To See Ourselves as Others See Us": Christians, Jews, "Others" in Late Antiquity*, 93–116. Chico, Calif.: Scholars Press, 1985.

Menahem ben Solomon ha-Meiri of Perpignan. *Bet ha-Beḥirah ʿal Massekhet Avot.* Jerusalem: Mekhon ha-Talmud ha-Yisre'eli ha-Shalem, 1967/68.

Mendels, D. "'Creative History' in the Hellenistic Near East in the Third and Second Centuries B.C.E.: The Jewish Case." *Journal for the Study of Pseudepigrapha* 2 (1988): 13–20.

Michael the Syrian. *La chronique de Michel le Syrien.* Edited and translated by Jean Chabot. 4 vols. Paris: Académie des Inscriptions et Belles-Lettres, 1899–1914.

Midrash Aggadah. Edited by S. Buber. Vienna: A. Fanto, 1894.

Mielziner, M. *The Jewish Law of Marriage and Divorce in Ancient and Modern Times.* New York: Bloch, 1901.

Migne, Jacques-Paul, ed. *Patrologia graeca.* Paris: Migne, 1857–66.

Miller, Philip E. *Karaite Separatism in Nineteenth-century Russia: Joseph Solomon Lutski's "Epistle of Israel's Deliverance."* Cincinnati, Ohio: Hebrew Union College Press, 1993.

Milliot, Louis. *Introduction a l'étude du droit musulman.* Paris: Recueil Sirey, 1953.

Mishkat Al-Masabih. Edited by James Robson. 4 vols. Lahore: M. Ashraf, 1973.

The Mishnah. Translated by Herbert Danby. Oxford: Clarendon Press, 1933.

Mishnah. Edited by Yosef Kafah. Jerusalem: n.p, 1955–56.

Mizraḥi, Elijah. *Sefer ha-Mizraḥi.* Venice, 1527.

———. *Sefer She'elot u-Teshuvot R. Eliyahu Mizraḥi.* Jerusalem, 1938 [Heb.].

———. *Sefer Mayim Amukim* (Book of deep waters). Jerusalem: N.p., 1969/70. Reprint of Berlin, 1778.

Moravcsik, Gy., ed. *Constantine Porphyrogenitus De Administrando Imperio.* Trans. R. J. H. Jenkins. Washington, D.C.: Dumbarton Oaks Center for Byzantine Studies, 1967.

Mordecai ben Nisan. *Dod Mordekhai.* Hamburg, 1714.

———. *Dod Mordekhai.* Israel: Hatzlahah li-vne mikra, 1966. Based on Vienna, 1830.

———. *Sefer Levush Malkhut.* In Adolf Neubauer, ed., *Aus der Petersburger Bibliothek*, 30–66 [Heb.].

Moore, George Foot. *Judaism in the First Centuries of the Christian Era: The Age of the Tannaim.* Cambridge: Harvard University Press, 1927.

Morony, Michael G. *Iraq after the Muslim Conquest.* Princeton, N.J.: Princeton University Press, 1984.

Moses ben Jacob of Coucy. *Sefer Miṣvot Gadol.* Rome, 1480.

Mowinckel, Sigmund. *He That Cometh: The Messianic Concept in the Old Testament and Later Judaism.* Oxford: Blackwell, 1956.

Nasrallah, Joseph. *Saint Jean de Damas: Son époque, sa vie, son oeuvre*. Harissa, Lebanon: Imp. Saint Paul, 1950.

Nemoy, Leon. "al-Qirqisānī's Account of the Jewish Sects and Christianity." *HUCA* 7 (1930): 317–97.

———. "Anan ben David: A Reappraisal of the Historical Data." In P. Birnbaum, ed., *Karaite Studies*, 309–18. New York: Hermon Press, 1971. Reprint of 1947.

———. "Ibn Kammūnah's Treatise on the Differences between the Rabbanites and the Karaites." *PAAJR* 36 (1968): 107–65.

———. S.v. "Karaites." In *EJ* 10:762–85.

———. "Mourad Farag and His Book, *The Karaites and the Rabbanites*." *REJ* 135 (1976): 87–112.

———. "The Pseudo-Qumisian Sermon to the Karaites." *PAAJR* 43 (1976): 49–105.

———. "Elijah ben Abraham and His Tract against the Rabbanites." *HUCA* 51 (1980): 63–87.

———. "Karaites." In J. R. Strayer, ed., *Dictionary of the Middle Ages*. New York: Scribner, 1982.

———. "Nissi ben Noah's Quasi-Commentary on the Decalogue." *JQR* 73 (1983): 307–48.

———. "Karaites." In Mircea Eliade, ed., *The Encyclopedia of Religion*. New York: Macmillan, 1987.

———. "Israel Maghribi's Tract on Ritual Slaughtering." *Henoch* 13, no. 2 (1991): 195–218.

———, ed. and trans. *Karaite Anthology: Excerpts from the Early Literature*. New Haven, Conn.: Yale University Press, 1952.

Nemoy, Leon, with W. Zajaczkowski. "Karaites." In *Encyclopedia of Islam*, 2nd ed.

Netanyahu, B. *Don Isaac Abravanel, Statesman and Philosopher*. Philadelphia, Pa.: Jewish Publication Society of America, 1982.

Neubauer, Adolf, ed. *Aus der Petersburger Bibliothek*. Leipzig: Oskar Leiner, 1866.

———, ed. *Medieval Jewish Chronicles*. Oxford: Clarendon Press, 1895.

Neuman, A. A. "Abraham Zacuto, Historiographer." In *Harry Austryn Wolfson Jubilee Volume*, 3 vols. 2:597–629. Jerusalem: American Academy for Jewish Research, 1965.

Neusner, Jacob. *A Life of Rabban Yohanan ben Zakkai*. Leiden: E. J. Brill, 1962.

———. *A History of the Jews in Babylonia*. 5 vols. Leiden: E. J. Brill, 1969–70.

———. *From Politics to Piety: The Emergence of Pharisaic Judaism*. Englewood Cliffs, N.J.: Prentice-Hall, 1973.

———. *Messiah in Context: Israel's History and Destiny in Formative Judaism*. Philadelphia, Pa.: Fortress Press, 1984.

———. *Judaism in the Matrix of Christianity*. Philadelphia, Pa.: Fortress Press, 1986.

———. *Judaism and Christianity in the Age of Constantine: Issues in the Initial Confrontation*. Chicago, Ill.: University of Chicago Press, 1987.

———. *Self-fulfilling Prophecy: Exile and Return in the History of Judaism*. Boston, Mass.: Beacon Press, 1987.

———. *Death and Birth of Judaism: The Impact of Christianity, Secularism, and the Holocaust on Jewish Faith.* New York: Basic Books, 1987.

———. "Judaic Uses of History in Talmudic Times. In A. Rapoport-Albert, ed. *Essays in Jewish Historiography.* Middletown, Conn.: Wesleyan University, 1988.

———. *Judaism and Its Social Metaphors.* Cambridge: Cambridge University Press, 1989.

———. "History Invented: The Conception of History in the Talmud of the Land of Israel." In Jacob Neusner, ed., *The Christian and Judaic Invention of History,* 181–208. Atlanta, Ga.: Scholars Press, 1990.

———. "History Transcended: The Mishnaic Uses of the Past." In *The Christian and Judaic Invention of History,* 175–80.

———. "The Theory of History in Genesis Rabbah." In *The Christian and Judaic Invention of History,* 209–32.

———. "The Historical Event as a Cultural Indicator: The Case of Judaism." *History and Theory* 30, no. 2 (1991): 136–52.

———. *Introduction to Rabbinic Literature.* New York: Doubleday, 1994.

———. *Rabbinic Judaism: Structure and System.* Minneapolis, Minn.: Fortress Press, 1995.

———. *The Presence of the Past, the Pastness of the Present: History, Time, and Paradigm in Rabbinic Judaism.* Bethesda, Md.: CDL Press, 1996.

———, trans. *The Talmud of Babylonia: An American Translation.* Vol. 25. A: *Tractate Abodah Zarah, Chapters 1–2.* Atlanta: Scholars Press, 1991.

Newby, Gordon D. *The Making of the Last Prophet: A Reconstruction of the Earliest Biography of Muhammad.* Columbia: University of South Carolina Press, 1989.

Newman, Louis I. *Jewish Influence on Christian Reform Movements.* New York: Columbia Univesity Press, 1925.

Nosonovskii, Mikhail. "The Karaite Community in Derazhnia and Its Destruction." *Shevut* 6, no. 22 (1997): 206–11 [Heb.].

O'Brien, Conor Cruise. *The Siege: The Saga of Israel and Zionism.* New York: Simon & Schuster, 1986.

Olszowy-Schlanger, Judith. *Karaite Marriage Documents from the Cairo Geniza: Legal Tradition and Community Life in Mediaeval Egypt and Palestine.* Leiden: E. J. Brill, 1998.

Origen. *Origen: Contra Celsum.* Edited and translated by Henry Chadwick. Cambridge: Cambridge University Press, 1953.

Osborn, E. F. *The Philosophy of Clement of Alexandria.* Cambridge: Cambridge University Press, 1957.

Ostrogorsky, George. *History of the Byzantine State.* New Brunswick, N.J.: Rutgers University Press, 1969.

Ovadiah, A. "Rabbi Eliyahu Mizraḥi." *Sinai* 5 (1939–40): 397–413; 6 (1940): 73–80 [Heb.].

Parkes, James. *The Conflict of the Church and Synagogue.* London: Soncino Press, 1934.

Paul, A. *Écrits de Qumran et sectes juives aux premiers siècles de l'Islam: Recherches sur l'origine du Qaraïsme.* Paris: Letouzey et Ané, 1969.

Pausanias. *Guide to Greece*. Trans. and ed. Peter Levi. 2 vols. Harmondsworth: Penguin Books, 1971.

Pelikan, Jaroslav. *The Christian Tradition: A History of the Development of Doctrine*, vol. 1: *The Emergence of the Catholic Tradition, 100–600*. Chicago: University of Chicago Press, 1971.

———. *The Christian Tradition: A History of the Development of Doctrine*, vol. 2: *The Spirit of Eastern Christendom, 600–1700*. Chicago: University of Chicago Press, 1974.

Perlmann, Moshe. "The Medieval Polemics between Islam and Judaism." In S. D. Goitein, ed., *Religion in a Religious Age: Proceedings of Regional Conferences Held at the University of California, Los Angeles, and Brandeis University in April, 1973*, 103–29. Cambridge, Mass.: Association for Jewish Studies, 1974.

Photius. *Bibliothèque*. Edited and translated by René Henry. 9 vols. Paris: Société d'édition Les Belles lettres, 1959–91.

Pines, Shlomo. "Nethanel ben al-Fayyûmî et la théolgie ismaelienne." *Revue de l'histoire juive en Egypte* 1 (1947): 5–22.

———. "Some Traits of Christian Theological Writing in Relation to Moslem *Kalām* and to Jewish Thought." *Proceedings of the Israel Academy of Sciences and Humanities* 5, no. 4 (1976): 105–25.

———. "Notes on Islam and Arabic Christianity and Judaeo-Christianity." *Jerusalem Studies in Arabic and Islam* 4 (1984).

———. "Studies in Christianity and in Judaeo-Christianity Based on Arabic Sources." *Jerusalem Studies in Arabic and Islam* 6 (1985).

———. "Gospel Quotations and Cognate Topics in ʿAbd al-Jabbar's *Tathbit* in Relation to Early Christian and Judeo-Christian Readings and Traditions." *Jerusalem Studies in Arabic and Islam* 9 (1987).

———. *Lickute Kadmoniot*. Vienna: Adalbert della Torre, 1860.

Pinsker, Simhah. "Mittheilung über einen arabischen Auszug aus dem Werke *Ḥovot ha-Levavot*," *Der Orient* 12 (1851): 737–49.

———. *Likkute Kadmoniyyot*. Vienna: Adalbert della Torre, 1860.

Polliack, Meira. *The Karaite Tradition of Arabic Bible Translation: A Linguistic and Exegetical Study of Karaite Translations of the Pentateuch from the Tenth and Eleventh Centuries C.E.* Leiden: E. J. Brill, 1997.

Popkin, Richard H. "The Marrano Theology of Isaac La Peyrère." *Studi Internazionali di Filosofia* 5 (1973).

———. "Les Caraïtes et l'émancipation des juifs." *Dix-huitieme Siècle* 13 (1981): 137–47.

———. "The Lost Tribes, the Caraites, and the English Millenarians." *JJS* 37, no. 2 (1986): 213–27.

Posselt, Alfred. *Geschichte des chazarisch-jüdischen Staates*. Vienna: Verlag des Vereines zur Förderung und Pflege des Reformjudentums, 1982.

Postel, Guillaume. *Linguarum duodecim characteribus differentium alphabetum introductio*. Paris, 1538.

Poznanski, Samuel. "Anan et ses écrits." *REJ* 44 (1901): 161–87; ibid. 45 (1902): 51–69, 176–203.

———. "The Karaite Literary Opponents of Sa'adiah Gaon." In Philip Birnbaum, ed., *Karaite Studies*, 129–234. New York: Hermon Press, 1971. Reprint of 1908.

———. S.v. "Tobias ben Moses ha-Ma'tik." In *Oṣar Yisra'el* 5:13b. New York: Ḥevrat moṣi l'or Entsiqolpedia 'Ivrit, 1907–13 [Heb.].

———. "Karaite." In James Hastings, ed., *Encyclopedia of Religion and Ethics*. New York: Scribner, 1913–27.

———. "Reshit hityashevut ha-qara'im bi-yerushalayim" (The beginning of Karaite settlement in Jerusalem). In A. M. Luncz, ed., *Jerusalem*, 10:83–116, 321–23. (1913) [Heb.].

———. *Babylonische Geonim im nachgaonäischen Zeitalter nach handschriften und gedruckten Quellen*. Berlin: Mayer & Müller, 1914.

———. "Zweiter Nachtrag zur Karäischen Familie Firuz." *Monatsschrift für Geschichte und Wissenschaft des Judentums* 60 (1916): 149–52.

———. *Esquisse historique sur les juifs de Kairouan*. Warsaw: N.p., 1919 [Heb.].

———, ed. *Zecher Caddikim, Kronika Historyczna Karaity Mordechaja Sultanskiego*. Warsaw: bi-Defus ha-Ṣefirah, 1920.

Prawer, Joshua. *The History of the Jews in the Latin Kingdom of Jerusalem*. Oxford: Clarendon Press, 1988.

Pritsak, Omeljan. "The Khazar Kingdom's Conversion to Judaism." *Harvard Ukrainian Studies 2*, 261–81. Cambridge, Mass.: Harvard Ukrainian Research Institute, 1978.

———. "The Role of the Bosporus Kingdom and Late Hellenism as the Basis for the Medieval Cultures North of the Black Sea." In Abraham Ascher, Tibor Halasi-Kun, and Béla K. Király, eds., *The Mutual Effects of the Islamic and Judeo-Christian Worlds: The Eastern European Pattern*. Brooklyn, N.Y.: Brooklyn College Press, 1979.

Psellus, Michael. *Fourteen Byzantine Rulers: The* Chronographia *of Michael Psellus*. Trans. E. R. A. Sewter. London: Penguin Books, 1966.

al-Qirqisānī, Ya'qūb. *Kitāb al-anwār wal-marāqib, Code of Karaite Law*. Edited by Leon Nemoy. 5 vols. New York: Publications of the Alexander Kohut Foundation, 1939–43.

al-Qūmisī, Daniel b. Moses. *Pithron Shenem 'Asār: Commentarius in Librum Duodecim Prophetarum*. Edited by Isaac Dov Markon, with notes by D. Z. Baneth and E. E. Urbach. Jerusalem: Mekiṣe Nirdamim, 1958.

Rabinowitz, Louis Isaac. S.v. "Ten Lost Tribes." In *EJ* 15:1003–6.

Ratzaby, Yehuda. "'Ezra ha-Sofer ve-ha-Temanim" ("Ezra the Scribe and the Yemenites"]. *Sinai* 15 (1945).

———. "Nosafot le-'Ezra ha-Sofer ve-ha-Temanim" ("Additions to Ezra the Scribe and the Yemenites"). *Sinai* 18 (1946).

Reuben Ahroni. *Yemenite Jewry: Origins, Culture, and Literature*. Bloomington: Indiana University Press, 1986.

Revel, Bernard. "The Karaite Halakah and Its Relation to Sadducean, Samaritan and Philonian Halakah." In P. Birnbaum, ed., *Karaite Studies*. New York: Hermon Press, 1971, 1–88. Reprint of 1913.

Richardson, Peter, ed. *Anti-Judaism in Early Christianity*, vol. 1: *Paul and the Gospels*. Waterloo: Wilfrid Laurier University Press, 1986.

Richter, Gerhard. *Die Dialektik des Johannes van Damaskos: Eine Untersuchung des Textes nach seinen Quellen und seiner Bedeutung.* Ettal: Buch-Kunstverlag Ettal, 1964.

Rieger, R. "The Foundation of Rome in the Talmud." *JQR*, n.s., 16 (1925–26).

Robinson, Chase F. *Empire and Elites after the Muslim Conquest: The Transformation of Northern Mesopotamia.* Cambridge: Cambridge University Press, 2000.

Robinson, Ira. "Jacob al-Kirkisani on the Reality of Magic and the Nature of the Miraculous: A Study in Tenth-century Karaite Rationalism." In Howard Joseph, Jack N. Lightstone, and Michael D. Oppenheim, eds., *Truth and Compassion: Essays on Judaism and Religion in Memory of Rabbi Dr. Solomon Frank*, 41–53. Waterloo: Wilfrid Laurier University Press, 1983.

Rosanes, Salomon. *Divre Yeme Yisra'el be-Togarmah* (History of the Jews in Turkey). Vol. 1. Tel Aviv: Dvir, 1930.

Rose, William J. *The Protestant Churches in Poland.* London, 1944.

Rosenthal, J. M. "Marcin Czechowic and Jacob Belzice: Arian-Jewish Encounters in Sixteenth-century Poland." *PAAJR* 34 (1966).

Rosman, M. J. *The Lord's Jews: Magnate-Jewish Relations in the Polish-Lithuanian Commonwealth during the Eighteenth Century.* Cambridge: Harvard University Press, 1990.

Rossi, Azariah, de'. *Sefer Maṣref le-Kesef ha-Mityaḥes la-Ḥibbur Me'or ʿEnayim.* Edited by Tsevi Filipovski. Edinburgh: N.p., 1854.

———. *Me'or ʿEnayim.* Edited by D. Cassel. Jerusalem: Makor, 1970. Reprint of Vilna: Y. R. Romm, 1864–66. 3 vols.

———. *The Light of the Eyes.* Trans. and ed. Joanna Weinberg. New Haven, Conn.: Yale University Press, 2001.

Roth, Ernst. "Ketaʿ le-Shalshelet ha-Kabbalah mi-Tekufat ha-Geonim" ("A portion of a chain of tradition from the era of the Geonim"). *Tarbiṣ* 26 (1956–57): 410–19.

Ruether, Rosemary Radford. "The *Adversus Judaeos* Tradition in the Church Fathers: The Exegesis of Christian Anti-Judaism." In Paul E. Szarmach, ed., *Aspects of Jewish Culture in the Middle Ages*, 27–50. Albany, N.Y.: State University of New York Press, 1979.

Saadia Gaon. *Saadia Gaon: The Book of Beliefs and Opinions.* Trans. Samuel Rosenblatt. New Haven, Conn.: Yale University Press, 1948.

———. *Sefer ha-Nivhar ba-'Emunot uva-Deʿot (ha-'Emunot veha-Deʿot) le-Rabbenu Seʿadyah ben Yosef Fayyumi.* Edited and translated by Yosef Kafah. New York: ha-Makhon le-Meḥkar ule-Hoṣa'at Sefarim Sura Yerushalayim, Yeshivah Universitah, 1969/70.

Safrai, Shmuel. "Talmudic Sources on Aliya and Pilgrimage." In Lee I. Levine, ed., *The Jerusalem Cathedra*, vol. 3, 188–89. Yad Izhak Ben-Zvi: Jerusalem, 1983.

Sāliḥ, Yeḥiyah. *Megillat Teman.* Edited by David Sassoon. *ha-Ṣofeh li-Ḥokhmat Yisra'el* 7 (1923): 1–14.

Salmon ben Yeruḥim. *Sefer Milḥamot Adonai: The Book of the Wars of the Lord.* Edited by Israel Davidson. New York: Jewish Theological Seminary of America, New York, 1934.

———. *The Arabic Commentary of Salmon ben Yeruham the Karaite on the Book of Psalms, Chapters 42–72.* Edited by Lawrence Marwick. Philadelphia, Pa.: Dropsie College for Hebrew and Cognate Learning, 1956.

Samson ben Isaac of Chinon. *Sefer Keritut.* Edited by Y. Z. Roth. Brooklyn: Hoṣa'at Sameaḥ, 1961.

Samuel al-Maghribī. *"Traktat" über den Sabbat bei den Karäern (al-Maqālah al-thānīyah min al-kitāb al-musamma bil-murshid fīl-shabbat).* Edited by Nathan Weisz. Pressburg: Alcalay, 1907.

———. *Die Incestgesetze bei den Karäern (al-Maqālah al-tāsī'ah fial-'arawūt min al-kitāb al-musamma bil-murshid).* Edited by David Weiss. Berlin: H. Itzkowski, 1911.

———. *Sefer ha-Miṣvot (Kitāb al-murshid).* Edited by Yosef ben 'Ovaydah Algamil. Ashdod, Israel: Mekhon Tiferet Yosef le-Ḥeker ha-Yahadut ha-Kara'it, 5762 [2001 or 2002].

Samuel ha-Nagid. *Divan.* Edited by Abraham Meir Habermann. Tel-Aviv: N.p., 1946/47.

———. *Hilkhot Hannagid.* Edited by Mordecai Margolioth. Jerusalem: Hoṣa'at Keren Yehudah Leb ve-Mini Epshtain, 1962.

———. *Divan Shemu'el ha-Nagid.* Edited by Dov Yarden. Jerusalem: Hebrew Union College Press, 1966.

Sanders, Paula A. "The Fāṭimid State, 969–1171." In Carl F. Petry, ed., *The Cambridge History of Egypt,* vol. 1: *Islamic Egypt, 640–1517,* 151–74. Cambridge: Cambridge University Press, 1998.

Saraf, Michal. "The 'Discussion between Wine and the Poet' by Kaleb Afendopolo the Karaite." In Zvi Malachi, ed., *Papers in Medieval Hebrew Literature Presented to A. M. Haberman . . . ,* 343–61. Jerusalem: R. Mas, 1977 [Heb., with Eng. summary].

Savage, Elizabeth. *A Gateway to Hell, a Gateway to Paradise: The North African Response to the Arab Conquest.* Princeton, N.J.: Darwin Press, 1997.

Schacht, Joseph. *The Origins of Muhammadan Jurisprudence.* Oxford: Oxford University Press, 1950.

———. *An Introduction to Muslim Law.* Oxford: Oxford University Press, 1964.

Schechter, Solomon. *Aspects of Rabbinic Theology.* New York: Schocken Books, 1961. Reprint of 1909.

———. *Documents of Jewish Sectaries,* vol. 2: *Fragments of the Book of the Commandments by Anan.* Cambridge: Cambridge Univesity Press, 1910.

Schedel, Hartmann. *Sarmatia, the Early Polish Kingdom: From the Original Nuremberg Chronicle.* Los Angeles: Plantin Press, 1976.

Scheiber, Alexander. "Manuscript Material Relating to the Literary Activity of Judah Hadassi." In *Jubilee Volume in Honor of Prof. Bernhard Heller on the Occasion of his Seventieth Birthday,* 2–33. Budapest: N.p., 1941.

———. "Eléments fabuleaux dans l' Eshkôl Hakôfer de Juda Hadasi." *REJ* 107 (1948): 41–62.

———. *Essays on Jewish Folklore and Comparative Literature.* Budapest, 1985.

Scheible, Heinz. *Die Anfänge der reformatorischen Geschichtesschreibung: Melanchton, Sleidan, Facius, und die Magdeburger Zenturien.* Gütersloher: Gerd Mohn, 1966.

Schiffman, Lawrence. *Who Was a Jew? Rabbinic and Halakhic Perspectives on the Jewish Christian Schism*. Hoboken, N.J.: Ktav, 1985.

Schminck, Andreas. S.v. "Antecessors." In *Oxford Dictionary of Byzantium*.

———. S.v. "Prochiron." In *Oxford Dictionary of Byzantium*.

Schoeps, Hans Joachim. *Philosemitismus im Barock*. Tübingen: J. C. B. Mohr, 1952.

Scholem, Gershom. "Sabbatian Documents Concerning Nathan of Gaza from the Archives of R. Mahallellel Halleluyah of Ancona." In *H. A. Wolfson Jubilee Volume*, 3 vols. Heb. Sec., 225–41. Jerusalem: American Academy for Jewish Research, 1965.

———. *The Messianic Idea in Judaism*. New York: Schocken Books, 1971.

———. *Sabbatai Ṣevi, the Mystical Messiah, 1626–1676*. Princeton, N.J.: Princeton Univesity Press, 1973.

Schorsch, Ismar. *From Text to Context: The Turn to History in Modern Judaism*. Hanover, N.H.: Brandeis University Press, 1994.

Schreiner, Martin. *Studien über Jeschuʿa ben Jehuda*. Berlin: H. Itzkowski, 1900.

Scott, James C. *Domination and the Arts of Resistance: Hidden Transcripts*. New Haven, Conn.: Yale University Press, 1990.

Seder ʿOlam Rabbah. Edited by Adolf Neubauer. In *Medieval Jewish Chronicles*. Oxford: Clarendon Press, 1895.

———. Edited by B. Ratner. Vilna, 1897.

———. Edited by A. Marx. Berlin, 1903.

Seder ʿOlam Zuta. Edited by Adolf Neubauer. In *Medieval Jewish Chronicles*. Oxford: Clarendon Press, 1895.

Seder Tannaʾim ve-Amoraʾim. Edited by Adolf Neubauer. In *Medieval Jewish Chronicles*. Oxford: Clarendon Press, 1895.

———. Edited and translated by Kalman Kahana. Frankfurt: Bayerische Julius-Maximilians-Universität Würzburg, 1935.

Segal, Lester A. *Historical Consciousness and Religious Tradition in Azariah de' Rossi's Meʾor ʿEinayim*. Philadelphia: Jewish Publication Society of America, 1989.

Segel, Harold B. *Renaissance Culture in Poland: The Rise of Humanism, 1470–1543*. Ithaca, N.Y.: Cornell University Press, 1993.

Seligsohn, Max. S.v. "Hadassi, Judah ben Elijah ha-Abel." *JE*, 6:132.

———. "Solomon." In *JE*, 11:446–48.

Shacht, Joseph. *An Introduction to Muslim Law*. Oxford: Oxford University Press, 1964.

al-Shāfiʿī, al-Imām Muḥammad ibn Idris. *al-Risāla fī uṣūl al-fiqh, Treatise on the Foundations of Islamic Jurisprudence*. Trans. Majid Khadduri. Cambridge: Islamic Texts Society, 1987. Reprint of 1961.

al-Shahrastānī, Muḥammad ʿAbd al-Karīm. *Kitāb al-milāl wal-nihāl*. London, 1846.

Sharf, Andrew. *Byzantine Jewry from Justinian to the Fourth Crusade*. London: Routledge & Kegan Paul, 1971.

Shaw, Stanford J. *The Jews of the Ottoman Empire and Turkish Republic*. New York: New York University Press, 1991.

Shmueli, Efraim. *Seven Jewish Cultures: A Reinterpretation of Jewish History and Thought.* Cambridge: Cambridge University Press, 1990.

Shunary, Jonathan. "Salmon ben Yeruhim's Commentary on the Book of Psalms." *JQR*, n.s., 73 (1982): 155–75.

Ṣiddīqī, Muḥammad Zubayr. *Hadith Literature: Its Origin, Development, Special Features, and Criticism.* Calcutta: Calcutta University, 1961.

Siddur ha-Tefillot ke-Minhag ha-Yehudim ha-Kara'im. 4 vols. Vienna, 1854.

Siddur Tefillot ke-Minhag ha-Kara'im. 4 vols. Ramlah, Israel: ʿAdat ha-Yehudim ha-Kara'im be-Yisrael, 1971.

Siddur Rav ʿAmram Ga'on. Edited by A. Frumkin. 2 vols. Jerusalem: Zuckerman Press, 1912.

Silver, Abba Hillel. *A History of Messianic Speculation in Israel.* 2d. ed., Boston, Mass.: Beacon Press, 1959.

Simon, Uriel. *Four Approaches to the Book of Psalms: From Saadiah Gaon to Abraham Ibn Ezra.* Albany, N.Y.: State University of New York Press, 1991.

"Sippur ʿAravi." JTS MS Mic. 3328, Jewish Theological Seminary of America, New York.

Sirat, Colette. "Judah b. Solomon ha-Cohen, philosophe, astronome et peut-être kabbaliste de la première moitié du XIIIe siècle." *Italia* 2 (1979): 39–61.

———. *A History of Jewish Philosophy in the Middle Ages.* Cambridge: Cambridge Univesity Press, 1985.

Sklare, David E. "Yūsuf al-Baṣīr: Theological Aspects of his Halakhic Works." In Daniel Frank, ed., *The Jews of Medieval Islam: Community, Society, and Identity.* Leiden: E. J. Brill, 1995, 249–70.

———. *Samuel ben Hofni Gaon and His Cultural World: Texts and Studies.* Leiden: E. J. Brill, 1996.

———. "Responses to Islamic Polemics by Jewish Mutakallimun in the Tenth Century," *The Majlis* (1999): 137–61.

Slutsky, Yehuda. S.v. "Krasnoye." In *EJ* 10:1242.

Southgate, Minoo S., trans. *Iskandarnamah, A Medieval Alexander-Romance.* New York: Columbia University Press, 1978.

Spitzer, S. "The Ashkenazim in the Ottoman Empire from the Middle of the Fifteenth Century until the Middle of the Sixteenth Century." In H. Z. (J. W.) Hirschberg, ed., *Mi-Mizraḥ umi-Maʿarav: Koveṣ Meḥkarim be-Toldot ha-Yehudim ba-Mizraḥ uva-Magreb*, 59–80 [Heb.]. Ramat-Gan, Israel: Bar-Ilan University, 1974.

Stark, Rodney. *The Rise of Christianity.* San Francisco, Calif.: HarperCollins, 1997.

Stark, Rodney, and William Sims Bainbridge. *A Theory of Religion.* Bern, 1987.

Starr, Joshua. "A Fragment of a Greek Mishnaic Glossary." *PAAJR* 6 (1935): 353–67.

———. *The Jews in the Byzantine Empire, 641–1204.* New York: Burt Franklin, 1970. Reprint of 1939.

———. *Romania, the Jewries of the Levant after the Fourth Crusade.* Paris: Éditions du Centre, 1949.

Steinschneider, Moritz. "Die Karaiten und die Grammatik Zur Richtigstellung der

Frage, Ein letztes Wort." *Magazin für Wissenschaft des Judentums* 20 (1893): 236–37.
———. "Kaleb Afendopolo." In *Gesammelte Schriften*, 1:184–96. Berlin, 1925.
———. *Die arabische Literatur der Juden*. Frankfurt: M. J. Kauffmann, 1902.
Stern, S. M. "A New Fragment from the 'Sepher Ha-Galuy' of R. Saadyah Gaon." *Melilah* 5 (1955): 133–47. [Heb.].
———. "Fāṭimid Propaganda among Jews According to the Testimony of Yefet b. ʿAlī the Karaite." In *Studies in Early Ismāʿīlism*, 84–95. Jerusalem, 1983.
Stillman, Norman A. *The Jews of Arab Lands: A History and Source Book*. Philadelphia, Pa.: Jewish Publication Society of America, 1979.
Strack, Hermann. "Abraham Firkowitsch und der Wert seiner Entdeckungen." *Zeitschrift der Deutschen Morgenländischen Gesellschaft* 34 (1880).
———. *Introduction to the Talmud and Midrash*. New York: Atheneum, 1969.
Stroumsa, Sarah. *Dāwūd ibn Marwān al-Muqammiṣ's Twenty Chapters* ('Ishrūn Maqāla"). Leiden: E. J. Brill, 1989.
———. "On Jewish Intellectuals Who Converted in the Early Middle Ages." In Daniel Frank, ed., *The Jews of Medieval Islam: Community, Society, and Identity*, 179–97. Leiden: E. J. Brill, 1995.
al-Suyūṭī, Jalāl al-Dīn Abūal-Faḍl ʿAbd al-Raḥmān, *al-Laʾālī al-maṣnūʿa*. Cairo, 1317 A.H.
Szyszman, Simon. "Gustaf Peringers Mission bei den Karäern." *Zeitschrift der Deutschen Morgenländischen Gesellschaft* 102 (1952): 215–28.
———. "Le Roi Bulan et le problème de la conversion des Khazars." In *Actes du X. Congres international d'etudes byzantines*. Istanbul: *Comité d'organisation du X. Congrès international d'études byzantines*, 1957.
———. "Die Karäer in Ost-Mitteleuropa." *Zeitschrift für Ostforschung* 6 (1957): 24–57.
———. "Les Khazares: Problèmes et controverses." *Revue de l'histoire des religions* 152, no. 2 (1957).
———. *Les Karaïtes d'Europe*. Uppsala: Centre d'études multiethniques de l'Université d'Upsal, 1989.
al-Ṭabarī, Abū Jaʿfar Muḥammad ibn Jarīr. *The History of al-Tabari (Taʾrikh al-rusul waʾl-muluk)*, vol. 4: *The Ancient Kingdoms*. Edited by Moshe Perlmann. Albany, N.Y.: State University of New York Press, 1987.
Talmud, The Minor Tractates of the. Edited by A. Cohen. London: The Soncino Press, 1965.
Tatakis, Basile. *La Philosophie Byzantine: Fascicule supplémentaire n° II de Émile Bréhier, Histoire de la Philosophie*. Paris: Presses Universitaires de France, 1949.
Tazbir, Janusz. *A State without Stakes: Polish Religious Toleration in the Sixteenth and Seventeenth Centuries*, translated from the Polish by A. T. Jordan. New York: Košciuszko Foundation, 1973.
al-Thaʿlabī, Abū Isḥaq Aḥmad ibn Muḥammad ibn Ibrāhīm. *ʿArāʾis al-majālis fī qiṣaṣ al-ʿanbiyāʾ, or "Lives of the Prophets."* Trans. and ann. William M. Brinner. Leiden: E. J. Brill: 2002.
The Shorter Encyclopedia of Islam. Edited by H. A. R. Gibb and J. H. Kramers. Ithaca, N.Y.: Cornell University Press, 1953.

Tobias ben Eliezer. *Midrash Lekaḥ Tov ha-mekhuneh Pesikta Zutrata, Genesis-Exodus.* Edited by Salomon Buber. Jerusalem: N.p., 1959/60. Reprint of Vilna, 1880.

———. *Midrash Lekaḥ Tov ha-mekhuneh Pesikta Zutrata, Leviticus-Numbers-Deuteronomy.* Edited by Aaron Moses Padowa. Jerusalem: N.p., 1959/60. Reprint of Vilna, 1880.

———. *Midrash Lekaḥ Tov ha-mekhuneh Pesikta Zutrata, Canticles.* Edited by A. W. Greenup. London, 1909.

Trevisan Semi, Emanuela. "A Brief Survey of Present-Day Karaite Communities in Europe." *Jewish Journal of Sociology* 33, no. 2 (1991): 97–106.

Trigland, Jacob. *Diatribe de Secta Karaeorum: Trium Scriptorum Illustrium de Tribus Judaeorum Sectis Syntagma* 2. Delft, 1703.

———. "Abhandlung über die Sekte der Karäer." *Literaturblatt des Orientes* 4 (1843).

Troki, Isaac. *Faith Strengthened: The Jewish Answer to Christianity.* Trans. Moses Mocatta. New York: Sepher-Hermon Press, 1970. Reprint of London, 1850.

———. *Rabbi Yitzchak, Sohn Abrahams Sefer Chizzuq Emunah: Befestigung im Glauben.* Edited by David Deutsch. Breslau: Commissionsverlag von H. Skutsch, 1873.

———. *Ḥizzuk Emunah.* Ashdod, 1972. Based on Brooklyn, N.Y., 1932.

Troki, Solomon ben Aaron. *Sefer Apiryon Asah Lo.* JTS MS Mic. 3325, Jewish Theological Seminary of America, New York.

———. *Sefer Appiryon ʿAsah Lo.* In Adolf Neubauer, ed., *Aus der Petersburger Bibliothek,* 1–29 [Heb.].

———. *Sefer ʾAppiryon ʿAsah Lo.* Bnei Berak, Israel, 1960.

———. *Sefer ʾAppiryon ʿAsah Lo.* Edited by Yosef ben ʿOvaydah Algamil. Ramlah, Israel: Mekhon Tifʾeret Yosef le-Ḥeker ha-Yahadut ha-Karaʾit, 5760 [1999 or 2000].

Trouillot, Michel-Rolph. *Silencing the Past: Power and the Production of History.* Boston, Mass.: Beacon Press, 1995.

Twersky, Isadore. *Introduction to the Code of Maimonides.* Mishneh Torah. New Haven, Conn.: Yale University Press, 1980.

Urbach, Ephraim E. *The Sages: Their Concepts and Beliefs.* Jerusalem: Magnes Press, 1979.

———. *Baʿale ha-Tosafot: Toldotehem, Ḥibburehem, Shitatam.* Jerusalem: Mosad Byalik, 1980.

Vajda, Georges. "Etudes sur Qirqisânî, vol. 1: La Magie, la Mantique, et l'Astrologie selon le 'Livre des Lumieres et des Vigies.'" *REJ* 106 (1946): 87–123.

———. "Etudes sur Qirqisânî, vol. 2: Les fondements speculatifs de la legislation religieuse." *REJ* 106 (1946–47): 52–98.

———. "Etudes sur Qirqisânî, vol. 3: Questions de méthodologie." *REJ* 108 (1948): 63–91.

———. "Etudes sur Qirqisânî, vol. 4: Questions de méthodologie (suite)." *REJ* 120 (1961): 211–57.

———. "La contribution de quelques textes judéo-arabes à la connaissance du mouvement d'idées dans l'Islam du III–IXe siecle." In *L'élaboration de l'Islam: Colloque de Strasbourg, 12–14 juin 1959.* 87–97. Paris: Presses universitaires de France, 1961.

———. "La finalité de la création de l'homme selon un théologian juif du IXe siècle." *Oriens* 15 (1962): 61–85.

———. "Etudes sur Qirqisânî, vol. 5: Les règles de la controverse dialectique." *REJ* 122 (1963): 7–74.

———. "Quelques aggadōt critiquées par Yefet ben ʿĒlī." In Sheldon R. Brunswick, ed., *Studies in Judaica, Karaitica and Islamica Presented to Leon Nemoy on his Eightieth Birthday,* 155–62. Ramat-Gan, Israel: Bar-Ilan University, 1982.

———. S.v. "Ananiyya." In *Encyclopedia of Islam,* 2nd ed.

———. *al-Kitāb al-Muḥtawī de Yūsuf al-Baṣīr.* Leiden: E. J. Brill, 1985.

van Rooden, Peter T. *Theology, Biblical Scholarship, and Rabbinical Studies in the Seventeenth Century: Constantijn L'Empereur, 1591–1648, Professor of Hebrew and Theology at Leiden.* Leiden: E. J. Brill, 1989.

Vernadsky, George. "Byzantium and Southern Russia: Two Notes. 1: The Eparchy of Gothia. 2: The Date of the Conversion of the Khazars to Judaism." *Byzantion* 15 (1940–41): esp. 76–86.

Vikan, Gary. S.v. "Education." In *Oxford Dictionary of Byzantium.*

Villagomez, Cynthia, "Christian Salvation through Muslim Domination: Divine Punishment and Syriac Apocalyptic Expectation in the Seventh and Eighth Centuries." *Medieval Encounters* 4, no. 3 (1998): 203–18.

Vryonis, Speros, Jr. *The Decline of Medieval Hellenism in Asia Minor and the Process of Islamization from the Eleventh through the Fifteenth Century.* Berkeley: University of California Press, 1971.

Wagenseil, Johann Christoff. *Tela ignea Satanae. Hoc est: Arcani, et horribiles Judaeorum adversus Christum Deum, et Christianam Religionem Libri* ANEKDOTI. Westmead, 1970. Reprint of Altdorf, 1681.

Walfish, Barry Dov. "The Mourners of Zion ('Avelei Siyyon): A Karaite Aliyah Movement of the Early Arab Period." In M. Mor, ed., *Eretz Israel: Israel and the Jewish Diaspora—Mutual Relations,* 42–52. Lanham, Md.: University Press of America, 1991.

Wall, E. G. E. van der "Johann Stephan Rittangel's Stay in the Dutch Republic, 1641–1642." In van den Berg and van der Wall, *Jewish-Christian Relations in the Seventeenth Century,* 119–33.

Walter, D. P. *The Ancient Theology: Studies in Christian Platonism from the Fifteenth to the Eighteenth Century.* Ithaca, N.Y.: Cornell University Press, 1972.

Wansbrough, John. *The Sectarian Milieu: Content and Composition of Islamic Salvation History.* Oxford: Oxford University Press, 1978.

Wasserstrom, Steven M. "Species of Misbelief: A History of Muslim Heresiography of the Jews." Ph.D. diss., University of Toronto, 1985.

———. "Who Were the Jewish Sectarians under Early Islam?" In Menahem Mor, ed., *Jewish Sects, Religious Movements and Political Parties,* 101–12. Omaha, Neb.: Creighton University Press, 1992.

———. *Between Muslim and Jew: The Problem of Symbiosis under Early Islam.* Princeton, N.J.: Princeton University Press, 1995.

———. "Šahrastānī on the Maġāriyya." *Israel Oriental Studies* 17 (1998): 127–54.

Waszink, J. H. "Some Observations on the Appreciation of the 'Philosophy of the Barbarians' in Early Christian Literature." In L. J. Engels, H. W. F. M. Hoppenbrouwers, and A. J. Vermeulen, eds., *Mélanges offerts à Mademoiselle Christine Mohrmann*, 41–56. Utrecht: Spectrum, 1963.

Watt, W. Montgomery. "Shiʿism under the Umayyads." *Journal of the Royal Asiatic Society* (1960): 158–72.

———. "Khārijite Thought in the Umayyad Period." *Der Islam* 36 no. 3 (1961): 215–32.

———. *The Formative Period of Islamic Thought.* Edinburgh, Scot.: Edinburgh University Press, 1973.

Wegner, Judith Romney. "Islamic and Talmudic Jurisprudence: The Four Roots of Islamic Law and Their Talmudic Counterparts." *American Journal of Legal History* 26 (1982): 25–71.

Wehr, Hans. *A Dictionary of Modern Written Arabic.* 3d ed. Ithaca, N.Y.: Spoken Language Services, 1976.

Weinryb, Bernard D. "The Beginnings of East-European Jewry in Legend and Historiography." In *Studies and Essays in Honor of Abraham A. Neuman*, 445–502. Leiden: E. J. Brill. 1962.

———. *The Jews of Poland: A Social and Economic History of the Jewish Community in Poland from 1100–1800.* Philadelphia, Pa: Jewish Publication Society of America, 1972.

Wellhausen, Julius. *The Arab Kingdom and Its Fall.* London: Curzon Press, 1973. Reprint of 1927 ed.

Wheatley, Paul. *The Places Where Men Pray Together: Cities in Islamic Lands, Seventh through the Tenth Centuries.* Chicago: University of Chicago Press, 2001.

Wheeler, Brannon M. "From Dār al-Hijra to Dār al-Islām: The Islamic Utopia." In Yanagihashi Hiroyuki, ed., *The Concept of Territory in Islamic Law and Thought*, 3–36. London: Kegan Paul International, 2001.

White, Hayden. *Metahistory: The Historical Imagination in Nineteenth-century Europe.* Baltimore, Md.: Johns Hopkins University Press, 1973.

———. "The Value of Narrativity in the Representation of Reality." In *The Content of the Form: Narrative Discourse and Historical Representation*, 1–25. Baltimore, Md.: The Johns Hopkins University Press, 1987.

Wieder, Naphtali. "The Dead Sea Scrolls Type of Biblical Exegesis among the Karaites." In A. Altmann, ed., *Between East and West: Essays Dedicated to the Memory of Bela Horovitz*, 75–105. London: East and West Library, 1958.

———. *The Judean Scrolls and Karaism.* London: East and West Library, 1962.

Wijnman, H. F. "Philippus Ferdinandus, Professor in het Arabisch aan de Leidse Universiteit . . . ." *Jaarbericht van het Vooraziatisch-Egyptisch Genootschap Ex Oriente Lux* 6 (1967): 558–80.

Wild, Joseph. *The Ten Lost Tribes.* Boston, Mass.: A. A. Beauchamp, 1919.

Wilson, Bryan R. *Magic and the Millennium: A Sociological Study of Religious Movements of Protest among Tribal and Third-World Peoples.* New York: Harper & Row, 1973.

Wilson, N. G. *Scholars of Byzantium*. London: Duckworth, 1983.

Wilson, Stephen G., ed. *Anti-Judaism in Early Christianity*, vol. 2: *Separation and Polemic*. Waterloo: Wilfrid Laurier University Press, 1986.

Wolfius, Johann Christophorus. *Notitia Karaeorum*. Hamburg, 1714 and 1721.

Wolfson, Harry Austryn. *Philo: Foundations of Religious Philosophy in Judaism, Christianity, and Islam*. 2 vols. Cambridge: Harvard University Press, 1948.

———. *The Philosophy of the Church Fathers*, vol. 1: *Faith, Trinity, Incarnation*. Cambridge: Harvard University Press, 1956.

———. "The Pre-Existent Angel of the Magharians and al-Nahāwandī." *JQR* 51 (1960–61): 89–106.

———. *Religious Philosophy*. Cambridge: Belknap Press of Harvard University Press, 1961.

———. *The Philosophy of the Kalam*. Cambridge: Harvard University Press, 1976.

———. *Repercussions of the Kalam in Jewish Philosophy*. Cambridge: Harvard University Press, 1979.

Wolohojian, Albert Mugrdich, trans. *The Romance of Alexander the Great by Pseudo-Callisthenes*. Introduction by Wolohojian. New York: Columbia University Press, 1969.

Yerushalmi, Yosef Hayim. *Zakhor: Jewish History and Jewish Memory*. New York: Schocken Books, 1989.

Yovel, Yirmiyahu. *Spinoza and Other Heretics: The Adventures of Immanence*. Princeton, N.J.: Princeton University Press, 1989.

———. *Spinoza and Other Heretics: The Marrano of Reason*. Princeton, N.J.: Princeton University Press, 1989.

Yūsuf al-Baṣīr. *al-Kitāb al-Muḥtāwī de Yusuf al-Basir*. Trans. and comm. Georges Vajda. Edited by David R. Blumenthal. Leiden: E. J. Brill, 1985.

Zacuto, Abraham. *Sefer Yuḥasin*. In Adolf Neubauer, ed., *Medieval Jewish Chronicles*. Oxford: Clarendon Press, 1895, 1:2–46.

———. *Sefer Yuḥasin ha-Shalem*. Edited by H. Filipowski. Jerusalem: N.p., 1963.

Zajaczkowski, A. *Ze Studiów nad Zagadnieniem Chazarskim: Études sur le problème des Khazars (avec résumé français)*. Kraków: Nakladem Polskiej Akademii Umiejetnosci, 1947.

———. "Khazarian Culture and Its Inheritors." *Acta Orientalia* 12 (1961): 299–307.

al-Zamakhsharī, Abū al-Qāsim Maḥmūd ibn ʿUmar. *Tafsīr al-kashāf ʿan haqāʾiq ghawāmiḍ al-tanzīl wa-ʿuyūn al-ʿaqāwil fī wujūh al-taʾwīl*. Edited by Mustafa Husain Ahmad. Cairo: n.p., 1953–55.

Zipperstein, Steven. *Imagining Russian Jewry: Memory, History, Identity*. Seattle: University of Washington Press, 1999.

Zlotnick, Dov. *The Iron Pillar—Mishnah: Redaction, Form, and Intent*. Jerusalem: Bialik Institute, 1988.

Zucker, Moshe. *Rav Saadya Gaon's Translation of the Torah: Exegesis, Halakha, and Polemics in R. Saadya's Translation of the Pentateuch*. New York: Michael Higger Memorial Publications, 1959 [Heb.].

———. "Responses to the Karaite Mourners of Zion Movement in Rabbanite Literature." In *Sefer ha-Yovel le-Rabi Ḥanokh Albek: Jubilee Volume in Honor of Hanokh Albeck*, 387–401. Jerusalem: Mosad Harav Kook, 1964 [Heb.].

General Index

Index to Citations from Biblical and Rabbinic Literature

www.ingramcontent.com/pod-product-compliance
Lightning Source LLC
LaVergne TN
LVHW050147080826
844660LV00002B/106
9781570035180